BUSINESS

FOR A LEVEL

Andy Mottershead,
Alex Grant and
Judith Kelt

BUSINESS
FOR A LEVEL

Orders: please contact Bookpoint Ltd, 130 Milton Park, Abingdon, Oxon OX14 4SB.
Telephone: +44 (0)1235 827720. Fax: +44 (0)1235 400454. Lines are open 9.00a.m.–5.00p.m., Monday to Saturday, with a 24-hour message answering service. Visit our website at www.hoddereducation.co.uk

First published in 2015 by

Hodder Education

An Hachette UK Company

Carmelite House

50 Victoria Embankment

London EC4Y 0DZ

Impression number	7	6	5
Year	2020	2019	2018

Typeset in Bliss Light 10.75/13.5 pt by Aptara inc.

Printed in Dubai

A catalogue record for this title is available from the British Library

ISBN 978 1471836152

Contents

Accounting and finance

Human resource management

Marketing

Introduction

This textbook has been written specifically to meet the needs of students taking OCR A Level and AS Business, which is 40 per cent of a full A Level. It provides a comprehensive coverage of the new specifications and uses a wide range of up-to-date examples. The order of chapters within the book reflects the 'Unit Content' of the OCR specification, which is available in hard copy or on the OCR website.

The specification refers to:

- an increased emphasis on decision making, noting how the size and scope of a business will affect how it operates
- the synoptic nature of all papers
- the case studies within the examination papers will be based on real businesses
- a need to apply mathematical skills in the context of business
- it is assumed the specification will be co-teachable for AS and A Level.

The actual content of the specification will concentrate on:

- the objectives of a business and its strategic decisions
- the external influences facing a business
- its operational strategy
- human resources
- accounting and financial considerations
- the global environment of business.

These areas are broken down into specific headings and the authors have tried to reflect these within the chapters of the book. However, in an attempt to enhance your understanding, some topics have been amalgamated where it is logical to do so.

Special features

AS and A Level

It is clearly shown which material within this book is for AS level and which is for A Level.

In addition, this book contains several other special features designed to aid your understanding of the concepts and examination techniques required by OCR.

Tips and techniques

All three authors have many years' experience of teaching for OCR, and use their experience to provide useful advice where appropriate. The advice concentrates on what students should do, and which common candidate mistakes should be avoided.

Your turn

To reflect the new specification, there are multiple-choice questions in the majority of the chapters. Each multiple-choice question will have four responses for you to choose from: A, B, C and D. The multiple-choice questions can be numerate or non-numerate.

Each chapter provides questions for the student (you) to tackle, either in the form of short questions, which are intended for reinforcement and revision purposes, or longer questions requiring more detailed answers.

The teachers' guide book, which is available separately, provides a mark scheme as a guide to the type of answer that is expected for each question and the amount of detail required (see answer style). Where appropriate, there are more numerical questions than in the previous textbook, in order to cover the new specification requirements.

Case studies

At the end of almost all of the chapters there is a case study, which requires you to apply the concepts you have been taught within the context of a business. The case study will also offer you an opportunity to practise your examination technique. The types of questions are aimed to be similar to those that may appear within the three examination papers. Marks are allocated as a guide and are, where possible, similar to those in the examination papers, as specified within the new specification.

The case studies also meet the requirements as stated within OCR's introduction to the specifications: 'The fundamental philosophy of the specifications is that the study of Business requires an integrated approach at all stages of the course.'

For this reason, some of the case studies include a wide range of material. Furthermore, they have been written to support OCR's requirements.

The specification requires an approach that views business behaviour from a variety of perspectives, namely an integration of the four main areas: marketing, operations management, (production), finance and HRM.

The case studies have also been chosen to try and reflect the range of businesses as stated within the specification; namely:

- Local businesses
- National (UK) businesses
- International businesses (global).

Group tasks

A few of the chapters feature group tasks. These are intended to stimulate debate and encourage you to learn the technique of justifying your view, a skill necessary for evaluation.

Further sources

The majority of the 'further sources' are websites for you to view and find additional up-to-date material and examples.

Key terms

These are included as a summary of the key concepts that you will need to know.

The examinations

A Level

Mark allocation and length of exam	Content overview	Assessment overview for full A Level Weighting of exam component
Section A Multiple choice 15 marks Section B Data response 65 marks 2 hour paper	01 Operating in a local business environment	33.3% of A Level
Section A Short answer 20 marks Section B extended response 60 marks 2 hour paper	02 The UK business environment	33.3% of A Level
Data response and extended response questions based on a case study 80 marks 2 hour paper	03 The global business environment	33.3% of A Level

None of the above components are pre-issued.

Unlike any of the previous specifications, it is very important to note that all three examination papers are synoptic; consequently, you will be expected to be able to draw on your knowledge from the whole of the specification for all components.

AS Level

Mark allocation and length of exam	Content overview	Assessment overview for AS level H031
Section A Multiple choice 20 marks Section B Case study: extended response 40 marks Sections A+B 1.5 hours	01 Local business environment	50% of AS level
Section A Short answer 20 marks Section B Case study: extended response 40 marks	02 The wider business environment	50% of AS Level

Examination advice

The 'Tips and techniques' feature contains useful hints on certain issues and topics. Remember, the authors are highly experienced teachers. There are several other important factors for you to remember, which apply to all three papers.

For ALL three papers, answering in the context of the case is very important.

Read the case with care to ensure you are familiar with:

- the type of business (its status, size, place in the market)
- the product or service
- the consumers
- the objectives of the business.

Read the question with care to ensure you have noted the trigger word: state, explain, outline, analyse, evaluate, to what extent. Questions beginning with these words require different types and lengths of answers. Writing too much for a 'state' question could lose time and therefore many marks. A 'state' question requires you to write perhaps no more than a couple of words, and in some cases just one word.

Mark allocation: noting the number of marks will help you to write an appropriate amount.

Be careful when phrases such as 'other than' are used. Many candidates miss the opportunity to gain marks by ignoring this instruction. For example: 'Other than by taxation, suggest how a business may be affected by the government.' Any references to taxation will not gain marks!

The quality of language *is* important. Examiners are aware of the pressure under which students write their answers. Nevertheless, using paragraphs and spelling certain words incorrectly such as 'business', 'interest' and 'their' (belonging to someone), are likely to mean that full marks are not awarded.

Always try to write specific points related to the case, rather than general points, which could apply to any business. In other words, answer in the context of the case.

Answer the actual question, rather than the one you prepared for or hoped would be there.

It is essential that you take careful note of your time allocation. Many of the large mark questions are at the end of the papers. Remember, you must give yourself enough time to read the case properly to ensure that you answer in its context.

Be careful how long you spend on any of the multiple-choice questions.

Ensure you read such questions with great care.

Assessment objectives AO1 –AO4

Level	Key word	Definition	Trigger words
AO1	Knowledge	Business knowledge/ facts.	State, List, Describe
AO2	Explanation or Application	Knowledge of the issues and or concepts. An explanation of the knowledge.	Explain, Outline, How
		For A02 your point MUST be in the context of the business.	
AO3	Analysis	The implication for the business.	Analyse
		How the business will be affected.	
		How the business reacts.	
		For A03, your point MUST be in the context of the business.	
AO4	Evaluation	Supported/ informed or justified judgements and/ or, weighting of arguments and/or consideration of long- and short-term issues. Offer a balanced view.	Evaluate, To what extent Discuss, Assess, Recommend

Ensuring you reach the highest assessment objectives as quickly as possible will ensure higher marks.

Analysis

There is not a magic number of points that need to be analysed before you have reached AO3. As long as you have shown how a particular point has affected the business or how the business is likely to react, you will gain AO3 marks.

Example

Analyse how a building company will be affected by demographic changes.

Answer

If there were changes in the demographics of a country, this may mean that the building company would have to change the type of housing that it built. As a result the business may have higher costs, as it would need to design different types of houses to meet the changes. As the population increased and there were more elderly people, land would become more expensive and therefore the builder's costs would rise, which in turn would affect its profits. If it wanted to keep its profits at the previous level, it may have to increase its prices.

This answer shows how the business would be affected and how it would react (including both is not essential; it depends upon the question) and therefore an AO3 mark would be gained.

Evaluation

The key element for evaluative comments is to ensure that you offer a 'justified judgement'. Questions where evaluation is required are asking you to suggest which factor is:

- the most important to that particular business
- most likely to benefit the business
- most likely to occur

- likely to damage the business the most.

To be evaluative, you will need to compare and weigh the evidence, having considered the positives and the negatives for the business in the case. It is always advisable to think about a balanced view.

In essence you are answering by making a decision which you justify.

Example

Evaluate how a change in technology could affect the business.

Answer

A change in technology may affect the business in several ways. If the new technology has to be bought in order to remain competitive, then business X will have to find the money and this may lead to an increase in its costs in the short term. However, once the new technology is bought, it may help to give the business a competitive edge and therefore increase its sales and its market share.

Depending upon the type of technology bought, there may be an additional opportunity cost, as employees may be made redundant if the technology requires fewer units of labour. This may mean that in the short term business X will have to pay out a significant amount of money in redundancy payments, reducing its profits for that year. However, in the long term, the technology will bring savings in labour and unit costs, which will yield higher profits in the following years.

In this answer, there is a clear judgement that has been justified and an attempt has been made to consider the short and long term. Consequently, this would gain an AO4 mark (marks for evaluation).

There is an assumption that there would be sufficient context by using references to the name of the business, the product or service involved, direct reference to the specific question, names of people mentioned within the case and any specific external factors affecting the cited business.

However, new to this specification is a change to the marking process.

The assessment objectives will be assessed at different levels. For example:

	Knowledge and understanding	Analysis	Evaluation
Strong		A fully developed argument demonstrating sequential links in relation to any causes, consequences and/or possible solutions	Conclusion is made weighing up both sides and reaches a fully supported judgement
Good	Accurate usage of terms and required concepts applied in the context of the question	Developed argument demonstrating sequential links in relation to causes, consequences and /or possible solutions	Conclusion drawn weighing up both sides and reaches a judgement which is not fully supported
Reasonable	Aware of the meaning of the required concepts and applied in the context of the question	Argument demonstrates some of the links to the causes, consequences and/or possible solutions	Some attempt to reach a conclusion showing some recognition of the influencing factors
Limited	Aware of the meaning of terms and required concepts within the question	Simple statement(s) of cause and consequences and /or possible solutions	An unsupported assertion

Throughout the specification you are expected to be able to evaluate; consequently this is a skill that you will need to practise. The guide above ought to help you see what the examiners are looking for in order to award the higher marks within a question.

Actual content of the specification

The authors have tried to mirror the headings used within the specification to ensure you know exactly what needs to be covered. However, to enhance your understanding we have tried to ensure topics fit in a harmonious manner and can be followed in a logical manner. Where there appears to be any obvious overlap within the specification we have highlighted clearly where such examples are, with marked cross references between relevant chapters.

Within the specification, it states that students will need to be able to evaluate the external influences on:

- accounting and finance
- human resource management
- marketing
- operations management.

Within separate chapters, the external influences are dealt with in considerable detail and can then be applied to any of the influences listed.

A and AS Level Business: notes for guidance on co-teaching

The following sample curriculum plans for AS and A Level Business are suggested examples of how the course could be taught. The design of the Business AS and A Level specifications mean that effective co-teaching is easily achievable. The new specification has been written so that there is a significant overlap between the content of the AS Business course and Components 1 and 2 of the A Level course. In addition, the assessment for Components 1 and 2 of both the AS and A Level course are similar. There is a greater demand at A Level but, due to the linear design of the course, there is some time to revisit earlier work and focus on the A Level demand in the latter part of the second year. In fact, preparation for the AS level exam is useful in terms of providing the first-year students with an opportunity to build their exam skills. Some centres may decide to enter their candidates for both the AS level and the A Level exams. If this is the case then the AS level exam will become useful practice for the final A Level exams in year 2. There will be an OCR Mock exam service available, which will help with the process of preparing students to practise unseen questions. This will also help teachers to understand the level of demand of both the AS and the A Level exams.

The significant change compared to the previous specification is the fact that the content, as in the case of a real-life business, is completely integrated into the two components at AS level and the three components at A Level. This means that any topic within the specification can be asked in any of the two or three components. The only difference is that for students taking these components to A Level, the demand will be higher in their final exams in year 2. This does mean that co-teaching is made much easier and allows for any number of ways of approaching the teaching of the course, in terms of the order of topics.

Continuity and themes

The key themes of the four business functions of human resources, marketing, finance and production run throughout the AS and the A Level course along with external influences, business objectives and decision making. These key themes can be introduced throughout the AS course and then revisited in a more strategic manner at A Level (notice in the specification how an emphasis is put on the link between the objectives, external influences and strategy, within each functional area). It is also vital that, as Component 1 at both AS and A Level contains multiple-choice questions, students have a sound understanding of basic concepts.

Other than in the methods of assessment (see below) the way in which the components are different is the focus on the market in which the business is operating.

In Component 1, for both the AS and A Level, other than the multiple-choice questions, the focus will be on the business operating in a local or regional market. This may be a small business which only has a local market or one part of a larger national or international business; for example, the actions of one branch, office or store.

In Component 2, for both the AS and A Level, the focus will be on the UK business environment. This may be a UK or non-UK business, but questions will concentrate on that business's operations ONLY in the UK market.

Component 3 (which only applies to the A Level) sees the global business environment as the focus. Again, this may be a UK or an international firm, but now the wider global activities of the business will be examined. This will also allow more synoptic/strategic questions to be asked.

In ALL components, the businesses will be REAL ones, using case material from sources such as the internet, company reports and newspaper articles.

Assessment

There are a number of different types of skills being assessed through a number of different question styles. Similar to the old specification, the new specification has a higher level of demand in the full A Level. Therefore, the AS level questions can be treated as preparation for the A Level skills.

Component 1 for both the AS and A Level contains multiple-choice and short-answer questions, as well as questions which will allow evaluative skills to be shown.

Component 2 for both the AS and A Level is made up of two sections. Section A contains short, theoretical questions, primarily assessing the knowledge and understanding of key business concepts. Section B will ask questions based on material about a real business provided in a resource booklet. These questions will include both short-answer and longer-answer questions.

Component 3 of the A Level will contain a few short-answer questions, although most marks will be available in three longer questions which will be of a decision making and/or strategic nature.

Sharing teaching within co-teaching centres

Sharing the teaching of the AS and A Level is very easy and there are suggestions of how to do this on the OCR website. The only difference is that if there are two teachers sharing one group, one of the teachers may be more likely to finish teaching the course slightly earlier than the other. This will leave them time to prepare the students for the A Level examinations.

Year 1	Content	
Autumn term Part 1	**Introduction to business**	
	The role of the entrepreneur; factors of production; stakeholders.	Ch.1
	Economic sectors; legal structure; private & public sector.	Ch.2
	The functions of business; methods of measuring the size of a business; factors affecting size & the importance of size.	Ch.4
	Human resource management	
	Organisational structure.	Ch.41
	Recruitment & selection; documentation, methods & impact.	Ch.44
	Training; methods, choice & impact of decisions made.	Ch.44
	Workforce performance measures; appraisal methods.	Ch.45
	Fair & unfair dismissal; redundancy; grievance procedures.	Ch.49
	Management; leadership styles & theories.	Ch.46
	Motivational theory; methods of motivation.	Ch.47
	Employment legislation; contracts, minimum wage, health & safety, equality, data protection.	Ch.49
	Industrial democracy; role of good employee relations; the changing nature of trade union membership.	Ch.48
Autumn term Part 2	**Marketing**	
	Identifying resources required to market a product; using a SWOT analysis to assess the current market position.	Ch.50
	Using market research to identify customer needs; sampling; using market share and market growth data.	Ch.51 & 52
	Customer & product orientation; niche v. mass marketing; market segmentation; b2b or b2c marketing.	Ch.53
	The marketing mix in a local, national & global context:	
	(i) Product: the product life cycle; Boston matrix; USP; branding	Ch.54
	(ii) Price: pricing strategies; price, income & cross elasticity of demand	Ch.55
	(iii) Place: physical & online distribution strategies	Ch.13 & 56
	(iv) Promotion: above & below-the-line methods.	Ch.57
Spring term Part 1	**Finance**	
	Sources of finance.	Ch.24
	Costs, revenue & profit; break-even analysis; contribution.	Ch.26, 27 & 28
	Investment appraisal; payback, ARR & NPV.	Ch.29
	The role of budgets; calculate & interpret variances.	Ch.30
	Cash-flow forecasts; the working capital cycle.	Ch.31
	Calculation & interpretation of income statements & statements of financial position.	Ch.33 & 34
	Ratio analysis (liquidity & profitability) as a way to evaluate the financial position of a business.	Ch.36 & 39

Spring term Part 2	**Production** What is added value?; productivity; economies & diseconomies of scale; capacity management. Methods of production; specialisation & division of labour; production in the service sector. Stock control methods; stock control charts; the impact of the production method on stock control. Lean production. Quality standards; quality control, quality assurance, TQM, external standards, benchmarking. **External influences** Demand & supply; equilibrium price; the degree of competition in the market place; market dominance & regulation to protect stakeholders. Globalisation; international trade. STEEPLE analysis; how social, technological, economic, ethical, political, legal and environmental factors affect business behaviour.	 Ch.60, 64, 65 & 66 Ch.62 Ch.67 Ch.68 Ch.70 Ch. 13 & 14 Ch.15 & 16 Ch.17–21
Summer term Part 1	**Business objectives & decision making** Aims & objectives; the influence of and impact on stakeholders; conflict between stakeholder groups. Business plans; the relationship between risk & reward; the role of uncertainty. Financial & non-financial measures of performance to help a business to make decisions. Revision for AS Level examination	 Ch.5 & 6 Ch.8 & 9 Ch.11
Summer term Part 2	**Managing change (A Level)** Causes of change; levels of change; barriers to change. Change management; Lewin, McKinsey & Kotter's models; role of leadership and/or external consultants; change strategies. Contingency planning & crisis management.	 Ch.22 Ch.22 Ch.8
Year 2	**Content**	
Autumn term Part 1	**Human resource management** Communication; formal & informal; group norms & the impact of groups; communication methods & media; models of communication; effective communication. Workforce planning; flexible working practices; goal-setting & excellence; theories of motivation; organisational culture. Training needs analysis (TNA); the usefulness of appraisal methods; evaluating employee contribution. Employment tribunals. HRM objectives, external influences and strategy. **Finance** Accounting conventions; GAAP. Cost & profit centres; stepped fixed costs; full, absorption & marginal costing methods; special order decisions. Cash-flow statements; depreciation. Solvency, efficiency & shareholder ratios. Finance objectives, external influences and strategy.	 Ch.42 Ch.43 Ch.44 Ch.49 Ch.41 & 45 Ch.25 Ch.26, 27 & 28 Ch.31 & 35 Ch.37, 38 & 40 Ch.23

Autumn term Part 2	**Marketing** Using normal distribution & standard deviation to help identify customer needs; explaining consumer behaviour; AIDA, DAGMAR, ATR; customer service; market segmentation strategy. Extension strategies; value analysis; justifying a product mix. The usefulness of income & cross elasticity of demand; justifying a pricing mix. The role of place in a marketing strategy. Drip & viral marketing; advertising elasticity of demand; justifying a promotional mix. Service marketing. Marketing objectives, external influences and strategy. **Production** Innovation, research & development; the importance of technology. Project management; CPA, Gantt charts & PERT; the importance of quantitative and qualitative factors. Managing capacity & capacity utilisation. The importance of service provision; improving customer service. Location; the importance of a suitable logistics strategy; outsourcing, subcontracting, offshoring & re-shoring. Production objectives, external influences and strategy.	 Ch.52 & 53 Ch.54 Ch.55 Ch.56 Ch.57 Ch.53 & 54–57 Ch.50 & 58 Ch.61 & 21 Ch.63 Ch.66 Ch.54 Ch.69 Ch.59
Spring term Part 1	**More external influences** Factors to consider when trading internationally; impact of exchange rate changes; supporting international trade; free trade & trading blocs. The EU & Single European Market; emerging markets; responses to increased globalisation. Government expenditure & policy; the business cycle; political stability and uncertainty. The digital revolution; usefulness of computer hardware & software to business. The consequences of complying or not complying with legislation; ethical trading and working practices; being an environmentally friendly organisation. The impact on a business of market forces & competition and its reaction to them.	 Ch.15 & 16 Ch.15 Ch.17, 18 & 19 Ch.21 Ch.17, 20 & 21 Ch.13 & 14
Spring term Part 2	**Business decision making & strategy** The franchise model; co-operatives; joint ventures & strategic alliances. Mission statements; the 'Plan-Do-Review cycle'; corporate social responsibility. Forecasting; structured (Delphi & expert opinion) & unstructured techniques of qualitative forecasting; quantitative forecasting; time series analysis. Decision trees; Ansoff's matrix; the use of decision making tools; conflicts in decision making. Porter's models of strategic choice; the relationship between objectives, tactics and strategy; developing & justifying a strategy. Problems associated with using financial & non-financial measures to assess performance.	 Ch.3 & 4 Ch.6, 8 & 17 Ch.10 Ch.11 & 12 Ch.7
Summer term Part 1	**Revision** Revise Components 1, 2 and 3 for A Level exams.	

Sample curriculum plan for AS and A Level OCR Business (one teacher)

Source: OCR website

Acknowledgements

The authors would like to express their thanks to numerous individuals who have contributed to the completion of this book.

We are particularly grateful to Beth Cleall and Caitlin Seymour. Their patience, continued support and ability to cajole gently without creating too many ripples are much admired. Such support has been most welcome and has been very much appreciated.

Andy is particularly grateful to JCB, Sweetarts and Secret Compass for their support.

We are grateful to several businesses that have allowed visits to enhance our knowledge.

Andy would like to thank, yet again, Sheila for her understanding (well, most of the time) during the writing period. I would also like to thank my fellow co-authors who have had to put up with me asking for chapters and elaboration throughout the writing process.

Alex would like to thank his wife Kate and sons James and Ben for putting up with his long absences in the study. Thanks also to MK Dons for being an inspiration in demonstrating that you do not give up when things become difficult and don't go as planned.

Judith would like to thank Tom for his help and encouragement while writing the book. His comments, constructive criticisms and IT support were invaluable, if not always well-received.

Chapter 1

Enterprise and business functions

AS / Year 1

Both AS and A Level students must know all of the content in this chapter.

Enterprise and the entrepreneur

'Enterprise' is a word that has two meanings in business studies. Firstly, 'an enterprise' is simply another term for 'a business' and it is common to read a statement such as 'Richard Branson's first enterprise was selling vinyl records'. The second meaning is used to refer to the actions of a risk taker who starts up his or her own business; such an individual is said to be 'an enterprising person' and is also referred to as an entrepreneur.

An entrepreneur is more than 'a businessman' or 'a businesswoman'. Essentially, an entrepreneur is 'a risk taker who sets up a business'. This is not the same as being self-employed.

For example, a person who is a carpenter or a hairdresser may have been made redundant and, not being able to find another job, sets up their own business. Many self-employed people will have had a job working for someone else. They may have become self-employed later in life, rather than earlier, and may not have wanted to. They may not like risk taking and would prefer to have 'a steady job' working for someone else.

An entrepreneur is different. An entrepreneur will usually have always wanted to run his or her own business and will be prepared to take risks.

Although the original concept of the entrepreneur was developed in an age when most businesses were small and owned by one person, the term is still in very common use. People such as Richard Branson and James Dyson, who come up with a new business idea or product, are still referred to as entrepreneurs even though the businesses they run are definitely not small.

Entrepreneurs are a very diverse group of people but they share similar characteristics, which are quite different from those of a person who is self-employed. There is nothing 'wrong' with being self-employed but the difference between a self-employed person and an entrepreneur is an important one. A self-employed person could be described as being:

- hardworking
- competent
- reliable
- diligent.

These are certainly important characteristics; however, as well as demonstrating these, entrepreneurs will have certain character traits:

Chris Oakley OBE, from the web design company Chapter Eight gives a lengthy, but detailed, definition of an entrepreneur:

> *An entrepreneur sees an opportunity which others do not fully recognise, to meet an unsatisfied demand or to radically improve the performance of an existing business. They have unquenchable self-belief that this opportunity can be made real through hard work, commitment and the adaptability to learn the lessons of the market along the way.*
>
> *They are not diverted or discouraged by scepticism from 'experts' or from those from whom they seek backing and support, but willing to weigh all advice and select that which will be helpful. They are prepared not just to work seriously hard but to back their judgment with personal investment at a level which will cause problems if they are wrong about the opportunity. They understand that achievements are the result of team work and know how to choose the necessary blend of talents and inspire them with their vision.*

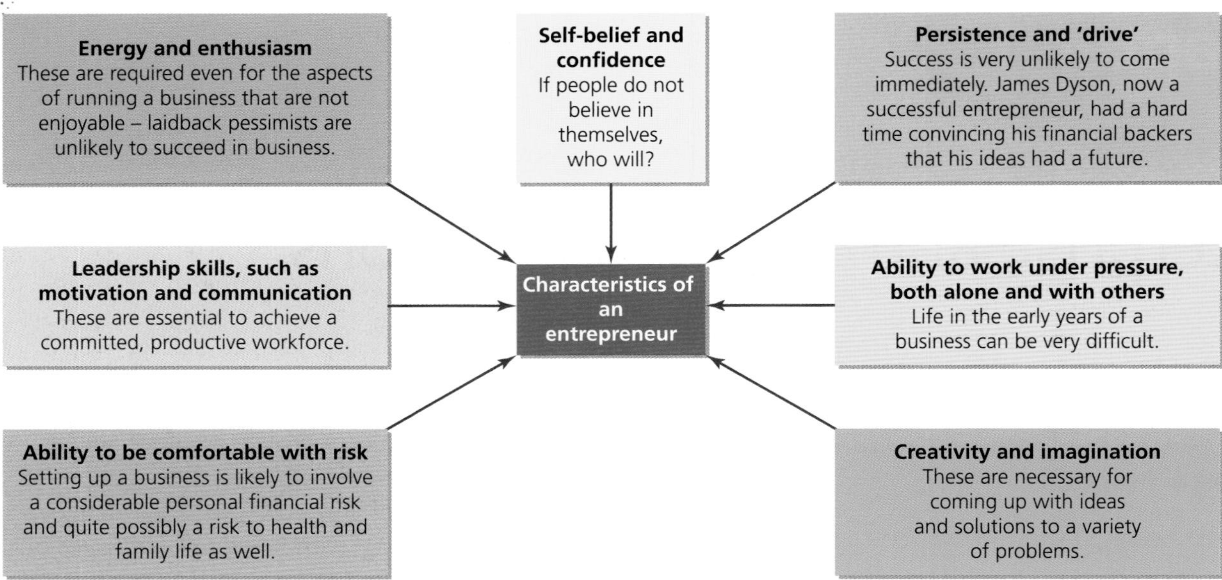

Figure 1.1 Character traits of an entrepreneur

Successful entrepreneurs can therefore bring a variety of benefits to the business's stakeholders. If the firm is profitable and growing as a result of the entrepreneur then it is more likely that its stakeholders will be able to reach their objectives (see **Chapter 5**). For example, more people are likely to be employed and employees will have more secure jobs and the chance of better pay and conditions, suppliers will receive larger and more regular orders, and the firm will pay more tax. A successful business may start to export goods to other countries and so help improve the UK's trade balance (see **Chapter 16**). The government will receive more tax revenue from sources such as income tax, corporation tax, national insurance, and VAT if businesses are thriving.

It is for these reasons that the government is very keen to encourage enterprise and entrepreneurship and why a variety of initiatives exist to help would-be and existing, entrepreneurs.

Factors of production

Using resources (inputs) a business can produce the products that consumers want to buy (outputs). These resources are sometimes referred to as the factors of production: land, labour, capital and enterprise. Each of these can be used in various combinations in order to produce goods and services. 'Land' is natural resources; not only fields, but what lies below them in terms of minerals, and land also includes what can be grown on it. 'Labour' is all of the human resources available (except the entrepreneur) whatever the age and skill of the worker. 'Capital', in this context, refers to buildings, machinery and tools rather than money. 'Enterprise' is the entrepreneur who organises the other three factors.

Key term

Factors of production: the inputs that are used in the production of goods or services. They are land, labour, capital, and enterprise.

For example, bread is produced using the following factors:

- Land is used to grow the wheat and build the bakery on.
- Labour is used to plant the wheat, drive the combine harvester and collect the wheat, to operate the ovens, to pack the bread and to deliver it to the shops where it is sold.
- Capital is a combine harvester used to collect the wheat, ovens and baking trays are used to cook the bread, packaging machines to pack the bread, and vans to deliver it.
- Enterprise is the entrepreneur, the owner of the farm or the bakery; the person who organises the other factors of production in order to make a profit.

The factors of production are essential inputs for a firm and their availability can affect the business and its stakeholders. If there is a shortage of a particular factor its price will rise. The factor's price is a cost to the business and any rise in factor costs is not going to be welcome since it potentially reduces profit margins. How might the firm react to a rise in factor costs? Raising prices is one option. The extent of the ability to do this depends on how many competitors there are in the market and the firm's brand loyalty. Alternatively, the business could try and lower some other costs; it may impose worse terms and conditions on its suppliers in an attempt to do so. If the supplier is a small firm with no market power it may just have to accept the situation. However, if it is a nationwide supplier of a well-known national brand there will be little chance of such an approach succeeding. If the business tries to cut back on non-essential areas of expenditure, the local community may suffer in terms of fewer community initiatives such as sponsorship. The business may well, in fact, adopt a combination of all three approaches. The entrepreneur has to manage and make decisions on these issues.

An entrepreneur also has to make decisions about which factors to use and in what quantities; for example, should a farmer harvest a large field by using ten men with scythes, or one man using a combine harvester? It depends on costs. The combine harvester option sounds cheaper in terms of labour costs, but what about the capital cost? The entrepreneur is usually trying to make a profit and so will make decisions based on factor costs and also the likely payoffs from the risks that must be taken by running the business (see **Chapter 9**).

Key term

Value added: what a business achieves by ensuring that the price of the finished good or service is in excess of the cost of the inputs.

Adding value

Adding value means that a business can sell the product at a price that is higher than the cost of producing it. Any extras that can be added to a product that are priced above the additional cost result in value added (see **Chapter 60**).

An entrepreneur is concerned with adding value in order to make a profit. Manufacturing raw materials into a product adds value. For example, a piece of wood can be burned and therefore could be sold as a fuel. However, if the wood is cut, made into a toy animal and then painted, its value will be much higher.

Similarly, value can be added by creating an image for a product, making it appear to be more valuable. That is the key function of creating a brand image (see **Chapter 57**).

Constraints on a business

The entrepreneur also has to decide how best to manage the constraints on a business.

A constraint is a restraining factor on a business: something that limits how a business operates. It often involves a cost that the business will need to pay, either directly or indirectly. If, for example, the government passes a law stating that all employees who work with a certain type of chemical must be trained in a new way of handling and storage then those businesses involved would have to spend money on training and storage facilities. There would also be an additional cost in terms of lost production time while the training takes place and also the management time spent organising it. This cost would either be passed on to the consumer in the form of higher prices or be paid for by the businesses, which would affect the level of their profits.

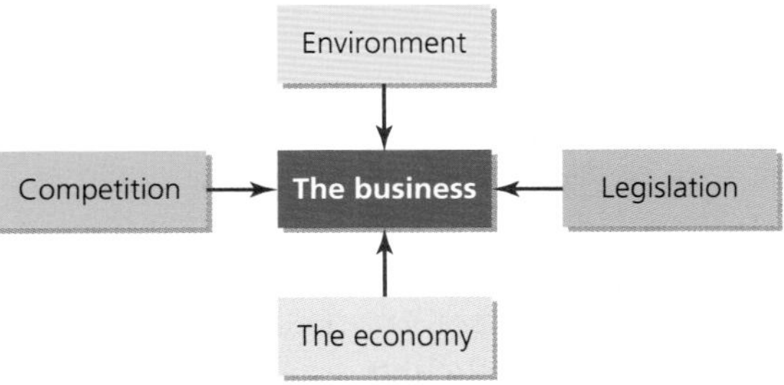

Figure 1.2 Constraints on a business

The functions within a business

The organisation of a business is often divided up into several functions or departments. In a large business each function will be staffed by specialists, whereas an entrepreneur starting up and acting on his or her own will have to be a 'jack of all trades' in carrying out different business functions

1 Accounting and Finance. This department monitors and controls the business's financial resources. The department keeps detailed records of all the products that the business has made and sold, the cost of the goods sold, and any tax due as a result of this. It has overall responsibility for ensuring that costs are kept under control and that there are sufficient funds available to pay all the day-to-day running costs of the business. It sets budgets in order to control the business and operates the business's payroll.
2 Operations management and production. 'Production' can be thought of as the process of transforming resource 'inputs' into finished 'outputs',

i.e. the products that the business sells in order to meet the demands of consumers. 'Operations management' is a wider term that refers to designing and controlling the process of production to make it as efficient as possible. It therefore encompasses maintenance of capital equipment, stock control, quality control, and managing technological change (see **Chapter 21** and **22**). In practice the two terms are sometimes used interchangeably – or together, as in 'Production and Operations Management' (POM).

3 Marketing and support services. As consumers have greater choice and an ever-increasing ability to purchase goods and services, the role of the marketing department is highly significant. It is the role of marketing to ascertain the needs of consumers by conducting market research and to attempt to satisfy the consumers in order to make a profit. Adding value and ensuring consumers are informed of the product or service in such a manner as to create a desire to buy (and then make repeat purchases) is all part of the task of marketing. Customer service may be considered as part of marketing since the way the product is sold can influence a purchase. This is particularly important when customers make expensive purchases such as a car, for example, and there is a requirement for clear advice on the nature of the product. Once a product has been bought, sales support is also important. It is reassuring for a customer to know that if help is needed with, say, tuning a new television or installing software on a new computer it is available – and this could encourage someone to make a purchase. Indifferent customer service at point of sale and/or sales support that is poor (either because of a lack of product knowledge or because the support is offered via a website that does not work, or a phone line that is always busy) loses the business customers and can attract poor publicity.

4 Human resource management (HRM). Sometimes referred to as personnel, this department is responsible for the wellbeing of the employees. This includes recruitment and training, and, if necessary, terminating employment. How much time and money is devoted to this department often depends on the size of the business. As a business grows, its need for a separate HRM department increases, as there are more employees to look after. Motivating the workforce and ensuring that the business complies with employment legislation is also part of the HRM function.

A business needs to pay careful attention to each function and ensure that all departments work together. There should not be a situation where (say) the production function produces quantities that are not carefully co-ordinated with marketing, since this could result in either disappointed customers or a build-up of unwanted stock. Both instances are damaging financially since the former means revenue is lost and the latter means funds are 'tied up' that could be used elsewhere. Where a function is given insufficient attention, or co-ordination between them is poor the business will not be as profitable as it could be and this will impact negatively on its stakeholders.

Tips and techniques

Unless the question is based upon a specific business function it is wise to consider how a decision made on a particular course of action, such as launching a new product, will affect all four functions, since for the business to reach its goals all areas need to work together. A knowledge and understanding of the role of the four business functions will be important in constructing an analytical and evaluative answer.

Further sources

www.gov.uk/government/organisations/department-for-business-innovation-skills

www.greatbusiness.gov.uk

Both of these websites offer information on the assistance available from the government for new and existing businesses.

Your turn

Questions in red are for A Level candidates only.

Multiple-choice questions

1 Which of the following is a correct statement?
- A An entrepreneur runs a profitable business.
- B An entrepreneur can see an opportunity that others cannot.
- C An entrepreneur is not happy with risk.
- D An entrepreneur does not take advice from others. *(1)*

2 Which of the following is not a factor of production?
- A enterprise
- B land
- C labour
- D money. *(1)*

3 Which of the following best describes the term 'value added'?
- A the value of output
- B the difference between the value of output and the value of input
- C the cost of the factors of production
- D the revenue the business gets from the sale of a product. *(1)*

4 Which of the following is not one of the functional areas of a business?
- A finance
- B marketing
- C production
- D the economy. *(1)*

Revision questions

1 State the two meanings of the term 'enterprise'. *(2)*

2 Identify three likely characteristics of an entrepreneur. *(3)*

3 Analyse two reasons why the government is keen to encourage enterprise and entrepreneurship. *(4)*

4A State what is meant by 'a constraint' on a business. *(1)*

4B Identify two likely constraints on a business. *(2)*

5 As a product passes through different businesses, value is added to a product. Calculate the value added by the activities of turning timber into wood pulp and the total value of output. Show your working. *(4)*

Business activity	Value of input (£)	Value added (£)	Total value of output (£)
Timber is forested	0	500	500
Turned into wood pulp	500	?	750
Turned into books	750	1000	1750
Sold by the retailer	1750	1000	?

Total *(16)*

Group task

In groups of two, you are required to make a 5–10 minute presentation on an entrepreneur. Select an entrepreneur and explain that person's achievements in terms of businesses that have been created, consider the entrepreneur's personal characteristics and evaluate why he or she has succeeded.

Case study

Specsavers Optical Group Ltd (better known as simply 'Specsavers') is a high street opticians, selling spectacles, contact lenses and hearing aids. The business was launched in 1984 by husband and wife team Doug and Mary Perkins in Guernsey. Now the group has over 1500 branches and employs around 25,000 people. Specsavers operates in Europe and has recently opened branches in Australia and New Zealand. It controls 42 per cent of the UK opticians market and had a turnover of £1.7 billion in 2012.

Specsavers is clearly a vast business. Yet it retains the feel of being a family firm, and this is one of its strengths. Dame Mary Perkins gives a sense that she is deeply involved in the company, and deeply interested in its operations on the ground. 'I never lose sight of the customers. We wouldn't have a business if it wasn't for them, so they... are my best friends, the most important people in my life.'

Among the many awards won by Specsavers since 1984 is being voted most trusted optician by British consumers for 10 years in a row.

After its slow first year, Specsavers has achieved growth year after year. It has never closed a store, and has no loans or outside investment. This is nothing to do with luck or timing, asserts Dame Mary Perkins, but the result of 'careful appraisal of everything'.

Specsavers rigorously researches aspects such as locations and partners, and its senior management style seems to be micromanagement in the best sense, with headquarters closely involved with the day-to-day running of each store. 'We have a close working relationship with all the stores, and we're very hands-on with them,' explains Perkins. 'We don't just give a manual and say this is how you do it. A board member will meet with all the opticians in every country every eight weeks. We sit down for the day and ask what's been happening, and whether something's worked ... It's not all done from behind a desk, we're very much involved at the sharp end.'

The optician chain's joint venture structure, whereby each partner (the optician in charge of the management of the store) has a 50 per cent stake in his or her store, offers partners a long-term incentive to perform well and grow. This structure, points out Perkins, offers greater rewards and motivation to each partner than a franchising arrangement. It's an excellent formula for growing a company and getting staff to buy into its vision.

The joint venture arrangement encourages opticians to nurture their own patch. Perkins explains: 'Reputation is ever more important with the new media around. Companies should stay close to their customers and be part of their communities.' It's an interesting paradox that in the days of global online purchasing, local engagement and individual customer care are more important for retailers than ever. A small local problem or small group of disgruntled customers can quickly become a national or even international story.

Perkins warns that the internet has also changed customer expectations, and the difficult economic landscape has exacerbated this. 'Customers are searching for more value – for more for less.

They're more demanding, and more knowledgeable, using the internet to find out things for themselves, and they want better service. So they need to be told why they should spend money with you.'

One of the challenges for Specsavers has been to keep growth at a steady and manageable rate. A common cause of failure, advises Perkins, is 'trying to run before walking, trying to get big in a hurry – there's no need to do that'. She warns against being too thinly spread, and of losing your culture, vision and values when you expand into other markets.

1. State two reasons why Mary Perkins could be considered as 'an entrepreneur'. *(2)*
2. Specsavers controls 42 per cent of the UK opticians market and had a turnover of £1.7bn in 2012. Calculate the total value of turnover in the market for 2012. *(2)*
3. Analyse two likely issues that Doug and Mary Perkins would have needed to consider before deciding to try to become entrepreneurs in the opticians market in the UK. *(6)*
4. Evaluate the reasons why Mary and Doug Perkins have succeeded as entrepreneurs. *(15)*

Total *(25)*

Chapter 2

Business sectors and types of business

AS / Year 1

Both AS and A Level students must know all of the content in this chapter.

It is important to recognise that businesses are not all the same; they vary in size, by the sector they operate in, and by the legal structure they possess. In addition, just as a market can be local, national, or international this is also the case with a business. It is unlikely that a small firm will have branches in other countries (although it may still sell products abroad) but many public limited companies (PLCs) have operations in other countries as well as nationally in the UK. These businesses are known as 'multinationals'.

Different stages of production

As products are made, they pass through the chain of production. For example, production of petrol starts with the extraction of crude oil from the ground; next the oil is refined and then the petrol is distributed to garages, where it is sold to the final consumer. In some industries, one firm is involved in all stages of the chain, as shown in Figure 2.1.

Key term

Chain of production: stages that a product passes through until it reaches the final consumer.

In other industries, the businesses involved at each stage of the chain are different. This textbook started out as part of a tree that was grown by one firm and possibly cut down by another. It was probably turned into wood pulp and then paper by another quite separate business. The paper was then printed with the text, which someone else had written, and made into a book, before being distributed (by yet another business) to a retailer where it was finally purchased by the consumer.

It does not matter whether one business or many are involved in the chain of production. What is important to note is that, as a product passes along the chain, it has value added to it – in other words, it becomes worth more because of the business activity at each stage of the chain (see **Chapter 60**).

Business activity

This can be classified by the nature of output into three broad sectors.

1 Primary sector. Businesses in the primary sector are concerned with the extractive industries. These include farming, forestry, fishing and mining, as well as oil and gas extraction.
2 Secondary sector. Businesses in the secondary sector are concerned with manufacturing — that is, turning raw materials into semi-finished and finished products. The pressing of steel into a chassis, the

Figure 2.1 Most petrol companies own their own oil fields, refineries and garages

production of an engine and then the final assembly of components into a complete car are examples of business activity in this sector. Secondary production also includes the construction industry — building houses, factories, office blocks and roads.

3 Tertiary sector. Businesses in the tertiary sector are concerned with the output of services; and services still count as production even if there is no actual finished product to see. They include a wide range of tertiary activities from retailing, banking and transportation, through the many services provided by the leisure industries, to the kinds of service provided by professionals such as teachers and doctors.

Figure 2.2 shows the proportions of each sector in the output of the UK.

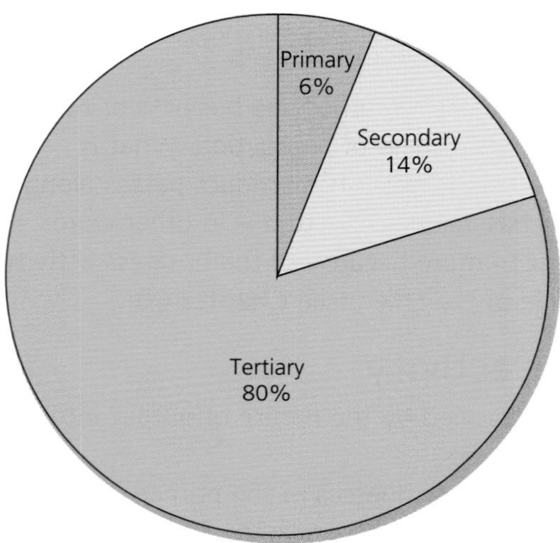

Figure 2.2 The composition of output in the UK

Different surveys measure GDP data in slightly different ways but it is clear how output is divided. The tertiary sector is by far the largest. This accounts for nearly 80 per cent of total output in the UK. The secondary sector accounts for around 14 per cent, while primary output is around 6 per cent of total GDP. A large tertiary sector is one of the features of an advanced economy. The decline in the level of secondary output and employment typical of advanced economies is referred to as deindustrialisation.

Key term

Deindustrialisation: the decline in the size of the secondary sector of the economy.

Structure of the economy

The structure of the economy and what businesses produce is important. Manufacturing does matter. The UK produces and exports high-value products especially in areas such as engineering, machine tools, electrical components, nuclear reactor components and aircraft. Chemical engineering and pharmaceuticals are also strong in the UK. If manufacturing is thriving then there is likely to be a positive effect on the other two sectors as well, since there will be a need for more raw material inputs and services to support the business. Furthermore, the UK needs a successful manufacturing sector to generate the export earnings.

Types of business

Businesses can also be classified by whether they are in the private sector or the public sector (see Figure 2.3). In the private sector, businesses are owned and run by individuals. These are referred to as 'private enterprise'. In the public sector, there are not many 'businesses' in the usual sense of the word. The term 'organisation' is more appropriate. In this sector, organisations are referred to as 'public enterprise' and are owned and run on behalf of the public by central or local government. Examples are the British Broadcasting Corporation (BBC), The National Nuclear Laboratory (NNL) and the National Health Service (NHS). At local level, libraries and (some) leisure centres are government owned.

Key terms

Private sector: businesses owned and run by private individuals — usually for profit.

Public sector: businesses and organisations owned and run by local or central government, whose objective is to provide a service rather than make a profit.

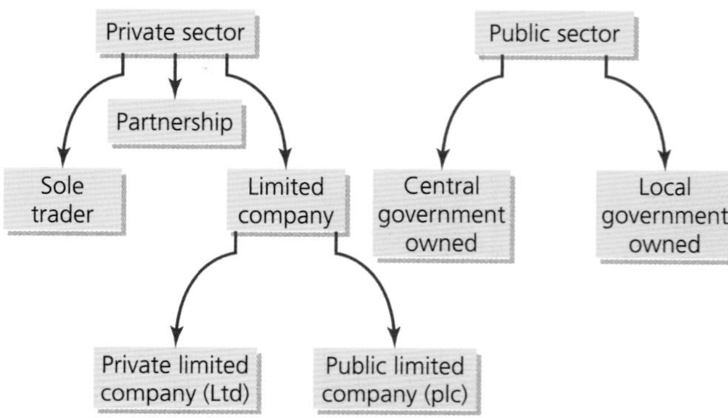

Figure 2.3 The private and public sectors

Businesses in the private sector

The legal structure of a business is important because of the ways in which it influences the firm's operation. Legal structure is particularly important for the effects that it has on:

- ownership and control of the business
- responsibility for any debts
- sources of finance available
- the objectives pursued.

Sole trader

The sole trader (also known as the 'sole proprietor') is the simplest form of business organisation. The sole trader owns the business and makes all the decisions affecting it. This does not mean that the business has only one person working there; the sole trader could employ a number of people, but he or she is in overall control. The most important legal aspect of being a sole trader is that, as far as the law is concerned, the business and its owner are inseparable. The business does not exist in its own right — it is said to be 'unincorporated'.

Advantages of being a sole trader

- There are few legal requirements when setting up as a sole trader, although some businesses may need a licence (e.g. to sell alcohol). It is therefore possible to start a business quite quickly and with relatively little capital.
- The sole trader does not have to consult with anyone and therefore making decisions (e.g. over the products on sale and the hours that the business will open) is quick and easy.
- A sole trader keeps all the profit (after tax).
- As a sole trader cannot issue shares, he or she cannot be subject to a 'takeover' in the way that a public company can.
- Apart from having to provide information for income tax purposes, the financial state of the business can be kept private. This is not the case with a company, which has to publish its accounts.

Disadvantages of being a sole trader

- The sole trader is 'the business' and is fully responsible for all its debts. If the business runs into financial difficulty, the sole trader may be forced to sell his or her personal possessions (e.g. house or car) to pay the debts. This is known as unlimited liability.
- Sole traders have to be a 'jack of all trades'; they must single-handedly perform all the business's functions, such as marketing the products, controlling finance and motivating employees. No matter how talented a person is, it is unlikely that he or she will be good at, or enjoy, all of these. Unfortunately, if any one of these is neglected or performed badly, the business is going to suffer.
- Successful businesses often want to grow. It can be hard to raise capital for expansion, because a small business is seen as risky, which can limit the opportunities for growth.
- Sole traders can easily get overworked. This is especially true in the first years of the business's existence when the sole trader is likely to be working long hours to build up the customer base and reputation.
- Sole traders are usually small businesses. Larger firms may not wish to deal with them because they may feel that they do not have the expertise or ability to 'deliver' in the way that a larger business could.
- Since the sole trader legally is the business itself, if he or she dies, then the business comes to an end. There is no continuity.

Partnership

Dentists often form a partnership

Whenever two or more people run a business together, as far as the law is concerned, they are partners. There does not have to be any formal documentation for a partnership to come into existence. Partnerships are common in the professions, among, for example, solicitors, accountants and dentists.

Just as is the case with a sole trader, a partnership is not a legal entity in its own right. The partners are 'the business'. The law requires a minimum of two and a maximum of 20 partners.

It is good business practice for partners to draw up a Deed of Partnership. This is a legal document that governs the running of this type of business. It sets out and clarifies matters such as:

- how much money each partner is expected to contribute
- how much income each partner can draw (i.e. take) from the business
- the responsibilities and duties of each partner
- the arrangements to cover absence, sickness or holidays
- how decisions are to be made within the partnership
- the arrangements for taking on new partners
- the arrangements if the partnership is to be dissolved
- the arrangements for finance (e.g. will partners have separate or joint accounts?).

If no deed exists, the business will be governed by the Partnership Act of 1890, which states that the responsibility for running the business and the distribution of profits and losses are to be shared equally among the partners.

Advantages of partnerships

- A partnership is easy to establish.
- Additional partners mean there will be more capital. Expansion is therefore likely to be easier than it is for a sole trader.
- Work is shared and different partners with different skills can be employed.
- Partners can specialise in what they do best.
- Losses are shared.
- Partnerships, like sole traders, pay income tax, which means that the financial state of the business can be kept private.

Disadvantages of partnerships

- Partners, like sole traders, have unlimited liability. Furthermore, an individual partner is liable for any debts incurred by other partners even if he or she had no knowledge of the decisions that led to them. Partners may have limited liability if they simply contribute money and take no active part in running the business. These people are known as 'sleeping' partners. However, a partnership must have at least one partner with unlimited liability.
- Decision making is slower and there is the possibility of disagreement.
- The legal restriction on the maximum number of partners means that the business can still lack capital for expansion.
- Losses are shared but so are profits.
- In law, a partnership can be automatically ended with the departure, resignation, or death of one partner. For this reason, partners should make provision by having a written agreement about what will occur if this happens; perhaps agreeing that a new partner can be taken on, or that the existing partners will convert the business to a company.

Limited liability partnerships (LLPs)

LLPs became legal in 2001. They combine some features of partnerships with some of those of limited companies. An LLP is a separate legal entity, so its owners have limited liability. The owners of an LLP are called members rather than partners.

Before 2001, if a group of people wanted limited liability (see **page 11**) they had to form a company. The creation of LLPs means that it is possible to have the advantages of a partnership combined with limited liability. However, this limited liability comes at a price: LLPs, like private limited companies, are required to file their annual accounts at Companies House. Their accounts are therefore available publicly for competitors to view.

Limited company

There are a number of important differences between companies and other types of business organisation:

1. Incorporation. In law, sole traders and partnerships are unincorporated — that is, they do not exist separately from their owners. A company, on the other hand, is 'incorporated' — the business exists in its own right. Those who own the company (the shareholders) are not the same as those who run it for them (the directors).
2. Shares. Companies can raise capital via the issue of shares, whereas sole traders and partnerships cannot. A 'share' is exactly what the term implies: buyers own a share of the company. They become one of its owners. Companies issue shares to raise money. Investors buy shares with two aims in mind: receiving a return on their money (which is known as a dividend) and making a capital gain — selling their shares for a higher price than they bought them at. The issue of shares is covered in **Chapter 40**.
3. Limited liability. If a company goes into liquidation (has to cease trading) because of financial problems, its shareholders have limited liability. This means that the shareholders only lose their shares.

This could mean the loss of a significant sum of money, but at least shareholders are not personally liable for the business's debts in the way that sole traders and partners are. The shareholders' liability is limited to the capital they have invested.

Private and public limited companies

There are two types of company: the private limited company and the public limited company. Private companies are often, but not necessarily, family businesses, where the advantages of being incorporated can be linked to the ability to keep control within a fairly small group of people.

It is usually the case that sole traders and partnerships operate in local markets because of their size and ability to supply. A private limited company may operate nationally, and a public company will operate nationally and often in international markets as well. If this is the case it is known as a 'multinational'. A small business may, of course, sell products abroad but this does not make it a multinational; a multinational actually produces in the foreign market rather than simply exporting to it.

Public companies are larger than private companies. Other differences are as follows:

- The name. A public company is a 'plc'. A private company's name must end with 'Limited' or 'Ltd'. Virgin Atlantic Ltd is an example of a private company even though it is part of the larger Virgin Group.
- Where shares can be traded. A plc can sell shares on the stock market. A private company cannot. A public company's shares can therefore be bought by anyone. In a private limited company, shares must be sold through private negotiation and cannot be advertised for sale to the public.
- The possibility of being taken over. As a plc's shares are available for anyone to buy, it can be quite legally taken over if an investor gains 51 per cent of its shares. A private company can 'sell out' to an investor but cannot involuntarily be taken over.
- The amount of share capital. A plc is required to have a minimum share capital of £50,000. A private company has no minimum.
- The way the company reports to shareholders. A plc is required to include more detail in its annual publication to shareholders (the 'Report and Accounts'). In a private company, reporting to shareholders and the accounting procedures that the company has to use are less complicated.

Private and public companies have a number of similarities too:

- Directors. Shareholders elect a board (a group) of directors to run the company on their behalf. In a private company, the directors may be the shareholders.
- Information. Shareholders must receive a copy of the company's Report and Accounts every year. They are also entitled to attend the annual general meeting (AGM). At this meeting, they receive a report from the directors on the state of the company. This includes information on the company's finances. The shareholders are entitled to vote at meetings (e.g. in the election of directors) and to question the directors about the way the company is being run.
- Voting. Voting by shareholders is 'one vote per share', not 'one person, one vote'. This means that an individual or a relatively small group of people can own enough shares to outvote all the others. Theoretically, to do this a person or group would need 51 per cent of the shares, but AGMs are often poorly attended and so it is possible to influence the business's decisions with a smaller percentage.

Smaller, family businesses tend to operate as a private rather than a public limited company

Advantages of companies

- The main advantage of a company is its access to large amounts of capital through the ability to issue shares. This means that there are greater opportunities for growth.
- Limited liability for shareholders encourages people to invest in the company.
- Investors such as banks often regard companies as less risky than a sole trader or partnerships. This could mean better terms for borrowing money.
- Continuity: a company is a separate legal entity and so does not come to an end when the original

owner(s) die. Unless a company has severe financial problems, it can exist forever.

Tips and techniques

The legal structure of companies is different from that of sole traders and partnerships. This has important implications for how they raise finance, how they are run and how they report to stakeholders. It is therefore a mistake to refer to every business as 'a company'.

Disadvantages of companies

- Setting up a company can be expensive. In order for a business to be established as a company, two important legal documents need to be completed to protect the interests of shareholders. These are known as the Memorandum of Association and the Articles of Association.
- The Memorandum deals with the company's relationship with the outside world (whether it will be a private or a public company, the nature of the products it will sell, etc.). The Articles deal with the internal running of the company (e.g. arrangements for the election and removal of directors). Completing these documents to the required standard means that establishing a company can be slower, more complicated and therefore more expensive than setting up as a sole trader or partnership.
- Running a company is more complicated than being a sole trader or partnership. Directors have certain legal responsibilities to the shareholders (e.g. holding the AGM, preparing the accounts in a certain way and publishing the Report and Accounts). This added complexity may mean that the company has to hire an accountant and a lawyer, which will be additional expense.
- Company accounts are not private. All company accounts, whether they are public limited companies or private limited companies, are on open access at Companies House. It is therefore difficult to keep the business's main financial details hidden from competitors.
- The danger of a takeover: in the case of a public company, the original owners could lose control if large blocks of shares are bought up by other investors. If the takeover is successful the company will usually continue to exist as an independent legal entity controlled by the acquirer. A takeover might go smoothly because the shareholders of both companies consider it to be beneficial. On the other hand, it may be resisted and so be regarded as 'hostile'. This is different from a merger, which is where two companies join together to form a new, larger business.
- Large companies can require complicated management structures. The more people there are to manage, the more difficult communication and co-ordination become.

Key term

Companies House: All UK companies must be registered. They must also submit details about themselves such as the identity of the directors, the number of shares and the latest 'Report and Accounts' every year. This is where these details are on open access to the public.

Tips and techniques

Remember that in law a company is a separate entity from its owners. This has implications for the way it raises capital and how it reports to its shareholders.

Public sector

At central government level, money that has been raised through taxation is spent on essential services such as healthcare, education and pensions. At local government level, a range of services, including street lighting, the fire service, and refuse and recycling collection, must be provided for all residents. In addition to these, councils also provide libraries, parks and leisure centres.

The nature of the services being provided by public sector organisations means that their objectives are different from those of businesses in the private sector. The National Health Service is clearly not a 'business' in the usual sense of the word and is not expected to make a profit. The priority of most of the public sector is to provide a value-for-money service.

However, there are likely to be certain similarities between an organisation in the private sector and one in the public sector: NHS managers may not have 'customers' in the sense that a business in the private sector has, but they are still expected to provide the highest quality of service possible. They are also expected to keep tight control on finances so as to eliminate wastage of scarce funds.

The fire service is financed by taxes paid to local government

Tips and techniques

Do not confuse the term 'public sector' with 'public company'. A public company is not the same as 'public enterprise'.

Third sector

A 'third sector organisation' (TSO) is one that is neither in the public sector nor private sector in the usual sense of the term. TSOs include charities, community groups, faith groups, self-help groups, social enterprises, and co-operatives. TSOs are motivated by the desire to achieve social goals (e.g. improving housing, the environment, helping people with social problems, or trying to reduce poverty) rather than the desire to maximise profit. A profit may be made (and indeed may be an important objective) but a key feature of a third sector business is that this profit is reinvested in order to improve the service being provided, rather than distributing it to shareholders.

TSOs can have a number of legal forms; a TSO is not a separate legal entity in itself. Some are just associations of people with shared values and objectives. Some operate as a company but with a not-for-personal-profit approach such as charities or co-operatives (see **Chapter 3**).

Tips and techniques

You could be asked to form a judgement on the most appropriate legal structure for a particular business, so it is essential that you understand the implications of each type. Remember also that an individual business is always referred to as 'it' not 'they'.

Further sources

www.companieshouse.gov.uk: All companies must be registered. They must also submit details about themselves such as The Report and Accounts every year. This is where these details are on open access to the public.

www.thirdsector.net: News and information about the third sector and the jobs available in it.

Your turn

Questions are suitable for all AS and A Level candidates.

Multiple-choice questions

1 Which of the following must have unlimited liability?
- A sole trader
- B private company
- C public company
- D business in the Third Sector. *(1)*

2 Which type of business does not have continuity?
- A private company
- B public company
- C sole trader
- D any business in the public sector. *(1)*

3 A public sector business:
- A has to publish an Annual Report and Accounts
- B is owned by central or local government
- C will have a large number of shareholders.
- D is likely to try to maximise profit levels. *(1)*

4 With regard to a company, which of the following is not true?
- A Shareholders have one vote per share.
- B Shareholders have to attend an annual general meeting.
- C The company is a separate legal entity from its owners.
- D Company accounts are on open access to the public. *(1)*

Revision questions

1A Identify the three sectors of economic activity. *(3)*

1B State an example of business activity in each sector. *(3)*

2 Explain the difference between the private sector and the public sector. *(4)*

3 Explain the difference between 'unlimited liability' and 'limited liability'. *(4)*

4A State two advantages of operating a business as a sole trader. *(2)*

4B State two disadvantages of operating a business as a sole trader. *(2)*

5A State two advantages of operating a business as a partnership. *(2)*

5B State two disadvantages of operating a business as a partnership. *(2)*

Total *(22)*

Case study

Pfizer and AstraZeneca

Until April 2014 you might have been forgiven for thinking that AstraZeneca (AZ) was a fading rock star from the 1970s. In fact, AstraZeneca is one of the UK's largest plc's; a multinational pharmaceutical company employing almost 7000 people. It has sites all over the country including ones for research and development, manufacturing and supply, sales and marketing, an environmental research facility and the head office in London. The company's website states 'Our focus is on developing new medicines to make a meaningful difference to patients' lives - and the UK is right at the heart of our efforts to do that.'

In April 2014 AZ was the subject of a takeover bid from Pfizer. If AZ is big, the American-based Pfizer is colossal. Why was this a major news item for weeks? After all, takeovers happen all the time. The issues focused on the motives of Pfizer and the likely consequences, not just for AZ, and its stakeholders but for the UK as a whole.

In the end, the takeover did not take place but if it had it would have been the largest in UK history; being worth around £69 billion. Shareholders would certainly have seen a premium on the value of their shares. Before Pfizer made its move, the company's share price was £37 a share. Pfizer indicated it would pay as much as £55.

The directors of AZ each owned around 300,000 shares and would have stood to share a figure in the region of £60 million. Pfizer made several bids for the shares, upping the amount several times. Why? There was some logic to the argument in favour of a takeover; Pfizer produces drugs to treat cancer and so do AZ – who have conducted a good deal of research and development in this area. There are also arguments in terms of cost advantages arising from economies of scale.

Others, at the time, were much less charitable and have said it was all about tax reduction. The likelihood was said to be that after the takeover a new company would be created in the UK, meaning the company's non-US profits would not be subject to US taxes – which are higher than those in the UK.

If the commercial logic was debatable, the consequences for AZ's operations and its employees could be questioned. There was concern that instead of 'sharing knowledge' the fact that there would be duplications of some company functions would mean closures and redundancies. The Chief Executive of Pfizer himself admitted this. AZ's trade unions were especially unhappy about the proposal, claiming that Pfizer has a history of takeovers and closures. These closures would have been significant, and not just for employees, because AZ is a leading company in its field with a worldwide reputation for developing and selling innovative pharmaceutical products especially those that treat cancer. AZ's Chief Executive went so far as to express concern that lives may be at risk if research into certain treatments are delayed or abandoned because of cost-cutting caused by Pfizer.

AZ's operations and investments create linkages with other UK firms in this fast-moving market. If the plants and research facilities are shut down, the UK as a whole loses out in one of the areas it has a competitive advantage. AZ's exports account for 2.3 per cent of the UKs total exports.

The takeover was eventually abandoned when AstraZeneca rejected Pfizer's £69 billion takeover approach, saying the bid undervalued the company and posed too many risks. AZ's shares tumbled 13 per cent to £42.04 on the news, wiping about £8 billion off the company's market value. However, perhaps the Pfizer takeover attempt has been a belated wake-up call. It fuelled wider debate about the whole nature of the ownership of public companies and how short term their focus often is – on profit.

1 AZ is a public limited company. Outline two differences between a private limited company and a public limited company. *(4)*

2 AZ was subject to a takeover bid. Outline the difference between a takeover and a merger. *(4)*

3 Other than the possibility of a takeover, analyse one disadvantage to AZ of operating as a public limited company. *(4)*

4A When the bid was abandoned, AstraZeneca's shares tumbled 13 per cent to £42.04. Calculate the figure for Astra Zeneca's share price before the 13 per cent fall. *(3)*

4B Analyse how the 'tumble in the share price' might affect one of its stakeholders. *(4)*

5 To what extent could the stakeholders of AZ have benefited from the takeover by Pfizer? Justify your view. *(15)*

Total *(34)*

Chapter 3

Franchises and co-operatives

Year 2

A Level students must know all of the content in this chapter.

This chapter is not applicable for AS students.

Franchises

A franchise is where a business with a well-known brand name (the franchiser) lets a person (the franchisee) or a group of people set up their own business using that brand. This is in exchange for an initial fee and continuing royalty payments (a certain percentage of turnover or profit) for as long as the franchise lasts.

A franchise is not a type of legal structure in itself. The liability for the person (or people) using the franchise depends on how the business is established. A franchisee can choose which legal structure to adopt, although the franchiser may recommend a particular type. Franchisees have unlimited liability if they are in business as a sole trader or a partnership, but have limited liability if they have set up the franchise as a company (see **Chapter 2**).

Franchisers can now be found in most sectors of the economy and quite a few of the best-known brand names operate some, or all, of their businesses as a franchise. McDonald's and Burger King are well-known examples of franchises in the fast-food market, as is the Body Shop in the cosmetics market.

Key term

Franchise: a business with a well-known brand name (the franchiser) lets a person (the franchisee) or a group of people set up their own business using that brand.

Advantages for the franchiser

- The firm does not have to spend large amounts of money (possibly getting into debt) in order to expand.
- The products necessary for the franchise to operate are under the franchiser's direct control. This can mean that franchisees are charged high prices for supplies.

Many of the UK's well-known businesses are franchises

- Applicants are carefully selected for their suitability to become franchisees. Issuing franchises should therefore generate a continuous stream of revenue from franchisees who are determined to make their business succeed.

Disadvantages for the franchiser

- Control issues. The control the franchiser has over the product is not as great as it would be if the business sold the product itself. Time has to be spent ensuring than franchisees are following procedures properly. Bad publicity from 'a rogue franchisee' could affect the brand image.
- The cost of supporting franchisees. One of the selling points of a franchise is that ongoing support, training, market research and product development are available to a franchisee. There are considerable costs to be incurred if these are to be provided. The support network has to grow as the franchise grows.
- The possibility of conflict. If there is a disagreement between franchiser and franchisee it may get quite acrimonious. If a product fails to sell, a franchisee may blame the franchiser and may claim that inadequate marketing support or product training

was given. This could lead to court action. There is also the chance that if a franchise closes down and the franchiser is seen as the problem, the franchisee may decide to disclose confidential information to others as a means of 'getting even'.

Should a business franchise its brand?

Whether a business feels that it is worth franchising its brand depends on its managers' attitude to such factors. There is also the initial cost of setting up the whole network and the risk that it may initially fail if the wrong locations and/or franchisees are chosen. A long-term view may need to be taken; franchising a brand is not a 'get rich quick' scheme. This means that the business's stakeholders are unlikely to see huge benefits immediately – and if the franchises perform poorly, for whatever reason, they may suffer as well. The loss of control issue may be a particularly important one for senior managers who may prefer to keep business decisions highly centralised.

Whether a franchise is an appropriate choice for someone wanting to start their own business depends on factors such as how much time and money they are prepared to invest in the business, the desired rewards, and their attitude to risk.

Advantages for the franchisee

- The franchisee is using a tried-and-tested brand name, so there is a greater chance of success than if they had gone into the same sort of business with their own brand.
- Specialist advice and training are available from the franchiser on an ongoing basis.
- The franchiser carries out market research and provides marketing support. Thus franchisees can spend more time actually selling products and making a profit for themselves.
- It may be easier to obtain a loan from a bank because of the factors mentioned above.

Disadvantages for the franchisee

- Supplies have to be bought from the franchiser, which may charge higher prices than those for similar products on the open market. This will lower profit margins.
- There will be continuing royalty payments (a certain percentage of turnover or profit) to the franchiser.
- The franchisee has less control over what it is selling, and how it sells it, than a person running their own business would usually have.
- The business cannot be sold without the franchiser's permission.
- A franchise is for a fixed period of time and is not automatically renewed.

Co-operatives

The Co-operative movement

The term 'stakeholder' might be a relatively modern one, but the concept of stakeholding is not. One business that has been applying it for over 150 years is the Co-operative movement. This began in Rochdale in 1844 when a group of workers who were fed up with poor-quality products and high prices set up their own grocery business. It was to be a 'co-operative business'; that is, one that existed for the benefit of its users rather than some distant and uncaring owner. The co-operative idea was a great success and The Co-operative Group ('The Co-op') went on to employ over 60,000 people and now operates in many different business areas, including retailing, wholesaling, travel, funerals, insurance and banking. Strict ethical principles upholding the 'stakeholder approach' have been applied in every area of operation. It has around six million members who receive a share of the profits that they help to create, based on how much they spend with any of its businesses in a particular year.

The group's website makes its approach clear under the heading 'Championing a new way of doing business for you and your communities':

> *Better way of doing business – we need to be commercially successful, building a sustainable way of doing business that is mutually beneficial, recycling our success into strengthening communities. Continuing our ongoing commitment to ethical values and sourcing*
>
> *For You – immediate and tangible benefits for our members and customers who are not yet members. Functional benefits – better prices; great quality; right location; excellent customer service; emotional benefit – feels good and feels right*
>
> *Your Communities – enabling and strengthening communities, being locally relevant and reinforcing reasons why members and customers should be loyal to us*

Source: http://www.co-operative.coop/corporate/aboutus/ourvisionandaims/

In theory, all stakeholders should get a better deal with this business model because the concern of those running it is not narrowly focused purely (or mostly) on the organisation's shareholders. Stakeholder conflict is not eliminated but hopefully it is minimised; all of those involved can benefit.

In 2013, however, it became clear that 'The Co-op' was in serious trouble. The Co-operative Bank, once upheld as an outstanding example of the stakeholder approach to operating a business had run into trouble following its merger with the Britannia Building Society. It had to be bailed out by hedge fund companies (companies whose aim is solely to make a short-term profit and who do not focus on ethical standards). This was a humiliation given the ethical heritage of the organisation. Worse was to come when its former chairman, the Reverend Paul Flowers, was charged with possession of illegal class A drugs.

Key term

Co-operative: a business that is owned and run by its members (employees and customers). Profits are shared between members rather than being distributed to shareholders.

Tips and techniques

Remember that co-operatives can take many different forms. Do not assume that any 'co-operative business' is the same organisation as 'The Co-op'.

The problems with the Co-operative bank in 2013 caused a major crisis for the whole Co-operative Group

However, it was not only the banking arm of the Co-operative Group that was in difficulty. A report in 2014 by Lord Myners, a former Co-op Board member said that the whole board was 'dysfunctional' and should be more concerned with making a profit. This led to outrage among some members who were implacably opposed to running The Co-op as if it were just another plc. Questions were raised about whether those running The Co-op had the necessary ideals, qualifications, experience, and skills. A debate began about the extent to which a business in the modern world can actually truly be ethical if it is to succeed. It was eventually agreed that there would be a new board governing The Co-operative Group, with executives being drawn from professional backgrounds. In the light of this, it is clear that the future running of The Co-operative Group will be very different to its past.

It should be recognised that not all references to 'co-operatives' refer to parts of The Co-operative Group. Co-operatives are very diverse; they can range from retail business, to credit unions, and housing co-operatives. They can be set up in different ways, using different legal structures. As is the case with a franchise, a co-operative is, in itself, not a separate legal structure. Whatever its legal form there are certain key elements to any co-operative business:

- It is owned by its members; the people who use it.
- It is run by its members who elect those managing the business and so help shape the decisions their co-operative makes.
- Profits are shared among members; this is important; a co-operative is not a charity, it is a business.

Advantages of a co-operative

- Establishing a co-operative is legally straightforward; the legal documentation is straightforward and inexpensive.
- All involved are working towards a common goal; employees can be expected to be motivated and therefore productive. Customers are usually loyal and supportive.
- Liability for members is usually limited.
- A high quality of service should be provided, since customers are likely to be members and also because profits made (from customers) are shared.
- The stakeholders in a co-operative should benefit because of the approach it adopts. However, there are also disadvantages.

Disadvantages of a co-operative

- Capital can be limited. Initially it is limited to what is contributed by members. Banks may be reluctant to lend as a co-operative might be regarded as 'not a normal type of business'. In any event, potential investors may be put off by the possibility of a limited return.

- Weak management. Those elected to manage may be well intentioned but ineffective because they do not have sufficient grasp of business principles. If this occurs it will mean lower benefits for members and other stakeholders.
- Employees may want more as they begin to feel that instead of profits being reinvested to further the co-operative's aim, they deserve more themselves.
- Slower decision making, since there is greater involvement by members.
- Co-operatives operate successfully all around the world, but there is no guarantee that operating a business in this way is necessarily going to generate more benefits for its stakeholders than an 'ordinary' business would.

Further sources

www.franchisedirect.co.uk: franchise opportunities available in the UK.

www.mcdonalds.co.uk/ukhome/Aboutus/Franchising.html: information about running a franchise from one of the world's leading franchisers.

www.co-operative.co.uk: homepage of the Co-operative Group. It contains information about the history and nature of the Co-operative movement and its stance on business practices and consumer issues.

www.uk.coop: information about the co-operative approach to running a business.

www.employeeownership.co.uk: The Employee Ownership Association. The voice of business in the UK with a significant amount of employee ownership.

Your turn

Revision questions

1A Explain what is meant by the term 'franchise'. *(2)*

1B Explain what is meant by the term 'franchisee'. *(2)*

2 Identify two likely costs a franchisee has to pay to the franchise. *(2)*

3 Explain what is meant by 'A franchise is not a separate type of legal structure'. *(2)*

4 State the three characteristics of a co-operative business. *(3)*

5A Analyse two advantages of running a business as a co-operative. *(4)*

5B Analyse two disadvantages of running a business as a co-operative. *(4)*

Total *(19)*

Case study

Co-operatives and franchises in the high street

Any shopper walking through a typical town centre might easily come across examples of both co-operatives and franchises. John Lewis, which operates John Lewis department stores, Waitrose supermarkets and a number of other services, is a common sight in a high street. Officially the business is 'John Lewis plc', but it is actually owned and managed by its staff who are called 'partners'. With thousands of staff, it is clearly not 'a partnership' in the legal sense of the term and, in fact, it is not a plc in the usual sense either. It is employee owned; a co-operative.

Its founder was John Spedan Lewis, an entrepreneur in the 1920s who wanted to create an organisation that (to quote from the business's website) 'would be both commercial allowing us to move quickly to stay ahead in a competitive industry, and democratic giving every Partner a voice in the business they co-own'.

The business was indeed once a company, but in 1949, Lewis signed a Trust Settlement, transferring his shares and making the whole business the property of the people employed by it. He made the trust settlement 'irrevocable', that is, permanent. Thus, although it is technically still a company, no one can actually buy shares in it. This is highly unusual.

The internal running of John Lewis is democratic; every employee has the opportunity to influence the business through local branch meetings. At the top of the business is the Partnership Council. The partners elect most of the representatives on this committee, while the chairman appoints the remaining ones. The councils have the power to discuss 'any matter whatsoever'.

The partnership believes in ethical standards of trading and there is a code relating to supplier expectations on issues such as pay, working hours, child labour, and employee rights.

Profits are reinvested into the business for modernisation and expansion and also into the business's pension scheme. Employees are expected to be smartly dressed, polite and very attentive to customer needs. High-pressure selling is forbidden. In return, employees get a variety of benefits and a bonus based on the business's profits every year. In 2014, even though the group saw its annual pre-tax profits fall by 4 per cent, to £329.1 million, it paid all staff a bonus of 15 per cent – the equivalent of around eight weeks' salary.

A rather different situation exists at McDonald's, another well-recognised retailer in the high street. McDonald's is known as a premier franchising company around the world and, in fact, more than 80 per cent of its restaurants worldwide are owned and operated by franchisees. Franchising has become very popular in recent years and a survey by NatWest and the British Franchise Association in 2013 found that:

- The annual turnover of UK franchises in 2013 was £13.7 billion.
- Franchise revenues have grown 20 per cent since 2008 (whereas the overall UK economy had contracted 2.5 per cent in the same time period).
- There are 930 franchisers in the UK.
- There are 39,000 franchise outlets.
- The number of franchisees reporting profitability (including new businesses) was 92 per cent.

How much does a McDonald's franchise cost? The cost of a restaurant ranges from £125,000 to £325,000. There is also a one-off franchise fee of £30,000 and a training deposit of £5,000 (which is refunded once training is complete) and on-going fees such as the fee for using the McDonald's brand and their system of retailing. There is also a contribution to the national marketing spend.

In return for this, the franchisee gets to use a globally known brand name and an established business model. On the issue of 'how much will I make?' the McDonald's website states 'Cashflow (before debt repayment) typically ranges from £95,000 to £200,000 per year for each restaurant but this isn't guaranteed: it could be more, it could be less.'

McDonald's are looking for people with a specific skill set to operate their franchises; strong leadership qualities, high personal integrity, and the personality to be an excellent ambassador for the brand are prerequisites – along with business experience. In addition, franchisees are encouraged to support the community in which they operate.

Source: www.thebfa.org/about-franchising/franchising-industry-research

http://www.johnlewispartnership.co.uk/about.html

1 Explain how two stakeholders in the John Lewis Partnership may benefit from its co-operative approach. *(4)*
2 Analyse one reason why it may not be possible for a business to operate using the co-operative principles of the John Lewis Partnership. *(4)*
3 Calculate the average turnover of a UK franchise. *(3)*
4 Calculate the minimum amount of capital a franchisee would need in order to purchase a McDonald's franchise. *(4)*
5 Evaluate why someone starting their own business might decide to operate a McDonald's franchise. *(9)*
6 Evaluate why McDonald's has chosen to franchise some of its operations. *(15)*

Total *(39)*

Chapter 4

Business size, growth and external growth

AS / Year 1 | Year 2

A Level students must know all of the content in this chapter.

AS students must know:

- Business size and growth

But they are not required to cover:

- External growth (pages 23–25)

Business size and growth

It is common to read statements such as 'the economy is dominated by large businesses' or 'small and medium-sized businesses are the future of the British economy'. In order to help evaluate whether these sorts of statements are correct, it is important to understand the criteria by which a business's size can be measured.

A number of factors need to be taken into account when making a judgement about the size of a business.

Number of employees

Normally it would be expected that a 'large' business will employ a large number of employees. However, it may not be appropriate to judge the size of a business purely on the number of employees. Many factories are highly automated and capital-intensive; they produce a lot of output, but do not employ a large number of people.

In the UK, a business with fewer than 50 employees is regarded as small, and a business with more than 250 employees is large.

A 'large' business usually has a large number of employees

Number of factories, shops or offices

The higher the number of factories, shops or offices a business has, the more it will be perceived as 'large'. A similar criterion is whether the business has factories, shops or offices in other countries – and, if so, how many.

Turnover and profit levels

Turnover is the value of a business's sales. A high turnover is usually associated with a large business. However, a jeweller may only own one shop but still have a high turnover because of the high value of the (relatively few) products sold. Similarly, the higher the profit level, the larger the firm is likely to be. However, a large firm may temporarily be having trading difficulties and therefore making a lower than usual turnover and profit, so this measure may not be completely accurate as a measure of size.

Tips and techniques

It is important to note that there is not necessarily a direct correlation between the size of a business and the level of profit made

Stock market value is one way of measuring the size of a public company

Stock market value

The value of a public company can be calculated by multiplying the current share price by the number of shares issued. The higher the figure, the larger the company is likely to be. There is, however, a significant drawback with this method; if the share price falls, it reduces the value of the company. This means that on this measurement of size the business has suddenly become smaller – even though a change in share price has no immediate impact on the number of factories, machines or employees. Throughout 2013 and most of 2014 Tesco's share price steadily fell as it struggled to cope with the competition from businesses such as Aldi and Lidl, but this did not change the size of the company. Since share prices can change daily, this method of estimating a business's size could be misleading.

Capital employed

Capital employed is the total value of a business's assets – its factories, machinery, offices, and so on. If the figure is high, it is reasonable to assume that the business is large. However, as with stock market valuation, prices, and therefore values, of factories and office blocks can rise or fall without any changes in the actual number owned. In addition, the geographical location of assets also affects their value. A factory unit in north London will be more valuable than a business of exactly the same type, in exactly the same sort of unit, in (say) South Wales. On this measure, the London business would be 'larger'.

Tips and techniques

Measures of size may seem obvious but be aware of the limitations of each measure.

EU definitions of business size

In the EU there is, in fact, a standardised way of determining the size of a business. The EU's chosen factors for this are the number of employees it has and either turnover, or the balance sheet total. As defined by the EU (EU recommendation 2003/361) the definitions for small and medium-sized enterprises (SMEs) are as shown in Table 4.1.

Table 4.1 EU definitions of business size

Company category	Employees	Turnover (€ m)	Balance sheet total (€ m)
Medium-sized	< 250	≤ 50	≤ 43
Small	< 50	≤ 10	≤ 10
Micro	< 10	≤ 2	≤ 2

These EU definitions are important since one of the objectives of the EU's regulation of businesses is that they are all 'operating on a level playing field': any financial support to small and medium-sized enterprises in member countries has to be given according to the same criteria. If 'small businesses' in EU countries are going to be allowed to be supported with (for example) grants from their national government or from the EU itself then there has to be a common definition of what 'a small business' actually is. Large companies (those with more than 250 people; turnover greater than €50 million; or a balance sheet greater than €43 million) usually have limited scope for any state or EU assistance.

Key term

Business size: the EU has a standardised way of measuring size based on the number of employees, and turnover or balance sheet value.

Factors affecting the size of a business

Market size

Where the market is small it is often dominated by relatively small businesses. This is because larger firms do not think they can gain the economies of scale and/or the level of sales to gain the desired level of profit. Consideration also needs to be given as to whether the market is expanding, static, or contracting.

Nature of the product

If a product is large and technologically complicated the firm will usually be larger because of the resources necessary to make, and upgrade, it. Where the product is highly standardised it is usually made by a large business since it can gain economies of scale from manufacturing it. A less standard product made, and marketed, with 'a personal touch' will often be supplied by a smaller business.

Personal preference

An entrepreneur may not want to expand nationally (or even regionally). He or she may not be particularly ambitious and may prefer to be 'a big fish in a small pond' than 'a small fish in a big pond'. Opening a new factory or office could mean a loss of control over the business, which the entrepreneur may not want. There may also be the consideration of whether the time and trouble that will need to be devoted to any expansion is 'worth it' in terms of risks (see **Chapter 9**) and personal sacrifices that may have to be made in terms of family life.

Ability to access resources for expansion

Are funds available? For example, the 'credit crunch' (the banks' reluctance to lend in the years following the 2008 crash) prevented many small and medium-sized firms from expanding.

External growth: the growth of a business

A business might want to grow for a number of reasons. These include:

- The entrepreneur wants a greater challenge.
- The owners want a higher return on their investment.
- Growth, through diversification into new markets, can help spread risk.
- A bigger, stronger business is better placed to fight any economic or competitive threats successfully.
- The opportunity to gain unit cost reductions through economies of scale.

The effect of a business's size on its stakeholders

There can be a tendency to assume that a large business is always better for its stakeholders than a small one because it is bigger and stronger. This is not necessarily the case; each business needs to be considered individually when examining the impact of its size on its stakeholders, but Table 4.2 indicates some of the possible stakeholder issues in a large business.

Table 4.2 Possible advantages and disadvantages for stakeholder in a large business

Stakeholder	Advantages	Disadvantages
Employees	Greater job security A large firm will have a specialist human resources department which will ensure compliance with legislation The business may recognise the trade union or have some other method of employee participation in order to improve communication and productivity	Feeling remote from those who make the decisions that affect them. Issue of poor morale and motivation that may affect productivity There may be problems of effective co-ordination and control that negatively impact upon the business's operation and profitability
Suppliers	Regular orders Large orders Security	May be offered a 'take it or leave it approach' to conditions of supply and payment Overdependence on a large customer can cause problems if the large firm decides to change supplier
Local community	Creation of jobs Local 'multiplier effect' (see **Chapter 19**) boosts economic activity Community initiatives from the large firm	Possible negative externalities such as pollution and/or congestion around the business A large business may drive the existing local firms out of the market, thus reducing choice and variety
Shareholders	The large firm may have some market power and so may have a degree of control over prices – leading to higher profits, dividends, and share prices Large firms can gain managerial economies of scale to improve performance	If managers make the wrong decisions they can have a significant effect on the business profits and therefore share price and dividends Large businesses can be organisationally inflexible. It can be hard to 'turn around' a large business that is failing. It may be some time before dividends rise (to acceptable levels) again
Customers	The business can 'seek out'/develop new products Economies of scale lower costs and therefore prices The business can be expected to treat customers well in order to maintain its image	Diseconomies of scale may raise costs, which will be passed on in the form of higher prices Customers might be swayed into buying products they don't want through contact exposure to marketing If point of contact with the firm is a call centre the business can appear remote and the consumer can feel powerless and neglected if there is a problem

Organic growth

Organic growth is that which is achieved by increasing the firm's sales. This comes from selling more to existing customers, finding new customers, or both. If a business constantly achieves high levels of organic growth this indicates that its managers are taking the right actions in terms of (say) marketing and are using the business's resources efficiently.

Mergers and acquisitions

Growth that comes from a merger or an acquisition is different to organic growth. A merger is where two companies join together to form a new larger business. A takeover involves acquiring control of another company by buying its shares. If the takeover is successful the target company will usually continue to exist as an independent legal entity controlled by the acquirer. A takeover might go smoothly because the shareholders of both companies consider it to be beneficial. On the other hand, it may be resisted and so be regarded as 'hostile'. In 2014, the American pharmaceutical giant Pfizer made a takeover bid for the UK company AstraZeneca, which did not succeed, but was the largest ever attempted takeover in UK corporate history – £69 billion (see **Chapter 2**).

Joint ventures

A joint venture is a formal business arrangement between two (or more) businesses who commit to work together on a particular project. Both parties invest money, time, and effort in the project. A joint venture is different from a merger because there is no change of ownership involved for either firm. A joint venture may only be in existence for a particular project, or it could be ongoing. A joint venture will often result in the creation of a new business to implement the venture.

The two companies forming the joint venture do not have to be in the same country. Virgin Mobile India is a joint venture between Tata Teleservices and the Virgin Group. Before the venture Tata did not have a developed mobile phone brand image and Virgin did not own any telecommunications infrastructure in India. The result was the joint venture. Virgin uses Tata's networks to offer its services under the brand name 'Virgin Mobile' and in turn it provides Tata Teleservices with experience and expertise in designing, marketing and servicing of mobile phone products.

In 2014 the UK-Dutch oil company Shell announced a joint oil exploration venture with Russia's state-owned oil business Gazprom. Both companies had already been co-operating on shale oil exploration and drilling since 2013.

Why undertake a joint venture?

- The capital cost of a particular project might be very high and may well be beyond the resources of a single business. Thus a joint venture allows both parties to share the cost burden.
- A single business may consider the venture too much of a risk. The construction of the channel tunnel was a joint venture for this reason.
- It also enables businesses to share strengths, and increase their competitive advantage against others.
- A joint venture can be an effective way of gaining access to markets or resources in another country.

However, a joint venture will mean drawing up a contract that specifies responsibilities and goals. This may be expensive due to the legal costs but will be crucial for avoiding disagreement in the future.

Strategic alliance

A strategic alliance is similar to a joint venture. In this context, 'alliance' means 'co-operation' rather than the sort of partnership that usually comes with a joint venture. It is typically less involved and less permanent than a joint venture, although the aim is similar – each party hopes that the benefits from the alliance will be greater than those that could be obtained from operating on its own. With a strategic alliance there will not be the creation of a new company and each party will clearly maintain its own identity.

The co-operation between the companies could come from the sharing of (say) technology, information, or risks. Apple, for example, partnered with Clearwell in order to jointly develop Clearwell's E-Discovery platform for the Apple iPad.

The concept of the strategic alliance is clearly demonstrated by the behaviour of many of the major airlines in what is known as 'a codeshare flight' (the code refers to the ticket's code), where a flight is operated by one airline, but is marketed and sold by others as well. It began in 1990 when American Airlines formed an alliance with the Australian-based Qantas. The two airlines reached an agreement that merged many of their flights. The alliance allowed American Airlines to sell tickets on some Qantas flights, and in turn for Qantas to sell tickets on some

American Airlines flights. This meant that each airline could book passengers to fly to more destinations without actually incurring the cost of expanding their service. Most major airlines now have alliances in the form of code-sharing agreements with other airlines.

The strategic alliance need not necessarily be for profit. The Global Alliance for Vaccines and Immunization is a public sector–private sector global health partnership which brings together donors, developing country governments, and national healthcare delivery systems to try to eradicate disease.

Are joint ventures and strategic alliances beneficial for a business's stakeholders?

Whether these types of growth impact in a positive manner on the business's stakeholders will depend on several factors:

- The venture/alliance could fail and the expected stakeholder benefits fail to materialise, for the same reasons that any business can fail; e.g. shrinking markets, inability to keep up with changes in customer needs, or poor economic conditions.
- The relative strengths of the parties when the contract or agreement is drawn up. If one party is more powerful than the other it could demand conditions, such as the division of profits, which are more advantageous to itself and its stakeholders than to the other firm.
- The terms of the agreement and the wording of any contract need to be clear; the parties must be very specific about their rights and duties. If the contract is vague or ambiguous it will be a recipe for trouble (and possibly legal action), therefore the expected benefits for the stakeholders will not appear.
- Much depends on the integrity of those working together and how problems that arise during the venture or alliance are resolved; are parties honest and helpful with each other, or is there simply an attempt to shift the blame? As with any agreement to undertake a project, if one party fails to honour the terms of it, it will fail to the detriment of all.
- Even if both parties are 'evenly matched' and work together in good faith, whether all stakeholders benefit from the venture or alliance depends on whether the business adopts 'the stakeholder model', which sees stakeholders as broadly equal, or sees one particular stakeholder (typically the shareholders) as the group that should benefit the most from it. If the joint venture or alliance results in worse conditions and terms for (say) employees and suppliers then clearly these stakeholders will not benefit from it. This is a particularly important consideration if the joint venture or alliance is taking place in a country in the developing world.

Further sources

www.ec.europa.eu/enterprise/policies/sme/facts-figures: The European Commission. Definitions of business size, EU policy towards small and medium-sized businesses and the types of legislation that impact on them.

Your turn

Questions in red are for A Level candidates only.

Multiple-choice questions

1 Which of the following is not one of the EU's criteria for measuring a business's size?
- A number of customers
- B number of employees
- C the balance sheet value
- D value of turnover. *(1)*

2 A firm is most likely to be 'large' if:
- A It produces a highly personalised product
- B It is hard for the firm to access capital via loans
- C It is experiencing diseconomies of scale
- D The entrepreneur is successful. *(1)*

3 Which of the following is a likely characteristic of a joint venture but not a strategic alliance?
- A There are diseconomies of scale
- B A new company is formed
- C The partnership ensures growth for both businesses due to customer loyalty
- D The businesses involved are large. *(1)*

4 A joint venture is most likely to be a success if:
- A Both businesses are large
- B The duties of each partner in the venture are clearly established
- C There are a large number of customers in the market
- D Sufficient capital is available. *(1)*

Revision questions

1A Identify two different methods of measuring a business's size. *(2)*

1B State one advantage and one disadvantage of each method identified. *(4)*

2 Explain how the size of the following businesses might be judged:
- A a supermarket chain *(2)*
- B a car manufacturer *(2)*
- C an online retailer *(2)*

3 Evaluate which, if any, of the businesses in the table below would, according to the EU criteria, change their size if the predicted percentage increases in employees, turnover, and capital employed actually occurred. *(3 × 6)*

4 Outline two reasons why small businesses continue to thrive in an economy dominated by large firms. *(4)*

Total *(34)*

	Number of employees	Predicted rise over next year (%)	Turnover (€ m)	Predicted rise over next year (%)	Capital employed (balance sheet total) (€ m)	Predicted rise over next year (%)
ABC Ltd	238	9	€42 m	11	€41m	3
LMN Ltd	41	18	€9 m	7	€9m	10
XXZ Ltd	9	35	€1.5m	50	€1.9m	20

Chapter 5

Stakeholders

AS / Year 1

Both AS and A Level students must know all of the content in this chapter.

Business activity creates jobs, prosperity and wealth. Who benefits from this? One way of considering this question is to look at the concept of stakeholders. A stakeholder is a person, or party, with an interest (i.e. 'a stake') in the success of a business. Stakeholders want to see a business succeed because they will benefit from this success.

Key term

Stakeholder: a person or party with an interest in the success of a business.

Stakeholders can be classified as internal or external. Internal stakeholders are found within the business and are the owners and employees, including managers. External stakeholders are suppliers, lenders, customers and the local community (see Figure 5.1).

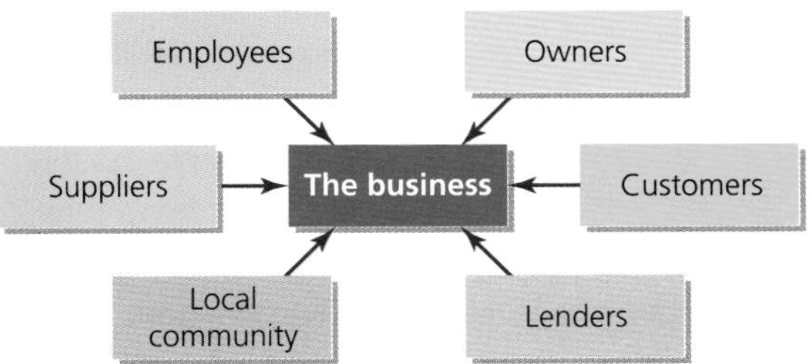

Figure 5.1 The stakeholders in a business

The concept of stakeholding can be used to create a useful framework to help analyse the operation of a business, the setting of a business's objectives and also the strategy it develops to reach them.

The business–stakeholder relationship is extremely important because the relationship is 'two way'; the business affects the stakeholders, and the stakeholders affect the business. The sorts of issues involved are:

- which stakeholders are the most important and/or powerful?
- how the objectives of the different stakeholder groups could affect the strategic decisions of the business
- how the different stakeholder groups' view may change
- the extent to which the stakeholders regard the business as a success.

Tips and techniques

It is important that you understand the relationship and the interaction between a business and its stakeholders. You need to be able to identify what each stakeholder wants from the business, and also evaluate the influence which each stakeholder can bring to bear on the business's strategic decision-making.

Stakeholder objectives

In theory, all stakeholders will benefit from a business's success, but in reality they may not. Furthermore, even if all stakeholders do benefit, they may not do so equally. It is very important to recognise the potential conflicts between the objectives of the different stakeholder groups. In order to analyse why, it is necessary to consider the objectives of each stakeholder in the business.

Owners

A business may have a single owner if it is a sole trader, several if it is a partnership, or thousands of shareholders if it is a public limited company (see **Chapter 2**). The owner(s) will want the best possible return on the money they have invested in the business. They are also likely to want to see the business grow so that these returns increase.

The owners' pursuit of profit seems obvious, but this does not necessarily mean that they want 'immediate maximum profit'. Although a high rate of return is certainly likely to be a long-run objective, in the short run a business may pursue the objective of growth via low prices. This will hopefully mean that it captures more of the market and that customers will stay loyal in the long term if the business increases prices. In the immediate future, however, this tactic may reduce profits. This will have implications for the other stakeholders.

Employees

As their livelihood depends on the business, it is not surprising that employees want the highest wage they can get, a bonus if possible and job security. Employees are also likely to want the business to offer more than the legal entitlement to holidays, sick pay, and so on.

Most employees would like managers to organise their work so that it is interesting, challenging and provides some job satisfaction. In addition, many will want to attend training courses to improve their skills and therefore their pay and promotion prospects.

Customers

Customers want the best-quality product(s) at the lowest possible price. They also want product innovation – each year's products should be better than the last. Other requirements are good customer service, such as helpful and polite staff or an easily accessible call centre with well-trained customer service representatives to answer any queries. They may want credit facilities if the product is expensive, such as furniture or carpets. As well as these factors, customers are increasingly aware of ethical issues and ask questions such as 'Were the products obtained from sustainable sources?' and 'Did any animals suffer in the making of the product?'

If consumers are fundamentally dissatisfied with quality, price, service or ethical behaviour, they will eventually stop buying from the business. If sufficient numbers of people do this, it can have a significant effect. Consumers may form pressure groups that try to influence the business by generating bad publicity.

Suppliers

If a business ceases trading, its suppliers lose a source of income. Therefore, a supplier would like to see its customers prosper so that it has a regular profit; it would like repeat orders rather than 'one-offs'. Furthermore, it hopes its customers will grow larger so that, in turn, it can increase its own sales to them. A supplier would also like to be paid as promptly as possible.

There is a difference between a supplier as 'a supplier' and a supplier as 'a stakeholder'. In the latter case, a business will try to build up a long-term relationship with its suppliers. This means using them regularly, paying them on time, and involving them in any plans for expansion. Suppliers who are treated as stakeholders are more likely to be loyal and committed because they have 'a stake' in the business in the true sense of the word.

A business that changes suppliers continually and tries to delay payment whenever possible may well be able to lower costs in the short term. However, a business should not be surprised when, if it needs supplies of a particular kind at short notice, the firms that it has treated as suppliers rather than stakeholders are not prepared to 'drop everything' in order to help out if they are already busy.

While it is sensible for any business to try to drive its costs down, this has to be balanced against the benefits of developing a long-term commitment with reliable suppliers who may be crucial to success in the future.

Lenders

Just like a supplier, a bank wants the agreed amount owed to it to be paid at the agreed time. These stakeholders do not want to receive less than expected or, alternatively, the correct amount but at a later date. The objective of a lender, such as a bank, is therefore to get its money back at the agreed time.

The community

Businesses are chiefly interested in what their costs of production will be and what profit they will receive from their sales. These are known as private costs and benefits. However, the community is also affected by business activity. This 'community' can be defined as the people living in the area around the business. While most people would welcome an increase in their quality of life, they may not all agree that business activity necessarily brings it about. On the one hand, businesses bring jobs and greater spending power. It may also cause property prices to rise and crime levels to fall. Furthermore, many businesses are actively involved in community projects such as sponsoring sports teams. As more businesses move into an area, the local authority may improve the roads, making it easier for residents to drive around. These positive factors are brought to the community by businesses and are known as external benefits.

Business activity can also create external costs. These are costs which are not paid by the business itself in the same way that labour and raw material costs are. These external costs are 'paid' by society. For example, if a business that produces chemical products locates in a particular area, there might be continual deliveries of raw materials. This will mean additional congestion and pollution on the roads, as well as noise pollution for nearby residents. There may also be a smell from the factory. Property prices may fall. None of these is a cost to the firm, but will be paid (i.e. imposed on) the community.

When making a judgement about the activities of a business the phrases 'social benefits' and 'social costs' are sometimes used. These terms are not quite the same as 'external benefits' and 'external costs'. Social benefits and social costs refer to the overall benefits and/or costs to society that are involved. They are calculated as follows:

Social benefits = private benefits (to the firm) + external benefits (to society)

Social costs = private costs (to the firm) + external costs (to society)

Suppose a recycling plant for household waste is built on some wasteland, what are the likely costs and benefits? The private benefits are going to be the profits created by the firm's operation and the external benefits will be the jobs created and the renovation of land and roads around land that was previously unused.

The private costs will be the construction cost to the business of the plant and the redevelopment of the area. The external costs could be the fall in house prices on any roads near the plant and any extra pollution and congestion created in the area.

The calculation of the full social benefits and social costs means allotting a monetary value to an external benefit or cost. Once this is done then a judgement can be properly made on whether 'benefits exceed costs' or not. This judgement would not be accurate if only the private costs and benefits were taken into account.

Key terms

Private costs and benefits: costs that a business pays (e.g. labour costs) and the benefits it gets from its activities (e.g. profit).

Social costs and benefits: the overall, or 'true cost' of a business's activities, taking into account external costs and benefits, as well as private ones.

Pollution caused by a business is a an external cost

The government

The government is not a direct stakeholder in the same way as the others, but nevertheless it has an interest in any business's success. This is because if more people are employed as a result of a business's activities, the government will pay out less social security benefits and receive increased tax revenue from the business and its employees.

Also, as a business grows larger, it may start to export (sell goods abroad). When this happens, it helps to improve the UK's trading position with other countries.

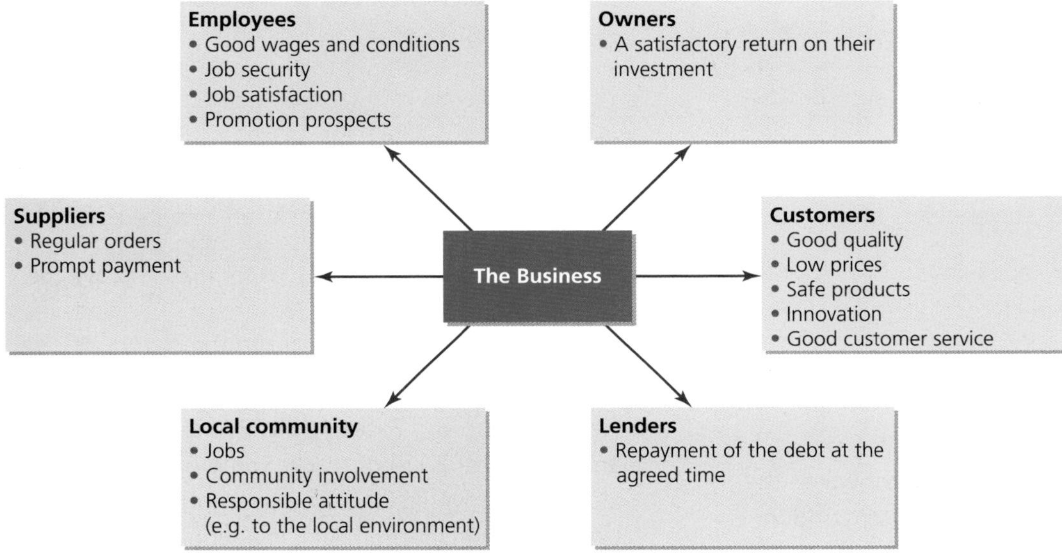

Figure 5.2 A summary of a business's stakeholders and their objectives

Tips and techniques

There is some debate as to whether a competitor is actually a stakeholder or not. It is true that a competitor has 'an interest' in a rival business, but it is unlikely that they have an interest in (i.e. want to see) that business succeeding. It would presumably rather see it fail and for its own business to succeed. You will not be penalised for adopting either point of view, as long as you make clear how you view 'a stakeholder'.

Further sources

http://www.companieshouse.gov.uk/: information about and the legal situation regarding companies in the UK.

www.gov.uk/company-and-partnership-law--2: information about the provisions of the Companies Act 2006.

Your turn

Questions are suitable for all AS and A Level candidates.

Multiple-choice questions

1 Which of the following is an example of an external cost?

- A Employees demand a pay rise because the rate of inflation has risen
- B A fall in the cost of raw materials sourced from abroad
- C A drop in house prices in a location near a business that produces smoke pollution
- D A new competitor emerges, causing market price to fall. *(1)*

2 Which of the following is an internal stakeholder in a business?

- A local community
- B managing director
- C suppliers
- D the government. *(1)*

3 A 'key stakeholder':

- A is the stakeholder group with the largest number of people in it
- B will always succeed in achieving its objectives
- C has influence over a business's decision making
- D is only a relevant concept in large businesses. *(1)*

4 Which of the following is not likely to be an example of a stakeholder conflict?

- A A rise in wages lowers profits
- B Community initiatives are reduced in order for funds to be spent on training
- C A reduction in dividends to fund employee bonuses
- D A supplier lowers costs and the business reduces prices. *(1)*

Revision questions

1 State what is meant by the term 'stakeholder'. *(1)*

2A Identify five likely stakeholders of a business. *(5)*

2B Identify two likely objectives of each stakeholder you have identified. *(10)*

3 Explain the difference between 'private costs and benefits' and 'social costs and benefits'. *(4)*

Total *(20)*

Case study

The London Underground

The London Underground (also known as the Tube) serves a large part of Greater London and parts of the counties of Buckinghamshire, Hertfordshire and Essex. It has 270 stations and around 402 km of track. Some of the track also runs above ground. The operator, London Underground Limited (LUL), is a wholly owned

subsidiary of Transport for London (TfL), which is the publically owned body responsible for most elements of London's transport network; it reports to the Mayor of London. Over a billion journeys a year are made on the Tube; passenger traffic was up from 1,089 m in 2008 to 1,229 m in 2013.

TfL's website states 'We are here to keep London working and growing, and to make life in the Capital better' and is funded in a variety of ways including central government grants, a proportion of London's business rates and income from fares and the Congestion Charge scheme.

Employer–employee relations at LUL have not always been positive. In 2014 there was a dispute concerning LUL's intention to close a number of ticket offices (replacing them by automated machines) and making 960 staff redundant. The RMT union announced its intention to call another strike lasting three days in May 2014, but after 'last ditch' talks the union announced that it was calling it off. This was good news for LUL's passengers; the strikes called by the RMT union in the past have been extremely disruptive. The RMT's acting general secretary Mick Cash said they had secured 'real movement and significant progress'. LUL's Chief Operating Officer Phil Hufton said he was 'pleased that Londoners will not have to endure further strike action'.

Mr Hufton added:

> Modernisation of the Tube means that it is our intention to close all ticket offices, used in less than 3% of journeys, and instead deliver a vastly better customer service by bringing more staff than ever before out on to the concourses of stations at ticket machines, ticket gates and platforms – just as we delivered during the London 2012 Games. This will also allow us to save £50m per annum to reinvest in better and more reliable train services and to keep fares down.

Source: www.oxfordmail.co.uk/news/11192118.print

1 Explain what is meant by the term 'stakeholder conflict'. *(2)*

2 Analyse two possible stakeholder conflicts that could arise within LUL. *(4)*

3 Identify two external benefits that could arise from the operation of LUL. *(2)*

4 Calculate the percentage increase in passenger numbers on the Tube between 2008 and 2013. *(3)*

5 Employees, customers, and managers are three important stakeholders of LUL. Evaluate the influence that each stakeholder has on the operation of LUL. *(9)*

Total *(20)*

Chapter 6

Different stakeholder objectives and mission statements

AS / Year 1 | Year 2

A Level students must know all of the content in this chapter.

AS students must know:

- Different stakeholder and business objectives

But they are not required to cover:

- Mission statement (page 32)

However, knowledge of the mission statement is useful, as it forms the basis for many business objectives.

A business needs some sort of target or sense of what it wants to achieve. To suggest that all businesses just want to make a profit is not enough; nor is it necessarily accurate. It may depend on what type of business is involved and how long it has been trading. Having a clear idea of its intentions is not only important in terms of providing a target, but it will also enable all who work in the business to be aware of where the business is hoping to go.

A company's intentions can be analysed in terms of its mission statement, its aims or goals, and its strategic and tactical objectives. These form a hierarchy of objectives, as shown in Figure 6.1.

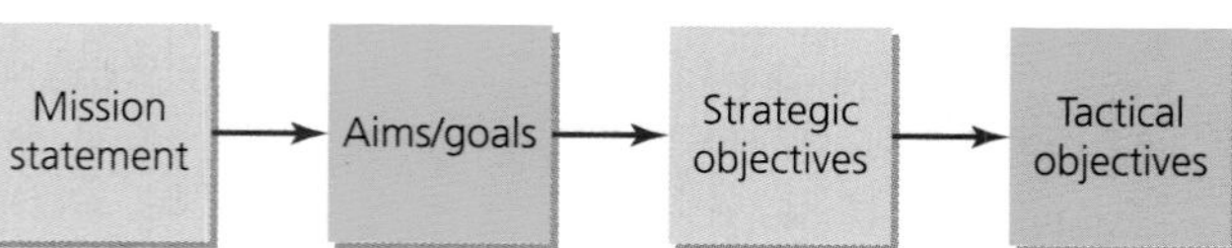

Figure 6.1 A company's mission statement, goals and objectives

Mission statement

A mission statement gives a general idea of what the business exists to do and its purpose is to set this down for the benefit of all stakeholders. Examples of mission statements from Unilever, Cadbury UK Limited and Ella's Kitchen are given below. The statement is intended to appeal to employees and customers alike. It is a qualitative statement, which contains no specific elements. The mission statement can be used as a form of marketing and it will usually state the overall organisational or corporate aims of the business.

Examples of mission statements

Unilever

'...the highest standards of corporate behaviour towards everyone we work with, the communities we touch, and the environment on which we have an impact...'

Cadbury UK Limited

'Our core purpose is working together to create brands people love.'

Ella's Kitchen

'At Ella's Kitchen our mission is to create healthy eating habits that will last a lifetime. With all our products we take simple, wholesome, organic ingredients that ooze goodness and have nothing else added at all.'

Aims/goals

Aims or goals are more specific than a mission statement, but they are sometimes confusingly used as alternative terms for the main objectives of a business. The principal aims of most businesses include:

- Survival. For a new business, the most important aim is survival, especially if the new business is trying to compete with well-established companies.
- Breaking even. It is not likely that a business will be profitable straight away. There are many costs to cover, especially those of the premises and all the fixtures (fixed costs or overheads — see **Chapter 26**).

Therefore, it is more realistic to set a target of breaking even within a given time period (see **Chapter 28**).

- Share of the market/growth. Much depends on the type of business and the market in which it operates. Capturing a larger share of the market not only increases sales with all the benefits that follow, but also puts the business in a position from which it can try to dominate the market.
- Profit. This is a longer-term goal than survival. The ability to make a profit depends on the type of products or services offered by the business and the amount of competition in the marketplace.

Cadbury UK Limited states that its main aims are to:

- deliver top-quartile shareowner returns
- profitably double its global confectionery share
- profitably maintain and grow its regional beverages share
- develop best-in-class capabilities
- grow as a company admired internally and externally.

Objectives

Companies seek to achieve their main aims or goals by setting various specific objectives. Setting objectives provides:

- a greater sense of direction for the business
- a possible motivational force for all employees
- an aid to controlling existing and future operations in the business.

Hierarchy of objectives

One way of looking at objectives is to see them as part of a hierarchy for the business of moving itself forward. The hierarchy will involve:

- the mission or overall purpose of the business
- its vision and where it wants to be in the future
- the aims the business has for achieving its mission and vision
- the objectives that are to be put in place to achieve all this.

Strategic objectives

In order to achieve its main aims, a business adopts a plan that contains several strategic objectives. For example, the business could aim to achieve a 10 per cent growth in sales within three years. To reach this goal, the business may decide that its strategic objectives are to:

- increase productivity within the business in order to reduce costs and thereby increase sales via lower prices
- sell its products in new markets.

> **Key term**
>
> **Strategic objectives:** how a business plans to achieve its aims or goals; often a long-term approach.

However, before deciding on the most appropriate strategic objectives, the business may undertake a SWOT analysis (see **Chapter 50**). This will help the business to decide the best way forward in order to achieve its aims.

Tactical objectives

These are the short-term objectives necessary to achieve the business's strategic objectives. They are likely to be concerned with the day-to-day activities of the business. If the company's aim is to achieve 10 per cent growth in sales and its strategic objective is to sell its goods in new markets, the tactical objectives will concentrate on how this is to be achieved. For example, the business may want to advertise and merchandise its products in a chosen area within six months. It may also decide that the best way of achieving the strategic objective is to reduce its prices in these new markets.

> **Key term**
>
> **Tactical objectives:** the day-to-day (short-term) objectives needed to ensure the strategic objectives are achieved.

Setting objectives: SMART

A useful set of criteria for setting objectives is SMART. According to these criteria, objectives should be as follows.

Specific

It is important that everyone understands what the target is.

Measurable

Normally, the objective statement should contain a type of measurement to ensure that success or failure can be ascertained.

Agreed

Agreement between different departments makes it more likely that objectives will be achieved. In practice, not only might different departments within a single business set different objectives, but some of these objectives might be conflicting. The marketing department may want to achieve an increase in sales of 10 per cent and therefore decide to run a larger advertising campaign. Meanwhile, the finance department may want to achieve cuts in costs of 5 per cent and therefore want to restrict the spending of other departments. To be successful, all departments need to work together in setting objectives. It is also useful for stakeholders, such as employers and workers, to agree on the firm's objectives. In practice, the stakeholders of the business have different needs and therefore often have different objectives (see **Chapter 5**).

Realistic

It is important to be realistic when setting objectives, in order to avoid employees becoming demotivated. How would you feel if you were set the objective of gaining an A grade for all your subjects? What objectives are realistic will vary according to the type of business. A large multinational plc will have achieving a certain level of profit in a given timescale as one of its major objectives. This is because it has shareholders to satisfy. On the other hand, a new business that is owned and run by one person will want eventually to make a profit, but in the short term will be more concerned with survival.

Time-bound

Often there is a timetable specifying the period over which an objective is to be achieved. A time constraint aids measurement and tends to focus people's minds.

Tips and techniques

SMART is a good starting point for a business when setting objectives.

Constraints

Once objectives have been set, it is not just a question of sitting back and waiting. The circumstances in which the business operates (the business environment) may hinder progress and, in some situations, may require a complete change in direction.

Constraints on a business can be either internal or external.

Internal constraints include:

- a lack of finance to meet the chosen objectives
- poor communication within the business
- a conflict of interests between departments within the business
- an industrial dispute with the workforce.

External constraints include:

- changes in the law that affect the operation of the business
- the state of the economy
- the behaviour of competitors
- the opinions and behaviour of external stakeholders.

Objectives and stakeholder conflicts

The constraints on a business mean that even when SMART objectives are set, those objectives are not automatically going to be achieved. Also, SMART objectives do not mean that all stakeholders are happy with those objectives, or the manner in which they are going to be reached. There are a number of conflicts that can occur between stakeholders (see **Chapter 5**).

Those who believe in the stakeholder approach to business argue that taking into account the needs of all stakeholders when setting objectives rather than only one group – usually the owners – will mean in the long run that all stakeholders will benefit. They say that concentrating on one group is counterproductive, as it will alienate the others. This may be true, but in the short term at least there have to be trade-offs between the various groups.

The objective of increasing company profits by £10 million over the next 18 months seems, on the face of it, to fit most of the SMART criteria. However, suppose it will be achieved through price increases and making employees redundant. The fact that in the future there is the possibility that all stakeholder groups will benefit from the greater profits will be no consolation to those who are about to lose their jobs, or to consumers facing a large price rise. It is therefore possible to see how conflict between these two groups and the shareholders is likely to arise as a result of this particular objective being chosen.

Corporate objectives

The mission statement gives an indication of the corporate objectives of the business, but often in vague terms. The aims or goals for the business are more specific and change over time. Such objectives give a sense of direction for the business and help to define the culture in which the business is organised and operates. The corporate culture of the business is clearly linked to its corporate objectives. Many Japanese companies operate a culture that tries hard to ensure that all employees feel they are part of a big family.

Social objectives

Today there is a greater desire to be seen as a business that cares. Having a social conscience is also seen by many businesses as an effective marketing tool. Being 'green' or environmentally friendly, or offering sponsorship in the local community, are all ways in which a business can satisfy its social objectives. Regardless of the size of the business, from a multinational petroleum company to a mobile road café, all businesses are now likely to have an awareness of, and a policy on, social issues.

Waste and its reduction are a good example of how businesses have realised that demonstrating social conscience can also save significant amounts of money – if there is a reduction in the amount of waste they create. With the rising cost of using landfill sites, reducing waste not only lowers costs but also satisfies the social objectives of the business.

There are instances when the corporate and social objectives may conflict. If one of the corporate objectives is related to profitability for its shareholders, spending money on social objectives that add to costs and therefore reduce profits may not be appropriate for the shareholders.

Changing objectives

Over time, as circumstances change, businesses may need to adapt their objectives. In particular, a firm's tactical objectives may alter, depending on priorities and circumstances, in order to achieve both the implementation of the strategic plan and the firm's main goals.

However, only in extreme circumstances will the strategic plan have to be changed. Following the Ebola epidemic in 2014 in Western Africa, companies in the travel industry had to alter their plans for flights and visits to that area. For some businesses, it even led to a change in their strategic objectives, such as their sales targets, as these were no longer realistic.

A business may have a plan in place to deal with such circumstances — this is known as its contingency plan. Airlines have plans to counter any event that is outside their control. For example, an airline like British Airways will have plans in place to deal with industrial action by cabin crews.

Communications and objectives

Businesses need to ensure that they communicate their objectives clearly to all stakeholders and that they adhere to their objectives. Miscommunication about objectives can have serious results; if employees feel that growth is going to be achieved at the cost of jobs, with workers replaced by capital equipment, this can result in serious unrest (see **Chapter 42**). The method chosen to communicate the objectives, particularly a change of objectives, will need to be chosen carefully. Employees are likely to be resistant to change and any new ideas will have to be explained carefully, paying particular attention to the reasons for the change (see **Chapter 22**). Miscommunication from employer to employee and vice versa can quickly escalate into industrial unrest and a lack of trust.

Further sources

www.learnmarketing.net
www.topachievement.com
www.maxwideman.com

Your turn

Questions in red are for A Level candidates only.

Multiple-choice questions

1 Which of these is not part of the SMART process?
   A Make sure the objective is stated specifically.
   B Make sure the objective is to be achieved in a set period of time.
   C Make sure the objective can be realistically achieved.
   D Make sure the objective is meaningful. *(1)*

2 A business sets an objective of growing 5 per cent a year for the next two years. If it begins with turnover of £100 million, what will its turnover be at the end of the two years?
   A £110 million
   B £105 million
   C £110.25 million
   D £110.5 million. *(1)*

Revision questions

1 Explain what is meant by a 'hierarchy of objectives'. *(2)*

2 Explain why a firm might have a mission statement. Give three examples of objectives that might be included in a mission statement. *(5)*

3 Explain the difference between strategic and tactical objectives. *(4)*

Total *(11)*

Case study

Time for tea

Jane James opened her tea shop in a small market town in 2010 when she was made redundant. She had always loved baking and, as she was still below retirement age, she felt that this would be a good use of part of her redundancy pay.

Jane found suitable premises to rent in a small building at the end of her local high street and opened her business in 2011. She served teas, coffees, and light lunches between 9.30 a.m. and 4.30 p.m. six days a week, working with one part-time helper. Jane made all the cakes and lunches herself, which meant that she often worked 14 hours a day.

When Jane was starting up the business she wrote a mission statement for herself and her other stakeholders. Her mission statement was as follows:

Time for Tea will:

- provide an outstanding service to customers
- use ethically produced ingredients and home-made products in the café
- try to ensure that every customer feels valued and not rushed
- provide a family friendly environment for both customers and employees.

Jane's café was an immediate hit in the town and Jane realised that she would need to employ more staff to cope with demand. She decided that she would offer part-time work to mothers with young children, mainly because this was a large part of her customer base, but also because the café's hours would suit this group of employees. She built up a team of part-time workers who usually did four-hour shifts. The fact that they appreciated the work and understood the problems of childcare meant that these employees were usually willing to cover for each other when problems arose and that they were very loyal to the business.

Jane now has a decision to make about the future of her business. Her success has come to the attention of a company that runs a leisure park for families offering children's activities. The organisation would like Jane to open a café on the side of the lake in the park. This would mean considerable growth for the business in terms of time, employment, production of food and financial commitment. Jane is not sure that she wants the business to expand and diversify to the extent that she loses day-to-day control, but she also knows that this is a huge opportunity for the future. At present she has no debts and Time for Tea is profitable; she needs to decide whether to risk expansion with all its problems.

1 State two features of Jane's business that can be gained from her mission statement. *(2)*

2 Analyse one possible conflict of objectives that could arise if Jane decides to expand to the leisure park. *(8)*

3 Evaluate the benefits that have resulted from Jane's 'stakeholder objectives' approach to running the business. *(15)*

Total *(25)*

Chapter 7

Strategy and implementation

AS / Year 1 | Year 2

A Level students must know all of the content in this chapter.

AS students must know:

- PEST analysis (pages 39–40)
- Stakeholder conflicts (page 41).

Strategic management and planning

Planning is an important tool in ensuring the future success of a business. It will involve using tools such as decision trees (**Chapter 12**), critical path analysis (**Chapter 63**) and investment appraisal (**Chapter 29**) in any discussion about strategic planning.

Successful businesses need to plan for the future in many ways, and they need to ensure that the objectives that have been set for the future of the business fit with planning. They need to consider new products, changes in their markets, cashflow and investment decisions in order to remain competitive. Managers may need to take risks in order to maintain or increase profits; effective planning will help to minimise these risks and ensure that the business knows clearly what its future course of action will be. Businesses that don't plan ahead are likely to find that they are overtaken by competitors and that profits are affected.

Objectives, strategy and tactics

These terms are often confused and used incorrectly in the everyday business matters, but each of them has a different meaning.

1 An objective is set by a business in an attempt to reach a particular goal. The main business objectives are survival, break even, profitability and expansion.
2 A strategy is the action plan that the business puts in place to reach its objectives. For example, a new children's clothing shop may want to achieve survival in its first year. Its strategy to do this may be to use marketing to increase customer awareness in the local area.
3 A tactic is a particular step that a business takes to achieve its strategy. The tactic the children's shop might use to achieve its strategy is to target all families in its local area with emails or flyers offering 10 per cent discount on sales.

So there is a flow from setting an objective into formulating a strategy and then determining the tactics to be used. Starting from the other end, the tactics make it possible to achieve a particular strategy and if the strategy or strategies are successful, a business will achieve the objective that it has set

Developing a strategy

In order to formulate a strategic plan, it is necessary to collect information on many aspects of the business. This will involve an internal and external audit of the business, which should be executed on a regular basis. The internal audit looks at the strengths and weaknesses of the business, and the external audit looks at the opportunities and threats in the trading environment of the business.

Figure 7.1 An internal audit

Internal audit

An internal audit allows a business to assess its strengths and weaknesses in relation to its competitors across the whole of the business. Many businesses employ external organisations to complete these surveys, although it is possible for management to do them for their own departments. The purpose of the audit is to provide accurate information about each particular department, and it is therefore best to use accounting or statistical data wherever this is possible. For example, the human resources department could provide figures for absenteeism and turnover, while the marketing department looks at market share and advertising elasticity of demand. In each case, the business should compare itself with its major competitors to see where it has strengths and weaknesses.

External audit

The external audit looks at the opportunities open to the business and the threats which it faces in its external environment. All businesses operate in a constantly changing environment. The business needs to be aware of these changes, and must then assess the extent and implications of them on future success. Figure 7.2 shows the range of external factors which might affect a business.

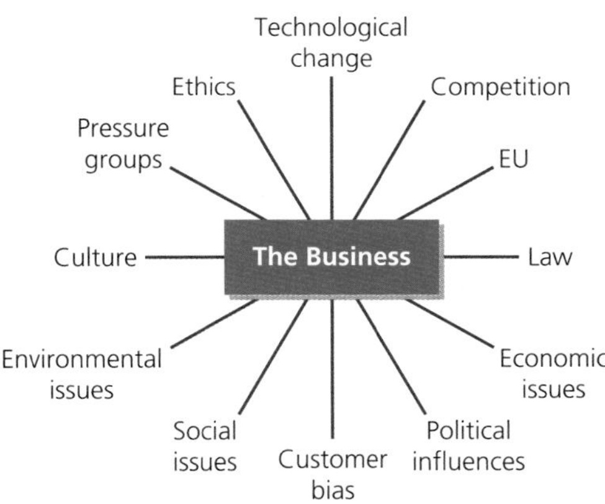

Figure 7.2 An external audit

Volkswagen and the car industry

Volkswagen (VW) has built up an image of quality and reliability for its cars, which is reflected across the whole range. This has been done in response to competition and customer demands. In recent years, VW has managed to transfer this image to its Eastern bloc brand, Skoda. The business acquired this make of car, and changed it from a car renowned for unreliability into one which is now still inexpensive but produced with a commitment to quality in the factory in the Czech Republic.

A car manufacturer may have to respond to any of the factors shown in Figure 7.2 at any particular time. In recent years, safety and carbon emissions have become increasingly important issues for the consumer when purchasing a new car, and manufacturers have had to address these consumer concerns in their specifications for new models. The environmental effects of transport are now at the centre of concerns about climate change across the globe; no car manufacturer can afford to ignore these issues if they are to succeed.

Factors included in the external audit are referred to by a variety of different acronyms, but the main ones are included in a PEST analysis, standing for political, economic, social and technological factors. PEST analysis now also covers a variety of other issues.

Political

The actions of government can have a major impact on the way in which a business operates. Legislation on employment, health and safety, competition and taxation are all examples of government policies that have an impact on employers and businesses. In addition, the government's influence is now moving into new areas of the business environment such as environmental and ethical issues.

Economic

The economy and government economic policy are key areas of concern for all businesses, because of the impact which they have on consumer demand. Inflation, interest rates, the value of the currency, unemployment and the economic cycle will play their part in influencing the success of the business and in determining its actions. For example, car dealers may need to offer low-cost finance terms, or lengthened periods of repayment in order to attract new customers at times when interest rates are high.

Social

The characteristics of the population are important factors for business demand. Changes in the distribution or spending habits of consumers are constantly changing, making it vital that businesses are aware of these changes and act accordingly. For example, an increase in the number of retired people, many of whom have higher disposable incomes and are physically active, has produced a large and growing demand for specialist holidays. This relatively new sector of the market is referred to as the 'grey economy'. Similarly, growth in the number of students in the UK has led to increased demand for rented accommodation in university cities.

Technological

Changes in technology offer businesses new opportunities, but also create new risks. A successful business must be ready to implement new procedures and train staff in their use. They also need to recognise situations where existing processes and machinery have become obsolete. The music recording industry has moved from tapes, through compact discs and on to internet downloads with increasing rapidity.

Successful and innovative businesses will already be preparing for the next product in such a cycle. For example, the Apple business is continually updating the specification of the ipod and the iphone, in order to generate new demand from customers to have the latest 'must-have' equipment.

Competition

The extent of the competition and the threat which it poses will have a considerable impact on the success of the business. It may be necessary to change the price or product range in response to competition; for example, the arrival of a 'Sainsbury's local' store will have an impact on local shops and newsagents.

Culture

Businesses need to take account of the characteristics of the local population and their shopping habits. Food stores in Indian, Chinese or Pakistani neighbourhoods often do not sell dairy products because they do not form part of their customers' diet.

Ethics

Businesses must be aware of the demand for ethical trading and its effect on customer demand (see **Chapter 14**). Television coverage of chicken farming in the UK by well-known presenters, like Jamie Oliver, has led to an increase in demand for free-range chicken in supermarkets.

Pressure groups

Pressure groups can exert pressure on businesses. Animal welfare organisations have put pressure on shops to sell meat products that are produced in humane conditions.

Environment

Environmental factors are becoming increasingly important. The high price of domestic fuel and an increase in awareness of global warming have led to a rapid rise in the demand for low-energy light bulbs and a consequent fall in their price.

Using the information

Once the audits are complete, the business needs to put the information into a summarised format. The usual way of presenting this sort of information is in a SWOT analysis (see **Chapter 50**) to show the strengths, weaknesses, opportunities and threats for the business.

In terms of formulating strategy, SWOT is only one of the tools that the business can use, and it is important not to use a SWOT analysis in isolation from all the other information which a business might gather. A SWOT analysis only gives part of the picture, and it should be viewed alongside information such as market research, ratio analysis and other financial data, sales figures and government economic statistics. For a business considering growth, Ansoff's Matrix (see **Chapter 11**) could also be another useful tool to use with a SWOT analysis, because it would help the business to consider the best direction for changes to achieve growth.

It is also important to remember that a SWOT analysis is not an end in itself. It is something for the business to use in determining objectives and strategy. For example, the knowledge that new competition is entering the market could lead a business to look at different opportunities in its environment that may help it to survive and grow. It is also vital to remember that the usefulness of all of this planning will depend on the information being gathered in a way that is unbiased and objective. To achieve this, it may sometimes be necessary for the business to use an outside agency.

Stakeholder objectives and strategic management

A stakeholder is a person or party that has an interest (i.e. a 'stake') in the success of a business. Stakeholders want to see a business succeed because they will benefit from its success. The objectives of stakeholders can be used to create a useful framework to help analyse the operation of a business. It can also be used to analyse the setting of a business's objectives and the strategy it develops to reach them.

The business/stakeholder relationship is extremely important and cuts both ways; the business affects the stakeholders, and the stakeholders affect the business.

The issues for consideration include the extent to which the stakeholders regard the business as a success, how the different stakeholder groups may view change, which stakeholders are the most important, and how the objectives of the different stakeholder groups could affect the strategic decisions of the business.

Tips and Techniques

It is important that you understand the relationship and the interaction between a business and its stakeholders. You need to be able to identify what each stakeholder wants from the business, and also evaluate the influence which each stakeholder can bring to bear on the business's strategic decision making.

Key term

Stakeholder: a person or party with an interest in the success of a business.

Stakeholder objectives

In theory, all stakeholders will benefit from a business's success, but in reality they may not. Furthermore, even if all stakeholders do benefit, they may not do so equally. It is very important to recognise the potential conflicts between the objectives of the different stakeholder groups. In order to analyse why, it is necessary to recall the objectives of each stakeholder in the business.

These stakeholder objectives have to be addressed by a business, for these reasons:

- Employees who feel valued will be more productive, be less resistant to change and less likely to leave. It should be noted that there are different types of employee. Directors and managers are certainly 'employees' but may have different objectives to 'front-line' workers. They may be expecting a greater element of career progression.
- Customers who do not feel exploited and like the standard of products and service will generate repeat custom.
- Suppliers who are treated as true stakeholders rather than 'suppliers' are more likely to be loyal and committed because they have 'a stake' in the business. This has important implications for the short term (i.e. needing a quick delivery) and also for the successful implementation of strategy.
- Owners will want a return that they feel is satisfactory. If the business is a company, shareholders will expect (at least) the sort of dividend that investors in a similar business have received. They will also be expecting a rise in the share price over time. If these are not forthcoming, they will sell their shares. This will drive the share price down and could leave the business open to a takeover.
- The local community, while not a single coherent entity, could generate negative publicity for a business if it creates social costs such as pollution or congestion. There are also examples of how a community can turn against a firm. A good example of this is *The Sun* newspaper's coverage of the 1989 Hillsborough football stadium disaster in Sheffield, where 96 people died and over 700 were injured. *The Sun* ran the headline 'THE TRUTH', claiming that some Liverpool fans stole from victims and others urinated on members of the emergency services when they arrived to help. This caused outrage among thousands of people in Liverpool, and even now the newspaper sells poorly in the city as many newsagents refuse to stock it.

Stakeholder conflicts

A business must take into account stakeholder objectives when making strategic decisions. However, this can lead to a variety of conflicts and, in the short term at least, there will probably have to be trade-offs between the various groups.

A business might set the strategic objective of increasing profits by £15 million over the next three years. This may seem to be valid, and meets some of the 'SMART' criteria (see **Chapter 11**). However, this objective is to be achieved through price increases and making employees redundant. The fact that 'in the future there is the possibility that all stakeholder groups will benefit from the greater profits' will be of no consolation to an employee who is going to lose their job, or a consumer facing a large price rise. It is therefore quite possible to see how conflict between these two groups and the shareholders is likely to arise as a result of this particular strategic objective being chosen.

Stakeholder influence

The influence that the particular stakeholder groups can exert on the business is not likely to be equal; in any given business some stakeholders will have a greater influence than others. Some issues for consideration are detailed below.

Employees

How many are there? Is there a union that the business recognises? If so, how many members belong to it? Are there a large number of 'career' employees (who could not easily be replaced), or is the workforce largely uncommitted with a high rate of labour turnover?

Shareholders

If the business is a company, is it private or public? In a private business, it can be hard to identify the actual price of the shares as they are not traded on the open market. However, in a public company shareholders will be very sensitive to changes in price, and indeed the dividend which they receive. They have the power to vote directors off the board, whereas employees and suppliers cannot. Therefore in a public company, directors may feel that shareholders are key stakeholders whose views must form a very important part of strategic decision making.

Suppliers

Is the supplier in a monopoly position, or could similar products be bought from elsewhere? If the latter is the case, then potentially it has considerably less power than if it supplies a unique, essential product.

Local community

To what extent might any bad publicity affect the business in the long term? Might bad publicity 'blow over' quite quickly?

Creditors

If a business is finding it difficult to keep up with its mortgage (or other loan) repayments, it may have to delay payments to suppliers to improve its liquidity position, so as not to default and run the risk of the loan being recalled.

Key term

Key stakeholder(s): One(s) with a large amount of influence on the business. A key stakeholder's views will play an important part in strategic decision making.

The legal situation

Faced with potential conflicts arising from stakeholders with differing objectives and influence, can those running a business look to the law for guidance? In the case of a company, it has until recently been the case that the objectives of shareholders (as the owners) were expected to be the main concern for directors and managers.

The Companies Act 2006 has altered this. It is an important piece of legislation that consolidates and updates existing law relating to the running of a company. It caused a lot of debate when passing through parliament. Section 172 is particularly important, putting into law for the first time a statutory statement of directors' duties and responsibilities. It states that each director must act in a way that they consider in good faith (i.e. honestly) would be most likely to promote the success of the company (although the term 'success' is not actually defined in the Act).

Directors must now 'have regard' for a number of factors that include the:

- likely consequences of any decision in the long term
- interests of the company's employees and the company's business relationships with suppliers and customers
- impact of the company's operations on the community and the environment.

In some ways the new legal position still leaves the issues regarding conflict unchanged. While 'having regard' for different stakeholders is now enshrined in law, this does not remove the likelihood of stakeholder conflict. It still will not be possible to satisfy all groups all of the time. If a plant has to close 'for the long-term success of the company' this will be obviously be against the interests of the employees that are made redundant and the company's suppliers. The concept of 'having regard' for stakeholders in a particular instance may need to be tested in court for the issue to be clarified.

Nevertheless, under Section 172 directors who make very unsuccessful decisions could be in breach of their legal duty. Any serious (e.g. fatal) health and safety failures, or a failure to protect the environment from significant damage, could result in prosecution. Directors will have to be more attentive to a wider variety of stakeholder interests than was previously the case.

Tips and Techniques

When approaching a question involving stakeholder needs, try to adopt a balanced view and then reach a conclusion as to which group(s)' needs are most important or significant at that particular time for that business.

Key term

Companies Act 2006: this has put into law for the first time a statutory statement of directors' duties and responsibilities. This includes 'having regard' for employees, suppliers, and the environment.

Porter's five forces model

Porter's five forces model is a system for analysing the level of competition in an industry. It looks at the forces that determine the level of competitive intensity and the attractiveness of the industry in terms of profitability.

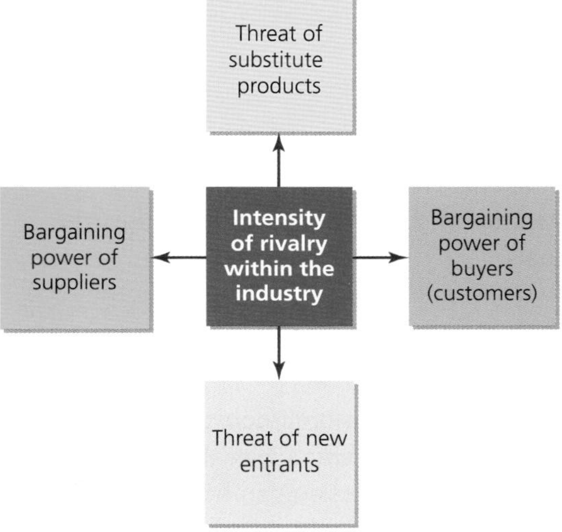

Figure 7.3 Porter's 5 forces

Porter's five forces are the:

1 threat of new entrants to the market
2 bargaining power of suppliers
3 bargaining power of consumers
4 threat of substitute products entering the market including changes in technology
5 degree of existing competitive rivalry

Using this diagram, Porter offers points under each of the items that make it possible to create an analysis of the competitive situation in any market.

1 The threat of new entrants. When new firms enter an industry they will take a share of the market and increase the competitive intensity. The greater the barriers to entry, as in a monopoly like Broadband supply from BT, the smaller the threat will be.
2 The bargaining power of suppliers. When an industry has suppliers who can force up the price of their products through their strong power to bargain, this will cut the profits that are available to the firms in the industry. The lack of bargaining power of suppliers to supermarkets in the UK increases the profitability of the supermarkets and lowers the competitive intensity.
3 The bargaining power of customers. If the consumers in an industry have strong bargaining power, this will force prices down and reduce likely profitability. Acting as consumers, the supermarket chains are able to negotiate low prices from suppliers like farmers when buying milk.
4 The threat of substitutes. In some sectors there is a threat of substitute products entering the market. This is particularly the case in markets with technological products like tablets, mobile phones and games consoles. A business that fails to keep up to date with new devices will quickly lose market share.
5 The degree of competitive intensity. Where there is high competitive intensity it is likely that the result will be innovation, price wars and higher spending on promotion. All of these things are likely to reduce the level of profitability that can be achieved.

Using the model

When a business is thinking of moving into a new sector, it is possible to use the model to see the situation clearly. For example, the threat of substitution in some sectors may come from individuals choosing to do the work themselves rather than employ a professional. During a recession, many people will choose to do jobs like decorating or home improvements themselves. If an individual or business is thinking of moving into this market they need to assess the likelihood of this situation arising. The decision to proceed into the industry may depend on the quality of the service offered, as well as the ability to offer good customer service and rapid delivery.

The problem with using Porter's model is that it is not always easy to obtain all the required information about the threats that exist and the market situation.

Models of strategic choice

Porter's generic strategies

Porter's generic strategies show how a company can achieve a competitive advantage in its industry. He suggested three strategies, together with a fourth, 'stuck in the middle' which is unlikely to result in any competitive advantage.

1 Cost leadership
2 Differentiation
3 Focus or niche

1 Cost leadership. This strategy involves the aim of being the lowest cost producer in the field. To achieve this, the firm will need to achieve economies of scale, particularly by reducing production costs and passing those savings on to the consumer.
2 Differentiation. This will involve the firm in producing a range of goods that is either different, or perceived as different from that of the competition. For example, a new lightweight and strong bike will attract consumers who need to take their bike on public transport. The differences in the product, if achieved, will allow the firm to charge a premium for the product and increase profitability. The risk in this strategy is that if a patent does not exist, the product can be copied and competitive advantage will be lost.
3 Focus or niche strategy. This involves producing for a particular sector of the market; usually consumers in such a sector will be prepared to pay a premium for the status of being different. This applies to the market for designer clothes and handbags. Mulberry charges prices in excess of £1,000 for some of its handbags and consumers are prepared to pay this.
4 'Stuck in the middle'. A business that tries to adopt all three strategies is unlikely to achieve success. It is impossible to please all consumers and trying to achieve everything suggests that there is no strategy at all.

If a firm wants to achieve a competitive advantage, it should look at each of these strategies to see if they can be applied to the business's particular situation. Although they are called generic (applicable in all situations), some firms will find that they cannot gain competitive advantage through any of the situations. They may be too small to achieve economies of scale; they may not have the possibility of creating a differentiated product or appeal to a niche market.

Management by objectives

Management by objectives (MBO) is a system by which managers and employees define and agree a series of objectives for the business. Peter Drucker worked on the system and outlined the term 'management by objectives'.

The process has to involve measuring the employees' performance against the standard set and, ideally, it should include the employee from the outset, particularly in setting targets.

The advantages of MBO are:

- It should improve the motivation of the employee.
- It involves management and employees in communication about the targets and increases interaction and involvement for both groups.
- The organisation should be working towards the same goals.
- If employees are involved in setting goals they are more likely to accept them and achieve them.

The disadvantages of MBO are:

- The goals can become more important as a focus than having a cohesive and achievable plan.
- MBO needs to be used taking an holistic view of the whole organisation.
- Meeting the targets at any cost may result in poor quality output.

Further sources

www.dfid.gov.uk: The Department for International Development (DFID) leads the UK's work to end extreme poverty.
www.businessballs.com
www.businesslink.gov.uk

Your turn

Questions in red are for A Level candidates only.

Multiple-choice questions

1 Which of the following are not always regarded as stakeholders for a business?
  A customers
  B shareholders
  C competitors
  D suppliers. *(1)*

2 What is meant by a niche market?
  A a small market
  B a market that supplies a particular sector of the population
  C a new market
  D a market that supplies only one geographic area. *(1)*

Revision questions

1 Explain two factors that would be included in an external audit. *(6)*

2 State three examples of stakeholders for a local garage run by a sole trader. *(3)*

3 Explain two examples of 'stakeholder conflict' for any well-known high street bank. *(6)*

Total *(15)*

Case study

Stone Country Butchers

Stone Country Butchers was opened in January 2012 by three friends, Stefan, Paul and Dan, from Hereford who had qualified in butchery and ran an online business supplying meat. They moved to Stone because they wanted a retail market in an area where competition was not as fierce as it was in the Hereford area.

The business quickly established a steady trade in the town, but after a year, two of the partners decided that they wanted to return to their home town, leaving Stefan running the business himself. Initially, Stefan's strategy was to continue to build up the butchery side of the business. However, he quickly realised that there was a market for him to expand, offering hog roasts and barbecues at parties, weddings and other events. This side of the business expanded quickly, creating a need for extra staff but giving a good return for the business.

Stefan is now considering expanding his business further by opening a delicatessen in the adjoining vacant shop. He feels that there is room for the business in the town, where his only competition would be from two medium-sized supermarkets. Stefan realises that he would need to employ extra staff and that he would aim his products at a niche market. This is not the case for the butcher's shop which is the only independent one in the town centre. Stefan realises that if he is to undertake this expansion, he needs to assess the situation through an external audit and to create a clear strategy for growth

1 Analyse two factors that Stefan could look at as part of an external audit. *(4)*

2 Analyse one problem that Stefan could face in expanding to provide a delicatessen. *(7)*

3 Evaluate how Stefan could use Porter's Five Forces to formulate his strategy and make a decision on growth. *(15)*

Total *(26)*

Chapter 8

Business plans and contingency crisis management

AS / Year 1 | Year 2

A Level students must know all of the content in this chapter.

AS students must know:

- the business plan

But they are not required to cover:

- the plan-do-review cycle (page 50)
- contingency planning and crisis management (pages 51–53)

Although not examined at AS, Strategic Review is a useful concept in understanding the formulation of business plans.

Business plans

As the saying goes, 'if you fail to plan, you plan to fail', and that is not what a business wants to do. A business plan is a formal written document that explains in detail how a business is going to achieve its objectives. Strategic planning is the process of identifying the long-term direction of the business in terms of objectives and initiatives to achieve them. It is usually conducted by senior managers. Tactical planning is usually undertaken by middle managers and is more centred on 'day-to-day operations' and so it has a rather more short-term focus. Business plans are therefore very important for all businesses, whether brand new start-ups or established companies.

Key term

Business plan: a formal written document that explains in detail how a business is going to achieve its objectives.

Business plans for start-ups

For a business which is starting up, the absence of a plan virtually guarantees failure. A proper plan proves that those who run the business 'know what they are doing' and also know what the potential of the business is. Without a plan, it will be almost impossible to obtain financial backing for a start-up because there is no formal indication of what the business intends to achieve and how it will attempt to do it. The ability to access funds is therefore a crucial reason for drawing up a plan; the same point also applies to an established business which needs capital for expansion. There are also a number of other important reasons to draw up a business plan, as shown later in the chapter.

Business plans for established companies

For existing companies, planning does not occur as an isolated activity; it usually follows a strategic review of the firm, which is about improving and sustaining business performance. It addresses questions such as 'where are we now?', 'where do we want to go?', 'can we get there?', and 'how?'

The benefits of a strategic review

A strategic review enables:

- analysis of the key performance indicators from all of the four functional areas in the firm; underperforming departments and products can be identified.
- analysis of SWOT and PEST to be undertaken (see **Chapter 50**) and so the current situation in the external environment (e.g. changes in competition, whether the market is growing or not, changes in technology); this means that the options for future action can be considered.
- identification of 'good practice' in the firm, e.g. how employees are kept motivated; also identification of 'bad practice', e.g. budgets being routinely exceeded.

- a consensus hopefully to be established among senior managers on exactly where the business is headed and what needs to be done to get there.

It is most likely that conducting a strategic review, by doing all of the above before planning, will lead to an improvement in the long-run profitability of the business. This means that stakeholders are more likely to be satisfied; shareholders will have greater dividends; employees will have more job security; suppliers will be in a more secure position; and there can be greater community involvement because more funds are available.

Why is a plan important for the business's stakeholders?

Whether the firm is just starting up or has been established for many years, its stakeholders will want to see its plan; and preferably they should be involved in some way in its construction. The reason for this is related to the objectives of the individual stakeholder. Consider a typical company and its stakeholders, as shown in Table 8.1.

Advantages of a business plan

Strategic planning involves the use of quantitative techniques such as forecasting (**Chapter 10**), decision trees (**Chapter 12**) and network analysis (**Chapter 63**). Even if the future is uncertain, some attempt should be made to consider what lies ahead and how it will impact upon the firm.

A business plan:

- requires that a strategic review of the firm is conducted; there will be an analysis and evaluation of how well each functional area of the business is performing
- gives a business a sense of direction
- forces an evaluation of current strategic and tactical objectives
- forces senior managers to explicitly consider the constraints faced by the business in reaching its objectives
- sets out the role of each department/section of the business and the part it has to play in the achievement of the overall strategic objectives
- encourages communication, co-ordination and co-operation between different departments and stakeholders of the business.

Table 8.1 Stakeholders and the business plan

Stakeholder	Main objectives	Reason for wanting to view the business's plan
Employees	Job security Pay rises Improved conditions of work and service	Are these likely to be forthcoming in the future? If so to what extent?
Suppliers	Regular orders, preferably of increasing size Prompt payment for products	Are these more or less likely to occur? There may be implications for expansion and gaining economies of scale if orders increase. Alternatively, if the supplier does not feature in the plan because new ones are being used it will need to seek new customers.
Investors, such as the bank	Interest on any loans (and the capital) repaid on time	Is there an 'excessive' degree of risk in the plan that might worsen cash flow and make this less likely?
Shareholders	Larger dividends A rise in the share price (both preferably in as short a time period as possible)	Will future plans jeopardise this? Or/and will the plan make it likely that any gains will be long term rather than short term?
Customers	A 'fair' price Ethical issues with how the product is made/sourced A product that can be 'trusted' Improvement in the product Good customer service	Will there be changes to products? Are they being sourced ethically? Is customer service likely to improve? Even if individual consumers do not look at the business plan, pressure groups and consumer groups will.
Local community	Jobs (preferably full time and permanent) Business involvement in the community Supply links to other local firms 'Responsible attitude' to those affected by the business' activities	Are jobs likely to be created or lost? Will more be 'put back' into the community/communities? Will (smaller) existing firms be adversely affected or will it create more business for them? Will the plans mean more negative externalities such as pollution, noise and congestion?

Many of the same benefits apply to those managing the business and making tactical decisions on a day-to-day basis, rather than at senior management level.

Disadvantages of a business plan

There is the opportunity cost of the time spent gathering the data for the planning process and then analysing and evaluating it. Furthermore, planning is an ongoing process and so this opportunity cost is also ongoing. This may not be a burden in a large established company with specialist managers but could be considerable for a small business.

There is a possibility of spending too much time on planning, rather than implementing that it reduces the initial enthusiasm for moving forward.

A plan may be too rigid and leave little room for individual employee creativity; this may demotivate those responsible for carrying it out.

The plan may be disregarded or altered by someone who does not like it. A plan is useless unless it is actually followed by those responsible for implementing it. It could be argued that this is not a disadvantage of the plan itself, but it does illustrate that if a business plan is drawn up in isolation from its key stakeholders, it has a lower chance of succeeding than one in which they have been involved.

There is a possibility that the plan may somehow get 'leaked'. If so, competitors will gain knowledge that could be used to undermine the business.

Key term

Opportunity cost: the cost of the next best alternative foregone. The opportunity cost of planning is that the time spent on it could have been spent on some other activity.

What should be included in a business plan?

The short answer is 'everything'. A business plan must answer these questions:

1 What are we aiming to achieve?
2 Why?
3 What will need to be done to achieve this?
4 By whom?
5 When?
6 Using what resources?

Planning must involve all of the functional areas of the business; and obviously the implementation of the plan needs to be carefully co-ordinated. Table 8.2 indicates the key issues that need to be considered and why.

Table 8.2 Key issues for consideration in a business plan

Business function	Key issues for consideration in a business plan	Reasons for planning
Accounting & Finance	Cash flow implications for the future, especially if the firm is expanding How to raise any additional funds needed, or simply to maintain existing levels of funding A projection of the costs involved in implementing the plan and the resulting revenue and profit The budget to be allocated to each department	To ensure an adequate cash flow which will avoid the need to borrow money at short notice on unfavourable terms To ensure that any funds to be raised are available and are raised in an appropriate way, e.g. preventing the business from getting too highly geared (see accounting ratios, Chapter 36) To identify and quantify the effects of the events being planned for. A plan without cost and revenue projections is not only worthless but positively dangerous for a business So that those with management responsibility for implementing the plan know what their budget will be; they can then prioritise actions To try to ensure shareholder objectives in terms of expected returns are met. If financial results are out of line with expectations the share price will drop
Human resource management	Whether the existing workforce is capable of carrying out the plan If any changes to recruitment and training are necessary The projected level of labour turnover If there is a need for any changes to company policies as a result of changes in the law (e.g. maternity and paternity rights)	To ensure employees have the right skills and competencies for what the firm is trying to achieve. If there are recruitment and training implications then there are issues such as 'who'? 'when'? and 'how'? Correct planning here can avoid hiring or training employees at the wrong time, either too early or too late There is a need for labour turnover to be calculated and planned for in order to avoid future staff shortages. Even if the plan is not for a significant change of direction, some employees will retire and some will leave To identify if there are any relocation or redundancy implications. These can cause anxiety and discontent and will need to be communicated to the workforce. What is the best way to do this? There will be a need to identify and negotiate redundancy payments

Operations management	Whether the existing capacity of the firm is correct, i.e. is it too big or too small? Is it underused or is there a need for expansion? If the existing production process can cope with any planned changes Are changes in technology necessary (even if the firm is not planning on making major changes) to stay competitive? If there are any new stock and quality control issues	To consider if there is a huge amount of unused capacity; if so, unit fixed costs will be higher than they could be. Alternatively, there needs to be an investigation into whether the business could achieve economies of scale by expanding To examine the implications in terms of the need for new capital equipment. There will need to be liaison with those responsible for accounting and finance To identify what will happen to costs as a result of the plan To avoid an 'out of stock' situation where customers are unsatisfied To consider whether the products can actually be made to the desired standard
Marketing	Are there any changes to the product or service as a result of (say) changes in demographics or income levels? The advertising and promotional plan The pricing strategies for different products Any changes to where the product is sold and/or the way that it is distributed? Likely sales and revenue levels. Overreliance on a single or a few products to be the business 'cash cow' (see **Chapter 54**).	Markets are dynamic. There is a need to identify if the products are those wanted by the consumers. Is the price 'correct'? If not then the business is going to suffer in terms of reputation and profit To see if new markets or market segments have emerged that can be exploited To avoid any mistakes from previous promotions and/or pricing strategies that have failed There is always a need to identify new threats and opportunities. Have new competitors emerged or have old ones disappeared? To ensure that sales levels are carefully co-ordinated with the amount being produced to avoid unsatisfied customers or a build-up of excess stock (As above) There is a need to identify what will happen to revenue from the product(s) as a result of the plan

Start up plans need to be particularly detailed, as shown in Figure 8.1.

What your business plan should include

1. **Company name, address and other contact details**
2. **Non-disclosure statement**
3. **Table of contents**
4. **Executive summary (easier to do after rest has been completed) to include:**
   - Summary of business, when formed etc., and what it does
   - The objectives of the business plan
   - The personnel involved in the business
   - The market the business is aimed at and how much this market is worth / what % the business expects to cover
   - Any development plans
   - Financial summary – showing sales in first year, gross profit margin, fixed costs and expected month of break even
   - Funding – how much required / received so far
5. **Business description to include:**
   - The business idea (what the business will be and why the legal trading format was chosen)
   - Brief history of the business
   - Current position
6. **Management and personnel**
   - Brief description of yourself (CV in appendices may be useful) and role of key personnel, details of roles
   - Reporting structures
   - Advisers to the business

7. **The products and services**
   - Description (range of products / services) include price list in appendices x Distinctions – why are you different?
   - Products / services development strategy
8. **The market**
   - Market sector positioning
   - Target customers
   - Market research (describe how gathered, who are competitors, what is your USP)
9. **Sales and marketing**
   - Marketing strategy (how you will find customers)
   - Sales methods (face-to-face / internet / telesales etc.)

10 Operations
   - Premises (now and in the future)
   - Production facilities
   - Suppliers
   - Distribution
   - Equipment
   - Business systems
   - Training requirements

11 Finance
   - Financial analysis
   - Explanation of assumptions used to produce P&L account

12 Risk analysis
   - Explanation of what could go wrong and how you would overcome it

13 Cash flow and profit and loss forecasts
   - Detailed forecasts for twelve months
   - Summarised forecasts for years 2 and 3

14 Appendices

Figure 8.1 A template for a business plan

The plan-do-review process

Once a plan has been drawn up it needs to be implemented and then monitored to make sure that it, and hence the business as a whole, is 'on track'. The plan-do-review process formalises this approach. It is a method used to achieve key departmental tasks which should mean that the business reaches its strategic objectives.

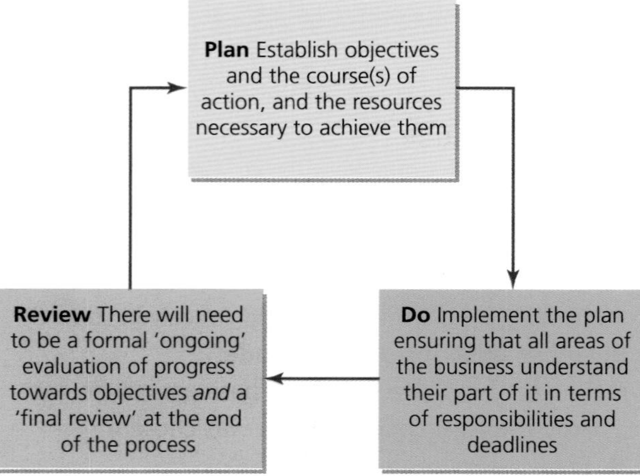

Figure 8.2 The plan-do-review cycle

Advantages

- The approach is methodical. It forces a strategic approach on those setting the objectives. They will need to consider carefully what the business should be trying to achieve and how likely it is that it will achieve the objectives. This process is as useful to a new, small business as it is to an established multinational.
- If those in each department of the business are clear about what they have to 'do' then employees should be more focused on achieving the desired results.
- Regular reviews of departmental and individual employee progress mean that deviations from the plan can be identified and corrected.
- A final strategic review offers the opportunity to evaluate the appropriateness of the objectives that were set and the methods used to achieve them. If there were problems, were they due to (say) human resource issues, unrealistic budgets, or were they due to external factors? After the final review the whole cycle can begin again, along with a consideration of how these problems could be avoided in the future.
- It encourages 'Kaizen' – continuous improvement in the business. (See **Chapter 68**.)

Disadvantages

- It is a lengthy process that will have a considerable opportunity cost in terms of managers' time, both at senior and middle level.
- Once the cycle has started it can be inflexible. If the whole organisation is set on a particular course with a specific set of objectives, then if a chance event occurs it could be difficult to change direction. This is especially true if contingency planning has not been conducted thoroughly.
- If employees have not been involved in the planning process they may feel less committed to the firm's

objectives, as they have no 'ownership' of them. This may make the achievement of the objectives slower.

- Some employees will dislike the ongoing review of their progress. They may regard it as 'spying' and an indication that management has a lack of trust in them.

Contingency planning and crisis management

Contingency planning

Strategic and tactical planning are important, but so too is realising that what has been planned does not always happen in the expected time frame, or even happen at all. It is crucial to consider what might go wrong with the plan, and the more risks that can be anticipated the better. Therefore, in addition to strategic and tactical planning, there is also planning for 'what will happen if things go wrong?' This means that an agreed course of action is in place and is ready to be used if necessary; this is known as 'contingency planning'.

While contingency planning is no doubt a useful exercise for a business, there can be disadvantages. These include the opportunity cost of the time involved in constructing the plan, as well as the possibility that the people who construct the plan may not be honest in their assessment of risk and the plan therefore not being a true reflection of the business's situation.

A contingency plan needs to be constructed with 'worst case scenarios' in mind. It also needs to be constructed methodically; 'brainstorming' the risks is all very well to start with but, as with strategic planning, it needs to be dealt with by considering the four functional areas. Therefore, the contingencies being planned for may include:

Key term

Contingency planning: planning for 'what will happen if things go wrong?' This means that an agreed course of action is in place and is ready to be used if necessary.

- Accounting and finance: sales levels being (far) below expectations and, quite possibly, causing cash flow problems as a result; products exported abroad being stolen or damaged in transit with the consequent loss of revenue and profit.
- Human resources: key employees leaving the business; key employees being absent through sickness or injury for a long period of time.
- Operations management: a supplier failing to deliver on time, delivering the wrong quantity, or the wrong quality; accidentally producing output to the wrong specification or quality level; an ICT failure that halts operations across the business.
- Marketing: a 'shock' to the economy, such as the banking crisis of 2008, causing an unexpected recession and a fall in sales; the emergence of a (possibly powerful) competitor arriving in the market; one of the firm's distributors going into liquidation.

There will be other issues to consider as well such as:

- a fire/flood or some other natural disaster that destroys a factory/office/distribution centre
- an employee or customer suing the business
- a complete ICT failure (or cyber-attack) that corrupts/destroys company and customer data
- a pressure group accusing the business of behaving unethically (whether true but never 'found out' before, or completely false)

Without a contingency plan if 'the worst that can happen' does indeed occur then it is likely to impact very negatively on the business's stakeholders. Consider the scenario mentioned above. There is a fire which destroys a factory. Assume that the business had no contingency plan. How will stakeholders be affected?

- Employees will have no livelihood. If it is not practicable to continue employing someone in these circumstances then they can legally be dismissed without following the usual procedures.
- Suppliers will receive fewer orders and will suffer a drop in revenue and profit.
- Customers will be let down. If the products the business sells are intermediate products that another business needs then that business will suffer a blow to its reputation because, in turn, it will let its own customers down. This will impact on its sales.
- The local community will experience a fall in income from the rise in the number of jobless and a fall in the level of funding for community initiatives.
- The government will lose tax revenue form corporation tax, VAT, income tax, and national insurance.

It could be argued that if a factory that processes chemicals, which caused a lot of negative externalities to nearby residents in the way of smell, pollution and congestion burned down, then there are benefits to the community in terms of a reduction in these externalities; but these may not outweigh the disadvantages imposed on other stakeholders.

The existence of a contingency plan reassures stakeholders that managers are aware of the main risks faced by the business and that they are ready to deal with a problem if it actually occurs. A contingency plan may take a considerable amount of time to construct, but the existence of such a plan will mean that managers spend less time and trouble 'firefighting' a crisis if it occurs because it has already been foreseen. Contingency planning is just as important as creating a strategic plan.

Key term

'Firefighting': where a manager spends time (and other resources) trying to fix unforeseen problems and 'emergencies'. With appropriate contingency planning this sort of situation can be avoided.

Crisis management

It should be remembered if the plan has not worked as it should, then it does not necessarily mean that 'a crisis' has occurred. Some deviations from the plan are always to be expected and some are less serious than others. If a contingency plan has been drawn up then these deviations should be manageable to a greater or lesser degree. What constitutes 'a crisis' is likely to be subjective and, obviously, some will be easier to solve than others. For example, a cash flow problem could indeed be a crisis as cash is 'the lifeblood' of the business. However, it may be resolved easily (if expensively) by an arrangement with the bank for a larger overdraft. On the other hand, an unexpected flood that affects a whole factory could be a very serious crisis indeed.

Crisis management is the process by which an organisation deals with an event that threatens to harm the business and its stakeholders. It is not the same as risk management (which considers potential risks and the ways to try and avoid, or at least minimise, them) because it deals with harmful events before (via contingency planning), during, and after it has occurred. By its nature, crisis management means having to deal with a potentially damaging event very quickly after it has occurred.

Some obvious solutions to the possibility of a crisis include:

- ensuring that insurance policies are up to date and that there is adequate fire cover, etc., for buildings
- keeping a 'cushion' of cash (although there is an opportunity cost to this)
- private health care for key employees
- establishing data monitoring systems to try and spot crises coming
- having 'trial runs' (e.g. of an ICT shutdown) to see if the plan 'works' – in the same way that a business has a fire drill to ensure that its evacuation procedure works.

Crisis management will differ from business to business, but in all cases the essence of crisis management is an effective contingency plan. The plan will need to be communicated so that everyone knows what to do if an event occurs. Crisis management should originate at the most senior level of the business, but middle managers and possibly employees should be involved as well, since they are at the 'sharp end' of the business's operations and know what the consequences are, from first-hand experience, if something goes wrong.

If there is a plan and it is followed decisively then potentially damaging effects can be avoided. The actions of the pharmaceutical giant Johnson and Johnson indicate this clearly.

> *The field of crisis management is generally considered to have originated with Johnson & Johnson's handling of a situation in 1982, when cyanide-laced Tylenol (a pain and fever reducing drug) killed seven people in the Chicago area. The company immediately recalled all Tylenol capsules in the country and offered free products in tamper-proof packaging. As a result of the company's swift and effective response, the effect to shareholders was minimised and the brand recovered and flourished.*

Source: http://whatis.techtarget.com/definition/crisis-management

What should be done in a crisis?

It is generally accepted an effective response to a crisis has three elements.

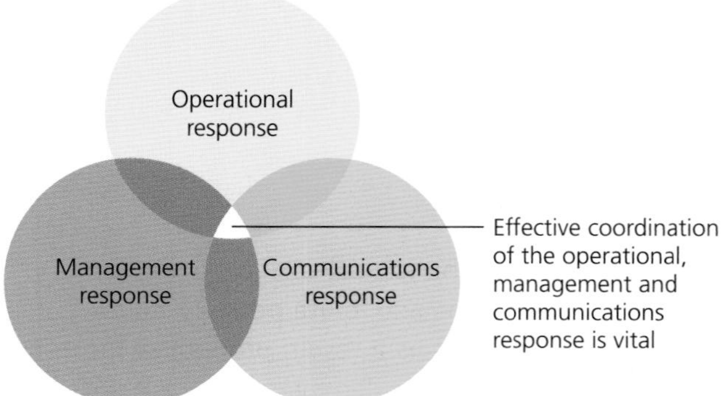

Figure 8.3 The elements of an effective crisis response

The management response would include:

- assessing the crisis' severity
- contacting the most senior executives of the business
- overseeing the implementation (and progress) of the contingency plan.

The operational response would include:

- implementing the contingency plan
- minimising the impact on stakeholders.

The communication response would include:

- contacting key stakeholders such as employees (and their families), suppliers, and customers
- media briefing – especially if the business is large and the crisis severe.

Your turn

Questions in red are for A Level candidates only.

Multiple-choice questions

1 Which of the following is **not** an advantage of a business plan?
  A It enables a business to assess its present position.
  B It provides a sense of direction.
  C It enables employees to better understand their role in the firm.
  D It encourages co-ordination of the different areas of the business. *(1)*

2 Which of the following is the correct wording?
  A can-do-review cycle
  B do-plan-review cycle
  C plan-do-review cycle
  D review-plan-do cycle *(1)*

3 Which of the following is NOT a reason for constructing a contingency plan?
  A Employees can make mistakes.
  B The market may change suddenly.
  C A new competitor may emerge.
  D The business has been in existence for a long time. *(1)*

4 Crisis management should originate from the business's
  A stakeholders
  B senior management
  C finance department
  D SWOT analysis *(1)*

Revision questions

1A Explain what is meant by the term 'strategic planning'. *(2)*

1B Explain what is meant by 'tactical planning'. *(2)*

2 Explain what is meant by 'a strategic review'. *(2)*

3A Explain two advantages of a business plan. *(4)*

3B Explain two disadvantages of a business plan. *(4)*

4 An independent online travel agent is constructing a contingency plan for dealing with a fire that would prevent it operating from its current office. Analyse one likely issue to be considered in the plan. *(6)*

Total *(20)*

Case study

Tesco – Born again in the USA?

It was not very long ago that one in every seven pounds spent in UK shops went through Tesco's tills. This was a phenomenal achievement. But all good things come to an end and in April 2014 there were increasing calls for the chief executive, Philip Clarke, to step down following a fall in the company's trading profit by 6 per cent to £3.2 billion. Unsurprisingly, its share price fell when this was announced.

To some, Tesco had lost its way. The good old days when it was run by Sir Terry Leahy seemed to have gone for ever, but Mr Clarke said that he 'wasn't going anywhere' and that there were plans in place to get the company back on track.

The Observer reported:

> There is no question that Clarke is trying to turn around the 3,000-store UK business at a difficult time. The industry is being rocked as shoppers turn their backs on big stores; the sprawling Extras that helped Tesco conquer Britain in the noughties are now a millstone around his neck.
>
> Clarke has sought to put the brakes on big store openings and focusing investment on convenience stores and its website. He still has the backing of big investors who accept a business of Tesco's size takes time to turn around. 'I know our business is getting better and there is a lag between it being better and people talking about it,' he said recently.

One issue that raised some eyebrows in 2014 was the announcement of the decision to start selling clothes from its clothing brand F&F in the USA. F&F, which was launched in the UK in 2001, opened seven 'affordable fashion' stores for men, woman, and children on the east coast of America in a joint venture with a franchise partner, Retail Group of America. Selling abroad is all very well and can be very profitable, but it is also risky. There is sometimes a tendency to think that just because America is the world's largest economy that just about any product launched there will be a success. Tesco had already discovered the hard way that is not the case. Less than a year previously, it abandoned its attempts to break into the American food market under the name 'Fresh & Easy', selling 'wholesome food that doesn't cost your whole paycheck'. It failed amid accusations of failing to plan a variety of factors properly from the location of the outlets ('in the wrong place') to the marketing ('insufficient TV advertising'). When selling abroad, there are also issues of the exchange rate to take into account.

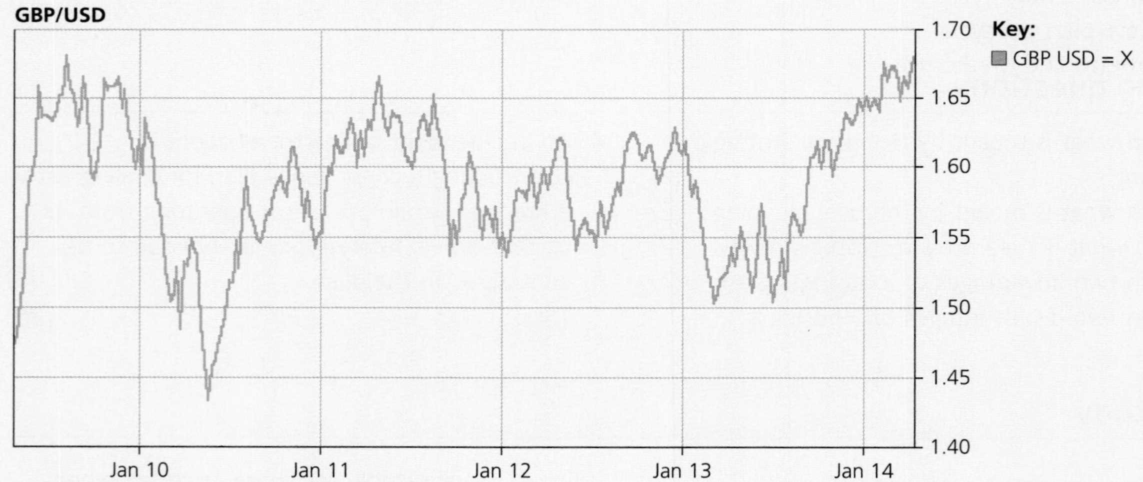

Figure 8.4 Changes in the £/$ exchange rate

Source: www.chartoasis.com/forex/1/gbp_usd/5_years.html

Should Tesco concentrate on what is going on at home? There are major challenges in the UK, never mind abroad. The discounters who have arrived in the shape of Lidl and Aldi have hit Tesco hard. Tesco has discovered that competing on price can be difficult even with the brand image it has. Clarke commented that 'If you try and get lower than them on price, they don't let you. I've learned that we have got to be different'.

Exactly what that difference will be and whether it is successful remains to be seen.

Source: (1) Zoe Wood, *The Observer*, 13 April 2014

1 Tesco's profits have fallen by 6 per cent to £3.3 billion for the period 2012–2013. Calculate the figure for Tesco's previous profit at the end of 2012. *(3)*

2 Tesco has decided to start selling its range of F&F clothes in the USA. The board of directors will have drawn up a contingency plan to help it manage any crises.
   - A What is meant by 'crisis management'? *(2)*
   - B Explain two possible crises that Tesco might face by deciding to start selling F&F clothing in America. *(4)*
   - C Analyse two benefits of the use of the plan-do-review process in this venture. *(4)*
   - D Evaluate the usefulness of a contingency plan for the launch of the clothing in America. *(15)*

3 Assume that the mark up on a range of F&F clothes is 8 per cent and they are bought from a supplier for a total of $58,000. If all of the clothes in the range are sold and the exchange rate is £1 = $1.6, calculate the profit in pounds. *(3)*

4 Evaluate the possible impact of exchange rate fluctuations on the success of the American F&F clothing venture. *(15)*

Total *(46)*

Group task

Tesco has decided to start selling clothes in the USA through its F&F brand.

Divide into four groups. Each group is to consider one of the functional areas of F&F: accounting and finance, human resources, operations management, and marketing.

A Each group must identify the planning issues to be considered by all of the functional areas of F&F as a result of this decision to sell abroad.

B Each group must then evaluate the two most important issues to be planned for if this venture is to be a success. This will then be presented to the other groups.

C Analyse two factors other than individual departmental planning at F&F that are likely to be important if the launch is to be a success.

Chapter 9

Risk and uncertainty and opportunity cost

AS / Year 1 | Year 2

A Level students must know all of the content in this chapter.

AS students must know:

- Risk and uncertainty

But they are not required to cover:

- Opportunity cost (page 59)

Anyone running a business, whether 'an entrepreneur', a director, or a manager, has to face uncertainties and take risks. Those running a business need to try to identify all the possible uncertainties and risks that they face. In general, the correlation between risk and reward is that if a 'big' risk is taken, then the expected reward is correspondingly large. Leaving a huge amount of money in the bank means that there is little risk involved for a business in terms of ability to pay debts, but the reward will be a very low rate of interest. Alternatively, starting to export abroad for the first time means taking a high risk but carries the potential for a high return for the business in the future. Risk-taking is what entrepreneurship is all about, but a risk should never be taken recklessly; risk needs to be managed and in order to manage a risk the nature of it needs to be understood. There are two types of risk: pure risk and speculative risk.

Pure risk is an event beyond someone's personal control. It can only result in a loss of some sort, never in a gain. Examples of such risk are the possibility of a fire at a factory, a natural disaster, fraud, a clerical mistake, and the unfortunate death of an employee who is key to running the firm. This does not, however, mean that nothing can be done about such risks; in these instances the solution is to ensure that premises and goods are adequately insured and a contingency plan constructed for the event of losing a key employee.

Speculative risk is different to pure risk because it carries the possibility of a gain as well as a loss. There is an obvious correlation between this sort of risk and reward; if entrepreneurs/managers take a large risk, then there is an expectation (but not a guarantee) of a high reward – and vice versa. When a business decides to take a particular course of action such as opening a new factory in order to increase output, it is taking a speculative risk. For this to occur, the costs and benefits of the decision will have been considered in great detail. The financial costs and benefits will be the easiest to quantify (i.e. measure) when making this decision; for example, cost of construction, equipping the factory and the likely increase in revenue and profit. However, not all of these costs and benefits will be readily measureable. Suppose the factory is built on an area that used to be a park; what about any negative publicity resulting from this? What if key employees will be required to relocate to the new plant and they do not really want to? How will morale and motivation be affected? Such 'costs' may not be completely unquantifiable and their effects are likely to be uncertain.

Uncertainty

'Uncertainty' is always an issue for a business and a failure to assess it can be a significant factor in success or failure. It is not, however, the same thing as 'risk'. Uncertainty could be described as 'a situation where the current state of knowledge possessed by a business's managers is imperfect'. This means that making a decision could be difficult because the outcomes of the decision are not fully known, that is, they are uncertain.

Tips and techniques

Do not confuse 'uncertainty' with 'risk'. The two are related, but they are not the same.

Key term

Uncertainty: the inability to calculate the costs and benefits of a decision precisely.

Risk: the chance or possibility of an adverse occurrence.

Reward: the possible return that a particular activity may make.

Uncertainty and the risks associated with it could arise from external or internal factors as shown in Table 9.1.

Tips and techniques

It is useful to be able to be able to identify the uncertainties in a specific business situation. For higher marks it is, however, more important to be able to judge how these affect the firm's objectives and decision making.

Uncertainty, risk and setting objectives

Where there is a high degree of uncertainty there will be a higher degree of risk, which can have a significant effect on a business's decision making. It is likely that a decision involving considerable uncertainty and risk will be associated with a greater degree of planning than one which is not. It needs to be recognised that although the analysis of data, planning, and forecasting (see **Chapter 10**) can help with making a decision, it cannot eliminate the risk associated with it. Suppose a board of directors is considering expansion as an objective; and it wants a growth in sales of 10 per cent within the next two years. It has to decide whether or not to try to achieve this by heavily promoting a product in a market that is growing fast but in which the firm has a low market share – the classic 'question mark' on the Boston Matrix (see page 394). A decision needs to be made about whether to do this or not. Uncertainty affects this decision because of the unknown responses from (for example) competitors, the firm's stakeholders and also the future direction of the economy.

Table 9.1 Risks associated with external and internal factors

External uncertainty		Internal uncertainty	
Economic uncertainty	The true state of the economy (or the market in which the firm is operating) in terms of consumer confidence, income levels and spending plans. It could also include uncertainty about government economic policy or The Bank of England's decisions on interest rates. If rates rise and the business has a number of large loans how will this impact financially?	Organisational and human resource uncertainty	Does the organisational structure of the business (its hierarchy and spans of control) support the decision? Does the culture of the business support the decision? Will change be opposed? Will the employees affected by the decision actually be capable of implementing it?
Political uncertainty	If an election is due, will the new government have a different attitude to business in terms of (say) employee rights, attitude to global warming, or the regulatory framework within which the business operates? Is this likely to increase costs? By how much?	Stakeholder uncertainty	How could stakeholders such as shareholders and employees react to a decision? Will any change cause a shareholder revolt at the next AGM? Could any change lead to (or worsen) industrial relations problems?
Competitive uncertainty	What are competitors planning to do? How will they respond to any decision your business makes? How should your business respond to the competitors' response? Does the business have the resources to react quickly and effectively?	Technological uncertainty	Will existing technology be able to cope with any decision the business takes. E.g., if the business decided to sell its product(s) abroad using agents, would its ICT be adequate for issues such as stock control and cash flow in a different currency? Another issue is whether to upgrade technology frequently to maintain a competitive edge; or whether to allow it to become obsolete and get the maximum return from it, but face the risk of falling behind competitors. There may therefore be uncertainty over whether an upgrade is 'worth it'.

Furthermore, not all of those involved in making the decision may agree on this course of action, since the perception of the severity of the risk and the uncertainty may vary from person to person on the Board. The perception may reflect personal preferences or prejudices; some directors will be, by nature, more cautious than others. Some may be coming up for re-election and do not want to jeopardise their chances by participating in a decision that may go badly wrong and reflect poorly on them.

If there is a good deal of uncertainty and the risk is perceived to be high, that may mean that the decision to adopt the objective of expansion is made but the nature and extent of the expansion is cautious rather than ambitious. Where uncertainty is low and the perception of risk is also low, the opposite is likely to apply.

Different risks are faced by different business. A large plc that has been trading successfully for 50 years does not face the same uncertainties and risks as a sole trader who has just started up his or her own shop. The plc has an established customer base, extensive knowledge of the market and a brand image. The new business does not. It could be argued that the risks they face may be similar in some respects, for example 'the risk of a competitor taking away their sales', but this risk will be of a completely different magnitude because the plc is much better placed to respond to this if it occurs. Similarly, 'the risk of failure' is not the same; the plc could make a loss for a period of time but still survive. The sole trader runs the risk of personal bankruptcy if this happens because of unlimited liability. The nature of the uncertainties and risks faced by a particular business will be a major influence on the objectives that are set. The plc will be expected by its shareholders to adopt the objective of maximising profits (in the long run if not the short run), whereas the new sole trader will probably have the initial objective of survival.

Management of risk

How may risk be dealt with? The management of risk is certainly going to be an essential part of an entrepreneur or manager's job, particularly at senior executive level. How the risk is managed depends on the nature of it. For example:

Economic risk could be managed by:

- analysis of a wide variety of economic indicators (not just GDP)
- use of Time Series Analysis to forecast trends in variables such as consumer demand, unemployment, imports, and investment; the use of these forecasts will make planning more reliable
- a recognition that some data may be national level and regional data may be more appropriate; also that some data, e.g. unemployment statistics, are 'lagged'; unemployment may not fall even if demand increases, as a business waits a few months to see if the rise is sustained.

Political risk could be managed by:

- managers being up to date and aware of the policy intentions of the main political parties; this knowledge will then make planning for alterations to existing policies more straightforward even if the government is a coalition – as occurred in 2010.

Competitive risk could be managed by:

- building a strategy based on regular and thorough SWOT analyses
- ongoing market research
- use of tools such as the Boston Matrix.

Organisational risk could be managed by:

- a clear understanding (especially at managerial level) of how one department's actions impact upon another
- fostering a 'change culture' where employees are encouraged to accept change rather than resist it; this will mean involving employees in planning; where there has been input into plan it is more likely to be accepted
- offering appropriate incentives for those adopting new roles where restructuring is necessary; careful consideration of the terms being offered for those facing redundancy.

Stakeholder risk could be managed by:

- consultation with any stakeholders likely to be affected by the decision well in advance; employees and suppliers could be especially important.

It has to be emphasised that even thorough risk management through actions such as the detailed analysis of data or considering the responses of stakeholders cannot guarantee success; risk will never be eliminated. The uncertainty involved with the use of quantitative techniques means it can be difficult to assign accurate values to costs, revenues, and profits. Also, the response from stakeholders may not be unequivocal. Furthermore, risk assessment is not a 'one off'; it is ongoing. Careful decision making based on risk is essential.

Unquantifiable risk

It is not always possible to put an absolutely precise figure on a risk because of uncertainty, but usually some figure, or a range of figures, can be arrived at and assigned to a risk. Some risks, however, are unquantifiable, that is, they can be risks that are completely unexpected. In the event of a factory burning down the amount involved in rebuilding and re-equipping it would be known, but the amount of revenue and profit that would be lost from future customers in the coming years is likely to be unquantifiable. Similarly, the loss of a key employee may be unquantifiable because although someone else could, no doubt, be employed the new person may not have the expertise and personality to 'get the work done' in the way that the previous person had.

Key term

Quantifiable risk: the likelihood of a predictable risk occurring. It is possible to put a value on this sort of risk.

Unquantifiable risk: the risk of an event that is unexpected. Sometimes referred to as 'the unknown unknowns'. It is not possible to put a value on this sort of risk.

Personal risk

Mention should also be made of the personal risk to anyone running a business. Entrepreneurs often take risks with their own physical and mental well-being by working long hours with few breaks or holidays, especially in the early stages of the firm's existence. Furthermore, if a person uses his or her house as security for a loan there is a risk to their whole family if the business collapses.

Decision making, risk and opportunity cost

The relationship between risk and reward has already been established; a decision to take a high risk is associated with the expectation of a high reward and vice versa. As well as risk-taking, decision-making involves another important concept – that of opportunity cost. This is not the financial cost of a decision but is what has to be 'given up' when a course of action is chosen. Businesses do not have sufficient resources to do everything they would like to do and so pursuing a particular course of action will mean that something else has to be forfeited.

Consider a situation where the marketing director of a company that makes dishwasher tablets wants to launch a nationwide television advertising campaign lasting several weeks, backed up by the distribution of extensive free samples. This, she argues, will boost the business's sales considerably and therefore seems like a sensible course of action. However, the finance director wants to install a completely new ICT system throughout the business's head office which will have not only a high initial capital cost, but also significant training implications in the short term as well. Assume that both options have about the same financial cost and that the business does not have the funds to do both. How will the board of directors decide what to do? They will certainly consider risk and reward and then decide on the basis of which is most likely to yield the most benefit to the business. If the board decides on the advertising campaign, then the opportunity cost of the decision is not the cost of the advertising campaign but the benefits from the new technology (in terms of better communication, faster processing of orders, etc.) that have been foregone. Opportunity cost is therefore the real cost of a business decision; time or money can always be put to an alternative use.

It is not only businesses who face the concept of opportunity cost. Consumers face it; if someone spends £50 on computer games then they cannot spend that £50 on clothes. The clothes have had to be forfeited. The government faces it as well. With the limited finance available it must decide whether (say) £100 million spent on schools will yield more benefits than £100 million spent on improving the health service. Both will clearly lead to benefits (over a period of several years) but these will be of different types: a more educated nation versus a healthier nation. If it cannot afford both then the benefits from one of these courses of action must be foregone.

In summary, when a business decision is going to be taken the concept of opportunity cost means that all possible courses of action have to be considered very carefully. Decision-makers need to bear in mind the business's current objectives, and the course of action with the most potential to help reach those objectives should be chosen – after all, why choose an option that does not contribute much to the objective(s) that the business is trying to achieve? This is a sound principle but it is not always straightforward because not all risks, costs and benefits can be measured precisely and there may well be disagreement over the extent and nature of them – and over what time period they may occur.

Key term

Opportunity cost: the next best alternative that has to be forfeited when a decision is made.

Your turn

Questions in red are for A Level candidates only.

Multiple-choice questions

1 A business does not have up-to-date figures on whether its market is growing or shrinking. This is an example of:
A risk management
B speculative risk
C quantifiable risk
D uncertainty. *(1)*

2 Where there is a high degree of uncertainty there will be:
A a large opportunity cost
B a higher degree of risk
C a greater return
D high expenditure in order to counteract it. *(1)*

3 The loss of £1 million due to a failed advertising campaign is an example of:
A customer risk
B personal risk
C speculative risk
D opportunity cost. *(1)*

4 Which of the following is an example of internal uncertainty?
A competitive uncertainty
B economic uncertainty
C employee uncertainty
D political uncertainty. *(1)*

Revision questions

1 State the relationship between 'risk' and 'reward'. *(2)*

2 State the difference between 'risk' and 'uncertainty' in business. *(2)*

3A State what is meant by 'uncertainty'. *(1)*

3B State one effect of 'uncertainty' on a business. *(1)*

4 Identify one example of an internal uncertainty and one example of an external uncertainty that a business has to face. *(2)*

5 State what is meant by 'opportunity cost' and give one example of an opportunity cost to a person who decides to start an apprenticeship when they leave school at 18. *(2)*

Total *(10)*

Case study

Ebac

In 2014 the business Ebac was featured as part of BBC2's 'New Troubleshooter' series. In this series (Lord) Digby Jones, an entrepreneur and former president of the CBI visited businesses to give advice on how they could improve and reach their potential. At the time, Ebac, which is based in County Durham, successfully made water coolers and humidifiers which it sold abroad as well as in the UK. The company was proud of its reputation as a major employer (around 200 employees) and as an example of British manufacturing. It was about to diversify into making chest freezers. There was certainly some synergy in this move, as the cooling technology used in these products is very similar.

The route chosen by Managing Director, Pamela Petty, to do this was to use an existing brand – Norfrost. Based in John O'Groats, Norfrost had gone into liquidation some months previously and the plan was for Ebac to buy the freezer-making equipment from Norfrost and transport it to a new production area near its existing factory. The advantage would be the considerable cost saving on buying the capital equipment, but there were clearly risks associated with the diversification. For a start, the equipment at the John O'Groats factory had not been tested to see if it actually still worked.

There was also an issue with marketing. The 'white goods' market in the UK is dominated by imported products with established brand names and Digby Jones wanted to know what 

Ebac's unique selling point for the freezers would be. There wasn't one. In fact, very little market research had been done at all into the likely customer base. Jones was incredulous and asked how they could possible target a customer effectively if they didn't know who the customer was. The marketing director's notion that 'people liked to buy British' and that 'the product was reliable and affordable' were deemed very generic statements and unlikely to make much of an impact in such a competitive market.

Ebac therefore had two massive tasks: first, uninstalling all the equipment, moving it several hundred miles and reinstalling it in a more efficient layout than before in order to save costs; and second it also had to resurrect a brand that had not been a spectacular success in the past. All the time, 'the clock was ticking' and money was being spent (in excess of £1 million) but no revenue was coming in.

It was described as 'the biggest gamble in the company's history'. If it succeeded, turnover could increase from £15 million to £50 million, but it appeared that there was only 'a basic business plan' in place for the venture. The move, the reinstallation, and the relaunch were all scheduled to occur over a six-week period. Could it succeed? The answer was 'yes' but the launch was delayed by several months due to Ebac's management underestimating the risks and challenges they faced.

1 The diversification was 'the biggest gamble in the company's history' and involved a considerable amount of uncertainty and risk. State the relationship between uncertainty and risk in business. *(2)*

2 Ebac's turnover 'could increase from £15 million to £50 million'. Calculate the percentage increase in turnover if the diversification was successful. *(3)*

3A Distinguish between quantifiable and unquantifiable risk. *(2)*

3B Using the example of Ebac's Norfrost diversification, identify an example of each type of risk. *(2)*

4 Analyse how Ebac might have used the concept of opportunity cost when making the decision to diversify. *(6)*

5 Evaluate how Ebac could reduce the level of risk it faces from the diversification into freezers. *(15)*

Total *(30)*

Chapter 10

Forecasting

Year 2

A Level students must know all of the content in this chapter.

This chapter is not applicable for AS students.

Forecasting is the use of existing data to predict future trends. Businesses need to use forecasting so that they can make plans for the future. For example, a bathroom supplier might forecast the growth in house building in order to assess the future demand for its products. A business can use forecasting for costs, market size, but the most important use for forecasting is sales. From this, the business will be able to look at its market share and the likely demand for labour, marketing and training. For example, if a business finds from forecasts that it is likely to experience growing sales in the next two years, it will need to recruit and train new workers and to ensure supplies of raw materials.

Methods of forecasting

A business can use quantitative (numerical) and qualitative (based on experience and understanding) methods of forecasting. Which is the best method to use will depend on the business and what it is trying to forecast. For example, quantitative methods require the use of good numerical data. However, any forecast will only be as good as the information it is based on. Even then unforeseen circumstances may arise that make the forecast inaccurate and useless.

Qualitative forecasting

As an alternative to forecasting using numerical methods, it is possible to use views and opinions in reaching decisions about the future. These will often be based on previous experience or on a systematic collection of opinions from groups like consumers or sales staff. Although some may think that this is a less accurate method of forecasting than the use of quantitative methods, it can yield good results. Quantitative methods may look more accurate, but they will only be as good as the information on which they are based. Sometimes a 'gut reaction' may give a better result.

1. Delphi technique: this is a form of structured qualitative forecasting that relies on information from experts. It usually takes the form of a questionnaire that is supplied individually to a group of experts, who are asked their opinions on the likely outcomes of particular business or economic situations. After the first round, the information from all the questionnaires is summarised anonymously and given back to the experts for a new set of forecasts, which will be revised according to the information provided. It is believed that over this process the opinions in the group will converge to a median or average. The process can continue over a number of 'rounds' depending on a predetermined stop point.
2. Brainstorming: this is a technique that brings together individuals to discuss their ideas for solutions to problems. It is believed that it is more effective to use group discussion to resolve problems than to have individuals working alone.
3. Sometimes, instead of using any structured techniques, managers will rely on intuition to forecast an outcome. In doing this, they will rely on their knowledge of their businesses, their knowledge of their markets and the economy and past experience.

Qualitative forecasting methods

- Consumer expectations: consumer expectations may differ from the views held by others in the economy. Consumers can often be pessimistic about the future despite what the trends from forecasting show for the economy. If consumers are pessimistic against the trends, it is likely that this will affect future growth. Market research can be used to assess consumer feelings and opinions. (See **Chapters 51–53**.)

- In some situations, sales staff may have the most accurate view of the way in which the market is moving. They are in daily contact with likely retailers, and possibly consumers, and they will be able to use this contact to assess the way in which the market is moving. Sales staff forecasts are particularly useful for short-term planning.
- It is possible to use the opinions of academics and business experts to forecast future market changes. This can be done through meetings or through the use of academic papers or by direct approach to experts or expert panels.

Possibly the best way to use qualitative forecasting is in conjunction with quantitative results. Sometimes quantitative data may be incomplete, ambiguous or misleading. For example, it can fail to give information about changes in the feelings of local populations about proposals on where to build a shopping centre. Using qualitative methods like local resident panels alongside quantitative methods will help to highlight this problem.

Quantitative methods: time series analysis

There are a number of quantitative methods that the business can use for forecasting, but this chapter will consider the use of time series analysis, which is a moving average. A moving average looks at data over a period of time and combines it over different periods to give averages. Time series analysis is the use of a moving average using past data, calculated over a period of time, which is then projected to give forecast figures for the future. It is particularly useful for a business that faces cyclical or seasonal changes in demand, because the analysis will iron out the variations and give a long-term trend for the data. The analysis makes the assumption that past performance can be used as an indicator for the future, which may not always be the case.

The business will want to find four components from the information given by time series analysis:

1. The trend: the raw data or actual figures that make up the data may fluctuate over a period of time. For example, an ice-cream seller will find that sales vary with the weather. These fluctuations may make it difficult to see whether the overall movement of sales is upward or downward. The trend figure will smooth out these fluctuations to give an overall picture.
2. Cyclical variations: these are the variations that occur as a result of the business cycle, and recessions and booms in the economy (see **Chapter 18**). For example, a house-builder may find that demand for properties change with the rate of interest and the availability of credit.
3. Seasonal variations: these are changes that occur over the year; they will affect some businesses more than others. For example, a toy manufacturer would expect sales to increase in the run-up to the Christmas period and holidays.
4. Random fluctuations: these are changes in sales that might be difficult to predict. For example, the ice-cream seller might find that sales increase at unexpected times if the weather is warmer than normal.

Finding the trend

Identifying the trend in sales figures will show a business whether the overall movement in its sales is upward or downward. In order to do this, the raw data must be used to calculate a moving average. This average can be calculated over any period of time, but the choice will depend on the cycle of sales which the business faces. For example, if a business has seasonal sales that fluctuate over quarters of the year, it would use a three-month average. If it faces variations over a three-year period, the average would be a three-point calculation.

Tips and techniques

It is very unlikely that you will be asked to calculate a moving average under examination conditions because the process is time-consuming. It is also important to understand the process and what the figures mean.

Table 10.1 Calculating the three-year periods

Year	Sales (£000)
2000	120
2001	110
2002	115
2003	130
2004	112
2005	121
2006	133
2007	121
2008	127
2009	145
2010	133
2011	138
2012	154
2013	144
2014	151

Table 10.1 shows the figures for a business where sales peak at three-year intervals. In this case, a three-period moving average should be used. To calculate the three-period average, add together the first three numbers and put the total alongside the middle of the first three years; in this case, 2001.

120 + 110 + 115 = 345

This number should be put in the total column as shown in Table 10.2. The first sales number then drops out and the following three numbers are added for 2001, 2002, and 2003. The total of these numbers is placed alongside 2001. This process is continued down the table, with the top number dropping out at each stage and the next three being added until the final three numbers are reached. The final total will be placed alongside 2014.

Table 10.2 Calculating the three-period averages

Year	Sales (£000)	Three period total
2000	120	
2001	110 (a)	(a) 345
2002	115 (b)	(b) 355
2003	130	357
2004	112	363
2005	121	366
2006	133	375
2007	121	381
2008	127	393
2009	145	405
2010	133	416
2011	138	425
2012	154	436
2013	144	449
2014	151	

This will be the fourth column in the table, and the figure is found by dividing the totals in the third column by three to find the average figure.

Table 10.3 Calculating the three-period moving average

Year	Sales (£000)	Three-period total	Three-period moving average
2000	120		
2001	110 (a)	(a) 345 / 3	(a) 115
2002	115	355	118.3
2003	130	357	119
2004	112	363	121
2005	121	366	122
2006	133	375	125
2007	121	381	127
2008	127	393	131
2009	145	405	135
2010	133	416	138.7
2011	138	425	141.7
2012	154	436	145.3
2008	144	449	149.7
2013	151		
2014			

To calculate the value of (a):

```
345/3 = 115
```

Plotting the information on a graph

If the sales figures are plotted on a graph, they will fluctuate as shown in Figure 10.1. This graph is not appropriate for forecasting because it is impossible to see any long-term trend in it.

When the moving average figures are plotted, they should not be joined together. Instead a straight line should be drawn through them, which is called the line of best fit (or correlation). This line will show a

Key term

Line of best fit: a line drawn through the points on a graph so that the points are distributed as evenly as possible above and below the line.

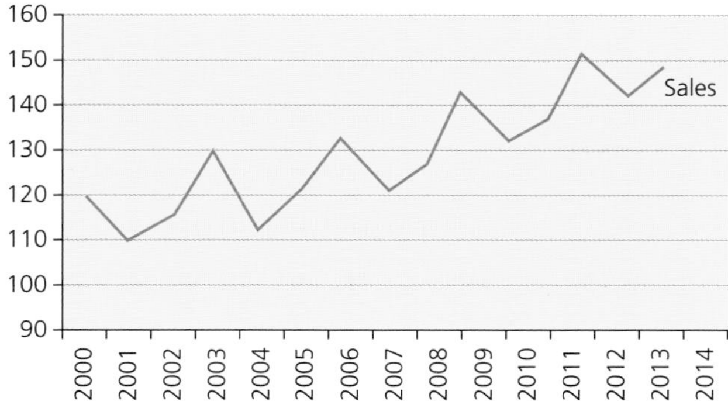

Figure 10.1 Sales information in a graph

long-term trend and can be used to forecast future sales; this is shown in Figure 10.2. This is now an appropriate graph for forecasting purposes because it can be used to predict a long-term trend. The data is extrapolated in this process; the line of best fit will be extended to show what might be expected to happen in the future.

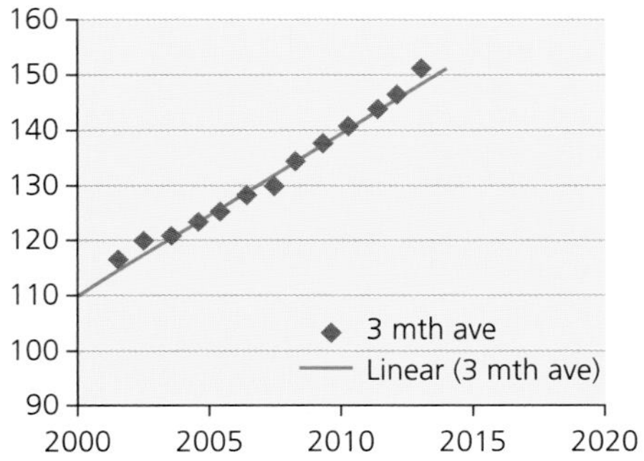

Figure 10.2 Line of best fit (or correlation)

Once this line has been drawn in, it is possible to extend or project it so that forecast figures for future sales can be read if the long-term trend remains the same; see Figure 10.3.

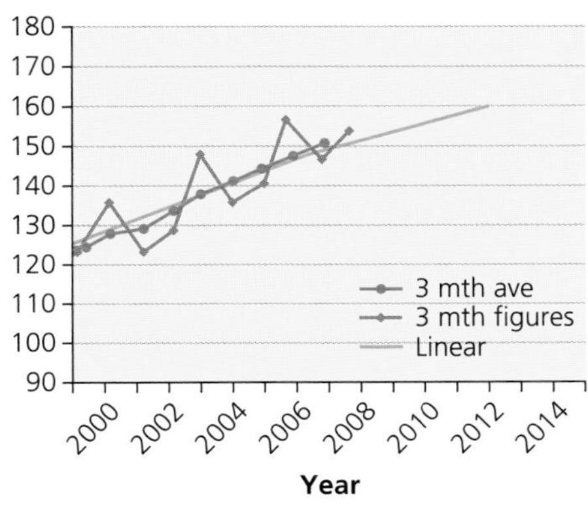

Figure 10.3 Sales graph

In Figure 10.3 the line of best fit through the moving average figures has been extended up to 2014. If the current trend in sales figures remains the same, it will be possible to read off the sales figures from this line for the next five years.

Calculating the cyclical variation

Although it is possible to read off the trend in sales from the moving average line on the graph, accurate figures for annual sales are not given. As Figure 10.1 shows, sales figures for each year will fluctuate. By calculating the average variation of sales in each of the periods (three, in this example) and applying this to the figures, it is possible to obtain a more accurate forecast of annual sales.

The cyclical variation is the amount by which the actual sales in a period vary from the moving average figures. In Table 10.4, the actual sales for 2001 are £110,000, whereas the moving average sales are £115,000. This means that the cyclical variation is:

Actual sales – moving average sales, so
110 – 115 = –5

It is important to show the sign in the calculation.

Table 10.4 Calculating the cyclical variation

Year	Sales (£000)	Three-period total	Three-period moving average	Cyclical variation
2000	120			
2001	110	345	115	–5 period 1
2002	115	355	118.3	–3.3 period 2
2003	130	357	119	+11 period 3
2004	112	363	121	–9 period 1
2005	121	366	122	–1 period 2
2006	133	375	125	+8 period 3
2007	121	381	127	–6 period 1
2008	127	393	131	–4 period 2
2009	145	405	135	+10 period 3
2010	133	416	138.7	–5.7 period 1
2011	138	425	141.7	–3.7 period 2
2012	154	436	145.3	+8.7 period 3
2013	144	449	149.7	–5.7 period 1
2014	151			

Each of the periods has been given a period number in the final column. This is a three-period average, so starting at the first year, 2000, with year 1, go through and allocate the period to each of the following years.

It is then possible to calculate the average of the cyclical variations for each period.

For Period 1, the average is:

$$\frac{-5 + (-9) + (-6) + (-5.7) + (-5.7)}{5} = -6.3$$

For Period 2, the average is:

$$\frac{-3.3 + (-1) + (-4) + (-3.7)}{4} = -3$$

For Period 3, the average is:

$$\frac{11 + 8 + 10 + 8.7}{4} = -9.425$$

Using these average cyclical variations with their signs to adjust the values taken from the projected line on the graph will help to make the figures a more accurate forecast of annual sales. For example, in Figure 10.3, the projected sales figure for 2012 is £160,000. The year 2012 is period 3 in the cycle and the average cyclical variation in period 3 from the calculation above is £9,425. This means that sales for that year are forecast to be:

£160,000 + £9,425 = £169,425

Similarly for 2011, which is period 2, the reading from the graph is £158,000. From this £3,000 must be subtracted because the cyclical variation for period 2 is a negative value of £3000:

158,000 – £3,000 = £155,000

Tips and techniques

Questions about moving averages are likely to ask you to calculate or apply cyclical variations to a set of figures or a graph of moving averages that has been given to you.

Summary for calculating a moving average and using it to forecast

- Find the trend period.
- Calculate the moving total.
- Calculate the moving average.
- Calculate the cyclical variation.
- Calculate the average cyclical variation.
- Plot the trend line on a graph and extrapolate the forecast from the projected line of best fit.
- Add or subtract the average cyclical variation to the forecast figures on the graph.

Use and limitations of forecasts

Forecasts are likely to be useful to businesses in showing the trend in figures such as sales, but they need to be used with caution.

- Any forecast will only be as reliable as the data that is used to formulate it. It is vital in preparing forecasts to use accurate and reliable information.
- Businesses need to be careful about making assumptions about the future based on the experience of the past. While past performance may be a reasonable indicator of the future most of the time, events in political and economic spheres can occasionally make forecasts less useful.
- The most recent information is often the most useful and relevant. The use of moving averages does not distinguish between recent and distant information in formulating the forecast.
- The forecast does not take account of any change in the objectives of the business. For example, the business may want to increase its sales by a larger percentage in the next few years or, if the economic outlook is not good, it may be happy simply to maintain sales at their current level.
- It is important, nevertheless, for businesses to try to estimate future revenue and costs so that they can take action to improve their overall performance. The use of a moving average will help to show the business how well it is likely to perform in the future, other things remaining equal.

Your turn

Multiple-choice questions

1 The cyclical variations for three time periods of sales are (-)4, (-)7, and (-)2 . The average cyclical variation is:

A 4.3
B (-)13
C (-)4.3
D 13 *(1)*

2 The line of best fit shows:

A the sales of a business over a period of time.
B the projected sales over a period of time.
C a line drawn through sales with points distributed evenly on either side.
D a line extended to show likely future sales. *(1)*

Revision questions

1 State two benefits of calculating a moving average. *(2)*

2 Explain how to draw 'the line of best fit'? *(2)*

3 State three limitations of forecasts. *(3)*

Total *(7)*

Case study

Petals and cakes

Nicola James set up her flower and cake business ten years ago, working out of a unit in her garage that had been fitted out to meet the health and safety requirements for catering. She specialises in producing cakes and flowers for special occasions like weddings, birthdays and anniversaries.

Nicola now finds that most of her business comes from wedding orders and these are becoming increasingly complicated and lavish as the wedding market continues to grow. This is now a successful market for Nicola, but it has the disadvantage of the work being cyclical. Most of the orders for wedding flowers and cakes come in the spring and summer months and around Christmas. January, February and November are very quiet times for the business.

Nicola has decided that she would like to see what the trend is for her business by using a time series analysis, which she can then project into future years. She hopes that this will help her to see what the demand for premises and staffing could be in the future. Nicola wants to know whether she should take on a new apprentice cake decorator and consider moving to a larger, purpose-built unit.

The figures for the business's sales for the past two years are shown in the table below.

Sales (£)	2013	2014
Jan	500	400
Feb	200	150
Mar	2000	3500
Apr	4000	4500
May	9000	10500
Jun	15000	17500
Jul	15000	14000
Aug	12000	12000
Sep	7000	8000
Oct	3000	4500
Nov	1500	1500
Dec	500	600

The table below shows the calculations for a three-month moving average with the last two months missing (October and November).

Year	Month		3 mth total	3 mth average
2013	January	500		
	February	200	2700	900
	March	2000	6200	2067
	April	4000	15000	5000
	May	9000	28000	9333
	June	15000	39000	13000
	July	15000	42000	14000
	August	12000	34000	11333
	September	7000	22000	7333
	October	3000	11500	3833
	November	1500	5000	1667
	December	500	2400	800
2014	January	400	1050	350
	February	150	4050	1350
	March	3500	8150	2717
	April	4500	18500	6167
	May	10500	32500	10833
	June	17500	42000	14000
	July	14000	43500	14500
	August	12000	34000	11333
	September	8000	24500	8167
	October	4500	?	?
	November	1500	?	?
	December	600		

1 Calculate a three-month moving average for October and November for the business. *(6)*
2 Plot the figures on a graph and show the line of best fit. (8)
3 Use the graph to forecast sales for the business for the first six months of 2015. *(2)*
Total *(16)*

Chapter 11

Decision making and conflicts in decision making

Year 2

A Level students must know all of the content in this chapter.

This chapter is not applicable for AS students.

Making effective decisions is one of the most important factors in achieving success and meeting targets. The process of decision making will involve skills like identifying the options available, consultation and taking advice, the use of decision making tools, clear vision, commitment and firmness in carrying the decision through and effective implementation.

Effective decision making is particularly important when it comes to winning over stakeholders. Workers will often be resistant to new ideas, whereas shareholders may be enthusiastic if it is likely to lead to a growth in profits. It is important that the effects on all stakeholders are considered in the decision making process from the outset. (See **Chapter 5**.)

Decision making is a process that can be learned by managers and others in the business. It is increasingly the case that employees at almost all levels are involved in the decision making process in some way. For it to be successful process, those making decisions need to be supported; the decision will not necessarily always be the correct one so it is important that decisions are not made in an atmosphere of fear and criticism. The success of the decision making process can be measured in a variety of ways depending on the decisions being taken. It could be reference to financial information (see **Chapter 34**) or labour turnover (see **Chapter 43/45**) or productivity (see **Chapter 64**).

There are a number of different types of decision made in business:

1 Strategic decisions are long-term decisions affecting the whole of the business; they are long-term decisions that are taken at board or senior management level. This could include a decision about growth of the business or diversification.
2 Tactical decisions are taken by middle management affecting a particular part of the business; they are medium-term decisions affecting a particular department. An example would be making a decision to increase the training given to a particular group of workers.
3 Operational decisions are those taken on a day-to-day basis; these decisions are taken by managers of departments. An example would be moving personnel to different jobs on a production line or in a supermarket.

One of the easiest ways to begin a decision making process is to look at and weigh the pros and cons of the change. For example, a business considering implementing a new computer system could start out by doing this simple exercise shown in Table 11.1 below.

Table 11.1 Example of weighing the pros and cons for a new computer system

New computer system			
Pros		**Cons**	
Fewer staff needed	3	Cost of the new system	4
Better results from the work	5	Cost of redundancies	2
Up-to-date, faster, more reliable	4	Cost of retraining staff	2
Good support system available	2	Teething problems	3
Total	14	Total	11

Although such a process is only a rough guide, it helps in looking at the process objectively; putting down all the concerns the decision raises before moving on to the next and more formal stages is also helpful.

The business may use a variety of decision making tools in the process of making a decision, particularly a strategic decision: some of the tools may be financial, others non-financial. Some decision making tools are quantitative, which means that they use numerical information; others are qualitative, which means that they are based on non-numerical data. The quantitative tools are more likely to be subject to value judgments and bias. The following is a list of some of the measures that the business may use. See the chapters referred to in this book to learn more about the measures and their advantages and disadvantages:

- SWOT analysis: qualitative (see **Chapter 50**)
- Financial accounts of the business: quantitative
- Financial information on the state of the local, national and international economy: quantitative (see **Chapter 18**)
- Market research information: qualitative and quantitative (see **Chapter 52**)
- PEST analysis: qualitative (see **Chapters 17 to 19**)
- Porter's five forces: qualitative (see **Chapter 7**)
- Advice from consultants: qualitative and quantitative
- Brainstorming or running a workshop: qualitative and quantitative
- Help from business advisers, for example at the bank: qualitative and quantitative
- Decision trees: quantitative (see **Chapter 12**)
- Time series analysis: quantitative (see **Chapter 10**)

Businesses also need to take into account factors such as risk, bias and the accuracy of forecasting when using any of the decision making tools listed above.

Obviously it will not be possible or even advisable for a business to use all of these methods when making a decision. It is likely that looking at too much information will only confuse the issue, making it almost impossible to reach an effective decision. Managers may also decide to ignore the information if they believe a particular course of action is desirable. This may sometimes be the case with investment decisions. The theory would suggest that when making investment decisions, managers should look at something like payback (see **Chapter 29**). Practice seems to show that decisions are often reliant on business confidence or lack of it amongst fellow business leaders. As a result, managers will sometimes make decisions to invest when there does not seem to be any concrete justification for it and vice versa.

The main objectives of a business are survival, breaking even, profitability and growth. Alongside these, there might be other lesser objectives such as a low environmental impact, market leadership, customer satisfaction and low labour turnover (see **Chapter 7**).

JCB and decision making

A JCB digger

JCB is a business supplying heavy earth moving equipment to the construction industry. In this sector, it is important to assess where the economy is going, not where it is at the moment, when making decisions about staffing and training. Although it will be possible to use some of the methods listed above, the decision about whether to expand and take workers on may also be the result of the use of past experience, rather than any quantifiable factor. JCB has been particularly successful at anticipating movements in the economy, both here and overseas. In 2014, despite signs of recovery in the UK and world economy, the business started to lay off workers. This would suggest that either by using decision making tools, or through on-the-ground evidence, they felt that the recovery was fragile and could stall.

For example, if a business decides to make its main objective growth, it might use the following tools to aid its decision making into the best way to achieve this:

- SWOT analysis to see where the business's strengths and weaknesses are and what the threats and opportunities may be
- bank business advisers to recommend credit or loans
- time series analysis to forecast sales
- market research to find out if there is sufficient demand in the market.

Decision making tools

There are various tools that managers might use when making decisions. One of these is decision trees, which are covered in detail in the next chapter. Another tool is Ansoff's matrix.

Ansoff's Matrix

Ansoff's Matrix is a strategic tool used to help a business that wishes to grow. Igor Ansoff worked for Lockheed Electronics before leaving to become a university professor. He was interested in ways by which businesses could identify their competitive advantage in existing and new markets.

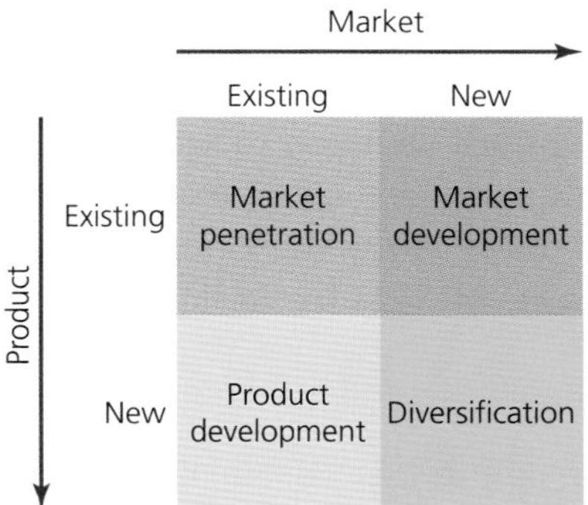

Figure 11.1 Ansoff's Matrix

The matrix looks at the business's markets in terms of existing and new products, and existing and new market opportunities. It identifies four possible strategies for growth: market penetration, market development, product development and diversification. Each of them will require the use of different elements of the marketing mix (see **Chapters 54–57**), together with market research.

Market penetration

This is a situation where the firm tries to sell more of its existing product in its existing market. To achieve this, the business may need to use more aggressive promotion, or it may need to price its product more competitively.

Market development

This involves selling the existing product to a new market segment. Careful market research will be required in the first instance to identify possible markets. The business then needs to ensure that it prices and promotes the product with the new market in mind.

Product development

Changes are made to the existing product, but it continues to sell in the same market. This might involve new packaging, new flavours or new formulation for the product.

Diversification

This entails selling a new product in a new market, and it is a high risk strategy for any business. Thorough market research will be needed so that the firm is aware of any threats that might exist, particularly in the form of competition.

Ansoff's Matrix in practice

Using Ansoff's Matrix makes it possible for the business to identify how it wants its market to grow and to formulate a strategy. For example, suppose that a business producing personalised office stationery decides it wants to grow. Having looked at the alternatives and completed market research, managers make a decision to move into the market for wedding stationery where opportunities exist because there are few competitors. This is an example of diversification in the matrix; the business will be selling a new product in a new market. The business will need to ensure that the new product range meets the needs of the market at a price that consumers are willing to pay. Promotion will also be needed to create awareness of the new range among potential customers. The strategy will therefore be based around price, promotion and product. In all growth strategies, businesses will need to use elements of the marketing mix to ensure that success is achieved. The extent to which Ansoff's Matrix will be useful to a business will depend on the nature of the business and the market it is operating in.

Tips and techniques

The advantage of using Ansoff's Matrix in a question on business strategy is that it encourages concentration on a combination of one or two factors from the marketing mix. This makes it less likely that the answer is a list of possibilities with little or no analysis or evaluation.

Conflicts in decision making

The process of decision making may create problems for a business if the information acquired from different sources is conflicting. Sometimes, one decision making tool may suggest one course of action while others disagree. The final decision will then come down to the manager's judgement.

Conflicts in reaching decisions may arise because:

- The information gathered might not reflect reality.
- Factors like customer satisfaction and staff morale are almost impossible to quantify and may prove unexpected in the face of change.
- When complex research is undertaken by experts it may prove inaccurate because the experts have little knowledge of the reality of the situation, or the problems faced by management in the business world.

On the other hand, good research used for decision making can be very useful. The use of sophisticated computer modelling, allowing the decision maker to look at different scenarios can be used very effectively. This is often the case with sales predictions.

Stakeholders and decisions

It is often the case that the result of a particular decision may be viewed differently by different groups of stakeholders. Conflict may arise for a number of reasons:

- Shareholders will be interested in profits and dividends.
- Customers will want quality, reliability, low prices and good customer service.
- Employees and unions may also want to see increased profits if it means better pay and more jobs. They will not want to see decisions that reduce employment prospects and result in redundancy.
- The local community might be interested in decisions for the firm to grow if it means more jobs, but not if it results in pollution.
- Environmental groups will be happy to see 'greener' production methods, but shareholders might object if they cause costs to rise in the short run.

Further sources

www.bbc.co.uk/education: Bitesize Decision making in business
www.businessballs.com
www.businessnewsdaily.com

Your turn

Multiple-choice questions

1 Which of the following statements is correct?
   A Strategic decisions are medium term and made by senior managers.
   B Tactical decisions are long term and made by senior managers.
   C Tactical decisions are medium term and made by departmental managers.
   D Strategic decisions are long term and made by departmental managers. *(1)*

2 Which of the following decision making tools is qualitative?
   A the profit and loss account
   B the balance sheet
   C SWOT analysis
   D time series data. *(1)*

3 In Ansoff's Matrix, the launch of a new product in a new market is called:
   A market penetration
   B market development
   C diversification
   D product development *(1)*

Revision questions

1 Explain two tools that a local bakery could use to help make a decision on introducing a new line of cakes. *(4)*

2 Explain two conflicts between stakeholder groups that could arise if a car hire business decides to relocate to a residential area. *(4)*

Total *(8)*

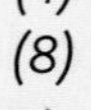

Case study

Transport for London (TfL) is responsible for the transport network across London. As a result it has large property holdings comprised of tube and train stations, bus stations, disused depots and surplus underground land, much of which it regards as underused. TfL is asking for input from groups such as architects, agents, structural engineers, developers and quantity surveyors to help it make decisions about how to maximise the value of its property holdings. At the same time it wants its decisions to take into account the Mayor's policies to improve London.

TfL is considering making much greater use of its stations for the retail and service sector. Most stations already have retail outlets and food providers; most of the bigger stations also have a wide range of larger shops and services, such as dry cleaners and shoe repairers. TfL is considering working with logistics firms and supermarkets to provide pick-up points at stations through the use of lockers. The idea is that customers could shop online and arrange to pick up their shopping on the way home from work. The shopping would be delivered to a locker in the station and the customer would be given a code to open the locker. A similar system would be used for parcel collection through logistics firms.

TfL is also closing many ticket offices in stations as the use of ticket machines rises. The idea is to take staff from behind glass and put them in ticket halls to assist travellers. This measure would free up more space in station concourses to be used for other revenue-producing schemes. This idea has met with considerable hostility from passengers, employees and the rail unions who feel that ticket offices are important for visitors to the capital and because employees fear redundancy.

1. Explain two decision making tools that TfL could use to help make decisions about closing ticket offices. *(4)*
2. Analyse the factors that TfL may need to take into account before making an agreement with a major supermarket to use its premises for delivery purposes. *(9)*
3. Evaluate the problems that TfL will face with stakeholders if it takes the decision to develop the retail possibilities of its station holdings. *(15)*

Total *(28)*

Chapter 12

Decision trees

Year 2

A Level students must know all of the content in this chapter.

This chapter is not applicable for AS students.

A decision tree is a technique that is used to aid the decision making process. Whenever a business is considering two or more options, decision trees can be used to show the likely financial return for undertaking each of the options. Decision trees combine the risk (costs) and the likely return (revenues) from a given undertaking. The 'decision' is based on two aspects:

1 The probability of a particular outcome (the risk)
2 The estimated monetary reward of a given option (the reward).

Decision trees consider the risk in relation to the possible level of reward. Each of the above factors is estimated and calculated in order to reach an amount.

One of the advantages of using decision trees is that the technique is usually drawn, allowing for a visual presentation of the choices and their likely returns. The visual approach allows the business to see the options available, along with the likely outcomes and their possible monetary values.

The diagrams

As for many techniques, particular symbols are used.

The symbols used in Figure 12.1 are:

1 The square represents a decision; to do something or not to do something, or to do one thing or another. The number of lines drawn from the square represents the number of options, from which one will eventually be chosen. In this example, the decision is between selling and not selling.
2 The circle represents the possible outcomes once an option is selected. The outcomes may be simple, such as success and failure. However the outcomes could be for different products, or even days on which particular goods are sold. Whatever the possible outcomes once a decision is made, a line represents each such outcome from the circle.
   In this example, if the decision were to sell, then the possible outcomes would be to sell online or sell at the market.

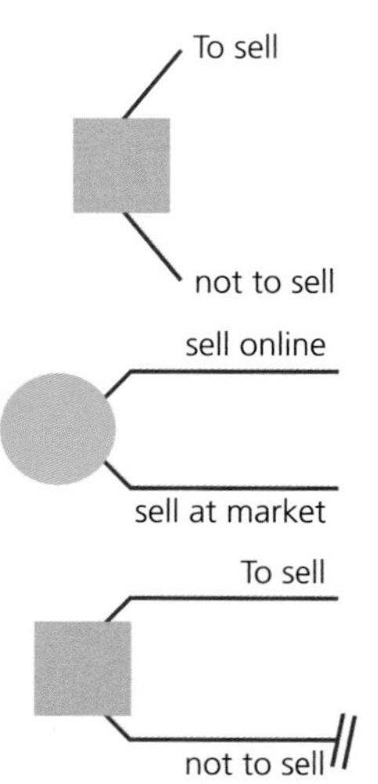

Figure 12.1 A decision tree

3 If a decision is made to sell, it is necessary to end the alternative choice. This is done by drawing parallel lines on the option that is not selected.
   To build a decision tree, the information available has to be 'converted' into a diagram.

Converting information into a diagram

For example, a building company has some land and it needs to decide whether to build some houses on the land or do nothing.

1 The first step is to draw the initial decision: to build or not to build. Action: draw a square to represent the decision (see (i) on Figure 12.2).
2 Now consider how many outcomes there are of building the houses. In this example there are two possible outcomes:
   The houses are built and successfully sold OR
   The houses are not sold.
   Action: draw a circle to represent the outcomes and label each option (see (ii) on Figure 12.2).
3 It is also important to state (usually below the outcome line), the probability of that outcome occurring (see (iii) on Figure 12.2).

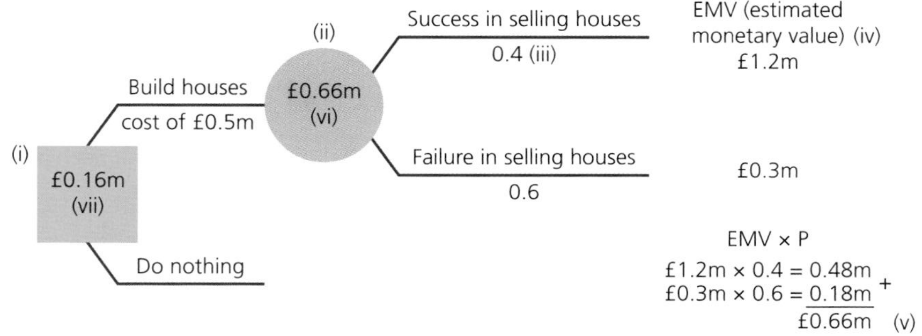

Figure 12.2 A decision tree

4 The final piece of information to be put on the diagram is the likely monetary value of a particular outcome. This is called the estimated monetary value or the likely revenue. This information is placed to the right of the outcome line (see (iv) on Figure 12.2).

Tips and techniques

It is important to ensure your diagram is clearly labelled. Remember that the addition of the probabilities for any decision is always equal to one.

Calculating the expected values

Figure 12.2 now has the complete picture of the decision to be made. The tree is now used to calculate the 'expected values'.

The expected value = EMV × probability.

For example:

Success in selling the houses = £1.2 million × 0.4 = £0.48 million

Failure in selling the houses = £0.3 million × 0.6 = £0.18 million

The two outcomes are added together to gain an expected value of £0.66 million (see (v) in Figure 12.2).

This expected value is then placed into the outcome circle (Figure 12.2, (vi)). If one of the outcomes is negative, then this figure is subtracted from the positive outcome.

Finally, the cost of the particular decision selected is subtracted from the expected value, to give an amount that is the likely result of taking the decision to build the houses:

£0.66 million – £0.5 million = £0.16 million or £160,000

This figure is then placed into the decision box (assuming it is a higher positive figure than any alternative), Figure 12.2 (vii).

This figure can be compared with any of the other possible decisions. In this example, there was no alternative apart from doing nothing. However, this could still be important. If to do nothing costs nothing and consequently yields nothing, this may be a better choice if the choice to build the houses had meant making a loss.

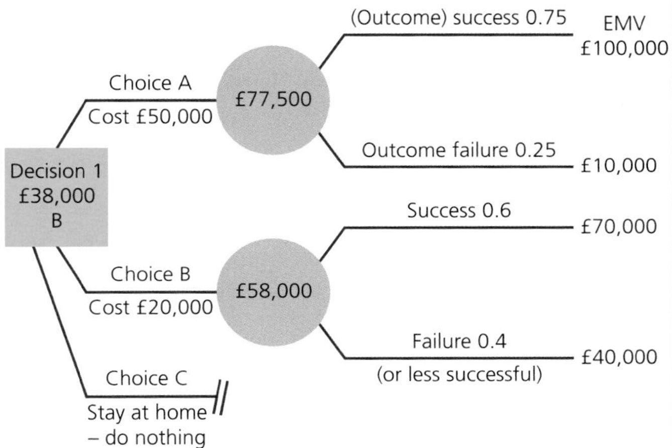

Figure 12.3 A decision tree

It is quite possible that there will be several options to decide upon.

In Figure 12.3 there are three possible options to be considered.

To choose the best option, the following calculations should be undertaken.

Choice A	EMV × p = £100,000 × 0.75 =	75,000
	EMV × p = £10,000 × 0.25 =	**2,500**
		77,500
Choice B	EMV × p = £70,000 × 0.6 =	42,000
	EMV × p = £40,000 × 0.4 =	**16,000**
		58,000
Choice C	no value or cost involved	0

Each figure would be placed in the circles and then the cost of each of the choices is subtracted.

Choice A £77,500 – £50,000 = £27,500

Choice B £58,000 – £20,000 = £38,000

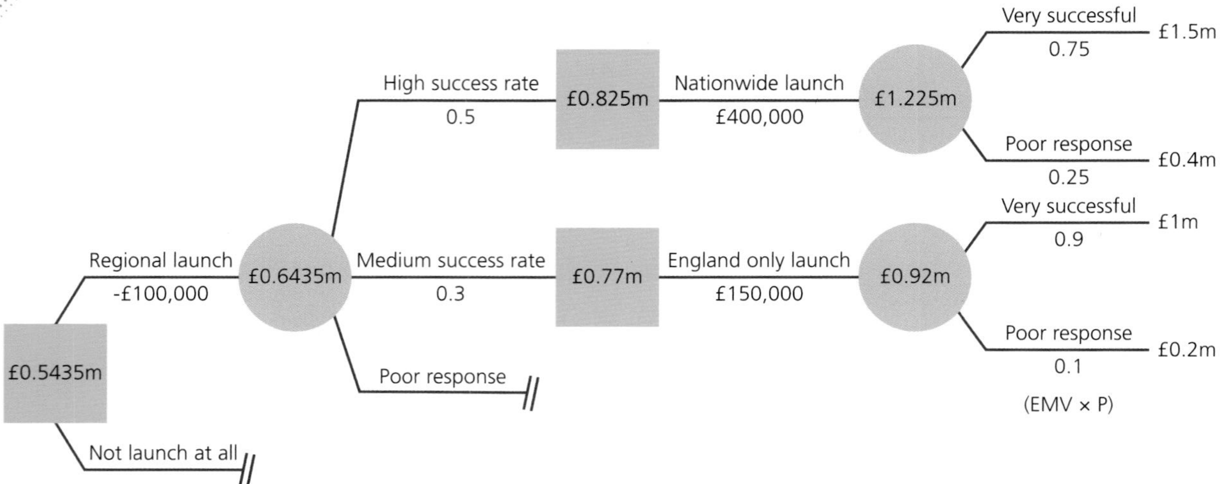

Figure 12.4 A decision tree

Therefore the 'best' choice would be B.

There are instances where there are a series of decisions to be made. It is important to remember that the process for calculating the expected values remains the same.

In Figure 12.4, the initial decision is to decide whether to launch a product on a regional basis, or not launch at all. If it is decided to launch on a regional basis, there are three possible outcomes:

1 high success with a probability of 0.5
2 medium success rate with a probability of 0.3
3 a poor response with a probability of 0.2.

The expected values for the nationwide launch and the England-only launch are:

Nationwide launch	£1.5m × 0.75 =	£1.125m
	£0.4m × 0.25 =	**£0.1m**
	Expected value =	£1.225m
Cost of launch	=	**−£.4 million**
		£0.825 million
England-only launch	£1 millliion × 0.9 =	£0.9 million
	£0.2 million × 0.1 =	**£ 0.02 million**
	Expected value =	£ 0.92 million
	Cost of launch =	**−£0.15 million**
		£0.77 million

Each of these final figures are written in the decision boxes and now become the EMVs for the outcomes of the initial regional launch.

The calculation process is now repeated with the new figures.

Regional launch		
High success	£0.825 × 0.5 =	£0.4125 million
Medium success	£0.77m × 0.3 =	£0.231 million
Poor response (no EMV)		£0
		£0.6435 million
Cost of launch		**−£0.1million**
		£0.5435

Based on the decision tree calculations, the answer is:

1 Undertake the regional launch and the nationwide launch if the regional one is a high success.
2 The overall expected value allowing for all costs will be £0.5435 million.

There may be other factors to consider that may be offered in a case study, which can be used as context. Such factors may include:

- The amount of finance available in the first instance
- If the launches fit with the objectives of the business
- The reliability of both the EMVs and the probabilities
- The business environment, such as the state of the economy
- If the £0.5435 million is a sufficiently high return on the investment
- What, if any, are the alternative investments that could be undertaken?

Tips and techniques

It is important to note that this process of using a decision tree, considers only the value of a choice and nothing else. A consideration of the affordability of the initial cost and whether the choice fits in with the objectives of the business is equally important. In other words, the context of the case is once again vitally important.

It does not matter how complicated the decision tree appears to be, the process for working out the best choice remains the same. It is quite possible that the decision tree diagram will be given to you, for you to calculate the best choice.

Be prepared to offer evaluative comments as to the reliability of the figures involved.

The benefits and limitations of using decision trees

Benefits

- It is a simplistic, visual method to aid the decision making process when faced with several alternatives.
- It is a relatively quick and therefore cost effective method of aiding the decision making process.
- By applying the probabilities, the technique does attempt to account for the level of risk involved, which other decision making techniques do not.
- May be accurate if a similar selection of choices has been considered before, making the figures more reliable.

Limitations

- Much depends upon the accuracy/reliability of the figures used. The probabilities are crucial to calculating the expected values on which a decision is based. Consequently, if these probabilities are only guesses, then the reliability of the technique is limited. This is especially true if the decision to be made relies on making 'guesses' for the probability of a certain outcome, when such an outcome has not occurred before. This prevents basing the probabilities on experience and the figures are therefore even more of a liability. (This is particularly true if such decisions are being made for the first time and therefore there is no experience to aid reliability of data.)
- When 'selecting' the probabilities, the management may be in favour of one particular choice and therefore be tempted to load the probabilities in the favour of that choice.
- Similarly, the ability to gauge the EMV (estimated monetary value) of an outcome may be difficult as there are so many variables that could affect the financial outcome.
- There is often no mention of a time period over which the decision is based. The longer the 'life' of the outcome, the less reliable the figures are likely to be.
- Decision trees concentrate on the quantitative and consequently, qualitative evidence is not considered, which may be crucial.
- There is no reference to the 'human element'. Even though a decision does not have a financial implication, it may affect how the business operates and therefore have an implication for employees.

Your turn

Multiple-choice questions

1 If the probability of the choices are 0.75 and 0.25 with estimated monetary values of £25,000 and £15,00 respectively; the expected value would be:

A £18,750
B £22,500
C £25,500
D £27,500 *(1)*

2 After the expected values have been calculated for all the possible choices there needs to be a calculation to take into consideration:

A The likely profit made
B The likely return on the capital employed
C The cost of each option
D The level of wages for each option *(1)*

Revision questions

1 State three benefits of using a decision tree in the decision making process. *(3)*

2 Calculate the expected value given the following information:
EMV of £50,000 and a probability of 0.8

EMV of –£10,000 and a probability of 0.2 *(3)*

3 Mario's, a local restaurant, is trying to decide if it should open on Sundays or remain closed. From research it has estimated that the chances of success by opening on Sundays are about 80% (0.8) with EMV of £600 and failure 20% (0.2) with an EMV of £200. The cost of opening on Sunday would be £200.
Draw and complete a decision tree using the information given above to decide if it is worthwhile opening the restaurant on Sundays. *(6)*

Total *(12)*

Case study (Group task)

Much in the news has been, and continues to be, regarding what should be done about expanding the UK's runway capacity. In September 2014, The Airports Commission shortlisted three options to help alleviate the problems of air congestion.

The three serious contenders that were shortlisted were:

1 A third runway at Heathrow
2 A second runway at Gatwick
3 An extension to one of the existing runways at Heathrow

The idea of building a completely new airport in the Thames estuary was dismissed by the Commission.

Various costings were put forward:

- Probably one of the reasons why the new airport in the Thames estuary was dismissed was the estimated cost, which was between £24 billion and up to £50 billion, whereas building an additional runway at Heathrow was estimated to cost around £15.6 billion. It was suggested that the proposed extension to one of the existing runways at Heathrow would cost in the region of £5 billion to £9 billion, although another estimate put the figure higher at £13 billion.
- The new runway at Gatwick was estimated to cost £7.8 billion.
- Various estimates were offered as to the economic benefits these proposals would yield to the economy. The additional runway at Gatwick was thought to yield an economic benefit of around £40 billion, whereas the third runway at Heathrow was estimated to yield benefits of around £30 billion.

1 By undertaking your own research, draw a decision tree adding any suitable costs of each choice and gauging a probability figure for each, enabling you to calculate the expected values. Also via research, ascertain the likely costs of each choice to enable you to make a suggestion as to which choice ought to be made.
2 Evaluate the reliability of your decision, having used decision trees.

Chapter 13

The market including physical and non-physical markets

AS / Year 1

Both AS and A Level students must know all of the content in this chapter.

The market

It is quite common to hear a statement such as 'that market is very competitive' but what exactly is a 'market', and what is 'competition'? The term 'competition' tends to be used rather loosely. 'A competitive market' usually means a market in which large numbers of producers actively compete with each other to satisfy the wants and needs of a large number of consumers. In practice, there are, however, different degrees of competition.

People tend to think of a market as a collection of stalls in a town centre with lots of traders selling fruit, vegetables and other products. This is a correct example of a physical market; another example of a physical market is a shopping centre.

However, buyers and sellers in a market do not have to be in face-to-face contact. In a non-physical market sellers compete with each other but do not meet or interact physically with buyers at all. The foreign currency market, for example, is not a market where people are moving around piles of notes and coins in a single building; it exists in the interaction of buyers and sellers in many different financial institutions all over the world. Transactions and movements of currency are made electronically. Another example of a non-physical market is ebay where the transaction is made online. Online markets are also known as digital markets and businesses in these markets are able to gain and process data very quickly about customers and buying habits, so can better manage their supply chain, production and distribution network.

Non-physical markets have grown rapidly in recent years. Convenience is a big factor in this; customers are pleased that they can make a purchase at any time without leaving their home and have it delivered to them directly. From the seller's point of view, operating from one or two locations, with a well-designed website, a secure payment system, and a reliable delivery network is far cheaper than operating a whole network of local or regional branches. High street shopping is not dead, however, and many retailers want to provide a more personalised service where goods can be physically examined. Naturally, they can typically charge a higher price for this, which the customer is usually willing to pay for the extra attention.

Some businesses offer products in both types of markets, for example Tesco. However, such an operation is not confined to food shopping. A process known as 'me-tailing' has emerged as part of the rise in popularity of digital marketplaces, whereby retailers in a physical market offer personalised products and customer service in the 'traditional way', but also go much further. The footwear-retailer Soletrader has in-store iPads that allow customers and sales assistant to search for products and then place the order online. The customer pays in the store and the shoes are delivered to their home address.

It has been suggested that:

> *Retailers are now expected to develop a mobile app for smartphones and tablets and to post promotions and ads to social networking sites. The need for self-service tools of various types has increased, as well as the establishment of a forum for like-minded consumers. In addition, post-purchase experiences are of greater significance. The ability to form an opinion about the retailer after the purchase has become so important that it could increase consumer satisfaction even if the pre-purchase experience was poor.*

Source: www.onsmb.com/2013/10/04/tailing-future-retail/

The important point is the interaction between buyers and sellers. 'A market' is therefore any situation where buyers and sellers are in contact in order to establish a price. The market price is something that affects all of the businesses trading in it and is important for two reasons:

Key term

A market: any situation where buyers and sellers are in contact in order to establish a price.

1 All businesses have competitors. No firm can charge a price that is too far out of line with the market price for the product that it is selling. Even large, powerful firms usually have competitors. Although there is no such thing as 'the market price', in the sense of a single price for a product, there is a price range in a market at which consumers are prepared to buy. A business tries, through advertising, to stress how good its product is, but even so, if its price is much higher than the market price, it will be hard to sell many products. Similarly, if one firm's price is much lower than others in the market, consumers may feel that something is wrong with the product.
2 Market price affects a business's mark-up. Mark-up is the difference between the cost of producing an item and the price at which it is sold. If the market price rises, so does the mark-up (assuming that unit costs remain unchanged), and this is a signal to businesses selling in that market to try to supply more because it is now more profitable to do so. If the market price falls, a business must lower its costs or else it will have to accept a lower mark-up and make less profit per item. The same would apply if a business's costs rose. A business cannot automatically pass on cost increases (e.g. from a rise in raw material prices) to consumers by putting up the price. Therefore, a business is, to a large extent, 'disciplined' into keeping costs down by the market price.

A failure to be aware of, and respond to, is that any change in market price is going to mean lower profits for a firm, which will affect all of its stakeholder groups negatively; and in the worst case may cause the firm to go into liquidation. The internet has meant that competition is no longer simply local, or even national; it is global as well.

In a market, the price of the product is established by buyers and sellers

How can a market be classified?

As well as the difference between physical and non-physical markets, there are differences between the structures of markets. There are several different types of market structure and a business's behaviour and decision making power in each structure is different.

Competitive market

A competitive market is a market structure in which there are a large number of firms producing a similar product who are competing to meet the needs of a large number of consumers. These firms have to accept the price in the market. They have little, if any, power in the market; it is difficult for any one of them to raise the price because consumers will simply switch to another supplier. In a competitive market, no single producer can dictate price. This is especially true if one product is almost exactly the same as all the others in the market. Competition in this market structure is therefore mainly on the basis of price. The foreign exchange market is an example of a highly competitive market. If someone wants $1000 to go on holiday to Florida they know that one dollar is exactly the same as another; it does not matter where the $1000 are purchased from. There is little point in a firm trying to promote the virtues of its dollars over another's. Firms in the foreign exchange market must compete on price since buyers will simply go to the business where 'the best deal' can be obtained, that is, they pay the lowest number of pounds for their $1000.

Monopoly

A market controlled by a single business is known as a monopoly and the firm is known as a monopolist. This is the opposite of a competitive market. The monopolist can control the market because it is the only supplier of the product and can therefore charge whatever price it likes. It can adopt a 'take it or leave it' approach to customers and is unlikely to benefit them through low prices in the way that a competitive market does.

There are not many instances of 'pure monopoly' in the real world, although most UK households face a monopoly supplier of water. Nevertheless, it is still possible to talk of a business having 'monopoly power' if it is sufficiently large. A firm that is dominant in a market might not act in the interests of consumers. In the short term, such a firm may charge low prices, which is beneficial for consumers but, in the long term, it may drive other firms out of business and then become a monopolist – and raise prices. This is why the Competition and Markets Authority (see **page 83**) may become concerned about the behaviour of large businesses. The Competition and Markets Authority defines a monopoly as a situation where a business has a 25 per cent (or more) share of the market. In 2014, Tesco controlled nearly 29 per cent of the grocery market and was therefore a monopoly on this definition.

Monopolistic competition

In some respects this market structure is similar to a competitive market; there are a large number of businesses (hence the use of the word 'competition') and a large number of consumers. The products in this market are essentially very similar and so there will not be much scope for trying to raise prices on the grounds that one product is hugely better than another. Unlike a competitive market, in monopolistic competition there is usually a lot of non-price competition; products are branded and then promoted by the business. Each firm has a monopoly over its brand name (hence the use of the term 'monopolistic') and it uses this to promote what are usually quite minor differences between it and another brand. Another typical example of how businesses in this sort of market use non-price competition is through the use of loyalty cards to gain and retain customers.

Oligopoly

An oligopoly exists where a market is dominated by a few large firms. There may be other, smaller businesses in the market that follow the lead of the oligopolists in terms of prices and products, but the oligopolists are the main players. It is sometimes suggested that oligopolists collude (secretly agree) to keep prices higher than they would be if the market was competitive. Such behaviour is illegal (but can be hard to prove) as it is anti-competitive. It is not hard to see why firms might do this; if one business raises its price and the others do not, it will lose revenue. Alternatively, if it cuts its price and the others follow, they are all likely to end up with the same market share and worse off in terms of revenue. There is an incentive for all not to 'rock the boat'. For this reason, the market price might be 'sticky', that is, it does not change very much in a particular period of time. If price competition can be damaging to all, it may therefore be better for firms to compete through non-price competition such as the loyalty card scheme mentioned above in monopolistic competition, through regular product upgrades, or through advertising. The energy companies, supplying gas and electricity, are an example of oligopoly.

Tips and techniques

In practice, markets often exhibit characteristics from several market structures. For example, the grocery market is dominated by several large firms (and so might be considered an oligopoly) but the firms within it compete actively on price (a feature of a competitive market) and also have branded products and use non-price competition such as loyalty cards (a feature of monopolistic competition). It may therefore be best to use a particular market structure as a starting point for the analysis of a business's decision making and its market power rather than regarding it as definitive.

Market size and growth

Markets can, and do, change over a period of time. A market may become more oligopolistic, or more competitive. The size of the market can change too. Market size is the number of individuals in a certain market who are potential buyers and/or sellers of a product or service. It is important for a business to have an accurate idea of a market's size, particularly if it is planning the launch of a new product. This is because in a small market a large volume of sales is not likely – unless the number of consumers in the market is about to grow dramatically. On the other hand, a large market would have more potential for sales but probably has a number of established firms in it to compete against.

'Market growth' should not be confused with 'market size'. Market growth refers to an increase in the demand for a business's product(s) over a period of time. In a recession when consumer spending falls, it is likely that market growth will fall as well. Alternatively, when incomes rise market growth should rise, especially if there is a strong brand image and loyalty.

Competition and market dominance

Competition is regarded as beneficial because it forces businesses to be efficient in terms of keeping costs as low as possible in order to keep prices down for consumers. It also encourages innovation and emphasis on meeting customer needs. However, if the firms in a competitive market are small they will not be able to gain economies of scale (reductions in unit costs) and therefore customers may be paying a higher price than they would if the firm was larger and able to gain these economies. There are other instances of why competition in a market does not necessarily mean that all stakeholders of the firms benefit:

- Employees: competitive pressure to keep costs down may impact negatively on conditions of service (wages, overtime payments, hours, holidays, etc.) and conditions of work.
- Suppliers: may be offered a 'take it or leave it approach' to the conditions of supply and payment in a bid to keep costs down. They may be little loyalty to a supplier if a business is under a lot of competitive pressure.
- Shareholders: a small firm that is subject to intense competition will have little market power and little, if any, degree of control over prices. This might mean dividends are relatively low, especially if it is not easy for the firm to cut costs.

Market dominance is a measure of the strength of a business and its product(s) relative to the competition. The most obvious way of calculating market dominance is to consider market share, that is, the share of the market that the product or business controls in a particular area.

There is a variety of ways in which a business may increase its market share and hence its dominance in the market. For example:

- being aware of customer needs – and meeting them
- selling more to existing customers
- finding out why 'old' customers no longer use your products
- having a clear marketing plan
- using a variety of marketing techniques – pricing, advertising, and promotion.

These marketing issues are dealt with in detail in **Chapters 51–53**. Alternatively, a business could increase market share by merging with, or taking over another firm.

In defining market dominance there needs to be a precise definition of what 'the market' actually is; a firm could be dominant locally but not nationally. Also, a firm could be dominant but limited in its actions due to regulation – the regional water companies are 100 per cent dominant in terms of market share but are subject to regulation by The Water Services Regulation Authority (Ofwat).

Generally, the less dominant a business is, the weaker its market power over price will be. Why is it that some markets are more competitive than others? Where it is easy for a firm to enter a market, it is likely to be competitive. Entrepreneurs obviously want to enter a profitable market or at least break into one where there is the potential for future growth. There are, however, a number of factors that can prevent this from happening. These are known as barriers to entry and include:

1. Large start-up costs. Typically these will be capital costs such as buildings and machinery. A firm simply may not be able to afford the necessary expense. Setting up as a landscape gardener may be relatively cheap in terms of capital outlay but setting up a company making mobile phones will not be.
2. Having to match the marketing budgets of those already in the market. Many customers are going to be loyal to existing firms and it may take a vast marketing budget to get them to alter their behaviour.
3. Legal restrictions such as a patent or government restrictions. Trying to copy another's success by making a similar product may lead to legal action if the product has a patent. Some markets have restrictions placed on them by the government; e.g. a business cannot just try to set up another national lottery.
4. The inability to gain economies of scale and so achieve low unit costs. Lower unit costs come from large-scale production and this may not be possible for a new business – at least not initially. With high unit costs, profit per item will be low.
5. The possibility that the existing firms in the market may start a price war. This would be illegal if the objective was to destroy the new firm, but it could be hard to prove that this was the intention. In any event, such a war could damage the new firm irreparably before it was properly established because it would reduce its revenue and profit at a time when it particularly needed them.

In the light of these, an entrepreneur may well decide that it is too much of a risk to even try to break into a market.

As well as barriers to entry there are also barriers to exit. It might be expected that if a business is not profitable and/or it sees little opportunity for future growth it will simply close down and leave the market. Sometimes this is not straightforward and a firm may have to continue trading even if is not very profitable. Barriers to exit include:

1 The difficulty of selling off expensive plant and machinery. If the business closes down, these 'sunk' costs may be huge. It may take many months to sell a factory and even then it may have to be sold at a small proportion of its original purchase price.
2 High redundancy costs. After two years' service employees are legally entitled to a redundancy payment. The firm may therefore face a very large bill for making employees redundant.
3 Contracts with suppliers. These have to be honoured or the firm will face a legal challenge and possible bad publicity from breaking the contracts.

Key terms

Barriers to entry: the factors that could prevent a business from entering and competing in a market.

Barriers to exit: the factors that could prevent a business from leaving a market, even if it would like to.

Where a market has significant barriers to entry and exit, this will deter new entrants because it is risky and expensive to enter a market and/or expensive to leave if the venture fails. Such barriers will make the market less competitive and strengthen the dominance and market power of the existing firms. Other than barriers to entry and exit, there are other ways that businesses can achieve market dominance: organic growth, acquisitions and mergers.

Organic growth

Organic growth is growth that is achieved by increasing the firm's sales. This comes from selling more to existing customers, finding new customers, or both. Assuming that other businesses are not growing at a similar rate, organic growth will help to lead to market dominance.

Mergers and acquisitions

Growth that comes from a merger or an acquisition is different to organic growth. A merger is where two companies join together to form a new larger business. This larger business will obviously be more dominant than the two individual businesses were. A takeover involves acquiring control of another company by buying a majority of its shares. If the takeover is successful the target company will usually continue to exist as an independent legal entity controlled by the acquirer. The 'parent company' therefore has increased market dominance, even though it might appear that there has been little change because the original company is still using its brand name. British Gas, for example, is owned by the multinational Centrica. A takeover might go smoothly because the shareholders of both companies consider it to be beneficial. On the other hand, it may be resisted and so be regarded as 'hostile'.

When a smaller business is operating in a market that has a dominant firm operating in it, it cannot hope to compete by matching the price that the dominant firm can charge, or through the sort of marketing it can use. Instead it will need to use strategies such as:

- Compete in a niche in the market rather than the market as a whole – at least to start with. Dominant firms often look for the 'easy pickings' of a mass market. They consider it too expensive or not worth the trouble to operate in the smaller market segments.
- Offer better customer service. Customers appreciate the personal touch with clear advice, rather than dealing with someone in the call centre of a huge corporate entity.
- Offer longer opening hours – making purchasing more convenient.
- Use local resources such as the British Chambers of Commerce (BCC) to gain expertise and customers. Members of the BCC can access a range of services, networking and support from their Chamber to help them.

Regulation and restriction of market dominance in the UK

Where a single business (or a group of businesses) becomes dominant in a market it may be investigated by the Competition and Markets Authority (CMA). Alternatively, a market may be regulated by another body. In the UK the responsibility for enforcing competition law lies with the CMA.

Both UK and EU competition law prohibit two main types of anti-competitive activity: anti-competitive agreements and the abuse of a dominant market position. The CMA therefore has powers to investigate firms and examine evidence to see whether there is an anti-competitive agreement in existence. It also aims to prevent actions that would allow the abuse of a dominant market position by a firm to the detriment of consumers in that market. It does not automatically assume that a large dominant firm is going to act in an anti-competitive manner, but it can consider (and rule on) whether certain types of mergers or takeovers would result in a substantial lessening of competition in a market. If a CMA investigation finds evidence of anti-competitive practices there are a variety of sanctions it can apply:

- The business(es) involved can be fined up to 10 per cent of their global turnover.
- Customers and competitors of the firm(s) involved can sue for damages as a result of being affected by the anti-competitive behaviour.
- Individuals can be disqualified from being a company director.
- The CMA can also fine an individual, such as a director, if that person fails to comply with the CMA's requests for information provision during a Competition Act investigation.

The businesses in the markets for utilities such as water, gas, and electricity need a license to operate and are not only subject to competition law, but are also regulated by an independent body.

Ofgem, for example, is the Office of Gas and Electricity Markets. One of its key responsibilities is the supervision and development of competition in those markets. Ofgem does not regulate the market by a simplistic formula such as only allowing prices to rise by a specified amount. Its website states:

We do not regulate energy retail prices – these are set by energy suppliers in competition with each other. Our role is to promote competition, which we believe acts as an effective mechanism to drive down prices and promote higher quality service. We aim to encourage suppliers to deliver: Simpler choices – by reducing the complexity and number of tariffs, clearer information for consumers and fairer treatment....Key to how we work is our responsibility to carry out investigations into company behaviour when we believe they may have breached a condition of their licence, or have breached the requirements of consumer protection or competition legislation.

Source: www.ofgem.gov.uk/about-us/how-we-work

Companies making such breaches face a large fine. Ofgem can also order businesses to repay money. For example, when someone switches energy supplier there is often a positive balance left in their old account. The energy companies had been very slow in returning this money after the switch and so in 2014 Ofgem ordered that £153 million of funds held in this way be returned to customers.

Further sources

www.britishchambers.org.uk: The BCC is a dynamic, high-profile and independent business network. It is especially useful for smaller businesses.

www.gov.uk/government/organisations/competition-and-markets-authority: the organisation that promotes competition for the benefit of consumers within and outside the UK.

www.ofgem.gov.uk: Ofgem is the regulator for the electricity and gas markets in the UK.

www.ofwat.gov.uk: Ofwat is the regulator of the water (and sewerage) sectors in England and Wales.

Your turn

Questions are suitable for all AS and A Level candidates.

Multiple-choice questions

1 Market price has a direct effect on a business's:
A delivery schedules
B costs
C mark up
D social costs. *(1)*

2 Organic growth comes from:
A a successful merger
B an acquisition of another company
C a management buyout
D an increase in sales. *(1)*

3 A business would be classified as a monopoly if it has a market share of at least:

A 20%
B 25%
C 40%
D 51%. (1)

4 In the UK, the organisation with the responsibility for enforcing competition law is the:

A BCC
B CBI
C CC
D CMA. (1)

Revision questions

1 Explain what is meant by 'a market'. (2)

2 State two characteristics of a competitive market. (2)

3 State two features of each of the following:

A monopoly (2)
B oligopoly (2)
C monopolistic competition. (2)

4 Outline what is meant by 'market dominance'. (2)

5 State the difference between a merger and an acquisition. (2)

6 Consider the following data. The two firms operate in different markets. On the basis of market share as a measure of market dominance, analyse which is the more dominant firm. (3)

Firm	Market sales achieved by firm (£m)	Overall market sales (£m)
ABC plc	19	186
XYZ plc	23	65

Total *(17 marks)*

Case study

The UK grocery market

Store Wars: A New Hope

There are unprecedented changes occurring in the UK grocery market. This change is structural rather than cyclical; in other words, permanent rather than temporary. Historically, the UK has had limited discounter heritage, but after initial hesitancy, increasing numbers of UK consumers are turning from The Big Four (Tesco, Sainsburys, Morrisons, and Asda) to Aldi and Lidl – and staying with them.

Collectively, Aldi and Lidl will add some £5.9 billion sales over the next five years and, by 2018, the value of the UK discount market will surpass £20 billion. By then, discounters will command a share of 8.5 per cent of the UK market, compared to 6.3 per cent at present. With both Aldi and Lidl earmarking substantial capital for investment in the UK, physical expansion will accelerate rather than recede – each will open 25–40 new stores per annum over the next five years.

However, the Big Four are not going to take this structural change lying down. For all their stellar growth, the discounters are not infallible, nor are they immune from downward pricing pressure from the larger multiples.

'The Empire May Yet Strike Back.'

Source: Adapted from 'Store Wars', Stephen Springham, Senior Retail Analyst, Planet Retail's UK Discount Grocery Report, 24 March 2014

http://www1.planetretail.net/news-and-events/press-release/discount-store-wars-%E2%80%93-reshaping-uk-grocery-landscape

1 If the value of the UK discount market does reach £20 billion and the discounters do have a market share of 8.3 per cent, calculate the value of their sales. (3)

2 Analyse one barrier to entry that might have affected Lidl. (4)

3 'The discounters are not infallible, nor are they immune from downward pricing pressure from the larger multiples.' Analyse one reason why market price is important to Lidl. (4)

Total (11)

Chapter 14

Demand and supply and market forces

AS / Year 1

Both AS and A Level students must know all of the content in this chapter.

Chapter 13 showed how markets and market prices are very significant influences on a business and its behaviour. It is therefore important to be able to analyse how markets actually establish a price and also what the effects of any change in market conditions are on a business.

How is market price determined?

In order to answer this question, it is necessary to look at what are often referred to as 'market forces' – demand and supply.

Demand

When economists talk about 'demand', they are not talking about what people would buy if they had an unlimited amount of money. They are talking about effective demand, which means the quantity that people in a particular market can and will purchase at each price.

Generally, if the market price is low, more people will purchase the product, and vice versa. Of course, there are exceptions to this: if someone sees a car or a mobile phone on sale at a quarter of its normal price, they might think that there is something wrong and therefore not buy it.

Suppose that there is a small grocer's shop situated on a housing estate, which sells cans of soft drink. Table 14.1 shows the quantities of cans that consumers in the market (in this case, the people living on the estate) would buy at various prices.

Table 14.1 Demand schedule for soft drinks

Price (£)	Quantity demanded
0.50	1,000
0.75	800
1.00	600
1.25	400
1.50	200

Figure 14.1 shows this information graphically. Quantity is always put on the x-axis and price is always put on the y-axis. A change in price moves a consumer up or down the demand curve.

At £1.25 consumers would buy 400 cans, but if the price fell to 75p, demand would increase to 800 cans. The curve slopes down from left to right. Note that, although the line in Figure 14.1 is a straight line, it is still referred to as a 'demand curve'.

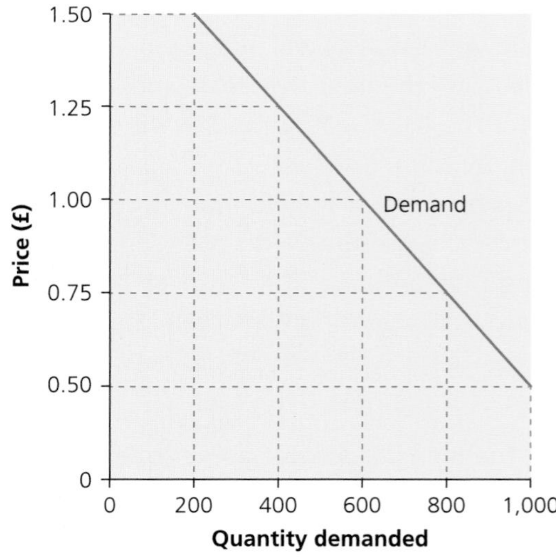

Figure 14.1 Demand curve for soft drinks

Supply

Supply refers to the quantities that are offered for sale by businesses at each price. Whereas the demand curve looks at the behaviour of consumers when price changes, the supply curve looks at price from the point of view of the business. If market price rises, businesses will try to supply more because (assuming the unit cost of producing stays the same) they can make more profit. This is shown for the grocer's supply of soft drinks in Table 14.2.

Table 14.2 Supply schedule for soft drinks

Price (£)	Quantity supplied
0.50	200
0.75	400
1.00	600
1.25	800
1.50	1,000

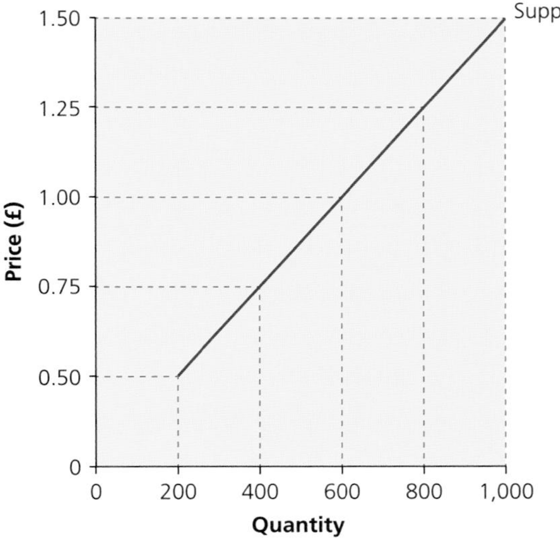

Figure 14.2 Supply curve for soft drinks

The terms 'cost' and 'price' should not be confused. If the market price of a can of soft drink rises and the cost to the shop of buying the cans from the supplier stays the same (or rises by a smaller amount than the price increase), it will be more profitable for the shop to supply.

Figure 14.2 shows the quantities supplied at the various prices. Once again, quantity is put on the x-axis and price is put on the y-axis. A change in price moves a business's supply plans up or down its supply curve.

At £1.25, for example, the shop will supply 800 cans, but if price falls to 75p, supply will become less profitable and will be reduced to 400 cans.

Equilibrium price

The price at which the consumers' demand coincides with what businesses are prepared to supply is known as equilibrium price. In Figure 14.3 it can be seen that this can only occur at one price – £1.

At the price of £1, the demand for soft drinks is equal to the supply of soft drinks. In this situation, consumers are able to buy everything that they want to buy; they are satisfied with the situation. So is the business, because at this price there are no unsold stocks of cans in the shop. When this is the case, the market is in equilibrium.

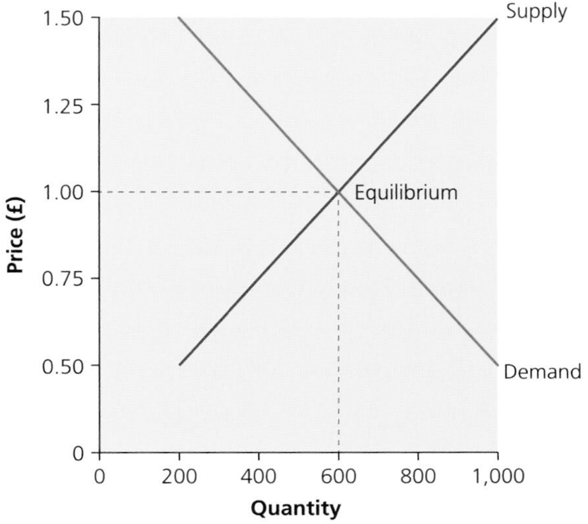

Figure 14.3 Equilibrium price

Key term

Equilibrium: the situation in a market when demand is equal to supply.

In any market, price is always moving towards equilibrium: in other words, it changes until both businesses and consumers are satisfied.

How is equilibrium established?

At first sight, this situation seems rather unlikely to occur. A business would like a high price for its products but consumers would like a low price. What happens if the plans of consumers and businesses do not coincide?

Suppose that the shop is trying to sell at a price that is quite high, say £1.25. If Tables 14.1 and 14.2 are put together, as in Table 14.3, it is obvious that demand and supply are not in equilibrium at this price: 400 cans are demanded, but the soft drinks firm is trying to supply 800.

However, this situation would not last for long. Where demand in the market is less than supply (and therefore there are unsold stocks of goods), this is known as a situation of excess supply. This is not something that businesses want because it means they have incurred costs making products (or, in the case of a shop, buying them from a supplier), but are not making any profit because they cannot sell them.

This means that if the price being charged in the market is too high, businesses have to lower their prices if they want to sell their goods. The fall in price encourages consumers to buy more. Price is pushed down towards equilibrium, as shown in Figure 14.4.

On the other hand, the price being charged may be particularly low, say 75p. Table 14.4 shows that, at a price of 75p, the firm is less keen to supply than it was at £1.25, but consumers certainly want to buy. In this situation, consumers are prepared to buy 800 cans, but firms are prepared to supply only 400.

In this instance there is excess demand – that is, more demand than supply. With people trying to buy more of the product than is on sale, the price rises. This encourages businesses to supply more because they are able to make more profit. In this way, excess demand pushes prices up towards equilibrium, as shown in Figure 14.5.

Table 14.3 Excess supply

Price (£)	Quantity demanded	Quantity supplied
0.50	1,000	200
0.75	800	400
1.00	600	600
1.25	400	800
1.50	200	1,000

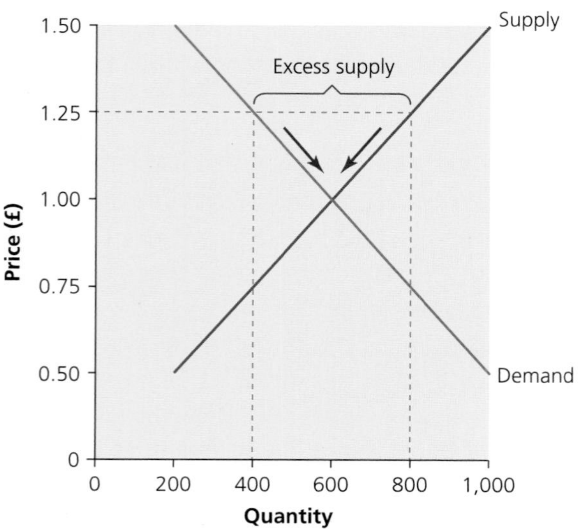

Figure 14.4 Excess supply

Table 14.4 Excess demand

Price (£)	Quantity demanded	Quantity supplied
0.50	1,000	200
0.75	800	400
1.00	600	600
1.25	400	800
1.50	200	1,000

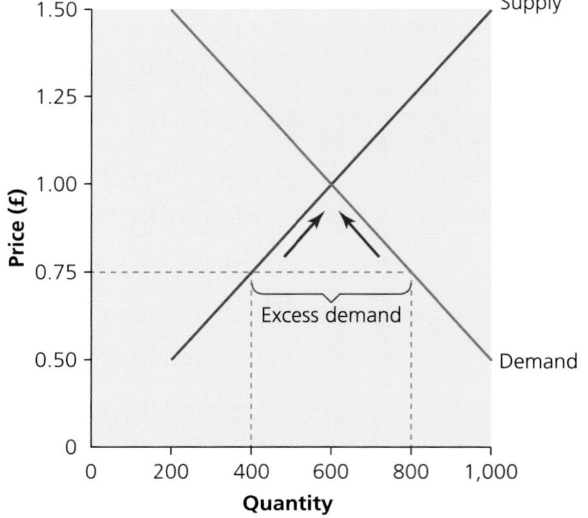

Figure 14.5 Excess demand

Both businesses and consumers 'read' the price in the market:

- Businesses respond to price changes by adjusting their supply plans: increasing or lowering output in order to maximise their profit.
- Consumers respond to price changes by increasing or decreasing demand so that they always buy the quantity they require. They will not buy products that they feel are too expensive.

These actions mean that market price moves towards equilibrium. At equilibrium, both parties are satisfied; there is no excess supply and no excess demand.

Once equilibrium has been established, it does not mean that it stays at this point for ever. If the conditions that influence consumers' demand change, a new demand curve is created because the market situation is now different. The same applies to businesses. If the conditions under which they supply change, a new supply curve is created.

What are the factors that determine demand?

Demand is determined by the following factors.

Price

The higher the price, the lower the quantity demanded, and vice versa. Figure 14.1 showed that a change in price moves a consumer along an existing demand curve.

If changes in other factors occur, a new demand curve will be created because the conditions under which consumers buy will have changed, and they will demand more or less of the product at every price.

Income

An increase in income leads to an increase in demand for most goods; economists call these normal goods. Figure 14.6 shows a rise in quantity demanded from 600 to 1,000, but this does not happen because of a fall in price – which has stayed the same at £1. The increase in demand has come about because of a change in another factor affecting demand – in this case, a rise in income. This change has created a new demand curve, D2, to the right of the old demand curve, D1. More is now being demanded at every price level.

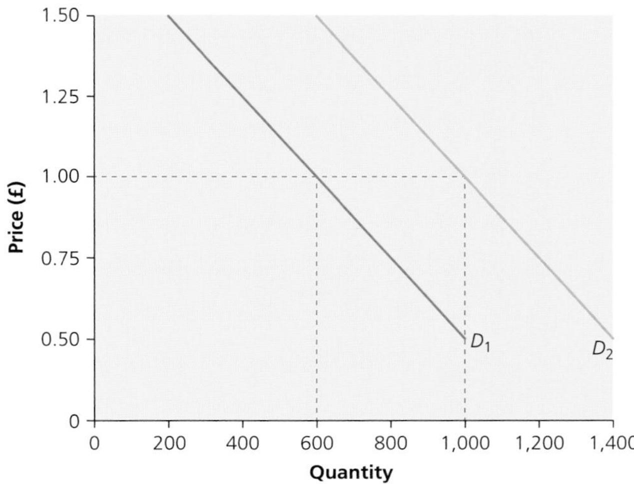

Figure 14.6 A shift in the demand curve

Alternatively, consider a fall in income. This will cause less to be demanded at every price level. At a price of £1, the quantity demanded will fall from 1,000 to 600.

Not all goods are 'normal'. There are some goods whose demand goes down when income rises. These goods are known as inferior goods. Products with names like 'value', 'budget' or 'discount' are inferior goods. This does not mean that there is anything wrong with them; it just means that there are other, similar goods of better quality. As their income rises, people tend to buy fewer inferior goods.

It is by no means a disadvantage for a business to produce or sell inferior goods. Most supermarkets supply both normal goods and low-budget goods that might be regarded as inferior. This enables the business to cater for two different sections of the market: those on a high income and those on a low income. Furthermore, in a recession, the demand for inferior goods will almost certainly rise, whereas the demand for better-quality goods will probably fall.

Wealth

Wealth is not the same as income. Wealth is the combined value of savings, shares owned, your house (if owned) etc. This last factor is important: there is evidence that when house prices rise, people feel wealthier even though they have not had an increase in income. They therefore feel confident about spending more. A business needs to be aware of consumer confidence and to consider how demand might be affected if this confidence changes.

Advertising, promotional offers and public relations

Television advertisements, 'two for the price of one' offers, and the sponsorship of sports teams all affect demand. That is the reason why firms spend so much money on them. A successful promotional campaign shifts the demand curve to the right, as was shown in Figure 14.6.

Taste and fashion

Some fashionable products, such as certain brands of clothes, or iPods, are seen as 'in' and some consumers regard these products as essential for their lifestyle.

Demographic changes

A larger population means more spending. Apart from considering the total population, businesses need to be aware of other demographic changes as well. These include:

- any shift in the age structure of the population, because young people tend to buy different products from older people
- a change in the gender ratio, because men buy different products from women

Government action

A campaign by the government – for example, to encourage a healthier lifestyle – will alter patterns of consumption. A 'keep fit' campaign by the government will affect the demand for both healthy and unhealthy food.

The price of other goods

As far as the price of other goods is concerned, two terms are important: substitutes and complements.

Substitutes

A substitute is a product that can be used instead of another one because it performs the same sort of function: for example, apples and pears are substitutes, as are electricity and gas for heating a home.

Consider apples and pears. What would happen if the price of pears stayed the same but the price of a substitute, such as apples, went up? If the price of apples rose, this would not only decrease the demand for apples, but also increase the demand for pears. This is shown in Figure 14.7.

Key term

Substitute: an alternative product that serves the same function.

An increase in the price of apples reduces the demand for apples. This is shown as a movement along the demand curve for apples from Q1 to Q2. As pears are a substitute for apples, there is a shift in the demand curve for pears. A new demand curve for pears is established because the conditions of demand for them have changed. The demand for pears increases to Q2 not because the price of pears has gone down, but because the price of a substitute (apples) has gone up.

How quickly will this occur? The changes in demand might happen quite fast; consumers who enjoy eating fruit and do not mind whether they buy apples or pears are likely to react to the price change the next time they go shopping. But will the same thing happen with the other example – gas and electric heating? The answer to this is no. If the price of gas rises, it is not easy for households to switch their heating systems to electricity. They would probably wait until their gas system broke down or wore out – which could be several years.

Apples and pears are examples of close substitutes; they are very similar products. However, not all substitutes are close. Consider travelling to work by car or by bus. Millions of people use their cars every day to drive to work. What might happen if the price of petrol rose? Logically, people should start to look for a cheaper alternative, such as bus travel. However, is waiting at a bus stop, having to queue, then stopping and starting throughout the journey really a close substitute for driving in the comfort of your own car? The answer might well be no. It could take a very large rise in the price of petrol to make commuters abandon their cars and start demanding, i.e. making, journeys by bus.

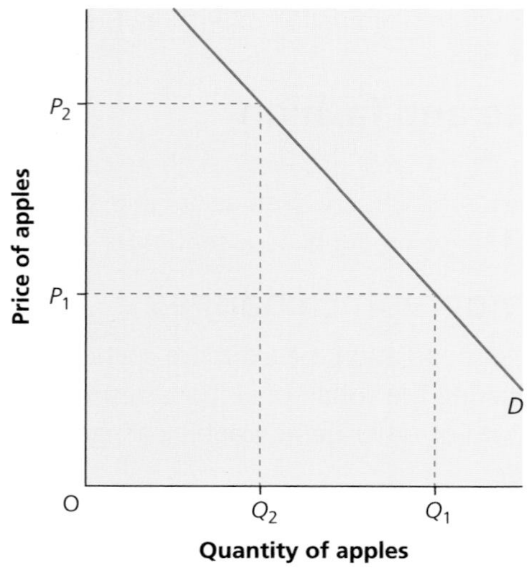

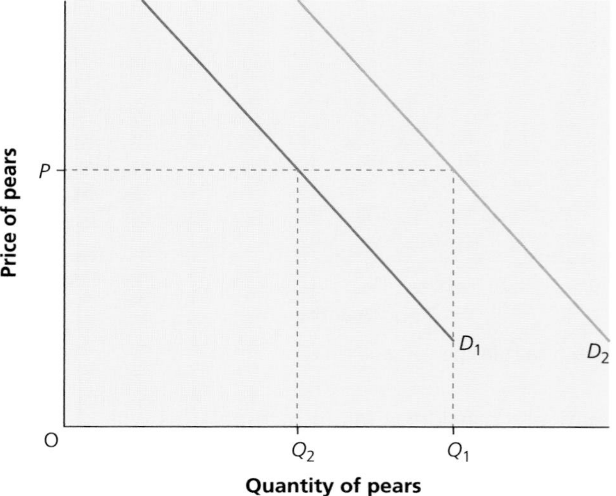

Figure 14.7 Substitutes

Brand names are used to distinguish one product from its substitutes

The relevance of this to a business is two-fold:

1 When considering any likely changes in the demand for its product that are caused by a change in the price of a substitute, a business needs to make a judgement on how close the substitute is.
2 It also needs to make a judgement on whether the price change in the substitute will be short term or long term. Is it a temporary 'one-off', or has a price war started?

Complements

Complements are products that are in joint demand: that is, when one product is bought, so is the other.

DVD players and DVDs show this relationship. If the price of DVD players falls, there will be an increase not only in the demand for DVD players – because they are cheaper – but also in the demand for DVDs, because more people now own the players. This is shown in Figure 14.8.

Key term

Complement: a product that is used, and is therefore bought, in conjunction with another.

The fall in the price of DVD players moves consumers along the existing demand curve for these. The rise in the demand for DVDs does not result from a fall in the price of DVDs — their price is still at P. It is because DVDs are a complement to DVD players, which are now cheaper. The opposite would apply if the price of DVD players rose.

A business can use the relationship between complements to maximise its revenue and profit over a period of time. A printer for a PC might be fairly low priced, say £85, but the ink cartridges that have to be used with it are likely to be quite expensive, say £20. The low price of the initial printer tempts consumers to buy, but they may be 'forced' to purchase the expensive complementary product thereafter.

The reverse is also true. Suppose a car manufacturer puts up its prices because it thinks that the effect on demand will be small. Even if it is correct, in the future, fewer spare parts, such as radiators, brakes and bulbs, will be sold. A business must therefore exercise caution when increasing the price of a product, as it may find that it decreases the demand for any complements that it sells as well.

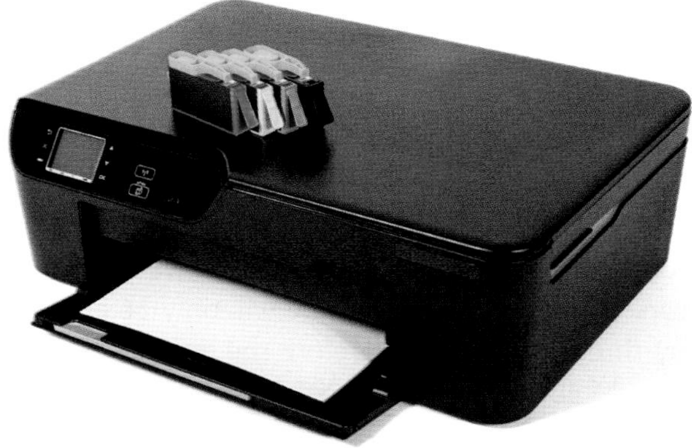
Complementary products such as ink cartridges increase the revenue that the company receives from the initial sale of the printer

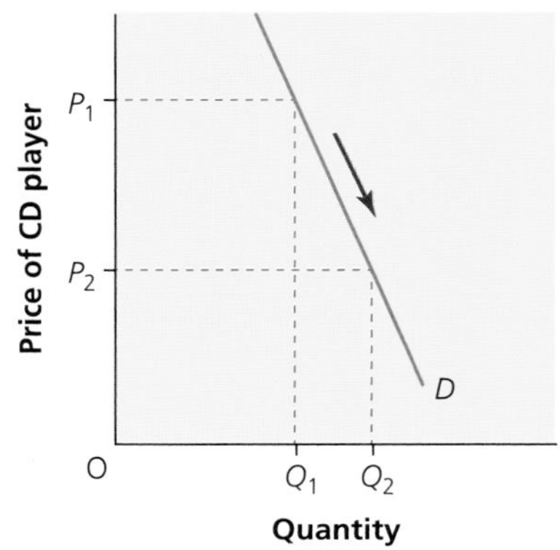

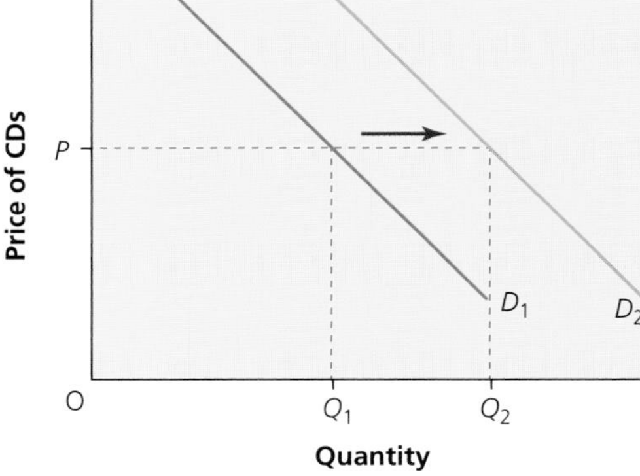

Figure 14.8 Complements

What are the factors that determine supply?

Supply is determined by the following factors.

Price

The relationship between price and supply is the opposite to that of price and demand. When prices are low, businesses supply less because it is less profitable to do so. Conversely, the higher the price, the more a business will try to supply. Figure 14.2 showed what happens when price changes. A change in price moves a business along an existing supply curve.

If changes in other factors occur, a new supply curve will be created because the conditions under which businesses supply will have changed, and they will supply more or less of the product at every price.

Costs

A fall in costs will cause supply to rise. Imagine a very simple situation in which the owner of a gravel pit employs people to dig gravel for him using spades. When he bought the gravel pit, he was given a free supply of spades as part of a special offer. This means that if he takes on extra workers there will be no increase in equipment costs.

Suppose the owner of this pit has a budget of £100 per week for labour. If the wage of his workers is £20 per week, he will employ five of them. If the wage falls to £10, he will employ ten workers and will be able to supply more gravel to market. Conversely, if the workers' wages rise to £30, he will only be able to employ three people and therefore the amount he can supply will fall.

Now consider another situation – a business producing furniture. Exactly the same reasoning as above would apply to the cost of any raw materials, such as wood or plastic. If the price of one of these falls, the firm will be able to supply more from its budget for raw materials. The same amount of money will now buy more raw materials because their cost has gone down.

Similarly, if the rate of interest goes down, the firm's cost of borrowing will fall, so it will have more money available to employ workers and buy raw materials. It can therefore supply more.

In both of these situations, the supply curve will shift to the right – more will now be supplied at all prices. This is shown in Figure 14.9 as a movement of the supply curve from S1 to S2.

Conversely, if a business's costs rise (e.g. if there is an increase in wages), it will supply less. This will shift the supply curve to the left. Less will now be supplied at all prices. This is shown in Figure 14.9 as a shift in the supply curve from S1 to S3.

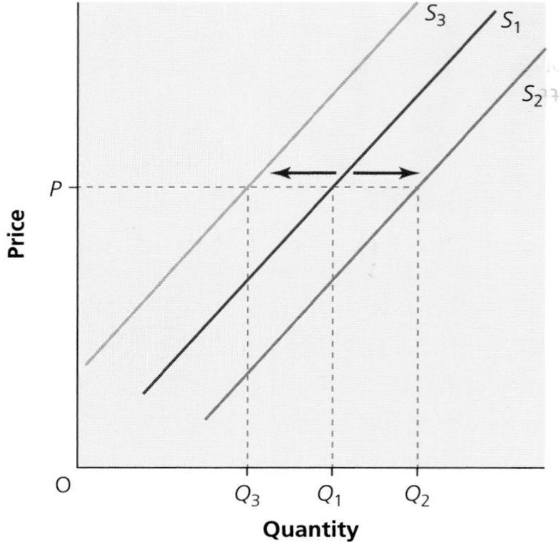

Figure 14.9 Effect of changes in costs on supply

Taxes and subsidies

Tax

The government may put a tax on a product in order to raise revenue, but it might also want to discourage the consumption of certain products, such as cigarettes and alcohol, because it believes them to be harmful. This sort of tax is known as an indirect tax because it is only paid if a consumer actually buys the product; it is not deducted directly from wages in the way that income tax is. How will a tax on a product affect a business's supply? It has exactly the same effect as an increase in costs – it shifts the supply curve to the left. This is because for every unit of the product sold, the business will have to pay a certain amount of tax to the government.

If the tax is £1 per unit and the firm sells 1,000 units a week, this means a rise in costs of £52,000 per year. This increase in costs means that the firm will supply less.

Any government legislation that lays down minimum standards, such as the minimum wage or health and safety laws, will have the same effect on a product as the imposition of a tax. As minimum standards increase costs, they will reduce supply. In Figure 14.9, the supply curve will shift to S3.

Subsidy

Alternatively, the government might want to encourage the supply of certain products, such as organic fertiliser, because it believes them to be beneficial. One way to do this would be to offer a subsidy to any business supplying this product. A subsidy is a payment from the government to the business for every unit supplied. This will have the opposite effect to a tax.

Key term

Subsidy: a payment from the government to encourage a business to increase supply.

The government might decide that for every bag of organic fertiliser supplied, a business will receive a subsidy of £1. Suppose, as in the previous example, that the business supplies 1,000 bags per week: this would mean an increase in annual income of £52,000. This payment has exactly the same effect as a fall in the business's costs, that is, the product is now cheaper to produce. The effect would be to increase the supply of organic fertiliser. In Figure 14.9, the supply curve would shift from S1 to S2.

Price of other products

This is sometimes known as competitive supply. Consider a business that supplies tinned foods, shown in Figure 14.10. A fall in the price of baked beans from P1 to P2 makes it less profitable to supply them (so supply falls to Q2) and more profitable to supply some other commodity – say, tins of spaghetti. The supply of canned spaghetti rises to Q2.

Tips and techniques

Examiners are not looking for the use of complicated theoretical concepts. They are looking for your ability to apply knowledge of economics to an actual business. Do not be frightened of drawing a graph; think of it as simply a quick, visual way of representing changes in the market that can complement your explanation.

Interaction of demand and supply

Change in demand

First consider the effect of a change in demand on the equilibrium price and quantity of a product.

Figure 14.11 shows the market for PCs. Suppose that there is an increase in consumers' spending caused by an income tax cut. The initial equilibrium (E1) is at price P1 with quantity Q1 being demanded and supplied. The rise in disposable income shifts the demand curve to the right. The result is a new equilibrium (E2) at P2 and Q2 – with a higher quantity now being demanded and supplied at a higher price.

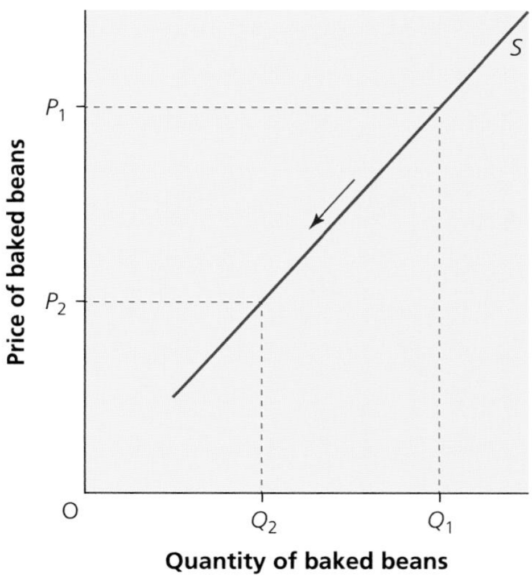

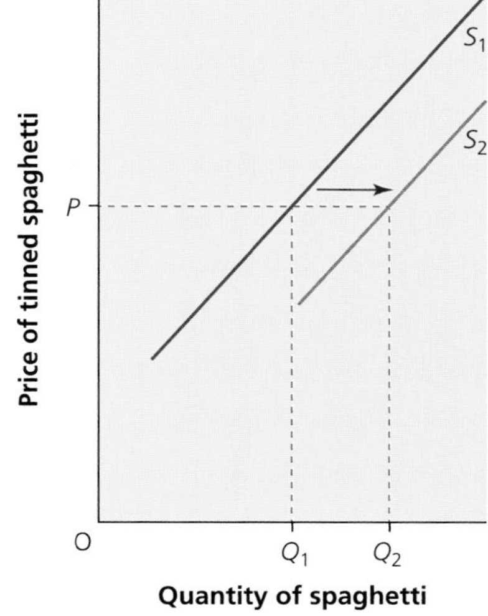

Figure 14.10 Competitive supply

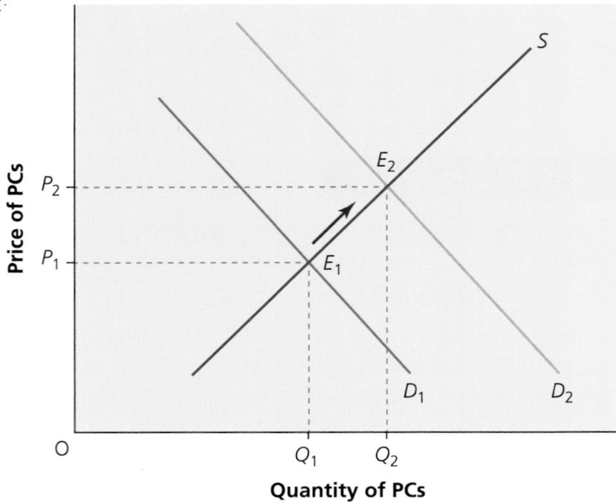

Figure 14.11 Effect of an increase in demand on price and quantity

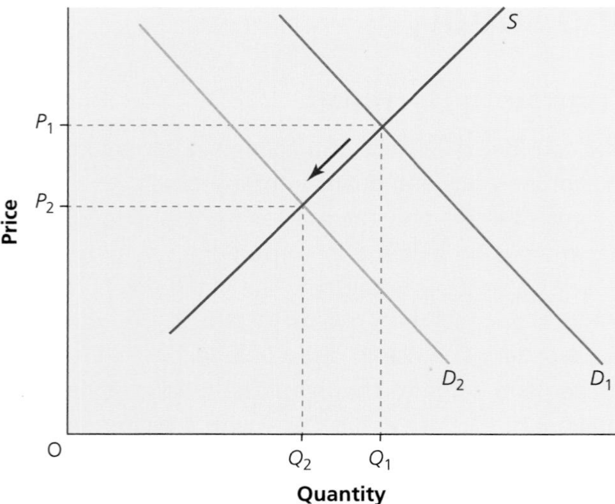

Figure 14.12 Effect of a fall in demand on price and quantity

Exactly the same result would occur following a change in any determinant of demand that caused a rightward shift of the demand curve.

Figure 14.12 shows the opposite. Consider the market for mobile phones. Suppose that a piece of scientific research proves that mobiles really are dangerous to health. The demand for mobile phones will change. There will be a shift of the demand curve to the left. A new equilibrium will be reached where a lower quantity is demanded and supplied at a lower price.

Exactly the same result would occur following a change in any determinant of demand that caused a leftward shift of the demand curve.

Change in supply

Now consider what happens when supply shifts and there is a movement along an existing demand curve.

Figure 14.13 shows the market for cornflakes. Suppose that the cost of corn to the manufacturer of breakfast cereal falls. Any fall in the cost of a raw material input will shift the supply curve to the right and cause an increased quantity to be bought at a lower price.

Exactly the same result would occur following a change in any determinant of supply that caused a rightward shift of the supply curve.

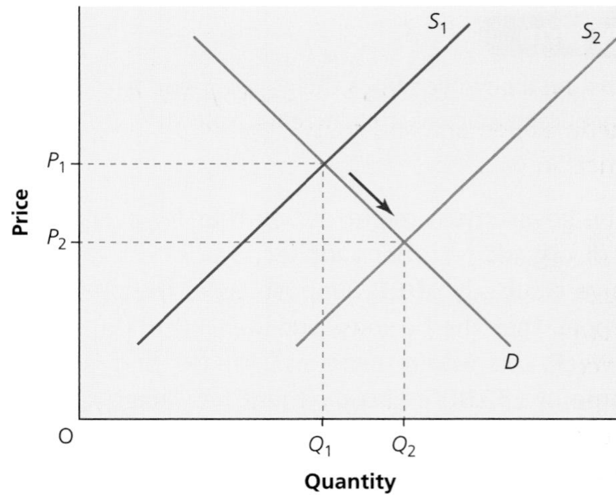

Figure 14.13 Effect of an increase in supply on price and quantity

Figure 14.14 shows the market for bread. Assume that bakery workers throughout the country negotiate a large pay rise. This will increase production costs for all bakeries. These rising costs will cause the supply curve to shift to the left. Less bread will now be demanded at a higher price.

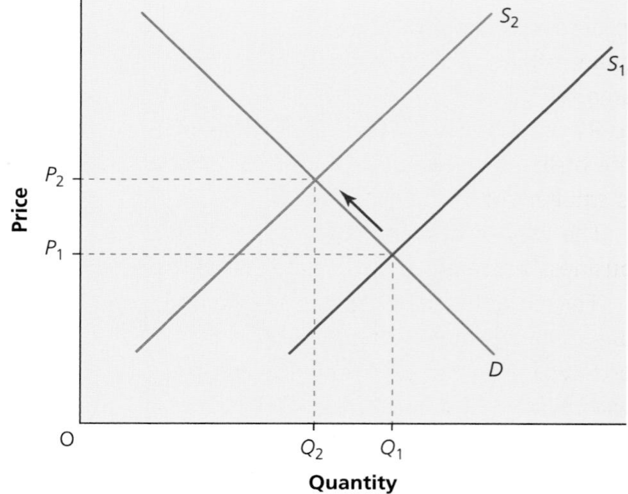

Figure 14.14 Effect of a decrease in supply on price and quantity

Exactly the same result would occur following a change in any determinant of supply that caused a leftward shift of the supply curve.

Elasticity of demand

Price elasticity of demand shows how responsive demand is to a change in price.

The demand and supply curves included so far in this chapter have been shown as sloping at about 45 degrees. Economists would say that these curves are quite elastic. In other words, they are quite responsive to a change in price. This is not always the case. Sometimes demand and supply are very unresponsive to price, in which case we say they are inelastic.

Key terms

Elastic: where the change in demand that results from a price change is greater than the change in price that caused it.

Inelastic: where the change in demand that results from a price change is less than the change in price that caused it.

If an economist says that a demand curve is quite inelastic, this means that the curve is quite steep and that demand will not change very much when price changes. This is shown in Figure 14.15.

If demand for a product is price inelastic, it means that when price rises (in this case, from P1 to P2), the quantity demanded falls, but not by a proportional amount. In this situation, a business can put the price of its product up and there will not be a large fall in demand. The firm's revenue (price multiplied by quantity) will rise because area OP2BQ2 is larger than area OP1AQ1. On the other hand, a price cut from P2 to P1 only generates a small increase in demand and the business's revenue actually falls because OP1AQ1 is smaller than area OP2BQ2.

The way to calculate elasticity and the effect on a business's revenue is shown in **Chapter 55**.

'Flatter' demand curves are said to be elastic. If a product has elastic demand, this means that a rise in price will generate a large fall in demand and revenue will decrease. In Figure 14.16, OP2BQ2 is smaller than OP1AQ1. On the other hand, if there were a fall in price, the opposite would apply. Lowering price will increase revenue because OP1AQ1 is larger than OP2BQ2.

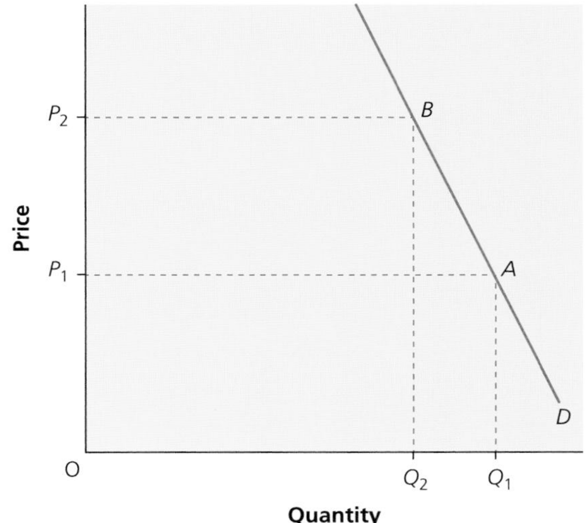

Figure 14.15 Inelastic demand curve

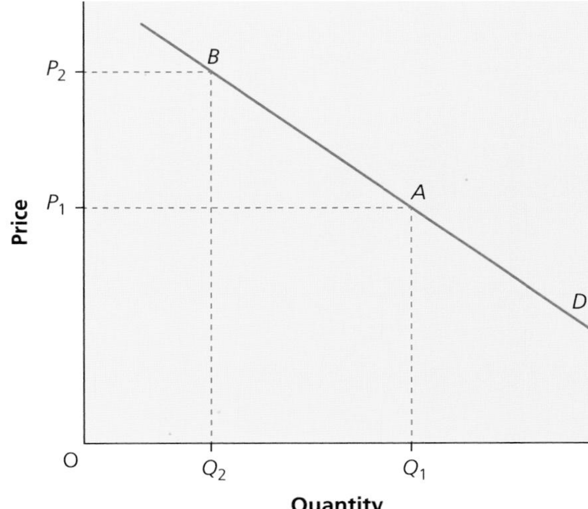

Figure 14.16 Elastic demand curve

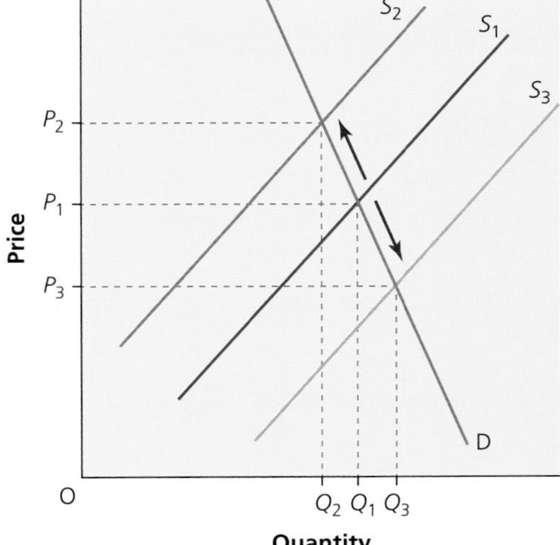

Figure 14.17 Effect of a change in supply on a product with inelastic demand

Elasticity is important because of the effect on market price. If demand is inelastic, the effect of a change in supply can be quite dramatic, as shown in Figure 14.17.

The demand for petrol is a good example. If garages run short of fuel, there is a distinct lack of substitutes for motorists to use and so petrol prices will rise sharply when the supply curve shifts from S1 to S2. If the supply of petrol rises due to lower production costs (S3), there will be the opposite effect.

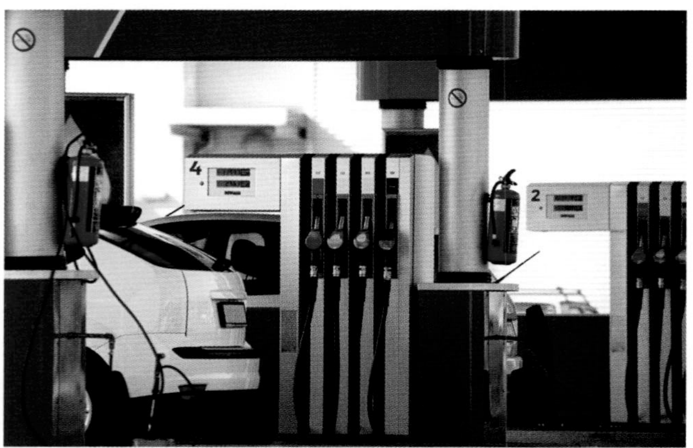

Products which are essential such as petrol have inelastic demand, and demand is relatively unresponsive to a rise in price

What makes demand elastic or inelastic?

If a business has few substitutes for its products, then if the price of the product rises, demand is likely to be inelastic as consumers cannot switch to another product. Where there are many alternatives, demand will be elastic as consumers will be able to switch to a substitute if price rises.

Another factor is the cost of buying the product in proportion to the consumer's income. For example, a 50 per cent rise in the price of a can of baked beans will not affect demand as much as a 50 per cent rise in the price of a product such as a car. More detail on what affects elasticity and how a business may use it can be found in **Chapter 55**.

Tips and techniques

If you can suggest how elastic or inelastic demand is likely to be (with the consequent effect on price) it will help to strengthen your answer.

Your turn

Questions are suitable for all AS and A Level candidates.

Multiple-choice questions

1 Which of the following are substitutes?
- A apples and oranges
- B knives and forks
- C guitars and guitar strings
- D electric fires and gas fires. *(1)*

2 A subsidy is likely to lead to:
- A a rise in supply and a rise in price
- B a rise in supply and a fall in price
- C a rise in demand and a rise in price
- D a fall in demand and a fall in price. *(1)*

3 If there both a rise in the price of petrol and in the price of motor insurance it is likely that:
- A The supply curve for cars will shift to the right
- B The demand curve for cars will shift to the right
- C The demand curve for cars will shift to the left
- D The two effects will cancel each other out and equilibrium will be unchanged. *(1)*

4 A product is likely to be demand inelastic if:
- A It has few substitutes
- B It is difficult to increase the supply of it
- C It is always readily available
- D Consumer tastes change quickly *(1)*

Revision questions

1 Explain three factors that affect the demand for a product. *(6)*

2 Explain three factors that affect the supply of a product. *(6)*

3 Explain the effects on price and quantity of:

A Excess demand in a market *(2)*

B Excess supply in a market. *(2)*

4 State what is meant by:

A Elasticity of demand *(1)*

B Elasticity of supply *(1)*

C State one factor that might make demand for a product elastic *(1)*

D State one factor that might make supply for a product elastic. *(1)*

Total *(20)*

Case study

The Thomas Cook Group

Thomas Cook Group plc (TCG) is one of the world's leading leisure travel groups with sales of over £9 billion and more than 20 million customers in the year ended 30 September 2013. The group is supported by around 27,000 employees and operates from 17 countries. It is perhaps best known as a travel agent but, in fact, the group owns a number of tour operators, as well as several smaller airlines and the booking website Hotels4u. It also offers foreign exchange services and travel insurance. TCG has a number of brands to satisfy customer needs. These include cheap package holidays, luxury holidays, city breaks, and cruises. The holiday market is competitive and, like any business, the TCG is subject to the market forces that affect it.

1 TCG offer foreign exchange services. Assume that an American hotel chain in Florida is prepared to offer rooms to TCG at $90 a night and TCG book 50 rooms per month, and that the exchange rate is $1.4 to the pound. If increased demand for hotel rooms in Florida raises the price to $105, and the pound falls in value to $1.3 calculate the monthly increase in cost in pounds for TCG. *(4)*

2 Assume that the government has decided to increase the tax on all flights from the UK. To what extent might the TCG be affected by such a tax? Justify your view. *(12)*

3 'The holiday market is competitive and, like any business, the TCG is subject to the market forces that affect it.' Evaluate the likely impact of market forces on the TCG. *(15)*

Total *(31)*

Chapter 15

The European Union, emerging markets and the global context

AS / Year 1 | Year 2

A Level students must know all of the content in this chapter.

AS students must know Global context (page 103).

AS students are not required to cover:

- The European Union (pages 98–103)
- Emerging markets and the global environment (pages 103–104)

The European Union (EU) is a group of 28 countries that aim collectively to improve the standard of living of their citizens. This is achieved by:

- creating a large market where businesses can compete, prosper and, in doing so, benefit their stakeholders
- generating economic and political stability
- achieving balanced economic growth across all of Europe
- protecting all EU citizens' rights via a common framework of law.

Membership of the EU has a significant effect on UK businesses.

Countries in Europe that are not yet members of the EU can apply to join if they wish. They must meet certain conditions to be allowed in.

Free trade and the single market

A thriving business community improves standards of living and promotes growth. One of the major goals of the EU is to create a large market where member states can trade freely. That is what 'single market' means: countries can trade freely with a common (i.e. single) set of regulations and rules on the movement of goods, people and finance, rather than having different regulations for each country.

This single market can help to make trade easier, and so businesses can sell more. This creates more wealth and jobs. The problem is that trade is not always free.

Key terms

Free trade: trade without tariffs or quotas being imposed when products are traded.

Single market: a market in which there is a single (i.e. common) set of laws and regulations relating to the movement of products, people and money; all businesses in the single market have to abide by these.

Trade barriers

Countries sometimes import more than they export. Many people think that the solution to this is straightforward: a country in this position should restrict the number of imports allowed in. This is known as imposing a quota. Another way to solve the problem would be to put a tax on goods entering the country from abroad. This would make imports more expensive and home-produced goods relatively cheap. This tax is known as a tariff.

The problem with these actions is that other countries will retaliate. This can result in a quota and tariff trade war that is damaging to businesses in all the countries concerned. Quotas and tariffs are trade barriers, and using them could mean that businesses in all countries that trade abroad end up selling less.

Any consideration of trade in a global context (and, for A Level students, emerging markets and the EU) must therefore involve an understanding of the nature of free trade. This is considered briefly in this chapter and it is then developed in more detail in **Chapter 16**, which is aimed mainly at A Level students, alongside

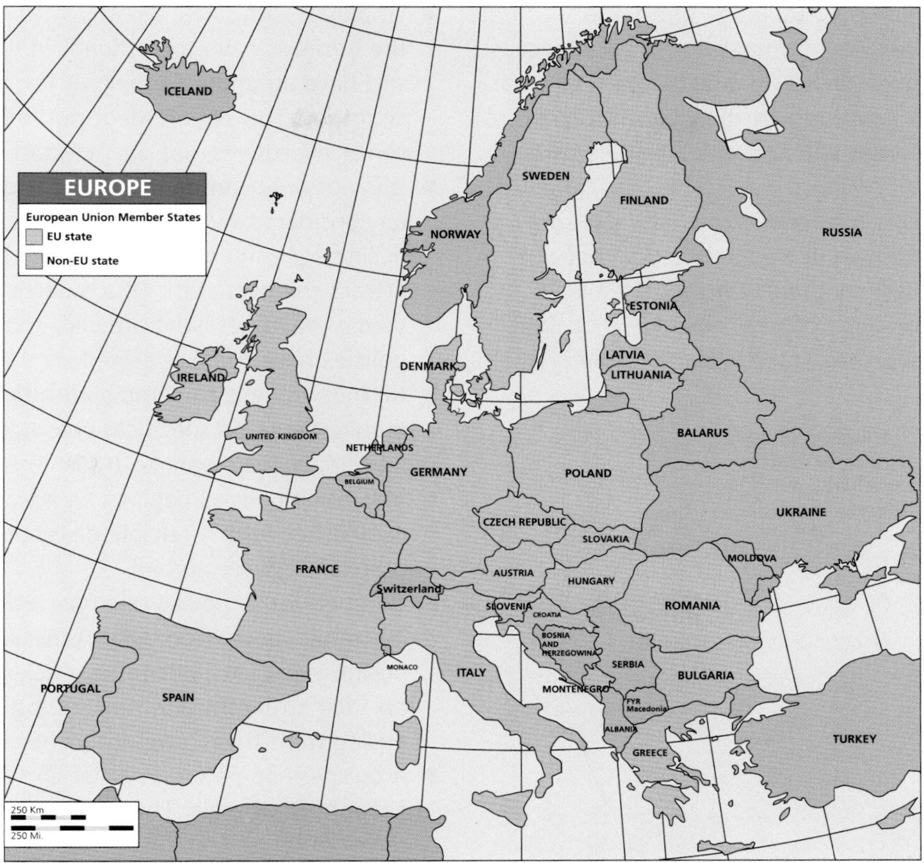

Figure 15.1 Member countries of the European Union in 2014

the other considerations involved when a business engages in international trade.

Removal of trade barriers

One aim of the single market is to remove trade barriers between member states. However, goods entering the EU from outside (e.g. from the USA or Japan) face a barrier called the common external tariff (CET), but it is thought that the negative effects of any retaliation from outside the EU are outweighed by the benefits for members of trading within the single market. Furthermore, many non-EU businesses are encouraged to build their own factories in EU countries to avoid the CET. This inward investment creates employment in the EU.

Another example of the removal of trade barriers is the harmonisation (i.e. adopting a similar set) of specifications, safety standards and testing requirements for products. Before the single market came into being (on 1 January 1993), these were different in each EU country. This meant that a UK business that sold electrical components and wished to export them faced considerable duplication of work, as it would have to meet its own standards as well as those of other countries. Moreover, different standards in different counties meant that it was expensive (or perhaps impossible) for some businesses to comply with all of them, and in some cases they did not even bother to try to trade. Now, a single set of rules makes trade easier and has opened up a larger market.

Labour market barriers are also being removed by changes such as the harmonisation of qualifications needed to do a certain job. Previously, a professional person might have needed a qualification gained in a specific country to be allowed to work there. Now, people with the appropriate qualification (e.g. doctors, teachers and social workers) have the right to work in any EU country, not just the one in which they were trained. In this way, people can improve their own lives and the lives of others in the country to which they move.

Finally, restrictions on moving money around within the EU have been abolished. This helps to encourage investment in profitable opportunities, and promotes competition. It should give both borrowers and savers a better deal.

All of these measures encourage free trade, and free trade brings competition. Competition is good because it brings down prices, drives up quality and improves customer service. Any business that does not strive to improve in these areas will find its customers taken by those who do.

The single market is intended to create the sort of virtuous circle shown in Figure 15.2. The hope is that the circle will continually repeat itself, with competition in the single market ensuring that the best businesses and their stakeholders prosper.

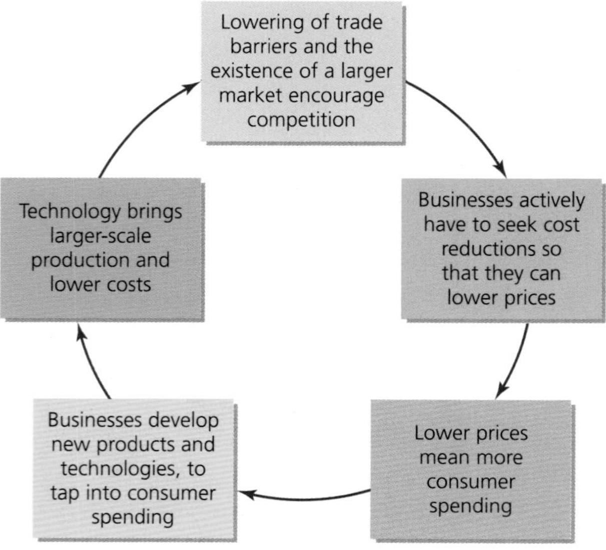

Figure 15.2 Benefits of free trade within the EU

Critics point out that EU laws and regulations are a huge burden and distract businesses by taking up a large amount of management time to ensure compliance.

What are the implications of trading in the EU for a UK business?

A business does not just start selling in Europe. There is an almost endless list of implications. Some of the most important are as follows:

- Someone in a senior position in the business must be put in charge of analysing the strengths, weaknesses, opportunities and threats in the proposed EU markets. They need to conduct and update market research, which takes up a lot of time and other resources.
- Employees who deal directly with other EU states in the business have to be fluent in different languages and have an understanding of the culture of other countries. This requirement not only applies to senior executives, but also to staff at all levels.
- It is not only competition for customers that has to be considered. With the free movement of workers, businesses offering the best employment package attract the best staff. This is particularly true for young graduates, who are very mobile. Recruitment policies have to be reviewed.
- Businesses have to comply with the common requirements on specifications, standards and labelling if they want to trade. This can be costly.
- Marketing policies need to be adapted, and links established with a reliable distributor, bank and, probably, lawyer abroad.
- Competition is not all one way. EU firms can take customers away from UK businesses. Therefore, UK businesses must fight to be efficient, concentrating on their strengths and maximising opportunities arising from their competitors' weaknesses.
- A business operating in other countries can gain economies of scale. These are the advantages in terms of lower unit costs that come from large-scale production. Lower costs per item mean a larger profit margin.
- Selling in other EU countries can increase a UK business's stability. It no longer has all its eggs in one basket.
- Customers in Europe may insist on paying UK businesses in euros, since that is the currency they use with all other European firms. If this is the case, the UK business has to bear the cost of exchanging the money into pounds.

Expansion of the EU

Many, but not all businesses have benefited from the expansion of the EU in the following ways:

- larger market for those who export
- opportunity to expand manufacturing into other countries
- availability of labour from migrants moving into the existing member countries; the service sector and the building industries in the UK have benefited particularly from these workers.

New EU legislation on vacuum cleaners

EU legislation on vacuum cleaners came into force on 1 September 2014. From this date companies in the EU were prohibited from producing or importing vacuum cleaners with power of more than 1600 watts. This news caused a rush of people buying powerful vacuum cleaners across the country before the law came into operation. From 2017, the maximum allowable wattage will be 900.

Hoover has most of its vacuum cleaners in the 'over 1600' watts category, whereas Dyson has none. Despite this, James Dyson has decided to challenge the change in the legislation.

Critics see this as yet another piece of ridiculous legislation thought up by bureaucrats in Brussels. Others point out that high wattage is not essential for good suction performance from a vacuum cleaner and that the rules will encourage the industry to produce more energy-efficient machines.

The euro

The euro came into existence because, to many people, it made no sense to have a single market with over ten different currencies operating in it. So, in 1999, most of the member countries gave up their individual currencies and adopted the euro as a common currency. The UK did not join the euro, but it is clearly still an important economic issue both for the UK as a whole and for its businesses.

Key term

Euro: the single currency that came into being in most EU countries on 1 January 1999.

Advantages to UK businesses of joining the euro

It would encourage trade

UK businesses would no longer have to pay commission for buying or selling euros. Going on holiday abroad means people have to pay commission to buy foreign currency and travellers' cheques, which may only have come to a few pounds but is still annoying. For a UK business buying from, and selling to, EU countries, the commission may be considerable. This extra cost may discourage some businesses from exporting, and so reduce trade.

Prices would be more transparent

Different currencies make it difficult for firms to compare prices. The euro enables businesses to compare prices of raw materials and components from other EU countries quickly. Finding the best deal is a lot easier.

Less uncertainty over costs and profits

With a single currency there is less uncertainty over costs and profits. The possibility of a changing exchange rate can mean a great deal of uncertainty for a UK business. At present there is the possibility of a fall in the exchange rate which will make imported raw materials more expensive. This causes lower profit margins for businesses that have to buy them. At present, while the UK is not a member of the Eurozone, if the exchange rate changes then this could disadvantage a UK company. Suppose this company agreed to buy 1 million components at €3 each and the exchange rate was €1.5 to the pound: the cost is €3 million. In pounds this would be £2 million. If the rate falls to €1 to the pound, the cost rises to £3 million. This could easily wipe out any profit that has been budgeted for.

Alternatively, the exchange rate may rise, making the euro price of exports rise (which will deter some foreign customers from buying). For example, a UK business could sell a product at £10,000. If the rate was €1.5 to the pound, the cost to a customer in the Eurozone would be €15,000. If the rate rose to €2 to the pound, the euro cost would now be €20,000. This increased price is likely to make the product produced by the UK business unattractive.

Such large changes are unlikely (in the short term at least), but they do illustrate how an exchange rate can 'move against' a UK business. If the UK joined the Eurozone, neither of these events could happen. Thus, it is often argued, EU membership should help to create greater business confidence in the likelihood of success when trading with other EU countries.

> **Key terms**
>
> **Eurozone:** the collective name for countries that have adopted the euro as their single currency.
>
> **European Central Bank (ECB):** the central bank that sets interest rates for the whole of the Eurozone.

Disadvantages to UK businesses of joining the euro

Loss of control over monetary policy

Decisions on interest rates are made by the European Central Bank (ECB). This could cause problems if not all economies in the EU are at the same stage of the economic cycle. Suppose that the UK joined the euro at a time when the UK economy was in a mild recession, while the rest of the EU was booming. The correct policy for the ECB to adopt would be to increase the rate of interest. This, however, would mean that economic activity in the UK would slow down further, perhaps even provoking a slump. This situation would clearly not be beneficial to UK businesses. Joining the euro could mean UK businesses suffering for the good of the others.

'Outer' countries may get left behind

Economic activity in a country is often concentrated around its capital and a few of its other important cities. Sometimes the regions 'get left behind', which is why governments have a regional policy. Exactly the same argument applies to the EU as a whole. Some people think that economic power, prosperity and decision making will become centred on the leading member countries, especially France and Germany. Businesses in other countries could suffer unless they received considerable financial assistance. Where, it is often asked, will the funds for this assistance come from? One source could be increased taxation on UK businesses. This would be an unwelcome burden.

At what exchange rate should the pound join the euro?

This is potentially the most significant problem. If the UK joins the single currency, on an agreed day, all pounds will be converted to euros. Suppose that, for a long time, the rate of exchange has been €1.5 to the pound. Now, as the day for joining approaches, the pound rises so that it is worth €3. Is this the correct rate?

At first sight, it would be a good idea to have as many euros to the pound as possible on the day of joining. If there were €3 to the pound, then a pound would have a lot of purchasing power in the rest of the EU; imports would be very cheap. This would be good for UK consumers, but bad for UK businesses because they might not be able to compete with the flood of cheap imports. However, the reverse of this would mean that businesses in other EU countries would have to pay €3 instead of €1.5 for every product that previously cost a pound. This would make UK products very expensive, and so all exporting firms would suffer. This could lead to unemployment.

Alternatively, if the pound fell in value to €1 just before the date for joining, this would make exports cheaper but would make imports from the rest of the EU, including raw materials, a lot more expensive, since £1 would only buy €1. This could also lead to inflation and unemployment.

Joining the euro would not be an easily reversible decision. It is therefore extremely important that the correct rate is agreed before the UK joins. It is essential that the pound is not locked into a rate that is permanently damaging to businesses. However, there is little if any agreement on what the 'correct' rate actually is.

> **Tips and techniques**
>
> There is no clear answer to the question of whether joining the euro is appropriate for UK businesses or not. It depends on an individual business's circumstances.

Continued EU membership

In recent years there have been increasing calls from UK citizens and some politicians for the UK to leave the EU. The emergence of UKIP, with its strong anti-EU bias, as a viable electoral party has led to fierce debate on this issue. As with everything concerned with the UK, there are many issues and many different points of view.

- Can the UK survive in trade terms outside the EU?
- Will some companies choose to leave the UK if they lose the benefits of free trade?
- Has the EU become too large and unwieldy?
- Has the day of the nation state finished; is it necessary to be a large political and economic unit to have an impact on a world stage?
- Is EU immigration taking UK jobs or are EU citizens essential to keep the UK economy running?

All these issues are likely to continue to be discussed at length after the 2015 election – whoever wins.

Global context

Key term

Globalisation: the process of growth in world markets through a process of integration where it is possible to trade in a global market in the same way as one would in a domestic market.

The process of globalisation has come about through the growth in transport, telecommunications and the internet; many regard it as a late twentieth century process, but others think it is a process that began with industrialisation in the eighteenth and nineteenth centuries. The process of globalisation is increasingly rapid as telecommunications improve.

The International Monetary Fund (IMF) identified four factors that have contributed to globalisation in 2000. These include:

1 increase in trade and the number of transactions taking place
2 increase in movements of capital for investment
3 increase in the movement of people across international borders for work
4 increase in the availability of knowledge, particularly through the internet.

The biggest companies in the world are now multinational corporations that operate on a global scale; they may produce in many centres in different countries and they are likely to sell in most countries as well. Examples of such businesses are Procter and Gamble, Shell, Microsoft, Sony, McDonald's and Ford Motors. These companies are global brands. Companies that are keen to operate on a global scale must also have a global strategy, and consider how to build competitive global advantage and which are the best locations to trade and produce products.

In developed countries, globalisation is often seen as a good thing because it allows firms to take advantage of economies of scale to reduce the process for the consumer. However, globalisation is not helping to reduce the gap between rich and poor countries; in many ways it is worsening the situation as a result of the low wages paid to vulnerable groups, in manufacturing businesses in the developing world.

Factory workers manufacturing clothes

Several factors have contributed to speeding up the process of globalisation:

- Trade is now freer on a world level than it has ever been as trade barriers between countries are reduced.
- Telecommunications have improved in all areas, from the use of mobile phones to teleconferencing and the internet. In developing countries new mobile phone networks have opened up communications to all; it is no longer necessary to install expensive landline systems.
- There are huge economies of scale possible now in transport of freight by air and sea.

Multinationals are increasingly moving to developing countries to take advantage of factors such as lower wages, fewer legal constraints, government grants towards setting up and the opportunity to sell in a new market with less competition. As the laws on selling cigarettes have increased in the developed world, the tobacco companies have looked increasingly to the developing world for their markets.

Some of the growth of multinationals has been to the benefit of the less developed countries (LDCs) in terms of providing jobs, infrastructure and training, all of which will have important multiplier effects (see **Chapters 18/19**) in these countries. However, there have also been problems in terms of the exploitation of vulnerable members of society and the plundering of resources to the benefit of the multinational and its shareholders.

Emerging markets

Emerging markets refers to developing countries that are achieving rapid growth and industrialisation and are quickly achieving the status of developed markets. The main countries in this category are India and China, although reference is sometimes made to the BRIC economies, which includes Brazil and

Russia as well. Reference may also be made to the Tiger economies of the Far East that includes South Korea, Taiwan, Singapore and Hong Kong. In general, emerging markets do not have the same efficiency and financial standards that would be expected from a developed economy, but they will have a unified currency and a banking sector.

For the developed world the emerging economies represent both an opportunity and a threat. The opportunities arise from:

- new markets with higher disposable income.
- opportunity to move production into these markets and take advantage of the new group of consumers
- investment opportunities in infrastructure and production.

The threats arise from:

- lower labour costs and the ability to produce more cheaply than in developed economies
- fewer exports from developed economies as the emerging economies become able to produce for themselves
- greater independence for emerging economies.

Advantages and disadvantages of globalisation

Advantages

- The incoming company brings investment, jobs and training.
- News and ideas are spread quickly and easily around the world so that we know about events such as natural disasters and environmental problems on a world scale.
- LDCs need foreign currency to enable them to buy the imports they need to develop further. This money can also be used to improve the lives of inhabitants by providing clean water, medical services and education.

Disadvantages

- The benefits of globalisation are mostly felt by developed countries, their inhabitants and their businesses. These businesses may repatriate their profits so that there may be little benefit for the LDC.
- The lack of a clear and robust legal framework in LDCs can often result in poor working conditions, lack of concern for the environment and pay that is too low to sustain a reasonable living standard.
- The multinational corporation might impose its ideas, morals and ethics on local populations in LDCs.
- There is always a fear in developed countries that jobs will be lost to LDCs. This has been the case with call centre workers when businesses such as Marks and Spencer moved part of their work to India.

Globalisation and the growth of multinational firms is now an inevitable part of life in the developed and developing world. However, it is not possible or even advisable for all companies to go down this route. There is always room for a small business that meets the needs of a local or national market, alongside the world brands that we all recognise.

Opportunities and threats of globalisation

At present, not all businesses are affected by globalisation. The newly industrialised countries are likely to concentrate their production in areas such as motor vehicles and textiles at first. However, the rate of expansion in these countries is very rapid because they are able to take advantage of technological developments throughout the world. This means that the threat of competition will soon be felt by businesses in all areas of the developed world. In the past it has been possible for businesses to use comparative advantage (see **Chapter 16**) and make changes to concentrate production in specialist areas or niche markets so that they were not facing direct competition from lower-wage economies; this will be increasingly difficult as the developing economies become more sophisticated. Globalisation brings with it all the opportunities created by larger markets and lower production costs; but it also brings the threats of high interdependence of nations and unemployment in those areas and businesses that cannot compete efficiently and economically.

Tips and techniques

The topics covered in this chapter are constantly changing. It is important to keep your information up to date by following these topics in the media.

Further sources

www.cbi.org.uk: The employers' lobbying organisation. Information on their attitude to the EU and many other business issues.
www.ecb.int: The European Central Bank

Your turn

Questions in red are for A Level candidates only.

Multiple-choice questions

1 Free trade means:
- A moving goods at no cost
- B absence of trade barriers
- C absence of legal constraints
- D absence of safety controls. *(1)*

2 An advantage of globalisation is:
- A greater diversity in product ranges
- B ability to take advantage of lack of legal controls
- C inward investment with multiplier effects
- D loss of jobs in developing countries. *(1)*

Revision questions

1 State what is meant by a 'free trade area'. *(2)*
2 State two advantages of membership of the EU for the UK. *(2)*
3 State what is meant by 'the Eurozone'. *(2)*
4 State three features of globalisation. *(3)*
5 State two advantages and two disadvantages of globalisation. *(4)*
Total *(13)*

Case study

Primark – Globalisation in action

Primark is an Irish clothing retailer that operates across Europe and from 2014 in the USA. All its clothing carries the Primark label, with many of its products being produced in the developing world. Primark has taken advantage of globalisation to keep its costs low by using factories in countries where labour is relatively cheap.

As a result of coverage in the press and TV programmes, Primark had to look carefully at its factories around the world to try to improve its working practices. However, much of its effort in trying to rebuild its image was shattered in 2013 when a building collapsed near Dhaka, Bangladesh, killing at least 1,127 garment workers and injuring over 2,000. As well as Primark, the factory produced clothing for Benetton and Monsoon.

Globalisation has made it possible for multinational companies to manufacture in countries where they can take advantage of cheaper labour. But sometimes this cheaper labour can turn into the exploitation of vulnerable groups. This is one of the disadvantages of globalisation; the benefits of cheap clothes in developing countries come at the expense of these groups in countries like Bangladesh and India.

Conscious of the need to redeem its image, Primark is now going out of its way to show that it is an ethical business. It signed an agreement in 2013 to compensate the victims of the factory collapse. In 2014, it published a code of conduct prohibiting child labour and started inspections of all its manufacturers to ensure that employees were of working age. In addition, Primark is working with local communities to promote the advantages of education for children and to identify risks that could arise in the supply chain.

1 Explain two ways in which Primark benefits from globalisation. *(4)*
2 Analyse two likely disadvantages for Primark of producing in developing countries. *(6)*
3 Primark's main market is in Europe. Discuss the likely benefits for Primark that arise from trading in the EU. *(20)*
4 Evaluate the likely benefits that will arise as a result of Primark's decision to promote an ethical stance in global markets. *(20)*
Total *(50)*

Chapter 16

International trade and free trade

AS / Year 1 | Year 2

A Level students must know all of the content in this chapter.

This chapter is mainly aimed at A Level students; however, AS candidates do need to cover:

- What is meant by, and reasons for, international trade (**page 106**)
- The nature and purpose of barriers to international trade (**page 106**)
- What is meant by an exchange rate (page 109) (but they do not need to cover how to calculate it or its impact)

International trade is the exchange of capital, goods, and services across the borders of different countries. There are a number of reasons why it is beneficial for countries to trade internationally:

1. Variety: trade enables countries to obtain products they cannot make themselves or could only produce at a vast resource cost.
2. Economic efficiency: the development of export markets can enable a business to gain economies of scale. Also, foreign firms competing in the domestic market helps force UK firms to be more efficient.
3. Growth: access to millions of new customers creates the potential for businesses, and therefore the economy, to grow.
4. International co-operation: trade leads to co-operation rather than conflict as nations become dependent on each other. A war between European countries is now incredibly unlikely as their economies are so interlinked.
5. Specialisation: the main advantage of international trade is that a country can specialise in what it does best, i.e. what its resources are most suitable for, and then sell these products to others. The UK as a post-industrial country specialises in (to name just a few) high-grade engineering parts, pharmaceutical products, and plastics.

The growth of globalisation over the last 30 years or so has meant there has been a huge growth in international trade. Globalisation can be defined in different ways but essentially it is a process of global integration. Products, capital, and labour – as well as ideas and culture – can now move much more freely around the world than before. It is a particularly important concept for businesses since they are able to sell finished products and source raw material inputs from all over the world, not just within a country or from countries nearby. This creates the potential for a larger market and lower costs.

Key term

Globalisation: the process of global integration; the ability of businesses to sell finished products and source raw material inputs from all over the world.

Free trade

'Free trade' is not the same as 'international trade'. Free trade occurs when there are no barriers or limitations to trade at all. Such trade should, in theory, bring the benefits already stated above. However, it is by no means the case that international trade always takes place in a situation where there are no barriers. There are a number of reasons why a country may decide that although it wants its economy to be open to trading internationally, it believes that free trade would be damaging. If this is the case it will take measures to try to influence the way the trade takes place, that is, it protects its industries by putting up trade barriers.

Likely reasons for erecting trade barriers are:

- Foreign competition can lead to unemployment if domestic industries are being undercut, or destroyed altogether, by cheap imports.
- A country may decide that its businesses have considerable potential for the future but are currently in no state to compete against well-established multinationals with their economies of scale and marketing expertise. This is sometimes known as the 'infant industry argument'; the infants need protecting until they have grown and are in a position to compete.

- When a country persistently runs a large balance of payments deficit (see **Chapter 19**) it might try to correct this by discouraging imports.

A country that is concerned about one or more of these reasons could restrict the number of imports of foreign products allowed in. This is known as imposing a quota. Another way to try to solve the problem would be to put a tax on goods entering the country from abroad. This would make the imports more expensive and home-produced goods relatively cheap. This tax is known as a tariff.

A subsidy (government payment) to a domestic industry also counts as protection since it lowers the production costs of the company receiving it. Another less obvious, but still effective, way to put up trade barriers is to insist that any goods entering the country have to conform to a variety of complicated regulations that foreign producers will find hard or/ and expensive to meet. The same regulations will not apply to domestic producers.

The problem with these actions is that other countries affected by the barriers are likely to retaliate in a 'tit for tat' manner. This can result in a quota and tariff 'trade war' that is damaging to businesses in all the countries concerned. Such retaliation could mean that businesses in all the countries affected end up selling less than they potentially could. This would mean a variety of negative effects on their stakeholders; fewer employees, lower orders for suppliers, a reduced range of products for consumers, lower dividends for owners, less in the way of community initiatives, and lower tax revenue for the government. For these reasons, free trade is usually encouraged and that is the reason for the existence of organisations such as The World Trade Organisation (WTO).

The WTO website states:

> *The WTO agreements cover goods, services and intellectual property. They spell out the principles of (trade) liberalisation, and the permitted exceptions. They include individual countries' commitments to lower customs tariffs and other trade barriers. They set procedures for settling disputes....WTO agreements require governments to make their trade policies transparent by notifying the WTO about laws in force and measures adopted.*

Source: World Trade Organisation website http://www.wto.org/english/thewto_e/whatis_e/what_we_do_e.htm

Key term

Free trade: trade without tariffs or quotas being imposed on products.

Free trade can also be encouraged through the creation of a trading bloc. A trading bloc is a group of countries within a particular geographical region that protect themselves from imports from non-members. There are several types of trading bloc:

- A free trade area: this is one in which two or more countries agree to reduce (or eliminate) barriers to trade on all goods being traded with other members in the free trade area.
- A customs union: this takes the concept of the free trade area a stage further; it not only involves the removal of tariff barriers between members, but there is now also a common external tariff against goods being imported into the bloc from non-members.
- A common market: in this situation all of the member countries trade all resources freely not just goods. This means that all barriers to trade in goods, services, capital, and labour are reduced (or removed).
- The EU is the world's largest trading bloc. The EU is far more than just 'a common market' because of the political, legal, and economic implications involved in those who join it (see **Chapter 15**). For example, any country wishing to join the EU now has to agree to join the euro at some point in the future. The EU is said to be 'a single market' – a large market where member states can trade freely with a common (i.e. single) set of regulations and rules on the movement of goods, people and finance, rather than having different regulations for each country. Easier access to each other's markets and competition for customers in a bloc like the EU means that trade between member countries is going to increase, which will hopefully bring benefits for consumers in terms of greater choice and lower prices.

For businesses the potential benefits are:

- Access to a potential market of hundreds of millions of people (and billions of pounds worth of sales). This is known as 'trade creation'.
- Selling in another country can increase a business's stability. It no longer has 'all its (sales) eggs in one basket'.

- Access to raw materials and components at lower costs (since tariffs have been removed).
- Access to capital from foreign financial institutions (which due to competition may be at a more attractive interest rate than the one on offer from a UK bank).
- The potential for economies of scale (lower costs per item mean a larger profit margin).

There are nevertheless some disadvantages for businesses operating within a trading bloc:

- Membership may hinder trade with countries outside of the bloc; the UK, for example, is sometimes said to have 'a special relationship' with the US but due to membership of the EU any US exports (say of manufacturing components) to the UK will have the same tariffs on them that they would face in any other EU country. This may raise the cost of imported components for the UK firm. If there is 'retaliation' from the US then a UK exporter will now find tariffs have been put on exports to the US and so may sell less. This is known as 'trade diversion' – although presumably a government taking its country into a bloc would have considered that the benefits of trade creation outweigh those of trade diversion. Any businesses which trade with countries that are not part of the bloc will now face these issues.
- If the trading bloc permits the free movement of capital it will be easier for domestic companies to be taken over by foreign investors.
- The scale of competition from the foreign firms that can now freely compete in any bloc country's market may be too great for the domestic businesses to cope with. They could lose sales or even be forced into liquidation. This is especially true when new members to the bloc have considerably lower labour costs than the existing members.
- Bloc members have to abide by 'the rules of the club'. This may not be too onerous in a simple free trade area but in a more advanced organisation such as the EU, businesses face a multitude of regulations and directives such as on how to produce, how to package, and how to treat employees. Those running a business lose the freedom to operate it in the way they would like. There are also the costs of complying with these regulations which could, at least in the short term, lower profits.

What are the implications of international trade for a UK business?

Whether trading with other countries in a free trade block or not, a business does not just 'start selling abroad'. There is a long list of implications to be carefully considered. Some of the most important are as follows:

- Someone (or several people) in a senior position must be put in charge of analysing the strengths, weaknesses, opportunities and threats of the proposed markets abroad. They need to conduct (and continuously update) market research. The business's marketing policies will need to be adapted. The buying habits of foreign consumers may be very different to those in the UK and it cannot be assumed that 'what works here, will work there'. One of the reasons for Tesco's failure in the USA with its 'Fresh and Easy' convenience stores was that US shoppers prefer to buy in bulk to save money but Fresh & Easy offered small pack sizes.
- Some of the employees in the business will have to be fluent in different languages and have an understanding of the culture of other countries. This requirement not only applies to senior executives, but also to staff at other levels. An inability to respond to a query from someone asking a question in another language will lose sales. Cultural norms differ between countries and it is important that respect for other cultures is maintained, for example, when communicating with someone or when marketing a product. Offence might otherwise be caused; again losing sales.
- Businesses have to comply with the requirements on specifications, standards and labelling in other countries if they want to trade abroad. This will mean redesigning packaging and researching into legislative requirements, which can be costly.
- The logistics of transporting the product needs to considered, especially if it is perishable or fragile. How will it reach its destination? A contract will need to be signed with another firm to transport the goods – unless the company wants to set up its own distribution network, which would be an additional expense. Insurance will need to be arranged for loss, damage, and theft. Once 'in country' the products will, obviously, need to reach the consumers. This means establishing a link with a distributor who understands the business's needs

and objectives and who can be 'trusted' to market the product effectively. A fee and commission will be charged for this and if prices are set low initially to penetrate the market then it may mean trading at a loss for a considerable period of time. A specialist lawyer will have to be hired (and retained) to ensure that the necessary purchases and contracts of sale are made correctly according to the law in the foreign country.

- It is not only competition for customers that has to be considered. With the increasingly free movement of workers, businesses offering the best employment package attract the most talented staff. This will apply to both attracting employees and retaining them. This is particularly true for young graduates, who are very mobile. Recruitment policies will have to be reviewed.
- Customers abroad may want to pay UK businesses in their own currency. If this is the case, the UK business will have to bear the cost of exchanging the currency into pounds. An insistence on being paid in pounds may lose sales and so foreign currency accounts will need to be established. There are also cash flow implications (see **Chapter 31**). The delay in payment for the sale of products can be problematic enough when selling in the UK, the issues and risks are multiplied when selling abroad and payment is received in a currency whose value may fluctuate.

Tips and techniques

Knowledge of the implications for a business of selling abroad is important, but more important is the ability to evaluate the implications in the context of a particular business. A large firm that is already exporting is likely to find expansion into new foreign markets easier than a small firm that is starting to sell abroad for the very first time.

Whether it is international trade or free trade which is being considered there will always be the issue of the exchange rate for UK businesses.

Exchange rate

The exchange rate is the value of one currency in terms of another. When UK citizens travel abroad, they usually take an interest in how much foreign currency each pound will buy, and how many pounds they are likely to get for any currency brought back. It is exactly the same for UK businesses.

A change in the exchange rate can be problematic. A business might make a sale of \$1m dollars' worth of goods at the start of January on the understanding that payment will be made at the end of February. Assume that the current rate of exchange is \$1.2 to the pound. The business is therefore expecting a sum of £833,333 (\$1m/1.2). If payment is delayed by a month and the pound rises against the dollar to \$1.5 the business will have a worsening cash flow situation and they will only receive £666,666 (\$1m/1.5) when the payment does come through.

UK businesses trade with many different countries and these countries use different currencies. It is therefore important to understand the nature and effects of the exchange rate. The exchange rate can have a significant effect on a business, which can drastically affect its operation. Before these are examined it is necessary to consider how the exchange rate is determined. It is not 'fixed' by the government, although the government can try to influence it. Currencies are traded in a market, in this case, the foreign exchange market. This market is global: wherever banks and other financial institutions trade currencies, they are part of the foreign exchange market.

Key terms

Exchange rate: the value of the pound in terms of another currency.

Foreign exchange market: the market for currency, which is not in a single location but exists globally whenever buyers and sellers deal.

How is the exchange rate determined?

As in any market, the price (in this case the 'price' of the pound, i.e. the rate of exchange) is determined by the interaction of demand and supply.

What determines the demand for pounds?

The demand for pounds on the foreign exchange market is determined by several factors, as shown in Figure 16.1.

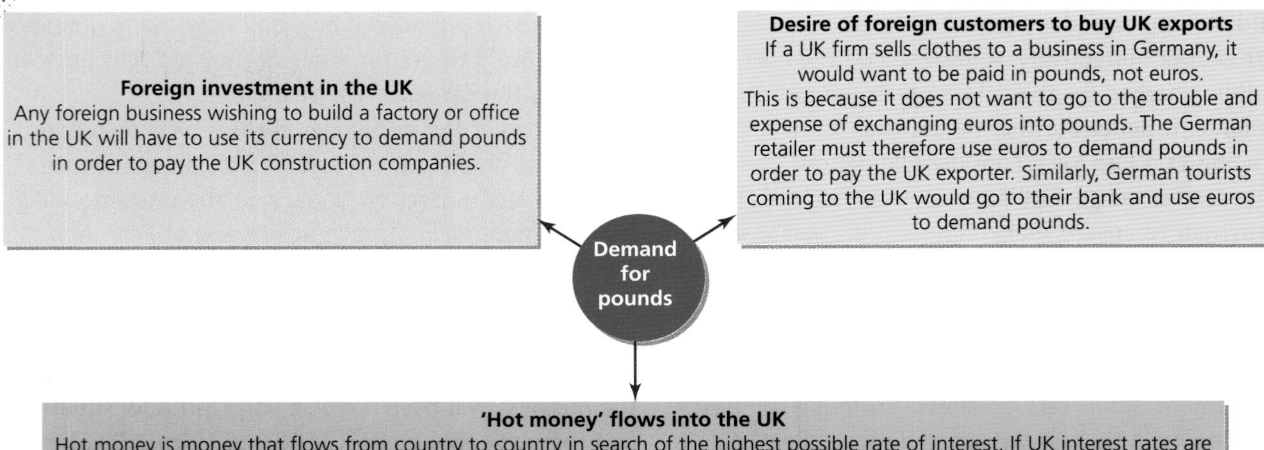

Figure 16.1 Determinants of the demand for pounds

What determines the supply of pounds?

The supply of pounds on to the foreign exchange market is determined by the factors shown in Figure 16.2.

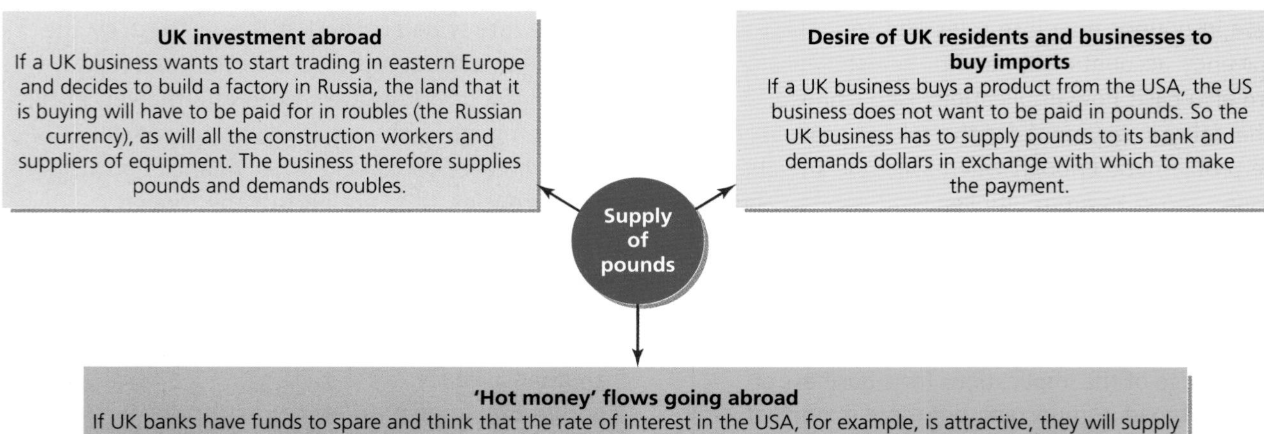

Figure 16.2 Determinants of the supply of pounds

The interaction of the demand for and supply of pounds establishes the exchange rate, as shown in Figure 16.3.

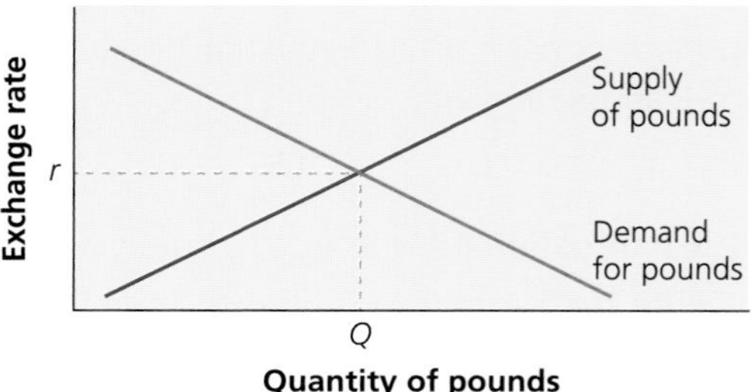

Figure 16.3 Determination of the exchange rate

What are the effects on a business if the rate of exchange changes?

Assume that there are 1.5 euros to the pound. This means that:

- for every £1 supplied, a business will receive €1.5
- for every €1.5 supplied, a business will receive £1.

An Italian pizza producer sells a box of 20 'Mama Mia' pizzas' for €100. A restaurant in London imports them from Italy. This transaction is shown in Figure 16.4.

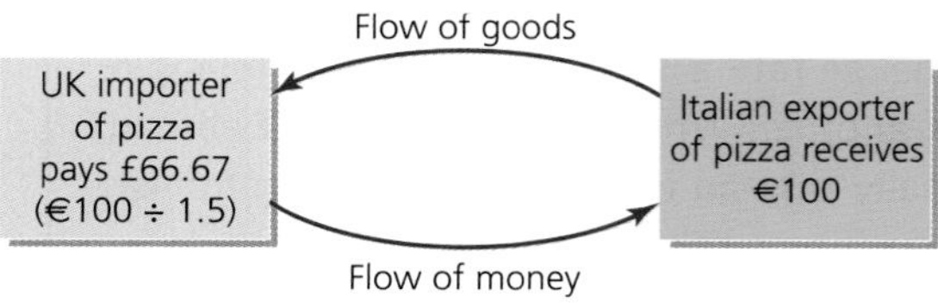

Figure 16.4 Cost to the UK importer of pizza

Near to the London restaurant is a business that sells fountain pens. It sells a box of five for £100. A lot of its business is in the EU. A stationery shop in Italy buys these for its more exclusive customers. This transaction is shown in Figure 16.5.

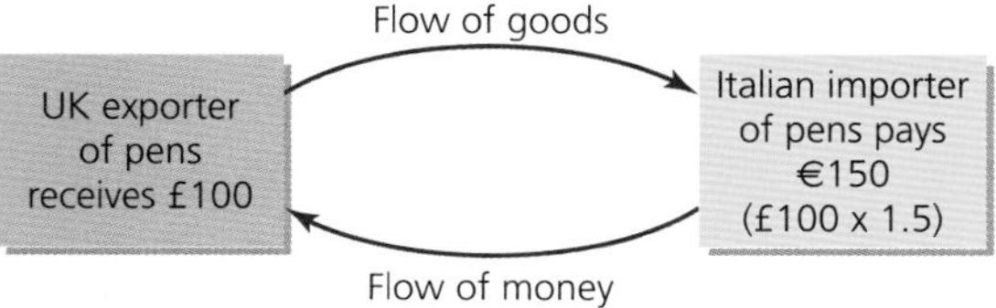

Figure 16.5 Cost to the Italian importer of fountain pens

What happens if the exchange rate rises?

Assume the rate is now £1 = €2. This means that the pound is now stronger and therefore buys more foreign currency than before. Both of the two businesses will be affected, as shown in Figures 16.6 and 16.7.

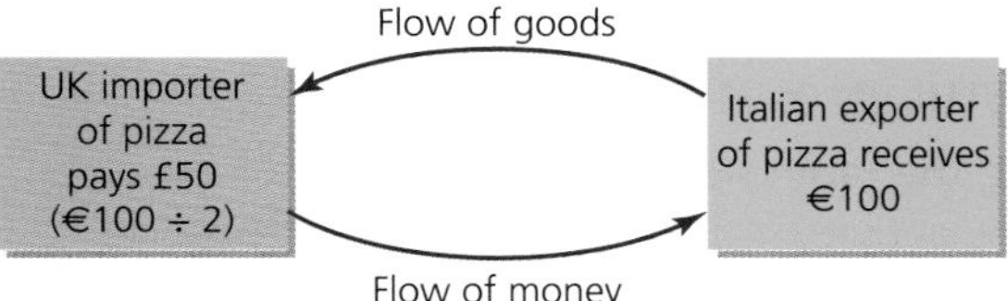

Figure 16.6 Effect of a higher exchange rate on the UK importer of pizza

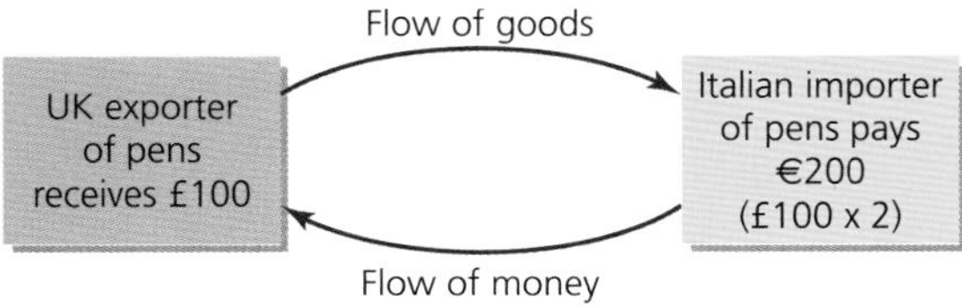

Figure 16.7 Effect of a higher exchange rate on the Italian importer of pens

The effect of a rise in the exchange rate is to make imports cheaper, but exports more expensive.

What happens if the exchange rate falls?

Assume that the rate is now £1= €1. The pound is now weaker: that is, it buys less foreign currency than before. Once again, both businesses will be affected, as shown in Figures 16.8 and 16.9.

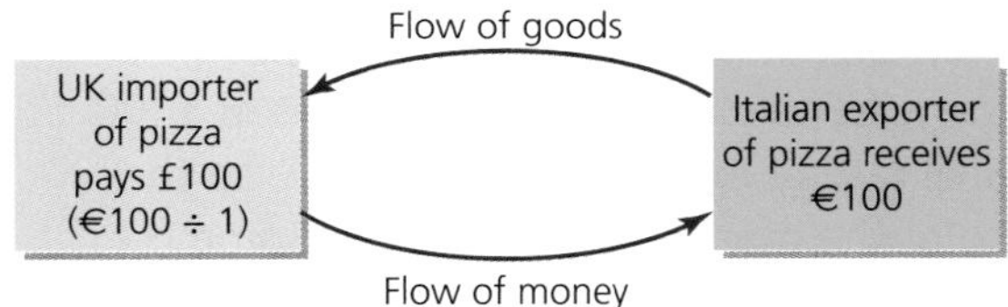

Figure 16.8 Effect of a lower exchange rate on the UK importer of pizza

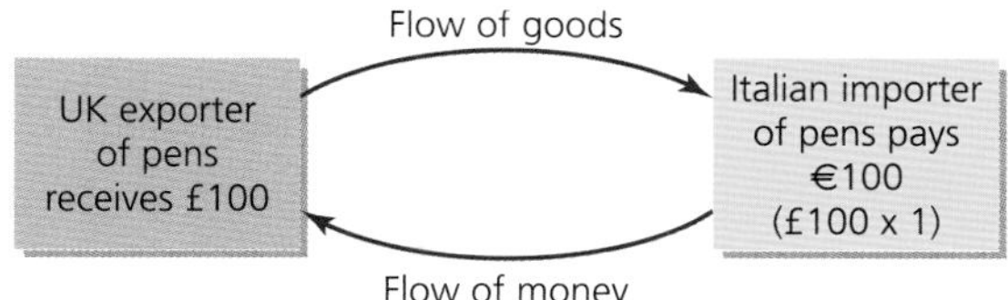

Figure 16.9 Effect of a lower exchange rate on the Italian importer of pens

The effect of a fall in the exchange rate is to make imports more expensive, but exports cheaper.

The interaction of the supply and demand for pounds causes the rate of exchange to change on a daily basis. Unless there is some factor that is out of the ordinary, such as terrorist attacks, a war or an unexpected change of government, these daily changes are minor. This is just as well because the changes in costs and prices caused by sudden large changes in the rate of exchange can be very destabilising and damaging to a business.

Bank of England and the exchange rate

The Bank of England is able to buy and sell currency whenever it is thought necessary in order to prevent potentially damaging changes in the exchange rate or to support the objectives of its Monetary Policy Committee. For example, if the bank thought the exchange rate was slightly too high, it would sell (supply) pounds and buy foreign currency or gold. This is shown in Figure 16.10; the sale of pounds lowers the exchange rate from r1 to r2. Alternatively, if it thinks the exchange rate is too low, the bank will buy (demand) pounds using reserves of foreign currency or gold to do so. However, the Bank does not seek to intervene in the currency market on a regular basis and when doing so, it does not attempt to engineer large changes in the exchange rate.

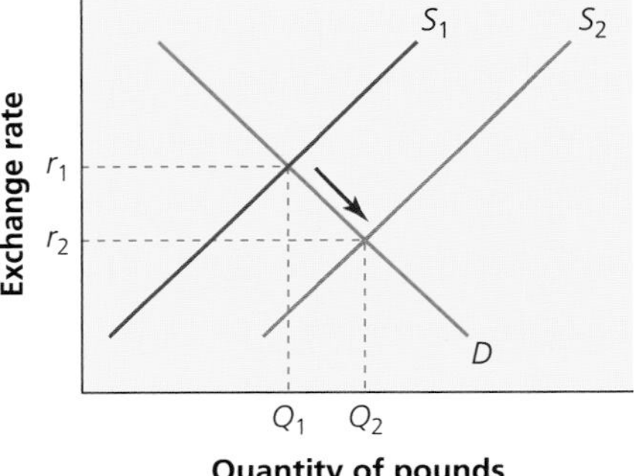

Figure 16.10 Effect of the Bank of England selling pounds

Hot money

Changes in the rate of interest affect the exchange rate via flows of what is known as 'hot money'. It is important to understand this relationship because hot money is a major determinant of the exchange rate. Consider the following: someone receives £100 as a birthday present and decides to save it rather than spend it. Naturally, they will look for the bank or building society that offers the best rate of interest. Exactly the same principle applies to international finance: hot money chases the highest rate of interest it can get. International banks are looking for the best rate of interest for their money. Suppose there is a Japanese investment bank in Tokyo and that interest rates are 2 per cent in Japan, while UK banks are offering 5 per cent. If the Japanese bank has some surplus funds, it will transfer them to the UK because the return is better. However, it will have to change its Yen into pounds first. This increased demand for pounds will raise the price of pounds, that is, the exchange rate.

So, if the Bank of England wants the exchange rate to rise, instead of buying pounds itself (using foreign currency or gold), it can put up the rate of interest. This will encourage inflow of hot money into the UK to take advantage of the higher returns. This will shift the demand curve in Figure 16.11 from D1 to D2 and raise the exchange rate to r2. Alternatively, if the bank wants the rate of exchange to fall, it can lower the rate of interest. This makes deposits of money in the UK less attractive and the rate of exchange will fall.

Key term

Hot money: flow of money from country to country, which is chasing the highest rate of interest it can possibly get.

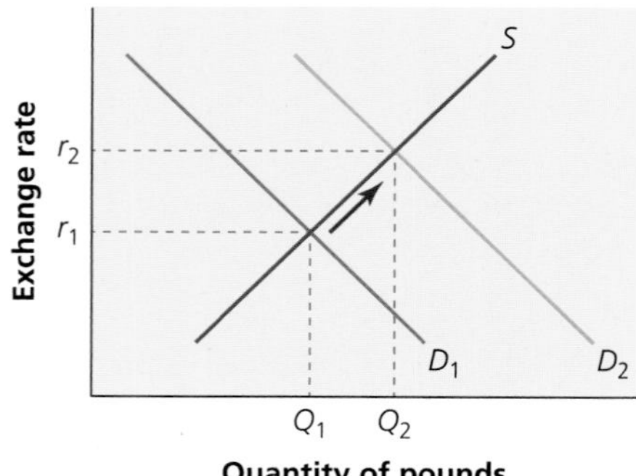

Figure 16.11 Using hot money to raise the exchange rate

The exchange rate as a tool of economic policy

What is the Bank of England trying to achieve when it intervenes? Apart from smoothing out temporary fluctuations, the bank may intervene for other reasons.

Inflation

Raising the rate of exchange can be a useful part of an anti-inflationary policy. Imports become cheaper, which lowers the cost of raw materials bought from abroad. This means that UK businesses can keep costs, and therefore prices, down.

In addition, an increase in the value of the pound means that the price of UK exports rises. The prices charged by any UK businesses exporting now appear uncompetitive, and they must try to cut their prices if they want to continue to export. This means they will have to keep control of wages and other costs. This will help to lower the rate of inflation.

Economic growth

Lowering the rate of exchange can help to increase economic activity. A lower rate makes UK exports cheaper, which is useful if the UK is not exporting enough. A fall in the rate helps to boost exports and in doing so creates employment and economic growth.

Unfortunately, a lower rate may cause imported inflation, as any raw materials purchased from other countries will become more expensive.

Are all businesses affected in the same way by changes in the exchange rate?

The answer is 'no'. Consider the following three examples.

UK business that exports but does not import

If the rate rises

Consider the business mentioned earlier that exports pens to Italy. It sells boxes of pens at £100. The original rate of exchange is £1 = €1.5, so the euro price of the box of pens is €150. Assume the exchange rate rises to £1 = €2. This means that the selling price has gone up in terms of what foreign countries must now pay: the price is now €200 per box. This may make the product uncompetitive when compared with pens produced in other countries. So why does the UK business not lower its selling price to £75, which would put the euro price back down to where it was before, at €150?

A price reduction of £25 per box of pens is quite substantial. If it wanted to keep profits per box of pens at the same level, the company would have to lower costs by £25 per box. However, it may not be able to find a cheaper supplier of the components that go into the pens, and its employees are unlikely to take a pay cut.

If the costs of production are £70 and the pens now sell at £75, this means a profit of only £5 per box. Worse still, if the total cost of making the pack in the first place was £80, the business will now make a loss if it sells them abroad.

The business is now faced with the issues of:

- selling fewer pens abroad because the foreign exchange price has risen
- trying to sell more pens in the UK to make up for reduced sales abroad
- trying to offset the rise in the exchange rate by lowering costs and therefore the selling price
- selling at a loss abroad because it is taking a long-term view of its relationship with its Italian customers (but how long can it keep this up for?).

If the rate falls

A fall in the exchange rate means that the foreign currency price falls, although the price in pounds is still £100 per box. The business is now faced with the issues of:

- increasing the profit per box (i.e. deciding whether it could raise the selling price in pounds); if the rate fell to £1 = €1, the selling price could be raised to £150; this would be equivalent to €150 (the same euro price as before).
- leaving the price unchanged at £100 (which is now equivalent to €100) and hoping the Italian importer will buy more because they are now cheaper.

UK business that imports but does not export

If the rate rises

UK businesses that do not export products will not be affected by the higher foreign currency price of exports. An example of this would be a hairdresser.

However, even if they do not export, many businesses will import raw materials or components. For example, a hairdresser may import shampoo and conditioner from Spain. If the pound rises, these imported products will become cheaper. What will the owner of the salon do? If her costs have fallen by 5 per cent, she is now faced with the issues of:

- passing this saving on to her customers in the form of a price cut, if she feels that this will generate a lot of extra business
- taking a larger profit margin, if she decides that she has enough customers already and wants to take advantage of the cost reduction.

If the rate falls

A fall in the exchange rate means that the cost of the imported shampoo and conditioner rises. The business's owner is now faced with the issues of:

- passing the cost increase on to her customers: will this be possible or will they go elsewhere?
- absorbing the increase in costs, accepting lower profits: this may be likely if the situation is not expected to last very long.

In both of these instances, if the shampoo and conditioner costs were only a small percentage of total costs of the business, the impact of the rate change would not be very significant. If they were a large part of total costs, the impact would be greater.

UK business that both imports and exports

Consider a business that imports various components in order to make tractors. It assembles them into finished tractors, which it then exports. If the exchange rate changes, whether it is 'good' or not depends on the relative magnitude of the two effects.

If the rate rises

Imported components are now cheaper, but this good news may be offset by bad news in the form of the higher foreign currency selling price of the product. Fewer finished tractors may be sold abroad.

If the rate falls

Exports are now cheaper and so, theoretically, more tractors should be sold abroad. However, the fall in the rate will mean that the imported parts that the business uses have become more expensive. This could mean a rise in the final selling price, and this bad news may offset the good news.

Summary

In conclusion, there will not be an exchange rate that is satisfactory for all UK businesses; it depends on their circumstances. The various effects of changes in the exchange rate are summarised in Table 16.1.

Table 16.1 Summary of the effects of a change in the exchange rate

Rise in exchange rate	Fall in exchange rate
The pound will buy more foreign currency than before	The pound will buy less foreign currency than before
UK exports become more expensive	UK exports become cheaper
Imports into the UK become cheaper	Imports into the UK become more expensive

Tips and techniques

You need to be able to calculate an exchange rate conversion (e.g. dollars into pounds) and you need to be able to form a judgement on the extent to which a business's strategy may be affected by a change in the exchange rate, if you want to gain marks for evaluation.

Analysing and evaluating the effects of a change in the exchange rates

The extent to which a business is affected by an exchange rate change depends on several factors:

- What percentage of sales are exports? If exports were only 5 per cent of a business's total sales, it might not be too concerned about a rise in the rate. However, if 50 per cent of its sales were made abroad, this would be much more significant. It may then decide to try to switch sales to UK customers.
- What percentage of inputs is imported? If this is only a small proportion of its total costs then it will not be badly affected by a fall in the rate. Another issue is whether any cost increases caused by a fall in the rate can be easily 'passed on' to customers.

The 'TED' framework from page 148 can also be applied again here: trend, extent, duration. 'TED' is important.

- Trend. Was the rate change part of a trend? If the rate fell and this fall had been expected then it may have little effect on a business's strategy. Its managers might have bought currency in advance, as explained above. Alternatively, an unexpected change against the trend (especially if it is a relatively large change) may be more problematic.
- Extent. Was the rate change large or small? In reality, large changes in the value of a currency are quite rare. The value of the pound against the euro, for example, tends to change by tenths of a cent at a time. This means that while a change from 1.434 to 1.432 euros to the pound is indeed 'a fall in the exchange rate', it will not produce the same reaction among businesses as a fall from 1.434 to 1.234.
- Duration. Is the rate change expected to be temporary or more permanent? Rates of exchange change every day and therefore 'a change in the exchange rate' in itself is not an unexpected event, and is unlikely to be the cause of any major strategic changes. However, even with a small rate change it is important for a business to try to take into account how long it could last for. Consider the change above. Suppose a business plans to invest 100 million euros in France in one year's time. At the rate of 1.434 euros to the pound, this will cost £69,735,007. If the rate falls to 1.432 and the business expects it to remain there then, if it is correct, the cost of the investment will now be £69,832,402 – almost £100,000 more. This may have an effect on the business's strategic plans.

What support is available for businesses that trade internationally?

Avoiding the effects of a change in the exchange rate

There is a way for a business to shield itself from exchange rate fluctuations. It is possible to sign a contract to buy (or sell) foreign currency in advance of when it is actually required (or received). The rate will be fixed at the agreed figure. The business will then be certain of what it has to pay, or what it will receive. However, the bank will charge a fee for this future trading, and this will be a further cost to a business. Managers must assess the risk of any rate changes and their impact and, in the light of this, decide whether it is worth signing up to the fixed rate.

Export factoring

A business which needs finance can factor its debts (see **Chapter 31**) and a similar service exists for exporters. Export factoring is provided by most banks.

This is a process in which the bank arranges to obtain payment directly from the importer and agrees to pay the exporting company the value of the invoice less a discount for commission and fees. This avoids the uncertainty for the exporting firm of whether it will be paid or not and enables it to gain most of the money without having to wait for payment.

Export insurance

In some circumstances the UK government offers assistance in the form of insurance to UK exporters against the risk of non-payment by overseas buyers.

Training and support for exporters from the government

Most banks will be able to offer guidance and support for business customers who are considering exporting, but a business can also apply for training and support from the government. The Passport to Export programme offers help to small and medium-sized firms that want to start exporting. Assistance includes:

- help with market research and selection of target market(s)
- help to visit potential markets
- a detailed assessment of the business's readiness to export
- an action plan for exporting.

This service is free. In addition, The Foreign and Commonwealth Office offers guidance on overseas business risks and political and economic updates for many countries.

Further sources

www.thebankofengland.co.uk: what the bank does and how exchange rate policy operates

www.x-rates.com: one of many websites that offer foreign exchange services; it is useful for explaining why currency values change, and offers a conversion table and the ability to plot rate changes over time in virtually any currency

www.gov.uk/government-help-for-exporters: the assistance that is on offer to exporters from the government

Your turn

Questions in red are for A Level candidates only.

Multiple-choice questions

1 The exchange rate is £1 = $1.4. This year a UK business has spent a total of $500,000 launching a product in America and is expecting a total revenue of $720,000. Assuming no change in the exchange rate, its profit in pounds is:

A £220,140
B £177,134
C £157,143
D £54,411. *(1)*

2 A UK business plans to import components from America, next month. It will assemble them, and then, in six months' time export the finished product to a country in the Eurozone. It will pay for the imported components and receive payment for the exports immediately. In the light of this, which of the following changes to the value of the pound is most likely to be beneficial to it? *(1)*

Option	Direction of change in the exchange rate of the pound to the dollar in the next month	Direction of change in the exchange rate of the pound to the euro in six months' time
A	Fall	Fall
B	Fall	Rise
C	Rise	Fall
D	Rise	Fall

3 Which of the following options is most likely to cause the largest rise in the value of the pound? *(1)*

Option	Demand for pounds on foreign exchange market	Supply of pounds on foreign exchange market
A	Rise	Fall
B	Rise	No change
C	No change	Rise
D	Fall	No change

4 Which of the following is a likely efficiency gain to a business resulting from exporting abroad?
A higher potential amount of revenue
B greater awareness of other cultures
C lower unit costs resulting from economies of scale
D the ability to sell globally. *(1)*

Revision questions

1 Outline two reasons why a government might want to encourage free trade. *(4)*
2 State the difference between 'international trade' and 'free trade'. *(2)*
3 Outline the difference between 'the rate of interest' and 'the rate of exchange'. *(4)*
4 State what is meant by the term 'hot money'. *(2)*
5A Outline two factors that could cause a rise in the rate of exchange. *(4)*
5B Outline two factors that could cause a fall in the exchange rate. *(4)*
Total *(20)*

Case study

Wheathills

Wheathills in Derbyshire has been a family-run business for nearly 200 years and maintains a long-standing tradition based on inherited skill and experience. It is one of the region's most highly regarded antique furniture and period property* interior restorers, supplying services to antique collectors and those renovating period homes worldwide. The company not only restores antique furniture, but also creates unique pieces of handmade furniture, especially Marquetry Boxes, which are made to the customer's own specification. Marquetry is the art of applying pieces of veneer to a structure to form decorative patterns, designs or pictures.

Wheathills are now selling Memory Boxes, a custom-made box for holding keepsakes designed to reflect the personality of the recipient, in various countries abroad. This came about with support from UK government's Passport to Export programme run by UK Trade & Investment's services (UKTI). As part of this programme, Wheathills' owner Nigel Heldreich attended a workshop covering all the practical elements of exporting.

'The passport to export workshop was incredibly informative. It covered everything we needed to know about exporting,' said Nigel. One particularly successful sale came from Switzerland – an order worth £250,000 for a one-off piece of furniture, the company's largest single sale.

Nigel was particularly interested in selling to the USA. A meeting was arranged for a Development Visit to Wheathills by a trade officer from the British Consulate in New York, to discuss how the company's advertising and website could be tailored to better suit this market.

Nigel said:

> The work we did to tailor our marketing for the US has proven particularly effective. We now receive three or four genuine enquiries from there every day. ... What I value most is that I know I'm getting independent and objective advice. Thanks to this support, we've come a long way in the last two years and are confident of a promising future.

*A 'period property' is a classic representation of an architectural style from a certain era, for example a Georgian town house

Source Quotes from Nigel Heldreich

www.gov.uk/government/case-studies/ukti-helps-wheathills-carve-out-a-future-in-international-trade

1 Wheathills sold a piece of furniture to a client in Switzerland for £250,000. The Swiss Franc is denoted by the letters CHF. If the selling price in Swiss Francs was CHF 380,000:

   A Calculate the number of Swiss Francs to the pound. *(2)*

   B Calculate the value of 1 Swiss Franc in terms of pounds. *(2)*

2 Outline two trade barriers that Wheathills may have to face when exporting to the USA. *(4)*

3 Analyse one possible reason why Wheathills might have decided to start exporting. *(6)*

4 Evaluate the factors most likely to ensure the continuing success of Wheathills when selling products abroad. *(15)*

Total *(29)*

Chapter 17

Political, social and ethical factors

AS / Year 1 | Year 2

Both AS and A Level students must know all of the content of the Political (**pages 118–123**) section of this chapter.

Both AS and A Level students must know all of the content of the Social section (**pages 123–126**) of this chapter.

A Level students must study the whole of the Ethical section, but AS students only need to:

- be able to distinguish between law and ethics
- explain ethical issues which influence a business
- recommend and justify ways a business could improve its ethical profile
- evaluate the advantages and disadvantages to a business and its stakeholders of behaving ethically

These are covered in the introduction to the ethics section on page 126.

The political and social environment in which a business exists will have an impact on its actions, performance and success. In the UK, the tiers of government include the European Union, national government and local authorities. The political ethos of these bodies will have an effect on the way the business can operate. It is also important to remember that the UK operates within the world's economic and political scene and, therefore, events in other countries may have an impact on the UK. For example, the crisis in Ukraine in 2014 had an effect on UK gas supply companies because of the Ukraine's strategic position in gas piping from Russia. In general, political instability causes uncertainty for businesses and is likely to reduce success. In situations of instability, mangers will be reluctant to invest or to make decisions on change. Currencies are likely to be volatile, which will have an impact on international trade and the making of contracts to import and export.

European Union

As a member of the EU, the UK is bound by all its rules. These include:

- Regulations which are legally binding immediately and imposed directly by the EU
- Directives which must be applied as law, but it is up to the country how to implement it
- Recommendations and opinions that express the view of the particular body.

For example, rules controlling driving hours and the use of tachometers on heavy goods vehicles are applied and enforced by the EU throughout all member countries.

The introduction of the Single European Market in 1999 brought a number of changes that had an impact on business and the way it operates. As a result of EU membership, UK businesses are now able to supply to a market of more than 459 million people (the third largest in the world after China and India), with all the opportunities and risks from competition that this market creates.

The main changes introduced by the Single European Market legislation were:

- freedom of movement for all EU citizens within member countries
- free movement of capital within the EU
- harmonisation of rules and regulations applied to products and services making it possible for businesses to sell in all member countries; e.g. the requirement to sell all electrical appliances with a moulded plug already attached
- removal of some of the checks on crossing frontiers between member countries
- harmonisation of tax rules for individuals and businesses
- removal of internal tariffs and a common external tariff.

The result of all these changes has been an increase in the competition faced by all businesses, regardless of the extent to which they trade in the EU. Managers have realised that efficiency is vital for success in such a huge market and this has resulted in specialisation, growth within and outside national boundaries and a drive to achieve economies of scale in areas such as marketing and production. Huge companies like Nestlé own production units and supply markets throughout the EU, taking advantage of the economies of scale that this brings to all sectors of the business. They can manufacture for a much greater market, achieving huge cost savings through long production runs.

European Monetary Union

The EU introduced the single currency in January 1999, and in January 2002 all monetary transactions for those countries in the system moved into euros. For a number of reasons, the UK chose not to be part of the single currency. The difficulties experienced by the eurozone from 2008 have made the UK decision to remain outside it seem to make good economic sense. By 2014, the UK economy was one of the fastest growing in the developed world, whereas in the rest of Europe, commentators were talking of the threat of deflation. The fact that the UK is outside the eurozone has the following implications.

Canary Wharf in London

All transactions between UK business and firms in the Eurozone create costs, because businesses need to change currencies into and out of sterling.

The exchange rates between the euro and pound with countries outside the EU may vary, leading to different trading conditions; for example, since the single currency was introduced, the pound has performed better than the euro against the dollar. This means that UK firms exporting to the USA find that their goods are relatively less competitive against those from EU countries using the euro (see **Chapter 16**).

There was always a possibility that some countries might choose to relocate from the UK, but this does not seem to have been the case. The cost of relocation is likely to be higher than the difficulties created from being outside the Eurozone. Japanese businesses such as Sony, Nissan and Toshiba have all discussed the possibility of moving their production out of the UK if it continues to remain outside the single currency. These businesses have so far remained in the UK, but would prefer a situation where the UK was a member of the single currency.

Financial sector businesses, with their large movements of money, are likely to be seriously disadvantaged by the existence of transaction costs. Although it was felt that this might have implications for London's future as a major financial market, the City of London has confounded predictions and become increasingly important in European and world markets as a major money and banking centre.

Tips and techniques

In case studies and questions, you may find that the UK currency is sometimes referred to as sterling and at other times as the pound.

Key term

Eurozone: those countries in the EU that are now using the euro as their currency.

Growth of the European Union

As the EU continues to expand its boundaries, it creates many new opportunities for business, while introducing new problems and risks. The new member countries of the EU have a population base that is much more diverse than the one that existed previously, and businesses need to be aware of these differences before they move into those markets. Many of the Eastern European economies have much lower standards of living than those in Western Europe, and their economic systems have only recently moved to becoming market economies after being centrally planned for many years. Care needs to be exercised in trading or moving production to these areas because the business framework is still very fragile and the risks for business are therefore large.

Most of these countries are keen to move their economies forward as rapidly as possible. They want to increase the range of consumer goods, to provide better jobs for their populations and to import from and export to other EU countries. This means that there are opportunities for UK businesses to move into the areas in many ways:

A number of UK firms have moved some or all of their production to the newer member countries to take advantage of their lower-cost labour, and to gain easier access to these new markets. For example, many of the big 'blockbuster' films requiring large numbers of extras are now filmed in Hungary and the Czech Republic to take advantage of lower production costs.

There is a demand for new infrastructure and technological development in these countries that UK businesses are well placed to meet. A number of UK businesses have taken the opportunity to set up joint ventures with firms in these countries. Europolis (a project run by a consortium of European universities) is working on a joint venture with Polish businesses to build the largest logistics centre in Central and Eastern Europe. This is attracting attention from large businesses in Western Europe such as IKEA and Unilever.

UK business has taken advantage of workers coming into the UK from the new member countries. These workers often move into areas where there are skill or labour shortages and therefore help the UK economy operate more efficiently. For example, fruit farmers in East Anglia rely heavily on overseas workers from Eastern Europe to pick their crops, and many areas of the tourism and catering industry are increasingly reliant on foreign labour from EU countries. The UK economy is now reliant on EU workers in several sectors such as fruit picking, the restaurant trade and the NHS. Nevertheless, despite the advantages they bring, the increasing migration from countries such as Romania has put an enormous strain on certain areas of the UK. The problems are usually related to access to benefits, health care, housing and demand for school places. This has increased tensions and contributed to the rise of UKIP as a political party fighting EU membership and immigration.

Management and the European Union

The decision to move into Europe is an important strategic one for management, and it needs careful consideration before any such move is undertaken. Although the EU is now a single market, this does not mean that it is uniform throughout; in fact, the opposite is the case. Within the EU there is a huge diversity in terms of consumers, competition, demand and production; these factors must be taken into account. If a business is trading in a market that is fragmented and geographically separated, it is going to experience difficulties in supplying to that market unless there has been a thorough investigation of the market, and the business is aware of the sectors in which it wishes to trade. For example, a business producing an item at the premium end of the market will not want to move into a low-income economy to sell its product, but it may be interested in producing in such an economy. Burberry has moved some its production to eastern European countries in an attempt to cut costs and increase profit margins.

Above all, the managers of a business entering Europe need to have clear objectives for the future, both in terms of the existing domestic market and the new overseas market. There are opportunities for managers to take in terms of higher sales; for example, Melton Mowbray Pork Pies will benefit from 'Protected Geographical Status' (see below). However, there are also risks involved in moving into the unknown. Managers need to minimise these risks through careful planning, an understanding of the new market and a willingness to be adaptable to the new situations they face.

Protection for Melton Mowbray's pies

Melton Mowbray The Melton Mowbray pork pie has finally joined Cornish clotted cream, Whitstable oysters and Welsh lamb on Europe's list of protected food.

After a ten-year battle, the world-famous pie has been given protected geographic status by the European Commission.

This means only producers making these pork pies to the traditional recipe and in the vicinity of the Leicestershire town of Melton Mowbray will have the right to use its name. The Melton Mowbray Pork Pie Association has fought hard for the status, which came into effect in 2009. Matthew O'Callaghan, chairman and local councillor, said: 'The award of [protection] for Melton Mowbray pork pies safeguards our regional food heritage, protects our local jobs and gives the consumer value.'

Central government intervention

The extent to which the government intervenes in the economy will vary, and depends on one or more of the following factors:

The political persuasion of the party in power will be significant. In general, Labour governments are more likely to intervene in the working of the economy than Conservative governments. The Conservative government has made numerous changes to the running of government and the benefit system during its period of office. Many of these changes have had effects on the day-to-day running of businesses.

The state of the economy may be an important factor. Governments are likely to feel the need to respond more when the economy is in difficult circumstances, such as a situation of rising unemployment. A government coming up to a general election, with an economy experiencing low growth, may try to stimulate demand through the use of fiscal policy.

Key term

Fiscal policy: the use of government spending and taxation, through the government's annual budget, to influence the level of demand in the economy (see **Chapter 19**).

The views of the electorate may also play a significant role in influencing government opinion. Successive UK governments have tried to reduce the burden of the NHS by privatising parts of its operations, but this has to be done carefully in the knowledge that public opinion is in favour of the policy of health care that is free at point of use for all.

Sometimes local governments intervene and affect the operation of businesses. The recession from 2008 has led to cutbacks throughout local government. This has had effects on grants and benefits in different parts of the UK. Businesses need to take a change in policy like this into account when making decisions on location or relocation and in the provision of vehicles for their employees or for distribution.

Competition policy

The UK's policy on monopoly is to allow it to exist, but to prevent the use of restrictive practices that operate against the public interest. The Competition and Markets Authority (CMA) considers any business with more than 25 per cent of the market to be a monopoly. If a proposed takeover bid or merger would result in a monopoly situation, it will be the subject of investigation by CMA, requiring permission from it to go ahead.

Key terms

The Competition and Markets Authority (CMA): the government organisation that makes markets work well for consumers.

Monopoly: in terms of UK and EU competition policy, this is any business that controls more than 25 per cent of the market share.

In some cases, a group of businesses may operate restrictive practices together, through a joint and secret agreement. This practice is called 'collusion'. It is easiest to collude where a few large firms dominate an industry. This is because the fewer people who know of the agreement, the more likely it is to be undetected. The operation of collusion between businesses is illegal in the UK and elsewhere in the EU. As a result of the Office of Fair Trading's (OFT) investigation into collusion, British Airways was fined in 2007 for price-fixing fuel surcharges with Virgin Atlantic; Virgin was not fined because they reported the offence to the American Aviation Authority.

Tips and techniques

The term 'monopoly' is also used in some cases to refer to a single supplier who controls a market. Microsoft could be used as an example of a monopoly in this situation.

Privatisation and deregulation

The main period of privatisation of public sector businesses took place in the 1980s and 1990s under Conservative governments, particularly those of Margaret Thatcher. Privatisation is the act of passing ownership of a business from the public to private sector by selling shares in the business. In general, the businesses being privatised were monopolies within the UK, although some, like British Airways, faced considerable foreign competition even before their privatisation.

The arguments in favour of privatisation are as follows:

- Private sector businesses are subject to market forces and therefore need to operate efficiently, being aware of supply and demand conditions.
- A business that is privately owned needs to be profitable and to satisfy its shareholders in order to be able to survive.

The arguments against are:

- Many nationalised industries, like that of electricity supply, were natural monopolies. If privatisation results in new suppliers, this may lead to the duplication of expensive investment, which is inefficient and not in the interests of the general public.
- In some cases, it was felt that the businesses were sold off too cheaply and that valuable long-term assets were turned into short-term cash, which was not used prudently by the government of the day. Harold Macmillan, a former Conservative Prime Minister, referred to privatisation as 'selling the family silver'.

- Private sector businesses will not trade in unprofitable areas, leading to a variation in provision across the country.

To avoid problems of overpricing after privatisation, the privatised utilities were put under the control of regulators such as The Water Services Regulation Authority (OFWAT) for the water industry. Regulators have the power to cap price increases and demand efficiency savings through investment. Their intervention has been particularly evident in the telecommunications market, where the Office of Communications (Ofcom) has been responsible for a number of pricing interventions to the benefit of the consumer.

The process of privatisation was also accompanied by that of deregulation in a number of sectors of the economy during the 1980s. It was considered that outdated rules and regulations were stifling competition and that the result for the consumer was high prices and poor levels of efficiency. For example, bus provision in most areas of the UK was subject to a number of local authority laws, most commonly ones that limited the number of providers, often creating monopoly situations.

The removal of these laws led to a rapid increase in providers, sometimes to unsustainable numbers in the short run. The effect of deregulation is shown on the supply and demand graph in Figure 17.1 with a shift to the right of the supply curve. This will result in lowering the price to the customer.

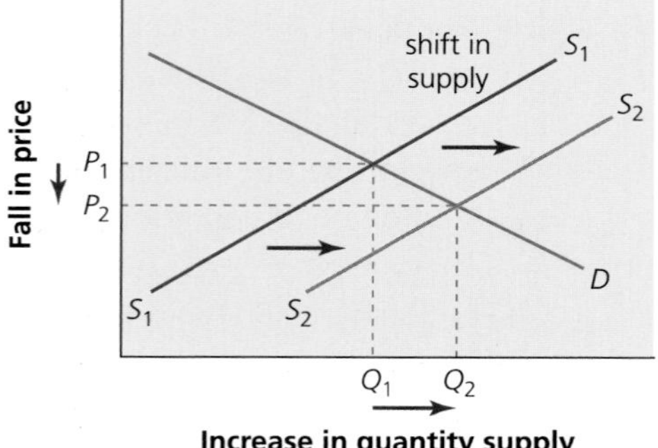

Figure 17.1 Supply and demand graph

In the longer term, there has been mixed results. Some areas of the market have better services, with more choice and greater efficiency; others face inadequate provision or a complete lack of services.

Labour markets

In recent years governments have shifted their intervention in labour markets from the demand to the supply side. They have used measures to try to encourage an increase in the number of people entering the labour market, but also to try to improve the skills and quality of that labour. These supply-side measures may take a long time to have an impact on the economy, but they are less likely to have the adverse economic effects that may come with demand management (see **Chapter 19**). At the same time, the government has removed some of the legislation and red-tape that affected the employment of workers. For example, although many UK employers now honour the working hours agreement, it is still possible to ask employees to work longer hours, provided that agreement is sought from the worker.

Labour market supply-side policies

Training and education are vitally important in any labour market, but this is more likely to be the case in a developed economy where there is likely to be less demand for unskilled workers. The government has tried to improve the skill level of the UK population through measures like the National Curriculum, access to university and training schemes for the long-term unemployed.

Employment regulations have been reduced to make it easier for employers to take on extra workers. Rules governing part-time work and the employment of women have changed, as have the rules about short-term contracts. At times these changes may create problems for the individual worker by giving them fewer rights than full-time workers, but they have benefited the UK economy in attracting overseas businesses, whose managers want to relocate to a country where employment practices are less restrictive for employers.

The overhaul of Trade Union legislation since 1980 has also helped to make the UK labour market much less restrictive. This legislation has covered issues like postal ballots and secondary picketing (see **Chapter 48**). The fall in working days lost through industrial action as a result of this legislation, together with the fact that UK employment laws are less restrictive than elsewhere in the EU, has also helped to attract inward investment to the UK.

Minimum wage

The use of a policy to guarantee a minimum wage for low paid workers has a number of advantages and disadvantages.

For the individual worker it means that they receive a reasonable rate of pay for their work and that the possibility of exploitation is removed; this should mean that all employees are guaranteed at least a basic standard of living.

For the employer, the effect of the minimum wage is to increase the costs of employing labour. This may mean that the employer reduces the number of workers employed to reduce the wage bill, which is not in the interests of the employees. Since the introduction of the minimum wage in the UK, there is little evidence that this is the case. However, there are still employers who are working outside the law, paying their employees below minimum wages; this is most likely to happen with home workers in industries such as textiles, where wages are paid in cash to workers who are isolated, unaware of the law and perhaps too reliant on the job to risk losing it.

There has also been a move to encourage employers to pay what is referred to as a 'living wage' to their employees. The amount of the living wage is more than the minimum wage and represents the basic cost of living in the UK. It is set independently and updated annually.

Tips and techniques

The legislation on employment and the rates of minimum wage are frequently changed. You can check for up-to-date information on www.direct.gov.uk/employment

Examples of effects of political factors on functions of business

1 Marketing: government legislation can have an effect on the nature of a product or the way it can be promoted and government policy could affect price. For example, new safety recommendations for children's products will have an impact on the toy industry.
2 Financial: government economic policy has a profound effect on the success or otherwise of a business. During a recession businesses may struggle to achieve growth and they may curtail investment if the political views of the party in power believe that government spending must be reduced.
3 People: the government's policy on employment and the extent to which it intervenes in the jobs and skills market will all impact on the behaviour of businesses.
4 Operations: political parties may announce plans before an election for price freezes on domestic energy suppliers.

Social issues

Any successful business will need to be aware of changes in the society in which it operates, so that the organisation of the business and the goods or services it produces will meet the demands of all stakeholders.

Demographic changes

The distribution and size of the UK population have undergone many changes since the Industrial Revolution in the nineteenth century. Similar changes will have occurred in major trading partners in Europe and North America. These changes have an impact on the nature of demand faced by business, as well as the size and characteristics of the workforce.

Source: Office for National Statistics, National Records of Scotland, Norther Ireland Statistics and Research Agency

The following demographic factors have an impact on the markets in which businesses operate.

Changes in the age of the population

From the late twentieth century onwards, there has been a growth in the number of old people in the UK and a fall in the number of young people. In addition, many of these elderly people now have access to large incomes through pensions and savings, together with better health and a longer life expectancy than was previously the case. All this has resulted in increases in demand for products such as specialist holidays and mobility aids.

Many businesses have had to revise their recruitment policies. A lack of young people entering the job market has encouraged some businesses to employ older workers with the necessary skills. Hardware store B&Q now has a policy of actively recruiting retired workers, whom they have found to be more reliable and knowledgeable in dealing with customer enquiries.

Tips and techniques

The term used to describe those in the population who are above retirement age is 'the Grey Economy'. This sector of the population is increasingly important for business because many of these elderly people have high disposable incomes as a result of private pensions, savings and the high value of their property.

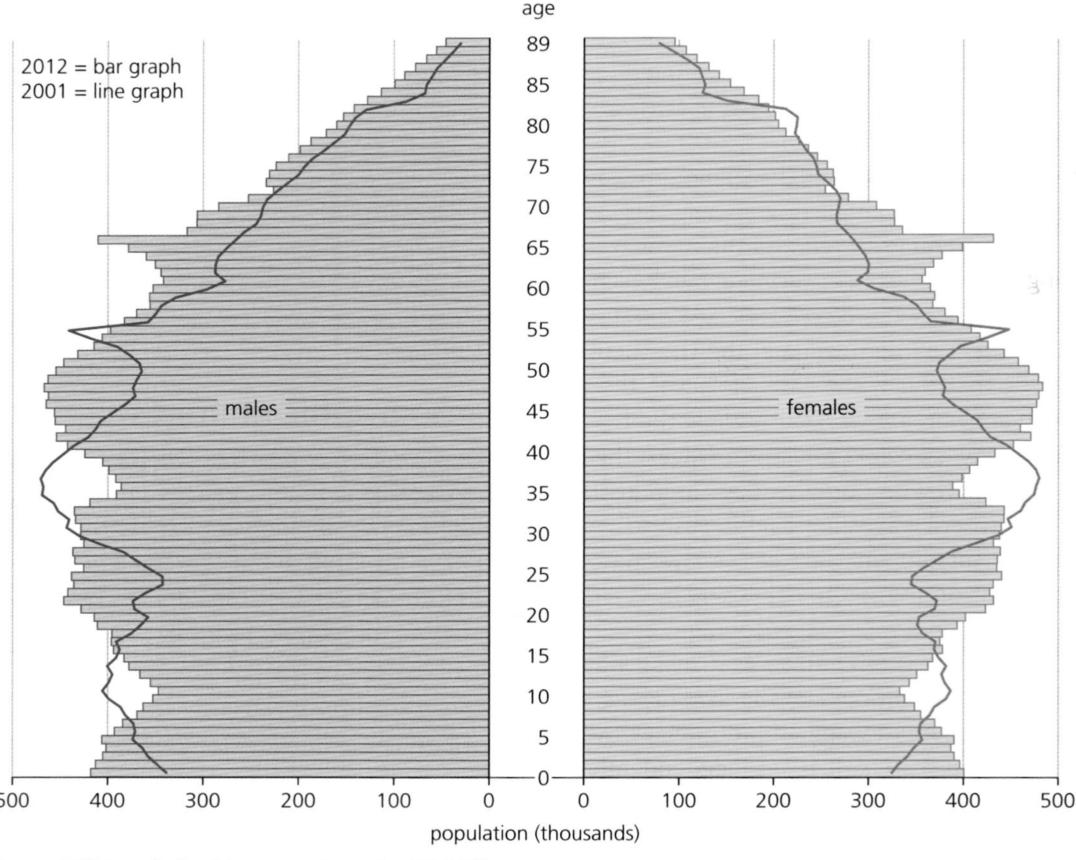

Figure 17.2 Population histogram from the UK 2011 census

Ethnic diversity

The UK has a more diverse ethnic mix now than previously. Part of this is a result of the free movement of labour in the EU and the increase in its size as countries from Eastern Europe have joined the EU in recent years. In many cases these different nationalities create demand for different ranges of goods and also bring aspects of their culture to existing UK residents. For example, most small towns and all cities have Indian and Chinese restaurants, and all the major supermarkets now carry ranges of the foods from these countries. Indian and Chinese food is now part of the British way of life.

Immigrants bring with them demand for different products and services, together with new ideas and customs. The influx of Polish workers has led to a demand for different foodstuffs, such as carp, in local supermarkets. The bus network in the West Midlands relies heavily on drivers of Polish origin. As a result of this the bus companies have had to introduce classes in English and local information to ensure that their Polish drivers can cope with requests for help from passengers.

Changing patterns of employment

Women

The role of women in society has changed considerably in recent generations. Before the Second World War, most married women would not have been in the workforce. Today, the opposite is the case; the vast majority of women of working age, even those with young children, are in paid employment, at least part of the time. This has increased demand for more flexible working patterns so that both women and men can fit employment around childcare. Businesses now have to offer maternity and paternity leave to their employees by law, but other businesses offer extended leave and flexible alternatives like job-sharing and home-working to ensure that they keep or attract the best possible female workers.

Education

A larger proportion of young people now stay on to pursue some sort of further education after the official school leaving age of sixteen. From 2015, young people will be required to remain in some form of education until they are 18, although this may be a practical or vocational course. This means that most young people now enter the workforce at a later age than previously and often with more qualifications. However, many of these young people will be involved in part-time working while pursuing their studies. The catering and retail sectors employ many of these students in temporary and part-time jobs, particularly in the evening and at weekends.

Flexibility

Businesses in the retail sector now need more flexibility in employment because of extended opening hours. Seven-day trading and twenty-four-hour opening require full- and part-time workers to cover the longer time period if they are to operate successfully. These jobs are often attractive alternatives for students or people with children.

Factors affecting the supermarket sector

Supermarkets face a perfect storm of challenges which goes well beyond the success of a couple of cheap German retail chains. They include:

- **Discounters** Aldi and Lidl, together with Poundland and B&M, are stealing trade as customers shop around to save money. Major supermarkets are being forced to cut prices.
- **Convenience** Shoppers are eschewing big edge-of-town stores: people are preferring to shop little and often.
- **Eating out** Breakfast on the go, take-aways, lunch in the canteen and more shoppers are buying ready meals.
- **Online** All the major supermarkets are having to invest in costly home deliveries or click & collect.
- **Cutting waste** Environmental concerns have merged with financial worries to get Britons shopping more carefully to avoid wasting food at home.
- **Eating less** The volume of food sold is declining.
- **Slowing inflation** Good harvests have meant lower prices on fresh food this year. Lower fuel prices have also helped reduce the cost of goods.

Source: Various news sources, including *the Guardian*.

Technology

The growth of electronic communication has made it possible for workers in some sectors to work either exclusively or partly from home. Meetings can be held using video-conferencing, and work can be circulated quickly around the globe. This type of working is more likely in jobs that rely on communication technology, like journalism, but it is an increasing feature of the business world. For the individual it removes the need for costly and time-consuming travel, and for the business it reduces the costs associated with providing office space.

Agency work

The use of agency workers has also increased in recent years. The businesses using these workers pay the agency for their use, and the employees are paid by the agency where they are registered. This gives the business the flexibility to vary their employment level from week to week to meet demand levels. It therefore also releases the business from responsibility for payroll, PAYE and National Insurance payments. Alternatively, businesses can outsource parts of their work to other organisations. This might be done because the other business has greater economies of scale, or because the business needs to free up labour to meet orders and commitments. For example, a clothing firm might outsource the design of its fabrics to businesses with expertise in this area.

Tips and techniques

Outsourcing means passing on all or part of a specific job to another firm. Outsourcing is used for the following reasons: greater efficiency in the outsource business, lack of capacity in the main business, ability to complete an order quickly.

Implications of social change on demand

All of these social changes have implications for the demand faced by businesses. An increase in demand, as a result of a change such as immigration, will shift the demand curve to the right; while a fall in demand, as a result of fewer babies being born, will shift the demand curve to the left (see Figure 17.3).

Increase immigration

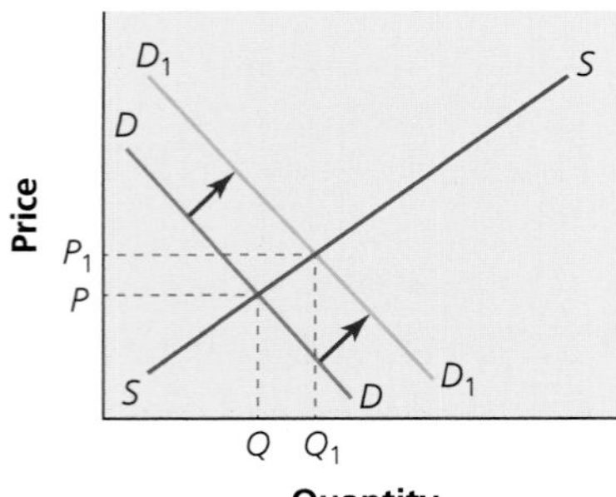

Lower birthrate

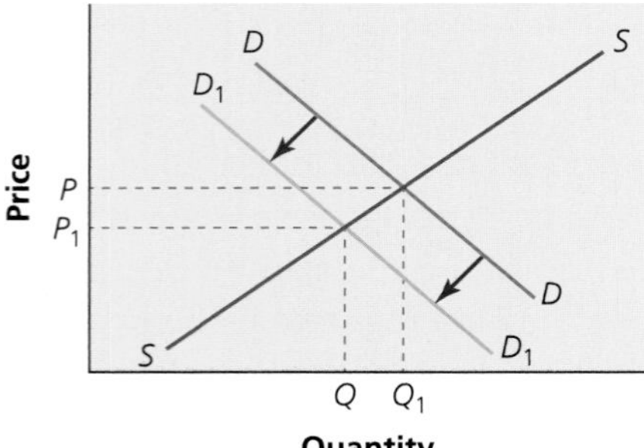

Figure 17.3 Demand and supply graph

Tips and techniques

It is important to remember that the issues discussed in this chapter are strategic for the business. It is useful therefore to try to include theory that you learned earlier in your course. The use of a demand and supply diagram in this section would show that you know how to apply your business studies knowledge in a strategic situation.

Examples of the effects of social issues on areas of business

1. Marketing: the age or income distribution in society will have an effect on the type of marketing a business uses and the products it sells.
2. Financial: changes in social habits, such as eating out more will have an effect on the business's success.
3. People: changes in employment patterns, like the increase in part-time working will have an effect on shopping habits and spending.
4. Operations: changing attitudes to work, such as increased holiday expectations or shorter working hours all have implications for business.

Ethical issues

Ethics is concerned with judgements about what is the right or wrong thing to do in a particular situation. Unlike legal issues, there is no requirement for a business or its employees to operate ethically and there will be no recourse to law if a choice is taken not to act ethically. The ethical issues that affect a business will include:

- treating workers well and paying a living wage
- not harming the environment through actions of the business
- behaving responsibly towards all stakeholders by being aware of the impact of production on others, such as the local community
- working with the community through sponsorship or charity work
- not discriminating in any way. Sometimes this may be a legal requirement, but an ethical business will go beyond what is required by law.

Benefits of ethical behaviour

Stakeholder conflict may make businesses worry about the costs of ethical behaviour. The requirement to make profits for shareholders and to pay wages to employees may take precedence over using ethical practices; yet in many cases, businesses employing ethical practices have shown there are benefits for the firm.

Ethical behaviour can:

- attract new customers to the business
- attract new and better quality employees
- encourage employees to stay with a business
- encourage investment
- create positive publicity
- result in increased sales and profits.

On the other hand, an absence of ethical behaviour or a lack of Corporate Social Responsibility (CSR) can harm a business's reputation, which may lead to falling profits and even possible failure. Businesses producing clothing in garment sweat shops in the Far East have suffered when their actions have been made public.

Corporate social responsibility

An important and relatively new area of awareness for the business world is that of corporate responsibility (CSR). Most businesses include profitability as one of their main objectives in order to satisfy stakeholders and shareholders. Corporate social responsibility goes further than this and includes the wider responsibility of the business to other stakeholders and society in general.

This is an extract from Barclays' statement on what corporate responsibility, which they call 'citizenship', means to them:

Finance and banking can play a critical role as a key enabler of social and economic progress when undertaken in the right way. This means considering how our day-to-day decisions impact on broader society and how we can create products, services and solutions that as well as delivering commercial value can also have a benefit in society.

Source: http://www.barclays.com/citizenship/our-approach.html

This approach is now typical of many industries in the UK. It stems from a recognition of the fact that business is no longer judged solely on its ability to deliver the good or service, but that the manner of the delivery is increasingly important. Businesses need to be aware of the wider concerns of the general public and of their impact on society and the environment.

Bad publicity in any area can bring a business to its knees. In recent years, McDonald's has responded to bad publicity about the problems of obesity in western economies by introducing ranges of healthier foods. It has undertaken to reduce the salt content and added sugar in their meals and signed a voluntary Food Pledge to advertise healthy options, like fruit, to children.

Amazon and Starbucks were in the media in 2013–14 because of their failure to pay UK taxes, through the use of 'creative accounting practices'. Although these businesses are not breaking the law, most people would regard their activities as unethical. Despite Starbuck's huge presence in the UK, it has managed to post a loss for its UK operations of £30 million. The company executives appeared before a committee of MPs to explain why the company had paid no corporation tax for the three years to 2013, despite having had total sales of £1.2 billion. The situation for Amazon is similar. (See case study below.)

Businesses have to consider their corporate responsibility in a number of different areas:

Environment and ethical issues

As the publicity about global warming, pollution and other environmental issues increases, businesses have had to respond to the demands of society and government to play their part in these areas. Most supermarkets now operate schemes to encourage customers to use fewer plastic bags, and producers are looking for ways either to reduce packaging or to make it biodegradable. Businesses can use their actions in these areas in promotion and publicity. Marks and Spencer now charge 5p for each food bag the customer uses; the money is donated to an ethical organisation.

Charity and fundraising

Most large businesses are now involved in charitable and community work to raise their profile. EDF Energy gives all of its employees one day off each year to work on projects in local schools; in addition, employees are encouraged to take part in the Young Enterprise Scheme with student businesses. Others businesses such as Tesco gain huge amounts of publicity and goodwill from schemes that pay for sports and computer equipment for schools and sports clubs.

Diversity

Many businesses feel that their operations should better represent and include the wide range of diversity of the population in the UK. Many are critical of the diversity of those in the theatre and television and Lenny Henry has fronted a campaign to improve this situation. The BBC has also been taken to task by MPs for the lack of women in all areas of it operations, both in front of camera and in its administration.

Financial responsibility

In recent years, UK banks and building societies have been criticised for their failure to lend money responsibly to customers. As a result of this, the financial sector has had to become increasingly aware of the need to exercise control of access to credit cards and loans, particularly to people who are more financially vulnerable.

Summary

It is therefore important for a business to use its corporate responsibility policy to show employees and the wider community that it cares about more than profit. The costs of doing this may be relatively small in monetary terms, in relation to the returns in the form of profit. It also helps to motivate workers and improve the image of the business projected to society in general.

Examples of effects of ethical issues on areas of business

1 Marketing: ethical behaviour can be used as a marketing tool for a business. For example, Marks and Spencer source all their coffee from fair trade schemes.

2 Financial: ethical financial behaviour means doing the right thing for society, not just obeying the letter of the law. For example, businesses that use tax avoidance schemes are not acting illegally, but their behaviour would be seen by many as unethical.

3 People: workers will often be proud to be associated with an ethical business which could increase sales and lead to positive publicity.

4 Operations: this might mean ensuring that all production is undertaken with a concern for its impact on the environment and society.

Further sources

www.marksandspencer.com (corporate responsibility)
www.natwest.com (corporate responsibility)
www.statistics.gov.uk
www.cityandguilds.com

Your turn

Questions in red are for A Level candidates only.

Multiple-choice questions

1 The Competition and Markets Authorities can investigate monopolies. In EU and the UK a monopoly is:
- A a single firm in an industry
- B a very large firm
- C a firm with 25 per cent market share or more
- D a firm with 20 per cent market share. *(1)*

2 The most recent change in food shopping in the UK has been for consumers to shop little and often. This has been caused by all of the following except:
- A difficulty in finding staff
- B the recession
- C oil and petrol prices rising
- D changing life styles. *(1)*

Revision questions

1 State three significant changes in the age distribution of the UK in the last 50 years. *(3)*

2 Explain two benefits for the UK of not being a member of the Eurozone. *(4)*

3 State two examples of a firm taking account of its corporate social responsibility. *(2)*

Total *(9)*

Case study

Amazon UK

Amazon UK paid £2.4 million in corporation tax in 2012, although its sales for the year were £4.3 billion. The UK corporation tax rate in the UK is over 20 per cent. During the same period, Amazon received government grants of almost £2.5 million. In 2013–14 the business had sales of £11 billion, yet only paid £4 million in UK corporation tax; on its UK earnings, Amazon paid tax at 0.1 per cent. The *Guardian* has estimated that Amazon avoided taxes of £100 million in the UK in the last three years

There is no suggestion that Amazon is breaking the law in paying so little tax; the company is registered in Luxembourg and pays tax there, but the business employs over 5,000 in the UK and approximately 400 in Luxembourg. The company, along with others that include Starbucks and Google, has been questioned by a committee of MPs and investigated by the EU, but it would seem that it is the tax laws that need changing if the situation is to be resolved.

Nevertheless, many would question Amazon's tactics on tax and point out that the business has no sense of its Corporate Social Responsibility. Amazon's tax policy creates problems in a variety of ways.

- It robs the government of tax revenue.
- It increases the burden of taxation on others – both private individuals and businesses.
- It suggests to the ordinary citizens that the tax system is unfair and that the strong and financially astute can beat the system.
- It disadvantages other retailers who pay their taxes, by making their prices less competitive.
- Authors and publishers are aggrieved because Amazon drives hard bargains and pays low royalties on sales of books, while raking in profits and paying little in tax.

As consequence of Amazon's tax stance, many have started to boycott its website and there have been demonstrations by authors from around the world at its headquarters. It would seem, however, that what is needed is the will by governments to confront Amazon and change the laws on taxation so that it is no longer possible for them to avoid paying tax on sales.

1 Explain two reasons why paying tax may be regarded as a social obligation for a business like Amazon. *(4)*
2 Analyse one way in which Amazon's behaviour could affect its future success. *(4)*
3 Discuss the possible effects of Amazon's tax behaviour on its stakeholders. *(12)*
Total *(20)*

Chapter 18

Economic factors: GDP and the business cycle

AS / Year 1 | Year 2

A Level students must know all of the content in this chapter.

AS students only need to know:

- The key economic indicators which influence a business (pages 131–133)
- What is meant by GDP (page 131)

The nature of economic activity

The economy is a major influence on all types of business; indeed, it could be argued that it is the most important influence. This chapter considers the concepts involved with macroeconomics, the study of the whole economy, rather than those in an individual market (see **Chapter 13**).

Key term

Macroeconomics: the study and analysis of the behaviour of the whole economy.

The main groups involved in the operation of the economy are highly interconnected and a business can find its situation considerably changed by economic events, such as a fall in consumer spending or a change in the interest rate. These economic events may force the business to change how it operates, in ways that might not be positive for some of the business's stakeholders.

For example, a UK firm has been exporting sports equipment to a large retailer in Germany. The German retailer subsequently finds that it can buy equipment of the same sort of design and quality from a new supplier in Poland at a much more competitive price. The German retailer therefore does not renew its contract with the UK business. The emergence of this new low-cost supplier will make the UK business's life more difficult, and it may have to make some of its employees redundant. Thus, an employee who thought he had a reasonably secure job in a business selling to a growing area of the leisure market suddenly finds himself made redundant by economic events entirely outside his control. The same sort of reasoning will apply to the UK business's suppliers.

What is 'the economy'?

The economy is not a single entity. It refers to the collective behaviour of a number of different groups. These are:

- the different businesses in the UK; ranging from sole traders to multinational companies
- people acting as both employees of businesses and consumers of their products
- the government, which sets the economic framework within which businesses have to operate, and is also a major provider of many goods and services which it finances through taxation and borrowing.

In addition to these, any study of the economy must also take into account the UK's trading relationship with other countries, especially the European Union (EU).

Key term

The economy: the collective behaviour of a number of different groups such as businesses, people as employees and consumers, and the government.

Tips and techniques

Although a clear understanding of macroeconomic issues is important, examiners are not looking for highly detailed explanations of how the economy works. What is much more important is for you to be able to analyse how the economic environment is likely to affect the behaviour of the business in the case study.

Nature of economics

The economy is dynamic; it changes over a period of time. This means that the effects of a particular policy at any one time may be different from the effects that occurred previously from the same policy. Consider a cut in the rate of income tax. Lowering the rate of tax to increase consumer spending on the grounds that it was successful in a similar situation some years ago, may not be a sensible policy now. Perhaps the UK businesses that used to provide many of the products that people bought in the past have gone into liquidation. This means that much of the increase in consumer demand may be on foreign goods. Comparing the economy today with the economy ten years ago is not comparing like with like. In addition, although economists would agree that a cut in the rate of income tax will increase consumer spending, the extent of the increase in spending could be the subject of considerable disagreement. Will it be a lot or a little? Also, when will it happen?

What is 'economic activity'?

'Economic activity' refers to the production of goods and services. Production can be primary, secondary or tertiary. 'The level of economic activity' refers to what is happening to output in all of these sectors (see **Chapter 2**). A term often used when discussing economic activity is gross domestic product. This is usually shortened to GDP. It means the total output of all goods and services produced, usually in a year. 'Gross' in this case means total and 'domestic' means within a particular country.

It is important to realise that part of any rise in GDP will be due to a rise in prices (inflation, see page 139) rather than a rise in the actual amount of products produced. The figure for GDP is therefore adjusted by deducting the rate of inflation to give 'GDP in real terms', that is, the true figure for the rise in output.

Key term

Economic activity: the level of output in all sectors of the economy – primary, secondary and tertiary.

Gross domestic product: the total value of all of the economy's output (measured quarterly or yearly).

Usually, a rise in GDP (i.e. a higher level of economic activity) is beneficial for everyone. There is likely to be a high level of employment, since if the demand for products is rising businesses will need to employ more people in order to produce them. Jobs are also more likely to be secure when GDP is rising and this, coupled with increasing incomes, means that people's spending power will increase. Businesses too will benefit: if spending is rising, there will be more demand for products and (assuming that their costs are not rising too much) profits will also rise. This is usually beneficial for a business's stakeholders (see **Chapter 5**). It also means that through retained profit, more capital is available for further expansion.

The government should also benefit from rising GDP, since high levels of spending and output caused by the rise in economic activity mean more tax revenue from people and businesses. This can then be used for spending in socially desirable areas such as the health service and education. Alternatively, the government could use this extra tax revenue for tax cuts. Both these measures will be popular and may help to get the government re-elected. Conversely, a fall in GDP is not normally welcomed by wage-earners, consumers, businesses or the government.

Factors that affect economic activity

To analyse how the whole economy operates is to divide it into two groups: households and businesses. In the households group, people go to work and earn income. There is therefore a flow of income from businesses to households as payment for the work done.

Most of this income will promptly be spent and therefore there is a flow of income in the opposite direction from households to businesses. Economists call this consumption. Of course, economists are not saying that people spend their income at the same business at which they work, although this could be true in some cases (e.g. if someone worked in a supermarket). They are saying that businesses in the economy pay their employees and then receive income back when people, acting as consumers rather than employees, spend it. Figure 18.1 shows this diagrammatically.

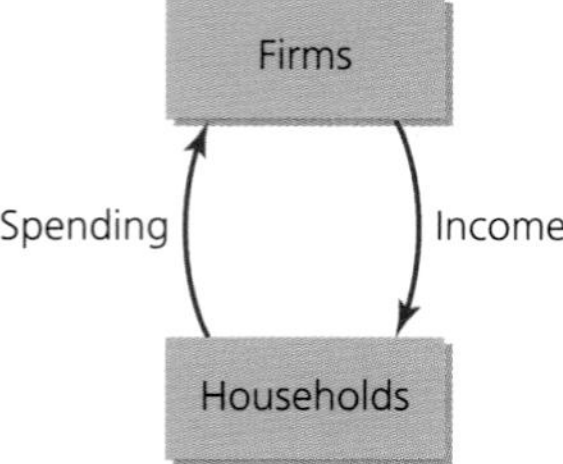

Figure 18.1 The circular flow of income

The circular flow of income begins with the flow of income that households have earned being spent on goods and services. This spending then enables firms to acquire the money they need to finance the next round of production. Assume a starting position where the level of economic activity is quite high and GDP has been rising. If consumption spending by households is sufficient to buy the whole output produced by businesses, this will please businesses because they will have made a profit and not have unsold stocks of goods. Businesses will continue to employ the same number of people and may even think of expanding output. However, this situation may not occur automatically because some of the income earned by households is not going to be spent. This means that businesses run the risk of not having all their output purchased by consumers. If this happens, they will have unsold goods that will not earn them any profit.

There are three reasons why all the income earned by households in the UK will not go directly to UK firms:

1 Taxes. The government takes a proportion of income through taxes.
2 Savings. Whatever remains after tax from an employee's wages is known as disposable income and people may decide to save some of this. Any income saved is obviously not spent.
3 Imports. Products that are made abroad and purchased by UK households are known as imports. When income is spent on products that are imported, there is a flow of income to foreign, rather than UK, firms.

These three reasons mean that there are leakages from the circular flow of income, which is why UK businesses do not receive back all the income that they have paid out to their employees. The diagram of the circular flow of income in the economy, including leakages, looks like the one shown in Figure 18.2.

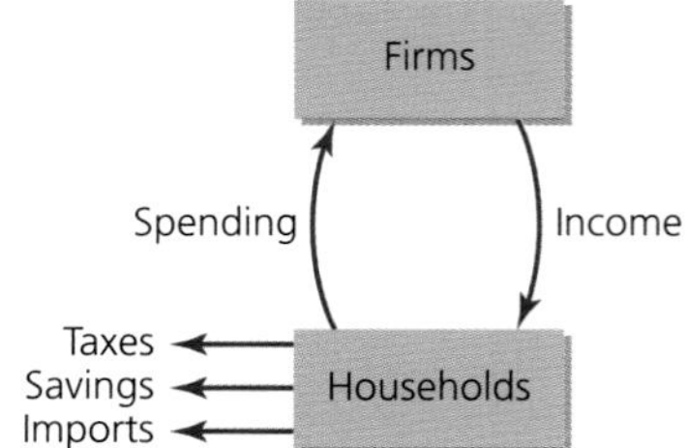

Figure 18.2 The circular flow of income, including leakages

Key term

Circular flow of income: the (continuous) flow of income from businesses to households as payment for work, and from households to businesses as payment for products.
Imports: purchase of goods from abroad.
Leakages: income that 'leaks away' from the economy and so does not get passed back to UK firms from households; this comprises taxes, savings and imports.

There are, however, a number of injections of income into the economy, which help to offset the leakages. These injections do not arise from UK consumers; they come from elsewhere. They are:

- Government spending. The government is a big spender in the UK on services such as schools, hospitals and defence. Many billions of pounds that businesses receive from the sale of their goods and services come not from household consumers, but from central and local government.
- Exports. The sales of products made by UK businesses to other countries are known as exports. The products go abroad, but income flows into UK businesses in payment.
- Investment. Investment is capital spending by businesses, i.e. businesses buying products such as new buildings, machinery and improved technology, in order to make themselves more competitive and productive in the future.

Tips and techniques

When economists talk about investment, they are not talking about a business (or a person) depositing money in a bank. That action would represent saving, which has the opposite effect on the economy to investing. Saving reduces total spending, while investment increases it.

Key term

Injections: income coming into the UK economy that does not come from UK households; this comprises investment, government spending and exports.

Exports: the sale of goods to other countries by UK businesses.

Investment: the purchase of capital equipment and/or buildings by businesses.

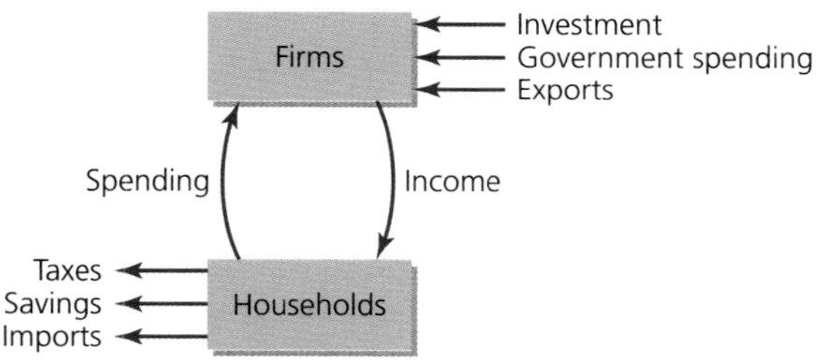

Figure 18.3 The circular flow of income, including leakages and injections

In summary, the circular flow of income is a continuous process. People are earning and being taxed, saving and spending (sometimes on imports) all the time. Businesses are continuously employing and therefore paying people income. They are also exporting products abroad and investing in capital equipment. The government takes in tax revenue and spends it.

What happens to GDP when the variables change?

Even though the circular flow of income never stops flowing, this does not mean that the level of economic activity stays the same. If there is a change in one of the variables, the level of economic activity is likely to change. In reality, several variables are likely to be changing at the same time, and what actually happens to the economy depends on whether a change in one variable is offset by another.

For example, a newspaper may report that 'imports rose by £10 billion last month'. On the face of it, this would mean a fall in GDP since imports are a leakage from the circular flow and £10 billion of income has been spent abroad. However, it may be that over the same period of time, businesses have invested £10 billion. In this case (since investment is an injection), the net effect on income and, therefore, the level of GDP will be nil.

This shows that when considering any news about the state of the economy, those running businesses need to consider what is happening to all of the relevant variables. When reading headline statements in the press, they must ask themselves 'Yes, but what else has happened?' before passing a judgement on the likely effects of a change.

What happens to economic activity if leakages do not equal injections?

The total amount of leakages from the economy in any given period of time is highly unlikely to be the exactly the same as the total amount of injections. Generally speaking:

- If total leakages are greater than total injections, the level of GDP will fall. This means that some businesses will experience a drop in the demand for their products, may make employees redundant, will invest less (as they are not very optimistic about the future) or may even close down.
- If total injections are greater than total leakages, the level of GDP will rise. This means that demand will rise and businesses will take on more employees and invest more. However, rising injections of income may mean that spending is increasing too fast, and that businesses cannot meet the rising demand for their products. The result will be that prices will start to rise rapidly and this can be very damaging for the economy.

In reality, small differences between leakages and injections do not matter much. Economic policy is not concerned with trying to balance them to the last pound, or even the last billion pounds. Economic policy is about creating a stable macroeconomic environment within which businesses can succeed. The government and the Bank of England are trying to prevent the potentially damaging effects of either a huge rise, or a huge fall in GDP.

Business cycle

The business cycle (also known as the economic cycle) refers to the changes that occur in the level of GDP over a period of time. An understanding of the concept is important because it makes possible an analysis of the macroeconomic variables that affect a particular business.

Key term

Business cycle: rises and falls in economic activity; these follow a pattern that can be identified as boom, recession, slump and recovery.

Economic activity in industrialised countries tends to proceed in cycles. GDP is rising and sometimes it is falling. A period of economic prosperity is followed by a period of slower or falling economic activity. Then, after a time, this gives way to a rise in GDP and the cycle starts again.

The business cycle is usually represented by the graph shown in Figure 18.4. The long-term trend (i.e. the general direction) in GDP is upwards, but the actual level of economic activity does not follow the smooth path of the trend; there is a cycle of rises and falls in GDP around it.

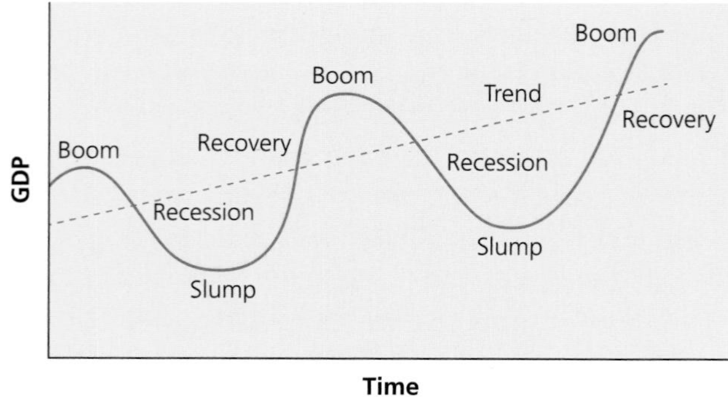

Figure 18.4 The business cycle is divided into four stages

What happens at each stage of the cycle?

Boom

In this stage of the cycle, there is a high level of employment and consumption, and therefore a high demand for products. Businesses are profitable and feeling confident about future sales. This may encourage them to invest in a new plant and machinery, which in turn leads to further rises in GDP. The boom eventually reaches a peak and GDP will not rise any further in that particular cycle.

Recession

A recession is defined as two successive quarterly falls in GDP: in other words, output falls for two consecutive three-month periods. In a recession, sales are falling and so business confidence about future consumer demand in some sectors is low. Initially, this may only happen in markets for luxury products, such as new cars and foreign holidays. This causes a fall in investment in those industries, since no business wants to invest in equipment and buildings that are going to be underused. The affected businesses make employees redundant, and this increased unemployment reduces consumer spending. This lowers demand and profits in other sectors of the economy, which is likely to depress investment even further. The government and the Bank of England will usually try to act before a recession becomes too serious, otherwise business confidence (in future sales) will collapse, which could lead to a slump.

In a recession, consumer spending is reduced, sales fall and some businesses will close down

Slump

The symptoms of a slump (also known as a trough or a depression) are similar to those of a recession, except that they are more serious and widespread. In a depression, almost all the economy is affected, not just a few sectors. This leads to high levels of unemployment in many different industries, low business confidence, low levels of consumer spending, low levels of investment and low profits for businesses.

Recovery

In the recovery phase of the cycle, economic activity rises. Consumers start spending again and demand increases. Business confidence starts to increase as profits rise. Businesses take on more employees, and higher employment in turn increases consumer spending. This is how the upturn in economic activity gets under way. This eventually leads on to the next boom.

The time taken to complete a cycle can vary, as can the length of each particular phase. Obviously, it would be better for businesses if recessions were as brief, and booms as long, as possible.

Effects of changes in economic activity on businesses

Not all businesses in the economy are affected in the same way by changes in economic activity caused by the business cycle. While it may be correct to assume that 'nearly all businesses are affected by a recession or a boom' the effects on businesses will differ. The effects of the cycle need to be considered on a case-by-case basis.

Consider the following examples.

Business selling computer tablets

How might this business be affected by a recession? To what extent are tablets essential for everyday life? If they are considered necessary, there may be little effect at all on demand. Presumably though, some people who are worried about losing their job will now cancel their planned purchase of a tablet. Others will keep using their old one rather than upgrade. Demand is therefore likely to fall. However, even if the market for tablets to be used at home suffers a fall in demand, they are often provided for people at work. To what extent will businesses cancel purchases or delay upgrading? If businesses continue to buy them in large quantities, the effect of the recession on the firm selling them will not be so severe.

Business selling mobile phones

Mobile phones have changed from being a luxury item to a necessity for most people. If there is a recession in the UK, to what extent will sales be affected? This could be an even more difficult question to answer than the one concerning ipads. This is because the groups who buy mobile phones are different. The business may find that demand from young people, who use mobile phones partly as a fashion statement and a means of shaping their identity, will be largely unaffected. This is because these consumers see mobile phones as essential for their lifestyle. They will almost certainly continue to buy the latest models. A business that sells mobile phones would need to consider demographics very carefully. If the proportion of younger people in the population is relatively small, the fact that they continue to buy mobile phones may not offset the decline in purchases (and upgrades) among other age groups.

Supermarket chain

If the economy moves into recession, will there be any change in demand for a supermarket's products? On the face of it, the answer is no, since people must eat in order to live. They also require other household goods, such as washing powder. However, if incomes are falling, there is likely to be an increased demand for 'value' products, so the supermarket will need to start stocking more of these if it is to meet consumer requirements. New suppliers may have to be found for some of these products. At the same time, the business may alter its advertising and promotional policies to reflect the change. Both these factors will involve additional expense.

Tips and techniques

Do not confuse 'the business cycle' with 'seasonal sales'. Seasonal falls in sales lasting a few months are a regular part of many business's annual trading pattern. In contrast, the business cycle will impact on a very wide range of businesses across the whole economy. Also, phases in the business cycle can last much longer than a few months.

How could a firm use the business cycle to its advantage?

Rising levels of GDP bring more sales for most firms but a business has to be ready to take advantage of any rise in income and spending. If the economy is in the recovery phase, it is important that the business ensures that it has sufficient capacity to meet future demand. This may mean that the firm needs to install new technology or/and extend the size of a factory or move to a larger location. If it can do this at the right time, it will be ready to take advantage of the upswing of the growth in GDP and so should be able to increase sales and profits.

In a recession, consumers' spending patterns change. Even though the sales of many products will fall, the sales of certain types of products will rise. These are often products at the 'discount' or 'budget' end of the market. If it is possible for a business to switch to making/selling such products then a recession may not necessarily be problematic and, in fact, could be very beneficial.

A similar logic applies to many other products such as DIY goods; people may decide to 'do up' their house themselves, rather than get a decorator in, or move. Thus DIY stores benefit. People may also take holidays in the UK rather than abroad and so whole tourist areas of the UK may get an unexpected boost in sales. People may keep their cars for longer instead of buying new ones, which generates more revenue for garages that carry out repairs.

The prices of many assets such as land and buildings often fall in a recession or slump. This means that a business – which has access to the necessary capital – may buy such assets in anticipation of a recovery in the near future and, in doing so, lower the cost of its future expansion. Employees (at all types of skill level) may be easier to find and cheaper to employ as well.

The same sort of analysis applies to financial institutions buying shares in other companies when (because of lower sales and profits due to the recession) the share price is low. They can then sell them when the economy and the share price recover.

Recessions can force those running a business to think about its operation in new and different ways. 'Business as usual' may no longer be an option. A recession can bring about much-needed change in an organisation, forcing it to become more efficient. It is therefore 'leaner and fitter' and its managers more resilient and creative when the recovery arrives.

Essentially, if a firm knows the current state of the economy and the likely path it will take in the future, then it can be proactive and will be in a much stronger position to use the business cycle to its advantage than one that is not paying much attention to macroeconomic data.

The economic indicators that influence a business are the current level of (and trend in):

- GDP
- employment
- consumer spending
- investment
- exports (and imports).

Businesses are, to a large extent, at the mercy of the state of these factors, but that does not mean that they can and should do nothing when one, or more of them, changes. The likely effect on a business of a change in the state of the economy from a boom to a recession depends on how it chooses to respond.

How may a business evaluate where the economy is on the economic cycle?

A business needs to know where the economy is in the cycle in order to plan ahead and make decisions about output, employment and marketing. Several sources of data should be used; a business should certainly not rely on just one. Possible sources of data include:

- output/sales trends from the business's own plant(s)/shop(s)
- news coming from managers' or directors' contacts with other (local/regional/national) firms about the state of their business
- national/local output and sales levels of other businesses in the same sector
- national/local employment levels
- national/local spending levels
- national/local sales levels
- professional journals/reviews of the economy, such as the Bank of England's Inflation Report
- the number of business start-ups and business failures nationally/locally.

Why does the business cycle exist?

There are many different views as to why the economic cycle exists. Figure 18.5 shows the cycle again, but this time includes an explanation for the various changes in GDP at each stage of the cycle.

There are other explanations for the business cycle. Some theories look at technological change and how it can increase GDP but also make employees redundant. Other theories look at the effects of businesses becoming either more pessimistic or optimistic about the future. Another possible cause is

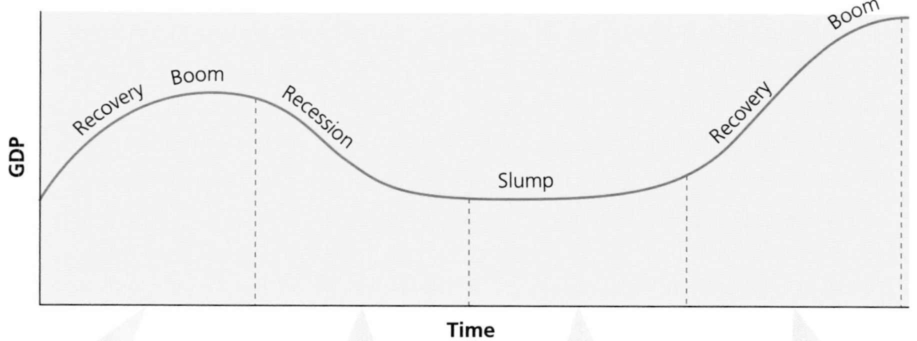

The high level of spending means that total demand in the economy exceeds supply. This starts to cause demand-pull inflation. The boom in spending may suck in a large volume of imports. This will worsen the UK's trading position. To counter these effects, the Bank of England puts up interest rates which slows down spending.

As spending falls, some sectors of the economy start to experience a fall in the demand for their products. These businesses then begin to lay off employees. Spending falls further.

Businesses are highly interdependent, so these falls in spending multiply across the economy, causing even larger falls in consumption. As a result, many businesses postpone investment in new plant and equipment.

The Bank of England will probably cut interest rates, as inflation is not likely to be a threat at this stage of the cycle. The government may also stimulate demand by its own spending. Businesses eventually have to undertake investment in the upkeep of buildings and machinery if they are to keep trading at all. These three actions cause spending to rise. Output and employment also start to grow – and the cycle begins again.

Figure 18.5 Reasons for the existence of the business cycle

a 'shock' from an event such as the the financial crash of 2008, or a rise in the price of oil because of a war within (or between) oil-producing countries. Whatever the cause(s), the business cycle is a feature of a market economy and is undeniably a major influence on a business.

Tips and techniques

Questions in the examination will centre around one specific business, not all the businesses in the economy, so you will need to apply your knowledge of the economic cycle and its effects to that particular business. How is it likely to be affected and why? You will need to consider the nature of the product and the nature of the consumer.

Further sources

www.statistics.gov.uk: data on the macroeconomic variables, the overall state of the UK economy and the different regions and sectors.

www.hm-treasury.gov.uk: a good source of economic data on taxation and public spending as well as other useful information about current fiscal policy.

www.entrepreneur.com/article/200342: ten reasons to start a business in a recession.

www.whystudyeconomics.ac.uk: information about the nature of economics and advice on how to study it.

Your turn

Questions in red are for A Level candidates only.

Multiple-choice questions

1 Economic growth is usually measured by:
   A improvement in consumer confidence
   B increase in secondary output
   C rise in GDP
   D level of public spending. *(1)*

2 Which of the following is most likely to lead to a fall in economic activity? *(1)*

	Public spending	Value of imports
A	Fall	Fall
B	Fall	Rise
C	Rise	Fall
D	Rise	Rise

3 If GDP in a country rises by 8% over the course of a year and inflation over the same period has been 4% the real rise in GDP is:
   A 2%
   B 4%
   C 12%
   D 32%. *(1)*

4 Which of the following is most likely to encourage an increase in investment? *(1)*

	Consumer spending	Rate of interest
A	Rise	Rise
B	Rise	Fall
C	Fall	Rise
D	Fall	Fall

Revision questions

1 State what is meant by 'GDP'. *(2)*

2 State two ways in which the government could benefit from a rise in GDP. *(2)*

3 State what is meant by 'the level of economic activity'. *(2)*

4 Outline the difference between imports and exports. *(4)*

5 Outline the difference between saving and investment. *(4)*

6 Outline two factors that could influence a business's decision to invest in new technology. *(4)*

7 Outline what is meant by 'the business cycle'. *(2)*

8 Outline the four stages of the business cycle. *(8)*

9 State three sources of data that could be used by a business to determine the position of the economy on the business cycle. *(3)*

Total *(31)*

Chapter 19

Economic factors: economic policy

AS / Year 1 | Year 2

A Level students must know all of the content in this chapter.

AS students only need to know:

- The nature and purpose of the main types of taxation in the UK (pages 144–145)
- Distinguish between direct and indirect taxation (pages 144–145)

Macroeconomic objectives

Most economists would agree that a government has four macroeconomic objectives: a low and stable rate of inflation; a high level of employment; economic growth; and balance of payments equilibrium.

Low and stable rate of inflation

People often say that inflation means rising prices, but this is only partly correct. At any one time, some prices in the economy will be rising but some will be falling. It would therefore be more accurate to say that inflation is a persistent general tendency for prices to rise. A high rate of inflation is bad for the economy and therefore bad for businesses. This is for several reasons:

- Inflation makes UK exports uncompetitive. As a result of globalisation (see **Chapter 15**), identical products (e.g. the same model of car, brand of clothes, can of soft drink) can be made almost anywhere in the world. If the UK has a rate of inflation that is higher than those in other countries, the price of UK exports will rise, making them less attractive to consumers abroad.
- Inflation can reduce investment. Multinational companies look to produce in the cheapest possible location. This means that when they invest in a new plant, they choose the country with the lowest rate of inflation. They do not want to locate in a country where the price of labour and raw material inputs is rising sharply, because this would make their products uncompetitive.
- Inflation creates uncertainty. Managers dislike uncertainty about what the return on an investment will be. It is one thing to estimate that the profits from an investment will be £500,000 a year for the next five years, but if inflation is accelerating, how much will this be worth in real terms: in other words, what quantity of products will this sum of money actually buy? Low inflation allows businesses to plan their investments with some degree of certainty about their financial return and so encourages investment.

Key terms

Inflation: persistent general tendency of prices in the economy to rise.

'In real terms': earnings (wages, revenue, or profit) adjusted for the effects of price rises. Price rises reduce the purchasing power of earnings.

Tips and techniques

Do not state 'When inflation falls this means that prices have gone down'. That is incorrect; it simply means that the rate of increase in prices has fallen.

High level of employment

The government wants a low level of unemployment for three reasons:

1 Unemployment is a waste of human resources. If unemployed people were at work producing goods and services, society as a whole would have more goods and services to enjoy. People would have a higher standard of living.
2 Unemployment is bad for the individual. Unemployment can be associated with social problems such as vandalism and drug abuse. The

lack of a job can also be damaging to a person's self-esteem.

3 Unemployment is bad for society as a whole. The social problems associated with unemployment have to be paid for. In addition, benefits have to be paid to people who have no job. 'Society' has to pay, in the sense that this money could be spent in other, more productive areas, such as education and health.

Economic growth

The main benefit of economic growth is that if more goods and services are produced, people have a higher standard of living. Over the past 30 years, or so, this objective has changed slightly. It is not just a continuous growth of goods and services that is desired; the growth should be sustainable. In other words, where possible, growth should come from the use of renewable resources, and damage to the environment resulting from growth should be minimised. Moreover, the needs of future generations should be considered. Issues such as the ozone layer and global warming have put this sharply into focus.

Key term

Economic growth: an increase in the volume of goods and services (GDP) produced each year.

Figure 19.1 Sustainable growth has become much more important in recent years.

Key term

Balance of trade: difference between the value of exports and imports. If exports exceed imports, there is a balance of trade surplus; if imports exceed exports, there is a balance of trade deficit.

Balance of payments equilibrium

'The balance of payments' is the term used to describe the financial records of the UK's trade with the rest of the world. For example, someone who stays in a hotel abroad makes a payment to the hotel, which is recorded as an outflow of income from the UK. If a UK company operating abroad sends its profits back to the UK, these are recorded as an inflow of money. The balance of payments is about the measurement of all these types of inflows and outflows, but the most important component of the balance of payments is known as the balance of trade. This is the record of all the UK's imports and exports. It is this figure that is usually used in the news. An excess of imports over exports is known as a trade deficit; an example is shown in part (a) of Figure 19.2. An excess of exports over imports is known as a trade surplus; an example is shown in part (b). It is important that the UK exports sufficient products to 'pay its way' internationally.

(a) Trade deficit

Imports £80bn | **Trade deficit £30bn** / Exports £50bn

(b) Trade surplus

Trade surplus £30bn / Imports £50bn | Exports £80bn

Figure 19.2 A trade deficit and a trade surplus

Economic policy and its effect on businesses

Economic policy is concerned with trying to meet the four objectives and in doing so create an environment in which businesses will thrive and grow. It is conducted in four ways: through monetary policy, fiscal policy, supply-side policies, and the exchange rate (dealt with in **Chapter 17**). All of these can be used to influence the economy. To speak of the government 'controlling' the economy would be wrong; a better phrase might be 'steering it in the right direction'. This is because the government cannot alter the behaviour of people and businesses simply by telling them what to do, so it has to use economic policy to try to alter their behaviour. The economic policy, or policies, that are used depend on what economic objective(s) the government or the Bank of England is trying to achieve.

Monetary policy

Monetary policy is concerned with manipulating the level of demand in the economy through the rate of interest. In reality, there is no such thing as 'the rate of interest' in the sense of there being a single figure. 'The rate of interest' has two different meanings. To borrowers it is the cost of borrowing; that is, what has to be paid back to the lender (in addition to the capital sum). To savers it is the reward for saving; the return on their money. Furthermore, there are different rates for different types of borrower (depending on risk and amount borrowed) and also different rates for different savers (depending on how much is deposited, how long it is deposited for and ease of access to the money once deposited). However, it is still possible to use the term 'the rate of interest' since when interest rates change, they all move in the same direction: when rates rise for savers, they also rise for borrowers.

Until 1997, monetary policy was decided by the Chancellor of the Exchequer and then put into effect by the Bank of England. One of the first actions taken by, the then Chancellor of the Exchequer, Gordon Brown, when Labour came to power in 1997, was to make the Bank of England independent and hand control of monetary policy to the bank's Monetary Policy Committee (MPC). The MPC is a panel of experts from the financial and business world, which meets once a month to decide whether to change the rate of interest. Although the government owns the Bank of England, the MPC is entirely independent.

Key terms

Bank of England: the central bank in the UK; as banker to the government and other banks, it conducts monetary policy and is not involved in personal banking.

Monetary policy: manipulation of the level of demand in the economy using the rate of interest.

Monetary Policy Committee (MPC): The committee at the Bank of England that meets once a month to decide whether to change the rate of interest.

At first sight this seems odd. Why would a government want to hand over one of the main policy weapons to another organisation? The answer is that when monetary policy was in the government's hands, there was always the temptation to use the rate of interest for political purposes. For example, a government might lower the rate of interest before a general election in order to induce a feel-good factor, even if the economy was at the wrong place on the economic cycle (i.e. a boom) for this to be the appropriate policy. If the level of demand was already rising too fast, a rise in interest rates would have been the correct policy. As a result of this, when interest rates were eventually raised, they would have had to go higher than would have been necessary, had the government acted economically rather than politically in the first place. High rates can be damaging to businesses. Virtually all economists now agree that giving the Bank of England control of interest rates was a good decision; governments can no longer meddle with the economy for political reasons.

Through use of the interest rate, the Bank of England tries to meet the government's target for the rate of inflation in the UK economy. This is currently 2 per cent. The MPC does consider factors such as the level of unemployment and output when assessing the level of demand (and therefore the possibility of inflation exceeding the target), but low inflation is its priority.

How does monetary policy work?

The rate of interest is essentially the price of money. The price of something affects its demand, and therefore the demand for money responds to changes in the rate of interest.

If the Bank of England wants consumers and businesses to spend less, it raises the rate of interest. Figure 19.3 shows that if the rate is increased from r1 to r2, this will discourage borrowing and spending. The demand for money will fall from Q1 to Q2. It may also encourage some people who have surplus cash to save. The opposite would apply if the bank cut the rate to r1.

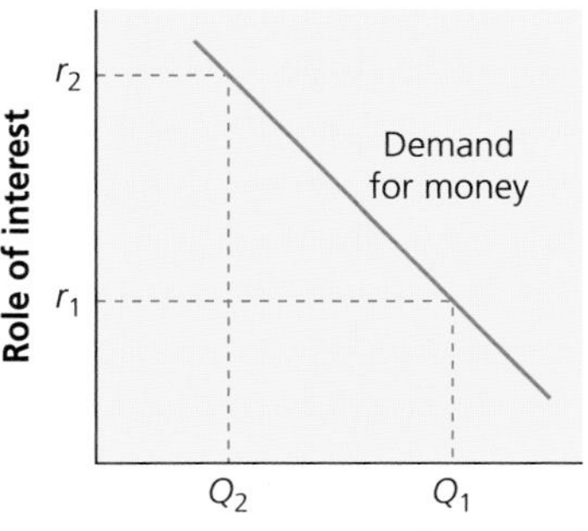

Figure 19.3 The rate of interest and the demand for money

To quote from the Bank of England's website:

> *When the Bank of England changes the official interest rate it is attempting to influence the overall level of expenditure in the economy. The Bank sets an interest rate at which it lends to financial institutions. This interest rate then affects the whole range of interest rates set by commercial banks, building societies and other institutions for their own savers and borrowers.*

Source: Bank of England website. http://www.bankofengland.co.uk/monetarypolicy/Pages/how.aspx

Therefore, if the Bank of England wants to slow down the economy and control inflation by lowering consumer spending and business investment, it puts up the rate of interest. If it wants to encourage people to spend and businesses to expand, it lowers the rate of interest.

Tips and techniques

To achieve a good mark for a question involving the rate of interest, you need to be able to analyse and evaluate the effects of any change; not all businesses and households are affected in the same way by interest rate changes.

Effects of a rise in the rate of interest on businesses

A rise in the rate of interest is likely to have the following effects.

- Investment will fall: If it is more expensive to borrow, businesses are more likely to make do with older, less efficient machinery and hardware because the cost of borrowing money to replace them has risen. This will have a knock-on effect on their suppliers who receive fewer orders. In addition, businesses know that a rise in interest rates will slow down consumer spending: this will make it even less attractive to invest. A fall in investment will slow down the level of economic activity, and if the fall in investment is severe enough, it may cause a recession.
- Consumer spending will fall. As the interest payable on mortgages, loans and credit cards increases, spending on other products will fall. The demand for luxury items, which are often bought on credit, will fall. It is often said that when rates rise, people save more and that this is what causes spending to fall. This is only partly true; it ignores the reality of the effect of a rate rise on a typical household with for example £2,000 in savings and a mortgage of £100,000.

Using these figures, let us consider this point in more detail. First, we make some assumptions to simplify the analysis, as shown in Table 19.1.

Table 19.1 The Smiths' family budget with a 3% interest rate

The Smiths have a disposable income of £1,500 a month.	+£1,500
The household has £2,000 saved in the bank, earning 3% interest. This means that the interest paid to them is £60 per year, or £5 per month.	+£5
The rate of interest on the family's £100,000 mortgage is 6%. This makes the monthly interest charge £500 (£6,000/12). the household also has to make a capital repayment of £400 each month towards the money it owes. The total monthly repayment is therefore £900.	−£900
The household's total monthly income available for spending is: £1,500 + £5 − £900 = £605.	**£605**

Table 19.2 shows what happens to the Smiths' finances when the rate rises.

Table 19.2 The Smiths' family budget with a 4% interest rate

Assume that disposable income is still £1,500. Employees do ask for higher wages when interest rates rise, but even if granted this will not happen at once.	+£1,500
At the bank the £2,000 savings now receives interest at 4%. This means a yearly return of £80. The monthly interest rate paid increases from £5 to £6.67.	+£6.67
As the rate of interest is now 7% repayments on the mortgage go up to £7,000 a year. This means a monthly interest repayment of £583 (£7,000/12). Add on the £400 capital repayment and that is a total of £983.	−£983
This means that income left for consumption is now £523.67. The Smith household is worse off by over £80. £1,500 + £6.67 − £983 = £523.67.	**£523.67**

So while it is true that some people (most likely those with no mortgages or other loans) can save more when the interest rate rises, the millions of people in the UK like the Smiths, with various loan debts, cannot do so. The main reason for the fall in consumer demand when interest rates rise is because of the rise in borrowing costs, not an increase in saving. Conversely, a cut in the interest rate will raise consumer spending, not so much because it is no longer worth saving, but because of the effect on consumers like the Smiths of having to pay less on their loans.

A rise in the interest rate will also slow down the rate of growth of house prices. When this happens, there is a wealth effect. As people see that the value of their property is no longer rising (and it may even be falling), they feel less confident about spending and this also acts to reduce consumer demand.

Exchange rate is likely to rise

When UK interest rates rise, the pound becomes a more attractive currency to invest in because the return on any sterling deposits has risen. This attracts an inflow of foreign currency into the country ('hot money'). This has to be exchanged into pounds and the increased demand for sterling causes the exchange rate to rise. This means that any business selling abroad will find that its exports become more expensive to foreign customers. It may well sell less. The other effect is on imports. These become cheaper. This will be beneficial if a business uses a large quantity of imported raw materials because its costs will now fall, but it will not be beneficial to a business if it is competing with foreign imports of a finished product. (The effects of exchange rate changes are dealt with in detail in **Chapter 16**.)

Effects of a fall in the rate of interest on businesses

A fall in the rate of interest is likely to have the following effects.

Investment will increase

A lot of investment is made with borrowed money. Any fall in the rate of interest means that it is now cheaper for businesses to borrow money to finance expansion and capital spending. They will therefore increase their purchases of new buildings, machinery and technology. Investment will raise the level of economic activity and this means more spending by consumers and a further boost to GDP. The installation of modern plant and equipment will also help UK businesses to be more competitive internationally.

Consumer spending will increase

Anyone with a mortgage (or any other type of loan) will now pay less interest and so their purchases of other goods and services from firms are likely to rise – although not all businesses will be affected in the same way. For example, a travel agent is more likely to expect an increase in demand as a result of a fall in interest rates than a baker. When it comes to spending on credit, consumers will now be more willing to borrow to buy consumer durables such as cars, DVDs and washing machines.

Exchange rate is likely to fall

How this occurs and the precise effects on businesses are explained in **Chapter 16**. For the moment, it is sufficient to say that a fall in the exchange rate makes UK exports cheaper abroad, so any business that sells abroad will find that its exports become more attractive. It may therefore sell more. It also means that imports become more expensive. This causes an unwelcome rise in costs if a business has to buy raw materials from abroad. On the other hand, a fall in exchange rates will benefit any UK firms that are competing with foreign imported finished products.

If interest rates are cut, consumer spending is likely to rise

'Credit crunch'

This term referred to the results of the problems in the financial sector that became apparent in 2008. Many banks in the UK became worried that a sizeable number of business and personal customers were so financially weak that they might fail to repay their debts and so, in an attempt to limit any further damage, they began to reverse their policy of 'easy loans for all' and increasingly started to lend only to those with very secure credit ratings. Mortgages and other loans began to cost more and were harder to obtain. This became known as 'the credit crunch'. One of the measures the Bank of England took to avoid this was to lower the rate of interest to make it easier (i.e. cheaper) for personal and business customers to repay loans. This meant that the banks could start to feel more confident about lending again.

How quickly do changes in interest rates take effect?

The Bank of England works on a timescale of around 18 months; this is how long it takes for changes in interest rates to have their full effect on investment, consumption and the exchange rate. Suppose that the bank increases the interest rate. Although some investment planned for the future will be cancelled or postponed, many projects will already be underway and cannot easily stop; once the construction of a factory or an office block has been started, it has to be completed.

Consumers also take time to react. Spending patterns do not change overnight and for millions of people it could be many months before their behaviour adjusts to the fact that they have less to spend. This is partly because there is a strong element of wanting to be seen to be 'keeping up with the neighbours' when buying goods such as cars and mobile phones. For quite a long time, people may run down their savings to maintain previous levels of spending.

This time-lag is not necessarily a disadvantage to the Bank of England. When it puts up interest rates, what it is hoping for is that the slowdown in economic activity is gradual rather than sudden; it wants a 'soft landing' rather than a recession. The bank hopes that as demand slows down, businesses will try to lower their costs and hence the prices they charge to their customers. If price rises slow down, that is precisely what the bank is trying to achieve in terms of its inflation target. Similarly, when interest rates are cut, the Bank of England is hoping for a steady, sustained increase in output, which will encourage long-term prosperity in the economy, rather than a burst of inflationary growth that has to be swiftly curbed by rate rises.

Fiscal policy

Fiscal policy is conducted through taxation and government spending. It is controlled by the government through the Chancellor of the Exchequer, the member of the cabinet responsible for the government's finances. The Chancellor works closely with the Treasury, which is the ministry responsible for helping to determine and implement the government's economic policy.

Key terms

Fiscal policy: economic policy conducted by the government through taxation and public spending.
The Budget: an annual statement of how much the government intends to spend in the next year and how this spending will be financed.

Fiscal policy affects the level of demand in the economy and so has a significant impact on businesses. In order to evaluate what is likely to happen to the demand for its products, a business needs to analyse the Budget. The Budget is a statement made by the Chancellor (usually in April) about how much the government intends to spend in the next year and how this spending will be financed.

Taxation

There are two types of tax: direct taxes and indirect taxes.

Direct taxes

Direct taxes are taken directly from either a person's income when they work (such as income tax), or from a company when it makes a profit (corporation tax). Sole traders and those in a partnership pay income tax.

There is another direct deduction from a person's income called national insurance. This is taken as a contribution towards the state pension and treatment under the National Health Service. It may not be called 'national insurance tax', but it is deducted by law directly from a person's income and so can be treated as a direct tax. A business also has to pay a certain amount of national insurance for every employee. The more employees a business has on its payroll, the more it has to pay. For this reason, national insurance paid by a business is sometimes called a payroll tax.

There is also direct taxation at local level. Households pay council tax to the local authority for services such as refuse collection, street cleaning and the fire service. Businesses have to pay the business rate to help fund the same services. This local authority taxation on a business is in addition to any national insurance payments and taxes that are paid to central government.

Indirect taxes

These taxes are not paid when a person or business earns money, but when they spend it; that is why they are 'indirect'. Most products have value added tax (VAT) put on them. This means that a percentage of the selling price is paid to the government as a tax. The standard rate of VAT is currently 20 per cent.

On many goods there is another indirect tax as well as VAT. The government puts excise duty on certain products. This duty is a fixed amount of tax on each item rather than a percentage rate, but the effect is the same: it makes the product more expensive and raises revenue for the government. Examples include car tax (the proper name of which is vehicle excise duty), tobacco, alcohol and petrol.

The treasury collects tax revenue comes from many sources. The main ones are:

- Income tax
- National insurance
- VAT
- Corporation tax
- Excise duties (e.g. from petrol, alcohol and cigarettes)
- Council tax (paid to local government)
- Business rates (paid to local government).

In addition to these, there are other taxes such as stamp duty (on the purchase of a house), capital gains tax (a tax on the rise in the value of an asset such as a second home), insurance tax (on many types of insurance policy) and flight duty (on those using air transport).

These taxes are levied ('put on') for three reasons:

1 To raise revenue: The government plays a major role in the economy, and the amount it spends amounts to around 40 per cent of GDP. Much of this spending comes from tax revenue. The rest is borrowed.

2 To affect the level of economic activity: In the years following the Second World War, the government often tried to manipulate the economy to achieve growth, full employment and low inflation through tax and expenditure changes. However, the idea that this can be done with any precision is no longer popular; experience shows that such policies may have the wrong effect. This is because there are time-lags before the effects occur. This means that when the effects of a particular fiscal policy eventually appear, the economy may have moved on to a situation in which the policy is no longer appropriate. For example, if taxes are cut to avoid a recession, by the time the extra spending starts to happen the economy may already be recovering strongly, which is likely to have the unintended consequence of a rise in inflation.

3 To influence the pattern of expenditure: The government tries to encourage certain kinds of behaviour and discourage others. Lower rates of indirect tax are placed on products that the government is trying to encourage people to buy; for example, unleaded petrol has a lower rate of tax than leaded. Taxes are put on products that can be harmful, such as cigarettes and alcohol. These indirect taxes raise the price of the product and discourage their use.

Public spending

The government also intervenes in the economy through public spending. This should not be confused with 'spending by the public'. A wide range of goods and services such as welfare, housing, health, education, the environment, transport and defence are provided for the public for several reasons.

To provide essential services that the private sector is unlikely to offer

'The market', that is, private businesses, will not want to supply services such as the police force, the army, or street lighting, as these will not make a profit. This means that central or local government has to provide them. In other cases, certain types of products may be provided by the private sector but not in sufficient quantities. These goods are known as merit goods. Merit goods are important for UK businesses. For example, if education were left completely up to people to buy privately, they might not buy 'enough' education for their children. This would not be good for an economy whose businesses need an educated workforce. The same argument applies to healthcare. The economy needs a healthy workforce because healthier workers are more productive. If the government thinks that people are not getting enough of these products for businesses to function effectively, it will increase its spending on them.

The government may also encourage the production and consumption of certain goods and services by offering a subsidy. A subsidy is a payment, or tax reduction, given to a firm/industry. Such a payment is equivalent to a reduction in costs (see page 92) and will increase supply to the market, which in turn lowers the price of the product. This will encourage people to consume/use it. The government subsidises various types of agricultural produce. Network Rail and the train operating companies also receive subsidy payments. Subsidies can be given to individuals as well as to businesses. These include home insulation grants and electrical charging points for vehicles. The government is also trying to encourage young people to develop a habit of consuming milk and milk products by subsidising the cost of milk and yoghurt products for school children so that it can be sold to them at a lower price.

To influence the level of demand in the economy

The government can influence the level of demand by its own spending as well as through taxation. If the amount of government spending rises, this will increase the level of economic activity. The reverse is also true. As was noted above, spending in the economy might be too high or too low. Changes in government spending can help to correct this.

This sort of fiscal policy is not as popular as it once was. Nevertheless, the principle of expenditure changes to 'nudge the economy in the right direction' is still accepted. The increases in spending on public services at the start of the millennium may well have helped to prevent a recession in the UK. Similarly, in 2008 with another economic crisis looming, even with the budget deficit larger than expected, some economists were urging the chancellor not to cut public spending because the outlook for the economy was so uncertain. Spending was maintained and the economy had started to recover by 2010.

If the government spends more than it raises in tax, it has to borrow. This is known as a budget deficit. If it raises more tax than it spends, this is known as a budget surplus. For many years the UK government has had a budget deficit. The coalition government of 2010–2015 put deficit reduction at the heart of its economic policy.

To assist certain regions in the UK

Some areas of the UK suffer from much higher levels of unemployment than others, while the more prosperous regions get congested, putting a strain on the transport infrastructure and creating pressure on facilities such as schools and hospitals. The government therefore targets some of its spending at specific regions of the country where industry has been in decline for a number of years. This is known as regional aid (or regional policy). It is administered through the Regional Growth Fund. Some of the funds for this aid come from the European Union. As well as trying to achieve balanced growth around the UK, the aims of Regional Aid are to:

- safeguard jobs in order to support communities
- encourage new businesses into the area and create jobs
- improve people's skills to make them more employable and productive
- minimise the loss of tax revenue (e.g. income tax and National Insurance) to the Treasury
- encourage investment and so boost the local economy
- help firms survive and/or grow, so they can compete more effectively abroad and also domestically against imported products
- help tackle social exclusion: this is where people (particularly young people) feel that they have little chance of participating in society and so turn to crime, vandalism and drugs; creating job opportunities will help prevent this.

The amount of assistance given to a business depends on the extent to which it will help meet these aims. A project that creates a lot of jobs that are likely to be permanent will receive more assistance than one that creates a few jobs that may only be short term.

Key term

Regional policy: government financial assistance to try to encourage businesses into regions of the country where economic activity is low.

Supply-side policies

Whereas fiscal and monetary policy operate by trying to manipulate the overall level of demand, supply-side policies aim to improve the economy's overall productive capacity, that is, they act on 'the supply side' rather than on demand. They are designed to make markets and industries operate more efficiently. If this occurs it will not only contribute to a faster rate of economic growth, but make it more sustainable as well. This is because there will be less danger of inflation from a rise in demand if total supply is also increasing. Supply-side policies also make a country more competitive internationally. There are a wide variety of policies that can be used to achieve this:

- Reducing welfare benefits: this may encourage the unemployed to take jobs, although the evidence for this is not clear cut.

- Income tax cuts: note that here the tax cuts are not acting as a means of boosting demand (although they might well have that effect as well) but as an incentive for people to seek work, if they are unemployed, or work more hours, if they are already employed, since they can now keep more of what they earn.
- Cuts in corporation tax: the same logic would apply here, to encourage a business to invest in new buildings, equipment and technology and also undertake research and development.
- Improved education and training: to improve the workforce's skills, flexibility, productivity and mobility.
- Removing unnecessary 'red tape', i.e. regulation and bureaucracy, which add to a firms costs.
- Encouraging business start-ups and expansion: encouraging 'the entrepreneurial spirit'.
- Improving the flexibility of the labour market and reducing trade union power: this makes it easier to 'hire and fire' workers and weakens the ability of organised labour to get pay rises that are not linked to productivity.

Supply-side policies are absolutely essential for the long-term 'health' of a country and the standard of living for those living in it. If a nation's employees have poor skills, if its entrepreneurs are not encouraged, if its benefit system discourages work, and if its businesses are tightly regulated, this is not going to result in a productive, flexible and innovative economy that is well placed to compete internationally.

Key term

The multiplier: the effect of changes in economic activity in one sector on other sectors; if one business experiences a rise or fall in demand for its products, this has a knock-on effect on businesses supplying it.

The multiplier

Put simply, 'the multiplier' means that if businesses experience a change in the demand for their products, this will have a knock-on (multiplier) effect on the businesses that supply them. The multiplier is a very useful concept for analysing not only the likely effects of economic policies, but also for considering other changes in economic activity. A cut in income tax will increase the demand for cars and this increase in

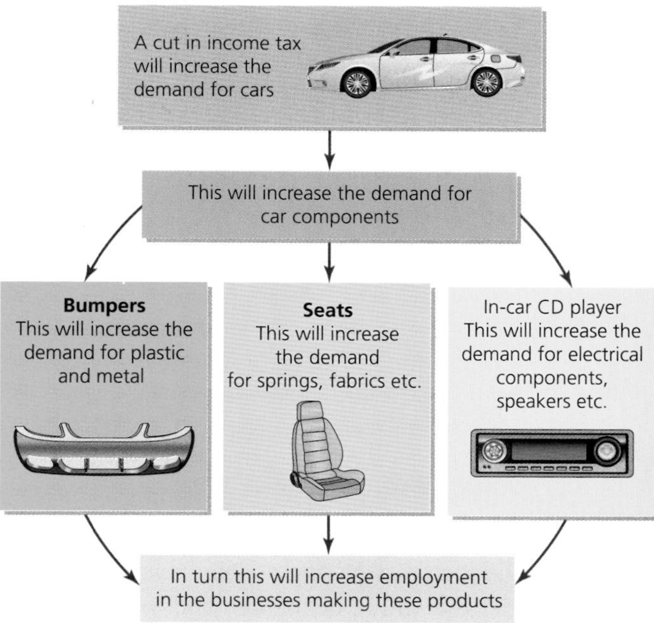

Figure 19.4 The multiplier effect of a cut in income tax

demand will cause a multiplier effect (see Figure 19.4). UK car manufacturers will order more of all types of components from their suppliers, some of which will also be in the UK – everything from brake shoes to bumpers, seats to CD players, and windscreens to wheels.

Income is being created at each stage of the process. This causes a rise in spending, and therefore employment is multiplied across the economy. The same would apply if there were an increase in UK exports of aircraft engines, for example. This would have a multiplier effect on the businesses that supply the exporter. Quite a small rise in spending in one or two industries can quickly generate increased demand for products elsewhere. The multiplier effect also operates in reverse. A fall in demand will cause spending to fall, which in turn has a multiplier effect across the economy. Any government putting up taxes to raise more revenue, or cutting public spending, must consider the multiplier effects of such a policy.

The multiplier also helps to explain why the closure of a large business or widespread redundancies can be so devastating to a local community. At best it suffers a fall in income and at worst loses a major source of employment. The (reverse) multiplier effect now means all the smaller firms that depended on the large business suddenly find themselves with vastly reduced order books. As unemployment rises, there is less spending in the local shops on all items, further lowering the level of economic activity. This is why the announcement of 2,600 job losses at Rolls Royce in 2014 caused concern.

Tips and techniques

A government has four policy weapons to use in order to achieve its economic objectives: fiscal policy, monetary policy, supply-side policies, and the exchange rate (for the last one, see **Chapter 16**). In order to score well, you will need not only the ability to explain these policies, but also to evaluate the likely effects of them on the business in the case study.

Evaluating the effects of a change in economic policy

A good starting point for evaluating the effects of a change in economic policy (or indeed a change in any of the factors affecting economic activity) is to consider the nature of the demand for the product. The demand for essential food items will be affected differently to that of the demand for new cars if spending changes, but this is only part of the evaluation. The remainder of the evaluation can be done by considering three issues. These can be remembered by the mnemonic 'TED':

- T: the trend in the variable
- E: the extent of the change
- D. the likely duration of the change.

Consider a question concerning the effects of a rise in the rate of interest on a business. It is tempting to say 'this will mean a drop in sales as consumers will spend less. Also the business will invest less as well because loan repayments are more expensive.' This is correct so far as it goes, but is not an evaluative approach. A better answer will consider 'TED'.

- T. If interest rates have been rising steadily for the past 12 months because the Bank of England has made it clear that it is concerned about inflation, the latest rise will not be unexpected. A business may already have anticipated it. This may mean that it has a marketing campaign ready to be launched to persuade consumers to buy, even if they have less to spend as a result of their mortgage repayments rising.

  On the other hand, if the rise comes unexpectedly and is against the trend (e.g. there has been no change in the rate for the last six months), this may come as more of a shock.
- E. Interest rates usually change by 0.25 per cent at a time. Thus although there has been 'a rise in the interest rate', this may not have a very large effect in the short run. Consumers may run down their savings, rather than cut down on consumption. It may be that several increases in the rate occur before there is a significant impact on spending. The effect on a business's ability to repay a loan will also be affected by an increase in interest rates. The result of this depends (again) partly on the extent of the increase and partly on how much finance has been raised by the business in the form of loans.
- D. Businesses and consumers are likely to consider how long the rate rise will last. If it is expected to be short term, it will have little effect as everyone expects economic life to return to normal quite soon. A business is unlikely to cancel the building of a strategically important factory just because the rate of interest has risen by a quarter of a per cent in one isolated change. If, however, it is expected that the rise will not be reversed for a year or more (with possibly more rises on the way), a business's reaction could be very different.

Therefore, a small rate rise in line with the trend, which is expected to be reversed shortly, will have much less effect on a business's decisions than an 'out of the blue' rise, against the trend, accompanied by the Bank of England making it clear that rates will have to stay high for a long period of time.

The same 'TED' reasoning can be applied to changes in tax rates, government spending and exchange rates. Remember, to evaluate any change in an economic variable on a particular business, use 'TED': Trend, Extent, Duration.

Further sources

www.thebankofengland.co.uk: the role of the Bank of England in the economy; how monetary and exchange rate policies operate.

www.hm-treasury.gov.uk: a good source of current economic data on taxation and public spending as well as other useful information about current fiscal policy.

www.statistics.gov.uk: data on the macroeconomic variables, the overall state of the UK economy and the different regions and sectors.

www.budgetresponsibility.org.uk: the Office for Budget Responsibility (OBR) was created in 2010 to provide independent and authoritative analysis of the UK's public finances. It is one of a growing number of official independent fiscal watchdogs around the world.

www.gra-ukgrants.com/Areas_red2.html: a map showing the Assisted Areas of the UK and information about the assistance that is available.

Your turn

Questions in red are for A Level candidates only.

Multiple-choice questions

1 Which of the following is an example of a monetary policy that is likely to reduce the level of economic activity?
  A rise in the interest rate
  B rise in income tax
  C rise in the exchange rate
  D rise in the government's budget deficit. *(1)*

2 Assume that the UK has a balance of trade deficit. Which of the following is most likely to help correct this deficit? *(1)*

	Exchange rate of the pound	Rate of inflation
A	Fall	Rise
B	Fall	Fall
C	Rise	Rise
D	Rise	Fall

3 Supply-side policies are intended to:
  A cause imports to become cheaper and therefore lower the rate of inflation
  B expand the productive capacity of the economy
  C increase consumer expenditure
  D reduce the government's budget deficit. *(1)*

4 A rise in the rate of interest in UK banks is likely to:
  A increase the demand for pounds and increase the value of the pound
  B increase the demand for pounds and lower the value of the pound
  C increase the supply of pounds and increase the value of the pound
  D reduce the supply of pounds and increase the value of the pound. *(1)*

Revision questions

1 State the four macroeconomic objectives of a government. *(4)*

2 Outline what is meant by the terms, 'fiscal policy', 'monetary policy', and 'supply-side policy'. *(6)*

3 State who is responsible for the control of fiscal policy in the UK. *(1)*

4 State who is responsible for the control of monetary policy in the UK. *(1)*

5 Outline what is meant by 'the multiplier principle'. *(2)*

Total *(14)*

Case study

Big Pit (BP) and The Snowdon Mountain railway (SMR)

In the nineteenth century, coal-mining was the main source of employment in South Wales. However, the twentieth century saw a steady decline in its fortunes, and the new competitors in the world market had a cost advantage that the Welsh mines could not match. The new millennium brought further job cuts and a once mighty industry was reduced to employing fewer than a thousand people. 'Ordinary' fiscal policy does not always work effectively when an industry is in decline and The Welsh Assembly is keen to regenerate areas of the country affected by the closure of the coal mines through supply-side policies.

Today there is one important reminder of the past glories of the Welsh coal industry. It is the oldest mine in South Wales, the 'Big Pit' in Blaenafon, which finally closed its commercial operations in 1980. The coal had run out and it seemed as if Blaenafon and the surrounding area were destined to suffer the same high level of unemployment as much of the rest of South Wales.

However, Big Pit was reinvented as a tourist attraction and it now houses the National Mining Museum of Wales. The main attraction at the museum is a 90 m-deep journey into the underground workings, using the same cages that once transported the miners. A former miner accompanies the tourists on a guided trip below ground, where they can see at first-hand what life was like for the men who worked at the coal face.

Like all national museums in Wales, admission is free. The museum has a number of interactive displays and a large collection of mining tools and equipment. There is a gift-shop selling souvenirs and books, meals are available, and there are facilities for disabled people.

Another well-known tourist attraction in Wales is the Snowdon Mountain Railway. Snowdon, at 3,560ft, dominates the landscape of Snowdonia National Park in North Wales and offers stunning scenery and awe-inspiring views. The railway has been operating since 1896. It is owned by Heritage Great Britain plc and is run as a commercial tourist attraction. It operates on a seasonal basis (weather permitting) from March to November. The return fare to the summit for an adult via steam train is £35.

1A Analyse one likely effect of a rise in VAT on the Snowdon Mountain Railway. *(6)*

1B Other than VAT, state two taxes that the Snowdon Mountain Railway will have to pay. *(2)*

2 Analyse one effect of an income tax cut on Big Pit. *(6)*

3 'The Welsh Assembly is keen to regenerate areas of the country through supply-side policies.' Analyse the suitability of one supply-side policy in regenerating the area of Wales affected by the decline of coal mining. *(4)*

4 Big Pit museum could be described as a merit good. Analyse why the Welsh Assembly has subsidised the provision of this merit good. *(6)*

5 Assume that the rate of interest rises. Evaluate which of the two businesses (Big Pit and The Snowdon Mountain Railway) is likely to be affected the most. *(15)*

Total *(39)*

Chapter 20

Legal factors

AS / Year 1 Year 2

A Level students must know all of the content in this chapter.

AS students must know:

- The nature and purpose of legislation
- The ways in which businesses can comply with legislation

This is covered on pages 151–155.

The law is a key aspect of the business environment and a very important constraint on strategic decision-making. It can be quite difficult for a business to keep up with legal changes (particularly a small business such as a sole trader). Nevertheless, it has to be done; in the event of a business doing something illegal it is no defence for a director or manager to say that they were not aware of the law. Time must be devoted to keeping up with legal changes. Also, where necessary, employees have to be informed and trained.

Types of law

There are two different types of law in the UK: civil law and criminal law.

Civil law

This law is concerned with the rules that govern the relations between businesses and/or people; for example, employment rights and consumer rights. A breach of civil law does not make a business or person a criminal. If the civil court's decision goes against a business or person, they are not fined or imprisoned but have to pay 'damages'. This is a payment to compensate the 'injured' party (business or person) for any loss or injury to restore them to the position that they would have been in, had the law not been broken.

Criminal law

This law defines the actions that the state has decided are 'wrong', and the punishment that will result from these actions. In a criminal court, if a business or person is found guilty the result can be a fine or imprisonment. Because of this, the 'burden' (standard) of proof is higher in a criminal court. The court has to be convinced 'beyond reasonable doubt' (i.e. certain) that the defendant is guilty, whereas in a civil court it is on 'the balance of probabilities'; that is, 'it is more likely than not' that one party is correct.

Key terms

Civil law: law concerned with the rules that govern the relations between businesses and/or people, for example employment and consumer rights.

Criminal law: this law defines the actions that the state has decided are 'wrong' and the punishment that will result from these actions.

EU law

Some laws affecting UK businesses have come from the European Union. Many of these have originated from the EU's Social Charter, which is a charter of rights for employees concerning areas such as working conditions, wages, and consultation of the workforce (e.g. the Working Time Directive, under which a business must not allow an employee to work more than 48 hours per week on average). UK businesses have to adhere to these EU laws just as if they had originated from the UK parliament. There are two types:

1. Regulations which have to be adopted and applied in a certain way.
2. Directives must also be applied as law, but it is up to the individual member country to decide how to implement it.

Why have laws?

The law aims to make individuals and businesses behave in a responsible way. Laws define the kind of behaviour that is unacceptable. Without laws a business could:

- dismiss employees at a moment's notice for any reason with no explanation

- provide dangerous and unhealthy working conditions that may lead to the injury or death of employees
- change the amount of money it had agreed to pay to a supplier for a particular delivery
- pollute and destroy the environment.

While employees could:

- turn up for work whenever they liked, completely disregarding the hours they had agreed to work
- remove products from their place of work and use facilities such as telephones or photocopiers for their own purposes
- ignore instructions about work from their managers.

A civilised society simply could not operate in this manner; there needs to be a framework for the protection of rights. Laws mean that there are legal minimum standards that must be adhered to by all businesses. If laws are to be effective they have to be enforced, which is why the state provides the judicial system.

Tips and techniques

At A Level it is important to know about three areas of legislation and their implications for business, governing the:

- relationship between one business and another
- way in which a business treats its consumers
- treatment of employees.

You also need to be able to identify the main pieces of legislation that affect a business's behaviour, particularly its strategic outlook. Be aware of the implications of a business complying (or not complying) with the law.

Laws governing the relationship between businesses

Contract law

A contract is a legally binding agreement between two or more parties. Most business relationships are of a contractual nature and so contract law sets out the basic framework of rights and obligations. A contract may be an offer to supply something at a particular time and/or of a particular quality.

A contract is binding on both parties; it is against the law for one party to change the terms of the contract without the other's agreement.

The breach (breaking) of a contract is a breach of the civil law and means that the aggrieved party (i.e. the person or business who has been wronged) can recover damages. Suppose a business that sells frozen desserts has signed a contract to deliver £10,000 worth of ice cream to a supermarket in one month's time. Its ability to do this depends on the ingredients being delivered one week before by its own supplier with whom it has contact. Suppose that the supplier failed to deliver the ingredients. This means that the dessert business is unable to make the product or deliver to the supermarket. Naturally, the supermarket does not pay because the goods did not arrive. The dessert business would be able to sue its supplier for damages, that is for the revenue lost as a result.

Key term

A contract: this is a legally binding agreement between two or more parties. Most business relationships are of a contractual nature and so contract law gives the basic framework of rights and obligations.

Competition law

Consumers benefit in terms of price and quality when businesses compete against each other for customers. In the UK (and the EU) it is illegal for businesses to restrict competition. This could occur in various ways:

- a relationship between businesses aiming to restrict supply
- businesses conspiring together to keep up prices (known as a cartel)
- a business charging an artificially low price in order to destroy a competitor, or to deter any new entrants into the market
- a business forcing its distributors to stock all of its products under the threat that if they do not do so, they will not be supplied at all.

The organisation that aims to ensure that UK businesses comply with the law is the Competition and Markets Authority (CMA). It will also consider whether a merger between two businesses is likely to result in any sort of anti-competitive behaviour.

Laws governing consumer protection

Sale of Goods Act (2012 and 1979)

This was an important Act when it was introduced in 1979, and remains important today. The Act was amended in 2012. The main change in this amendment was to state that if a fault was found within the first six months of the life of a product, it would be assumed in law that the fault existed at the point of purchase. The original rules of the 1979 Act would then apply.

Under the Sale of Goods Act, all goods must be:

- of 'satisfactory quality' (i.e. the product must not be damaged or defective)
- 'as described': this applies not only to advertisements but also to any explanations given by a shop assistant
- 'fit for the purpose for which they were intended'.

If any of these conditions is not met, a business must provide consumers with a replacement or their money back. A business cannot avoid the law by saying that it has a policy not to accept returned goods. The Act also imposes a duty on businesses to ensure that their products are safe to use.

In addition to these civil laws, there are a number of criminal laws.

Consumer Protection from Unfair Trading Regulations (CPRs) (2008) and Trade Descriptions Act (1968)

A consumer cannot be expected to understand everything about a product. The purpose of this Act is to prevent consumers from being intentionally misled when they buy goods. The 1968 Act states that any description of the goods on sale must not be false or misleading. The Act refers to all types of description – sign, advertisement or verbal.

The new legislation introduced in the 2008 Regulations replaced the original Act, but went much further in the rules it imposed on sellers. CPRs provides protection for consumers from unfair or misleading practices. The legislation has three main sections.

1. a ban on unfair practices.
2. a ban on misleading or aggressive practices.
3. a blacklist of unfair practices.

The legislation is intended to stop the following types of activity by businesses:

- claiming an item is 'free' when that is not the case
- aggressive doorstep selling
- refusing to 'take no for an answer' by a salesperson
- persistent cold calling
- time limited offers that are not limited at all.

Weights and Measures Act (1985)

It is an offence to give 'short measures' or an incorrect indication of the amount of a product on sale. If a product is labelled as containing 1 litre, that is what it should contain.

Unsolicited Goods Act (1971)

It is illegal to demand payment for services that have not been ordered. If a publishing business delivers a quantity of books that have not been ordered to someone's house, and then demands payment for them, the business is breaking the law.

The Trading Standards Authority is a public body that investigates breaches of consumer laws. It also assists consumers in taking a business to court if the business refuses to comply with its legal obligations.

Intellectual property

This is a legal term that applies to anything created out of the intellect of an individual or organisation. It could be literature, design, music, inventions, logos or advertising slogans. Most intellectual property rights are protected either by patents, or copyright.

Data Protection Act 1998

This Act controls how personal information on groups such as employees and customers is stored and used by a business. Any personal information held by a business must be used for lawful purposes, for a limited time and it must always be kept securely.

Laws governing the treatment of employees

See also **Chapter 49** for further details of these laws.

Prevention of discrimination

Discrimination occurs when an employer treats a person less favourably than another employee without any justification. This discrimination can occur in various ways; employing someone, promoting someone, or allowing them access to training courses.

Acts such as the Sex Discrimination Act (1975), the Race Relations Act (1976), and the Employment Equality (Age) Regulations 2006 and the Disability Discrimination Act 1995 mean that a business is breaking the law if it refuses to employ or promote a person on the grounds of race, sex, age or disability. For disabled people, a business has to make 'reasonable adjustments' to the way in which products and services are delivered so that disabled people can use them. Since 2003 there has been similar legislation applying to a person's sexual orientation and religion. There may be cost implications for complying with these rights, such as permitting extended leave for religious holidays or ensuring that any canteen facilities meet religious dietary requirements.

The implications for a business are:

- There needs to be a clear equality policy to ensure fair and consistent treatment of all employees.
- This policy needs to be clearly communicated to all staff. Managers should ensure that all employees are aware of this policy and its implications (i.e. that it is unlawful for someone to be discriminated, bullied or harassed on the grounds of sex, race, sexual orientation, etc.) and that disciplinary action will follow if they engage in any such behaviour.
- Employees should know about the business's procedures and who to speak to if they think that they are not being treated in accordance with the policy.
- The policy needs to be reviewed and monitored. The Acts make it clear that it is not a 'one-off' but a continuing duty on a business.

Tips and techniques

It is necessary to have a working knowledge of employment law, but it is also very important to be able to recognise the implications to the business in the case study. This approach will score higher marks.

National Minimum Wage Act

This Act which came into effect in 1999 lays down the minimum level of pay to which all employees in the UK (except those under 18) are entitled. It does not matter if the employee works part time or full time. If employees are paid on a piece rate (a certain amount for each item produced), the business has to ensure that the system of work is sufficient for enough items to be made for the employee to earn at least the minimum wage.

Health and safety

The Health and Safety Act 1974 was a very important piece of legislation. It has been extended to take account of new issues and hazards, such as repetitive strain injury or possible damage to the eyes from working at computer screens that people were not fully aware of, or did not exist, when the original Act was passed.

Not only do businesses have 'a duty to take reasonable care' of employees, but the criminal law lays down minimum safety requirements. There is a positive obligation to create a safe and healthy working environment; breaches of the law can lead to criminal prosecution as well as civil proceedings for compensation.

The provisions of the Act relate to the:

- place of work
- system of work
- working environment
- machinery used
- use and storage of substances
- employees.

The business must comply with the following regulations:

- Ensure that the building itself is safe. Entry to it and exit from it must be safe.
- Co-ordinate the whole system of work so that it is safe.
- Ensure that the temperature in the working environment is within certain limits; the atmosphere must be safe to breathe, the floors must be safe to walk along.

- Fit guards onto machinery to prevent accidents. Employees must be provided with the correct safety equipment (and clothing), and trained to use it.
- Provide training to guard against any hazards associated with the work; e.g. lifting loads and handling substances. A business that failed to provide any training 'because it was common sense for an employee not to lift a heavy load' would not have a legal defence if the employee injured him or herself.
- Draw up a written safety policy, making clear who is responsible for safety issues. This policy must be clearly communicated to employees.

Employees must also comply with the Act. They must:

- take reasonable care of their own health and safety and of others who could be affected by their actions
- comply with lawful instructions relating to safety matters; an employee who was trained and told to use lifting equipment could not try to sue the business for an injury to his back if he ignored the instructions
- not interfere or misuse anything provided for health and safety purposes; e.g. letting off a fire extinguisher for malicious purposes or 'in fun' is a serious matter, for which an employee can be summarily dismissed.

The Act says that a business must comply 'so far as reasonably practicable'. A business may dispute that it can afford to comply with every single part of the Act, claiming that the expense is not 'reasonably practicable'. If an accident occurred and the business was prosecuted, the court would decide whether it was 'reasonably practicable' or not.

Smoking in the workplace

On 1 July 2007, workplaces in England became smoke-free environments; legislation was already in place in Scotland, Wales and Northern Ireland. This includes offices, factories, shops, bars, restaurants, and work vehicles that are used by more than one person. Indoor smoking rooms are no longer allowed; anyone wishing to smoke must go outside the premises.

The 'anti-smoking law' will need to be taken seriously by a business. A business ignoring this law or failing to prevent smoking inside the premises will be liable for prosecution and a fine. An agreed policy (including disciplinary procedures for employees breaking this law) should be in place, and this needs to be carefully monitored to ensure compliance. If a business recruits a smoker then that person should be informed of the implication of the Act so that any breaches of the law are unlikely.

The Health and Safety Executive (HSE)

This is the organisation responsible for the regulation of risks to health and safety at work. If a breach of the Act is serious enough or there is repeated disregard for the law, the HSE can close down a business.

Termination of employment

This could occur through redundancy or dismissal. It is important to be clear about the difference.

Redundancy

An employee is not made redundant because they have done something wrong. Redundancy arises from a situation where the job that used to be performed no longer exists and so the employee is surplus to requirements.

Dismissal

Dismissal usually occurs for reasons of discipline or capability. Any dismissal has to be justified and must be 'fair' if it is to be legal. If an employee has accrued one year of continuous service with an employer then summary ('on the spot') dismissal is only 'fair' in two instances:

1. gross misconduct (e.g. an employee physically assaulting a customer)
2. gross negligence: a reckless or wilful disregard for the safety of others (e.g. a manager at a theme park allowing a ride to remain open when he knows that a safety fault with it exists).

For more detail about the law of termination of employment, see **Chapter 49**.

What happens if a business breaks the law?

Breaches of employment law are heard in an employment tribunal, a special court that deals with employees' claims for matters such as unfair dismissal, discrimination, breach of contract and victimisation by their employer. If the tribunal rules in favour of the employee, it will order the business to make a payment to the employee to compensate for what has occurred.

> **Key term**
>
> **Employment tribunal:** a special type of court that only deals with employment-related issues such as victimisation by an employer, unfair dismissal, and discrimination.
>
> For more details of employment law, see **Chapter 49**.

For breaches of criminal law, the business will be prosecuted in the criminal courts; either a magistrate's court for the more minor offences or the Crown Court where the penalties are more severe for the more serious matters. If a business is found guilty, it can be fined and/or those responsible for the breach could be imprisoned. Any breach of the civil law will be heard in the County Court where the business can be sued for damages.

If a business fails or refuses to pay damages or compensation, the business or person that is owed the money can apply to the County Court for payment to be enforced. The Court will not be impressed with a business that has failed to pay someone what is due to them. County Court judgments against a business can generate a lot of bad publicity and the hearing will be expensive. Furthermore, an adverse County Court judgment can affect a business's ability to obtain loans and other forms of credit in the future.

Strategic approach to complying with the law

It is usual for the government to announce changes in the law well in advance so that compliance with the change can be built into a business's strategic planning process. Discussion of the government's stated proposals should start at a senior level as soon as possible. Changes in the law are likely to affect one or more stakeholder groups, especially employees, and their views should be sought. Management of any change in the law must start from 'the top'; employees cannot be expected to know how they are to behave without guidance.

The actual detail of the legislation may be complicated, and it may be necessary to contact a lawyer for advice in the first instance (many websites including that of the Advisory, Conciliation and Arbitration Service (ACAS) offer advice and publications), and/or when the business has a plan in order to ensure that it actually does comply.

With legislation affecting employees (such as the prevention of smoking in the workplace), it is advisable to involve them at the earliest stage and to build their views into any plans. However, the consultation needs to be meaningful if the law is to be complied with effectively. Where possible it is useful for employees to have some 'ownership' of the changes. The manager that 'consulted' by asking the employees where they wanted the outside smoking shelter is not likely to have been as successful as the one who not only asked this question, but negotiated exactly how 'cigarette breaks' were to be taken: deducted from existing breaks or introduce extended breaks for non-smokers to ensure fairness? In addition, some managers brought in health professionals to offer guidance and support on how to give up smoking to minimise problems resulting from the change.

When there are changes to employment law (such as the Equality in Age Regulations) it is necessary to revise the business's existing employment policy and to ensure that employees (especially those in authority) are clear about the change. Someone at senior level needs to have responsibility for this; matters cannot be allowed to 'drift'. There are therefore resource implications such as, who will do this? When? Will the communication with employees and any necessary training be in work time, or will some employees have to be paid to attend a training session?

Compliance must be carefully integrated into the business's strategic plan.

Strategic benefits of complying with the law

The strategic benefits of complying with the law include the following:

- avoidance of fines (these can be large especially in matters of health and safety) which will lower profits

- avoidance of claims for compensation, which will lower profits
- avoidance of bad publicity (e.g. from discrimination, illegal safety measures or breaches of consumer law) that may deter potential employees and so leave important posts in the business unfilled
- avoidance of bad publicity that may deter customers and so lower sales and ultimately profits. There are, for example, over eight million people in the UK with disabilities, and compliance with the law may attract disabled customers to the business.

The poor treatment of employees means that they will not achieve their full potential. Where a business adopts practices to avoid discrimination, it should benefit all employees.

Compliance with health and safety legislation means fewer accidents and days off through injury or sickness. This may also result in a better relationship between managers and employees, which could make objectives easier to achieve, such as implementing change.

Examples of effects of legal factors on areas of business

1 Marketing: businesses need to be aware of the rules on advertising and must ensure that they adhere to the rules of the Advertising Standards Authority. (See **Chapter 58**.) Failure to do so could result in bad publicity.
2 Financial: businesses are required to meet certain financial obligations. All businesses are liable for tax and companies are required to lodge financial information with Companies' House.
3 People: there are numerous laws that employers have to obey when it comes to employing labour. Employers must ensure that workers are paid the minimum wage; they must provide them with a contract and a payslip. Employers are also responsible for paying tax and National Insurance contributions for their employees. They must also ensure that they do not discriminate in terms of age, gender, race and disability.
4 Operations management: employers must ensure that there is no risk of accident or injury for their employees.

Further sources

www.hse.gov.uk
www.businesslink.gov.uk/regulationupdates
www.legislation.hmso.gov.uk/acts.htm
www.cma.gsi.gov.uk

Your turn

Questions in red are for A Level candidates only.

Multiple-choice questions

1 What is the difference between civil law and criminal law?

A Criminal law may result in a fine, whereas civil law can result in imprisonment.

B In civil law there is a higher burden of proof than in criminal law.

C A person guilty of a civil offence is a criminal, whereas this is not the case in criminal law.

D A civil offence will usually result in a fine, whereas a criminal offence can result in imprisonment. *(1)*

2 Which of these conditions is not required by the Sale of Goods Act?

A The goods must be of satisfactory quality.

B The goods must be sold at the price stated by the manufacturer.

C The goods must be as described.

D The goods must be fit for the purpose intended. *(1)*

Revision questions

1 State two advantages for businesses in complying with the laws relating to employment. *(2)*

2 Explain one advantage and one disadvantage of the minimum wage. *(4)*

3 Explain two situations where on-the-spot dismissal is allowed. *(4)*

Total *(10)*

Case study

Health and Safety Executive (HSE) prosecution of Derbyshire firm

A Derbyshire firm was fined £1,300 with £7,353 costs after being found guilty of failing to install proper guards on a moving machine.

The firm, in the food packaging and processing industry, was prosecuted after a worker suffered a serious hand injury in an accident. The worker had been trying to free a jar while the machinery was still running by reaching around an existing guard. In doing so, his hand came into contact with a moving part of the machinery, severing part of his index finger and thumb. The court was told that there had been a similar incident previously that had been reported to HSE. New guards had been fitted, but it was still possible to reach round these. After the case an HSE spokesperson said that they were surprised that the firm had not responded more adequately to the previous incident. Better risk assessment would have prevented this serious accident.

Since the accident, the company has improved its safety systems. The employee eventually returned to work after one year.

1 Analyse one issue that would be required from a risk assessment in this business. *(6)*

2 Analyse one cost to the business of this incident. *(6)*

3 Evaluate the significance of this incident for the stakeholders of the business. *(15)*

Total *(27)*

Chapter 21

Environmental and technological factors and external factors and influences

AS / Year 1 | Year 2

A Level students must know all of the content in this chapter.

AS students must know all of the content in the Technological factors section of this chapter, however, in the exam AS Level students will not be asked to:

- Evaluate computer hardware and software to aid a business.

Whereas A Level students may be examined on this point.

AS students must be able to:

- Describe the environmental issues that influence a business
- Explain why a business needs to consider environmental issues
- Recommend and justify ways in which a business can address environmental issues.

Technological issues

People have come to expect an ever-increasing rate of change in technology, both at home and in the workplace. Keeping pace with what is available can be time-consuming and difficult for the individual, but is even more daunting for the manager of a business.

Effects of technology on business

Perceived disadvantages

Technological change at work is often felt to be threatening because of its possible effects on the individual worker. There are a number of reasons for this.

- Employees often associate technological change with unemployment. Computer-aided design and robotic processes in manufacturing have led to a reduction in the number of workers employed in those areas. Workers in sectors where new technology is being introduced may feel that their job is threatened; for example, the use of robotics instead of employees on assembly lines.
- New technology makes it necessary for workers to acquire new skills; those involved in this process may feel that they do not have the ability required to learn the skills, or that they are too old to take on the task.
- The changes caused by new technology may require employees to move to different departments or to work with new colleagues and managers. Many people will find such changes difficult, particularly if they have worked with one group of people for a long time, or there is someone in the new group whom they have found to be difficult. These types of changes often require a change of culture or way of thinking; many employees find it difficult to adapt in this way.

Tips and techniques

Look at the work done by Mayo in this area (see **Chapter 47**). You are encouraged to use theory to justify your answers.

In countries such as Japan and the USA, the 'new' is regarded as exciting and desirable. In the UK we have a tendency to cling to the 'old' ways and to regard new products and ideas with suspicion. This is particularly so in established manufacturing industries such as the production of china and glass tableware.

Benefits of technological change

On the other hand, new technology may bring numerous opportunities and advantages with it.

- Rather than creating unemployment, the introduction of new technology may bring a net increase in employment by increasing demand for the product or service. The introduction of internet banking may have reduced the demand for counter cashiers, but it has made the huge growth in the financial services sector possible and created thousands of new but different jobs as a consequence.

- New technology creates new demand among consumers. Japanese industry built its success in the late twentieth century by identifying the next product or trend and then making sure that they were first to bring it to market. This helped make their businesses successful and created employment for Japanese workers.
- Learning new skills and implementing the changes involved in introducing new technology can have positive benefits for the morale of the workforce and the self-esteem of individual workers. The result may be better motivation and an increased willingness to accept change in future. However, it is also important to remember that these situations may result in redundancy for some workers.
- Managers and employees need to understand that continuing to do the same thing is the highest risk of all. This might not be the message that employees and unions want to hear, but they need to be convinced. There are numerous examples of businesses where the need for change was either not recognised or ignored and the results were a failure to compete effectively.

The pottery industry

Stoke-on-Trent has been the centre of pottery manufacture in the UK since the industrial revolution, building its success on craftsmanship, design and the skills of its loyal workforce. However, by the 1980s, the threat of competition from countries such as China and Taiwan was increasing rapidly; these countries could compete with much lower prices as a result of lower labour costs. Many of the traditional firms in Stoke did not see this as a threat because the pottery from the Far East was of much poorer quality. UK firms such as Wedgwood and Royal Doulton failed to realise that lifestyles were changing and that the demand for long-wanted dinner sets and fine china was falling. The sector could arguably have survived more successfully if firms had invested in new technology at this stage and reduced their costs with computer-aided design and robotic production lines. Having failed to seize this opportunity, many of the larger firms went out of business, leaving those producing in niche markets, for example Moorcroft and Emma Bridgewater, as the survivors.

Implementing technological change

One of the major difficulties in implementing technological change is the timing. If a business holds back too long before introducing new technology, it may begin to lose markets and market share, and run the risk of being out of date. This may happen if a business wants to wait until new technology becomes cheaper or until the equipment has proved its worth. On the other hand, moving too soon may mean that a business has to pay higher prices and that it becomes involved in the inevitable teething troubles of new equipment. The situation is exactly like that of buying the newest games console. Do you buy it now when it is more expensive and there are not many games to play on but you are ahead of the curve, or do you wait until it is cheaper but everyone has already bought it and there are lots of games? There is no right answer.

Businesses considering the introduction of new technology must also look at the way it will fit into their overall situation. Too many businesses buy new equipment in a piecemeal fashion, a little at a time, having failed to make a strategic assessment of the complete situation. In order to make a reasoned decision, it is important to look at the investment in terms of its ability to reduce costs and its potential to improve the business's capability to respond to changes in the market place.

The costs and benefits of installing new technology in a business may not be immediately obvious, particularly in the area of human resources. Installing new technology in isolation, without training or organisational change, is unlikely to bring the benefits that the business may expect or want. The more complex the organisation, the more comprehensive the cost-benefit analysis needs to be in its scope before any decision is taken.

In some cases, it may make more sense for a business, particularly a small or new one, to choose not to invest in the newest technology and to use resources outside the business instead. For example, small businesses considering putting in new e-business systems may find that the benefits at this stage of their existence do not justify the expense that would be required. In these circumstances it would be sensible to look at external suppliers of such systems to see if they offer a better and cheaper alternative in the short term. Going down this route may also mean that the risk of rapid obsolescence is minimised because the supplier has to upgrade to the new technology.

Key term

Obsolescence: existing capital equipment is replaced by new developments in technology; for example, the replacement of the typewriter by the word processor.

Rapid technological change is a key factor in the business world. Its existence creates a situation of uncertainty as well as the possibility of dealing with an increasingly complex market. Any decision in this area needs strategic planning and investigation. Managers should not assume that new technology will always be better or more useful in their business, but neither can they afford to ignore possibilities that may improve the performance of their businesses and their competitiveness in the market.

Driverless cars

It will soon be possible for drivers to get into their cars and give a computer its instructions for the journey before sitting back. The technology for this already exists; what is now needed is to convince the public that this is a good idea. Some of this technology is already in cars at the higher end of the market; automatic braking; automatic parking; lane departure alerts; automatic handbrake and pull away – no more hill starts. For the future, technology could also see an end to traffic lights and even a reduction in car ownership, if drivers can order up a car that delivers itself to their doors. The move to driverless cars will change lives but it will also bring many ethical questions. Who is at fault if a driverless car fails to respond appropriately?

Advantages and disadvantages of using computer hardware and software

Advantages

- Systems are faster.
- Storage is easier and storage costs are reduced.
- Communication is easier and faster.
- Analysis of large amounts of data is possible to aid business processes.
- Modern banking and financial systems would not be possible without computer technology.
- The internet has increased the availability of knowledge.
- Workers do not have to be in the workplace – home working or off-site working is possible.
- Meetings can be held remotely without the need to gather groups of people together in one location with all its associated costs.
- New technology, like 'Click and Collect' and contactless cards have made life easier for consumers.

Disadvantages

- Money needs to be spent on effective training for all involved in new systems.
- The public may be resistant to changes. For example, telephone menus to direct callers to the right department are still not popular with consumers.
- System failure or breakdown may mean that the whole business is affected.
- New computer technology is costly. The NHS data storage system has been affected by its multi-billion pound cost and the unwillingness of the government to meet the spiralling costs.
- Systems need to be carefully tested before they are rolled out to the public. There are numerous examples of systems that have been introduced and then failed, catastrophically; for example, the baggage handling system at Heathrow Airport's new terminal.
- Security of data is a problem when storing information in computer systems. Safeguards and passwords for access need to be robust to prevent hacking.

Examples of the effects of technological issues on business

1 Marketing: new technology makes it possible to introduce new products to the market, e.g. smart phones and automatic vacuum cleaners.
2 Financial: the use of technology in the business can speed up accounting practices and make it possible to store data electronically.
3 People: new technology on the production line can result in redundancy or the need for retraining of staff, e.g. robotics on assembly lines.
4 Operations: new technology can improve productivity and make the business more efficient.

Digital technology

The digital revolution encompasses the shift from analog and mechanical technology to digital technology.

In the 1990s the World Wide Web had been introduced, and by the early 2000s television was digital. The vast growth in mobile phone technology saw a huge advance in digital technology, with smartphones having access to the web and apps in abundance. Growth in tablets has already started to surpass the usage of desk computers.

Such technology has enhanced the application of communicational media within the business world.

The impact of the digital revolution

The use of 'cloud' computing has advanced searches and access to services throughout the business environment.

The use of platforms such as Freenet, Wam!net, bulletin boards, and so on, have all made sharing and communicating information that much quicker and easier.

This has afforded businesses cost savings, as communication and access to data is easier, and research and market information is cheaper.

The impact on businesses of the digital revolution will vary according to:

- the type of business
- the market in which a business operates
- the budget of the business to utilise digital technology
- the level of digital technology used
- the type of consumer (age, socio-economic group, location, etc.).

The evidence of this revolution can be seen in all areas of business and among most customers.

- In production the revolution has led to the use of robotics and digital control systems.
- Both the public and private sector now use digital storage methods, e.g. patient records in GP surgeries.
- Communication has changed through the use of mobile phones, video conferencing, texting and emailing.
- The use of the internet is now widespread throughout the business sector. It is used to gain information, to advertise, to manage and access bank accounts, to sell and to communicate, to expand markets and become more efficient.

The growth of digital systems has helped industries to expand their markets and become more efficient but it brings problems with it such as secure data storage and the difficulty of keeping up with the speed of change. In addition, those businesses that fail to realise the significance of new technology are likely to be left behind and face falling sales.

Opportunities and threats for businesses that have arisen due to the digital revolution

Opportunities

- Cost savings as information has become more readily available and such information can be accessed quickly.
- The range of information has increased as access to websites has grown.
- Market research can be carried out using a larger sample as responses may be conducted online.
- Feedback from customers can be accessed more easily as using digital technology means it is more convenient for customers to respond. More responses increase the reliability of the information gained.
- Access to a much wider market of potential customers.
- The use of digital technology allows banks to introduce more types of online banking (and therefore cuts staff costs) in an attempt to be competitive.
- Digital technology has led to the development of driverless cars. This should enhance safety, as the automatic 'drivers' will not 'tailgate', for example, which often leads to accidents and consequential delays for many motorists.

- The digital revolution means there will be more employment opportunities in this particular sector of the economy.

Threats

- Digital technology is relatively new and consequently is changing and improving at a fast rate. The ability to 'keep up' with such technology may be expensive, particularly for smaller businesses.
- Certain examples of digital technology involve sires such as review sites, which, sadly, can be used to provide false reviews that are critical and damage a business – for example, a falsely critical hotel review could damage the reputation of the hotel.
- Increased access to information allows consumers and customers to make informed choices, and therefore businesses will need to be more competitive.
- Any adverse publicity will travel more quickly to consumers via websites and comparison websites, which may significantly damage the goodwill of a business.
- Businesses will need to be aware that both consumers and employees may be reluctant to grasp the virtues of the digital revolution. Consequently, training for its employees may be necessary, which in turn adds to its costs. Similarly, businesses have to spend money on educating its customers in the use of digital technology. Banks are spending huge sums of money on the implementation of digital technology in branches, replacing counter staff with machines. However, there are many customers who are reluctant to grasp the new technology.
- The fear of systems crashing or fraudulent activity has meant businesses have had to spend large sums of money installing protective systems to prevent fraudulent access to sensitive sites.
- There will be a need to customise any software packages to ensure the business provides the service that consumers expect. This may lead to additional expense or the risk of the software failing to deliver what is required.
- Newspapers have lost sales as a result of the web, by allowing access to news without the need to buy a newspaper, for example. In turn this may affect the level of advertising revenue that a paper may earn.
- Similarly, newsagents are finding it a lot harder to survive as news is instant and constantly updated via websites and apps.
- The overall threat to jobs is of note, as capital substitution will inevitably lead to a loss of jobs in certain sectors of the economy.

Tips and techniques

It is important to read the actual question carefully as it may ask for the threats and opportunities for a particular stakeholder, or ask for only the advantages of the digital revolution and not the disadvantages.

Environmental factors

Consideration of the environment is another external factor that affects the working of a business. Damage to the environment (a social cost, external cost or negative externality) is moving higher up the agenda for politicians and the general public. Consequently, businesses cannot afford to ignore the problem.

Key term

Negative externality: a cost that arises out of production or consumption which is not paid for by the producer or consumer, e.g. pollution, congestion or litter.

It is not just an issue for the UK economy; throughout the world the demand for energy resources has serious environmental repercussions. China consumes 17.5 per cent of the world's energy resources, second only to the USA. With only modest oil reserves, China relies on coal, which causes huge environmental damage.

The type of cars we produce and drive have changed considerably in recent years as a result of government intervention and legislation and because of pressure from consumers and environmental groups for 'greener' vehicles. Most car manufacturers now put economical energy consumption near the top of their list of necessities in producing a new car. The rising price of oil has also made this and fuel consumption an important consideration in a new car purchase.

Tips and techniques

This topic is highly controversial and you should guard against 'banging a drum' with emotive language and political dogma. It is better to put forward a balanced view, highlighting both the positives and the negatives of a business that may or may not be responsible for a particular form of pollution. Marks are awarded for the way in which you write your points and not for any particular viewpoint.

Environmental issues and their consequences

Air pollution

Much publicity was given to the level of air pollution in Beijing, the host city for the 2008 Olympics. The fact that smog descends upon the city at regular intervals forced some athletes to withdraw for fear of damage to their health. In an attempt to reduce the smog during the Olympics, the Chinese government stopped industrial production in the area and took over one million cars off the road.

Since 2013, Paris and Athens have faced similar problems, with air pollution at levels regarded as damaging to human health.

Our air continues to be polluted by a wide range of industrial processes. The power stations that generate our electricity and incinerators which burn some of our rubbish, are major causes of air pollution according to experts.

It is not only industry that creates the pollution. Cars and planes used by consumers are another major source of air pollution. The Environment Agency is responsible for monitoring the amount of air pollution caused by industry.

Noise pollution

Living close to a motorway or an airport will mean experiencing a considerable amount of noise pollution. House values are usually reduced as a consequence of their proximity to the source of noise pollution. Expensive anti-noise measures have been fitted to houses close to the runways of some airports (double- or triple-glazing), while large fences are erected on motorways to deaden the constant noise. Such measures add to the expense of the transport system, but are essential if the social costs are to be tolerable.

The fear of further noise pollution has caused serious opposition to another runway at Heathrow.

River or sea pollution

Water can be easily contaminated by industry when discharging its waste. Chemical plants have in the past been guilty of causing environmental damage as a result of careless disposal of waste, or insufficient treatment prior to disposal. Oil is spilt into the seas around the world on a regular basis; for example, the BP oil spill in the Gulf of Mexico in 2010. Some of the spills have been due to accidents as ships have run aground. The consequences of these accidents are significant. Oil spills are expensive to clear up and the damage to wildlife and the land is enormous. Money spent clearing up such spills could be better spent providing more hospitals or new schools.

Land pollution

Deforestation and land scarred by industrial quarrying or mining is a form of pollution. Brazil has continued to fell millions of its hardwood trees, leaving the land bare as there are no trees to hold the soil in place. Once the land is reduced to a barren state, nothing can be grown on it and therefore another resource has been lost.

Congestion

Traffic congestion is an environmental issue because cars in traffic jams are still using petrol and polluting the atmosphere. In addition, such traffic often leads to a call for more roads to be built, which erodes the amount of land for other uses.

Key term

Sustainability: the endurance of systems and processes. It refers particularly to preventing a negative impact from economic systems and production on the earth and its environment.

Government measures

Sustainable Development Strategy

The government introduced its Sustainable Development Strategy, which aims to deliver a better quality of life for everyone. It proposed the following:

- a reduction on vehicle excise duties for cars with low emissions
- an increase in the standard rate for the landfill tax (a charge for disposing of waste related to the amount disposed)
- tax allowances for industry which invests in environmentally friendly technology
- recycling schemes operated by local governments; many households now have additional bins and containers for plastic waste and papers.

Climate change levy

This is a tax on the use of energy in industry and commerce.

Carbon Trust Standard

Launched on 24 June 2008 by Environment Secretary, Hilary Benn and businesswoman Deborah Meaden, this is a kitemark for being environmentally friendly. The kitemark proves that the company has reduced its carbon footprint. B&Q and Morrisons have already gained their kitemarks.

The Carbon Trust

This government-funded body offers advice to firms on carbon-emission reduction.

Congestion charges

The government has also allowed local governments to introduce road congestion charges. In 2014 the London congestion charge was £11.50, each time a vehicle entered the congestion zone. Professor Begg, a government adviser on road issues, stated that the London congestion charge would have to be increased to £15 per vehicle before it would have a significant effect on the levels of traffic. This is due to the fact that car usage is highly inelastic and therefore the charge needs to be significant if it is to have any real effect.

Alternative sources of energy

The government has invested money into alternative sources of energy. The number of wind farms has escalated in the last few years, but face problems from local residents who object to them because they are unsightly. At present, wind farms only generate a single figure percentage of our total energy generation.

Harnessing the power of the tides (tidal energy) has not been prolific, which is perhaps surprising considering that the UK is an island.

Pressure groups

Environmental damage is not only expensive for businesses to reduce, but may bring unwanted publicity. Pressure groups such as Greenpeace and Friends of the Earth exist in order to highlight environmental issues. Negative publicity may affect sales or damage the image of the business.

Business has had to respond to demands for environmental issues to be addressed. Car manufacturers have responded by meeting the changing demand for cars. Consumers have been switching to smaller, more fuel-efficient vehicles, as a result of environmental concerns and the rising costs of petrol and diesel.

Conflict between environmental and ethical concerns and other objectives

For some firms the decision to follow an environmentally friendly, sustainable or ethical stance in the business is an easy one, often because the business has built a reputation for its actions in those areas. Businesses such as The Body Shop were at the forefront in developing products that were not tested on animals and it received a great deal of positive publicity for its actions. Pret a Manger has an ethical policy of giving all unsold sandwiches to charities for the homeless at the end of each day. The business uses this fact together with the information that all its sandwiches are made fresh each day within individual stores as a marketing tool. It is able to show that it is taking the problems of food waste and helping the homeless, while meeting consumer demand with fresh food.

For other businesses there may be concerns about taking an ethical or environmentally friendly stance. How much will it cost? Will it affect the product or sales? Will profits be lower? These questions may result in conflict between different stakeholders of the business.

For example, if a cosmetics business decides to stop testing its products on animals there will be a number of consequences that may be advantageous or not.

The nature of any new products may have to change.

- The price of new products could be higher.
- Customers may be attracted by the end of animal testing or put off by higher prices.

- There is likely to be good publicity.
- Workers may be pleased to be working for an ethical business.
- Shareholders will be pleased if sales or profits are affected positively, but will not be happy if there is a negative effect on sales and prospective dividends.

In other businesses, such as the example of Adnam's Brewery in the case study below, following an ethical and environmentally friendly route may have higher costs at the outset, but the end result may be lower costs and higher profits. These results will be achieved if the new production methods are more efficient in terms of inputs of raw materials and other factors of production; more efficient in use of time; and gain free publicity for the business in terms of marketing.

The business will need to weigh up the effects of all these factors before making decisions and it may need to put effort into convincing shareholders that such policies are likely to be worthwhile in the end.

Examples of the effects of environmental issues on business

1 Marketing: products can be marketed by reflecting a business's environmental concerns and awareness.

2 Financial: the use of electronic storage results in less paper use, reducing costs to business in terms of storage and paper usage.

3 People: workers are often proud to be a part of a business that has concern for the environment; it can encourage loyalty and commitment in employees. Adnam's Brewery workers are always keen to talk about the success of the business in reducing water usage.

4 Operations: the use of energy and water-saving measures is likely to reduce production costs, as well as making workers aware of their use of these scarce resources.

Further sources

www.boagworld.com (opportunities and threats of digital technology)

www.greenpeace.org.uk Website of a well-known 'green' pressure group

www.defra.gov.uk Information from the government on food and rural affairs

Your turn

Questions are suitable for all AS and A Level candidates.

Multiple-choice questions

1 Each of the following is an example of a negative environmental externality except:
A litter
B noise from a motorway
C poor air quality
D poor living standards. *(1)*

2 Technological change is not likely to result in:
A lower productivity
B higher productivity
C higher unemployment
D retraining. *(1)*

Revision questions

1 State two likely costs for a business of technological change. *(2)*

2 Explain two ways a business is likely to benefit from pursuing an environmentally friendly policy. *(4)*

3 Explain two reasons why car manufacturers are trying to make vehicles more fuel efficient. *(4)*

Total *(10)*

Case study

Adnams Brewery

Adnams Brewery was founded in 1872 in the Suffolk coastal town of Southwold. It is still best known for its beer and pubs, but has diversified into other areas in recent years. It now owns and runs two hotels in Southwold, as well as

distilling spirits and running a number of cellar and cookware stores around the country.

On its website Adnams says: 'We want to make sure our impact on society is a positive one. Our company values are rooted in making great products without costing the earth.'

The business works closely with the local farming community using local suppliers where possible; it has recently installed an anaerobic digestion plant that is used to turn all the brewery and food waste that the business produces into biogas. The mash produced by the brewing process is fed to local pigs, which in turn provide meat for the hotels and shops.

In 2006, a new eco-distribution centre was opened, with a living roof and a facility for harvesting rain; the reduction in water and energy usage achieved by the firm recently is significant for an industry requiring large amounts of both water and energy.

In more recent years, Adnams has put great efforts into reducing the amount of water that it uses in all its processes. In 2007, the brewery introduced the lightest-weight glass bottles into its process. The weight of the bottles for 500 ml of beer was reduced from 455g to 299g; at the same time a new energy efficient brew house was opened. In 2010, Adnams opened its distillery, taking great care, as with all its expansions, to meet the needs of the Conservation Area the business occupies. For many companies, environmental concerns and an interest in the local community are seen as an unnecessary cost; Adnams take the opposite view in all it does.

The company won the Queen's Award for Enterprise – Sustainable Development in 2012. The panel made the following comments 'Adnams wins this award for pursuing a values-based approach to management within its business. As a result it has reduced its negative environmental impact and made significant contributions to the well-being of its surrounding community. It provides an excellent example to its industry.'

1 State two examples of positive environmental initiatives at Adnams. *(2)*
2 Analyse a likely benefit of Adnams' environmental initiatives for one of its stakeholders. *(4)*
3 Evaluate the costs and benefits for Adnams of its commitment to 'values-based management' and concern for the environment in its operations. *(15)*

Total *(21)*

Chapter 22

Causes and effects of change and managing change

> **Year 2**
>
> A Level students must know all of the content in this chapter.
>
> This chapter is not applicable for AS students.

Change is an inevitable fact of life for everyone, including the business environment. Over recent years, the pace of change has become increasingly rapid, as scientific and technological development makes it possible to do things in new ways and to introduce new products and techniques into the industrial process and the market. Each of these changes makes it necessary for us to learn new skills in our home and work environments. Some of us will make the changes and learn the skills more easily and quickly than others.

Whatever the case, change creates uncertainty in the workplace. A failure to manage change without careful strategic planning and an appreciation of the problems that may arise will mean that the business is likely to suffer.

The main responsibility of managers is to manage change because any business will also be facing situations of change either internally, or externally. Even if the business carries on doing the same thing as far as production is concerned over long periods of time, the economy, the market and the customer base will be changing and managers will need to be aware of this if businesses are to thrive.

Communication and change

In his book, 'Making it happen', Sir John Harvey Jones says the following:

> *I have never understood why some managers are so terrified of telling their people the full economic facts. In a situation where there are inevitably going to be some job losses it is surely better to try to reassure as many people as possible, even if you cannot reassure everyone, than to end up with everyone in the outfit being anxious.*

In his opinion and that of many other successful and enlightened managers, it is always better to give everyone as much information as soon as possible. At ICI, managers always ensured that employees were the first people to hear of possible redundancies, and gave help to those involved from the beginning to the end of the process – and sometimes beyond their leaving the business. In general, people can cope better with a situation where they know the facts, however bad they may be, than one where there is secrecy and rumour. Inevitably, in the latter case, people begin to work in a climate of fear and suspicion, which does not create an atmosphere where change will be accepted. In addition, if the rumours are incorrect, a great deal of time and effort will be wasted in putting things right.

Communication of information in a clear way from the top to the bottom of the hierarchy is essential; it must be done in an appropriate way, with the opportunity for workers to talk further with those who can allay their concerns, particularly if they involve job losses. It is equally important in the process of change to communicate good news to people; all too often this aspect of change is overlooked. Workers need to be told that they have done a good job, they have succeeded in a particular task, the profits have improved and the business is doing well. If these things are said and all good news is communicated, the atmosphere in the workplace will be more positive, workers will see the benefits of the changes they have implemented and be more likely to embrace change in the future.

Causes of change

Changes in a business can arise from internal or external sources, and the business's ability to control them may vary accordingly. A strategy should be in place to identify likely problems and deal with them before they start to create difficulties for the business.

Internal change

Objectives

As businesses grow, it is likely that their objectives will change. In its early years a business will focus its efforts on surviving and ensuring an adequate cashflow, but gradually, if the business is viable, this focus will begin to change to profitability and possible growth in the long term. At each stage, the new objective will result in a change of emphasis for the running of the business that is likely to impact on everyone associated with it. A new business will need to keep tight control over costs in order to survive, whereas a business looking to grow may need to spend large amounts of money to achieve this objective.

Personnel

Changes in personnel are always likely to have an effect on the running of the business, and the more senior the personnel, the greater the possibility of major changes. New people bring their own ideas and methods of working, so that even though it may take time and the scale of the effects may vary, their priorities and methods of working will eventually permeate through the business to colleagues. New management appointments in Ryanair in 2014 have helped change the public perception of the business and have improved the company's profits.

Skill levels

The skill level of staff will also change over time as society's attitude to education and learning changes. This is likely to have an effect on the business, depending on the number of personnel it employs and the skills they require to do their job. Companies like Microsoft have experienced difficulties in recruiting high-level software workers in recent years because of the low number of graduates coming out of IT courses at UK universities.

Finances

The financial status of the business may also force it to make changes. New procedures, products or legislation may force a business to undertake large-scale investment. Trading losses or a drop in profit levels may make it necessary to reorganise the workplace with the possible need for redundancy.

In recent months, Tesco has faced profit warnings and a fall in its market share for the first time. This has forced the business to look more carefully at its market position and to take account of new customer patterns and shopping habits.

Conversely, improved trading conditions may make it necessary to take on new staff and to alter the responsibilities of existing employees. Changes like this are likely to result in uncertainty, disappointment and friction.

Innovation

If the business is innovative in its market, it may develop new products that result in changes in the processes it uses or the markets it supplies. This is particularly evident in sectors such as pharmaceuticals, electronics and communications, where the pace of change is very rapid. Companies such as Sony and Dyson continually innovate and change their product base in order to stimulate new demand. For Dyson this may involve a relatively small electronic adaptation of a new colour used for the vacuum cleaner, to signal a new model; for Sony it is likely to involve ground-breaking new technology in products such as its Play Stations.

External change

Globalisation

One of the most significant contributors to the change faced by all businesses in recent years is that of globalisation. The growth of China and India as major industrial nations has had huge implications for the business world. These countries are now significant both in terms of their production and consumption. Their low-cost labour also makes them attractive to businesses in the developed countries for outsourcing or relocation. The improvements in communication and the growth of cheap air travel bring these countries increasingly closer to the rest of the business world. Businesses in the developed world need to find markets where they can maintain an advantage over lower-cost producers. As these newly industrialised countries develop and increase their capabilities, this is becoming increasingly difficult.

> **Key term**
>
> **Globalisation:** the growth of the world so that it can be viewed as a whole place rather than a number of separate countries. The result for business is increased interdependence and the ability to trade in the world as if it were one market.

Environment

Environmental issues are becoming an increasingly important factor in the market, forcing changes on business either because of dwindling and expensive fossil fuel supplies or because of the threat of global warming and carbon emissions. Consumers now expect businesses to make major changes in their products and production because of the perceived threats to the planet; these changes may be to do with packaging, energy efficiency, recycling or production methods. Failure to respond may have dramatic consequences for future demand levels for some businesses. Electricity providers such as EDF Energy now provide 'green' tariffs, where the electricity is generated by renewable sources to meet a demand for environmentally friendly products from customers who want to reduce their carbon footprint.

The desire for renewable energy will bring great change to the energy industry

Technology

The speed of technological change has become increasingly rapid in recent years. New products, production methods and changes in information technology are increasingly significant factors in changing the business environment. Any business failing to take account of such changes is likely to find difficulty in maintaining success and profitability, particularly in the long term. An example of this can be found in the market for mobile phones, where consumers want to change their handset at regular intervals to take advantage of new features and styles.

Customer base

The customer base itself may change. There may be a change in its composition; for example, the age and ethnic distribution of the UK population has changed greatly throughout its history and is continuing to change as eastern European countries enter the EU and their workers enter the UK workforce. Supermarkets in Coventry and elsewhere in the West Midlands now sell a range of products for the Polish customers who have recently settled in the area.

At the same time, the demands of the population may also change, forcing business to react, as is the case with the growth in demand for exotic fruits and vegetables. This has forced the major supermarkets such as Sainsbury's and Tesco to stock a wide range of these items, where demand is growing rapidly and profit margins are high.

Economy

The economic situation and the stage of the economic cycle (see **Chapter 19**) in the UK and world economy may also inflict change on a business. A downturn in economic activity will force a business to look at its markets and finances, and to take steps to minimise any adverse effects. Globalisation also has an impact here because businesses are increasingly dependent on international markets, both for supplies and for customers.

Competition

Businesses may also have to change in response to competition and once again globalisation makes this a more serious threat; any business now faces competition on a worldwide basis. Businesses need to be aware of the actions of their competitors, and must introduce measures to secure their market share. Marks & Spencer's failure to take account of the growth of competition from retailers like Next, Topshop and Zara and to change its product range accordingly, had a serious impact on it profits in recent years. Businesses that have been market leaders can sometimes feel that they do not need to change. This may make a fall in their market share more disastrous and difficult to cope with. Small supermarket and convenience stores have responded to the threat of competition from larger chains by satisfying the needs of a local market. They have also diversified into areas such as utility bill payments and parcel collection to attract customers to their stores.

Government

The government and its policies can also impose change on businesses. This is most likely to come in the form of new legislation, either at a national or local level. For example, the government has recently increased maternity leave to one year. Changes in the rights to paternity and maternity leave may force a business to reorganise its deployment of staff. The government's policy on taxation may have a significant impact on the financial situation of the business, and could create a need for financial stringency and redundancy.

Management change models

Lewin's 3-step change management model

This model helps to explain the basic method of putting change management into operation. Its three steps are:

1. Unfreeze: this involves trying to remove the forces that are creating inertia in the business by putting forward new ideas and persuading people of the need for change.
2. Transition: at this stage, management will develop new ideas either in the production process or organisation of the business. This stage may create uncertainty and confusion in the business.
3. Freeze: at this stage, the business needs to ensure that the new processes are reinforced; otherwise there might be a tendency to revert to the 'old' methods.

The Lewin model is a straightforward one to use when managing change, whether the changes are strategic or tactical. It makes it possible for the manger to identify the problems and see where change is needed. It also benefits from including the workforce in the process.

McKinsey's 7-S model

This is a model that can be used to assess internal change in a business. The model can help management identify where there is need for change in the business; it can be used in any situation of change including growth, mergers, organisational change, new management and new working processes. For success, a business needs to make sure that all seven components are aligned.

The 7S framework is made up of:

- Strategy
- Skills
- Structure
- Style
- Systems
- Staff
- With an overall goal of shared values by using all elements together

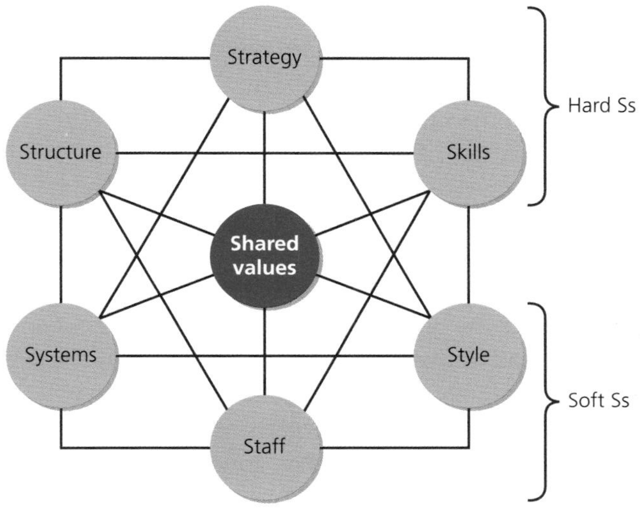

Figure 22.1 McKinsey's 7-S model

The objective of the model is to improve business performance, look carefully at the effects of change in all areas and to show how best to put change into operation with effective change management.

Kotter's 8-step change model

This model helps managers to understand and manage change in a business; each stage helps to show people's response to change and shows the process from seeing the need and then changing.

The 8 stages are:

1. Increase urgency: encourage people to make changes.
2. Build the team for change: put in people who have commitment to change and a range of skills.
3. Have a vision: establish a vision of what is to be achieved.

4 Communicate: use communication to get everyone to accept the change, involving as many people as possible in the changes.
5 Empower action: remove anything that will stop the change happening. Make sure that any progress is recognised and rewarded.
6 Create short-term wins: don't expect to be able to do everything immediately. Set achievable goals.
7 Don't let up: keep up the momentum
8 Make the change stick: don't let things go back to what they were because of lack of management of the change or control.

Management of change

The management of change is likely to be one of the most difficult roles facing managers or owners of a business. Human nature generally prefers stability and is suspicious of change. However, change in any environment is inevitable and continuous, and with forethought, planning and consideration for the feelings of others, change can be introduced effectively. Unfortunately, there are numerous examples of the opposite scenario; for instance, when workers read in the media about the closure of their factory and forthcoming redundancies rather than being informed of it by management, it is obvious that the management of change has gone badly wrong.

Anticipated change

Experienced managers may be able to anticipate changes in some areas of the business and respond in ways that minimise the adverse effects. For example, if a business has an efficient market research and forecasting department, it may be possible to anticipate a fall in demand and develop a new product or find a new market. Similarly, if labour shortages are expected, the business can begin to train new workers or offer training schemes to existing staff. This sort of change is referred to as anticipated change. A business should always be in a state of incremental change where managers are responding to the day-to-day changes in their trading environment. The benefits of incremental change are that its effects are less dramatic and staff can contribute to its introduction; employees are therefore less likely to be unsettled by it, and its implementation is likely to be smoother.

Unfortunately, not all change can be anticipated. Events such as the terrorist attacks in New York in 2001 and London in 2005 can create major problems for a business. In these cases tourism and travel businesses, such as major transatlantic airlines, were particularly badly affected in the aftermath to both events. Similarly, the discovery of horsemeat in the UK supply chain created major problems for supermarkets like Tesco, who found that its sales in all product areas were affected by its involvement in the scandal.

Unanticipated and catastrophic or crisis change

Although the business has no control over unanticipated or catastrophic change such as a terrorist attack like 9/11 or a natural disaster such as the Japanese tsunami, it needs to have contingency plans for worst-case scenarios.

Contingency plans to deal with catastrophic change are likely to be the responsibility of a small department. For example, the debate on childhood obesity in the UK has had a huge impact on the catering industry, with significant falls in demand for products like burgers and pizzas. McCain, the food company, used its contingency planning to fight back when there was bad publicity about the quantity of chips that children in the UK were eating. McCain encouraged discussion and debate to gain press coverage and give them the opportunity to emphasise the low-fat aspects of many of their products. McDonald's has also had to look closely at the range of products it offers, both in the USA and the UK, in response to consumer interest in healthy eating.

In doing this, both businesses managed to gain valuable publicity from numerous articles and features where their name was mentioned. Specialist companies working in contingency management encourage businesses to be ready to respond to criticism in an immediate and positive manner, exactly like the approach taken by McCain.

Strategic, tactical and operational change

Change may occur as a natural part of the operation of the business. The setting of strategic and tactical objectives by management will mean that change has to occur at a business and departmental level. This will require operational changes in the way the business is run on a day-to-day basis. (See **Chapter 46**.)

Factors for successfully managing change

The effective management of change in any business situation will depend on the extent to which the managers have been successful in managing the following.

Managers need to have created an environment of mutual trust between themselves and their employees. If either group feels that their credibility or efforts are being undermined by the other, the introduction of change is unlikely to go smoothly. Suspicion is counter-productive in any working relationship and will almost certainly create a climate where change results in difficulties in managing the business.

Communication is vital to any process of change. If the communication is timely, clear and truthful, appropriately delivered and gives a complete picture, it stands a much better chance of receiving a positive hearing. It is never going to be possible to counter all resistance to change, but if employees feel that management are being honest with them, a source of friction is removed, giving change a better chance of success.

In a fast-moving business which has experienced change many times, employees will become used to change, realise its necessity and view it as less threatening. It will always be more difficult to introduce change to a business that has remained static over a long period of time. For many years, companies such as Wedgwood and other pottery businesses resisted change because they thought the consumer wanted a traditional product. This resulted in inefficiency and a lack of investment. When the need for change became imperative, it was difficult to introduce the changes needed because of the resistance of the workforce.

The inclusion of employees in the process of change is always more likely to give a successful outcome. They will feel that they have 'ownership' of the changes and they may suggest helpful ideas. Participation often allows the changes to go further than management would have dared to consider if they were acting by themselves.

Tips and techniques

This is an example of the work of Mayo (see **Chapter 47**). If you can refer to different areas of business theory in your answers, it will show that you are aware of different aspects of a topic.

Whenever employees become involved in the process of change, management need to be prepared to listen to them and they must also be willing to compromise if the requests are appropriate and sensible. Making small changes to a plan to satisfy the concern of employees will often make it possible to introduce the much bigger changes.

Above all, management needs to have a clear strategic plan of the process for change which they must be able to explain and justify to those involved in its implementation.

Change within the business

For change to be successful, management and employees need to work together and co-operate at every stage of the process. There are many ways in which this atmosphere can be created and encouraged in the workplace by both groups. Some situations will involve managers and employees, but others will involve outside agencies such as unions and government bodies. If any of these situations does not exist, it will create a barrier to change which will hold back the growth of the business.

Effects of motivation and leadership on change within a business

Most of these measures will have been covered elsewhere in this book. See **Chapters 46** and **47**.

Teamwork

The use of teamwork in the workplace has expanded greatly since the 1980s, particularly with the introduction of Japanese work practices into UK industry. Making groups of workers responsible for particular tasks, allowing job sharing and encouraging worker participation in development with Kaizen methods (see **Chapter 68**) all make workers more involved in and more responsible for the final output of the business.

Co-operation

Enlightened management should understand that a well-motivated workforce will be more likely to work effectively in a climate of co-operation. There are many ways of motivating workers (see **Chapter 47**). It is important to ensure that the motivation used is appropriate for the circumstances and the group of people involved; this is where management skills are vital. To use motivation effectively, managers need to know and understand employees, to engender a spirit of trust at work and to create good two-way communication channels.

Organisational culture

An organisational culture where issues relating to change are considered to be important is likely to be one in which it is easier to introduce change. The atmosphere is likely to be one of co-operation and a common understanding of the needs of the business. This does not mean that the introduction of change will be easy; problems will inevitably be raised. What it does mean, however, is that there will be an ethos and culture that makes it possible to discuss problems and deal with them to mitigate their adverse effects wherever possible.

Role of employer/employee relations

Every business will have a different way of managing the relationship between employer and employee. These relationships will change over time through changes in the law, employment practices and social trends. Whatever the system, the processes should be clearly understood and trusted by all parties.

Individual relations

On a day-to-day basis, communication between management and workers on an individual level is vitally important. The more distant individual workers are from their managers, the more likely it is that problems will arise. Management need to know about the situations that their employees face in their jobs, and workers need to realise that managers have many different constraints that affect their actions. If there is mutual understanding and a climate in which people can discuss their roles and the situations they face, the need for change will be better understood and accepted, albeit reluctantly.

Collective relations: trade unions

At a collective level, many businesses have workers who are members of trade unions. The role of trade unions and the legislation which governs them is covered in **Chapters 48** and **49**. This situation has changed considerably since the 1980s when the then Prime Minister Margaret Thatcher introduced a wide range of legislation to reduce the power of the unions. At the time, this caused increased tensions in a number of industries, notably with the National Union of Mineworkers, but after the initial conflicts of opinion the situation has improved greatly. The UK now has a much better record on industrial relations than was previously the case. Nevertheless, any introduction of change where the workforce is unionised should include union representatives in their discussions from the outset.

The role of the trade union is ultimately to protect the rights of their members. This will often put them in conflict with management, particularly if planned changes will result in redundancy or the reduction of workers' rights. This sort of conflict has been experienced at London Underground. It has suffered a number of crippling strikes as a result of changes in workers' rights and the move to close ticket offices at underground stations.

Sometimes a more sympathetic approach to the management of change might help avert a strike, but at other times action takes place despite the best efforts of management. In these circumstances, outside, independent help is needed.

As a result of the trade union legislation of the 1980s and the entrance to the UK economy of Japanese businesses and their work practices, many businesses started to introduce single union agreements for their workers. A single union agreement means that workers and management will agree on one union that will represent any worker who wishes to belong to a union. Before this, many large businesses often found themselves in situations where change had to be agreed with a number of unions representing different groups of workers, often with different views on the proposed changes. It was sometimes the case that there was more disagreement between different unions than between management and workers. The single union deal makes negotiation easier and reduces the conflict in any situation of change. Toyota in Derby has operated such a scheme since first coming to the area. Other businesses have moved into different schemes to avoid conflict and confrontation.

No-strike deals

A number of businesses have adopted no-strike deals with their employees in return for certain benefits and guarantees. This type of system is in place at the Toshiba factory in the UK. For obvious reasons the trade union movement is not happy with these agreements, and complains that they put too much power in the hands of management. On the other hand, they often encourage positive discussion and negotiation, rather than forcing groups into conflict situations.

Arbitration

No-strike agreements often use a system of pendulum arbitration. In such a system an independent arbitrator is appointed to help in the negotiation of agreements where the two sides are in conflict. The arbitrator will in the final instance make a straight choice between the different positions. Those who support pendulum arbitration feel that it makes workers and management more realistic and aware of the opposing group's view. Those who oppose it feel that it creates a climate of winners and losers, which is not good for relations between managers and workers.

ACAS (Advisory, Conciliation and Arbitration Service)

During an industrial dispute, if employers and employees have reached a stalemate situation or have stopped talking, ACAS can be called in to help them in reaching a compromise situation. As its name suggests, the organisation will try to bring the two sides together and mediate in order to reach an acceptable conclusion for both groups. It will try to find common ground and move groups to a closer and more realistic stance, using trained negotiators.

Key term

Conciliation: the act of bringing parties together with an independent conciliator to find common ground and a solution to the problem. It differs from arbitration, in that it has no legal standing. Arbitration is a legal process outside the courts where both parties are bound by the decision of the arbitrator.

As well as being involved in resolving disputes, ACAS also produces a wide range of resources to help managers avoid the need for their services. They would prefer to be involved by giving assistance before a situation of conflict arises.

New working practices

In the past 20 years there have been a number of changes in employment practices, some of which have been introduced as a result of pressure from workers and others to satisfy the demands of management. Much of the pressure has come as a result of the changing pattern of family life and particularly the changes in the retail sector. Twenty-four-hour opening and Sunday working have changed the working lives of many people, and such changes require consultation and co-operation to ensure that they can be introduced successfully and operate effectively.

Flexible working is now common in many businesses. This may be a situation where each employee is allowed to vary the hours they work as long as they are in the office for certain core times; for example, an employee may work longer days without taking lunch-hours, but then take time off at the end of the day. This is usually called flexitime. In other cases, workers may be allowed to work from home for some part of the week; this practice is particularly useful for parents with young children, but its use is increasingly widespread, especially in IT-based firms. Reuters, the news agency, have found that allowing some home-working makes it easier for it to retain qualified and experienced staff, because workers enjoy the flexibility. Both of these systems are usually introduced in response to employee pressure, and the change is usually welcome. However, zero hours contracts are less popular with workers. This is a situation where the workload varies throughout the year or week, and workers are only called into work when they are required. The result is uncertainty about earnings in any particular time period. This is rarely a welcome change for the workforce.

Further sources

www.acas.org.uk
www.gov.je: The A–Z of work
www.flexibility.co.uk
www.direct.gov.uk/employees

Your turn

Multiple-choice questions

1 A supermarket has a 28 per cent share of a market where sales are £4 million. What are the supermarket's sales?
A 1 million
B £1.12 million
C £3.57 million
D 30.38 million. *(1)*

2 Changes in the economic cycle might create the need for management of change. Which of the following is not a stage in the economic cycle?
A Recession
B Boom
C Growth
D Saturation. *(1)*

Revision questions

1 Explain the term 'globalisation'. *(2)*
2 Explain what is meant by 'conciliation' in industrial relations. *(2)*
3 Explain the difference between anticipated and catastrophic change. *(4)*
4 Explain the term 'innovation'. *(2)*
Total *(10)*

Case study

Tesco

For many years Tesco has dominated the supermarket sector in the UK, with the largest market share in a seemingly ever-growing market. However, the situation has changed considerably in the last few months. In 2014, Tesco's market share fell to 28.7 per cent, its lowest level for over ten years. At the same time, possibly as a result of the recession, growth in the supermarket sector started to slow.

Over the past 20 years Tesco has bought up land around the UK with a view to building large out-of-town supermarkets. It now seems that the customer has fallen out of love with the big weekly supermarket shop at a superstore, preferring instead to shop at smaller stores on a more regular basis. The cost of fuel, the recession and the appearance of low-cost supermarkets like Aldi and Lidl, in the UK have all contributed to this change, a change that Tesco does not seem to have anticipated.

This may mean that Tesco will have to sell off some of its land holdings, with the possibility of selling them at a loss. This may mean other future problems, together with consequent shareholder dissatisfaction, will face Dave Lewis the new CEO in the near future. Many had become convinced that Tesco could do no wrong; the current situation shows that there are no certainties in the business world.

The following article on the change in shopping habits, which appeared in the *Guardian*, highlights current problems facing supermarkets:

> Supermarkets' seven problems
>
> Discounters
>
> Customers are shopping around more to save money. German chains Aldi and Lidl now control 8.3% of the £175bn UK grocery market, up from 6.7% a year ago, with sales growing at up to 30% a year. Major supermarkets are being forced to cut prices to keep customers. Industry research body IGD predicts that sales at discounters will double in the next five year.
>
> Convenience stores
>
> Shoppers are deserting big edge-of-town stores, preferring to shop little, local and often. IGD forecasts that sales in small neighbourhood stores will increase 31%, to 49bn, by 2019.

Eating out

Eating out is no longer an occasional treat, but a way of life, with breakfast on the go, lunch in a coffee shop and takeaways for dinner. Every pound spent in those establishments means less cash in supermarket tills.

Online

All the major supermarkets are having to invest in costly home deliveries or 'click and collect' services. Online grocery sales are up 17% on last year and now account for £1 of every £20 spent on food. Fashion sales – once a big profit centre for out-of-town grocers – are also shifting online.

Big stores

Nearly 75% of groceries are still bought in large supermarkets, but they're in decline; analysts say sales through big stores are down 10% on last year. Tesco is bringing in other retailers, opening restaurants and soft play areas to fill unwanted space and has started mothballing unwanted stores.

Waste reduction

Environmental concerns and financial worries have got Britons shopping more carefully to cut down on waste. The volume of food sold is also declining as people consume fewer calories. Household food waste dived by a fifth between 2007 and 2012, saving UK consumers almost £13bn, according to government-backed waste reduction quango Wrap. But we still throw away more than 7m tonnes of food and drink a year.

Slowing inflation

Food price rises are virtually zero – which hits sales growth. The cost of fresh produce is down about 5% this year as the result of good harvests. Potato prices are down 20%, according to Sainsbury's. Changes in exchange rates and cheaper fuel prices have also helped reduce the cost of goods.

Source: the *Guardian*, Tuesday 2 October 2014, Sarah Butler.

1 Analyse one problem that Dave Lewis is facing at present. *(4)*

2 Evaluate the threats that Aldi and Lidl pose for Tesco. *(9)*

3 Evaluate the alternatives available to Tesco's management in dealing with the changes in its market situation. *(15)*

4 Discuss how Tesco management could use change management to address the problems of slowing growth and new competition. *(15)*

Total *(43)*

Chapter 23

Accounting and finance objectives and strategy

Year 2

A Level students must know all of the content in this chapter.

This chapter is not applicable for AS students.

Accounting and finance objectives

All businesses from inception and throughout their existence ought to have some sort of financial objectives.

For a new business the financial objective will often simply be to survive, ensuring it has sufficient funds to stay in business and produce the goods or services required. It may quickly, depending upon the nature of the market it is operating in, move on to achieving 'break even' and beyond to a specific level of profit, or share of the market.

Regardless of what kind of objective the business sets itself, a financial consideration will have to be in place.

Ensuring the business has sufficient working capital, enough cash to keep the business operating, will be vital. Even businesses that have been in existence for a long time need to make sure they have enough cash to keep the business operational. In 2014, two Formula 1 teams went into administration due to a lack of cash required to be able to keep on trading and racing.

The significance of having accounting and financial objectives is the fundamental way of measuring the performance of a business. The level of profit or loss may be an obvious indicator of success or failure. It is something many of the stakeholders of a business will look at. By having financial objectives and the reports from the income statement and balance sheet allows the business to see where the main problems may be and therefore enables the business to prioritise its strategies to improve the situation.

These financial objectives are used by the various stakeholders to measure the performance of the business and can help management to judge the progress of the business in terms of meeting its targets within a given period of time. Having such objectives also allows those within the business to judge its performance when compared to others within the same market (benchmark). Potential investors will want to see how the business is performing prior to investing. Similarly, potential creditors will want to judge whether the business is performing sufficiently well in order to pay back any borrowing. These objectives can also be used to compare the performance of the business over time, whether to last year's results or over a longer or shorter period of time.

Comparing the financial results of the business may also allow the management to alter its financial strategy in order to put the business on a better course and, if successful, bring it closer to achieving its objectives.

However, care needs to be taken when making financial comparisons:

- Are financial comparisons being made in the same way to avoid bias or any form of misrepresentation as it was alleged Tesco may have done in 2014 (see **Chapter 22**).
- Are assets of the business valued in the same manner?
- Have allowances been made for either depreciation or appreciation (see **Chapter 35**)?
- Financial results are just figures and do not necessarily offer any indication on why the figures are as stated.

- There is also no indication as to the state of the economy; whether it is favourable or unfavourable for trading.

Only by being aware of the points above and ensuring a business has clear accounting and financial objectives can the business operate in such a manner that it can ensure there is sufficient accountability to the stakeholders of that business.

Tips and techniques

It is always worth noting any special circumstances before making judgements when comparing one year of financial data with another. There may be specific external factors that impinge upon the financial situation within a business. These may be stated within the case study, which you need to look out for.

Setting financial objectives

When setting financial objectives it is important to note the following:

- The legal status and size of the business: the level of profit which is set for a plc may be substantially different from that of a sole trader.
- The other objectives of the business: whether it is a production target or a marketing target, all will have a financial implication for the business.
- In almost all instances a budget will have been set and one which ought to 'fit' with any financial objectives set.
- The state of the economy: a growing economy, as in 2014, will make it easier to achieve financial targets or objectives than if the economy is in recession.
- The level of competition within the market in which the business operates: a highly competitive market may mean that prices have to be lower in order to compete and consequently profit margins may be lower, which in turn will affect the ability of a business to achieve a higher financial target.
- The government of the day: the government may encourage or discourage business as part of its political agenda. The level of taxation imposed upon business will impinge upon the ability to achieve any financial target set, or even the size of the target in the first place.
- The work of the Monetary Policy Committee (MPC): the MPC sets the level of interest rates that govern the economy. In turn, this rate will affect a business in terms of borrowing money, calculating certain financial ratios (ROCE), interest cover and the ability of a business to pay back any 'trade and payables' (creditors).
- Legislation may also affect the financial target set, or the ability of a business to meet its financial targets/objectives.
- Assuming any financial statements are set within the agreed guidelines for this country (see Accounting concepts in **Chapter 25**).
- That the financial information provided is timely to support any decision making within the business.

It is therefore essential that a business is able to see the value of having accounting and financial objectives, having noted the important factors listed above and their effects on a business and its ability to measure and compare in an accurate manner.

The financial objectives must, as for all objectives, be measurable, realistic and reliable to be of benefit to the business.

Tips and techniques

A variety of terms will be used within the next few chapters relating to accounting and finance. It is important to try and utilise the appropriate terminology wherever possible.

However, there will be instances when there is more than one term that can be used to explain or name a particular concept. It is therefore important to be aware of this to avoid being 'thrown 'by this in an examination question if a slightly different term is used. With this in mind, reference will be made to financial data and information, which is the same as referring to the 'accounts' of a business.

A vital part of all businesses is the financial information and the financial objectives that are set.

From the financial objectives and data, a stakeholder can ascertain a wealth of information which is useful for many reasons:

- Members of the board of directors or managers of the business will use the financial information to make important decisions and consequently plan for the future by setting objectives for the business.
- Prospective shareholders/investors will look at the financial information contained in the accounts of the business to decide whether to invest in the business.

- Banks will look at the accounts of a business to check if the business is able to afford the repayments if money is borrowed, or even whether the business ought to be lent the money in the first place. The banks can also look at the financial data and compare it with the objectives set by the business.
- Potential or existing suppliers may use the financial information and financial objectives of a business in order to assess whether it is 'safe' to trade with in terms of judging its ability to pay for any supplies provided.
- Directors or managers will use the accounts as a measure of success (or failure) in terms of how profitable the business is, assuming that is one of the objectives of the business or organisation.
- Financial information can be used to look at the amount of cash flowing in and out of the business in order to rectify any financial cash flow problem.
- There is a legal requirement to provide accounts depending upon the legal status of the business.
- Issuing such accounts is often referred to as the 'disclosure requirement'.
- Financial information is often looked at by competitors in an attempt to assess how a particular business is performing in comparison to itself.
- The state of the accounts may even be used by other businesses within the same industry as a 'benchmark'.

Given the large number of uses and interested stakeholders in the financial information of a business, it is essential that such information is accurate. To ensure this, there are several 'principles' that are used when formulating the financial accounts (see **Chapter 25**).

Setting clear financial objectives allows the business or stakeholders to:

- have targets to aim for.
- assess/monitor the progress of the business in meeting these objectives.
- have access to information that sets out the financial situation of the business.
- ensure the departments within the business understand the financial constraints it may face.
- provide the employees and trade unions with the financial objectives and therefore they will have a better understanding of what the business is trying to achieve.
- formulate their own departmental objectives in light of the financial situation. For example, the marketing department can plan its strategy knowing what the financial situation is and therefore be realistic in its targets and strategies.
- plan expenditure in a realistic manner. Investments can be planned to 'fit' within the financial situation of the business.
- assess the business in terms of its liquidity, via ratios (see **Chapter 36**).
- monitor and assess the likely impact of any changes within the economy that may impinge upon the objectives of the business.

There will of course need to be a clear link between the overall objectives of the business and the financial objectives to ensure compatibility.

Like all other information that is collected by a business, such information is not used in isolation. The accounts department will need to liaise with the other departments within the business in order to collect all the required data. Similarly, the production department will need the help of the accounts department in order to check that the necessary funds are available to finance any additional production or pay rises to employees.

As the accounts are 'used' by so many stakeholders, there are occasions when the figures are presented in a 'favourable' light. Some may suggest that the figures presented are massaged in order to show the business in the best possible manner. However, such 'window dressing' must be undertaken within the principles and regulations related to the collection and presentation of accounts (see **Chapter 25**). Window dressing may occur to:

- encourage shareholders to continue to hold or purchase more shares.
- encourage potential shareholders to buy its shares and thus enhancing the value of the shares and therefore the value of the business.
- suggest the business is able to borrow money.
- indicate that the business is able to repay any potential loans.
- deter or attract takeover bids.
- prevent employees from being concerned about the long-term security of employment.

All the above are legitimate reasons for wanting to create a favourable impression of the business. However, adhering to the principles of accounting is essential and is more important than presenting the business in a favourable light, especially when the favourable light might be inaccurate.

Your turn

Revision questions

1 Analyse how any two stakeholders of a business may find the business's financial information useful. *(4)*

2 Explain two reasons why a business may want to 'window dress' its accounts. *(4)*

3 Explain two reasons why financial objectives are set. *(4)*

Total *(12)*

Chapter 24

Sources of finance

AS / Year 1

Both AS and A Level students must know all of the content in this chapter.

When determining strategy, finance is a key business resource and sources of finance must be carefully considered. For example, imagine that a private limited company, making sports equipment, is operating from an old factory and wants to raise £1 million for a major new product launch. The board of directors have to consider how to raise it. If the company takes out a ten-year loan, it is committing itself to repayments over a substantial period of time and there is obviously an opportunity cost to these payments (e.g. the amounts involved could be spent on something else such as further product development). If the board is considering the issue of more shares, then there will be reduced control over future decisions since shareholders are entitled to a vote. This issue (unlike the interest payments) will not simply last for ten years but will exist for as long as the company continues to trade – as will the expectation of dividend payments. If there is a discussion about 'going public' then there are other issues as well as control to discuss; not least that if the shares are bought by financial institutions, these will tend to have a short-term focus on share value and dividends rather than long-term growth. As shareholders, these organisations will vote for the directors most likely to achieve these short-term objectives and therefore will have a major influence on company strategy.

The different types of sources of finance have different implications for a business, and the short-term finance needed for the day-to-day running of the business (working capital) will not be raised in the same way as the finance required for growth. Finance for growth will be needed for several years, so how a business decides to finance each stage of its development makes a great deal of difference.

Key term

Working capital: short-term finance required for the day-to-day running of a business.

Tips and techniques

At A Level it is essential not only to know and understand the different sources of finance, but to be able to analyse and evaluate their strategic implications as well.

Short-, medium- and long-term finance

A business might originally have been started using the owners' own capital. Apart from the owners' own funds, there is a variety of sources of finance available. These sources can be short term, medium term or long term.

Short-term finance

Short-term finance (working capital) is needed for the day-to-day running of a business, and is usually for a period of up to three years. In order to understand short-term finance, it is necessary to understand the concept of cashflow (see **Chapter 31**). There must be a sufficient inflow of cash (revenue) to meet cash outflows (bills, wages, etc.). If this is not the case, it has a cashflow problem and so needs short-term finance to overcome this.

Key term

Cashflow: a business needs sufficient inflows of cash to finance its day-to-day outgoings (e.g. wages and interest repayments); if cash receipts are insufficient, the business is said to have a cashflow problem.

When considering the sources of short-term finance, an obvious source is a bank. All of the commercial (high-street) banks offer various methods of finance for businesses.

Overdraft

There are two types of bank account: deposit accounts (also known as savings accounts), in which money deposited earns interest; and current accounts, which are used to make and receive payments. A debit card is used with a current account.

A deposit account usually requires a period of notice before funds can be withdrawn, and is therefore not suitable for a business to use to make payments. With a current account, funds can be 'drawn' (i.e. taken out) whenever it is necessary. Current accounts therefore tend to earn less interest than savings accounts, and some pay no interest at all.

When an overdraft is granted, no money is actually credited to the current account, but the business is allowed to run the account down to zero and then a further pre-arranged amount can be withdrawn, hence the term 'overdrawn'.

It is usual for a bank to permit a certain level of overdraft when a current account is opened. If a business wants a larger overdraft, it has to negotiate one, for which it may be charged an arrangement fee. If it fails to do this and simply tries to overdraw more than allowed, the bank may refuse to release the money and any attempted payment written will not be paid. The business will then not be able to make its payments, which could damage its reputation as a customer of the bank.

Interest on an overdraft is only paid on the amount actually overdrawn. If the overdraft that has been granted by the bank is for £2,000 and the business only uses £1,500 of it, the interest is only charged on this lower amount and not on the full amount of the overdraft. If a business quickly returns its current account to a credit balance, it will not have to pay much interest.

An overdraft is therefore a safety net for a business; it should not be used for the purchase of capital items such as computers or photocopiers.

Loan

Another source of finance available from a bank is a loan. Short-term loans tend to be used to buy specific pieces of equipment or to purchase a particular consignment of raw materials in order to fulfil a contract.

A separate account (for the amount of the loan) is opened and the full amount is credited to the business's current account. When repayments are made, they are taken from the business's current account and paid into the loan account. This reduces the amount of the loan that is outstanding, and this continues until the balance owing on the loan account falls to zero (i.e. the loan is repaid).

A loan is not a safety net in the same way as an overdraft. There is little point in a business borrowing money in the form of a loan and keeping it in its current account 'just in case anything happens', because this would mean paying interest on funds that it was not using.

There is another important difference between an overdraft and a loan. If a business exceeds its overdraft limit, the bank has the right to demand the whole amount back at once. This cannot happen with a loan. The loan is granted for a particular period of time and can only be demanded back by the bank if the business fails to pay the interest due.

It is sometimes asked why a business would want to take out a loan and pay the full amount of interest when it could negotiate an overdraft and only pay for the amount of money actually used. The answer lies in the concept of an overdraft as a safety net.

An overdraft should not be used for the purchase of capital items such as vehicles or office equipment. Suppose a business plans to expand. It is granted an overdraft and uses it for purchasing capital items such as computers. Assume that it does indeed sell a lot of extra products. If these are sold on credit, it will promptly run into a cashflow problem and have to ask for an even greater overdraft. The bank will not regard this as financially responsible. If this extra overdraft is granted, it will be at a high rate of interest.

It is also likely that the amount of interest payable on an overdraft will be higher than the amount charged on a loan. A business therefore needs to use its short-term finance in the proper manner.

Factors influencing a bank's decision to lend

When deciding whether or not to lend, a bank will consider the following factors:

- what the finance is to be used for
- the company's past trading record, or the business proposal if it is a new business
- the type of product being sold – is it a luxury purchase or one that consumers will always require?

- the business's current financial position, including existing debts. What does it already owe? Who has 'first call' on the business's revenue?
- financial projections – revenue, profit, cashflow, etc. The preparation of a business plan is essential.
- the nature of the market and forecasts of sales. Is the market growing or shrinking? At what rate?
- the role and experience of the business's managers. Are they steering the firm in the right way, so that it will be profitable and generate the returns to repay any money borrowed?

In addition to these considerations, the bank will want to know what sort of security will be offered by the business: that is, what can be offered if the business becomes unable to pay back the money borrowed. This may not be so important with a small overdraft or a loan, but it becomes important when large sums of money are lent for long periods of time. The bank may want to take possession of the title deeds to the business's factory or office as security. These deeds are the documents that give legal ownership to a particular piece of land, perhaps the land that the factory or office is built upon. If the business fails to repay the loan, the bank (as holder of the deeds) is legally entitled to sell the factory or office in order to recover any amount outstanding on the loan.

> **Key term**
>
> **Security**: something that acts as assurance to a lender that it will receive its money if a business is unable to pay back money it has borrowed.

Trade credit

This means making use of an opportunity offered to defer payment to a supplier. For example, a business called Soundrive makes high-quality audio equipment for luxury cars, some of which it sells to a company called Maximotors. It receives the majority of its components from a firm called Wireright. It assembles these components immediately into finished products, delivers them and receives payment one month later.

Wireright allows a six-week period of trade credit to all its customers. Soundrive would therefore be foolish to pay for the components as soon as they are delivered. If it does not have to pay immediately, this means that it can wait until it receives payment from Maximotors, and so use the funds it would have used to pay Wireright for other purposes in the meantime. Thus, Soundrive's use of trade credit is a form of short-term finance, one that does not incur any interest charges.

Why would Wireright offer this sort of credit period? Surely it wants its money as soon as possible; after all, it has its own debts to pay. The answer is that it is common business practice, and any business not offering trade credit and insisting on immediate payment is likely to find itself at a considerable disadvantage when marketing its products. If trade credit is offered, a business should use it.

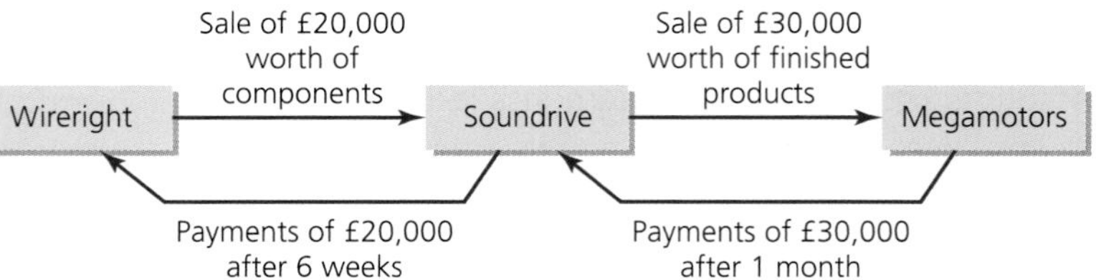

Figure 24.1 The use of trade credit means that Soundrive has £20,000 worth of finance to use, as necessary, for two weeks

Factoring

This means that a business sells its debts to raise finance. Debt often takes the form of an 'IOU'. This debt can be sold to a factoring company. Specialist companies exist for this, although most banks offer factoring services. The factoring company will offer a certain percentage of the debt to the business that needs the funds immediately and will now legally own the debt. When the payment becomes due, the factor collects the debt, not the original company. The advantage to the firm selling the debt is that it receives most of the finance at once, instead of having to wait for it. On the other hand, the drawback is that it has lost a percentage of the money it is owed.

Hire-purchase

Hire-purchase is a method of paying for an item in instalments over a period of months or years. As the name implies, the item is being hired by the business while the payments are being made, and does not actually become the business's property (i.e. is not actually 'purchased') until the last payment is made. Like all forms of credit, hire-purchase has the advantage that a large sum of money does not have to be found all at once, and the repayments can be spread over a period of time.

This method of finance can certainly help improve cashflow, but it means that at the end of the contract, more money will have been paid out than if the business had paid cash in the first place.

Medium-term finance

Medium-term finance is normally for a period of between three and ten years. The most likely purposes for obtaining medium-term finance are to:

- replace expensive pieces of equipment that have broken down or become out of date
- expand; if a business decides on the objective of growth, it will need larger premises, more equipment or more modern machinery
- convert a business's persistent overdraft into a formal medium-term loan; the overdraft will then be cleared and, although a loan will have been created, this means that the overdraft can then achieve its proper purpose, as a safety net for cash-flow problems.

Various different forms of medium-term finance are available to a business.

Medium-term loan

As is the case with a short-term loan, an agreed amount is credited to the business's current account. For a medium-term loan (and indeed a long-term loan), the rate of interest charged by the bank is particularly important. Suppose that Soundrive wants a loan to finance some new technology in order to expand. The amount of interest payable on a medium-term loan depends on several factors:

- how much is borrowed
- how long the money is wanted for
- the security that is provided.

Soundrive has the option to choose either a variable rate or a fixed-rate loan. The former means that the amount of interest which Soundrive pays varies, according to the Bank of England's decisions on interest rates. A fixed-rate loan has the advantage of certainty: if Soundrive takes out a fixed-rate loan, then those running the business will know what the repayment costs are going to be. This will make financial planning easier. Soundrive will not be financially disrupted by a rise in interest rates.

The disadvantage of a fixed-rate loan is that if rates fall, Soundrive still has to pay the rate that it has agreed. It will therefore be paying more than if it were on a variable rate loan. It is usually possible to end the fixed-rate agreement with the bank, but there is a penalty clause that could amount to several months' interest payments.

What happens if a business does not repay the interest due on a loan?

Organisations who lend money (typically a bank) in the form of a loan to a business are creditors not owners and, as such, are not entitled to any voice in the business's decisions. However, the lender is entitled to the repayment of the loan with interest. Imagine that a business takes out a loan for £50,000 for a five-year period, and that it defaults (i.e. fails to pay) on its monthly loan payment after three years. Technically the bank is entitled to call in the whole of the remaining balance on the loan at once. In practice, it is unlikely to do so as this might cause the business to cease trading. At best, this would mean the loss of a customer that might well become profitable to the bank again in the future. Alternatively, at worst, it might mean that the business is liquidated (i.e. sells off its assets), and there are insufficient funds from this for the bank to receive all of its outstanding money.

It is usually possible for a business to negotiate a 'payment holiday' to ease its cashflow problems. This means that no interest is paid for a specified number of months; this of course does not mean that the interest is 'written off' – exactly the opposite. It is being added to the amount outstanding on the loan.

Also, it may be possible to renegotiate the loan and agree to repay it back over a longer period of time. In this case, instead of repaying it at the end of the agreed term in two years' time, the bank might agree to allow the remaining balance to be repaid over the next four years. The monthly payments will therefore be reduced, and so financial life will be easier for the business. This will, of course, mean that more interest will have to be paid in the long run than was originally the case.

It is much more likely that the bank will agree to these new conditions if the person responsible for finance at the business informs the bank of the impending problem in advance of the default. It may be difficult and embarrassing to admit to this, but it shows that the business is prepared to face up to its financial responsibilities. The bank will not be impressed with a business which has taken few or no steps to sort out its financial problems ahead of a 'crash'.

Leasing

Hire-purchase, which has already been mentioned as a source of short-term finance, can also be considered as a method of medium-term finance. Leasing is similar in that it also allows payment to be made in instalments, thus spreading the cost over a number of years. However, as with hire-purchase, this means that the total amount eventually paid will be (perhaps considerably) in excess of the cash price.

Leasing, however, differs from hire-purchase in two important aspects. First, leasing an item is basically the same as renting it. This means that a business that leases something never actually owns it, unless the leasing company offers to sell it to the business when the agreement comes to an end.

If Soundrive wants a new network with specific facilities for computer-aided design and computer-aided manufacture, but cannot afford to pay for it all at once, it could contact a leasing company with the proposal to lease the equipment for six years. If the leasing company agrees, the equipment will be installed. Payments are made monthly but, unlike with hire-purchase, the items leased do not become the property of Soundrive at the end of the six years.

The second way in which leasing differs from hire-purchase is that, as the equipment is leased and not owned, if it breaks down, the leasing company must fix it at its own expense.

It may be part of the agreement that the leasing company updates Soundrive's computers and/or software. This would reduce the risk of the business getting left behind in technological terms. If this is the case, the lease will be more expensive.

Long-term finance

Long-term finance is usually for a period of time in excess of ten years. This finance is for securing the resources for long-term growth. For the long term, a business essentially has the choice of raising finance by borrowing or through the issue of shares.

Long-term loans

Long-term loans are used for expensive pieces of machinery, the cost of which needs to be spread over a lengthy period of time, perhaps as long as 20 years.

Loans for buildings are known as mortgages and can vary in duration of between 20 years and 30 years, although they usually run for 25 years. The amount of finance involved is large and the bank will certainly require the title deeds of the land as security. As with the medium-term loan, it is possible for a business to opt either for a variable or a fixed-rate mortgage. However, in the latter case, the rate would not be fixed for the whole length of the loan. Twenty years is too far ahead for either the bank or the business to judge whether the rate fixed at the beginning would be beneficial or not. It is much more likely that the option to renew on a fixed rate basis will be offered every few years.

Debentures

These are a special type of long-term loan that are only available to a public limited company. There are two differences between debentures and other types of loan. First, the company does not borrow money from a bank in the usual way, but sells debentures to investors in order to raise finance. The debentures carry a fixed rate of interest, which the company must pay to the debenture holders every year. Second, the debentures can be resold to someone else if the investor needs his or her money back before the debenture matures (is paid back). Debentures are sometimes called 'loan stocks' or just 'stocks', as in the term 'stocks and shares'. Like other long-term loans, debentures will almost certainly be secured on a specific asset of the company, so that if there are financial problems the debenture holders can force the company to sell the asset in order to get their money back.

Issue of shares

Share issue is also known as equity finance. When investors use the term 'equities', they are talking about shares. This type of finance is only available to a company (see **Chapter 2**).

In the case of a private company, there may be restrictions on the transfer of shares, and their value is not readily obvious because they are not traded in a market. With a public company, once shares are issued they are then traded on the stock market, the place where debentures and shares are bought and sold. Public companies are able to raise more capital than private limited companies, but in either case the shares are issued for ever; they are not like debentures or loans, which are paid back.

Shareholders are entitled to a dividend (a share of the company's profits), but it is not a legal requirement that a dividend is paid every year;

Key term

Stock market: a market where shares and debentures are bought and sold; only public companies have their shares traded on the stock market.

theoretically, a company could retain all its profit. The shareholders cannot demand their money back in the way that a bank can if interest on a loan is not paid. However, this would not be very popular and would result in some interesting scenes with the directors at the annual general meeting. Moreover, once knowledge of the company's action became public, the share price would be bound to fall.

When a company wants to issue more shares, this is known as a rights issue. Existing shareholders are offered the opportunity ('right') to buy more shares at a price that is lower than the current market value. This makes the shares tempting to buy, and the shareholders know that control over the company is being kept among the same group of people as before.

Tips and techniques

A common mistake is to assume that when shares are resold they are sold back to the company. This is not the case; they are sold to other investors. It should be apparent why. A company issues shares to raise large amounts of finance in order to purchase expensive buildings and equipment. If investors were entitled to sell their shares back to the company, it would either need to have a huge amount of cash constantly ready (which would be earning no return) or have to sell the very equipment it has bought in order to pay them back.

Sale and leaseback

A business can raise finance by selling off an asset such as a building or a piece of land. This can raise a considerable amount of finance and is a sensible course of action if the asset is no longer needed.

Sale and leaseback is where the asset is sold but then leased back, usually for a long period of time. Soundrive, the audio business mentioned above, could sell off one of its factories and then agree to lease it back for 20 years. If it needs finance in order to fund an expansion, it can raise a large amount in this way in the knowledge that it can operate from exactly the same site as previously for many years.

There are disadvantages. Soundrive no longer owns the asset it is leasing. When the lease expires, there is no guarantee that it will be renewed; the business that owns the factory may want to sell it. Soundrive would then have to vacate the premises and go elsewhere.

Retained profit

Once a business has been operating profitably for several years, it is likely that some of the profit will be retained for the purpose of using it in the future. When this has happened, the retained profit can be a useful source of finance, which does not incur debt for the business. As these retained profits have been used to finance the business and not distributed to the owners, there will be an entry on the liabilities section of the business's statement of financial position (see **Chapter 34**) under the heading 'retained profit', or alternatively 'profit and loss account', since this is where the profit was originally recorded in the accounts.

Table 24.1 Sources of finance: a summary

Short term	Medium term	Long term
Overdraft	Loan	Loan
Loan	Hire-purchase	Sale of assets
Trade credit	Leasing	Sale and leaseback
Factoring	Retained profit	Retained profit
Hire-purchase		Shares (if the business is a company)
		Debentures (if the business is a plc)

Other sources of finance

Government assistance

Certain areas of the UK are designated as 'Assisted Areas', which means that if a business is located in such an area, or is prepared to locate there, it will qualify for UK government assistance. The Department for Business Innovation & Skills provides guidance on the assistance that is available for a business if it can demonstrate that the assistance will safeguard and create jobs or that it will help the business compete more effectively at home or abroad. This does not, however, come with 'no-strings attached'. A business has to apply with a specific set of proposals. The sort of assistance that is on offer includes incentives to locate in a particular area such as:

- tax incentives which lower the amount of tax a business has to pay
- sale of land or property to businesses at a discounted rate
- lower than usual rents for buildings and factories.

In addition, there are grants to businesses for:

- investment in equipment to improve competitiveness
- training/retraining their employees to improve skills and productivity
- research and development into new products to keep ahead of foreign competition.

As a member of the EU, any UK government assistance has to comply with the EU regional aid guidelines, which set out the rules under which member states can give state aid to businesses. Aid (similar to that available from the UK government) is also available from the EU itself; for example, from the European Regional Development Fund and the European Social Fund.

Different initiatives from the EU and the UK government are announced every so often. In 2014 The Department for Business Innovation & Skills announced that a further £100 million was to be provided to help companies strengthen their domestic supply chains and create and safeguard jobs in UK manufacturing.

Depreciation

Over a period of time some of a business's assets will wear out or become obsolete. They become worthless each year; that is, they depreciate. Eventually, new ones will have to be bought. HMRC (the tax authorities) permit the business to claim an allowance for this depreciation each year and to treat it as a cost to the business. Since profit equals revenue minus cost, any increase in cost will lower the business's (pre-tax) profit. This may seem a rather odd thing for a business to want to do, but a lower profit will lower the amount of tax which it has to pay. It can therefore retain the amount 'saved' as a result of the depreciation allowance, in order to purchase new equipment.

It is important to understand that depreciation is not a source of finance like most other methods detailed in this chapter. Sources such as loans and overdrafts mean that the finance is available, and can be accessed, as soon as the paperwork and any other formalities are completed. With depreciation, the finance is not a sum of money that becomes available to spend; it is a reduction in the business's tax bill at the end of the financial year. It means that in the following year, the business has more funds available because it has not had to pay so much tax, but this does not become apparent until the business submits its tax return to the tax authorities and the figures are accepted. There are regulations as to what can and cannot be claimed as depreciation. For depreciation calculations see **Chapter 35**.

Venture capital and business angels

Venture capitalists are individuals or firms who lend money, known as venture capital, to small and medium-sized businesses that require finance for starting-up or expansion. Venture capitalists often take a gamble in doing this, because it is quite likely that the business requiring the funds has been refused finance by other lenders as the risk of failure is high. However, a high risk is associated with the expectation of a high reward. A venture capitalist may agree to provide a certain amount of finance in exchange for 20 per cent of a new company's shares and may adopt a 'take it or leave it' approach. If the company accepts and does well, then in a few years the venture capitalist will look forward to large dividend payments and a substantial capital gain from the shares if it chooses to sell them.

Key term

Venture capital: finance from individuals or firms who lend money to, or buy shares in, small and medium-sized businesses that require finance for starting-up or expansion.

Business angels are similar to venture capitalists, but they usually offer management advice as well. They can also bring knowledge of useful contacts, such as suppliers and potential customers, to a business.

The owner(s) of a small business need to evaluate carefully the use of this source of finance. An angel will require a financial return for its capital and time, and may insist on becoming actively involved in the running of the business in order to safeguard its investment. This may cause problems and conflict.

Internal and external sources of finance

Finance can also be classified according to whether it is internal or external.

If finance is raised internally, it does not increase the debts of the business. Internal sources include the funds available from the sale of any unwanted assets, from retained profit and from the use of trade credit. Internal sources are more likely to be available when a business is well-established.

External finance is provided by people or institutions outside the business in the form of loans, overdrafts, shares and debentures. The use of external sources of funding creates a debt that will require payment.

A business's choice of finance

There are advantages and disadvantages to every method of finance. The actual choice depends on several factors, as shown in Figure 24.2:

- The length of time involved. If equipment is purchased in order to expand the business, how long will it take to generate the funds to pay back the investment? If the answer is several years, short-term finance is not appropriate.
- The legal structure of the business. Sole traders and partnerships cannot issue shares and so are restricted in the types of finance available for growth.
- Quantitative factors such as existing levels of debt. A quantitative factor is one that is measurable. If a business has already been granted several bank loans and then applies for another, the bank will think twice about authorising it because of the amount of interest that the business already has to pay. If yet another loan is allowed, the bank may wonder if the business will be able to repay all of them. If a company decides to try to raise the finance it wants via the issue of shares, it will find this difficult to do if it already has several loans. Potential investors will know that interest payments on the existing loans have to be met before any dividends are paid. If a lot of revenue is 'disappearing' into interest payments, this will reduce the amount of profit, and dividends might be low as a result. This will make the proposed issue of shares unattractive to investors.
  Furthermore, a business with a high proportion of its finance raised in the form of debt compared to the amount raised by equity is said to be 'highly geared'. (See **Chapter 37**.) A highly geared business is clearly going to be susceptible to the effects of a rise in the rate of interest. For these reasons, a business has to be careful about obtaining too much finance in the way of loans.
  Another quantitative factor is the existence of any internal funds. If the business has reserves of cash, should it use them for finance? On the one hand, there will be no interest to pay; but on the other, once these funds are used, the business has no financial cushion to fall back on.
  Another issue is whether a company should hold back some of the funds available for dividend payments in order to finance a project. If it is a public limited company, it needs to consider how the stock market is likely to react to such a decision; the share price will probably fall.
  A fall of a few pence does not matter, but a large drop would be a sign of concern that the wrong decision had been made, and might tempt another firm into making a takeover bid.
- Qualitative factors such as the amount of control desired. A qualitative factor is not measurable, but this does not mean it is unimportant.
  Becoming a partnership (or taking on a new partner if the business is already a partnership) will increase the capital available but reduce the control over decisions. In the case of a company, all shareholders have a vote (one per share), so becoming a company or issuing more shares will weaken control. If the company is a plc and it pays a dividend that is out of line with stock market expectations, the share price will fall, which may leave the business open to a hostile takeover.

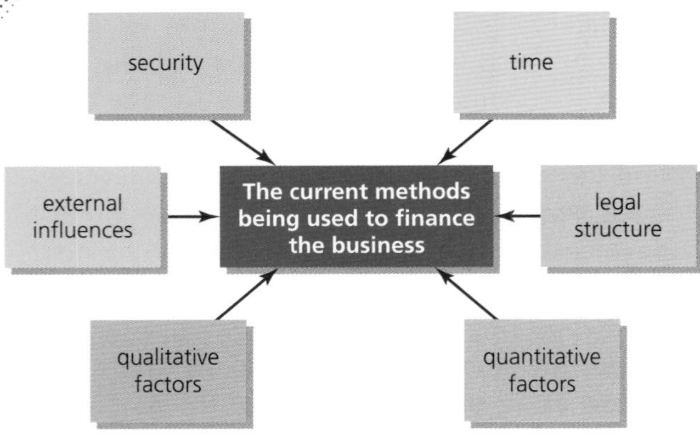

Figure 24.2 Factors influencing the choice of finance

- External factors such as the state of the economy. The economy can be an important external influence on the choice of finance. If business is booming for the firm's products because the economy is doing well, this will help to ensure a healthy cash flow which would mean a loan is less difficult to pay back.
- Security. A lack of security may mean that banks are unwilling to grant a loan, in which case some other form of finance must be found.

Further sources

www.gov.uk/government/organisations/department-for-business-innovation-skills: guidance and support from the government on starting up and improving your business.

www.barclays.co.uk/business: a website giving examples of the sort of banking services available to business customers (e.g. financial advice and 'start up packs' for new businesses).

www.londonstockexchange.com: the London Stock Exchange is at the heart of the UK's financial markets. This site contains lots of information about the stock exchange and the companies whose shares are traded on it.

- The current methods being used to finance the business. Inappropriate financial management, such as poor cashflow management or using an overdraft in the wrong way, will not impress a bank and will discourage it from lending.

Your turn

Questions are suitable for all AS and A Level candidates.

Multiple-choice questions

1 Which of the following sources of finance would not be available to a sole trader?
A a debenture
B factoring
C hire-purchase
D leasing. *(1)*

2 Which of the following is an internal source of finance?
A a short-term loan
B an overdraft
C equities
D retained profit. *(1)*

3 All of the following could be considered as a short-term source of finance except:
A an overdraft
B factoring
C trade credit
D sale and leaseback of assets. *(1)*

4 A business has a medium-term loan, of which £25,000 is still outstanding. Every month it makes a capital repayment fixed at £750 and also interest of 7 per cent on the amount outstanding. The total repayment it will make next month is therefore:
A £2,200
B £2,300
C £2,400
D £2,500. *(1)*

Revision questions

1 Explain the difference between internal and external sources of finance. *(4)*

2 Explain the difference between 'debt' and 'equity' finance. *(4)*

3 Explain the purpose of a business having an overdraft facility at the bank. *(2)*

4 Explain the difference between a loan and an overdraft. *(4)*

5A Explain one advantage to a business in factoring debt. *(2)*

5B Explain one disadvantage to a business in factoring debt. *(2)*

6 Analyse three factors that will influence a business's choice of finance. *(6)*

Total *(24)*

Case study

DDR Copiers Ltd (DDRC)

Most large and medium-sized businesses have at least one photocopier and these are often leased rather than owned outright. This has the advantage that a sum of money does not have to be found to buy the copier and that leasing payments can be spread over a period of time. The company leasing the copiers out to others is usually responsible for the maintenance of copiers and also fixing any breakdowns. At the end of the leasing period it will usually offer customers the chance to renew the contract with an upgraded model. This means that it has to do something with the 'old' models that have been replaced. Apart from the fact that the technology is slightly outdated, there is usually nothing wrong with the old copiers at all. However, a leasing company does not want capital tied up in what it views as obsolete stock. It needs to find a buyer.

DDR Copiers (DDRC) was established in 2001 by two brothers; Dan and David Roberts. Both men are now in their early 50s. They are the directors and sole shareholders of the company which operates from a leased unit on an industrial estate in Bedford. DDR has an authorised share capital of 30,000 £1 ordinary shares; 10,000 have been issued and each brother owns 5,000 of these. The growth of the business has been achieved without incurring any external debt. The business balance sheet has been built on retained profit and the brothers are very proud of this.

DDR's core business is the purchase of photocopiers from leasing companies. All copiers are serviced, checked for electrical safety and then sold on to other businesses.

Dan is good at buying. He has an encyclopaedic knowledge of copiers and their market price but he has to be careful to ensure that the right models are bought for resale and that they are bought at the right price. David concentrates on selling copiers and their activities have to be carefully co-ordinated; excess supply of stock can be an expensive issue.

Since it began trading, DDRC has seen a steady growth in its business although there were some difficult years following the financial crash in 2008. At that time, many businesses tended to stick with their existing copier when the lease was renewed, rather than upgrade to a more expensive new one. Since the economy began to recover in 2014 there has been a return to copier upgrading – and hence a new supply of copiers to be bought and sold on. There has also been a tendency for many of the new businesses that have been established since then to buy a small copier rather than simply use the copying facility on a printer.

Recently the brothers have been taking about expanding. The Bedford site is now too small for their growing volume of business. It is also right in the heart of the industrial estate and there are sometimes lengthy delays getting copiers in and out because of the congestion created by deliveries and sales from the other units. There are, however, no suitable sites nearby. Milton Keynes is a city about 25 miles away and there are a number of new developments of industrial units in the process of construction. A suitable unit is for sale at £160,000.

The bank has indicated that a 7 per cent, ten-year loan would be available for the full amount. Alternatively, there is a 25 year, 6 per cent mortgage available – again for the full amount.

1A Explain what is meant by hire-purchase. *(2)*

1B Explain what is meant by leasing. *(2)*

2 Dan is considering asking the bank for a loan. Outline two issues that a bank will consider when considering authorising a loan to DDRC. *(4)*

3 Using quantitative and qualitative information, evaluate the sources of finance that DDRC could use for the move to the new unit. *(15)*

Total *(23)*

Chapter 25

Accounting concepts

> **Year 2**
>
> A Level students must know all of the content in this chapter.
>
> This chapter is not applicable for AS students.

Accounting is a process of control on the expenditure of a business, and is a vehicle for the publication of figures for profit, value and cash.

Categories of accounting

The two main categories of accounting are financial accounting and management accounting.

1. Financial accounting: concentrates on the assets, profits and levels of cash within the business. The main purpose of this type of accounting is to satisfy the external stakeholders of a business, such as the shareholders and financial institutions. This information will be issued in the annual report of the business.
2. Management accounting: concentrates on the internal financial accounts, allowing the business to monitor and evaluate its performance. It also enables the business to set targets and therefore achieve its obectives.

Principles of accounting

Accounts are constructed in line with seven principles. These principles are used to ensure that the figures are produced in a standardised manner so that the accounts can be analysed, knowing they have been constructed in a recognised manner. All of these principles are 'guides', which exist in order for stakeholders to view accounts with some degree of confidence.

Consistency

The principle of consistency operates on the basis that all accounts will be produced in the same way. It is expected that a business will have a policy for the formulation of its accounts, and will apply this policy consistently.

By having a principle of consistency, any person using the accounts can be confident that the information within the accounts is more likely to be accurate.

Going concern

This principle assumes that the business is operating as normal and that there is no reason not to expect it to operate as normal in the foreseeable future.

This is important, because if the business was about to close, be put into administration or liquidated, then a different set of rules would apply on the way in which the accounts are prepared and presented.

Matching (accruals)

The timing of information put into the accounts is another important principle. The dates used to record financial transactions are those when the transaction occurred and NOT when the actual payment is made. This may appear slightly strange but is more realistic. In terms of producing an accurate statement of financial position (a method of recording the value of a business at a given point in time), it is important to record which sales have been made or which materials have been sold, regardless of when they are actually paid for.

Similarly, with a cashflow statement, recording the date of the transactions and not the payments is more realistic for the level of liquidity within the business at that moment in time.

For example, a business sells a product to a customer in January but is not paid for it until March. The transaction (what is owed to the business) is recorded in January and not March.

This is a more realistic approach and allows comparisons of trading to be made from year to year. This comparison will be more realistic because payment periods may alter (e.g. offering extended credit terms as a promotional tool) and therefore distort the level of actual trading within a given period of time.

There is a 'match' between the date of the transaction, not when the payment is made.

Materiality

Accounting is concerned with the big picture. Calculating the value of the business requires a realistic figure to be reached. But a business would not spend time calculating every single asset if it is of little or no value, and would therefore make no real (material) difference either to its balance sheet or profit and loss account. For example, counting the number of paper cups that a business such as BP has will make no material difference to the value of the business. The sorts of assets BP would count are oil, tankers or refineries. However, for a manufacturer of paper cups, their value would be important (material).

Objectivity

This principle is based on the idea that the accounts must be realistic and therefore based on facts, not opinions or guesses. It is very important to avoid any false statements or values. Similarly, bias must be avoided even if such bias would improve the figures. To ensure that this realistic picture is given, it is important to state the real value of the assets listed. Being optimistic is not the appropriate approach. For example, valuing a piece of machinery or factory highly because it is estimated that inflation would increase the company's value within a couple of months is not an objective valuation.

Prudence (conservatism)

This principle of prudence is similar to that of objectivity, in terms of not overstating the financial situation. Where there are any uncertainties as to the levels of profits or losses or valuations, then this principle suggests that it is right to understate the level of profits and overstate the level of losses. In other words, it is appropriate to take a pessimistic view. Being prudent is to be cautious and therefore the business will not be affected by figures that are less than expected. The principle of prudence in accounting can compensate for the over-optimism of directors or managers within the business.

It could also be argued that prudence involves being realistic with valuations of assets within the business. Refusing to take the value of fixed assets at their purchase price but considering their depreciation (see **Chapter 35**), is considered a prudent measure.

Realisation

Realisation is similar to matching, in that realisation takes place when the legal ownership changes hands and not when payment is made. Goods or services are 'realised' (become the property of the buyer) when any legal entitlement is exchanged. The seller has passed the legal title to the buyer; this process may take place several weeks before the buyer actually pays for the goods or services. Nevertheless, the article bought would now appear as an asset of the buyer's business, even if payment has not been made. For example, a buyer sells a product to the seller on 11 July; and consequently the buyer becomes the legal owner of the good (as legal title is transferred). Payment is not made until 5 August, but the product for accounting purposes is now owned by the buyer.

Generally Accepted Accountancy Practice (GAAP)

GAAP is a framework of accounting rules or principles. Some are identical or very similar to the principles already stated above.

The Financial Reporting Council (FRC) suggested there was a need to change and subsequently published three new financial reporting standards. These are: FRS 100, FRS 101, and FRS 102, which set out the rules for different businesses. For example, if a business is to use GAAP it will utilise FRS 102.

Tips and techniques

It is not expected that you need a working knowledge of any of the FRS details. You are, however, expected to know the principles that businesses ought to adhere to.

The new reporting framework or set of rules for accounting was due to be mandatory from January 2015. It is assumed that the following principles are adhered to:

- **Economic entity assumption**: separate records for each business entity.
- **Accrual basis accounting**: see 'matching' above.
- **Monetary unit assumption**: to include only quantifiable transactions.
- **Full disclosure assumption**: disclosure of all relevant information.
- **Time period assumption**: using a set period of time (usually one year).
- **Revenue recognition assumption**: revenue recorded when earned, i.e. when delivered not when paid for.
- **Matching principle**: see principles above.

- **Cost principle**: assets to be recorded at cost of acquisition.
- **Going concern principle**: see principles above.
- **Relevance, reliability and consistency**: see principles above.
- **Conservatism**: a less optimistic approach to be adopted.
- **Materiality**: see principles above.

Why comply with GAAP?

Stakeholders will often view the accounts of any given business in order to make decisions as to, for example, invest, check progress of a business's performance, ensure it is creditworthy in order to trade with it. By having GAAP, it allows stakeholders to make comparisons on the basis that the businesses all use the same set of principles in the manner in which accounts are formulated and presented.

Tips and techniques

Examination questions may well ask you to consider the principles in the context of a given business and expect you to be able to discuss and evaluate such accounting procedures. Such questions may or may not have numerical data alongside.

To have some critical awareness of these conventions or principles is essential.

Further sources

www.cliffnotes.com
www.investopedia.com
https://sage-exchange.co.uk

Your turn

Multiple-choice questions

1 Concern with the overview of a business and not minute detail is an explanation of which principle of accounting?
A realisation
B matching
C materiality
D accruals. *(1)*

2 The two main categories of accounting are management and:
A cost
B profitability
C logistical
D financial. *(1)*

3 The principle of realisation is similar to:
A matching
B objectivity
C prudence
D consistency. *(1)*

Revision questions

1 Explain what is meant by 'materiality'. *(2)*

2 State one example of a business that would not be classed as a going concern, and therefore different accountancy rules would be applied. *(1)*

3 State which principle best describes:
A the concept of avoiding bias or over-optimism? *(1)*
B the concept of conservatism? *(1)*
Total *(5)*

Case Study

Tesco

When Dave Lewis, the chief executive who had recently taken over from Philip Clarke, was shown a copy of a report written by a manager from the accounts department, it highlighted what appeared to be irregularities in the manner in which some of the accounts had been presented. Some payments from suppliers had been pushed forward and some costs pushed back, consequently enhancing the level of profits.

Subsequently, four executives of Tesco were suspended.

'Britain's biggest grocer admitted it had inflated forecasts of half-year profits by £250 million by bringing forward payments due from suppliers for promotion, and pushing back costs.'

Managers of Tesco's 3,400 stores were under intense pressure, as sales had weakened and targets were being missed.

Competition from Aldi and Lidl was an issue, due to the amount of price undercutting.

Previously, Tesco suppliers had to pay for small services such as promotional activities, which were, it is suggested, put forward on the accounts to inflate earnings. *(1)*

Dave Lewis, the new chief executive stated:

'We all expect Tesco to act with integrity and transparency at all times...' *(2)*

The Financial Conduct Authority began an investigation into Tesco following Tesco's admission that its book-keeping was flawed.

The FCA has the power to prosecute anybody who provides misleading financial information to investors. This investigation came soon after the Groceries Code Adjudicator informed Tesco it may face a large fine.

Source: (1) Adapted and quoted from *The Sunday Times* 28 September 2014, Oliver Shah.

(2) Adapted from www.thisismoney.co.uk

You may want to undertake some research before answering the questions below.

1 Explain what the term 'transparency' means in terms of accountancy principles. *(2)*

2 Explain one other accounting principle that may have been 'broken'. *(2)*

3 Evaluate how the Tesco 'irregularities' in September 2014 may have affected its stakeholders. *(9)*

Total *(13)*

Chapter 26

Costs, revenue and profit

AS / Year 1 | Year 2

A Level students must know all of the content in this chapter.

AS students need to cover all the material except for:

- Stepped fixed costs (page 196–197)
- Cost centres and profit centres (pages 201–202)
- How costs may be allocated: full, absorption, marginal (pages 201–203)

To make a profit, a business has to ensure that its revenue (the income from the sale of its products or services) exceeds its costs. Many people think that to increase profit, it is necessary for a firm to sell more goods and therefore gain more revenue. However, careful control of costs may be just as effective as higher revenue in adding to a business's level of profit.

Careful control of costs is essential if the business is operating in a competitive market where it is not easy to alter prices. Unfortunately, one of the most common ways for a business to cut costs is to reduce its number of employees. Headline news in November 2014 included statements referring to Lloyds bank making possible redundancies as it aimed to close more than 100 branches.

EasyJet can charge low prices because it keeps costs to a minimum

EasyJet has become a household brand because of its careful attention to costs, which has enabled it to charge low prices. Other products and services under the 'Easy' name, such as the company's ventures into cruises and hotels, have relied on keeping costs to a minimum.

In order to keep a check on the level of costs, it is useful to classify them. This chapter looks at costs under a number of headings.

Fixed costs

Fixed costs are costs that do not change as output or sales change. They have to be paid whether sales are 10 or 1,000. For example, factory buildings have to be paid for, usually in the form of interest on a loan. This interest is a fixed amount that the business pays regularly (probably monthly), irrespective of the level of production. Similarly, the costs of the machines used to make the products are a fixed cost. Those who administer the business (e.g. the managers and secretaries) all have to be paid even before production has begun. Marketing activities are also a fixed cost because the advertising has to be paid for irrespective of the level of sales that is achieved.

Fixed costs are sometimes called overheads or indirect costs although this can be misleading as some overhead/indirect costs may vary.

Key terms

Fixed costs: costs do not vary with the level of output (e.g. the factory, machines, business rates)

Overheads/indirect costs: costs that can not be attributed to a particular unit of output.

Stepped fixed costs

Although these costs are referred to as fixed costs, it is more accurate to suggest that they are fixed in the short term. If production continues to increase, it might be necessary to purchase an additional machine to cope with the extra production required. In this instance, the

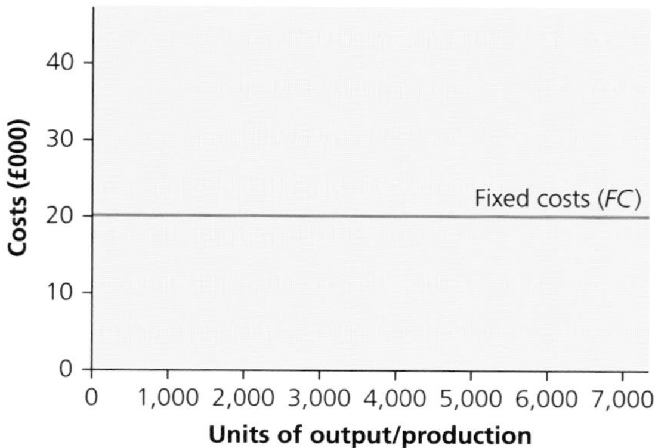

Figure 26.1 Fixed costs remain constant as output changes

fixed costs have increased, but only in order to meet the increase in production. The actual cost of purchasing the machine remains the same, regardless of whether the increase in production is 1 or 1,000. The fixed cost line will change, as shown in Figure 26.2 (FC_2). This increase in fixed costs is referred to as a 'stepped fixed cost'.

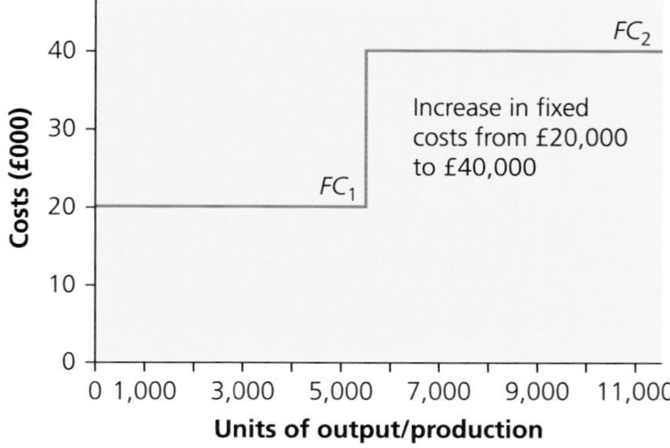

Figure 26.2 An increase in fixed costs

Variable costs

Variable costs are costs that are directly related to the level of output or sales. Variable costs increase when output increases and fall when output falls. A bakery will incur variable costs for the ingredients used in making bread. These raw materials, such as flour and yeast, change in proportion to the quantity of bread produced. Variable costs are often stated per unit, as the cost for each item produced. Unlike fixed costs, when production is zero, the variable costs are zero. Such costs can be shown as a straight line which slopes upwards as output increases (see Figure 26.3).

Variable costs are sometimes known as direct costs. This can be confusing, however, as there are some direct costs that don't change in proportion to the level of output.

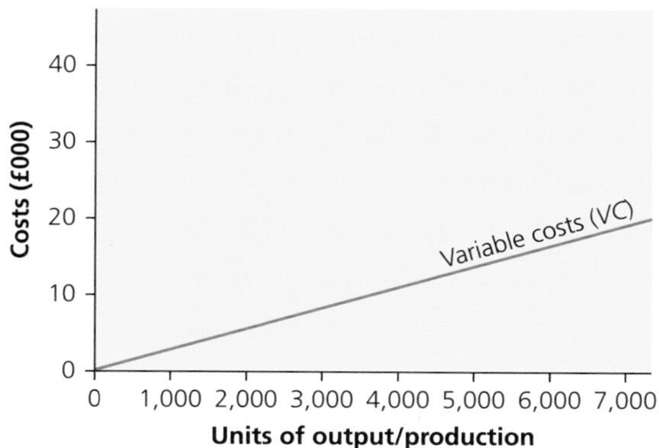

Figure 26.3 Variable costs

Key terms

Direct costs: costs that are directly attributable to a unit output (the raw materials).

Variable costs: costs that change in proportion to the level of goods or services a business produces.

Tips and techniques

Ensure you are familiar with the alternative names for costs, as an examination question could use any of those mentioned here.

Total costs

Having identified fixed and variable costs, it is possible to calculate the total costs for a business producing a particular product. The formula is:

Total costs = fixed costs + variable costs

Or

Total costs = direct costs + indirect costs

Key term

Total costs: fixed costs + variable costs.

The total cost line starts above zero because of fixed costs, as shown in Figure 26.4.

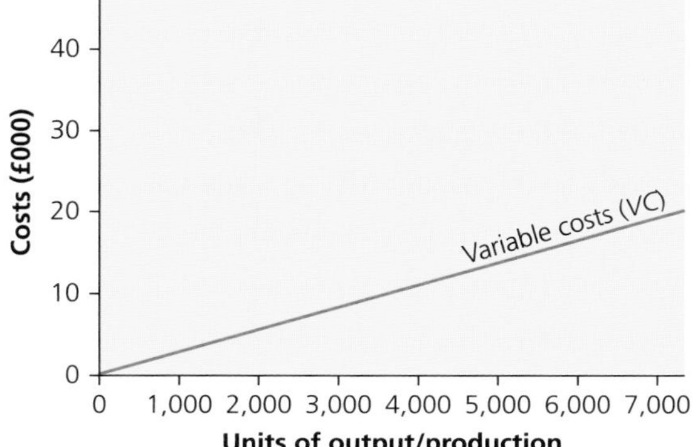

Figure 26.4 Total costs

Table 26.1 shows how total costs are derived from fixed and variable costs. Notice again that, even when no output is produced, costs are incurred. The fixed costs, probably for the factory, machines and administration, all have to be paid for. These costs do not change even as the output increases.

Table 26.1 Calculation of total costs

Units of output	Fixed costs (£)	Variable costs (£)	Total costs (£)
0	100,000	0	100,000
100	100,000	1,000	101,000
200	100,000	2,000	102,000
300	100,000	3,000	103,000
400	100,000	4,000	104,000
500	100,000	5,000	105,000

Unit cost and average cost

Table 26.1 helps to explain the significance of falling unit costs. The unit cost is the cost of producing one product and can be calculated using the formula:

$$\text{Unit cost} = \frac{\text{Total cost}}{\text{output}}$$

Key term

Unit cost: the cost of producing one unit = total costs ÷ output.

Reducing unit costs is a useful way for a business to survive in a competitive market. Using the figures in Table 26.1, when production is at 100 units:

$$\text{Unit cost} = \frac{\pounds 101{,}000}{100} = \pounds 1{,}010$$

Whereas, when 500 units are produced:

$$\text{Unit cost} = \frac{105{,}000}{500} = 210$$

The average costs have the same formula, namely,

$$\frac{\text{FC + VC (TC)}}{\text{Output}}$$

This fall in the unit cost is mainly due to the fixed costs being spread over a greater number of units.

An understanding of these costs will be useful when we come to consider the concepts of contribution and break-even in **Chapters 27** and **28**.

Marginal cost

Marginal cost is the cost of producing one additional (extra) good. Using the information in Table 26.1, the total cost of producing 201 goods is:

£100,000 fixed costs + (£10 × 201 = £2,010) variable costs = £102,010

As fixed costs do not change, the marginal cost is the increase in variable costs, which is £10.

Key term

Marginal cost: the cost of producing one extra unit.

Social cost

The implications of a business decision are not always included in the business's own costs. There might be a significant cost to other stakeholders or to the country as a whole. For example, a tobacco company producing cigarettes has to pay for the manufacturing process and the marketing and distribution of its cigarettes. However, it does not pay the negative costs of treating people who are diagnosed with cancer as a result of smoking.

Similarly, every time you or a member of your family drives a car, although some costs are paid by you, such as the cost of petrol, the damaging carbon dioxide emissions and the problems resulting from them are not charged to an individual driver, but are borne by society as a whole.

Opportunity cost

The opportunity cost is related to what a business could have spent money on. If a business such as McDonald's spends money on a new advertising campaign to highlight its range of healthy salad foods, it cannot spend that money on helping franchise owners improve the standard of their seats. The opportunity cost is the next best alternative (money towards new seats) that had to be given up in order to spend the money on its first choice (the advertising campaign).

Price, revenue and total revenue

Revenue is the cash that flows into a business from the sale of goods or services.

The amount of revenue will be determined by the number of sales of a product or service and the price that is charged for the products or service.

If the price is constant, the total revenue line will be a straight line as shown in Figure 26.5.

However, if the price is increased, the gradient of the total revenue line, TR2, also increases (see Figure 26.6).

This change in the gradient of the total revenue line will also have an impact upon the break-even levels (see **Chapter 28**).

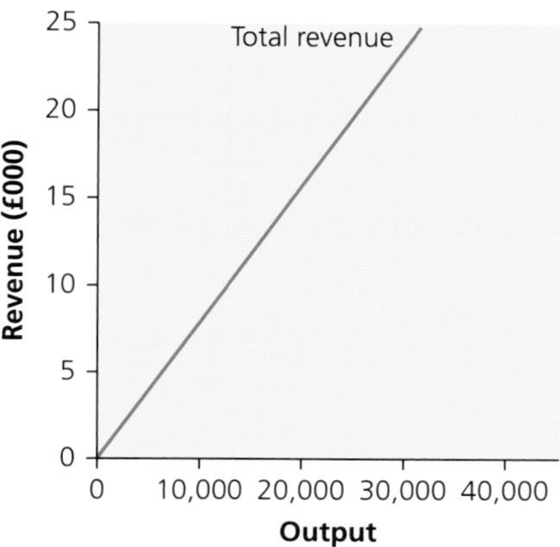

Figure 26.5

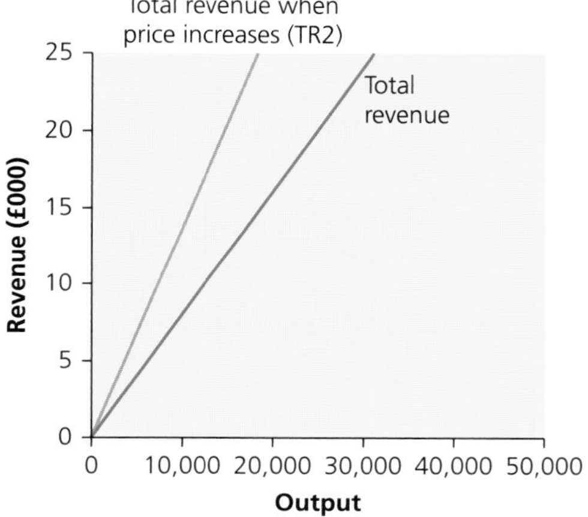

Figure 26.6

Average revenue

To calculate the average revenue, it is simply:

$$\frac{\text{Total revenue}}{\text{Number of sales}}$$

Table 26.2

Sales	Price (£)	Total revenue (£s) (Sales x price)	Average revenue (£) (Total revenue /sales)
10	25	250	10
50	25	1250	25
100	20	2000	20
150	15	2250	15

Using Table 26.2, it is possible to see that as the price is reduced, sales increase and that the sales revenue increases, although in order to achieve the additional sales the average revenue for each good sold falls. Much will depend upon the level of costs: if the costs fall due to increased sales, it will allow profits to be maintained; however, if not, profits will fall.

Much will also depend upon the elasticity of demand of the product or service sold. (See **Chapter 14**.)

It will be helpful for you to answer these questions before reading on.

Your turn

Questions are suitable for all AS and A Level candidates.

Multiple-choice questions

1 If variable costs are £3.50 and fixed costs are £1,200, producing 600 units will mean average costs are:
A £3.50p C £ 5.50p
B £ 2 D £ 5 *(1)*

2 Using the information in Q1, if price is £5 the level of profit/loss is:
A Loss of £300 C Profit of £300
B Loss of £600 D Profit of £600 *(1)*

3 Using Table 26.3 the total costs for 20 units is:
A 60,000 C 200,000
B 260,000 D 240,000 *(1)*

Revision questions

1 State two alternative names for indirect costs. (2)

2 Suggest which type of cost best fits each of the following items. For example, raw materials are direct or variable costs.
A cost of machinery
B fuel for an airline such as British Airways
C cost of an advertising campaign
D salaries
E wages of production workers. *(5)*

Total *(7)*

Tips and techniques

It is important to remember that the market and the economy change very rapidly. Businesses need to be prepared to adapt policies to changes in the market. The most successful firms are those that identify and predict changes and are prepared to adapt their policies to the changes.

Costing methods

Impact of costs and revenue on a business

Costs influence both the price that a product may be sold for and the level of profit for the business. If costs are high and there is an assumption that a profit is required, then the price must reflect the costs and be higher to ensure a profit is made.

Reducing costs allows a business to increase its profit margin and subsequently gives it the ability to deliver higher profits.

However, the degree of competition within the market will also influence the level of the price and subsequent profit margin. In a highly competitive market the profit margins may be small and therefore every reduction in costs allows the business to be more competitive.

Costing is the act of measuring the effects of any business activity in financial terms. In costing an activity, a business can work out whether it is likely to be worthwhile and profitable, or not worth pursuing. It can also help the business to plan for the future and find ways to reduce costs and maximise efficiency.

The level of costs for a business may well affect its decision making as it will want to remain competitive, possibly increase its market share and maintain a satisfactory level of profit to satisfy its stakeholders which will include the shareholders, employees, managers and any creditors.

Revenue provides the business with the cash to purchase raw materials and pay for other costs such as overheads, or, at least a contribution to such overheads. The revenue will provide the much needed positive cash flow for the business (see **Chapter 31**).

Standard costing

Standard costing is the cost that the business would normally expect for the production of a particular product, or to complete a particular activity. The setting of a standard cost is a target for the business to achieve.

Example

A hairbrush manufacturer may say that the standard cost for a hairbrush is £3. This is what the business expects the final cost of production to be, and is the standard cost. This can be compared with the actual cost to see whether it has been achieved. The difference between the standard cost and the actual cost is called the variance (see **Chapter 30**).

The use of standard costing helps a business to monitor its performance. If the hairbrush manufacturer finds that it has actually cost £3.50 to make a hairbrush, it will be able to investigate why the target is not being achieved, identify the area that is causing the negative variance and put processes into place to resolve the situation. It may find that the raw materials for the bristles were more expensive than anticipated and that this increased the actual cost. The manufacturer could either try to find a cheaper supplier or negotiate a better price with its existing supplier. If no solution is possible, the manufacturer may need to reassess the standard price for the future.

Table 26.3 The standard and actual costs of producing a hairbrush

	Standard cost	Actual cost
Raw materials	80p	130p
Labour	90p	90p
Indirect costs	130p	130p

In Table 26.3, the manufacturer needs to find out why the cost of raw materials is so much higher than was anticipated. This could be as a result of a change in the value of the currency affecting import prices, or because an increase in oil prices has increased the price of the materials used.

The advantages of standard costs

Standard costs can:

- Give a business a good idea of the target cost they should be aiming for. They can use their own estimates combined with information from outside the firm.
- Give employees a target to aim for and can alert them to problems as and when they arise.
- Be used within the reward and motivation policy of the business so that bonuses could be offered when positive variances are achieved.
- Encourage workers to look for better and more efficient ways of completing a job so as to achieve positive variances.

The disadvantages of standard costs

- Collecting information to arrive at a standard cost may be time-consuming. The process will need to be repeated at regular intervals, especially in periods of rapid inflation and in changing business environments.
- The use of standard costing, especially when tied to bonuses for workers, may result in a situation where quality is sacrificed to keep costs of production down. This will not be helpful to the business in the long term.
- If the business is not careful in reassessing the figures used periodically, it may find that standard cost has become an inaccurate measure of the actual cost because so many factors have changed.

Cost centres

A cost centre is a specific part of a business where costs can be identified and allocated with reasonable ease.

Example

The Curtain People is a business which provides an interior design and manufacture and fitting service for customers. Their business is divided into three cost centres: interior design; the making of soft furnishings; and the fitting of soft furnishings and carpets. The costs of the business are allocated between these three divisions in relation to the number of employees in each division.

The total costs for 2014 for The Curtain People were £4,500,000. The numbers of employees for each department are as follows:

- Design department: 3
- Making: 12
- Fitting: 5
- Total: 20

The allocation of costs for each centre is calculated using the proportion of the 20 workers in each department. For example, the design department employs 3/20 of the workforce, so it will be allocated this proportion of £4,500,000 as its costs. The other allocated costs are as follows:

- Design: £675,000
- Making: £2,700,000
- Fitting: £1,125,000.

There are a number of ways in which a business can choose to allocate costs to cost centres. These include:

1. The product being produced: The Curtain People could split the costs instead between curtains, carpets and other soft furnishings.
2. The individual department: this might be appropriate for a larger business with departments for marketing, human resources, finance, etc.
3. The location: a business based on different sites is likely to use each of its sites as an individual cost centre.
4. The capital equipment used in each department: this may be used in businesses such as electricity generation, where one department may have most of the costs and capital equipment employed.
5. The physical size of the department in terms of space.

Benefits of using cost centres

The use of cost centres can benefit a business and makes its performance more efficient in a number of ways:

- The information will help to highlight those departments that are performing well and those that are not, making it possible for management to make the necessary changes. If the only information available was for the business as a whole, it would be difficult to pick out the problem areas.
- The information gained can be used to help motivate the workforce. For example, achieving a stipulated reduction in costs in a department could be tied to a bonus payment for the workers in that department.
- The availability of the information may encourage management to look for new suppliers or more efficient production techniques to bring costs down. Without this information, managers may be unaware of rising costs and their implications on the performance of their departments.

Disadvantages of using cost centres

The use of cost centres may result in conflict and a lack of motivation.

- As previously, the act of collecting and separating out the information into different cost centres is likely to be expensive in terms of time and money.
- In some businesses it is difficult, if not impossible, to separate out the costs into different departments. There may be an overlap in the production process; some costs may apply to the business as a whole. Suppose that a large business like a building society decides to sponsor a local premiership football team. How should the cost of this be split amongst its different cost centres? Should branches close to the team ground have more of the costs allocated because they are likely to benefit most, or should the costs be allocated according to the size of the branch?
- The way in which costs are allocated can have a significant effect on the performance of a particular cost centre. In the previous example of the building society, some branches may not benefit at all in terms of business, and therefore an allocation of the cost would make their performance worse.
- Some of the costs for a business may be outside its control. The large rises in oil prices during 2008 pushed up the costs of all businesses to a greater or lesser extent.
- If the allocation of costs is felt to be unfair or unreasonable by some departments, this may lead to conflict between departments. Instead of motivating employees, it can have exactly the opposite effect.

Profit centres

A profit centre is similar to a cost centre, except that in this case the profits coming in are ascribed to different parts of the business. From this, management can judge which products, outlets or divisions are the most profitable parts of the firm's operations. The firm may use the same criteria for dividing the business into cost and profit centres. Sometimes, however, a department (such as marketing) may generate costs for the business but will not receive profit directly, so this will not be possible.

Absorption costing

In this costing method, all the indirect costs or overheads of a business are absorbed by different cost centres (see **Chapter 26**). The methods used for allocating overheads to different cost centres will vary. The easiest method is to use the output of each unit or its proportion of direct costs, to allocate the overheads.

Example

A business produces two types of kettles, electric and hob kettles; see Table 26.4 The overheads are £250,000.

Table 26.4 Output and direct costs for electric and hob kettles

	Electric	Hob
Output per annum	60,000	20,000
Direct costs	£200,000	£100,000

To use output to allocate overheads, work out the percentage of total production for each product.

For electric kettles: $\frac{60{,}000}{80{,}000} \times 100 = 75\%$

For hob kettles: $\frac{20{,}000}{80{,}000} \times 100 = 25\%$

The overheads will be allocated:

75% of £250,000 to electric kettles = £187,500

25% of £250,000 to hob kettles = £62,500

If instead the business decided to allocate overheads in relation to direct costs, then the division would be different.

To use direct costs to allocate overheads:

For electric kettles: $\frac{200{,}000}{300{,}000} \times 100 = 66.7\%$

For hob kettles: $\frac{100{,}000}{300{,}000} \times 100 = 33.3\%$

The overheads of £250,000 will now be divided as follows;

66.7% of £250,000 = £166,750 to electric kettles

33.3% of £250,000 = £83,250 to hob kettles.

This costing method will be time-consuming and expensive to complete. There is also a risk that the information is old and does not represent the current situation. The alternative is to use full costing, which takes all the overheads of the business and divides them using one simple criterion.

Example

A business has overheads of £50,000 a month made up of rent, salaries, clerical costs and depreciation. The firm produces four different products. These overheads can either be split:

- Equally: so that each production centre is charged £12,500.
- By revenue: one product brings in revenue, so it is allocated twice the overheads of the other three. One product will be allocated £20,000 and the others will be allocated £10,000 each.

The main benefit of using absorption costing is that it ensures that all the overheads are covered somewhere in the business. This therefore means that if price exceeds the cost for each unit of the good or service, a profit will be achieved. In addition, the overheads will not have been allocated in an arbitrary or haphazard manner.

Contribution or marginal costing

Contribution or marginal costing is a method whereby fixed costs or overheads are ignored and the business considers only the variable costs of production (see **Chapter 27**). Contribution is the selling price of a product minus the variable cost of producing it. This can be calculated as a total across all production or the contribution made by each extra unit produced. Once the variable cost has been covered, anything left over can be used as a contribution towards fixed costs.

Contribution per unit (cpu) = price – variable cost per unit

Total contribution = sales × cpu

It is important that contribution is not confused with profit. Output making a positive contribution may increase profits, but this is not necessarily the case. Businesses are most likely to consider contribution costing when they are considering accepting an order that will not increase their overheads (see **Chapter 27**).

For example, an airline like British Airways may consider filling the last few seats on a plane by costing them to cover the extra variable cost or marginal cost of carrying that passenger. These marginal costs will be the cost of food, the extra fuel to carry an extra passenger and the costs of the ticket itself. All the other costs like the crew, the fuel and services and parking slots at the airports will already have been paid. Any extra income can then be used to contribute towards the overheads of the business. Therefore, BA will be happy if the price it achieves for the last few seats gives a positive contribution.

The business will not cost so that revenue fails to cover variable cost because in this situation the business will make a loss on each unit sold.

Example

Middleport Mugs has been approached by a large supermarket and a department store with a request to produce a special edition mug as a limited addition. The business has some spare capacity over the summer and could therefore satisfy one of these orders. The figures are shown in Table 26.5.

Table 26.5 Potential order figures for Middleport Mugs

	Supermarket	Department store
Size of order	20,000	10,000
Price per mug	£1.00	£2.00
Variable costs:		
Raw materials	40p	50p
Labour	40p	40p
Other variable costs	30p	30p

The supermarket is only prepared to pay £1 for a mug that will cost £1.10 in variable costs to produce; therefore it is not worth accepting this order. The department store will pay £2 for a mug with variable cost of £1.20, so each mug sold will contribute 80p towards the firm's indirect costs and the business's profits will be increased or its losses reduced. If the business has the capacity to meet this order it will be worth accepting. The business does not have to take its fixed costs into account, because they will not be affected by the acceptance of this order.

Usefulness to stakeholders

For all of the costing methods, there are advantages and disadvantages in terms of their usefulness, which have been highlighted above. A consideration of how the methods described and explained will affect the various stakeholders of a business in differing ways is set out below. For example:

- Shareholders will look at the 'bottom line' (level of profit) as it will affect their dividends.
- Employees may be affected by the accuracy and relevance of the method used and therefore this will impinge upon sales and therefore the likelihood of retaining their job, or gaining any bonuses that may be linked to profits.
- Management decisions will be made on the basis of the costing methods used and therefore their reputation may be affected.
- Suppliers will be affected by how much a business is prepared to pay for its supplies, which in turn will be influenced by the method of costing used.
- Banks and other loan sources will look at the level of profits to help assess the ability of a business to pay back any such loan.

Further sources

www.labspace.open.ac
www.is4profit.com
www.accountingcoach.com

Your turn

Questions are suitable for all AS and A Level candidates.

Multiple-choice questions

1 If fixed costs are £2,000 and variable costs are £22 per unit, the average cost when 140 units produced is:

A £5080 C £22
B £36.3 D £22.4. *(1)*

2 Assuming all 140 goods are sold at £38, the profit will be:

A £5320 C £ 238
B £ 240 D £1.7. *(1)*

3 Using the information given in Table 26.6 the total costs for 30 units is:

A £520 C £120,000
B £520,000 D £400,000. *(1)*

Table 26.6

Units of output (000)	Fixed costs (£000)	Variable costs (£000)	Total costs (£000)
0			400
10		40	
20			
30		120	

Revision question

1 A business with overheads of £60,000 a year decides to allocate them between the two products it makes, in proportion to the output of each product. The business produces 2,000 units of product X at a direct cost of £3 each and 5,000 units of product Y at a direct cost of £5 each. Calculate:

A The amount of overheads allocated to product X and product Y. *(3)*
B The total cost of producing the output of product X and product Y. *(4)*
Total *(7)*

Case study

The price of milk has fallen by 50 per cent recently. Consequently, this has meant that the suppliers (farmers) have also seen the price they are paid for the milk fall by up to 30 per cent.

Meurig Raymond, President of the National Farmers Union described this as 'extremely worrying'. Farmers in many instances are being paid less than the cost of producing the milk or squeezing margins to breaking point.

There are also other knock-on effects of the supermarket price wars for the dairy industry. For example, Dairy Crest announced in September 2014 that it was to close its bottling plant in Hanworth, West London, which meant that its 1,400 milkmen would no longer deliver milk in bottles. Sales of milk in bottles now accounts for approximately 4 per cent.

Given that supermarkets are charging less than 50p a pint (half a litre) it makes little sense to pay to have milk delivered to the door anymore.

Doorstep deliveries now account for around 7 per cent of all milk sales.

Source: Adapted from 'Milkmen victims of supermarket price war', *The Telegraph*, 9 October 2014, Graham Ruddick.

1 Evaluate the likely consequences of the price war for the retailers and suppliers of milk. *(12)*

Chapter 27

Contribution

AS / Year 1 | Year 2

A Level students must know all of the content in this chapter.

AS students need to cover all of the content except:

- special order decisions (page 207).

Given the importance of this concept, a whole chapter has been dedicated to it to ensure students fully understand and are able to utilise it in calculating, for example, break even.

A business needs to cover its costs in order to make a profit. A profit is not made as soon as goods start to be sold, and contribution analysis can help the business to decide whether a product is making a profit, that is, contributing towards a profit.

Contribution is the revenue received from selling a product minus the variable costs of producing that good. Assuming that the revenue is greater than the variable costs of making the good or providing the service, there is a contribution to the fixed costs. In some cases, if the fixed costs have already been paid for, any contribution will be making a profit. Contribution costing is also sometimes called marginal costing.

Contribution or marginal costing

The contribution per unit (cpu) is the contribution of each unit of production to the overheads. To calculate it:

Cpu = price – variable costs

Example

Ahn and Shivan decided to run a disco for their GCSE business enterprise. They had fixed the price of the tickets at £7. This price included entrance to the disco and some food. The cost of the food to be provided for each person was £3, whereas the hire of the hall and the fee for the DJ came to £175 (the £175 in this case is the fixed cost). To calculate the contribution for each ticket sold:

Cpu = price – variable costs
= £7 – £3
= £4.

To calculate the total contribution (how much in total is contributing to the fixed costs), multiply the cpu by the sales. Therefore if 70 tickets were sold:

Total contribution = cpu × sales
= £4 × 70
= £280.

The profit of the disco is the revenue left over after paying the fixed costs:

Profit = total contribution – fixed costs
= £280 – £175
= £105.

Tips and techniques

Remember to show your working clearly so that the examiner can follow what you have done. By doing so, marks can be awarded even if your answers are incorrect. It is also important to write out any formula/equation you use, as this will show the examiner you know what to use, even if the figures you have used are wrong.

The principle involved in the contribution method is illustrated in Figure 27.1.

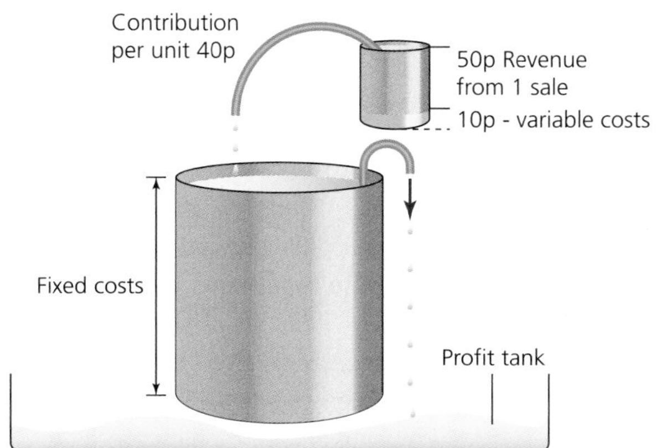

Figure 27.1 The contribution model

The contribution method can be used to calculate how much an individual product contributes to the fixed costs or profits (Table 27.1), and to compare how more than one product within a business contributes to the fixed costs of that business (Table 27.2).

Table 27.1 Calculating the profit for a given product

Product: Sunshield glasses	Value (£)
Price	100
Variable costs	30
Contribution per unit (price – variable costs)	70
Sales = 520	
Total contribution (Sales × Cpu)	36,400
Fixed costs	35,000
Profit (total contribution – fixed costs)	1,400

Table 27.2 Calculating profit for three products

Products: Sunshield glasses	Model 1 Sunshield shades	Model 2 Sunstops	Model 3 Sunseekers
Price	100	120	180
Variable costs	20	25	35
Contribution per unit (price – variable costs)	80	95	145
Sales	500	300	150
Total contribution (sales × cpu)	40,000	28,500	21,750
Fixed costs £30,000	10,000	10,000	10,000
Profit for each model: (total contribution – fixed costs)	30,000	18,500	11,750
Total profit (Model 1 + 2 + 3)			

Contribution allows a business to assess the level of profit for each product it makes:

- Model 1, £30,000
- Model 2, £18,500
- Model 3, £11,750.

The method also allows the business to see which products or models are contributing the most to cover its fixed costs. In Table 27.2, Model 1 contributes the most, £40,000. All three models are contributing in a positive manner because the revenue is greater than the variable costs.

In Table 27.2, the fixed costs of the business have been shared equally between the three models. There is no reason why the business cannot allocate as a percentage of sales or any other means it chooses.

The advantage of contribution costing is that the fixed costs do not have to be allocated at all.

In most cases, a business will not worry about the individual model in terms of how much of the fixed costs it should pay. Instead, the contribution from all three models can be added together:

£40,000 + £28,500 + £21,750 = £90,250

Then the fixed costs can be deducted to calculate the profit:

Profit = total contribution for all three models – fixed costs

= £ 90,250 – £30,000

= £60,250.

The table would normally look like Table 27.3.

Table 27.3 Calculating total profit from all three models

Products Sunshields	Model 1	Model 2	Model 3	
Price	100	120	180	
Variable costs	20	25	35	
Contribution per unit (price – variable costs)	80	95	145	
Sales	500	300	150	
Total contribution per model (sales x cpu)	40,000	28,500	21,750	
Total contribution (Model 1 + 2 + 3)				90,250
Minus fixed costs				–30,000
Total profit				60,250

Table 27.3 shows how contribution is usually used by business. As long as the fixed costs are covered, it is not important which of the products pays for them. What is important is that products are making a contribution to the fixed costs. For many businesses, it is almost impossible to work out which product should pay what percentage of the fixed costs as sales and variable costs vary, and therefore the best method of ensuring that the fixed costs are paid is for all products to contribute.

Tips and techniques

Most of the exam questions will concentrate on calculating the total contribution of products and then subtracting the value of the fixed costs (see Table 27.3) to ascertain the level of profit or loss. In some questions, there may be reference to labour costs and the cost of materials. Both are classed as variable costs unless otherwise stated.

Special orders

If the business were to be offered an additional or special order, the calculation of contribution is very helpful.

Example

Energise Drinks is a business which produces energy drinks that are sold to a range of fitness centres. It has fixed costs of £105,000. The business has not been trading for long but has already managed sales of 200,000.

The manufacturer already sells a range of drinks (five different types in total, but with almost identical costs), but is keen to attract an order from a supermarket chain. The price of the drinks to the retailer is normally 90p, with variable costs of 30p. Table 27.4 shows the sales and costs of the drinks.

Table 27.4 Sales and costs of energy drinks when price to the retailer is 90p per drink

Energise drinks	2008 figures
Price of drink	90p
Sales	200,000
Fixed costs	£105,000
Contribution per unit (price – variable cost) (price 90p – dc 30p)	60p
Total contribution (sales × cpu) 200,000 × 60p	£120,000
Profit (total contribution – fixed costs) £120,000 – £105,000	£15,000

Tips and techniques

Take care when calculating the total contribution as the sum may involve the multiplication of pounds and pence, which may cause confusion.

The supermarket wants to place an order for an initial amount of 25,000 drinks for one region, but is only prepared to pay 40p per drink. What should the owners do? For this type of business decision, contribution is particularly helpful. Calculating the contribution is done in exactly the same way as before.

Table 27.5 Calculating the contribution when the price of energy drinks to the retailer is 40p per drink

Energise Drinks	Special order	
Price of drinks for supermarket	40p	
Sales for special order	25,000	
Variable costs	30p	
Contribution per unit (price – variable cost) (40p – 30p)		10p per drink
Total contribution (cpu x sales) (10p x 25,000)		£2,500

It is necessary to ascertain whether the total contribution from its existing sales covers its fixed costs. Table 27.4 shows that the total contribution of £120,000 covers the fixed costs of £105,000 and therefore the business makes a profit of £15,000. By taking on the additional order, although the business is only making a contribution of £2,500, it is an additional contribution and will therefore add to the profit of the business because the fixed costs have already been covered.

This example assumes that the business does not incur any additional fixed costs to meet this extra order and has enough capacity spare to produce the 25,000 extra drinks. If this is only an initial order, there are other factors to consider:

1 How many drinks will the supermarket want in the future?
2 Will Energise Drinks be able to produce the number of drinks that may be ordered in the future?
3 How will its existing customers be affected?
4 Will additional fixed costs be incurred?
5 Will the business have enough staff to take on the potential increases in production?
6 How keen is Energise Drinks to gain the supermarket order as a long-term source of business?

A business is often willing to take on a special order even if it appears to be unprofitable or produces only a small level of profit. This is because of an expectation of profits in the future. In the example above, Energise would be able to undertake the special order because it may lead to substantial increases in orders in the future. Increasing the number of drinks sold may enable the business to benefit from economies of scale and consequently reduce its variable costs per unit. Although the supermarket has offered a lower price than its other customers, the potential reduction in unit costs will compensate to some extent.

Careful consideration will need to be given to the potential increase in fixed costs. Additional machines and extra labour may be necessary which would increase fixed costs overall, in turn affecting the profit levels.

However, even an initial 'loss' may be worthwhile in the long term if additional orders are a possibility. Table 27.6 shows the figures for Energise and an alternative special order. For this additional order, another supermarket wants Energise to package the drink slightly differently, which will mean Energise buying an additional machine to package the cartons. The cost of the additional machine is £1,500.

Table 27.6 The figures for Energise and an alternative special order

Energise drinks	Special order	
Price of drinks for supermarket	35p	
Sales for special order	25,000	
Variable costs	30p	
Contribution per unit (price – variable cost) (35p – 30p)		5p per drink
Total contribution (cpu × sales) (5p × 25,000)		£1,250
Additional fixed costs	£1,500	
Profit (total contribution – fixed costs) £1,250 – £1,500		Loss of £250

It would appear from the information in Table 27.6 that the additional order is not worthwhile as a loss of £250 is incurred. However, whether the order is taken will still depend upon the list of factors raised above.

Tips and techniques

Sometimes examination questions require you to work out less obvious figures. For example, questions have stated that the variable costs are 20 per cent of the price. In other words, there is an additional stage to be undertaken before you have the figures in the format that you require. Remember to always show your working so that what you have done is clear.

Key terms

Contribution: revenue – variable costs.

Contribution per unit (cpu): price – variable costs per unit.

Profit: total contribution – fixed costs.

Tips and techniques

Be comfortable with using correct terms, keep to the term(s) used within a question.

Your turn

Questions in red are for A Level candidates only.

Multiple-choice questions

1 A business sells 5,000 goods at £5 each. The variable costs are £3.50p per good. The contribution per unit equals:
A £2.50
B £3
C £1.50p
D 0.50p. *(1)*

2 If 2,250 goods sold and using the information from 1, the total contribution equals:
A £2375
B £3375
C £3250
D £2250. *(1)*

3 Profit equals:
A contribution per unit minus variable costs
B contribution per unit minus fixed costs
C total contribution minus fixed costs
D total contribution minus total costs. *(1)*

4 Special orders are only viable if:
A all costs of the order are covered
B at least the fixed costs are covered
C at least all the variable costs are covered
D none of the above. *(1)*

Revision questions

1 State the formula for calculating contribution per unit. *(1)*
2 Total contribution – fixed costs = ? *(1)*
3 Explain two reasons why contribution is an important decision making tool for business. *(4)*
4 If a business sells 100,000 magazines at £2.50 each and the variable costs are 80p and fixed costs are £125,000, discuss whether the business should stop selling magazines. *(12)*
Total *(18)*

Case study

Jurassic Paddle Sports (JPS)

Jurassic Paddle Sports operates on Sidmouth beach in Devon. It hires out paddleboards and kayaks and the necessary safety buoyancy aids and wetsuit equipment for a safe and exciting experience. Paddleboarding is said to be one of the fastest growing water sports.

It operates throughout the summer season and closes near the end of September and opens daily from 9 a.m. to 7 p.m. The new season starts again in the spring. The business is run by Toby and Guy who are enthusiastic paddleboard trainers. They also operate a standup paddleboard yoga class twice a week. This involves undertaking yoga on the paddleboards while on the sea!

The weather is a factor that Toby and Guy cannot control. If the wind is too strong the service cannot operate as the sea becomes too rough and dangerous.

The prices, or hire charges, are stated in Table 27.7

Table 27.7 Jurassic Paddle Sports price or hire charges

	Per hour (£)	Per half day (£)	Per day (24 hrs) (£)
Standup Paddleboard (SUP)	10	40	70
Kayak	10	40	70
Tandem Kayak	15	-	-
Wetsuit only	-	-	10
Bodyboard	10	-	-

For all of the above, the hire charge includes wetsuits and buoyancy aids.

Jurrassic Paddle Sports offer discounts for school parties of 10, at £250 for a half-day session.

1 If Jurassic Paddle Sports' variable costs were calculated to be only £2 based on an hour's hire, calculate the total contribution if seven customers hired SUPs during the hour. *(2)*
2 If JPS were contacted by a local group of people wanting to hire both paddleboards and kayaks for the day but wanted a heavily discounted rate of £20 for a half-day hire for 20 people, discuss whether it should take the order? *(15)*
Total *(17)*

Chapter 28

Break-even analysis

AS / Year 1

Both AS and A Level students must know all of the content in this chapter.

Break-even analysis

Break-even analysis is another tool which businesses can use in order to aid the decision making process. The break-even point or level can be found by:

- using a chart
- calculating (using a formula)
- using a graph.

It is used to find the level of output necessary to cover all costs. Break-even is the point where total revenue covers (is equal to) the total costs.

Finding the break-even level by chart

In its simplest form, the break-even may be found using a chart, where the total revenue (TR), is equal to the total costs (TC). A table of figures may be shown to enable you to find the break-even level of output in this manner.

Table 28.1 Example of a table of figures given to find the break-even level of output

Units of output	Sales revenue	Fixed costs	Variable costs	Total costs	Profit/ loss
0	0	50,000	0	50,000	–50,000
100	12,000	50,000	2,000	52,000	–40,000
200	24,000	50,000	4,000	54,000	–30,000
300	36,000	50,000	6,000	56,000	–20,000
400	48,000	50,000	8,000	58,000	–10,000
500	60,000	50,000	10,000	60,000	0
600	72,000	50,000	12,000	62,000	10,000
700	84,000	50,000	14,000	64,000	20,000

The break-even level of output (TR = TC) is at 500.

Tips and techniques

When looking at such a chart, be careful to read the correct amounts, whether they are in millions or thousands of pounds. Getting the right formula and calculation, but writing out the wrong answer because you have not carefully noted the denominations, may cost valuable marks.

It may be time-consuming to produce a chart in order to find the break-even level. There is a quicker method available which uses a formula for calculation. It may also be the case that within the chart, there is no obvious break-even level as it falls between two numbers within the chart (see Table 28.2).

Table 28.2 No obvious break-even level as it falls between two numbers within the chart

Units of output	Sales revenue	Fixed costs	Variable costs	Total costs	Profit/ loss
200	40,000	45,000	5,000	50,000	-10,000
400	80,000	45,000	10,000	55,000	25,000

It is clear from Table 28.2 that the break-even level of output is somewhere between 200 and 400 units. In this situation, the chart is of little value and using a formula is more beneficial.

Finding the break-even level by formula

To calculate the break-even point, contribution can be used (see **Chapter 27**).

$$\text{Break-even} = \frac{\text{Fixed costs}}{\text{Contribution per unit}}$$

(Remember: contribution per unit equals price – variable costs per unit.)

Tips and techniques

When using the contribution formula for break-even, it is important to remember that total fixed costs (or non-current costs) are divided by unit contribution. It is a common error to put the formula the wrong way round, or put total contribution.

Example

A business making wooden puzzles has non-current costs of £20,000 and the variable costs are £1.50p for each puzzle made. The intended selling price is £2. The number of wooden puzzles that need to be sold to break-even is:

$$\frac{£20{,}000}{£\ 0.50\ (£2 - £1.50)}$$

= 40,000 wooden puzzles

This break-even figure can now be used to assess whether it is possible to achieve this number of sales.

Tips and techniques

It is always worth commenting upon an answer for break-even. Is it very high or low? Do you think it is possible to sell this many?

This formula can also be used to show the likely consequences for total revenue and the break-even point if there is a change in price. Increasing the price will mean that the contribution per unit increases and, as a consequence, the number of goods that need to be sold to break-even will be less.

If the selling price for the wooden puzzle increases to £2.50:

$$\frac{£20{,}000}{£\ 1.00\ (£2.50 - £1.50)}$$

= 20,000 wooden puzzles

The small increase in price led to a large fall in the number of puzzles that need to be made in order to break-even. Pricing strategies can be measured as to how they will affect the break-even level and the margin of safety (see below).

Similarly, if there is an increase in the variable, the formula quickly enables the new break-even level to be calculated.

Tips and techniques

It is quite possible that in a question, you may have to calculate the figures you require before applying the formula.

Example

Calculate the break-even when the fixed costs are £10,000 and the contribution is 20 per cent of the price, which is £2.

$$\text{Break-even} = \frac{\text{FC}}{\text{cpu (p–vc)}}$$

$$= \frac{£10{,}000}{20\%\text{ of }£2\ (40\text{p, therefore cpu} = £2 - 40\text{p} = £1.60\text{p})}$$

= £6,250

Finding the break-even level by graph

Break-even can also be shown graphically. It is important to understand how the various lines are calculated.

Fixed costs

Fixed costs do not alter with the level of output, and are therefore represented with a horizontal straight line.

Fixed costs will exist even if no output is taking place, and therefore are drawn starting at 'x'.

If a business uses a machine (a fixed cost) which costs £10,000, the fixed cost when output is zero is £10,000 (see Figure 28.1).

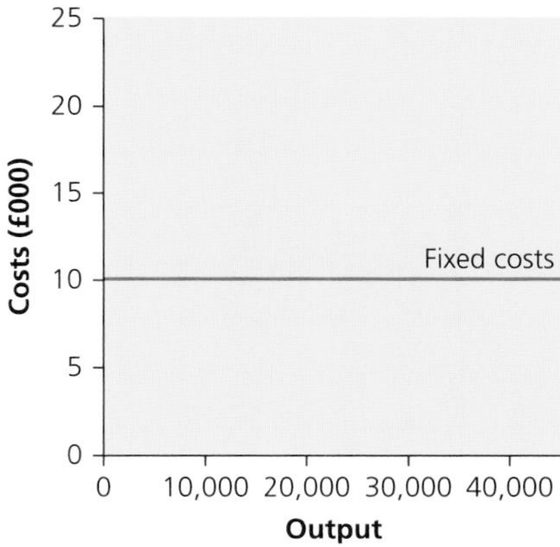

Figure 28.1 Fixed costs

Variable costs

Variable costs vary directly in proportion to the level of output. As output increases, the level of variable costs increases (see Figure 28.2). It is possible to use the graph to read off the particular total variable costs at any given level of output.

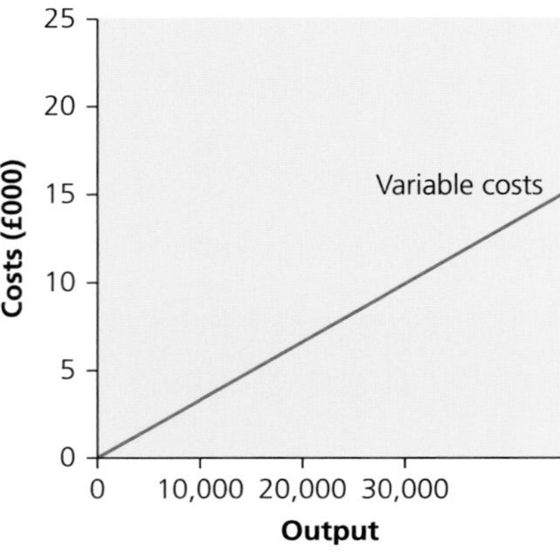

Figure 28.2 Variable costs

> **Tips and techniques**
>
> If an examination question asks you to work out a given variable cost for a certain level of output, the graph would be clearly marked to allow you to give an exact answer, rather than guess/estimate the level.

Total costs are the addition of fixed and variable costs. Note that the total cost line does not start at zero. Even when a business is not producing any goods, it still has costs (fixed costs). The business will have bought the factory premises and the machines necessary to produce the goods. The total cost line therefore starts at £10,000; see Figure 28.3.

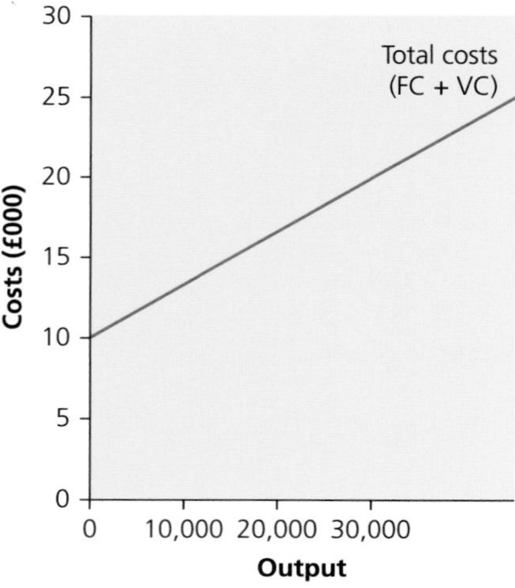

Figure 28.3 Total costs

Revenue line

Total revenue = price × level of output

The total revenue line will be a line with the same gradient, as it is assumed that there is only one price which does not change (see Figure 28.4).

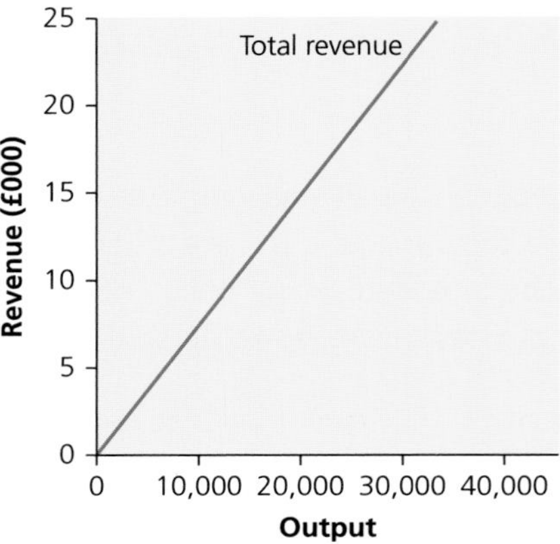

Figure 28.4 Total revenue

The level of the price will determine the gradient of the total revenue line; the higher the price, the steeper the total revenue line will be (see Figure 28.5). Similarly, if the price falls, the gradient of the total revenue line will fall.

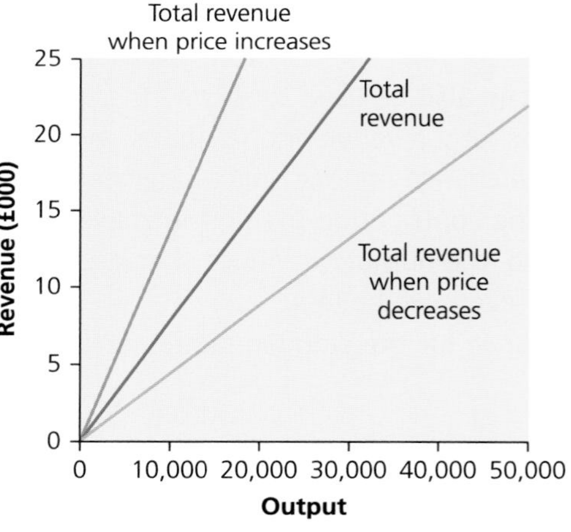

Figure 28.5 Total revenue line changes when price changes

Once the individual lines are known, the break-even point and level can be established. This is where the total revenue line cuts the total cost line; see Figure 28.6.

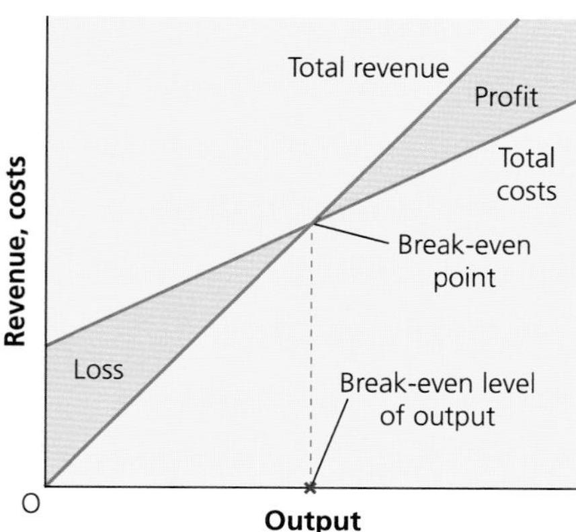

Figure 28.6 Break-even, profit and loss

Knowing the break-even level of output will enable a business to assess profit if output is above the break-even. Looking at the diagram below (Figure 28.7) any output level to the right of the break-even level will be profitable, whereas any level of output to the left of the break-even level will mean that a loss is incurred.

The break-even level of output is shown as 'x'. Once the break-even level of output is known, a business can easily assess its level of profit or loss by looking at its particular level of output (see Figure 28.7).

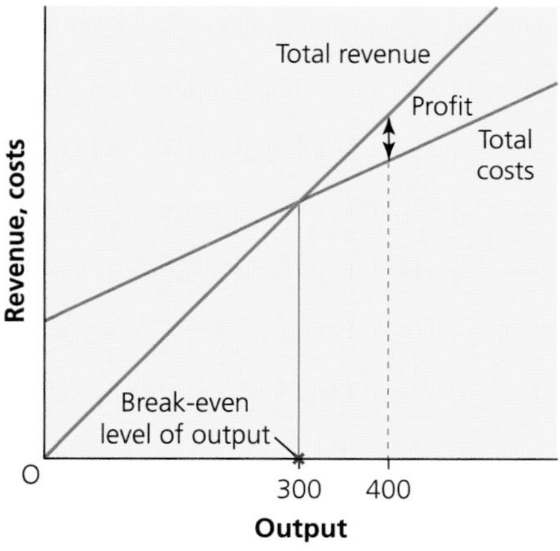

Figure 28.7 Comparing output for break-even

Using Figure 28.7, if the break-even level of output is 300 units and the actual level of output is 400, it is clear from the graph that the business is making a profit. If the scale is clear it will be possible to show the actual level of profit when 400 units are produced.

It is also possible on a break-even graph to show the consequences of a change in price. It has already been shown how the total revenue line changes when the price is changed (see Figure 28.5); but it is also possible to show what happens to the break-even level of output when the price is changed (see Figure 28.8).

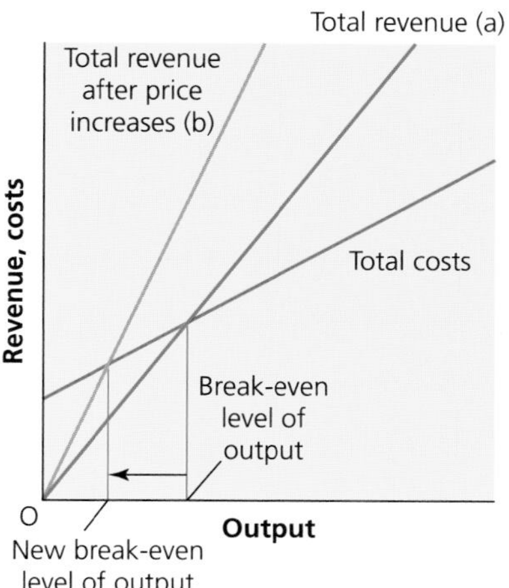

Figure 28.8 Consequences for profit if price is increased

In Figure 28.8, following a price increase, the total revenue line becomes steeper (total revenue b) and, as a consequence, the break-even level of output falls.

It is worth noting that although the break-even level of output falls, which means a profit will be earned at an earlier/lower level of output, there is no guarantee that the output will be sold at the higher price.

Tips and techniques

It is important to realise that any of the costs may change and therefore need to be shown on a diagram.

Margin of safety

The graph also allows a business to see its margin of safety. This is calculated by subtracting the actual level of output from the break-even level of output; that is, the difference between the actual and break-even level of output (see Figure 28.9).

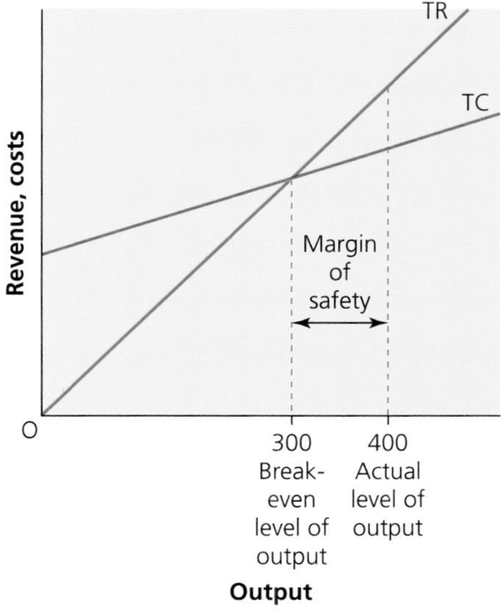

Figure 28.9 Margin of safety

The margin of safety allows a business to assess the consequences of any change in its circumstances that may affect its output, its prices or its costs (see Figure 28.10).

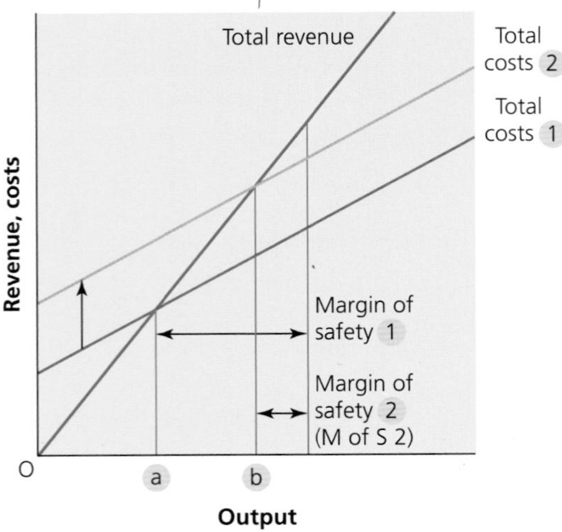

Figure 28.10 Changing margin of safety

In Figure 28.10, an increase in costs moves the total cost line upwards and as a consequence the break-even level of output increases from a to b. This in turn means that the margin of safety falls in size from margin of safety (M of S) 1 to M of S 2.

A business will find this useful because it can assess the impact of any changes in either the actual level of output, or the break-even level. As a consequence, the business will know the significance of any change in output. The smaller the margin of safety, the less flexibility the business has to deal with any change in circumstances. The margin of safety allows a business to know the likely effects on the profit of the business; the lower the margin of safety, the lower its profits.

Example

Table 28.3 shows the figures for a business producing ice cream.

Table 28.3 Figures for an ice-cream producing business

Actual level of output	Break-even level of output	Margin of safety
a) 1,200	900	300
b) 1,000	900	100
c) 900	900	0

At a), the difference between the actual and break-even level of output is 300 units of ice cream (1200 – 900).

At b), there has been a fall in the level of output due to a shortage of labour, and therefore, assuming all other variables are constant, the margin of safety will fall.

At c), a further fall in actual output due to one of the machines breaking now means there is no margin of safety, and therefore any other disruption to output will mean a loss being incurred. With no margin of safety, there is no difference between the actual level of output and the break-even level of output; hence no profit is being made.

Tips and techniques

Always state the formula in any question that requires a calculation. Any mistakes you may make subsequently will be marked using your own answer. There are usually some marks for stating the formula even if your answer is incorrect.

Target level of profit

This is a goal for a business. Once the break-even level is calculated it is possible for a business to decide on a required level of profit (the target level).

This is done in the form of a calculation using the formula for break-even.

For example:

If the target level of profit is £20,000, in order to calculate the number of goods which will need to be produced to achieve this target level of profit, the formula will be:

$$\frac{\text{Non-current costs (fixed costs or overheads)} + \text{target profit (£20,000)}}{\text{Contribution per unit}}$$

However, its value to a business is debatable as there are so many variables that can change while achieving this level of output. As a decision making tool it still depends upon predictions in terms of the numbers to be used (see below for limitations of break-even).

Benefits and limitations of break-even analysis

Benefits

1 Tables and diagrams that show break-even analysis are easy to view, comprehend and interpret. This makes it a valuable tool, as it does not take a long time to calculate or use.

2 Break-even analysis is a beneficial management tool to aid the decision making process. This is especially true for new businesses, which can use break-even analysis as part of their business plan. It will offer an opportunity to consider the level at which break-even occurs, and decide how realistic the chances are of such a level of output or sales being achieved.
3 It can be used to show the level of profit at a given level of output, and to set targets for achieving profits.
4 The margin of safety can be established.
5 It is possible to assess the consequences of changes in circumstances by looking at the margin of safety.
6 Similarly, a business can use break-even to consider the impact of changes for a particular product.

Limitations

1 The overall problem with break-even as a decision making tool is that it is based on using predicted figures. There is no certainty that the actual fixed costs, variable costs and prices will be accurate or constant. The cost of raw materials such as fuel can quickly render any break-even calculations almost worthless. The huge increases in the cost of oil and, subsequently, gas and electricity had a dramatic effect on the costs of industry in 2008.
2 The direct or variable costs may change, depending upon the quantities involved. A manufacturer is likely to be able to negotiate a discount for buying in large quantities. This will alter the variable cost line and therefore the total costs, which in turn will affect the break-even position. A new diagram or table would have to be drawn, which is time-consuming.
3 As the level of production increases, the opportunities to gain the benefits of economies of scale will have an effect on the unit costs.
4 If batch production (see **Chapter 62**) is being used, which may involve the production of fixed quantities for each batch, the break-even level of production may not be obtainable. Producing batches of 50 units with a break-even level of 840 will mean that the business must decide whether to produce 800 (which will mean a loss) or 850 (which is beyond the break-even but may be more than the demand for the product).
5 If there is more than one product or service involved, it may be difficult to allocate the fixed costs (see absorption, **Chapter 26**). Calculating the break-even may be very difficult.
6 Calculating the total revenue relies on just one price. In business, this is unlikely as discounts may be offered for large purchases or promotional offers may be used, especially in the early stages of the product life cycle.
7 For many businesses, trade discounts and prompt payment schemes make calculating the price and therefore the break-even difficult.
8 There is an assumption that if the price increases, total revenue will also increase. This is often not the case as an increase in price can lead to a fall in sales and therefore a fall in revenue. This in turn will affect the actual ability to break-even and the margin of safety.
9 There is sometimes some uncertainty as to whether costs are fixed or variable (labour is an obvious example).
10 There is no certainty that all goods will be sold. Circumstances change within the business environment and therefore may affect sales.

Key terms

Break-even: the point where total revenue is equal to total costs (TR = TC). At that point all costs have been covered.
Fixed costs: costs that do not alter with output.
Variable costs: costs that do vary with output.
Total costs: the addition of fixed and variable costs.
Total revenue: price multiplied by sales or output.
Margin of safety: the difference between the actual level of output and the break-even level.

Tips and techniques

Whenever you include a diagram in your answer, ensure that you explain what has happened. Do not just draw it and assume it is obvious. Ensure that all parts of your diagram have clear labels.

Your turn

Questions are suitable for all AS and A Level candidates.

Multiple-choice questions

1 Given a selling price of £8 and with fixed costs of £32,000 and variable costs of £2 per unit the break-even level of sales is:
   A 5334
   B 5333.3
   C 4000
   D 4200. *(1)*

2 Given the information from Q1, if sales are 6,000 the margin of safety is:
   A 720
   B 4,000
   C 666
   D 640. *(1)*

3 Given the information from Q1, with sales of 6,000 the level of profit is:
   A £12,000
   B £32,000
   C £4,000
   D £6,000. *(1)*

4 If the price of a product were to increase the break-even level would:
   A increase
   B decrease
   C remain constant
   D increase in the short term. *(1)*

Revision questions

1 State the formula for calculating the break-even level of output. *(1)*

2 Faye sells handbags at £40. Her direct costs per item are £10, with fixed costs of £7,500. Calculate the break-even level of sales. *(3)*

3A If Faye sold 320 handbags, calculate the level of profit made (remember to show your working). *(4)*

3B Calculate her margin of safety? *(2)*

4 If Faye were to increase her prices, use a diagram to explain what would happen to her break-even level of sales. *(4)*

5 Fill in the missing figures for each line in Table 28.4 *(5)*

Total *(19)*

Table 28.4

Actual output	Price £	FC £	VC £	Profit loss £	Breakeven level	Margin of safety
a) 15,000	4	6,000	3	9,000		
b) 5,000	10	2,000	6			

Case study

Secret Compass

Secret Compass runs pioneering expeditions to a wide range of remote places around the world such as Afghanistan, Ethiopia, Kamchatka, Panama and Madagascar. If adventures into deserts, jungles, and mountains are required, Secret Compass will provide them for its customers. Its website suggests that Secret Compass 'has redefined adventure', creating bold journeys for adventurous people.

Secret Compass is able to plan and operate remote expeditions using its extensive military background (both its owners were in the army) and its understanding of remote environments. It also provides a service to TV and film crews that wish to gain access to the remote parts of the world.

Its website states

'Secret Compass leads pioneering and exploratory expeditions to the world's last undiscovered places. We invite adventurous and independent-minded people to explore the most isolated and wild regions on the planet with us.'

As each expedition is unique, ascertaining a break-even number of adventurers for any one such expedition may appear to be difficult. However, the information given below is used to ascertain a price and a break-even for any given expedition.

	£
Fixed costs:	
Expedition leader fees	2,100
Leader flights	800
Leader insurance	75
Vehicle hire	1,000
Local guides	550
Contingency fund	750
Variable costs:	
Hotel rooms for adventurers, per person	200
Food, per adventurer	150
Porters	150

The final decision on the price rests with the owners of the company, although the mark-up varies depending upon the expedition and the level of competition from other companies. In this instance, the price to be charged per person for the expedition is £1,800.

1 Given the information in the case study, calculate the break-even number of adventurers for the proposed expedition. *(4)*
2 If the number of adventurers who actually paid is nine, calculate the margin of safety. *(2)*
3 Evaluate the likely effects on Secret Compass, if it decided to increase the price of its expeditions. *(9)*

Total *(15)*

Chapter 29

Investment appraisal

AS / Year 1

Both AS and A Level students must know all of the content in this chapter.

Investment appraisal

This chapter explores how a business can decide whether to undertake a particular capital investment, such as building a new factory or buying an additional machine.

Should a business invest?

The business needs to establish whether the investment is appropriate or worthwhile. It will have to consider the level of risk involved, how quickly the investment will pay for itself, and whether the investment will be profitable.

Investments can include a range of activities or products such as:

- purchase of machines
- building extensions or new factories
- buying another business (acquisitions)
- undertaking a large marketing campaign.

Before the new Airbus 380 airbus was built, investment appraisal techniques would have been applied to decide if it was a worthwhile investment

Investment appraisal techniques are quantifiable methods of deciding if an investment should go ahead. The three methods of investment appraisal are:

1 payback
2 accounting rate of return (annual average rate of return)
3 net present value.

Tips and techniques

Although you may be asked to use one, two or all three investment appraisal techniques, there are also qualitative factors to consider, which will be looked at within this chapter.

Payback

This technique measures how quickly the cost of the investment can be paid back. The faster the payback, the better is the investment. Payback is sometimes seen as a way of measuring the amount of risk involved. The longer the payback period, the greater is the degree of risk involved.

This technique is often the first to be applied, because the length of time for the investment costs to be covered (paid back) is regarded as a more important factor at this stage, than the level of profit it may yield in the longer term.

Payback can be used to assess the viability of a given investment and to compare alternative investments. Both examples will be covered within this chapter. It is not a technique to ascertain whether a business is able to borrow the money needed for any investment, nor is it a technique to help decide if the business can afford to pay back interest on a loan used to pay for such an investment.

Payback terminology

1 EOY: end of year.
2 EOY 0: a nought is added to indicate the year when the investment takes place.
3 EOY 1: one year after the investment.
4 Net cash inflow: the likely return on an investment in a given year.
To calculate net cash inflow: revenue – direct costs.

5 Cumulative cash inflow: the net amount of cash taking into consideration the initial investment and the net cash inflows (see Table 29.1).

Tips and techniques

It is important to understand that the net cash inflow does NOT take into consideration the cost of the investment or any of the overheads within the business.

Example 1

Table 29.1 Example of payback

Year	Net cash inflows (£)	Cumulative cash inflows (£)
EOY 0	0	(100,000) (cost of the investment)
EOY 1	20,000	(80,000)
EOY 2	30,000	(50,000)
EOY 3	30,000	(20,000)
EOY4	20,000	0

Tips and techniques

The layout of an answer when using an investment appraisal technique is important. You will be credited for any formula used and clearly showing how you did any calculations. This is vital because if you make a mistake in any of the calculations, the 'own figure rule' will be used, which is to your advantage!

Similarly a clear layout, preferably within a table, will make it easier for the examiner to see what you have done. It may also help you to see what you have done.

It does not matter if you use brackets or a minus sign for the negative values, as long as you are consistent.

With reference to Table 29.1:

- EOY 0: there is no net cash inflow; only the actual cost of the investment will appear in the cumulative cash flow column.
- EOY 1: the net cash inflow was £20,000 (revenue – direct costs); this is then subtracted from the cost of the investment (£100,000), leaving £80,000 still to be paid back.
- EOY 2: the net cash inflow is now £30,000 and again is subtracted from the last cumulative cash inflow figure (£80,000), to leave £50,000.
- EOY 3: the net cash inflow is another £30,000, which is subtracted from the previous year's cumulative cash inflow (£50,000), which leaves only £20,000 still to be paid back.
- EOY 4: the net cash inflow is £20,000 and this covers the remaining outstanding cumulative cash inflow.

The payback is therefore at the end of the fourth year. There has been a sufficient amount of net cash inflows to cover (pay back) the cost of the investment of £100,000. Sadly, not all payback calculations work out so easily!

Example 2

Table 29.2 Example of payback

Year	Net cash inflow (£)	Cumulative cash inflow (£)
EOY 0		(150,000)
EOY 1	50,000	(100,000)
EOY 2	40,000	(60,000)
EOY 3	40,000	(20,000)
EOY 4	30,000	10,000

In order to calculate the payback when it is within a given year, it is necessary to look at the year in which the payback occurs. Table 29.2 shows that the payback occurs within year 4. In order to calculate exactly when the payback occurs, it is necessary to look at how much is still to be paid back in the cumulative cash inflow column from the previous year (£20,000) and the amount of the net cash inflow for the next year (£30,000).

Dividing the amount still to be paid back (£20,000) by the net cash inflow for the following year (year 4, £30,000) will tell you exactly when within this year payback occurs:

$$\frac{20{,}000}{30{,}000} = \frac{2}{3} = 0.66 = \text{two thirds of a year} = 8 \text{ months}$$

Therefore the payback in example 2 is 3 years and 8 months.

The payback can be calculated in days if you prefer (depending upon what you are asked to do in the question):

$$\frac{20{,}000}{30{,}000} = \frac{2}{3} \times 365 = \text{payback of 3 years and 243.3 days}$$

Example 3

There are two possible investments:

1 Investment A which will cost £50,000
2 Investment B which will cost £35,000.

Table 29.3 Example of payback

Year	Net cash inflow A (£)	Cumulative cash inflow A (£)	Net cash inflow B (£)	Cumulative cash inflow B (£)
EOY0	0	(50,000)	0	(35,000)
EOY1	15,000	(35,000)	10,000	(25,000)
EOY2	20,000	(15,000)	10,000	(15,000)
EOY3	20,000	5,000	10,000	(5,000)
EOY4			10,000	5,000

Using the information in Table 29.3:

- The payback for investment A is 2 years and 9 months.
- The payback for investment B is 3 years and 6 months.

Therefore, investment A appears the better option because the payback period is shorter.

However, there are other factors to consider:

1 How easy will it be to borrow £35,000 or £50,000? There is no information on the business's ability to borrow money, so all that can be said is that normally £35,000 would be easier to borrow than £50,000.
2 There is no indication of how many years each of the investments could last, beyond the payback period. A vehicle bought for the business may not last as long as an extension to the factory.
3 The table does not show how accurate the two sets of figures are for the net cash inflows.
4 It is not clear whether the two options would face competition that may affect the net cash inflows.
5 The nature of the two investments is not clear; one may pay back earlier but in the long run lead to a far greater level of sales and subsequent profit.
6 It is for the last reason that another investment appraisal technique is used. Table 29.4 offers a summary of the advantages and disadvantages of the payback method of investment appraisal.

Table 29.4 Advantages and disadvantages of the payback method of investment appraisal

Advantages of payback method	Disadvantages of payback method
It is easy to calculate and understand, and is therefore a cost-effective way of assessing an investment.	It ignores the value of money over a period of time; the purchasing power of money falls as prices rise. Inflation erodes the spending power of money.
It is a quick and useful guide to the level of risk involved in an investment. The longer the payback, the greater is the risk.	It does not take into consideration any cash inflows after the payback period.
Because payback puts an emphasis on how quickly an investment is paid back, it is an effective method for companies in markets which are constantly changing.	There is no indication of when within any given year the cash inflows will occur.
	It does not measure the level of profits from the investment.

The last disadvantage in this table explains why it is wise to use an additional method of investment appraisal.

Accounting rate of return (ARR)

This method of investment appraisal measures the profitability of any investment. The profit is expressed as a percentage of the cost of the investment. By taking the annual average return, this method also takes into consideration the life of the investment, unlike payback.

The higher the rate of return, the better is the investment. Alternatively, another way to judge the success of the investment is by comparing the rate of return with the interest rates within the economy. If the percentage rate of return covers the percentage interest rates, then the investment may be seen as worthwhile. Similarly, if the percentage rate of return is more than the percentage interest rates that could be obtained from putting (investing the money into a bank savings account), then the investment is worth while.

The rate of return may need to be higher than the rate set out in the objectives of the business.

Tips and techniques

This method of investment appraisal is often known as average rate of return or annual average rate of return. It is vital that you are familiar with any of these three terms, even though they mean the same thing.

Example 1

An investment in a new digital printing machine which lasts for five years costs £15,000. The cash inflows (revenue – direct costs) from this printer are shown in Table 29.5.

Table 29.5 Cash inflows

Year	Cash inflows (£)
EOY 0	(15,000)
EOY 1	10,000
EOY 2	11,000
EOY 3	13,000
EOY 4	15,000
EOY 5	11,000

Step 1: Total cash (EOY 1 to 5) inflows = 60,000

Step 2: Total cash inflows – cost of investment = profit

60,000 – 15,000 = 45,000

Step 3: Average annual profit

$$= \frac{\text{profit}}{\text{life of printer (five years)}}$$

$$\frac{45{,}000}{5} = £9{,}000$$

Step 4: Return on investment $= \frac{\text{annual average profit}}{\text{cost of investment}}$

$$= \frac{9{,}000}{15{,}000}$$

= 60%

To formulate:

- Calculate the total cash inflows (add each year for life of investment) = £60,000
- Subtract the cost of the investment (15,000) to gain the profit = £45,000
- Divide the total profit by the life of the investment (5 years).
- Divide the answer by the initial cost of the investment (£15,000) to gain the percentage ARR.

Table 29.6 Advantages and disadvantages of the accounting rate of return (ARR) method of investment appraisal

Advantages of ARR	Disadvantages of ARR
It takes into account all of the cashflows throughout the life of the investment.	There is no indication of when the cash inflows occur within any given year.
It measures the profitability of the investment.	It ignores the value of money over time. The purchasing power of money falls as prices rise.
It is relatively easy to calculate and understand.	The life of the investment needs to be known and may alter over time.
It allows for a simple comparison between two or more investment opportunities or the opportunity cost of the investment.	It is harder to calculate than the payback and therefore will cost more in time and money to appraise potential investments.

Key term

Oppportunity costs: consideration of the next best alternative the money could have been used for (see **Chapter 9**).

Net present value

Both methods (payback and ARR) have the disadvantage of not taking into consideration the value of money over time. In order to gain a realistic measure of any investment, the net present value (NPV) method needs to be used. This method of investment appraisal considers the value of money over time. It converts all monetary values into today's values to allow for a realistic assessment of the returns in the years ahead.

Such a technique overcomes the problems of looking at cash inflows for three, four or even ten years' time, and being able to realise that £100 in ten years' time will not buy £100 worth of goods at today's prices. One only has to look at the changes in the price of oil in 2008/09 to realise the significance of such changes, and how they may affect the actual decision on whether to undertake an investment.

Although the rate of inflation, which affects the purchasing power of inflows over time, is at present low, it nevertheless still has an effect on the value of money over time.

Consequently, this method works on the assumption that any inflows will be worth less than the same amount today. The technique discounts the value of money over time by a given percentage rate. This discounted value allows the calculation of the discounted cash flow (DCF).

For example: if you invested £1,000 in your bank and interest was paid at about 5 per cent a year, after one year there would be £1,050; after two years, £1,102.50. Consequently, £1,000 in two years' time is worth £1,102.50; or £1,102.50 in two years' time is only worth £1,000 in today's money.

Tips and techniques

There is no need to worry about the particular percentage discounts or the actual figures as these will be given to you in a chart or table. There are examples for you to consider below.

The actual percentage discount rate will depend mainly on the likely level of inflation within an economy. Although this rate is not easy to forecast, it is better than not allowing for changes in the value of money at all. Other factors which affect the discount rate to be used are:

- The opportunity cost: the return on the investment must be better than the next best alternative.
- Some discount rates are determined by the business itself. It may have undertaken similar investments in the past and therefore have a set figure in mind.
- The length of the investment may also be a consideration. The longer the life of the investment, the higher the discount factor in order to take account of the fall in the value of money over a greater period of time.
- The amount of risk: if an investment is riskier, the required return will increase and therefore be reflected in the discount rate (higher).

However, it is also important to note that during the life of an investment, interest rates may change which means the discount rate ought to change. This of course is not possible as the rate chosen determines whether the investment is undertaken in the first place.

Example 1

Table 29.7 Example of net present value

Year	Discount rate 3%	Discount rate 5%	Discount rate 7%	Discount rate 10%
0	1.0	1.0	1.0	1.0
1	0.971	0.952	0.935	0.909
2	0. 943	0.907	0.873	0.826
3	0. 915	0.864	0.816	0.751
4	0.888	0.823	0.763	0.683

Table 29.7 shows the discounted figures for various rates: 5%, 7% and 10%.

It is interesting to note how the value of £1 falls over four years. If discounted by 10%, £1 in four years will be worth 68p.

Using the information in Table 29.7, a business can now calculate the net present value of an investment.

If a business wanted to buy a new machine which costs £10,000, and applied a discount factor of 5%, the net present value is shown in Table 29.8.

Table 29.8 Example of net present value

Year	Net return (£)	Discount factor 5%	Present value (£) (net return × discount factor)
0	(10,000)	1.0	10,000
1	4,300	0.952	4,093.6
2	3,100	0.907	2,811.7
3	2,650	0.864	2,289.6
4	1,850	0.823	1,522.5
Total (returns –cost)	1,900		10,717.4 – 10,000 717.4

The original figure of £1,900 after the discounted factor of 5% is now only £717.40. However, the net present value is still positive and is therefore considered worthwhile.

Tips and techniques

Again, although there is no need to put the figures in a table, ensuring that the information is clear both to you and the examiner is important.

Example 2

For the same investment, but with a discount factor of 10%, the figures are shown in Table 29.9.

Table 29.9 Example of net present value

Year	Net return (£)	Discount factor 10%	Present value (£) (net return × discount factor)
0	(10,000)	1.0	(10,000)
1	4,300	0.909	3,908.7
2	3,100	0.826	2,560.6
3	2,650	0.751	1,990.1
4	1,850	0.683	1,263.5
Total	1,900	0.621	(277.1)

With a negative answer, the investment is not worthwhile. This means that although the cost of the investment takes place immediately, the returns from the investment (the inflows) come in over four years, and during this period of time, the value of money is being eroded; so much so that in today's values, the investment will not cover its costs.

The examples in Tables 29.8 and 29.9 clearly show how significant the discount factor is in the decision process. The higher the discount factor, the greater the returns need to be to cover the falling value of money.

Table 29.10 Advantages and disadvantages of net present value method of investment appraisal

Advantages of net present value	Disadvantages of net present value
It takes account of the value of money over time.	It is more complicated to work out than payback and ARR.
All cash inflows are accounted for (not so for payback).	Because it is more complicated, it takes longer to make a decision and is therefore more expensive.
	Its value as a decision making tool is limited by the selection of the discount factor, which is at best only an educated guess about the value of money over time.

Although all of the three investment appraisal methods have their limitations, collectively they are a valuable method of deciding if a particular investment ought to go ahead. All of the methods considered are based only on financial data and, as a consequence, do not take into consideration any other factors that may be important in the decision making process.

Non-financial factors affecting investment decisions (qualitative): objectives of the business

There are occasions when a business will know what sort of return it requires on any investment but just as importantly, whether such returns satisfy the objectives set by the business.

Resources available, productive capacity, labour, finance

Although a particular investment may be financially attractive, the business may not have the required labour to operate the new machine. A significant amount of training may be required that would be too costly when added to the cost of buying the new machine.

Although the potential investment is worthwhile, the finance to purchase the new machine may not be available, either because there is no funding available or the business cannot afford to borrow sufficient funds.

The economy

The state of the economy can have a dramatic effect on investment decisions.

- The level of inflation may affect the discount factor used, which in turn may lead to an investment no longer being worthwhile.
- If the economy is moving towards a recession, there may be insufficient demand in the future to justify the investment. The lack of demand would affect the likely cash inflows and therefore affect the likely return or payback period.
- If a UK business sells goods or services abroad, the value of the pound could greatly affect sales and consequently affect the cash inflows of the business. Furthermore, the value of different currencies can fluctuate daily, making any forecast for inflows almost impossible.

All of the above creates uncertainty, and just because the economy may be flourishing at a particular moment in time, this does not mean that that state will be sustained in the future.

The data sources

The ability of the business to forecast accurately the demand for its products or services may depend upon the validity of its market research and other available data.

Who is making the decision?

Although the investment appraisal techniques are a useful method of deciding if an investment should go ahead, the person who is responsible for making the decisions may have his or her own agenda. There may be some status or kudos in going ahead with a project (look at the Millennium Dome debacle in 2000, or the HS2 rail line debate and the discussions over a third runway at Heathrow) even if the figures do not support such a decision. Self-interest for a particular department of the business or government service may mean that the financial evidence is ignored.

Hospitals have only a certain budget at their disposal, but may spend money on a renal unit rather than a physiotherapy unit, because there is more need for renal therapy in the area, even though the latter is a better option financially.

Internal rate of return

The net present value does not yield any specific information on the actual return on the investment. The internal rate of return is a method of investment appraisal that does allow the return to be calculated. However, the net present values are used in determining the internal rate of return.

Method of calculation

Two discount factors are used: the first where a positive net present value is produced, and the second where a negative net present value is produced. Using two discount factors and therefore having two net present values, one positive and one negative, means that a discount factor that produces a net present value of nought (zero) is found.

The net present value of zero means that this is, in fact, the rate of return on the project in question.

Tips and techniques

If the NPV is positive, the rate of return is higher than the discount rate. When the NPV is negative, the rate of return is lower than the discount rate.

Finding the discount factor at which the NPV is equal to nought will provide the rate of return (see Table 29.11).

Table 29.11 Calculating the internal rate of return

	Cashflow	Discount factor 8%	DCF	Discount factor 15%	DCF
EOY 0	-75,000	1	-75,000	1	-75,000
EOY 1	40,000	0.93*	37,200	0.87	34,800
EOY 2	30,000	0.86	25,800	0.76	22,800
EOY 3	20,000	0.79	15,800	0.66	13,200
EOY 4	5,000	0.74	3,700	0.57	2,850
		NPV**	7,500	NPV	- 1,350

* To calculate the DCF: 40,000 × 0.93 = 37,200

** To calculate the NPV, add the DCF for each of the four years and then subtract the initial investment of 75,000.

Therefore: 37,200 + 25,800 + 15,800 + 3,700 = 82,500

82,500 – 75,000 = 7,500

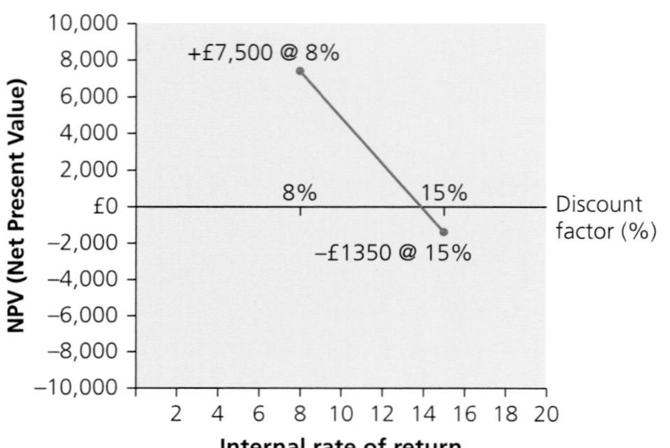

Figure 29.1 Calculating the internal rate of return

The internal rate of return can be found by plotting the NPVs on to a graph (see Figure 29.1). The positive NPV is plotted above the line of the discount factor, and the negative NPV is plotted below the discount factor line. The point where the line cuts the discount factor line (where the NPV is zero) represents the approximate return on the investment. In this example the return on a project is approximately 14.2 per cent. Whether that figure is acceptable will depend upon the objectives of the business and any possible alternative investments.

Key term

Internal rate of return: the discount rate at which the NPV is equal to zero.

Your turn

Questions are suitable for all AS and A Level candidates.

Multiple-choice questions

1 Which of the following techniques takes into account the value of money over time?
   - A payback
   - B net present value
   - C average annual rate of return
   - D cashflow forecasts. *(1)*

2 Using the table below, which is the correct payback period?

Year	Net cash inflow (£)
0	(55,000)
1	15,000
2	20,000
3	30,000
4	40,000

   - A 3 years
   - B 3 years 8 months
   - C 2 years 8 months
   - D 2 years 6 months. *(1)*

3 Which one of these is not an advantage of ARR?
   - A It measures the profitability of the investment.
   - B It is relatively easy to calculate and understand.
   - C It allows for a simple comparison between two or more investment opportunities or the opportunity cost of the investment.
   - D It is easier to calculate than the payback and therefore will cost less. *(1)*

Revision questions

1 Calculate the payback period from the following information:

Year	Net cash inflow (£)
0	(20,000)
1	6,000
2	9,000
3	10,000
4	12,000
5	10,000

(4)

2 Calculate the ARR and net present value (5% discount factor) from the following information:

Year	Project 1 (Net cash flows) (£)	5% discount rates
EOY 0	(50,000)	1.0
EOY 1	12,000	0.952
EOY 2	15,000	0.907
EOY 3	20,000	0.864
EOY 4	13,000	0.823

(4)

3 Explain two reasons why using net present value is useful when attempting to appraise a potential investment project. *(4)*

Total *(12)*

Case study

PhotoboothPlus

PhotoboothPlus was started in 2013 by Ben Barraclough, who, while at a wedding, was intrigued by a photo machine that was operating and attracting quite a bit of attention. Ben, rather than spending his time putting on the false noses and silly hats and subsequently having his photo taken, spent his time asking the person who was running the photo booth lots of questions about the business.

Ben felt the actual machine being used was okay but could be improved upon. He had all sorts of ideas in his head and decided he could do better and subsequently set up his own business. The idea was to rent out a photo booth for weddings and corporate events, in order to provide an additional piece of entertainment for those attending such events. However, he wanted to buy a better machine that not only looked the part, but also would ensure a better experience for his potential customers.

Having sourced such a machine, which he purchased for approximately £10,000, he set about marketing his new business both online and within his local area.

It did not take long for the word to spread that having a photo booth at a wedding would be really good fun for all the guests, regardless of age. Ben also approached some companies suggesting his photo booth would be good fun for a corporate day and was delighted with the response he got, with bookings being made quite quickly.

Due to such a demand for his photo booth, Ben was able to purchase a second machine within six months of purchasing the first one.

He offered three packages for clients:

Table 29.12 Photo booth packages for clients

Package 1 (2 hours' hire)	Package 2 (3 hours' hire)	Package 3 (4 hours' hire)
£395	£475	£595

A similar type of machine used in Ben's business

All packages include delivery and set-up charge, friendly booth attendants, prop box and a variety of backdrops within the booth. The rest of the facilities could be bespoke to meet the particular needs of the clients.

For weddings, Ben includes an album with the package for the bride and groom; once a person or usually a group of people have had their snaps taken, they may have one copy to keep and another copy is stuck into the album by one of the attendants and subsequently given to the bride and groom as a fun memento. Most of the guests write a comment under the photo, which adds to the fun.

Such has been the success of his business, Ben is now contemplating purchasing another photo booth, to meet what he hopes will be a continual growth in demand for his booths. He decided to ask his friend, an accountant, to do some calculations to test the viability of such a purchase.

The new photo booth would cost £10,500 with an expected life of five years, assuming it is well maintained. Ben's accountant friend said he would undertake a couple of investment appraisal techniques and asked Ben to provide him with some financial information. (See Tables 29.13 and 29.14.)

Table 29.13 Discount rates @3% for 5 years

Year	Discount rate
1	0.97
2	0.94
3	0.91
4	0.88
5	0.86

Table 29.14 Net cash inflow

Year	Net cash inflow (£)
0	(10,500)
1	5,500
2	6,000
3	7,500
4	9,000
5	8,500

Ben provided the information in Table 29.14, based on his sales forecast figures for the next five years for one photo booth machine and the prices of each of the three packages currently offered.

Using the case study:

1 Identify two advantages of payback to PhotoboothPlus as a method of investment appraisal. *(2)*

2 Explain two factors that may affect the 'discount factor' that would be used to ascertain the NPV for an investment. *(4)*

3 Using quantitative and qualitative information, suggest whether Photobooth should invest in another photobooth machine. *(15)*

Total *(21)*

Chapter 30

Budgets and variance

AS / Year 1

Both AS and A Level students must know all of the content in this chapter.

Any attempt to make strategic plans for the future of a business should include the use of budgets. A budget is a plan for the future that takes into account the resources that are available to the business. In most cases it will apply monetary values to different aspects of business activity, such as revenue, output and costs. Managers can then monitor the performance of the business with respect to the budgeted figures. Budgets are normally used in those parts of the business where it is possible to exercise some control.

Therefore, the main areas for budgeting involve the costs and revenues of a business.

It is possible for a business to operate effectively in terms of production, communication, and efficiency, but unless all of these things are measured effectively the business will not know how successful it is or, in some cases, whether its future is viable. This is all part of the ongoing strategic planning process for a business.

All businesses need to set objectives in a quantifiable form for the coming time period. For example, an improvement of productivity for labour of 10 per cent and a return on capital employed of 20 per cent for the coming year may be the target. Similarly, the marketing department may set a target for an improvement in sales as the result of an advertising campaign. To make all of this possible, the business must put a system in place for the collection of the data that it needs. This information needs to be used in assessing performance and setting targets for the next time period. The setting of budgets is the first part of a process that will enable a firm to review and monitor its progress and consider the need for change in the future.

The process and reasons for budgeting in a business are similar to those of a family working out a budget for the coming month or year. The act of budgeting encourages the production of inflows and outflows and helps the organisation to confront problems and act on them. It will also show which areas of the business are likely to be successful, and those that need extra attention, or which may need to be changed or dropped. Therefore, there are many reasons for undertaking budgeting in the firm. These include:

- measuring the money entering and leaving the business in all areas, using this information to indicate the level of efficiency and effectiveness of the business's activities
- giving information on the productivity levels of staff and providing one possible means of appraising and rewarding workers
- providing information for current and prospective shareholders and investors
- ensuring that the cashflow is adequate to meet the day-to-day needs of the business
- providing managers with the information they need to manage their departments and monitor their performance
- giving the whole business a strategic perspective and target that focuses on where it is now and where it would like to be after a specific period of time
- providing the basis of control and meeting objectives.

Budgeting for cashflow

The use of cashflow information is one of the most important budgeting exercises for a business. (Also see **Chapter 31** on cashflow.) Many businesses exist for relatively long periods of time while making losses. A situation where insufficient cash is entering the business to make it possible for it to meet its payment commitments is the one that most often forces a business to cease trading. The need to pay workers, either at the end of each week or month, makes it essential for the business to ensure adequate cashflow. It may be possible to delay demands from suppliers for payment without difficulty, but if wages payments are missed, the plight of the business will immediately become obvious to the outside world.

For many businesses, cashflow varies greatly from month to month, making it necessary to have overdraft facilities with the bank or cash reserves to call on. Chester Zoo is open to the public all year round, except for Christmas Day. Whatever the number of people who pass through the turnstile each day, it still has to feed the animals and pay the wages of keepers and administrative staff. The variation between cashflow in the school summer holidays and the cold dark days of January is enormous. This has to be budgeted so that plans are in place to ensure that sufficient cash is available during the winter months.

Tips and techniques

Be careful not to confuse cashflow with profit. Cash is the money entering and leaving the business. Profit is the difference between revenue and costs.

Key term

Overdraft facility: an agreement with a bank to be able to overdraw on an account up to a stated limit. This overdraft facility will usually have an agreed rate of interest (in relation to the Bank of England base rate) charged upon it.

Uses of cashflow information

The example below shows a cashflow chart for a business. These charts are calculated by adding in receipts for each time period and then deducting payments. This will give a closing balance. The closing balance for one time period will then become the opening balance for the next.

Example: Sally's Sweets

Sally Fordham runs an old-fashioned sweet shop in a holiday resort on the North Wales coast. She is often busy in the period running up to Christmas, but the main part of her business comes from holidaymakers and her busy time begins around the Easter holidays and runs through to the end of October. Since opening the shop, Sally has made a point of calculating her cashflow monthly to ensure that she can meet all her payments.

Table 30.1 Cashflow forecast for Sally's Sweets

	September (£000)	October (£000)	November (£000)	December (£000)	January (£000)	February (£000)
Opening balance	11	11	10	6	4	–1
Receipts (sales revenue)	7	5	4	10	2	2
Total (inflows)	18	16	14	16	6	1
Payments (expenses)	7	6	8	12	7	3
Closing balance	11	10	6	4	–1	–2

Tips and techniques

The terms shown in accounts may vary. Terms such as sales revenue and receipts can be used interchangeably.

Sally's payments are relatively high in October, November and December because she has to order and pay her suppliers for special Christmas stock well in advance of the Christmas period. She also has to pay for extra staff during the Christmas period. Sally knows that February will be her worst month of the year, with fewest sales and the need for an overdraft at the bank. Business will then begin to pick up as Easter approaches.

Preparing the cashflow forecast will help Sally in a number of ways. It will help her to see what her cash requirements are in any month, so that she can pay the part-time worker who helps her out during her busiest periods. She will also take this statement to her small business adviser at the bank to discuss her overdraft facilities with her. Sally knows that if she has shown that she is organised and planning ahead for all eventualities, this will reassure the bank that she is running the business effectively and that she is aware of problems that might arise in the future. The bank will also realise that over the summer months, Sally's account with them will have a substantial credit deposit. (See also **Chapter 34**.)

Decision making and strategic planning

As the example in Table 30.1 shows, the calculation of cashflow is an important tool for the business to use in preparing for the future and making strategic decisions about policy. Cashflow information can be useful in all the following budgeting situations.

Need for liquidity

The first thing a business needs to assess from a cashflow forecast is what the demand for cash is likely to be at any time, to allow the business to meet the demands for payments. Once these figures have been calculated, the manager/owner can start to think about how that cash could be generated. This will be one of the most important aspects of running a new business, when the outgoings are likely to be large and immediate but the revenue generated is small and takes time to arrive.

Improving liquidity

The most obvious source of cash for a business may be a loan, but this is not necessarily the best option. Cashflow can be improved significantly by delaying payments to suppliers and demanding payment from customers. Unfortunately, this option is often not available to new businesses because of their weak bargaining position with larger and more established firms. The larger business will know that it can delay payment and the small business will have to wait. This sort of business is often vital to the survival of the small business, and they cannot afford to do anything that puts future business at risk. Businesses can also limit outgoings by hiring or leasing equipment rather than buying it (see **Chapter 24**).

Dealing with the bank or other lenders

The preparation of a cashflow chart will highlight the need for borrowing, and will ensure that the business takes action before the event rather than when forced to react to unforeseen circumstances. Borrowing from a bank is never easy because they are effectively lending money to their customers and they must, therefore, be cautious. The bank will require other information such as accounts and projected sales figures, but much of this information will be historic. The advantage of cashflow from the bank's point of view is that it looks into the future and assesses need. A realistic estimation of future needs will also show the bank that the owner of the business is aware of fluctuations in movements of money and will therefore take a realistic and honest view of the business's performance.

Making changes

Sometimes the cashflow forecast may highlight the fact that changes need to be made. For example, a theme park may decide that it is not worth opening at certain times of the year because the revenue generated is insufficient. In another situation, a business may find that introducing longer opening hours solves some of its cashflow problems, because it will bring in larger revenue without the need for an equivalent increase in costs.

In all of these situations, the business needs to take account of the costs and benefits of its actions. For example, reducing the credit period given to customers might seem like a good way of improving cashflow, and it may work in the short term. It will reduce the debtor days' ratio for the business (see **Chapter 38**). There is always the risk, however, that the customer will find another supplier willing to give better credit terms, and that the order is lost for the long term. The need to ensure adequate cashflow is vital to the organisation, but decisions about generating cash need to be taken within the context of the whole commercial situation.

Budgeting in other areas

Budgeting is used in all areas of an effective business to ensure that spending is controlled and to provide forecasts of likely costs and returns. Budgeting by department makes it possible to split the business into smaller units and to pass responsibility to departmental heads for their own performance. This delegation of responsibility will be useful in a number of ways. Individual managers are likely to have a better immediate knowledge of their department, and should be able to ensure that their budgets are realistic and achievable. In addition, the responsibility for budgeting may be a motivator, showing that senior management trust the judgement of their more junior managers (see **Chapter 47** for information on motivation theory).

Key term

Delegation: the passing on of responsibility, usually to someone at a lower level in the organisation.

The success or otherwise of the budget may also be used to judge the performance of a particular department, its employees and its managers. It may be necessary, however, to use caution and common sense in the use of this information. Sometimes departments will fail to meet budgets for reasons outside their individual control. The figures should not be used in isolation from the performance of the rest of the firm, the market and the economy. For example, the eruption of the Icelandic volcano and the subsequent ash cloud in 2010 had an effect on air travel and airlines around the world. This event, which could not have been predicted, meant that prepared budgets were no longer valid. Far less serious events may also make it impossible to meet budgeted targets. Management need to use common sense in these situations.

Eyjafjallajökull erupting in Iceland, an event that caused global air travel disruption

Zero budgeting

An alternative to traditional methods of budgeting is zero budgeting. This involves setting all budgets at zero, requiring managers to justify any requirement for funds. The advantage of this system is that it prevents a situation where the same money is given each year without any consideration of actual need.

For example, the Head of the Business Studies department might have an annual budget this year of £500. This will be increased by 3 per cent to £515 because of the current rate of inflation. The department has had very few outgoings this year because there were sufficient books and equipment for all its students, so there will be money left at the end of the year, unless the Head of Department can find a way to spend it. Next year, however, there will be a problem because £515 will not be sufficient to buy all the books required for the new specification. It is easy to see that this system is inefficient and wasteful, particularly if the first year's money is used to buy non-essential supplies. That money could have been better used elsewhere. In this situation, zero budgeting would have worked well.

A business might use zero budgeting where it has a number of potential developments planned but is only prepared to proceed with those that are cost-justified. In this situation, it would be wrong to budget for all alternatives because of the amount of management time that would be taken in preparing the budgets.

The main problem with zero budgeting is the amount of time it takes for budget holders and financial co-ordinator to manage the system. The need to review items of expenditure and decide whether to pass them will be ongoing and may become tiresome for the person responsible. It may also mean that the business has a short-term perspective of the situation.

Flexible budgets

Flexible budgets allow a business to make allowances for changes in the level of sales volume so that adverse variances (see below) are avoided. If a business's sales rise by 5 per cent in a particular time period, the business will expect some of its costs such as raw materials and direct labour to rise. This can be taken into account immediately by increasing the budget to take account of the higher figures in these areas. For example, if a cake manufacturer finds that sales have increased by 10 per cent in the last month, the budgeted figures for ingredients would have to be adjusted to take account of this.

Variance analysis

The variance is the amount by which the actual financial results for an item differ from the amount in the budget. Variance can be adverse or favourable. For revenue, if actual sales exceed the budgeted figures the variance will be favourable, whereas for cost if actual costs exceed the budgeted figure the variance will be negative. A positive variance improves profit and a negative variance reduces actual profit.

Table 30.2 Variance analysis

Department	Budgeted figure (forecast) (£)	Actual figure (£)	Variance	
Sales	20,000	22,000	(+)	Favourable
Sales	20,000	17,000	(–)	Adverse
Labour	7,000	7,500	(+)	Adverse
Raw materials	3,000	2,900	(–)	Favourable

Tips and techniques

Great care needs to be taken when deciding whether a variance is favourable or unfavourable and in putting the correct sign in front of the number. With an inflow such as sales, an increase in the figure will result in a favourable variance and a positive sign. With an outgoing such as labour costs, an increase in the number will mean there is more money leaving the business than has been budgeted for. This means that there will be a negative variance, but a positive sign. In each case it is important to think about whether the change will make the business's circumstances better or worse for determining whether the variance is favourable or unfavourable.

Variance analysis is useful because it allows managers to see where there are problems in meeting budgets and where departments are doing particularly well, but the business needs to exercise caution in using it and should also view it alongside other relevant data. Budget targets may not be reached for a variety of reasons: some of these might be the responsibility of workers or management, like poor productivity or a breakdown in the production process. On other occasions, failure to meet the budget might be because of circumstances outside the business's control. The heavy flooding in Somerset in 2013 meant that many businesses in the tourist sector were hit by falling demand.

When variance analysis has been completed it will be necessary to assess the situation in the light of the business's current position. Managers will want to know what has happened to make variance adverse so that they can stop the problem arising again, and they will want to look at favourable variances to see if there are lessons that can be applied to other departments. Managers need to bear in mind that the variances might have occurred because the budget was unrealistic to start with. It is possible for forecasts to be too optimistic or pessimistic about future trends, or for managers to have unreasonable expectations of what employees can achieve.

In large businesses, it will not be possible for senior managers to analyse and review every budget for the business. In these situations, a system called 'management by exception' will be used. Senior managers will only become involved if the variance analysis shows a particularly serious adverse variance or a particularly good favourable variance. This means that the rest of the business can be left to run without the need for intervention as long as the variances are within defined limits. This passing of responsibility for day-to-day managers helps in encouraging responsibility and motivation as well as a responsibility for outcomes. When further action is required, it is vitally important that the manager who is dealing with the problem is in full possession of all the facts. Attributing blame to workers for failure to meet a budget target when the circumstances were outside his or her control is likely to lead to a feeling of grievance at best, or industrial action at worst.

Summary

This chapter has shown that the use of budgets is important in any business and particularly the preparation of cashflow information. As with all financial information, however, the figures are historic and managers need to remember that past experience is not always a good indicator of the future. If anything, it is the actual preparation of the budget that is important in the way it encourages a group of people to sit down and plan for the future. The alternative of leaving things to chance and good fortune is likely cause problems at some point. In addition, the budgeting process can help in making managers responsible for their departments, encouraging discussion and delegation of authority and preventing overspending.

Key term

Historic information: information that already exists from past years. For example, any figures included in a balance sheet will be historic figures, recorded at the point at which the account was dated.

Budgets cannot be used in isolation. Each business will need to consider the impact of the UK and world economy; it should look at its markets, its consumers and its competitors, and it should have contingency plans for difficult or disastrous situations (see **Chapter 8**). The budget should be used alongside information on sales, customer satisfaction and customer loyalty for the business to have a good idea of its future prospects.

Further sources

www.businessstudiesonline.co.uk
www.entrepreneur.com

Your turn

Questions are suitable for all AS and A Level candidates.

Multiple-choice questions

1 If a company has budgeted labour costs of £5,000 a month and its actual labour costs are £5,500, the variance is:
A (+) £500 (Adverse)
B (+) £500 (Favourable)
C (–) £500 (Adverse)
D (–) £500 (Favourable). *(1)*

2 A business has an opening balance in its cashflow of £12,000. Its receipts for the year are £20,000 and its payments are £17,000. What balance will it carry forward?
A £49,000
B £9000
C £15,000
D £17,000. *(1)*

Revision questions

1 State three reasons why cashflow is so important to the survival of businesses. *(3)*

2 State what is meant by 'zero budgeting' and give one feature of a zero budget. *(2)*

3 State three benefits for a firm from setting budgets. *(3)*

Total *(8)*

Case study

Gatehouse Catering

Sheila Stephens started her own catering company, working from home when her children were growing up. Starting small, Sheila catered for family celebrations, small dinner parties and the occasional wedding – if there was time. She soon built up a reputation for excellence and she had to make a decision about whether or not to expand the business.

The start-up costs for the business had been quite small so Sheila and her husband had used savings to fund this. To grow the business, Sheila would have to extend her property, put in catering equipment on a larger scale and take on extra staff. All of this would require a bank loan and possibly the help of a small business adviser from the bank. In order to apply for the bank loan Sheila had to prepare accounts for the business and a cashflow forecast. With the help of her husband, who is an accountant, Sheila was able to secure the bank loan she needed for expansion.

Sheila is now able to offer full catering facilities for weddings and other family parties, as well as catering for the local agricultural show and some business users. The business has achieved widespread success and excellent word-of-mouth promotion in an ever-expanding area.

Despite the growth in business, Sheila and her husband still manage all aspects of the business including preparing cashflow forecasts. This places an enormous strain on them, but they are reluctant to hand over any control or to pay for the services of an accounts manager. Their children have now left home, but Sheila feels that the imminent arrival of grandchildren may force them to reassess this situation.

In addition, cashflow is becoming an increasing problem for the business. At the outset, orders were paid for when delivered. This is not the case with the new corporate orders. Sheila has to pay for catering supplies and staff, but may not receive payment for the order for one or two months from these customers – and sometimes longer. Sheila is beginning to think that they should employ a part-time accounts manager who could prepare budgets, cashflow forecasts, send bills out more quickly and chase debts.

1 State three likely examples of items that would be included in a budget forecast for Sheila's business. *(3)*

2 Analyse one way by which Sheila could use budgeting to improve the performance of the business. *(6)*

3 Discuss the benefits for Sheila of preparing a budget. *(15)*

Total *(24)*

Chapter 31

Cashflow and working capital

AS / Year 1

Both AS and A Level students must know all of the content in this chapter.

Although AS students are not required in the specification to cover cashflow statements, it gives them a better understanding and is necessary for calculating variance (see **Chapter 30**); however, AS students will not be specifically examined on cash-flow statements.

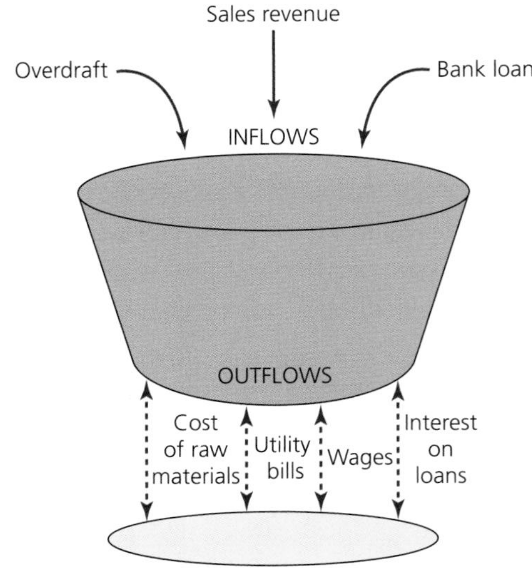

Figure 31.1 Cashflows

Cashflow

Significance of cashflow

Cashflow is the lifeblood of the business, as its circulation is essential if the business is to survive. Cash is constantly moving through and around the business. It comes into the business as a result of sales and borrowing (inflows), and leaves the business to pay for materials, labour, marketing, interest payments on loans (outflows).

Without cash, wages cannot be paid, loans cannot be repaid and raw materials cannot be bought. Without all of these inputs, there will be no business!

Cashflow differs from profit in that the former considers the inflows and outflows of cash for a business, whereas profit is a measure based on the difference between revenue and costs. Just because a business has a negative cashflow doesn't mean it has negative revenue (or profit).

Unfortunately, for many businesses, the outflows occur before the inflows are received and consequently the business fails. Both large and small businesses can run out of cash and subsequently go into liquidation. For example:

- Car manufacturers running out of cash: In 2008 some of the largest car manufacturers suffered severe cashflow problems as the demand for cars fell drastically. General Motors of the United States and its UK Vauxhall plants at Luton and Ellesmere Port were in serious danger of collapse as cash was running out.
- As reported in *The Times* (see the case study at the end of the chapter). The majority of small businesses have cash savings to last only two weeks. 'A survey by YouGov on behalf of Simply Business revealed that more than half of small businesses have a cash reserve of £10,000 while three in ten have £500 or less.'
- MFI: At the same time as Woolworths experienced problems, MFI was heading for administration. It too had run into a cash crisis. MFI had asked its landlords for a rent-free period in order to reduce its cash crisis. However, with falling sales, such action on its costs was not enough to avoid administration.

Cashflow forecasts and statements

Cashflow forecasts are estimates of the likely inflows and outflows of cash into and out of the business, over a given period of time. The forecast shows the amounts of cash that will flow in and out and the likely timing of such inflows and outflows. The timings of cash movements are just as important as the actual amounts.

For many businesses, it is not the amount of cash that creates the problems but the timings of the movements of cash.

Cashflow statements are the actual figures produced once transactions have occurred.

Reasons for cashflow forecasts

1. Preparing a cashflow forecast is a valuable planning procedure. It allows the business to put into place strategies to deal with any forecasted negative cashflow, such as organising a loan or an extension to its overdraft facilities.
2. Similarly, the forecast is useful for helping the business to set its prices.
3. The level of payment terms can be assessed or fixed to take account of any forecasted problems. A business will often alter its payment periods to its suppliers and the discount rate it offers to its customers, for prompt payment in order to help alleviate any cashflow problems.
4. If the forecasted sales revenue is low, the marketing team may consider promotional pricing in order to boost sales revenue.
5. Cashflow forecasts are looked at by potential investors. Venture capitalists and potential shareholders will be interested in the figures in order to assess its likelihood of success.
6. Suppliers may want to see such figures to assess if the business will be able to pay for the supplies on time.
7. The managers of the business will use the cashflow information to monitor the business and react accordingly.

The figures for the cashflow forecasts and statements are usually shown for each month of the year. This is because it will allow the business to see its cashflows throughout all the trading period. There may be seasonal variations in sales, and certain costs are paid quarterly and not monthly. It is therefore more accurate and reliable to show forecasts for all months.

Table 31.1 Cashflow forecast for ABC Ltd 2014

Item		January £	February £	March £	April £	May £	June £
Opening balance	A	0 H	(1,500)	(22,700)	(21,600)	2,000	28,600
Sales revenue		500 J	1,200	15,000	36,000	44,000	48,000 M
Bank loan	B	20,000	0	0	0	0	0
Total inflows	C	20,500	(300)	(7,700)	14,400	46,000	76,600
Raw materials		20,000 K	20,000	10,000	10,000	15,000	20,000
Wages		2,000	2,000	2,000	2,000	2,000	2,000
Utilities	D	0	0	1,500	0		1,700
Interest + repayments on loan			400	400	400	400	400
Total outflows	E	22,000	22,400	13,900	12,400	17,400	24,100
Net cash inflow	F	(1,500) L	(22,700)	(21,600)	2,000	28,600	52,500
Closing balance	G	(1,500)	(22,700)	(21,600)	2,000	28,600	52,500

Tips and techniques

The presentation of cashflow forecasts will vary, but the fundamental elements of inflows, outflows and net cash inflows remain the same.

As for all calculations, as long as what you have done is clear to the examiner, marks can be allocated even if you make mistakes with the actual calculations. It is also very important to note the denominations, whether it is £s or £000s, and so on.

Take care to note if the figure is within brackets, denoting it is negative.

Notes for guidance

See Table 31.1:

- A Opening balance: there is a need to ascertain if the January figure is the first ever month of the business trading, or if it is just the first month of a new forecast. If it is the latter, it is more likely to be a more accurate forecast. The opening balance may include a positive cashflow for the previous month's closing balance, or it may take account of a loan.
- B Bank loan: as well as an entry for a bank loan, there may also be a separate entry for an overdraft. Whatever is stated, it is important to remember that although the loan is a positive flow (an inflow), there will need to be outflows to pay back the loan with interest payments.
- C Total inflows: this is simply the addition of all inflows into the business (positive).
- D Utilities: this includes costs for gas, electricity, telephones and water. It is important to note that in some instances such bills are paid quarterly (every three months).
- E Total outflows: this is simply the aggregate of all the outflows (negative).
- F Net cash inflow: cash inflows – cash outflows.
- G Closing balance: the final figure (net cashflow + or –) that will be carried forward as the opening balance for the next month.
- H As the figure is 0, this shows that the business started with nothing and then gained a bank loan.
- J To gain sales revenue in the first month may be noteworthy; is it likely? Consideration of the actual product would be needed to comment on this.
- K It could be argued that the stock purchases are excessive. Too much money is tied up in stock, which will contribute to the negative cashflow.
- L The brackets indicate a negative cashflow, which could allow the business to cover the shortfall with an overdraft. The negative cashflow is set to continue into March and therefore will need to be addressed if wages are to be paid.
- M Sales revenue is set to continue growing throughout the first six months, but the rate of increase starts to decrease.
- N The comparatively large positive cashflow in June may suggest that there is more than enough cash in the business, and that some of it could be used to pay off the loan early or pay for further marketing or expansion.

Interpreting the data

Using Table 31.1:

1. Only the first six months of the year have been given. If the product or service is seasonal, these particular months will not necessarily show a true overall picture of the cashflow of the business.
2. It does not give any indication of how long the business has been trading, though the opening balance clearly suggests it has just started. The level of sales revenue compounds this.
3. The source of the sales revenue is just a total and gives no indication of whether it is from one or several products.
4. It is important to note that although sales may be agreed, they should not be counted until payment is received.
5. The type of business is not given and therefore it may be difficult to judge the significance of the cashflow forecast.
6. There is no indication of what is happening to prices (inflation) within the period for the forecast. (In 2014 the rapid increase and decrease in oil prices would have had a significant effect upon the accuracy of the forecast.)

Tips and techniques

Interpretation of cashflow forecasts and cashflow statements is a useful skill. Evidence of trends will be helpful, but the interpretation needs to be undertaken with care.

Extracts from cashflow statements

Table 31.2 Example 1: Extract from a cashflow statement

	January	February	March	April	May	June
Sales revenue (£)	200,000	180,000	130,000	80,000	30,000	10,000

Table 31.3 Example 2: Extract from a cashflow statement

	January	February	March	April	May	June
Sales revenue (£)	200,000	180,000	130,000	80,000	30,000	10,000

Table 31.4 Example 3: Extract from a cashflow statement

	January	February	March	April	May	June
Sales revenue (£)	200,000	180,000	130,000	80,000	30,000	10,000

Example 1 shows a falling level of sales revenue. It may be tempting to suggest that the business ought to think of ways to increase its cash inflows or reduce its outflows to compensate for the falling inflows. However, it would be more sensible to find out the reason for the apparent fall in revenues. The sales were for ski holidays, so a fall would be expected as the table shows a seasonal change in sales revenue.

Example 2 also shows declining sales revenue. However, reasons for the declining cash inflows are different and therefore will need a different interpretation and response. In this example, the business is faced with the recession and therefore the declining sales revenue is due to a lack of demand and not necessarily because of a fault within the business. The business is involved with selling a luxury product, so it will be more likely to feel the effects of a recession than if it were selling a necessity product. In this instance, the business may need to address the problem and take action to improve the revenue, which will in turn improve the cash inflow for the business.

Example 3 again shows a declining level of sales revenue (cash inflow). In this instance, the business is actually in decline and has genuine liquidity problems as a result of the declining sales. The competition has superior products and therefore drastic action may need to be taken.

Tips and techniques

It is important to realise that only the sales revenue has been shown in these three examples. The outflows would need to be considered before any action could be decided upon.

The three examples show that the same figures can reveal very different things about a business depending on the type of business and the state of the economy.

Limitations of cashflow forecasts

Changes to the interest rate

Circumstances within the business environment can change very quickly. Not many people would have been able to forecast the fall in interest rates that had taken place. The Bank of England had previously changed interest rates modestly, usually by only half of one per cent at any one time. However, in November 2008, in response to the effects of the credit crunch and in an attempt to stimulate the economy, interest rates were cut significantly. By 2014, interest rates were still at an all-time low of 0.5 per cent. No cashflow forecast would be able to assume that such cuts would be made, or that the rate would remain so low for so long.

The consequences of such low interest rates for businesses could mean a much lower level of costs in terms of repayments on overdrafts and loans. However, it is quite likely that the interest on loans will have been fixed when the loan was taken out.

Changes in economic policy

Being able to predict economic policy has always been difficult for businesses. What the government decides to introduce in its annual budget can have a significant effect on cashflow forecasts. Increases in taxation and national insurance contributions all affect the disposable income of consumers and therefore their ability to purchase products. Consequently, sales revenue forecasts can swiftly appear too optimistic or pessimistic.

Changes in the economic climate

The economic climate can affect a business very quickly. Although such changes in the value of shares may not affect the cashflow of a business immediately, in time the effects may show when sales fall or rise, or a business may have to pay a higher rate of interest because its asset values have fallen, making a loan more of a risk. For example:

The housing price boom in 2013/14 meant that fewer sales were achieved, which meant that home furniture businesses such as MFI suffered falls in sales, as there were fewer people moving home.

As a result of the economic upturn, car manufacturers were producing large amounts of cars in order to meet the increase in demand. Any cashflow forecast could not have gauged the significant increase demand for its cars.

Huge fluctuations in the price of a barrel of oil made forecasting costs for businesses using large amounts of fuel almost impossible. The knock-on effect on the cost of petrol, gas and electricity made cashflow forecasts very difficult.

Forecasts are estimates

If a new business is putting together its first cashflow forecast, much of the forecast will be based on assumptions, guesswork and objectives, but with no certainty as to how potential consumers will respond in purchasing its products. The sales revenue forecasts are therefore at best 'guestimates'! The time of the year in which the business is launched will influence the forecast. For example, the main sales period for many businesses is linked to Christmas and therefore the forecast for sales may be higher for this period.

Forecasting seasonal demand

Gauging demand for seasonal products is difficult. The sales of ice cream, soft drinks, alcohol and barbecues are all examples of goods that may be dependent upon the weather in the UK. The summer weather of 2008 was poor and subsequently sales revenue for many drinks businesses was much lower than their predictions.

World events

World events can have a dramatic effect on cashflow forecasts: For example, earthquakes, floods, tsunamis, plane crashes (Malaysian airlines 2014), terrorist attacks or uncertainty about events in Iraq, Israel and Gaza. All of these events can and have greatly affected sales revenues. In 2014, the Ebola virus outbreak which emerged in West Africa, affected airline flights to certain countries and consequently had a significant effect on any cashlow forecasts for these airline companies.

Competitors' behaviour

How competitors act and react can also have an effect on the accuracy of any cashflow forecast. If competitors reduce their prices, this may affect the sales revenue of another business. A business may respond to competitor price changes with its own price changes, which in turn affect its sales revenue. To what extent sales revenue will be affected will depend upon the elasticity of the product or service and the degree of competition within the market. Supermarkets, in an attempt to either protect or actually increase their market share engaged in a 'price-war' in 2014, which had a significant effect upon their cashflow.

Changes in technology

Changes in technology may affect sales revenue and costs. Competitors may launch a technologically superior product which makes the business's products inferior and therefore leads to a rapid fall in sales revenue. The business may need to respond by launching its own updated product in order to compete, resulting in higher investment and marketing costs to compete in the market place.

Given the large number of variables, the accuracy of any cashflow forecast is always in doubt. However, that does not mean that it is worthless as a decision-making or planning tool. On the contrary, planning can help alleviate problems in the future.

Cashflow statements

Table 31.5 Cashflow statement for ABC Ltd 2014

Item	January (£)	February (£)	March (£)	April (£)	May (£)	June (£)
Opening balance	0	3,000	(13,000)	(4,600)	14,900	32,200
Sales revenue	500	1,000	12,000	32,000	40,000	43,000
Bank loan	20,000	0	0	0	0	0
Overdraft			10,000	0	0	0
Total inflows	20,500	4,000	9,000	27,400	54,900	75,200
Raw materials	15,000	15,000	10,000	10,000	15,000	16,000
Wages	2,000	2,000	2,000	2,000	2,000	2,200
Utilities	500	0	1,600	0		1,900
Interest + repayments				500	700	700
Total outflows	17,500	17,000	13,600	12,500	17,700	20,800
Net cash inflow	3,000	(13,000)	(4,600)	14,900	32,200	54,400
Closing balance	3,000	(13,000)	(4,600)	14,900	32,200	54,400

To have a positive cashflow immediately is unusual but certainly not impossible, especially if the cashflow forecast has been considered carefully. It should be noted that the level of raw materials purchased has been reduced (when compared to the forecast), to avoid having a negative cashflow. However, gaining payment for goods sold in the first month should indicate that there was no 'debtor allowance' to its customers. This may also indicate the type of business and products that are being sold. By February, there is a negative cashflow which requires an overdraft to cover the cost of purchases. There is some overestimation of sales, but nevertheless a positive cashflow soon follows in April.

For many businesses, a negative cashflow is more likely, and this can be a serious issue.

Impact of cashflow forecasts and statements on a business

- They are used as a measure of performance.
- Management are able to monitor by comparing the forecast with the statement.
- They allow management to correct any problems that may occur (see below).
- Employees (if they see such documents) may be able to judge the ability of the business to offer higher levels of pay.
- Potential lenders may ask to see forecasts to assess viability of business to be able to repay any such loans.

Causes of cashflow problems

Level of sales

If a sudden fall in the level of sales revenue coincides with a heavy period of payments that are due, a negative cashflow may be inevitable.

Business environment

A change in the business environment caused by a range of factors, such as ethical issues or new legislation, may lead to a fall in sales and an increase in costs. In 2014, the conflict within Ukraine led to the EU introducing economic sanctions on Russia, who in turn retaliated, pronouncing a blockage on imported foodstuffs. This in turn affected sales for EU producers and consequently the cashflows literally overnight.

Changes in health and safety legislation may lead to additional costs for businesses, which have to implement the new laws and may face additional costs of safety equipment and further training for its employees.

Excess stock

Holding too much stock is a cost burden. If a large amount of stock in the form of raw materials, work-in-progress or finished goods are held in the factory, costs have been incurred without revenue being received. This in itself is a negative cashflow. The raw materials may have been paid for, wages will have been paid and the finished goods are costing money to be stored. All of these costs mean that the outflows will be considerable but, as yet, there are no inflows. This is one of the reasons why many businesses have adopted the just-in-time system of production (JIT), in order to reduce stock levels and therefore the amount of cash outflows.

Late payments from debtors (receivables)

Any delay in payments by the debtors of a business will have a negative effect on the cashflow. Sales revenue is the lifeblood of the business and therefore debtors should be encouraged to pay on time. Unfortunately, offering delays to such payments is often used as a marketing ploy by businesses to gain trade. This is a classic example of where different departments of a business will have differing views on required strategies.

The marketing department will regard offering late payments to its creditors as a viable incentive, while the finance department would encourage payment to be made as soon as possible.

Paying creditors too quickly

In some ways it is better to delay payment to the creditors of the business. However, there may be a delay in receiving attention to problems with supplies if payment to the suppliers (creditors) is delayed. It is therefore a balancing act between not paying immediately and keeping cash within the business, and ensuring that the relationship between the business and its suppliers is not damaged. If additional materials are required at short notice to satisfy an additional order, the business will want the supplier to help immediately. Being a 'prompt payer' may mean the business will be viewed as a preferential customer and gain an efficient service.

This is another example of a possible confrontation between departments within a business. The accounts department will want to delay payment, while the production department will want suppliers to be paid promptly to maintain a punctual supply of materials.

Over-trading

When a business grows very quickly, its need to buy materials and increase its productive capacity puts a strain on the cashflow of the business. The cost of such expansion is often greater than the present level of sales, and therefore there is a negative cashflow.

Holding the right amount of cash (working capital)

There is no right amount of cash that should be held by a business. It will depend upon the nature of the business.

Having enough cash to keep the business working (working capital) is essential to the survival of all businesses.

For example:

1 Business A (a supermarket) will receive large amounts of cash because it is selling food, and a large number of customers pay by cash. (It is not intended to suggest that 'cash' can only be notes and coins, but the use of debit and credit cards delays the actual flow of money into the business.)
2 Business B (a restaurant) will have less cash than a supermarket, but after an evening's takings may have a large amount of cash. It is also likely that many of its staff will be paid in cash.
3 Business C (a local garage repairing cars) may have little cash, as the number of customers may not be high.
4 Business D (a money lender) will of course have a very high level of cash, as this is the 'product' of the business.

Tips and techniques

It is essential that all cashflow forecasts and statements are viewed with care and the type of business noted.

Liquidity ratios

The use of liquidity ratios such as current ratio and acid test are simple ways to assess the level of cash within a business. (See **Chapter 36**.)

Too little cash

1 This creates an inability to meet creditors' requests for payment. Terms of purchase may be less favourable in the future. It may also mean that it becomes difficult to buy stock or raw materials. For some creditors, such as the bank, the consequences of not paying could be much more serious, as any loans may then be foreclosed.
2 A lack of cash may mean that additional funds will need to be borrowed from the bank, possibly at higher rates of interest.

Too much cash

1. There is a wasted opportunity to purchase more stock.
2. There may be a loss of interest if the excess cash was not put into an account.
3. Any borrowing costs are being paid unnecessarily as the excess cash could be used to reduce debts.

Improving the cashflow of the business

Increase sales

This is easier said than done, especially in periods of an economic downturn. There may also be financial implications of gaining increased sales.

In the short term, there will be additional cash outflows to pay for the marketing needed to increase sales. The increased sales may only be achieved by reducing the price and therefore, although inflows will increase, the aggregate amount of revenue will not.

Reduce stock levels by selling off stock or buying less stock

The utilisation of JIT will reduce the level of stock held, though the same amount of stock has to be paid for at some stage. By holding less stock, the cost of storage and the time gap between the usage of stock and the sales revenue may be reduced.

Factoring

Factoring is the 'selling' of the debts of a business. It allows for revenue from debtors to be received earlier, although there is a 'price to pay'. The factoring company will take a proportion of the value of the debt as payment.

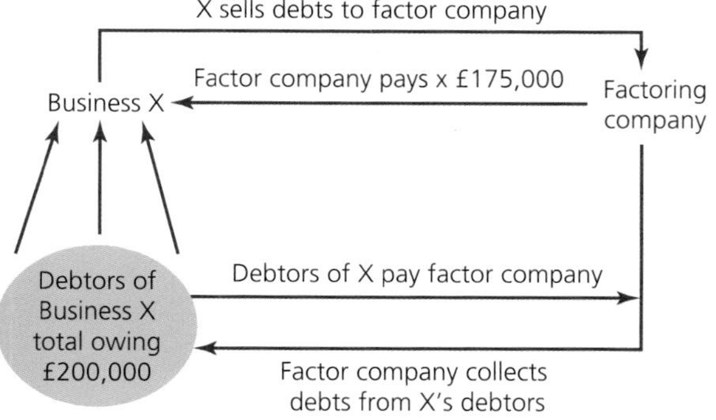

Figure 31.2 Factoring

In Figure 31.2, Business X has several debtors. If there is likely to be a delay in these debts being paid, X can sell the collective debt to a factor company.

The factor company will pay X a proportion of the total debt (£175,000 of the £200,000) immediately. X is satisfied as it will gain an injection of cash (£175,000) although it has had to 'lose' £25,000 of the debt in the form of a fee.

The factor or factoring company will now own the debt and be entitled to collect the money from the debtors.

Business X has to decide if the greater benefit is to have the majority of what it is owed immediately and pay a percentage of the debt to gain the cash now; or collect all of the outstanding debt (£200,000) at some time in the future.

The main criteria for deciding what to do will probably depend upon how much X needs the cash immediately, and if it can afford to lose a proportion of cash to this end.

Leasing not buying

This is a form of borrowing. It is similar to renting in that ownership is not gained, but usage is exclusive during the period of the lease agreement. A company may decide to lease an expensive new machine it needs rather than buying it outright.

The amount of cash required is obviously much less, and the cash paid out is spread over the period of the leasing agreement. Consequently, a large amount of cash is not needed, as it would be if payment for the machine was made immediately.

Loans

Although a loan allows a business to stagger the repayments over a given period of time, in the long run it is more costly because of the interest that has to be paid. However, a loan means that a large amount of capital is not required in one sum to pay for the required machine or building.

Changing creditor and debtor days

To improve the liquidity of a business, the number of debtors could be reduced. If the business no longer offered its customers a delayed time to pay for the products supplied, cash would flow into the business much sooner. However, the level of sales and therefore the amount of cash could fall, as the customers are reliant on a delayed payment.

Alternatively, the amount of time offered to customers could be reduced, to shorten the period between sales and the cash being paid. However, the marketing department may not be prepared to lose an effective promotional tool.

Creditor days could be increased. Delaying payment to creditors will allow cash to remain within the business for a longer period of time, and may mean that less cash is needed to cover any subsequent negative cashflow.

Cut operating costs

Expensive cash outflows in the short term can be alleviated by outsourcing. It may actually cost more to outsource, but on the other hand there may be an opportunity to reduce overheads and therefore reduce outflows.

Tips and techniques

All of the ways to improve the cashflow of a business are appropriate, but some are better strategies than others. It depends upon the actual business involved, its circumstances, its performance over time, and the nature of the market in which it competes. In other words, the context of the case is essential when selecting a method to improve the cashflow of a business.

Your turn

Questions are suitable for all AS and A Level candidates.

Multiple-choice questions

1 The following are all methods of improving the cashflow of a business, except:
   A factoring
   B decreasing creditor days
   C increasing sales revenue
   D increasing loans. *(1)*

Using the information in the table below answer questions 2, 3 and 4:

Cashflow item	January 2014 £000	February 2014 £000
Inflows		
Sales revenue	250	280
Bank loan	50	0
Outflows		
Raw materials	180	185
Wages	80	80
Utilities	30	32
Net cashflow		
Opening balance	(25)	
Closing balance		

2 The closing balance for January 2014 is:
   A (25)
   B 10
   C (15)
   D 15. *(1)*

3 The closing balance for February is:
   A (32)
   B (297)
   C 255
   D (25). *(1)*

4 The sales revenue from February increased by 15%; therefore the sales revenue for March 2014 is:
   A 56
   B 346
   C 295
   D 322. *(1)*

Revision questions

1 State three sources of cash inflows. (3)
2 State how to calculate net cash inflow (working capital). (2)
3 Analyse two consequences on the cashflow forecast for a business if fuel costs increase and unemployment rises. (4)
4 Explain two ways a negative cashflow could be improved by extending the number of creditor days. (4)
5 Explain two ways factoring could improve the liquidity of a business. (4)

Total (17)

Case study

As reported in *The Times*

Most small businesses have cash savings to last only two weeks if unforeseen circumstances were to force them to cease trading temporarily.

A survey by YouGov on behalf of Simply Business revealed that more than half of small businesses have a cash reserve of £10,000 while three in ten have £500 or less.

In recent years, independent businesses in the UK have battled unexpected problems ranging from riots to floods, leading many to cease trading permanently. Jason Stockwood, the chief executive of Simply Business, said:

'Even after last year's storms and flooding, which cost over £830million of damage to firms nationwide, small businesses are woefully under prepared for unforeseen circumstances, which will prevent trading'.

Source: 'Third of tiddlers have just £500 in reserve', *The Times*, 11 August 2014.

1 Apart from riots and flooding, list two examples of likely 'unforeseen circumstances' which may have an adverse effect upon the cashflow of a business. (2)
2 Explain two reasons why a small business may only have a cash reserve of between £10,000 and £500. (4)
3 Analyse the likely effect on a small business if a larger company were slow to pay for materials supplied by the small business. (6)
4 State four possible methods that a small business could use to improve its cashflow. (4)

Total (16)

Chapter 32

Index numbers

AS / Year 1

Both AS and A Level students must know all of the content in this chapter.

To allow for comparisons to be made, index numbers may be used. Index numbers convert values or numbers from different years into a 'value' based on one particular year (the base year).

By converting the numbers from different years into one year as a common denominator, this allows for meaningful comparisons to be made. This means a business can make judgements about whether there have been genuine improvements or a decline in, for example, sales.

Table 32.1 Sales of iPhones in a shop

Year	Number of sales in a given shop
2012	120,000
2013	130,000
2014	135,000

Using the formula of:

$$\frac{\text{Number in year required}}{\text{Number in base year}} \times 100$$

If the base year is viewed as having a value of 100 this enables a clear way to make valid comparisons.

Therefore, if the base year is 2012 and year to be compared with is 2013, the index number would be:

$$\frac{130{,}000}{120{,}000} \times 100 = 108.3$$

Therefore the sale of iPhones has increased by 8.3 per cent. Seeing a percentage allows for a quick and easy comparison rather than trying to ascertain between large numbers.

If a comparison is necessary for actual values in terms of money, the process is the same and the formula would be:

$$\frac{\text{Price in year}}{\text{Price in base year}} \times 100$$

Chapter 33

Income statements

AS / Year 1

Both AS and A Level students must know all of the content in this chapter.

The income statement, previously known as the P&L, reports the level of profit or loss that a business has made in a given period of time (usually one year), often known as the trading or accounting period.

The income statement is a measure of the performance of the business, and is used to inform shareholders and other potentially interested stakeholders of how well the business has performed. The layout of the income statement is important as the reader is able to see quickly the levels of revenues and costs within the business. This may be helpful when it comes to assessing the level of performance or considering how such performance can be improved.

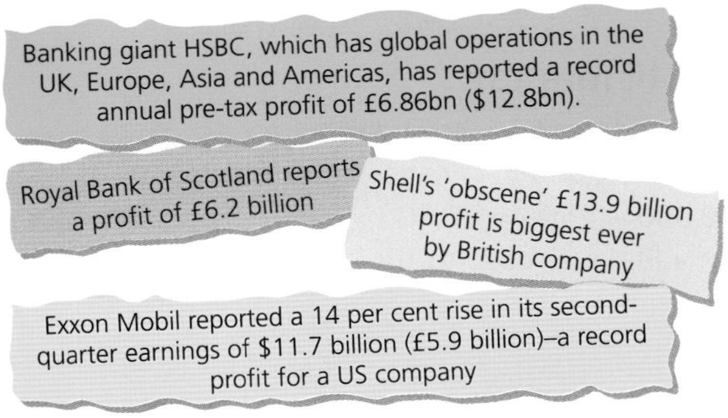

Banking giant HSBC, which has global operations in the UK, Europe, Asia and Americas, has reported a record annual pre-tax profit of £6.86bn ($12.8bn).

Royal Bank of Scotland reports a profit of £6.2 billion

Shell's 'obscene' £13.9 billion profit is biggest ever by British company

Exxon Mobil reported a 14 per cent rise in its second-quarter earnings of $11.7 billion (£5.9 billion)–a record profit for a US company

Figure 33.1 Newspapers report the profits of large companies

Profit

It is important to establish exactly what is meant by the term 'profit'. Profit is:

- the difference between the level of income generated and the costs incurred by the business. In its most simplistic form, profit is calculated by subtracting the total costs from the total revenue.

  Profit can also be defined as:
- return on an investment
- reward for taking risks
- source of income for the business
- measure of performance and noted by stakeholders such as the shareholders, employees and suppliers.

Key term

Gross profit: revenue minus cost of sales.
Operating profit: Gross profit minus expenses.
Profit before tax: Operating profit minus finance costs.
Profit for the year: Profit and dividends minus tax.

What does an income statement contain?

The income statement always states the trading period (e.g. 'Income statement for the year ending December 2014') so that stakeholders know that this information will tell them how the business has performed in a given time period. Profits for public limited companies are normally declared every six months. Some of the larger companies declare their profits quarterly. The half-year profits are known as the 'interim results'.

The financial year can start at any time but the majority of businesses use either the tax year, which runs from April to April, or the calendar year, January to December.

Table 33.1 Income statement year ending December 2014

	Expenditure (£000)	Income (£000)
Revenue (or turnover)		300,000
Minus cost of sales	120,000	
Gross profit		180,000
Minus expenses	100,000	
Operating profit		80,000
Minus finance costs	7,500	
Profit before tax		72,500
Minus tax	15,000	
Minus dividends	30,000	
Profit for the year		27,500

Table 33.1 shows that the figures for income start off as high, but become smaller as deductions are made. The first deduction is for the cost of the sales, which is calculated in a special way.

Revenue (turnover)

This is a simple calculation based on the level of sales and their value: price × sales.

It is important to ensure that the figures used are realistic, as in many instances the price of the goods or services will include VAT and possibly excise duties. The taxes included in the price of the good will have to be deducted to gain an appropriate figure.

Tips and techniques

It is not likely that any question would ask you to deal with taxes (they will be included in the price), but an awareness of this may be useful when commenting on such figures.

It is also important to note when the actual sale of the goods took place, to ensure that the figures are counted within the right year.

Cost of sales

The cost of sales describes the direct cost of producing the goods. Only direct or variable costs are counted and subtracted. Once the cost of sales has been calculated and subtracted from the sales revenue, the residue is the gross profit.

Knowing how much stock has actually been sold, and therefore needs to be costed, must be calculated with care.

To calculate the cost of sales:

Opening inventory (from previous year) + purchases in this year – closing inventory (what stock is left) = Cost of sales

Only the cost of the stock that was actually sold in the financial year must be counted. For example: if the business started with stock worth £95,000, bought £45,000 and at the end of the year had £20,000 left, the cost of sales would be:

Opening inventory	£95,000
+ purchases	£45,000
– closing inventory	£20,000
Cost of sales =	£120,000

In the year, the actual amount of stock sold cost £120,000. That is the amount that has to be taken off the total sales revenue of £300,000 to calculate the gross profit for that year.

Gross profit

This is calculated as shown here:

Sales revenue – cost of sales

300,000 – 120,000 = 180,000

Gross profit only considers the direct costs of production.

Operating profit

This is calculated as shown here:

Gross profit – expenses

180,000 – 100,000 = 80,000

Operating profit is a more realistic measure of profit as it accounts for both direct costs (variable costs) and expenses (overheads or fixed costs).

Profit before tax

This is calculated as shown here:

Operating profit – finance costs (interest paid)

80,000 – 7,500 = 72,500

An additional 'cost' to the business is interest on loans; these are treated separately as they are not related to the actual costs incurred with the production of the goods.

Profit for the year (retained profit)

Profit for the year is calculated as shown here:

Net profit – tax and dividends

72,500 – 45,000 = 27,500

Finally, the shareholders may be paid a dividend (their reward for holding shares in the business), and the government will want to deduct tax on the profits (corporation tax).

The profit for the year is the money which the business can use after all deductions have been made. The business can decide how best to use this profit. It may be invested into the business in the form of new capital equipment, or it may be used to pay off some of the debts of the business.

Non-operating income/expenses

On some income statements there may be reference to 'interest received or earned'. This is an additional source of income that has been generated within the period of time for that particular income statement period. The figure is simply added to the accounts, usually after operating profit and before net profit. Another source of income could be rents or dividends which the business has earned from its investments in other businesses.

Similarly, money may have to be subtracted from the accounts due to interest payable on loans which the business has taken out.

Tips and techniques

Amounts to be deducted can be put in brackets to signify it is a negative quantity, but in an income statement this is not essential. Again, the layout of your work is crucial to help both yourself and the examiner to see what you have done. It is not essential to have two columns for the figures; however, by doing so it is easier for you to know what a deduction is and identify a running total. It is less likely that you will be asked to undertake any significant or detailed calculations under examination conditions; you are more likely to be asked to use the figures. There may be instances where you will be asked to complete an income statement and then analyse it. Nevertheless, you should understand how the figures are deduced, as this will make it easier for you to analyse the income statement.

Divisions of the income statement:

The income statement can be divided into three divisions or sections:

1 trading account
2 income statement
3 appropriation account.

The trading account

This part of the income statement concentrates on the figures that are used to calculate the gross profit. The trading account considers just the sales revenue and the cost of sales.

This part can be used to judge the efficiency of the business in terms of its ability to convert its factors of production into finished goods; in other words, its ability to change the raw material into saleable goods.

The income statement

This account concentrates on the calculation of the operating profit for the business. It considers not only the sales revenue and the cost of sales, but also the overheads of the business such as machinery, salaries, and expenditure of the accounting and marketing departments. This account is a more accurate reflection of the success of the business. This account will enable the business to assess its efficiency in ensuring that overheads (expenses) are kept under control.

Tips and techniques

There is often some confusion between operating profit and net profit. The latter takes into consideration all deductions from the business. There may be one-off payments that would not usually appear (extraordinary items) as they would offer a misleading picture of the business. Operating profit only takes into consideration direct and indirect costs, before dividends and tax are paid. Taxes and dividend payments are included in the profit and loss section/division.

The appropriation account

This part of the accounts concentrates on what actually happens to the profits (if any) that are made. In some texts these are references to 'profit utilisation', which is how the profits are used.

The appropriation of accounts looks at how much is distributed to the shareholders in the form of dividends, and what proportion is retained by the business for future investment.

Tips and techniques

Care needs to be taken when assessing what amount of the profit goes to the shareholders. It may appear obvious in the short term that shareholders would want as much of the profits to be distributed to them in the form of dividends. However, limiting the distributed profits to the shareholders, in order to have more retained profits to aid investment, may mean higher profits in the long term.

Tips and techniques

Interpretation of income statement

Table 33.2 Income statement for E&T Ltd 2013 and 2014

	Figures for 2014 (£000)	Figures for 2013 (£000)
Revenue (turnover)	130	140
Cost of sales	85	83
Gross profit	45	57
Expenses	27	35
Operating profit	18	22
Finance costs	6	9
Profit before tax	12	13
Tax and dividends	8	9
Profit for the year	4	4

Be careful when commenting on any form of financial statement. Ensure that you refer to the correct amount involved. In Table 33.2, the value is in thousands of pounds.

Comparing two years of accounts

An income statement will often refer to at least two years of accounts. This will enable a comparison to be made. Analysing how the two years (2013 and 2014) differ is of interest. Although the amount of retained profit is the same (£4,000), the activities between the two years are different.

- The sales revenue has decreased by £10,000, while the cost of sales has only increased by £2,000; therefore the gross profit has decreased by only £8,000.
- The cost of sales has not fallen even though sales revenue has fallen. This may be due to a loss of the benefits from economies of scale; or perhaps the actual costs have risen because of increased cost of raw materials or direct labour. It may also be due to an increase in the number of goods sold, albeit at a reduced price.
- The operating profit has also decreased by £4,000 (although expenses decreased by £8,000).
- The fall in expenses may be because fewer machines were bought, as sales may have been expected to rise in 2014, and therefore additional overheads were incurred in 2013.
- Interest payable may support the point above. The need to borrow may have fallen, or some of the previous loans have been paid in full. Alternatively, the rate of interest may have fallen, but it is less likely that the amount paid in interest would fall if on a fixed-interest loan repayment.
- The retained profit is the same, possibly because the dividend paid has decreased (although the amount of tax paid could have decreased).

Tips and techniques

Be careful when assessing what has happened without knowing the actual facts. Although tax and dividends are down, it is impossible to state clearly why this is the case. It is a good idea to offer possible reasons for the changes, which may include:

- less profit made and therefore less tax to be paid
- a fall in the rate of corporation tax
- a reduction in the amount of dividend paid to shareholders as a result of falling profits.

Points to watch out for

- It is important to ensure that you comment on income statements in the context of the case information. Is the business new or well-established? The level of profit could vary according to the age of the business. Similarly, the level of profit could be affected by the nature of the product or service, and how competitive the market is in which the business is operating. A new business is more likely to want purely to survive, rather than expect to make a huge profit.
- A good student will try to evaluate and suggest the most likely reasons for the changes in the figures, with justification from the case study.

- If the case study states that the business is hoping to expand, then it is quite possible that the level of profit in the short term may be low, due to the cost of expansion. In the long run, profits will be higher, once the benefits of the expansion (assuming it is successful) have managed to increase production and therefore profits.
- For a case study that includes an income statement, much information can be gained from the figures. Ratios can be calculated, or trends established and measured against the objectives set by the business.

The usefulness of income statements

- The income statement enables the business to make decisions. Being able to see the amount of profit made may affect any decisions on future expenditure.
- Management can use the income statement to monitor the progress of the business in terms of targets. It allows comparisons to be made between financial years.
- The figures can be used to calculate particular ratios to help assess the performance of the business (see **Chapter 39**).
- It can help the business in formulating its objectives for the future.
- A healthy profit may encourage a business to buy back shares from the shareholders. It may also encourage expansion plans.
- It provides other stakeholders with valuable information. A bank may be interested to note the amount of profit a business has made in order to assess the amount of risk involved, and therefore help it decide whether to lend money to the business.
- Investors will look to see whether they should invest their money in the business. A profitable business is more likely to attract further investors.
- H M Revenue & Customs will be able to see that the correct amount of tax is paid.
- The employees are able to see how much profit the business made, and therefore note whether the business is in a strong position to increase its wages and salaries.
- It is a legal requirement to maintain and publish financial records for certain types of business (the Companies Act).
- Suppliers may want to see the income statement as evidence of an ability to pay for materials supplied.

Further sources

Company Reports, which are available from the *Financial Times*
www.ftannualreports.com
www.mulberry.com
www.mulberry.com/investor-relations/index

Your turn

Questions are suitable for all AS and A Level candidates.

Multiple-choice questions

1 If the sales revenue for 'Shirts 4 all' in 2014 was £158,000 and the costs of sales were £69,000, the gross profit is:
A £189,000
B £89,000
C £227,000
D loss of £69,000. *(1)*

2 The costs of sales is equal to:
A stock – revenue
B opening inventory + purchases – closing inventory
C opening inventory – purchases + closing inventory
D opening inventory – closing inventory. *(1)*

Revision questions

1 What is the difference between gross profit and operating profit? *(2)*

2 Outline two ways in which the income statement may be useful to external stakeholders. *(4)*

3 Explain two ways in which internal stakeholders would be affected by a fall in the level of profit made by a company. *(4)*

Total *(10)*

Case Study

Mulberry bags (Somerset)

Mulberry produces and sells premium handbags and bags of high fashion.

Table 33.3 shows a summary of its income statements for three years.

Table 33.3 Group Summary 31 March 2014

	2012	2013	2014
Revenue	£168.5m	£161.1m	£165.5m
Operating profit	£35.4m	£25.5m	£13.7m
Profit before tax	£36m	£26m	£14m
Dividend per share	5p	5p	5p

1 Using Table 33.3, calculate the percentage change in revenue from 2012 to 2014. *(2)*

2 Analyse how any one stakeholder in Mulberry will benefit from the results in the income statement shown in Table 33.3. *(4)*

3 Evaluate the value of the information contained in Table 33.3 to Mulberry and its stakeholders. *(12)*

Total *(18)*

Chapter 34

Statement of financial position

AS / Year 1

Both AS and A Level students must know all of the content in this chapter.

A statement of financial position, formerly known as the balance sheet, is a statement about the value of a business at a given point in time, showing what it owns (assets) and what it owes (liabilities). All private and public companies issue statements of financial position for their shareholders.

The amount of detail and some of the terminology may vary slightly for companies when compared to sole traders and partnerships.

The statement of financial position is normally headed: 'statement of financial position for (the name of the business/company), year ending (or 'as at') (insert date).'

Key terms

Statement of financial position: a method of recording the value or wealth of a business at a given moment in time.
Assets: what the business owns.
Liabilities: what the business owes.
Current liabilities: less than one year.
Non-current liabilities: money owed for more than one year.
Liquidity: the ability to convert assets into cash.
Depreciation: an allowance for the wear and tear on the fixed tangible assets.

Contents of a statement of financial position

Assets

Assets are what the business owns. Assets are a positive number on the balance sheet. There are several types of asset.

Non-current (fixed) assets

A non-current asset may be the factory or buildings owned by the business. It also includes the fixtures and fittings of the business, such as the machines and equipment used. These are the assets that are necessary to enable the business to function. It is important to realise that the business can only count what it actually owns; rented facilities are not owned and therefore would not be counted.

Tangible assets

These are assets which can be seen. The factory and machines will be both fixed and tangible fixed assets.

Intangible assets

These assets are not visible, such as a patent or the goodwill of the business, a value for its reputation or a good brand name.

It is very difficult to put an accurate value on intangible assets. The better known a business is, the more likely it is that its intangible assets (goodwill, see below) will be higher.

It will of course depend upon the 'health' of the business, as a business may be well known for negative reasons! (After the alleged financial irregularities published in October 2014, Tesco may well have lost some of its goodwill as its reputation may have been damaged.)

Goodwill may only be specifically mentioned if the business is involved in a takeover or merger. Nevertheless, it is a valued asset.

Goodwill

If a business is valued at £500,000 and the value of the tangible assets is £450,000, assuming there are no other intangible assets then the value of £50,000 is the value of the goodwill. The goodwill of a business is of value if a business is being sold and explains why there are occasions when a business is bought for what appears to be well in excess of its net asset value.

Patents

It is often very difficult to put a valuation on a patent.

- It will depend upon the length of the patent, its type and what the patent is actually for. The more technological the patent is, the more likely its value will be higher.
- Getting the valuation accurate is not easy and it is important to remember this, because a patent may be and is used as security when applying to borrow money.
- Scientific and technological businesses protect their research, techniques and products, in order to have the time and opportunity to generate sufficient income over time to compensate for the possible high level of expenditure on research and development.
- In an attempt to put a value on a patent it is common to value according to both the quantitative and qualitative elements.
- For the quantitative aspect there may be measurable data which can be used; however, for the qualitative, the characteristics and uses of the item in question need to be considered. The patent is often referred to as protecting the 'intellectual property' of the business.
- Putting a value on these is usually based on the amount in terms of costs that is spent on the R&D. Or the level of likely income the invention is likely to generate – its expected revenue inflows.

All of these factors are in the main guesswork; nevertheless, a patent has real value and therefore needs to be represented within a statement of financial position.

Prudence

This is an accounting phrase, used to indicate that there is a need to be cautious when valuing a business. Overestimating the value of a business is inappropriate, and hence to gain a realistic value of the fixed assets, depreciation needs to be considered.

Depreciation

Depreciation is an allowance for the wear and tear on the fixed tangible assets. As the factory and machines age, their value decreases. Depreciation reflects this, usually as a percentage of the assets, to give a realistic value of the business. (See **Chapter 35**.)

Financial non-current assets (fixed assets)

Occasionally the statement of financial position refers to investments that are made by the business in government bonds. Investing in long-term bonds or shares is considered as a fixed asset.

Current assets

Current assets describe everything owned by the business which is not a non-current (fixed) asset. These assets are capable of being converted into cash within the accounting period. The easier these assets can be converted into cash, the better. (This ability to covert assets into cash is known as liquidity.)

It is now normal practice that the current assets are listed in order of:

- inventories
- trade and other receivables (debtors)
- cash.

Key term

Liquidity: the ability to convert assets into cash.

Inventory

Inventory (stock) can be in the form of materials, unfinished goods (work in progress) and finished goods. The liquidity of stock very much depends upon the type of stock.

- Finished goods are usually easier to convert into cash.
- However, raw materials may also be converted into cash if there is a market for such materials.
- The least liquid type of stock is unfinished goods, which are neither raw materials nor finished goods, and therefore of little value to anyone until finished.
- Finished goods will vary in terms of their liquidity. Perishable goods with a short shelf-life will be less liquid than goods with a longer shelf-life. The latter has a better chance of being sold and subsequently generating cash.
- Fast moving consumer goods (FMCGs) are more liquid than other goods as there is a frequent and regular demand for such products.

Trade and other receivables (debtors)

This category includes money that is owed to the business. Assuming that the debts owed to the business are due for payment within one year, they are counted as a current asset.

As for the inventory, the liquidity of debtors will depend upon how quickly the debt is due to be paid, and the likelihood of the debt actually being paid.

The business may offer a period of credit, either 30 or 60 days, in which goods have to be paid for. (Any period can be offered. Offering a business time to pay is often used as a marketing incentive in order to gain business.)

Cash

Money is obviously the most liquid of the current assets, as it is already cash.

Bad debts

However, not all debtors (trade receivables) will pay and this is known as a 'bad debt'.

It is therefore important for a business to make allowances for such bad debts, in order to gain a more realistic valuation of assets (current assets).

There are several ways of estimating the level of likely 'bad debts' a business will incur:

- allowance method
- aging method
- credit sales.

Each of the above is an attempt to gauge a figure for the likely level of 'bad debts' and therefore provide a realistic figure for the trade receivables (debtors).

Allowance method

This is calculated by taking the figure as a percentage of the receivables (debtors).

A business will look at its records and take an average percentage of bad debts, for example 4 per cent. Therefore, if the business has for the present financial year £200,0000 in receivables then the bad debt allowance will be:

£ 200,000 × 4% = £8,000.

Or

£200,000 × 0.04 = £8,000

This amount is an allowance for bad debts, therefore giving a more realistic receivables figure of £192,000.

Ageing method

This assumes in a simplistic manner that the longer an account is overdue for payment, the more likely it will not be paid at all. If a business has sold goods to another business and has yet to be paid, it would be classed as receivables (debtors). However, based on historic records the business that sold the products will know the likelihood of receiving any payment at all. The business will also be able to factor into its thoughts the likelihood of being paid, based on its records of that particular business that has received the goods. The business that has yet to pay may always pay late or be one that needs several reminders to pay or, even worse, has failed to pay previously. The business supplying the products will have to decide whether to continue trading with such a business!

Credit sales

This is another method used in assessing the likely level of bad debts based on the historical records of a business.

If a business has £400,000 sales which use credit (credit sales), and based on previous records the average bad debt on credit sales is 2 per cent, then the bad debt calculation will be:

£400,000 × 2% = £8,000.

Or

£400,000 × 0.02 = £8,000

Some businesses calculate the likely level of bad debts on total sales (turnover and not just credit sales).

Tips and techniques

It is important not to become confused between debtors (those that owe the business) and when a business offers credit. If a business offers credit to another business, the latter will become a debtor of the former. For example: business A offers a credit facility to business B to pay for goods in 30 days' time. Business A will have debtors (business B).

Liabilities

Liabilities are what the business owes. They are negatives on the statement of financial position.

Tips and techniques

Negative amounts are usually shown by putting the figure in brackets; a minus sign can also be used, although this is not the norm.

Current liabilities

Current liabilities are negatives on the statement of financial position. They describe what is owed by the business and due for repayment within one year.

They are the opposite of current assets and may consist of overdrafts and short-term loans.

Overdraft

An overdraft is an agreement with the bank to borrow money to avoid cashflow problems. Overdrafts may be used when a payment needs to be made and sufficient funds are not available until days or months later. An overdraft may be agreed for anything from one day to just under a year.

The amount to be borrowed will vary according to the needs of the business and is usually for up to an agreed sum.

Short-term loan

This is a loan for a fixed amount over a fixed period of time, less than one year.

Trade and other payables (creditors)

Creditors are the opposite of debtors. They refer to other businesses (suppliers) who have not yet been paid. The business will have received raw materials or components but does not have to pay until an agreed time.

Net current assets (working capital)

To calculate the net current assets, or working capital, subtract current liabilities from current assets.

However, there are instances where within the statement of financial position it will show net current liabilities (as the assets) if the figure is negative.

Non-current (long-term) liabilities

These are loans for more than one year. They can be in various forms.

1. Mortgage: associated with the buying of property.
2. Debenture: only issued by a company that is a plc. A debenture is a long-term loan with a fixed rate of interest.
3. Bank loan: a loan of more than one year.

Net assets

To calculate the net assets, add the value of the net current assets to the non-current assets, minus the non-current (long-term) liabilities. This figure reflects the value of the business at a given point in time.

It may be calculated as follows:

Total assets (current assets +non-current assets) – Current liabilities – non-current liabilities

It is important to ensure the net assets of the business 'balance' with the funding of the business; this is normally shown via the total equity of the business.

Shareholders' equity or total equity (capital and reserves)

This is the value of funds tied up in the business, in the form of shares and retained profits. The shareholders' funds may have arisen from different types of shares issued.

Ordinary shares

These are the shares that show an ownership of the business. Each share allows the holder a vote at the annual general meeting (AGM) of the business. The value of these shares may change, reflecting the wellbeing of the business.

Preference shares

Preference share have priority (preference) over ordinary shares when the profits are distributed. The share of the profit is usually based on a fixed percentage rather than the size of the dividend declared, as is the case for ordinary shares.

Reserves and retained earnings (profit and reserves)

This refers to money that has been retained in the business in order to help it grow, rather than being distributed to the shareholders. It represents money that has been ploughed back into the business.

It is not cash, as cash appears as an asset under current assets.

Reserves are a balancing item to show that when a business increases its assets, some of the profit that did not go to shareholders has been invested in the business.

Tips and techniques

The presentation of your figures is vital; the use of columns should help you make the right additions and subtractions, and therefore gain the right answer. It is highly likely you will be presented with the figures and have to complete, interpret and offer some analysis of the figures shown.

Reading the statement of financial position

The statement of financial position will balance in terms of the calculations.

- Net assets (what the business owns) will always be equal to (balanced by) total equity, which includes the shareholders' funds (sometimes written as 'financed by'), also referred to as the source of funds.
- For negative amounts (money that is owed), the figure is often shown in brackets. This makes it easier for you to remember that the figure is negative and needs to be subtracted to gain a realistic value of the business.
- Regardless of the headings used, which may vary to some extent, the calculations you use should be clearly shown.

Looking at the statement for financial position for Pods Galore Ltd, much information can be gained about the value of the business.

- The owner may want to state that he or she owns a shop, which is worth £120,000. However, because the shop is quite old and some of the fixtures are in need of replacing, the true value is less than this. Depreciation takes into account this aging factor.
- The current assets of the business total £47,000. This does not mean that the owners spend this amount of money, even though this represents assets.
- Some of the £47,000 is tied up in inventory (stock) (£30,000), which may or may not be sold soon. (A business selling food may have a lot of current assets tied up in stock that will not sell, perhaps due to the sell-by-date being reached.) In this business, its stock of iPods may be out of date in terms of the latest versions/technology.
- Trade and other receivables (debtors) represent some of the current assets. This is money that is

Table 34.1 Statement of financial position for Pods Galore Ltd, year ending 31 December 2014

	Values and calculations in (£)	Running totals (£)	Comments/calculations
Non-current (Fixed) assets	120,000		
Less depreciation (10%)	12,000		(10% of 120,000 = 12,000) 120,000 – 12,000 = 108,000
		108,000	
Current assets			
Cash	2,000		
Inventory	30,000		
Trade/receivables	15,000		
Total current assets		47,000	(Adding cash, stock and debtors)
Current liabilities			
Overdraft	9,000		Overdraft is the only current liability stated
Total current liabilities		9,000	
Net current (liabilities) assets		38,000	(Current assets – current liabilities) 47,000 – 9,000
Non current liabilities	75,000		
Net assets		71,000	(Fixed assets + net current assets – long-term liabilities) 108,000 + 38,000 – 75,000 = 71,000
Shareholders' funds			
Ordinary shares	50,000		
Retained profit	21,000		These amounts should balance (be equal to) the net assets
Total equity		71,000	

owed to the business. However, it is not certain that this money will be paid to Pods Galore.

- Even after noting these points, there are current liabilities to be taken into account. Liabilities represent money that is owed by the business, in this case, £9,000.

As a consequence, the true value of Pods Galore's current assets is £38,000 (assuming stock can be sold and that debtors will pay).

To gain a more realistic value of the business, any non-current liabilities (money that is owed for more than one year) has to be taken into consideration (this is often in the form of a long-term loan). For Pods Galore Ltd, the actual value of the business is £71,000. This is calculated by adding the assets and deducting the liabilities:

Non-current assets (after depreciation)	108,000
Net current assets	38,000
(Current assets – current liabilities)	47,000 – 9,000
Minus non-current liabilities	75,000
Net assets	71,000

How useful is a statement of financial position?

It is important to be able to look at a statement of financial position and understand what is being stated. Do the figures make sense for this type of business selling this particular product? As the business is Pods Galore Ltd, a small retail outlet selling iPods and similar equipment, the figures appear realistic. However, the make-up of the assets may vary depending on the type of business. A large supermarket chain store such as Tesco would have a high proportion of its current assets in stock and cash, whereas a furniture chain store such as DFS, which often promotes its products with tempting offers of 'buy now pay later with three years' interest-free credit', will have much less in stock (products are made to order) and a high proportion of debtors.

The statement of financial position will be helpful if a business wants to obtain a loan from a bank. By looking at the statement of financial position, the bank would be able to assess if the business had sufficient assets that could be used for security against the loan.

The statement of financial position is also helpful to a business, as it can assess if it has enough cash to keep itself afloat. By looking at the current assets and liabilities, it can calculate its net current assets to see if it has enough cash (working capital) to keep the business going. All businesses need money on a day-to-day basis to be able to buy raw materials, and pay bills and wages.

The statement of financial position also provides a lot of information which can be used to calculate several ratios (see **Chapters 36–40**).

Interpretation of the statement of financial position

In summary, it is always important to avoid only looking at the figures. Although it is necessary to look at the components of a statement of financial position in the first place, to interpret an actual statement of financial position requires taking an overview. It is tempting to look at the figures and reach a conclusion about the value of the business at a particular moment in time. However, it ought to be looked at in the context of the business, its objectives and its business environment.

Further sources

Company reports from the *Financial Times*.

Your turn

Questions are suitable for all AS and A Level candidates.

Revision questions

1 From the list below, state whether each item is an asset or a liability.
   A trade and other receivables (debtors)
   B overdraft
   C loan for three years
   D machines. *(4)*

2 State how to calculate net current assets. *(2)*

3 The figures below are part of a statement of financial position for two retail outlets. Analyse two differences between the businesses using the figures. *(4)*

Table 34.2 Statement of financial position for two retail outlets

Current assets (£000)	Business A	Business B
Cash	130	15
Inventory	580	110
Trade and other receivables (Debtors)	15	600

4 Using the information in Table 34.3, calculate the following:
   A net current assets *(2)*
   B net assets. *(2)*

Table 34.3 Statement of financial position for Juicy Fruit Lollies Ltd, as at 31 March 2014 (£000)

Non-current assets				275
Current assets				
Cash				15
Inventory				120
Trade and other receivables (Debtors)				45
Current liabilities				
Trade and other payables (Creditors)				65
Net current assets				
Net assets				
Shareholders equity				390

Total *(10)*

Case study

Extract from easyJet Statement of financial position 31 March 2014 and 30 September 2013

£m	31 March 2014	30 September 2013
Non-current assets	3080	2964
Current assets	1281	1448
Current liabilities	(1808)	(1379)
Net current (liabilities) assets	(527)	69
Non-current liabilities	(892)	(1016)
Net assets	1661	2017
Shareholders equity	1661	2017

1 Evaluate how successful easyJet has been between September 2013 and March 2014. *(12)*

Chapter 35

Depreciation

> **Year 2**
>
> A Level students must know all of the content in this chapter.
>
> This chapter is not applicable for AS students.

What is depreciation?

The concept of depreciation allows for the simple fact that a fixed asset will be of less value over time. Machines wear out due to usage, or are replaced by technologically improved versions. Consequently, it is important that the accounts of the business reflect this.

Fixed assets, for example the machines or the factory, may have a 'life' of several years, but are not worth the same value throughout their lifetime. Depreciation takes this into consideration and spreads the cost of the assets over its lifetime.

Depreciation allows for an element of realism within the accounts of the business. If the business entered the cost of a fixed asset within just one year of its accounts, this expenditure would have a significant effect upon the profit in that year. The profit stated would be below its true figure. However, in the following years the profit of the business would appear inflated because no cost of the asset has been put against revenues. Therefore, spreading the cost of the fixed assets over the life of the asset allows for a more realistic statement of the financial status of the business, in terms of its profits and its value.

The value of fixed assets appears in the statement of financial position as a fixed asset, from which is subtracted the depreciation (sometimes written as 'less depreciation').

Depreciation terminology

Net book value

The net book value of an asset is its cost minus the amounts that have been written off as it wears out (depreciates). By allowing for depreciation, the 'net book value' is calculated.

Table 35.1 Calculating the net book value

	2011	2012	2013	2014
	(£)	(£)	(£)	(£)
Initial cost of machinery	20,000			
Less depreciation	5,000	5,000	5,000	5,000
Accumulated depreciation	5,000	10,000	15,000	20,000
Net book value	15,000	10,000	5,000	0

Life of an asset

The life of an asset will be affected by:

- amount of 'wear and tear', which depends upon the level of its usage
- whether or not the product or machine becomes technologically obsolete
- demand for the product or machine (market obsolescence).

The actual life of an asset will vary considerably, due to the reasons suggested above. The Channel Tunnel was built to last for many decades, while an office photocopier and computer will last for a much shorter period of time. Buildings tend to have a longer life than machines, but for each of these categories of assets there are large variations.

Accumulated depreciation

This is the addition of the depreciation for each year. In Table 35.1, the accumulated depreciation in 2013 is equal to £15,000 (following three years of depreciation of £5,000).

Residual value

The residual value represents the value of the asset at the end of its useful life. It is the estimate of what the asset could be sold for at this time.

Historic cost

The initial cost of the asset is calculated as an historic cost, because the actual cost at the time of purchase is used.

Tips and techniques

Questions may refer to the historic cost or the initial cost.

Methods of measuring depreciation

Measuring the depreciating asset may vary. The two main depreciation methods are:

- straight-line, in which an equal amount is taken off the value of the asset on an annual basis; and
- declining balance, where the asset is reduced in value by a constant percentage on an annual basis.

Straight-line method

This is the simplest method of depreciation to calculate and apply. For this reason, it is the method that is used most frequently.

The cost of the asset is equally spread over its life. For example, if a machine that costs £120,000 has an expected or estimated life of ten years, and a residual value of £20,000, the depreciation for each year would be:

$$\frac{\text{Initial cost} - \text{residual value}}{\text{life of asset}}$$

$$= \frac{£120{,}000 - £20{,}000}{10}$$

$$= \frac{£100{,}000}{10}$$

$$= £10{,}000$$

As a consequence, the £10,000 would be written off the value of the asset for the ten years of its life.

See Table 35.2 for a presentation of this rate of depreciation.

Table 35.2 Straight-line methods of depreciation

Year	Initial cost in £	Minus depreciation of £10,000 per year	Minus accumulated depreciation (£)	Equals net book value (£)
1	120,000	10,000	10,000	110,000
2		10,000	20,000	100,000
3		10,000	30,000	90,000
4	15,000	10,000	40,000	80,000
5		10,000	50,000	70,000
6		10,000	60,000	60,000
7		10,000	70,000	50,000
8		10,000	80,000	40,000
9		10,000	90,000	30,000
10		10,000	100,000	20,000

Table 35.2 shows the subtraction of the same amount of depreciation for each year of the asset's estimated life. After ten years of depreciation, the net book value is also the residual value.

Figure 35.1 shows the same information presented in a graph format.

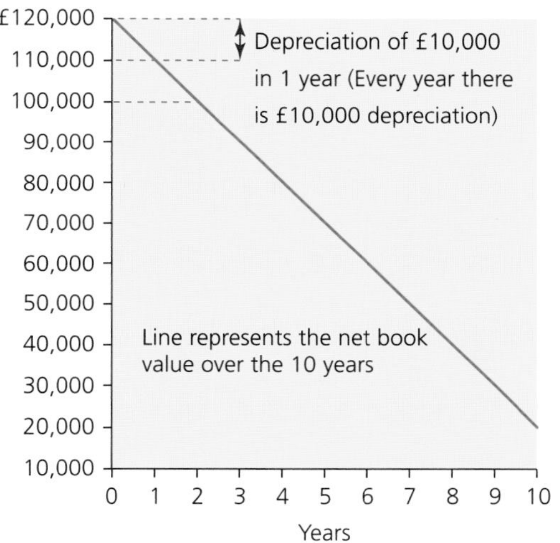

Figure 35.1 Straight-line depreciation

In Figure 35.1, the rate of depreciation is constant at £10,000 per annum; this is why the depreciation line is a straight line. Each year the asset is depreciated by £10,000.

After one year, £10,000 is the amount of depreciation from the asset that had an initial cost of £120,000 and is therefore 'worth' after that one year, £110,000.

After ten years, the asset is 'worth' £20,000. Using the straight-line graph it is easy to see the net book value at any time during the life of the asset.

Tips and techniques

As with all calculations, it is important to show clearly your formulae and workings.

Advantages of straight-line depreciation method

- The amount of depreciation is lower in the first few years.
- By having a lower level of depreciation, there is a higher valuation of the asset on the statement of financial position, suggesting that the value of the business is higher.
- Because less is deducted for depreciation, the profit of the business will be higher in the early years of the asset.

Disadvantages of straight-line depreciation method

- An estimate of the residual value is required, which for many assets is difficult to gauge.
- It assumes that the life of the assets is known, which may not be the case.
- Having a lower amount of depreciation in the first few years can be misleading; the value of the business may appear inflated.

Reducing (declining) balance

The declining balance method of depreciation applies a constant percentage rate of depreciation each year. This is not the same as a constant amount – straight-line method (see Table 35.3).

Applying this method of depreciation means that a higher amount of depreciation is subtracted from the value of the asset in the early years of its life.

A higher amount is more realistic and allows for the fact that in the later years in the life of the asset additional costs may be incurred to help maintain it and repair possible breakdowns. The declining balance still allows the business to spread the costs throughout the life of the asset.

Table 35.3 The declining balance method of depreciation

Year	Initial cost	Value after depreciation (net book value)	Minus depreciation of 20% per year	Minus accumulated depreciation	Equals net book value
	£	£	£	£	£
1	£120,000		24,000	24,000	96,000
2		96,000	19,200	43,200	76,800
3		76,800	15,360	58,560	61,440
4		61,440	12,288	70,848	49,152
5		49,152	9,830	80,678	39,322
6		39,322	7,864	88,542	31,458
7		31,458	6,292	94,834	25,166
8		25,166	5,033	99,867	20,133
9		20,133	4,027	103,893	16,106
10		16,106	3,221	107,114	12,885

Note: Some of the figures have been rounded up for simplicity.)

Although the rate of depreciation is constant (20%), the actual amount taken off for depreciation is falling (unlike in the straight-line depreciation method).

It should be clear that the level of depreciation is significantly higher in the first five years when compared to the level of depreciation for the straight-line method (£80,678 compared to £50,000 after five years). Figure 35.2 converts the information from Table 35.3 into a graph.

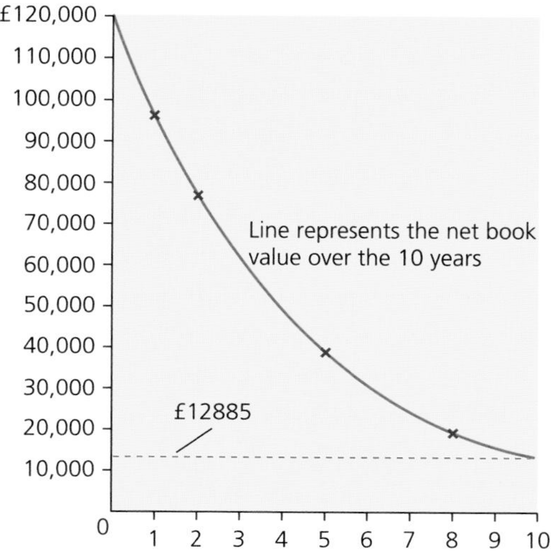

Figure 35.2 Declining balance

The difference between the two methods is demonstrated in the gradient of the graph line in Figure 35.2, which shows the net book value throughout the life of the asset (ten years). For the straight-line method the graph line is literally a straight line because the amount of depreciation is the same. For the declining balance, the gradient is not constant and is much steeper in the early years.

Advantages of declining balance

- This method reflects more realistically the value of assets that lose value significantly in the early years (such as lorries, cars, aeroplanes).
- No estimate of the residual value is required.

Disadvantages of declining balance

- With a higher level of depreciation in the early years, the valuation of the assets is lower on the statement of financial position.
- Lower valuation of assets may make it harder to borrow against assets.

Further sources

www.investorwords.com

Your turn

Multiple-choice questions

1 Depreciation using the declining balance method is where:
 A Every month a set amount is deducted from the value of the asset
 B On an annual basis an equal amount is deducted from the value of the asset
 C The asset is reduced in value by a constant percentage on an annual basis
 D The asset is reduced in value by the historic cost. *(1)*

2 A business buys an asset for £560,000 with a residual value of £80,000 after eight years. The straight-line depreciation for each year will be:
 A £480,000
 B £60,000
 C £70,000
 D £10,000. *(1)*

3 An asset is depreciated by 50,000 per annum from £600,000 to £100,000; the expected life of the asset will therefore be:
 A 12 years
 B 10 years
 C 15 years
 D 20 years. *(1)*

Revision questions

1 State two reasons why assets depreciate. *(2)*

2 State which method of depreciation has a constant percentage of depreciation. *(1)*

3 An asset is bought for £12,000 and has a residual value of £3,000. The life of the asset is expected to be three years. Calculate the rate of depreciation. *(3)*

4 An asset is depreciated by £20,000 per year from £240,000 to £80,000. Calculate the expected life of the asset. *(3)*

5 A hire-car business buys a new Ford Focus for £15,000. The business wants to keep the car for four years and has calculated a depreciation charge of £2,750 a year. Calculate the residual value of the hire car. *(3)*

Total *(12)*

Chapter 36

Introduction to ratio analysis and liquidity ratios

AS / Year 1

Both AS and A Level students must know all of the content in this chapter.

Ratio analysis

Ratio analysis is a method of measuring the performance of a business from various perspectives for the benefit of a range of stakeholders of the business, such as:

- directors and managers
- employees
- banks
- suppliers
- customers
- shareholders
- competitors
- government.

All stakeholders require information about a business, and can gain that information from some or all of the ratios.

The main sources of data for the calculation of the ratios usually come from the income statement and the statement of financial position of the business (see **Chapters 33 and 34**). Ratio analysis enables the business to:

- measure its performance over a given period of time
- make comparisons to be made over time and between other businesses (assuming they are of a similar size and nature)
- make comparisons between different departments within a business (intra-business).

Tips and techniques

It is vital that you are selective in the ratios that you use. This will depend upon the wording of the question and the nature of the business.

Ratios are usually divided into various categories:

- liquidity
- profitability (performance)
- financial efficiency (A Level only – not relevant to AS students)
- shareholder (A Level only – not relevant to AS students)
- gearing (A Level only – not relevant to AS students)

Tips and techniques

Do not be too concerned about which category some of the ratios belong to. There is some overlapping between financial and profitability ratios. What is important is that you clearly:

- state what a particular ratio shows
- show the formula for the ratio
- show the actual figures used (and where you found them)
- comment (analyse) your answer in the context of the case
- compare ratios for different years; it is dangerous to make conclusions based on just one year
- offer reasons for the figures you have calculated.

Whether you cover all of the above will, of course, depend upon the actual question. Nevertheless, this provides you with a worthwhile list of possible areas to cover.

Table 36.1 Ratio classification

Type of ratio	Ratios included	Concerned with
Liquidity	1 Current ratio 2 Acid test	The ability of a business to cover its short-term (current) liabilities.
Profitability	1 Gross profit margin 2 Net profit margin 3 Return on net assets 4 Return on capital employed	Sometimes referred to as performance ratios, these consider the level of profit in relation to the actual business. The ratios simply consider how profitable the business is in relation to its sales, its assets, or the capital invested.
Financial efficiency	1 Asset turnover 2 Stock turnover 3 Debtor days 4 Creditor days	These ratios concentrate on the efficiency of the business in terms of its ability to move stock (1 and 2) or how efficient it is at collecting money it is owed or paying money it owes (3 and 4).
Shareholder	1 Dividend per share 2 Dividend yield Price earnings ratio	These ratios allow shareholders to judge how their investments in the shares of the business are performing, compared to alternative investment opportunities.
Gearing	1 Gearing 2 Interest cover	Gearing concentrates on the long-term liabilities of the business and its ability to borrow money (1), and its ability to cover the cost of borrowing (2).

Liquidity ratios

Liquidity measures the ability to convert assets into cash. The most liquid asset is cash. However, other assets of a business vary in their ability to be converted. Following the 'credit crunch' of 2008, it was very difficult to sell assets such as houses and therefore they were viewed as very illiquid assets.

Some debts and other current assets (see **Chapter 25**) may be difficult to convert to cash. The debtor's ability to pay for goods will determine how liquid the business can regard that debtor. Stock, the other current asset, also varies in its ability to convert to cash. It is more likely to be possible to convert fast-moving consumer goods (FMCGs) into cash quickly, whereas other luxury or expensive goods may be much harder to sell and therefore convert into cash.

Liquidity is all about having sufficient cash to keep the business working (working capital). The liquidity ratios focus on the ability of a business to have sufficient current assets in relation to the amount of current liabilities.

Cashflow problems are one of the main reasons for a business to fail; therefore the liquidity ratios are very important. There are two liquidity ratios: current ratio and acid test.

Current ratio

This ratio considers the current assets and the current liabilities. The ratio between the assets and the liabilities indicates the level of liquidity within the business. In other words, it considers the level of liabilities in relation to the level of assets, to ensure that there is sufficient working capital (enough cash to meet the short-term debts of the business).

This is a very important ratio as no business can survive without sufficient liquidity.

Formula

$$\text{Current ratio} = \frac{\text{current assets}}{\text{current liabilities}}$$

The information for this formula may be found in the statement of financial position.

Example:

Current assets: £300

Current liabilities: £200

$$\text{Therefore the current ratio} = \frac{\text{current assets}}{\text{current liabilities}}$$

$$= \frac{300}{200} = 1.5$$

The significance of the answer of 1.5 is that for every £1 of liabilities, the business holds £1.50 in assets. In other words, there are 1.5 times as many assets as there are liabilities. It implies that there are sufficient assets to cover the liabilities.

Tips and techniques

What is the ideal current ratio? It is often thought to be 1.5. However, it all depends upon the type of business, its circumstances and its objectives; therefore any such 'ideal' should be treated with caution.

Nevertheless, if the current ratio falls to 1 or even below 1, this can raise concerns because it indicates that there are insufficient assets to cover the liabilities.

It is difficult to rely on a current ratio to provide an accurate measure of a business's liquidity position: see Table 36.3.

Table 36.2 Extract from the statement of financial position of Business X, year ending 31 December 2014

Statement of financial position	Value in £000
Current assets	
Cash	50
Inventory	300
Trade and other receivables (debtors)	50
Current liabilities	
Overdraft	200

$$\text{The current ratio} = \frac{\text{current assets}}{\text{current liabilities}} = \frac{400}{200} = 2$$

This business has a current ratio of 2, which implies that for every £1 of liabilities there is £2 of assets. This may suggest that Business X has a healthy liquidity ratio. However, the current ratio is a broad measure of liquidity. In this example, the assets include a large proportion of stock. There may be no certainty that the business will be able to sell this stock, and therefore the liquidity position is not as good as first appears. To alleviate such problems, there is a second ratio for liquidity. This second ratio is more stringent and ignores the stock as an asset. This ratio is the acid test.

Acid test

Because a business cannot be certain that it will be able to sell all of its stock, the acid test takes this fact into consideration. For certain businesses, this is a much more reliable test of liquidity. Selling perishable goods with a short shelf-life may mean that not all of the stock will be sold and therefore converted into cash (the most liquid asset).

Formula

$$\text{Acid test} = \frac{\text{current assets} - \text{inventory (stock)}}{\text{current liabilities}}$$

The information for this formula may be found in the statement of financial position.

Example:

Table 36.3 Extract from the statement of financial position of Business X, year ending 31 December 2014

	Value (£000)
Current assets	
Inventory	150
Trade and other receivables (debtors)	200
Cash	25
Current liabilities	
Overdraft	150

$$\text{Acid test} = \frac{\text{current assets} - \text{inventory (stock)}}{\text{current liabilities}}$$

$$= \frac{375 - 150}{150} = 1.5$$

The answer shows that for every £1 of liabilities, the business has £1.50 in assets, sufficient to meet its liabilities. Some experts suggest that the ideal ratio for the acid test is 1, though this again depends upon the type of business and the business environment in which it operates.

Tips and techniques

If the exam question asked you to comment on your answer, you should state the above and probably comment on the fact that although the acid test is positive (assets greater than liabilities), the level of debtors could be a problem depending on the type of goods being sold and the nature/standing of the debtors.

Value of ratios

Ratios are only as good as the figures that have been used. Assuming the figures used to calculate the various ratios are accurate, whether from the income statement or the statement of financial position, then the answers can be of value.

- Comparisons from year to year can be made (assuming figures are collected in the same manner).
- Stakeholders may be able to use ratios in order to assess if business is worth/safe to trade with. Shareholders can ascertain viability of investing in the business.
- Management of a business will want to consider certain ratios as a measure of performance and whether financial objectives have been met (profitability ratios and solvency ratios).
- Suppliers and potential creditors will want to know the business is worth trading with (solvency and liquidity ratios).
- Employees will be interested to see how the business is performing to ascertain if their jobs are secure and the potential for a pay rise (profitability ratios and shareholder ratios).
- Ratios are useful for providing a source of information in order to spot and possibly solve problems within a business.
- Ratios may help management in their decision-making process and choosing the strategy to adopt.

Limitations of ratios

- Inflation may distort figures such as revenue, profits and return on capital employed (see **Chapter 39**).
- The state of the economy may mean that a fall in certain ratios is not due to the poor performance of the business. On the other hand, a strong economy may show an improvement in the performance of a business, which actually has not occurred as a result of the business itself.
- It is assumed that the figures used within the ratios are calculated in the same way over time to enable comparisons to be made.
- The external factors may distort the figures which are outside the control of the business (government legislation, political factors, and international competitors).
- Some caution needs to be used as there are no set benchmarks for judging ratios. Although guidelines are offered for liquidity ratios, the business will need to decide whether it has sufficient liquidity.

Further sources

www.timesonline.co.uk/business: (for company results)
Company reports

Your turn

Questions are suitable for all AS and A Level candidates.

Revision questions

1 Using the information in Table 36.4, calculate the current ratio and the acid test ratio for 2013. *(4)*

2 Using the information in Table 36.4, analyse the implications for the business when considering the changes in the current ratio and the acid test ratio for 2014. *(6)*

Total *(10)*

Table 36.4 Statement of financial position for X Ltd.

	2013 (£000)	2014 (£000)
Fixed assets		
Current assets		
Trade and other receivables	67	94
Cash	15	30
Inventory	35	40
Current liabilities		
Overdraft	55	39
Net current assets	162	191

Accounting and finance

Chapter 37

Gearing ratios

Year 2

A Level students must know all of the content in this chapter.

This chapter is not applicable for AS students.

Solvency ratios

Table 37.1 Solvency ratios

Type of ratio	Ratios included	Concerned with
Gearing	1 Gearing 2 Interest cover	Gearing concentrates on the long-term liabilities of the business and its ability to borrow money (1), and its ability to cover the cost of borrowing (2).

Gearing

This type of ratio considers the level of risk for a business. It measures the level of risk by comparing the levels of debt and the amount of equity (capital employed) within the business; in other words, the proportion of the business that is financed through long-term borrowing.

Gearing is the percentage of long-term finance that is made up from loans, rather than shareholders' funds and retained profits. The gearing ratio is deemed to be high if the long-term borrowing (non-current liabilities) is more than 50 per cent of the capital employed (total equity) and low if below 50 per cent.

Tips and techniques

It is rather simplistic to talk about a business being highly geared because its non-current liabilities are above 50 per cent of the capital employed. It will depend upon the circumstances facing the business.

If the proportion of borrowing (debt) is high, there is more interest to pay, and any fall in sales revenue and subsequently profit will make it harder for the business to finance this borrowing.

The higher the proportion of assets financed through long-term borrowing, the greater is the risk for the business.

Similarly, if the business is highly geared (has a high proportion of debt), then a potential lender to the business is less likely to be willing to make further lending; the business is at greater risk of not being able to meet the interest charges and therefore the risk may be too high.

Banks are keen to know the level of gearing that already exists within a business before making any additional loans. If the business is already highly geared, the bank will be less likely to lend the money. If a high proportion of the capital within the business is borrowed, the business owns less capital to use as security on any additional loan.

Formula

Tips and techniques

There are several formulae for measuring the gearing of a business. Consequently, if you are making comparisons, ensure that you state the formula used and are consistent in its use.

The gearing ratio is used to judge if a loan should be granted.

$$\text{Gearing ratio} = \frac{\text{non-current liabilities}}{\text{capital employed}} \times 100$$

The information for this formula may be found in the statement of financial position.

OR

$$\frac{\text{Non-current liabilities (debt)}}{\text{Shareholders' funds (equity)}}$$

Example 1:

Table 37.2 Extract from the balance sheet

Non-current liabilities	£000
Creditors (more than one year)	5,200
Capital	
Share capital	3,100
Retained profit/reserves	10,200
Total capital employed (equity)	18,500

$$\text{Gearing ratio} = \frac{\text{long-term liabilities}}{\text{capital employed}} \times 100$$

$$= \frac{5{,}200}{(5{,}200 + 3{,}100 + 10{,}200)} \times 100$$

$$= 28.1\%$$

This indicates that 28.1 per cent of the total capital employed in the business is financed by long-term borrowing. This would be considered a company with low gearing.

Example 2:

Table 37.3 Extract from the statement of financial position

Non-current liabilities	£000
Creditors (payables)(over 1 year)	215
Capital and reserves	
Shares	150
Retained earnings	420
Shareholders' equity (capital employed)	785

$$\text{Gearing ratio} = \frac{\text{long-term liabilities}}{\text{capital employed}} \times 100$$

$$= \frac{215}{(215 + 150 + 420)} \times 100$$

$$= 27.4\%$$

Debt to equity ratio

The difference between the gearing ratio and the debt to equity ratio (which is sometimes used for gearing) is interesting; remember to state your formula.

This ratio compares the long-term liabilities with the share capital and retained profits.

Formula

$$\text{Debt to equity ratio} = \frac{\text{debt}}{\text{equity}} \times 100$$

Example: using Table 37.3

$$\text{Debt to equity ratio} = \frac{\text{debt}}{\text{equity}} \times 100$$

$$= \frac{215}{(150 + 420) \times 100}$$

$$= 37.7{:}1$$

There are benefits to being highly geared (having a high proportion of long-term liabilities to shareholders' funds and retained profits):

1 It may be a cheaper alternative source of funds when compared to shares, though much depends upon the level of interest rates and the level of profits.
2 If the gearing is high, perhaps there are fewer shareholders to be concerned about and therefore control of the company may be easier.
3 Being highly geared may be deliberate; some companies have bought back shares when profits are high to reduce dividend payments.

However, there are also benefits of having a low gearing ratio:

1 There are fewer funds that require repaying, helping to keep costs down. This could be significant if interest rates are high.
2 It is easier to gain future borrowing from banks.

Interest cover

Interest cover is used to help decide if a business can afford to repay any loan. This ratio measures the number of times in which a business can pay its interest charges with the operating profit it makes.

An answer of 3 means that there is sufficient profit generated to cover the cost of interest to be paid on a loan three times. The higher the number the better, as this indicates that the business can easily afford the interest payments.

Formula

$$\text{Interest cover} = \frac{\text{operating profit}}{\text{interest payable (finance costs)}}$$

The information for this formula may be found in the income statement.

Example:

$$\text{Interest cover} = \frac{\text{operating profit}}{\text{interest payable}}$$

$$= \frac{120{,}000}{30{,}000}$$

$$= 4$$

An interest cover of 4 means that the business is generating sufficient profit to cover the cost of the interest on a loan four times over. Judging if four times is sufficient, or given other years' figures to compare with, can only be decided in the context of the given business.

Further sources

Company reports

www.timesonline.co.uk/business: (for company results)

Your turn

Multiple-choice questions

1 If non-current liabilities are £315 million and shareholders' funds are £1,200 million, the gearing ratio is:
A 62.5%
B 26.25%
C 63.12%
D None of these (1)

2 If the operating profit of a business is £42 million and the finance costs (interest payable) is £2.5 million, the interest cover is:
A 68 times
B 44.5 times
C 16.8 times
D 2.5 times (1)

Revision questions

1 Explain two likely benefits of being highly geared. (4)
2 State the formula for interest cover. (1)
3 Calculate the gearing ratio in Table 37.4. (4)
Total (9)

Table 37.4 Extract from the statement of financial position, accounts year ending 2014

Statement of financial position	£ m
Non-current liabilities	50
Share capital	45
Reserves	15

Task

Prepare a table listing the stakeholders of a business and suggest which ratios will be of value to that particular stakeholder.
For example:

Stakeholder	Which ratio is interesting?	Why is it interesting?
Bank	Gearing ratio	To ascertain proportion of loans to assets to help decide if able to lend money to the business. To assess risk involved.

1 Using the information given in Table 37.5 and with the use of appropriate ratios, suggest whether the bank is likely to lend additional finance to this business. (4)
2 Analyse the impact for any future plans of the business shown in Table 37.5, given its present liquidity situation. (6)
Total (10)

Table 37.5 Extract from statement of financial position

Statement of financial position	2014	2013
Non-current assets	170	190
Current assets		
Cash	15	30
Inventory	135	106
Receivables	67	94
Total current assets	217	230
Current liabilities		
Overdraft	55	39
Payables	50	62
Net current assets	112	129
Non-current liabilities	110	130
Net assets	172	189
Shareholders' funds		
Shares	120	120
Retained profit	52	69
Total equity	172	189

Chapter 38

Efficiency ratios

Year 2

A Level students must know all of the content in this chapter.

This chapter is not applicable for AS students.

Financial efficiency ratios

Financial efficiency ratios measure the ability of a business to manage its assets and liabilities efficiently. The ratios include non-current asset turnover, stock turnover, debtor turnover (days) and creditor turnover (days.)

Tips and techniques

Different types of terminology have been included for terms such as inventory (stock), accounts receivable (debtors), accounts payable (creditors). This will also allow you to answer a question regardless of which terms are used.

Table 38.1 Financial efficiency ratios

Type of ratio	Ratios included	Concerned with
Financial efficiency	1. non-current asset turnover 2. inventory turnover (stock turnover) 3. debtor days (turnover) 4. creditor days (turnover)	These ratios concentrate on the efficiency of the business in terms of its ability to move stock (1 and 2) or how efficient it is at collecting money it is owed or it owes (3 and 4).

Asset turnover

This ratio measures how efficiently a business is able to use its non-current assets to generate sales revenue.

The higher the ratio, the better, as it implies that the assets are being used in a more efficient manner to generate sales revenue. This ratio is heavily used to make intra-business comparisons, such as between different branches or shops or productive units.

Formula

$$\text{Non-current assets turnover} = \frac{\text{revenue (turnover)}}{\text{non-current assets}}$$

The information for this formula may be found in the income statement for the revenue and the statement of financial position for the assets.

Example:

Table 38.2 Income statement

Income statement 31 December 2014	£000
Revenue	275
Costs of sales	95
Gross profit	180
Expenses	50
Operating profit	130
Finance costs	10
Profit before tax	120
Profit for the year	116

Table 38.3 Statement of financial position

Statement of financial position year ending 31 December 2014	£000
Non-current assets	800
Current assets	355
Current liabilities	295
Net current assets	60
Statement of financial position year ending 31 December 2014	**£000**
Non-current liabilities	240
Net assets	620
Share capital	400
Reserves	220
Total equity	620

$$\text{Non-current asset turnover} = \frac{\text{revenue}}{\text{non-current assets}}$$
$$= \frac{275{,}000}{800{,}000}$$
$$= 0.344$$

This suggests that the business is not very efficient in terms of the sales revenue generated from the non-current assets of the business. For every £1 of non-current assets, only 34p of sales is generated.

Tips and techniques

Such a comment as above could be misleading, as the result will very much depend upon the type of business. A capital-intensive business is less likely to have a high asset turnover, when compared with a business that does not possess many assets. It is, however, another ratio that can be used to help make a judgement about the efficiency of a business.

Stock (inventory) turnover

This ratio measures how quickly the stock is turned over (sold).

Formula

$$\text{Stock (inventory) turnover} = \frac{\text{cost of stock (or sales)}}{\text{average stock}}$$

(Average stock (inventory) can be easily calculated by adding the opening stock to the closing stock and dividing by 2.)

The information for this formula can be found in sales figures and the income statement for cost of sales.

Example:

$$\text{Stock (inventory) turnover} = \frac{\text{cost of sales}}{\text{average inventory (stock)}}$$
$$= \frac{25{,}000}{10{,}000}$$
$$= 2.5$$

This means that the stock was sold 2.5 times within the trading period of one year. If the business needs to find out how many days it takes to turn the stock over, this can be calculated by:

$$\frac{\text{Stock (inventory)}}{\text{cost of sales}} \times 365$$
$$= \frac{10{,}000}{25{,}000} \times 365$$
$$= 146 \text{ days}$$

This means that if the stock turnover is 2.5, the stock is turned over (sold) in 146 days. This may be helpful in assessing reorder and delivery patterns.

There are many factors to note before passing judgements on the answer obtained. A high turnover may appear to be a good sign, but the business may be running stock levels down and therefore it is more likely to turnover a lower stock level more quickly. This may be due to poor sales and therefore holding less inventory (stock). However, a high inventory (stock) turnover may be due to the usage of JIT (see **Chapter 67**). If inventory (stock) is delivered just-in-time, less inventory/stock is held, and therefore the stock will be turned over more quickly.

Alternatively, the rate of turnover may fall, which may be due to increased levels of inventory (stock) in order to ensure that there is sufficient inventory (stock) to meet a predicted increase in demand.

Debtor days (trade receivable days)

This ratio measures how quickly debts are turned into cash; in other words, how quickly the money owing to the business is paid.

It represents the average amount of time (days) which the debtors of the business take to pay. Alternatively, the ratio can be used to measure how efficiently a business collects its debts. Much will depend upon who owes the money. Often, the larger the business that owes the money, the longer it will take to pay.

Keeping debtor days as low as possible will help the cashflow of the business. However, it may be a deliberate strategy to extend the period before a customer has to pay. This may be part of a promotional campaign, but the consequences of such a strategy will be to increase the debtor days and subsequently damage the cashflow of the business.

Formula

$$\text{Debtor days} = \frac{\text{trade receivables}}{\text{revenue (sales)}} \times 365$$

The information for this formula could be found in the sales figures and sales agreements with its customers, the income statement account (sales) and the balance sheet (current assets).

Example:

$$\text{Debtor days} = \frac{\text{trade receivables}}{\text{revenue (sales)}} \times 365$$

$$= \frac{105{,}000}{980{,}000} \times 365$$

$$= 39.1 \text{ days}$$

Deciding if this is a satisfactory number of days will depend upon the normal trading (sales) agreements for the products involved. A business that sells furniture may have a higher level of debtor days than a newsagent.

There may be some businesses where debtor days do not exist at all. A fish and chip shop is unlikely to offer any form of credit sales.

Even when the number of debtor days is established, it will not necessarily be helpful information because the answer does not give any indication of the distribution of the debtor days. One outstanding long-term debt may be hiding the fact that the majority are paid promptly.

Creditor days/turnover (trade and payables)

This ratio measures how quickly a business pays its suppliers. It shows the number of days which a business takes, on average, to pay money it owes to its suppliers.

This is a useful ratio because a business needs to be mindful of how long it is taking to pay its debts. If the business takes too long to pay its suppliers, they may restrict the level of credit available or, even worse, cease to do business. By delaying payment, the credit rating of the business may be adversely affected.

However, being able to delay payment to its suppliers helps the cashflow of the business. It is therefore a careful balancing act between holding on to its cash and delaying payment without upsetting its suppliers; in other words, a careful balancing act between the debtor and creditor days.

$$\text{Creditor days} = \frac{\text{trade payables}}{\text{purchases (cost of sales)}} \times 365$$

The information for this formula may be found in the statement of financial position (creditors) (receivables), income statement (cost of sales) and sales agreements.

Example A:

$$\text{Creditor turnover} = \frac{\text{trade payables}}{\text{purchases (cost of sales)}} \times 365$$

$$= \frac{115{,}500}{890{,}850} \times 365$$

$$= 47.3 \text{ days}$$

Alternatively,

Example B:

If sales are £200 million and receivables are £20 million

Therefore,

Debtors turnover = 10 times

$$\frac{\text{365 days per year}}{\text{10 times}} = 36.5 \text{ days}$$

The answer (for creditor turnover or creditor days) in Example A means that the business takes, on average, 47.3 days to pay its creditors. Whether this is acceptable or not will depend upon any agreement the business has with its suppliers. If the agreement is normally for a supplier to be paid within 30 days, then there are problems.

Whereas the answer for Example B indicates the debtor turnover (receivables turnover) is 36.5 days.

Tips and techniques

Always show your formula and your workings, as the terminology used may vary. It is very important for you to show the terms you have used, the formula, and your workings.

Again care needs to be taken before making any conclusions. The information in the case may offer a reason why the creditor days are longer than expected. Use the context of the case and consider any trends before commenting on your answer.

Your turn

Multiple-choice questions

1 Using the information in Table 38.2, the finance costs refers to:

A level of debt

B amount owed

C interest on loans

D interest received on investments. *(1)*

2 By reducing the debtor turnover (days) a business will:

A improve its cashflow

B worsen its cashflow

C increase its creditors

D reduce its creditors. *(1)*

Revision questions

1 State the difference between receivable (debtor days) turnover and payable turnover (creditor days). *(2)*

2 Calculate the stock turnover (inventory turnover) for year 1 for the following business:

A Year 1: sales of £45,000, average stock of £10,000

B Year 2: sales of £35,000, average stock of £15,000. *(2)*

3 Explain two likely reasons for the change in stock turnover in Year 2. *(4)*

Total *(8)*

Chapter 39

Profitability ratios

AS / Year 1

Both AS and A Level students must know all of the content in this chapter.

Profitability (performance) ratios

Table 39.1 Profitability ratios

Type of ratio	Ratios included	Concerned with
Profitability	1. gross profit margin 2. net profit margin 3. return on capital employed (ROCE) 4. return on equity	Sometimes referred to as performance ratios, these consider the level of profit in relation to the actual business. The ratios simply consider how profitable the business is in relation to its sales, its assets, or the capital invested.

As the names of the ratios imply, they are concerned with the level of profit measured against various aspects of the business. Profitability ratios compare the profitability with the size of the business either by looking at the assets of the business, or at its level of sales.

Gross profit margin

This ratio looks at the level of profit as a percentage of the sales or turnover. The gross profit margin considers only the direct costs and not indirect costs (overheads). In other words, gross profit is the sales revenue minus the cost of sales (see **Chapter 33**).

Formula

$$\text{Gross profit margin} = \frac{\text{gross profit}}{\text{sales}} \times 100$$

The answer will tell you (as a percentage) how many pence from every pound of sales is gross profit.

If the answer is 40 per cent, this means that for every £1 of sales, 40p is gross profit.

The information for this formula may be found in the P&L account.

Example:

Table 39.2 Income statement year ending 2014 (£ million)

Income statement	£ m
Revenue	25
Less cost of sales	10
Gross profit	15
Expenses (overheads)	12
Operating profit	3

$$\text{Gross profit margin} = \frac{\text{gross profit}}{\text{sales (revenue)}} \times 100$$

$$= \frac{15}{25} \times 100 = 60\%$$

This means that for every £1 of sales, 60p is gross profit.

Net profit margin

This measures the net profit (or operating profit) as a percentage of sales or turnover. This takes into consideration the direct and indirect costs, and is therefore a more realistic measure of the profitability against sales than gross profit margin.

Formula

$$\text{Net profit margin} = \frac{\text{net profit (operating profit)}}{\text{sales}} \times 100$$

The information for this formula can be found in the income statement.

Example:

Using Table 39.2 above:

$$\text{Net profit margin} = \frac{\text{net profit}}{\text{sales}} \times 100$$

$$= \frac{3}{25} \times 100 = 12\%$$

This means that for every £1 of sales, 12p is net profit.

Tips and techniques

It is important to note that a high percentage figure for this profit margin does not necessarily mean that the business is more or less successful; much will depend upon how many products are sold at this margin.

It is also important to note that the figure used for the net profit margin was operating profit, as this was the figure given. However, if in addition the income statement offers profit before tax (a more accurate net profit figure) then this should be used.

This again demonstrates the importance of showing your formula and figures.

Return on capital employed (ROCE)

This is a frequently used ratio for performance. The return on capital employed (ROCE) measures the net profit as a percentage of the capital employed.

Formula

$$\text{Return on capital employed} = \frac{\text{operating profit}}{\text{capital employed}} \times 100$$

The information for this formula can be found in the income statement (profit) and statement of financial position (capital employed).

ROCE shows the amount of money earned by the business in terms of profits in relation to the amount invested by the shareholders. Capital employed refers to the shareholders' funds and the profits earned before tax and dividends.

Tips and techniques

There may be some debate about which 'profit' ought to be used for this ratio. Profit before tax or operating profit can be used as long as you state which you are using. However, using profit before tax allows comparisons to be made within different countries that may have differing tax levels.

Example:

Table 39.3 Extracts from income statement and statement of financial position for year ending 2014

Income statement	£000
Revenue	275
Cost of sales	95
Gross profit	180
Expenses	50
Operating profit	130
Finance costs	10
Profit before tax	120
Tax	4
Profit for the year	116

Table 39.4 Statement of financial position for year ending 2014

Statement of financial position	£000
Non-current assets	800
Current assets	355
Current liabilities	295
Net current assets	60
Non-current liabilities	240
Net assets	620
Ordinary share capital	400
Reserves	220
Total equity	620

$$\text{Return on capital employed} = \frac{\text{profit}}{\text{capital employed}} \times 100$$

$$= \frac{116{,}000}{620{,}000} \times 100$$

$$= 18.7\%$$

Whether this is an efficient return depends upon the type of product and how competitive the market is. This ratio can compare different values:

- year-on-year
- the results of different investments
- departments or products (if capital not shared)
- financial objectives.

Return on equity

This is another profitability ratio and it measures the ability of a business to generate profits from its shareholders' investments into the business.

In other words: how much profit is generated for every pound of shareholders' funds invested.

It may also be seen as a measure of how effective the management of a business is in generating profits from its investments (equity).

Formula

$$\text{Return on equity} = \frac{\text{profit for the year}}{\text{shareholders' equity}}$$

Tips and techniques

Again there are various ways to calculate this ratio and therefore it is important to show the formula you are using and, as always, show your working.

The difference between ROCE and ROE

Simply, return on equity (ROE) considers the amount of profits generated from equity (shares) whereas ROCE (return on capital employed) is the more comprehensive measure, as it takes into consideration shareholders' funds and liabilities (loans); in other words, all sources of capital employed within a business.

Further sources

www.timesonline.co.uk/business (for company results)
Company Reports

Your turn

Questions are suitable for all AS and A Level candidates.

Multiple-choice questions

1 If the gross profit = £720,000 and the sales are £1,200,000, the gross profit margin is:
A 60% C 72%
B 70% D 12% *(1)*

2 If ordinary share capital is £210 million, reserves are £40 million and profit for the year is £25 million, ROCE is:
A 10% C 30.9%
B 11.9% D 15% *(1)*

Revision questions

1 Using the information in Tables 39.5 and 39.6 calculate the ROCE. *(3)*

2 Evaluate whether the ROCE figure from question 1 indicates that this business is a success. *(9)*

Total *(12)*

Table 39.5 Statement of financial position for year ending 2014

Statement of financial position	£000
Non-current assets (Fixed assets)	800
Current assets	355
Current liabilities	235
Net current assets	120
Long-term liabilities	240
Net assets	680
Ordinary share capital	400
Reserves	280
Total Equity	680

Table 39.6 Income statement for year ending 2014

Income statement	£000
Revenue/turnover	275
Cost of sales	95
Gross profit	180
Expenses	70
Operating profit	110
Interest payable	10
Profit before tax	100
Tax	4
Profit at end of year	96

Chapter 40

Shareholder ratios

Year 2

A Level students must know all of the content in this chapter.

This chapter is not applicable for AS students.

Table 40.1 Shareholder ratios

Type of ratio	Ratios included	Concerned with
Shareholder	1. dividend per share 2. dividend yield 3. earnings per share 4. price earnings ratio	These ratios allow shareholders to judge how their investments in the shares of the business are performing, compared to alternative investment opportunities.

Shareholders buy shares for a variety of reasons. Some people buy shares for the perks attached to certain shares. Other companies offer discounts on their products or services for their shareholders. The building company Persimmon offers a 5 per cent discount on the price of its new homes to its shareholders.

The majority of people buy shares as a form of investment. When deciding which shares to buy, a potential buyer will consider not only if the price of the shares will increase, but also if the shares will yield a dividend (i.e. share of the profits that is distributed to the shareholders).

Being able to measure the success or potential success of a business may lead a potential buyer to look at the ratios below.

Dividend per share

How much of the profits are distributed to the shareholders will depend on a range of factors. However, once the company has retained some of the profits for future investments, some may be distributed.

Formula

$$\text{Dividend per share} = \frac{\text{total dividends paid}}{\text{number of shares issued}}$$

The information for this formula may be found in the P&L account (dividends to shareholders), balance sheet (number of shares issued) and company report (shares issued).

Example:

A company declares a distributed profit of £70 million and has 800 million shares.

$$\text{Dividend per share} = \frac{\text{total dividend}}{\text{number of shares}} = \frac{£70\text{m}}{800\text{m}} = 8.75\text{p}$$

Although this shows the dividend per share, it does not show how much the shares cost to buy in order to receive this dividend. Knowing the share price will help to assess the value of the investment in the shares. It is also worth noting the trend in terms of the dividend payable.

Tips and techniques

As always, show the formula you are using and all workings.

Dividend yield

In order to resolve the problem of not knowing the price of the shares, the calculation of the dividend yield will provide a clearer picture for the potential shareholder.

The dividend yield measures the return (the dividend per share) on the investment (the cost of buying the share). It is similar to the ROCE (return on capital employed) in that the potential return of the investment can be compared to test its viability.

Formula

$$\text{Dividend yield} = \frac{\text{dividend per share}}{\text{market price of share}} \times 100$$

The information for this formula may be found in the company report, press (*Financial Times*) and websites.

Example:

$$\text{Dividend yield} = \frac{8.75\text{p}}{655\text{p}} \times 100 = 1.33\%$$

Tips and techniques

The answer shown in the example is 1.33 and is the one you should give unless the question asks you to state to the nearest 2 decimal places. In that instance the answer would be 1.34 as actual answer is 1.335877 and therefore rounds up to 1.34.

This is not a high return on the price of buying the shares, especially when compared to the rate of interest that could be gained by depositing money into a savings account. However, potential investors may buy the shares because they will receive a dividend and possibly some perks for owning the shares, and because they are hoping for an increase in the price of the shares.

Any increase in the price of the shares will reduce the dividend yield for new shareholders, but may mean a shareholder can sell the shares for a capital gain. Similarly, any fall in the price of the shares will increase the dividend yield, but possibly discourage investors from wanting to buy the shares in the first place.

There are several variables that affect the purchasing of shares; the dividend yield is only one of those factors.

Although this ratio allows for a comparison to be made (the return on the investment of buying the share), it does not take into consideration other reasons why investors buy shares.

Tips and techniques

It is once again important to use the context of the case before passing judgement on the level of the yield.

Earnings per share

This ratio shows what each share earned in a financial year; however, it is highly unlikely that the shareholder will receive this amount when a dividend is declared because the business may want to use some of the profit for future investment.

Formula

$$\text{Earnings per share} = \frac{\text{Profit for the year}}{\text{number of shares issued}}$$

Example:

A business's profit for the year is £2.5 million and the number of shares issued is 5.5 million. Therefore the earnings per share are:

$$\text{Earnings per share} = \frac{\text{Profit for the year}}{\text{number of shares issued}}$$

$$= \frac{£2.5}{£5.5}$$

$$= £0.45$$

This means that each share has earned 45p profit.

Price earnings ratio

This ratio is concerned with the expectations which potential investors hold. It is a measure of confidence about what the shares will earn. The ratio compares the current market price with the earnings for that share. If the price earnings ratio is 10, this means that the market price is 10 times the latest earnings per share. However, the earnings per share are not the same as the dividend per share.

Dividends per share refer to the distributed profits in the form of dividends.

Earnings per share represent the profit after tax. Not all of this profit will be distributed to the shareholders, as some of it could be retained by the company for investment purposes.

Formula

$$\text{Price earnings ratio} = \frac{\text{market price of share}}{\text{earnings per share}}$$

The information for this formula may be found in the company report, press (*Financial Times*) and websites.

Example:

$$\text{Price earnings ratio} = \frac{\text{market price of share}}{\text{earnings per share}}$$

$$= \frac{655\text{p}}{40\text{p}} = 16.4$$

In this example, the market price is 16.4 times the earnings of the share. If earnings were constant, it would take 16.4 years to cover the cost of buying the shares!

An alternative way to consider this answer of 16.4 is in terms of the shareholder, who is willing to pay 16.4 times the earnings of the share in order to own such a share.

Tips and techniques

As for all of the external factors that influence any of the four main areas of a business (which include accounting and finance), ethical, economic and international factors, for example, to name some of them, will vary in terms of the degree of influence they may have on the financial aspect of the business.

How much influence these external factors have will depend upon:

- the type of business
- the objectives of the business
- the type of ethical issues involved (Tesco, banking)
- the exchange rates
- which countries are being traded with
- the existing financial situation within the business
- the state of the economy.

There is no right answer when either analysing or evaluating how the external factors impinge upon any one business. It is important to read the evidence within the question and/ or the case to ensure any such question is answered in context.

Further sources

www.timesonline.co.uk/business (for company results)
Company reports

Your turn

Multiple-choice questions

1 If the market price of a share is 120p and the dividend per share is 6p, the dividend yield is therefore:

A 5
B 6
C 5%
D 6% *(1)*

2 The total dividend paid for the year is £82 million and the number of shares is 750 million. The dividend per share is:

A 9.1p
B 61.5p
C 10.9p
D 11p *(1)*

Case study

1 State the formula for:

A earnings per share
B dividend per share. *(2)*

UDG Healthcare

Table 40.2

	2012	2013	2014 e
Pre-tax profit	59m euros	33.8m euros	125m euros
Earnings per share	25.5c	26.8c	28.9c
Dividend per share	9.04c	9.56c	10.1c

Source: Extract from News for investors, *The Sunday Telegraph*, 23 November 2014, edited by J Ficenec.

2 Using the information in Table 40.2 evaluate the success of UDG Healthcare. *(9)*
Total *(11)*

Chapter 41

Organisation

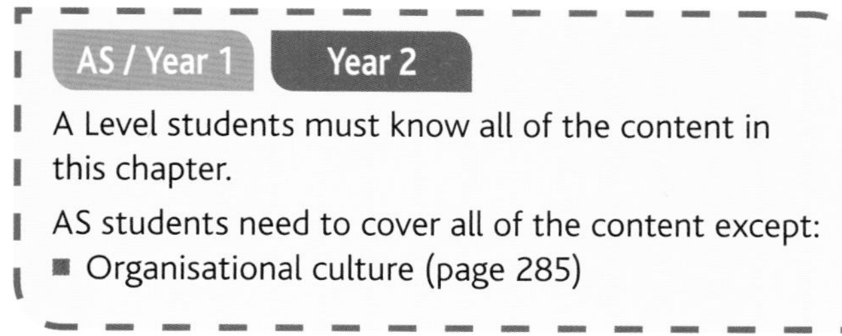

The simplest way to show how a business is organised is by using an organisational chart. This is a diagram that shows the hierarchy in a business, usually from top to bottom or from the board of directors to the shop-floor workers or operatives.

From this chart, it easy to see at a glance the other key concepts related to the organisation of a business. These include types of hierarchy, span of control, communication, line management, chain of command and accountability.

Tips and techniques

It is important to remember that every time you have to analyse an organisational chart, you should consider the key concepts listed here.

A typical organisational structure of a business may look like the one shown in Figure 41.1. It is a hierarchy, with the managing director at the top and the workers at the bottom. Senior management followed by middle management are in-between.

Figure 41.1 A traditional organisational structure: hierarchy with four and five levels

Organisational concepts

Span of control

The span of control is the number of employees for whom a manager or superior is responsible. A great or wide span of control means that the manager is responsible for many employees. A narrow or thin span of control means that the manager is responsible for relatively few employees.

Key terms

Organisational structure: the way in which a business is organised.

Span of control: the number of employees (subordinates) for whom a manager is responsible.

Traditional approaches suggest that the best span of control is four or five. This is because as the number in the span of control increases, the number of channels of communication increases rapidly, and therefore effective communication may break down. This is the dilemma for organisational structures. If a small span of control is required, the number of layers or levels in the hierarchy will increase. This means that there will be more layers for communication to pass through, thus making effective communication less likely.

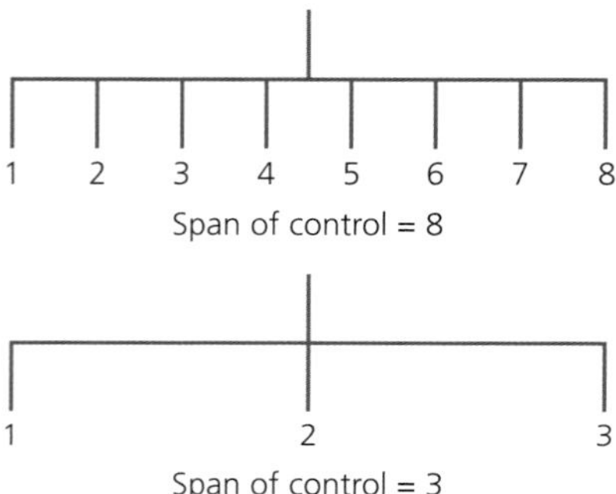

Figure 41.2 Spans of control

There is no correct number, even though four or five are often quoted, for an effective span of control. How many people are involved will depend on:

- the personality of the manager/superior
- the skill and experience of the employee or subordinate
- the size of the business
- whether or not the business is centralised (see below)
- the degree of competition in the market; if costs are an issue, this will encourage a wider span of control, which is often achieved through the process of delayering (see below)
- the extent to which the business has agreed and well-defined objectives; if all the employees are clear about the direction of the business, less supervision will be required and therefore a wider span of control can be used.

Chain of command

The chain of command is concerned with the way in which responsibility for employees is organised within a business. The organisational chart in Figure 41.3 shows that Judith is responsible for Tom, Harry, Francis and Sarah. It can also be seen that, in turn, Tom is responsible for Albert and Joe. Similarly, the chart shows that Tom, Harry, Francis and Sarah are accountable to Judith.

The chain of command can often serve as a useful guide to the lines of communication in an organisation.

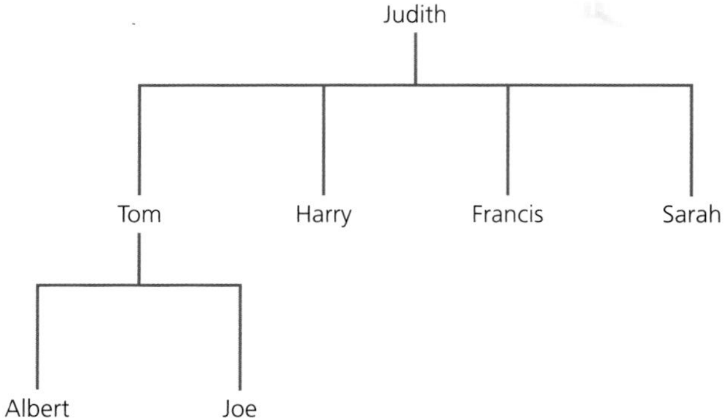

Figure 41.3 Chain of command

Levels of hierarchy

This refers to the number of levels or layers in a business organisation. In Figure 41.1 there are five levels or layers. The number of levels or layers will depend on the type of organisational structure chosen by the business. A horizontal or flat structure will have fewer levels than a vertical or tall structure.

Too many levels or layers in the hierarchy may not be good for a business. Addressing the annual conference of the Institute of Professional Qualified Secretaries (IPQS) in London, Chief Superintendent Helen Ball of the Metropolitan Police told delegates that hierarchical workplaces such as the police force and many 'old school' employers were in danger of stifling talent.

Delayering

Delayering often takes place as a result of rationalisation in a business. If the business is in a competitive market, it needs to ensure that its costs are kept under control, and one way to reduce costs is to remove a layer or tier of management.

A further advantage of delayering is that it provides an opportunity for employees to have more responsibility, which may be beneficial in terms of motivation. Delayering may also mean that the decision making process is quicker, as there are fewer layers for decisions and messages to go through.

However, it is important to note that if delayering takes place, the span of control in the business will increase. There will also be implications for costs in the short term, as redundancies may be necessary to achieve the delayering. This may demotivate employees if they are fearful of losing their job, as it will reduce their sense of security (Maslow, see **Chapter 47**).

Key term

Delayering: reducing the number of levels in the hierarchy of an organisation.

Tips and techniques

When you look at a case study, note the implications of delayering for the business. Notice also how your points can be justified by making reference to a motivational theorist.

Delegation

The more delegation in an organisation, the bigger the span of control will be and the wider the organisational structure. How much delegation takes place will depend on:

- leadership style: a democratic style will mean more delegation
- how busy the manager or leader is: if the leader is very busy, delegation is more likely to occur
- ability and willingness of employees to take on additional responsibility
- type of task that is to be delegated.

Empowerment

Empowerment means giving employees responsibility for the tasks they perform. It is a form of delegation. By enriching employees' jobs, it is hoped that they will be more motivated (Herzberg and Mayo). Offering empowerment may also give a business the opportunity to reduce the number of levels in its organisational structure (delayering).

Types of organisational structure models

Looking at an organisational structure chart can be misleading. However, each type of structure has implications for the likely style of leadership and the role of employees in such an organisation.

Tips and techniques

It is worth noting that the type of organisational structure may well be influenced by the type of leader that the business has. A centralised organisational structure may be more likely to have autocratic leadership, whereas a decentralised organisational structure is more likely to have a leader with a democratic leadership style, that is, one who is not afraid to delegate responsibility.

Organisation by system

Here, the business is split into specialist areas which operate together to make the business function efficiently, rather like the parts in an old-fashioned clock. This means that each part of 'the system' has some input into the output of the business's product(s).

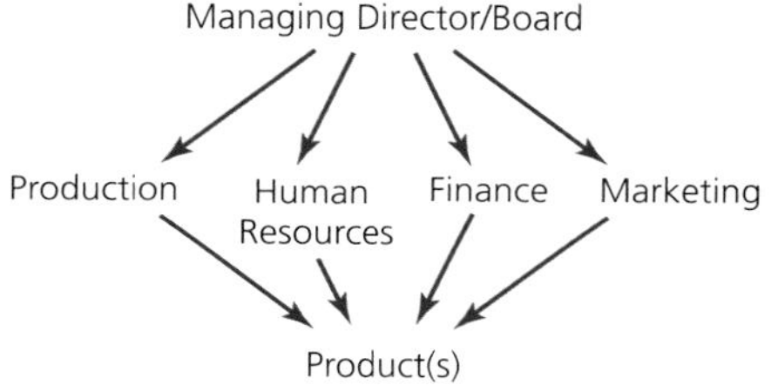

Figure 41.4 Input into the product

The achievements (or failures) of the business arise from the outcome of the interaction of a number of different departments. This seems very sensible; each part of the system (i.e. department) contains specialists who can concentrate on what they do best. Specialist functions (departments) are not duplicated but there are several points to bear in mind:

- There can be a tendency for each department to operate as a separate entity or/and to treat itself as the most important part of the business. If this occurs, managers in such a department fail to operate with the strategic objectives of the whole business uppermost in their mind.
- Without a high level of integration, co-ordination and some degree of compromise (e.g. over timescales and deadlines), the business will become fragmented with each department working largely to its own agenda. Such fragmentation will damage the overall productivity of the business.
- It can be difficult to evaluate performance and identify whether or not a particular product is particularly successful, since there are several

departmental inputs affecting performance. Some departments may try to take most of the credit for success and/or may blame others for failure.

- It is not always easy for managers in one department to see a direct result between their contribution and results.

Organisation by product

Alternatively, the company could be organised by product, that is, the business is organised around recognisable individual products. These are known as profit centres.

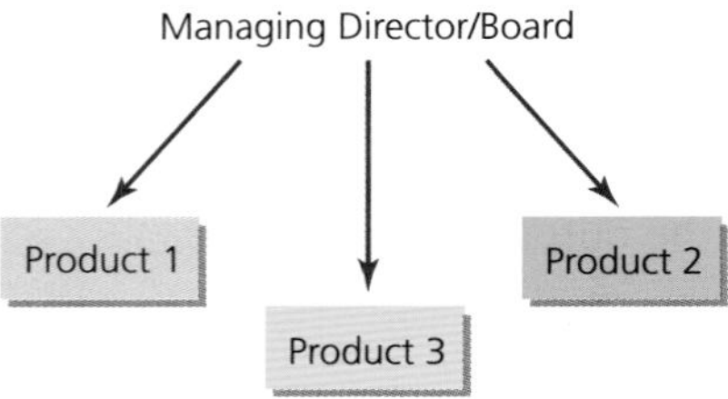

Figure 41.5 Organisation by product

Each product is 'a company in miniature' with its own finance, marketing department, and so on. This too seems a sensible way to organise for the following reasons:

- It is easier to see which products are performing well. Each profit centre can be easily evaluated.
- Managers of each product can concentrate their energies on one product rather than several.
- Each centre has considerable autonomy, which can increase motivation.
- Managers can see the direct result of their decisions and so may be more motivated.

Needless to say, there are also drawbacks with this form of organisation:

- Different products compete for resources (such as finance); this can create winners and losers and so can lead to conflict.
- Are resources wasted? Would it be better to have one finance department, one marketing department and so on, (thus achieving managerial economies of scale) rather than several?

It is for management (board of directors in this instance) to decide on the most appropriate method of organisation, given the business's situation and its objectives. Once a choice is made to change from one method of organisation to another, it will not be easy to change back.

The choice as to what type of structure to use may well be taken in the light of the ability and preferred style of leadership.

Organistic (horizontal or flat) structure

The organistic structure is flat and has a large span of control (see Figure 41.6). Each manager is responsible for a large number of employees (subordinates). This type of structure is associated with a democratic style of leadership. Delegation is encouraged, allowing for a more motivated workforce.

Figure 41.6 Organistic (horizontal or flat) structure

Mechanistic (vertical or tall) structure

The mechanistic structure is more vertical than the organistic and consequently has a smaller span of control (see Figure 41.7). The style of leadership is less democratic than under the organistic structure. As there are a large number of layers in the structure, it is also more bureaucratic. An example is the civil service in the UK.

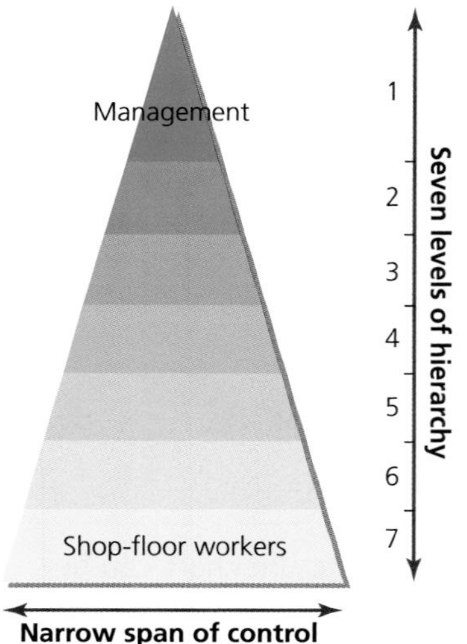

Figure 41.7 Mechanistic (vertical or tall) structure

Centralised or entrepreneurial structure

Weinshall classified organisations as either centralised or decentralised. A centralised structure is associated with autocratic leaders who want to keep firm control of the business (see Figure 41.8). The leader is involved with everything and all communication goes through him or her. The decision making process takes place at the top of the hierarchy.

Figure 41.8 Centralised structure

> **Key terms**
>
> **Organistic structure:** a flexible, flat organisational structure, with a wide span of control.
>
> **Mechanistic structure:** a bureaucratic, vertical structure, with a narrow span of control.
>
> **Centralised structure:** the decision making process is undertaken by the leader at the top of the hierarchy.

Decentralised structure

A decentralised structure allows the decision making process to take place away from head office. The structure may be decentralised either by product, where each product has its own organisational structure (see Figure 41.9(a)), or by area, where each area or region has its own structure (see Figure 41.9(b)). Under a decentralised structure, the span of control will be wide. The style of leadership that is likely to be associated with this structure is democratic, as more employees will have responsibilities delegated to them.

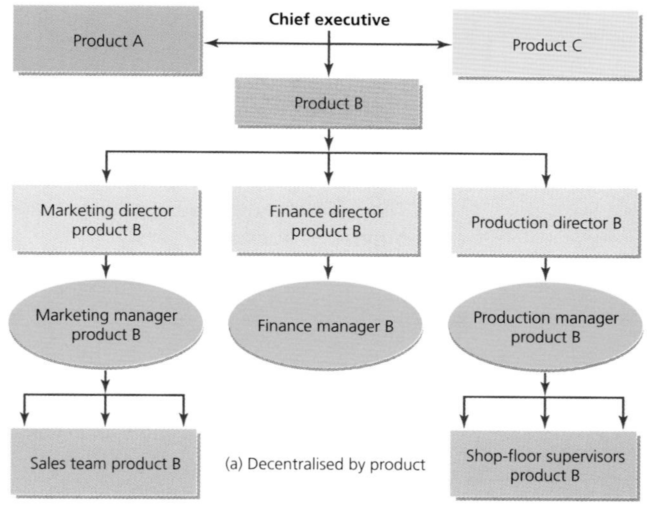

(a) Decentralised by product

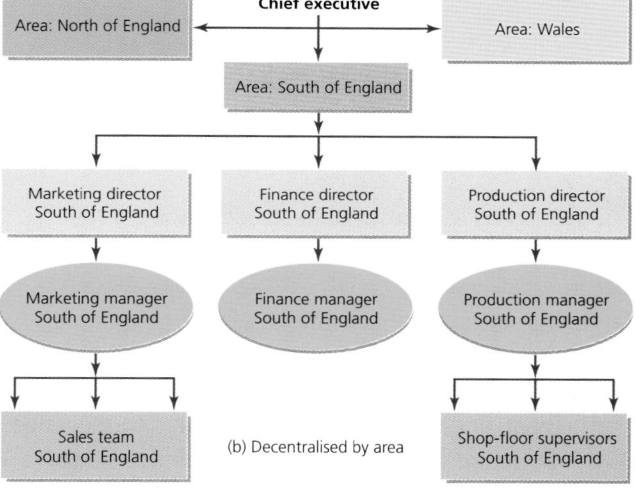

(b) Decentralised by area

Figure 41.9 Decentralised structure

> **Key term**
>
> **Decentralised structure:** the decision making process is delegated and undertaken on a regional or product basis.

Marriott hotels are often quoted as an example of a successful decentralised structure. In addition, after the privatisation of the railways, the industry became a decentralised network as the ownership of the track went to Network Rail. While the ownership of running the routes was split up into franchises, which were bought by businesses such as Virgin.

There is considerable debate about whether a centralised or decentralised structure is the more appropriate. The main arguments on both sides are presented in Table 41.1.

Table 41.1 Advantages and disadvantages of centralised and decentralised structures

Type of structure	Advantages	Disadvantages
Centralised	Decisions are quicker because there is no need to consult all areas or branches. In the event of a crisis, there will be strong leadership. There is a standardised approach in the way the business is operated. Consumers will recognise the standardised approach and consistent organisation. There is less duplication of resources, which may reduce costs.	Decisions are made without the benefit of local knowledge. Lack of involvement in the decision making process is demotivating. Experts in a region may be ignored, resulting in mistakes. Loss of goodwill in the regions may occur, as consumer needs are not met by centralised decisions.
Decentralised	Local regions or areas are better informed for some decisions. Regions will know local consumer needs and trends. Being able to make decisions is a motivator (Mayo and Herzberg). This delegation or empowerment will mean there are opportunities for local initiative to be used. This is a more flexible approach, as decisions can be made for individual areas or products rather than having a standardised approach for all. Less time is spent on communication and arguing a case for a specific region.	Consumers may not recognise the corporate identity as regions introduce variations. Some decisions made at regional or product level may be appropriate for that region or product but not appropriate for the business as a whole (no overview). Duplication of resources occurs, which could be reduced if centralised.

Historically, organisational structures were rigid and had many layers in the hierarchy. As businesses became larger, more layers were added, leading to large, bureaucratic organisations. These large, rigid organisations lacked the flexibility to cope with change and consequently suffered.

The changing nature of business has led to a change in the structure and organisation of businesses. More businesses today have flatter structures, which suggests that the levels of hierarchy have been reduced in an attempt to give more employees a chance to take responsibilities. This delegation and empowerment, along with decentralisation, have altered the span of control and the lines of communication in businesses, making them more capable of adapting to the ever-changing business world.

Matrix organisational structures

This type of organisational structure is where employees with similar skills are put together to complete tasks or projects, but with more than one manager supervising (see Table 41.2).

There needs to be a substantial amount of co-operation for this type of structure to work as working for various managers may be confusing nevertheless it can work with effective communication.

Such an organisational structure will have several lines of communication and reporting.

Table 41.2 Matrix organisational structure

Project/ task	Finance	Marketing	Operations management	Human resources
1	Group 1 (Finance)	Group 1 (Marketing)	Group 1 (Operations management)	Group 1 (Human resources)
2	Group 2 (Finance)	Group 2 (Marketing)	Group 2 (Operations management)	Group 2 (Human resources)
3	Group 3 (Finance)	Group 3 (Marketing)	Group 3 (Operations management)	Group 3 (Human resources)

Value of organisational structure

Having an organisational structure brings a sense of 'organisation' or order to the business. It is then plain to see who is responsible for whom, and who reports to whom; the lines of responsibility and communication are clear for all to see and may be of benefit within an induction programme.

The various spans of control can be viewed and possibly used to ensure there is a fair distribution for the spans of control for the directors and managers within the business.

It may be possible to ascertain whether 'delayering' is possible or beneficial to a business that may need to cut costs. Having an organisational structure may also allow the business to plan for the future; it is possible to see whether the business can cope with expansion, or take on new orders or even where efficiencies can be made.

The various stakeholders within the business can also see at a glance where the strengths and weaknesses may be with regards to the levels of manning within the business.

Employees may be able to see where there may be possibilities for promotion; the HR department should be able to ascertain where certain departments are being over-stretched and likely to suffer stress or a lack of motivation. Employees will also be able to clearly see their role and where that role fits in the business as a whole.

The level of authority within the organisation is clear by viewing the chain of command and the span of control. All within the business will be able to see who to pass information to.

Organisational culture

The organisational culture of a business reflects the values, attitudes and beliefs of a business.

The culture of the business will strongly influence the manner in which the business operates.

Another definition suggests the organisational culture of a business is the collection of values and behaviour which are unique to the environment of the organisation.

Many businesses have a mission statement (see **Chapter 6**) which will give an indication of the culture of that business.

Some mission statements highlight the ethical stance and/or how a concern for the environment is high on its list of priorities, which may be reflected in the way the business operates.

Many businesses today try to mirror their organisational culture with that of society. Offering equality for its employees, operating in a transparent manner are values that all can relate to and agree upon.

Writing in the *Harvard Business Review*, J Coleman (6 May 2013) stated that 'a strong corporate culture can account for approximately 20%–30% improvement in the performance of the business'. It is also suggested that the main components of a good organisational or corporate culture are:

- Vision – starting with a mission statement.
- Values – the values of a business are the core of its culture.
- Practices – actually acting and operating in such a way as to match its values.
- People – employees who share the values of the business.
- Narrative – viewing the history of the business and its heritage.
- Place – locating a business within, for example, the Silicon Valley if technology is the core part of the business. It also refers to the layout of the business – such as having open-plan offices to enhance communication with all within the business.

Although these may not be the only components, these six, it is suggested, form the foundation of the organisation culture of a business.

Ensuring all within the business understand these and are able to recognise these will help to shape the culture within the business.

The corporate or organisational culture of a business can be seen within a business by the manner in which it:

- conducts its business
- treats its customers
- reacts or shows concern for its local community
- allows its employees to be involved in the decision making process
- communicates within the organisation
- views the commitment of all within the business to the values, objectives and mission statement.

The organisational culture of a business may be seen (according to B. Tharp, April 2009) by:

- the way employees dress: often to enhance a sense of belonging employees will have corporate clothing (dress code or even a set uniform).
- the manner in which the building is designed, equipped and decorated.
- the publications of the business (in-house magazines).
- the degree of training offered.

These are all 'signs' that can give an idea of the culture of the business. Stakeholders of the business will be able to clearly see how the values of the organisation are put into practice.

Further sources

www.businesslink.gov.uk/bdotg/action

C. Handy (1990) *Understanding Organisations*, Oxford University Press.

www. Blogs.hbr.org (*Harvard Business Review*)

www.forums.digitalspy

Your turn

Questions marked in red are for A Level students only.

Multiple-choice questions

1 The following are all advantages of a centralised organisation except:
   A Decisions are made quicker
   B In a crisis, there is strong leadership
   C Less duplication
   D Higher motivation for employees *(1)*

2 For a tall (vertical) organisational structure, the following are true except:
   A high number of levels of hierarchy
   B smaller span of control
   C the civil service is a good example
   D communication will be quicker throughout the structure. *(1)*

Revision questions

1 Explain the term 'organisational structure'. *(3)*

2 State four pieces of information that can be found about a business by looking at its organisational structure. *(4)*

3 State what is meant by the term 'decentralisation'. *(2)*

4 Explain two reasons why a flatter organisational structure is more likely to provide more opportunities to motivate employees. *(4)*

5 Using Figure 41.10:
   A State the number of levels in the business. *(1)*
   B Whom is the marketing director responsible for? *(2)*
   C What is the span of control for the production managers? *(1)*

Total *(17)*

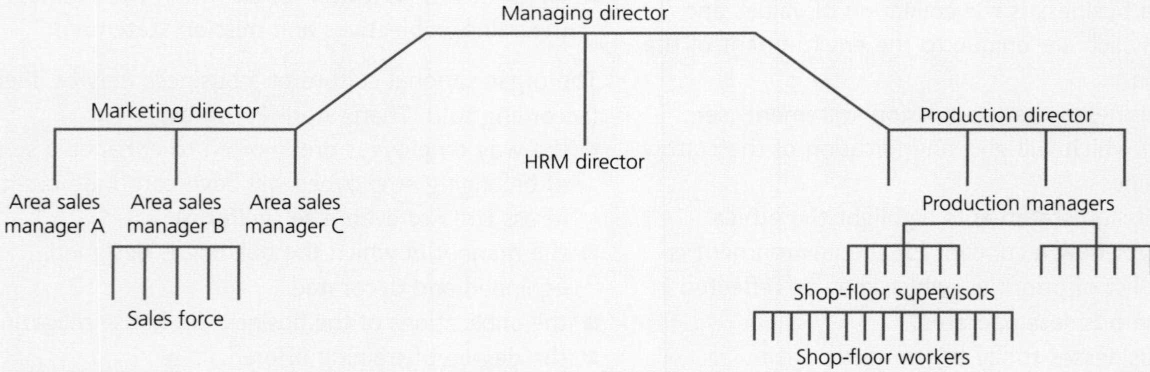

Figure 41.10 Organisation structure

Case study

Tesco's plans, in October 2014, to restructure the organisation with a round of redundancies of store team leaders, caused concern within the ranks of the employees. The role of team leader within the stores is a supervisory role, which Tesco suggests can be eliminated except for those involved with checkouts and online activities.

Some of the team leader roles may be replaced by other management positions although these would be rationalised as well. Further restructuring will be based around the merging of retail and warehouse activities. It is unclear whether managers affected by a fusion of managerial roles within retail and warehouse will have to reapply for their jobs.

It has also been reported (www. groceryinsight.com) that some deputy store managers' jobs may be cut.

There are to be several consultations taking place in several stores within the East Midlands. It is thought that redundancy packages will be offered for the team leaders, or they will be given an opportunity to take up lower paid roles within the stores.

The elimination of many of the team leaders and possible elimination of deputy store managers may be viewed as a partial 'delayering'.

1 If Tesco activate these changes, evaluate the likely implications for its organisational structure. *(9)*

2 If Tesco undergo this form of partial 'delayering' explain the possible consequences for the organisational culture of the business. *(4)*

Total *(13)*

Chapter 42

Communication

Year 2

A Level students must know all of the content in this chapter.

This chapter is not applicable for AS students.

Tips and techniques

When answering examination questions, it is a good idea to try to justify your points by relating any specific theory to them. The comments about the importance of effective communication have been justified by mentioning motivational theorists.

Effective communication is vital for a business to operate in an efficient manner. Regardless of what needs to be communicated, it is essential that the information given is clearly understood. Imagine being an employee on the production line at a car plant, where the level of noise may be significant, and needing to hear what the supervisor is trying to explain about a particular task. If the employee fails to hear the message correctly, serious errors may occur. Similarly, if a pilot aboard a jumbo jet fails to understand an instruction clearly about which course to fly, this inability to understand the instruction may have fatal consequences.

Communication is important to a business for a number of reasons:

1 Effective communication will ensure that the number of mistakes made within the business is reduced. If such mistakes can be reduced then this will have an effect upon the costs of the business, in time and consequently money.
2 If the level of communication within the business is clear and effective, then the employees within the business will feel a sense of belonging (Maslow's theory) and involvement (Mayo's theory).
3 If communication can take place quickly and effectively, this will enhance the decision making process of the business. As a consequence, the business will be able to progress and be more competitive.
4 Effective communication can be a marketing tool for the business; if communication reaches its target market successfully, via higher sales, the business should be able to generate additional income.

Communication involves the transmission of information from one person to another. The information or the message may take many forms and can be transmitted in numerous ways. Communication involves:

- the information to be imparted (the message)
- the transmitter (whoever sends the information)
- a form of transmission (a form of signal using sound or vision)
- a receiver.

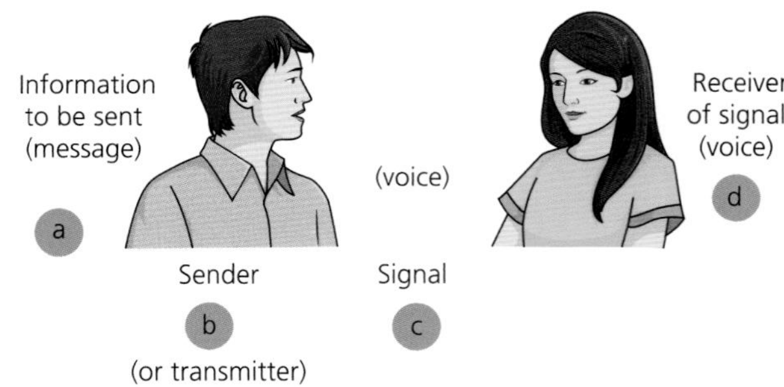

Figure 42.1 The communication process

Types of communication

There are several different types of communication:

- one-way and two-way
- formal and informal
- open and closed
- vertical and horizontal.

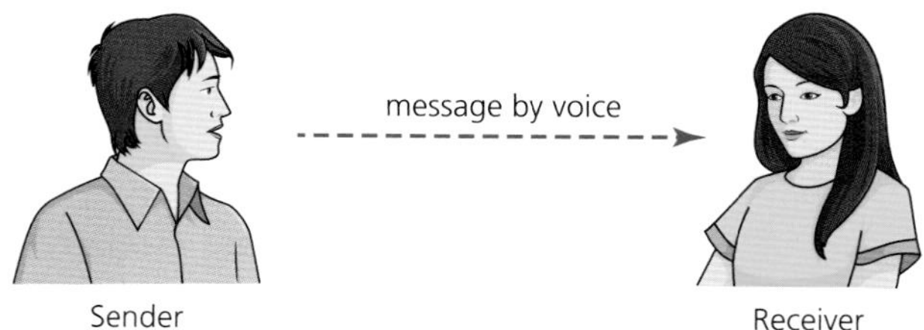

Figure 42.2 One-way communication

One-way communication

One-way communication is the simplest form of communication and usually comes in the form of an order, where the receiver has no right of reply.

Table 42.1 Advantages and disadvantages of one-way communication

Advantages	Disadvantages
Easy to use	Less reliable as there is no way to check message (no feedback)
Cheaper than two-way	May cause frustration for the receiver
No pressure on the sender to justify what is being communicated	

Two-way communication

Two-way communication involves both a sender and a receiver of information.

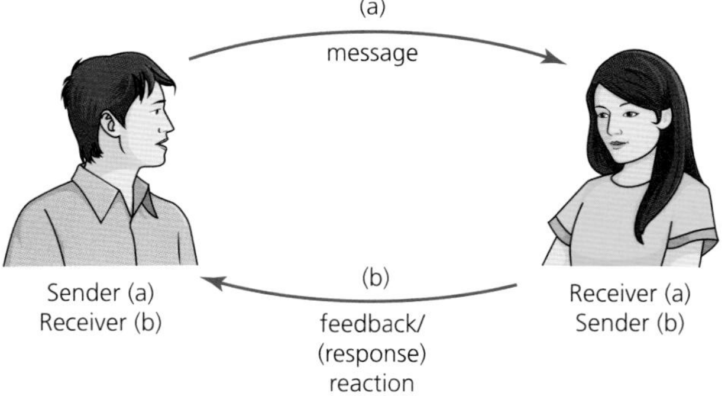

Figure 42.3 Two–way communication

Table 42.2 Advantages and disadvantages of two-way communication

Advantages	Disadvantages
More effective/reliable, because the receiver is able to gain clarification (feedback)	Takes more time and is therefore more expensive
Receiver feels more involved because he or she is able to seek clarification	Puts the sender of the information under pressure to justify/explain the information being sent

Formal communication

Tips and techniques

One of the easiest ways to distinguish between formal and informal communication is the location or environment in which the communication takes place.

This type of communication is often associated with how information is communicated, often using agreed rules or procedures. The 'house' style of communication is usually something that is made clear in an induction process, when a new employee joins a business.

- Formal communication will have been officially sanctioned by the business.
- The formality may refer to the type of language that is used, to whom one speaks or the media that is used to communicate.
- Many businesses insist on an established procedure for answering the phone or laying out letters or emails. Most businesses will also establish a procedure for communicating with staff higher up the hierarchy. Similarly, there will be 'pro forma' (a document with a specific purpose and layout) that is to be used for various activities such as requests for holidays, appraisals or training, and salary information.
- Many of the legalities that a business has to deal with use formal language. Documents such as the Memorandum of Association and the Articles of Association, which are necessary for the incorporated process, use formal terms and, in many cases, a formalised layout. Contracts between businesses will also use formal language.
- Information stored by a business such as sales figures or employees' details are examples of formal communication.

Informal communication

As the word implies, the type of communication in this instance has little or no established rules for how communication takes place. This applies to the type of language used, the procedures for communication and how such information is communicated. The setting for informal communication usually takes place outside of a work environment. There is usually no strict programme for communication and no particular rules on how such communication can take place.

The language and type of information passed on is unique to the people involved in the communicating process. If a group of friends are talking in a school dining room, what they communicate about and how is entirely their decision.

In the majority of cases, informal communication is not written down but passed on verbally. There are exceptions to this, when people are communicating by email or by text message, where a 'form' of the written word is used.

Open communication

This involves the use of language that will be understood by the vast majority of the population. Such communication tends to be free of technical language and jargon.

Open communication is very important if the business intends to reach a large audience. Using language that is not easily understood will reduce the number of people who can understand what the business is trying to state. This is particularly true within marketing. Often a clear, simple message will yield better results than a detailed, complicated and technical message.

If effective communication is to take place between the various stakeholders of the business, then an appropriate type of communication needs to be used. In most cases, open communication is required for any communication with the stakeholders outside the business. If the stakeholders of the business are internal (within the business), then it is more likely that closed communication will be used.

Closed communication

A business may have its own language for activities, procedures and components within the business. Such communication, once learnt, will be understood by those within the business, but not by anyone outside the business.

Students and teachers understand the significance of a 'U' grade at A Level, but there will be some people within the population who have no idea at all!

Such language may well be a form of slang or a convenient abbreviation in order to save time. Many of the terms used within government and the civil service are a series of initials, which are quicker to use than having to state in full the exact title of a particular body. The examination board, OCR, is in itself, a form of closed communication, as most people do not know what the initials stand for.

Closed communication may also include formal language relating to the business.

Vertical communication

This is normally associated with communication from the management being passed down to the employees on the shop floor. However, any communication between the different layers of the business is referred to as vertical communication. Such communication can take place in an upwards direction as well. Employees at the lower end of the business hierarchy may pass on vital information to the management about difficulties with production, or useful information about consumer attitudes to a specific product or service. This type of communication may just involve the day-to-day discussions between management and those who have to implement the business's strategies.

Being able to communicate with different levels of the organisational structure within a business may be highly beneficial to all concerned. It provides an opportunity for employees to feel involved (Mayo's theory) and helps alleviate any frustrations within the working environment (Herzberg, hygiene factors).

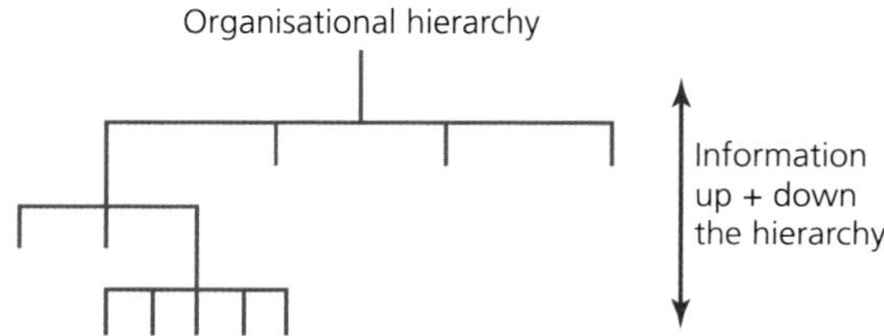

Figure 42.4 Vertical communication (information between different layers of hierarchy)

Horizontal communication

This type of communication involves communication between people on the same level of the organisational structure. Communication between two employees involved with the research and development of a product, or employees discussing a marketing plan for a new advert, or two people within the finance department looking at a cashflow forecast, will all be undertaking horizontal communication.

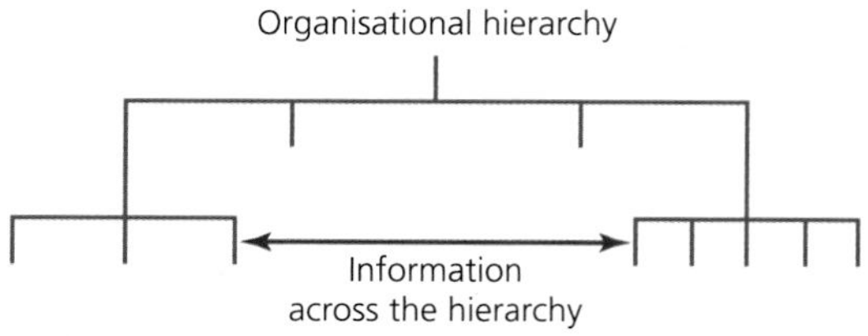

Figure 42.5 Horizontal communication (information between the same layers of hierarchy)

Tips and techniques

The difference between vertical and horizontal communication is not what is being said, but the route or channel of communication that is used.

Channels of communication/ networks

Different businesses may operate different communicational networks of channels. The channel or network will vary for different reasons:

- type of leader
- size of the business
- experience of the employees
- type of organisational structure.

All of these may be important, but there is no set rule on which network or channel is used. There is a link with the type of organisational structure, however; the more centralised the structure, the more likely is the business to use either a 'wheel' or 'chain' network.

Chain

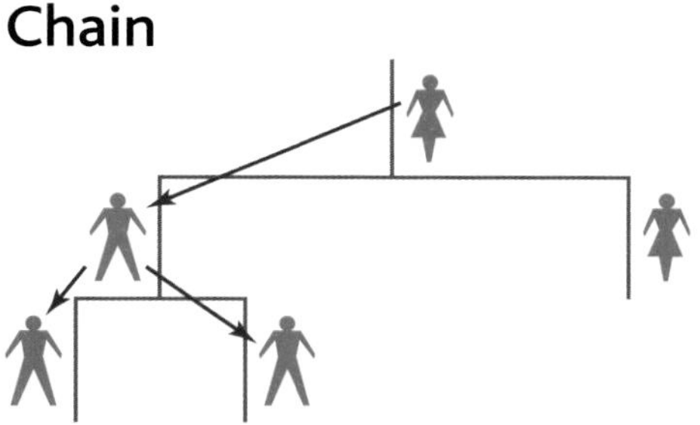

Figure 42.6 The chain

This type of network is normally associated with a formal and vertical hierarchy (see **Chapter 41**). Information can be communicated up and down the hierarchy, although it is more likely that much of the communication will be sent down the hierarchical structure. A typical organisation that would use this type of communicational network is a large one, such as the civil service or a local authority. There is likely to be a lack of opportunity for those employees at the lower end of the hierarchy to feel involved or be able to communicate with higher levels of the hierarchy directly. There is also the possibility of information becoming distorted as it travels through several layers of the hierarchy.

If communication is to be two-way, there is likely to be a problem in terms of the length of time it takes; any message that has to travel through every level of the hierarchy will take time, which is costly for the business.

Wheel

Figure 42.7 The wheel

The 'wheel' has the leader, chief executive, or board of directors at the centre. All communication goes through the leader (centralised structure, see **Chapter 41**), and this type of network enables the leader to keep in touch with everything that is taking place within the business. However, this network may discourage employee initiative and responsibility, as the leader is involved with all communication. This type of network is not associated with delegation.

Circle

This is a restricted network for communication, which can take place between employees, usually within a department or on the same level of a hierarchy. As communication takes place between two people, it will be time-consuming and therefore expensive.

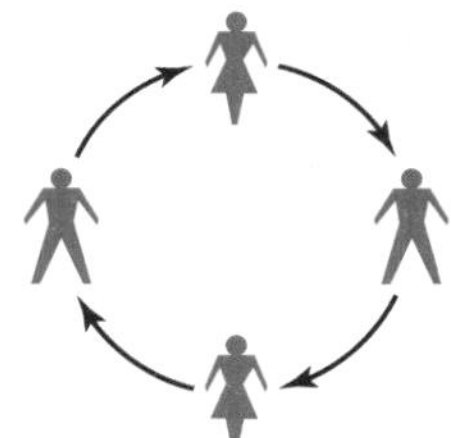

Figure 42.8 The circle

All networks

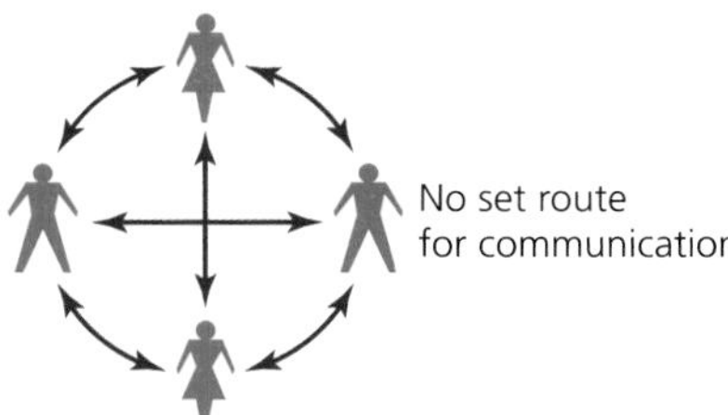

Figure 42.9 All networks

This network, as Figure 42.9 shows, has no set route and allows communication between anyone within the business. This informal network means that communication may be quicker, as those who need to communicate with each other can do so without going through a formalised network. Such a network is more likely to be appropriate for a smaller business, which does not need a highly structured process of communication.

Communication media

The communication media refers to how the message is imparted to the receiver or receivers. Television and radio (mass communication), text message, telephone, noticeboard, fax, memo, email and face-to-face video conferencing are some of the most frequently used media.

All of the above have their advantages and disadvantages, in terms of accuracy, speed, cost and formality.

The use of information communication technology (ICT) has speeded up the process of communication considerably; however, there may be problems with regards to the clarity and therefore the reliability of the information being imparted. Nevertheless, business has invested in ICT in a big way, as the cost of communication, coupled with its speed, has led to significant savings, even allowing for considerable set-up costs (particularly for the hardware).

The usage of ICT is not always successful; the National Health Service has spent billions of pounds on computer systems that have not managed to provide the required benefits. Whether this is due to inappropriate software or technical hardware issues is difficult to ascertain, in spite of the Freedom of Information Act.

Video-conferencing has had a significant effect upon costs for businesses. Sales teams no longer need to meet, but instead can 'link up' and hold a meeting with each person, even in different countries.

Tips and techniques

It is important to be consistent in your usage of terminology. Communication media (or medium if just one) is what is used to impart the message. The channel of communication or network is concerned with the route of the message. The types of communication are concerned with the manner in which the message is imparted.

Barriers to effective communication

Effective communication can be hampered by 'barriers'.

Shannon and Weaver's theory of communication highlights three main barriers to effective communication:

1 Technical: this barrier is concerned with the ability of the receiver to receive the information being communicated. If there is too much noise, the information will not be heard. You have only to think about the difficulty of hearing some of the announcements made at a railway station as a train approaches. Similarly, if a written message is sent but cannot be read by the receiver, this too would be a 'technical' barrier.

Tips and techniques

Any interference that prevents the receiver from being able to receive a message is described as a technical barrier.

2 Semantic: this barrier relates not to the ability to receive the message, but to the receiver's ability to understand what is being sent.

A text message may well be received by a parent from a son, but may not be understood, especially if predicted text has been used. The message may use closed communication that will not be understood by someone outside the family.

3 Effectiveness: if there are no technical or semantic barriers, the final barrier is whether the information being communicated has been acted upon in an appropriate manner.

If the message asked for an employee to contact his or her manager, the employee's act of contacting the manager suggests effective communication. The employee has received the message, understood the message and acted upon the request within the message.

Tips and techniques

Technical and semantic barriers are both relatively easy to identify, although ensuring that semantic barriers are removed may be harder to achieve. Dealing with the 'effectiveness' barrier is significantly harder because there may be several reasons why the message has not been acted upon. In other words, there may exist additional barriers to effective communication, not covered by Shannon and Weaver's theory.

Additional barriers to effective communication

Skill of the sender of the message

The ability of the sender may affect the effectiveness of the communication process. If the sender is inexperienced and has not given sufficient thought to the media for the communication or the nature of the message, these factors will act as a barrier to effective communication.

Similarly, the sender's ability to choose the right words or the right timing could also affect the reliability of the communication.

Ability of the receiver

Irrespective of the ability of the sender, communication can be ineffective due to the lack of ability of the receiver. If there is an inability to read or understand the significance of the message, problems may occur.

Body language

Regardless of the content of the message, body language may affect the effectiveness of communication; a serious message will not be received in the right way if the body language is contradictory. It is little wonder that undertakers are not known for their constant smiling and laughter, given the nature of their work and the information that needs to be imparted.

Body language can be used to put a greater emphasis on a message. Similarly, the tone of the voice can be used to help express a message. A phone call may enable the receiver to gauge feelings by the message and the tone of the voice, something that is not possible if emails or text messages are used.

Inappropriate medium used

Communication may be ineffective if the wrong medium is used. Informing an employee that he or she has been made redundant by a sing-a-gram would be totally inappropriate.

Similarly, there would be no need to formalise an invitation to a meal after work from one employee to another. Using text messages to your parents, even for a simple message of 'c u latr', may not be received clearly.

Cultural differences

Communication between different cultures may run into difficulties because the words used or the tone of the message are not perceived by the receiver in the same way as the sender intended. This is true regardless of whether any actual communication between the two parties was intended. In 2007, an English teacher working in Sudan allowed one of her pupils to choose the name Mohammad for a class teddy bear. This act caused offence to the Muslim population, which resulted in the teacher being prosecuted and sentenced to prison; such was the perceived level of offence caused by the 'innocent' act.

Size of the business and the number of layers in the business hierarchy

Communication becomes harder as a business grows. There will be more layers within the organisation (see **Chapter 41**), more messages issued and more employees to receive such messages. There may be more links in the chain of command and a higher number of employees within the span of control (see **Chapter 41**).

For the very large multi-national companies, communication will become even harder due both to language differences, with meaning being lost in translation, and cultural differences (see above).

The greater the number of layers within an organisation, the more opportunities there are for the communication to break down. A message may become distorted as it passes through the various layers within the business. You may be able to think of instances when your friends have passed on a message and managed to confuse it; or where a friend has not heard the information correctly and passed on information that is no longer accurate.

As the size of a business increases, there may be a greater degree of decentralisation, which will reduce the communication chains and therefore improve the effectiveness of any communication.

Amount of information

If there is a lot of information to pass on, and particularly if the media used is verbal, there is a much greater risk of errors occurring, making the communication ineffective. How easy it is to absorb a large amount of information will also be affected by the skill of both the sender and receiver.

Once a particular media becomes popular, there is a tendency to present too much information, which is sometimes known as 'information or communication overload'. Users of email are often guilty of this, sending a mass of information which could be better presented by alternative media.

Tips and techniques

It is important to note that no single factor can be considered in isolation. It is essential that you think about the context of the case and a range of factors when considering how effective any communication will be.

Table 42.3 Summary of communication aspects

Type of communication	One-way	Two-way
	Formal	Informal
	Open	Closed
	Vertical	Horizontal
	Internal	External
Communication channels/networks	Chain	Wheel
	Circle	All networks
Communication media	Text Email	Telephone Fax
	Letter/printed word Conversation	

Group norms

Group norms are a set of 'rules' which may be written, unwritten, spoken or even just implied. The rules will vary according to the type of group, the setting/environment, and the type of people involved.

The 'rules' or guidelines or standards that are expected in terms of behaviour within the group can vary enormously.

The norms may be either:

- Implicit: where there is an assumption that there is a set way to behave, operate or interact with members within the group; or
- Explicit: where there is a written set of rules on such matters as to how to answer the phone, respond to a customer, or the manner and language that ought to be used when addressing a superior.

Explicit norms are often referred to as the corporate approach and may well be explained in an induction course for new employees.

Having the group norms, whether implicit or explicit, allows the group to function and allows all stakeholders to know the right 'approach' within the group.

The group may be:

- Formal: the workplace is the most obvious example. The workplace is where people are performing set roles or tasks. Such groups have been set up deliberately in order to achieve the objectives of the business or fulfil particular goals.

  This type of group will have a sense of shared purpose, a set membership, where the relationships within the group are functional, task orientated and usually have a specified leader.
- Informal: where a group may consist of friends, and is usually formed for social occasions. There is less likely to be any leader and agreement is by consensus. The informal group may be more fluid, changing as social occasions change and the membership will also be more likely to be fluid.

Whether there is consensus within a group or whether an individual conforms to the group norms will depend upon:

- whether there is a shared view within the group
- the extent to which the individual needs the group
- the purpose of the group
- the formality of the group – a formal work group will have a heavier influence on an individual than an informal group.

R. Bales (group observation) was Professor of Social Relations at Harvard University. His study (1951) concentrated on the interaction within groups and attempted to classify such interactions. His conclusions suggested that:

- Over time a formal leader becomes disliked, whereas an informal leader tends to be liked by the group.
- The size of the group influences the level of contributions. The smaller the group the higher the contributions by its members.
- Those who contribute a lot will initiate ideas.

Tannenbaum and Schmidt considered how a group would have power over its members as conformity to the group is important for its members. As members want to remain in the group and be accepted they are more likely to conform.

Individual objectives will take second place to meeting the objectives of the group.

The membership of a trade union is a good example of where the group objectives will usually outweigh the objectives of the individual.

Your turn

Multiple-choice questions

1 Which of the following is not, according to Shannon and Weaver, a barrier to effective communication?
A semantic
B receiver skills
C technical
D effectiveness. *(1)*

2 All of the below are communication networks except:
A circle
B chain
C central
D wheel. *(1)*

Revision questions

1 Identify four different types of communication. *(4)*

2 Suggest an appropriate type of communication for each of the following, and justify your answer.
A An instruction from the manager to a shop floor worker.
B Communication between two friends planning a night out.
C Communication in the form of an advert aimed at its consumers.
D Communication between two technical experts discussing a new machine. *(4)*

3 For the following circumstances, suggest an appropriate communicational media:
A communication to employees, informing them that Fred is having a retirement party. *(2)*
B communication to employees, informing them that a new prospective customer will visit the factory next week. *(2)*

4 Explain two ways that effective communication may improve employee motivation. *(4)*

5 Explain the difference between open and closed communication. *(2)*

Total *(18)*

Case study

Midwives to strike October 2014

In October 2014, industrial action was taken by midwives, nurses, paramedics, ambulance crews and hospital porters. The Pay Review Body had made a recommendation of a 1 per cent pay rise for all, whereas the government of the day decided not to accept the recommendations in full.

A vote was instigated as to whether strike action should take place on 13 October. It would be the first time midwives had gone on strike over pay in 133 years.

Matthew Taylor from University College Hospital London stated:

'Nurses and midwives at UCH seem angrier than I expected. They are very "conflicted" about striking.'

Members of the Royal College of Midwives had voted 'yes', with a total of 82.2 per cent of those who took part in the ballot saying they would be prepared to participate in a strike. However, 94.6 per cent said they would take part in industrial action short of striking. The turnout for those who were eligible to vote was 49.4 per cent.

Cathy Warwick, the Chief Executive of the RCM, which has 26,000 members stated:

'This is a resounding yes from our members.'

The strike action would be for four hours. Picket lines, although present, did not include huge numbers of midwives attending.

Liz Coollings from Royal Hampshire county hospital stated:

'I never thought I'd be standing in front of a hospital saying 'Enough's enough ....'

Louise Hughes, a midwife for 19 years stated:

'We are striking with heavy hearts.'

Many felt the dilemma between strike action and the thought of leaving parients.

Caroline Abernethy stated:

'I don't take leaving patients and interrupting their care lightly, it took some thought to come out.'

Eleri Bates suggested that;

'As a group midwives are caring . . .'

Source: adapted from rmc.org.uk, Rob Dabrowski, 29 September 2014 and the guardian.com

1 Simplifying the numbers quoted within the case to a turnout of 50 per cent, and a yes vote of 82 per cent, calculate the number of midwives that voted to participate in a strike. *(2)*

2 Explain, using examples from the case, two types of communication that may have been used within this dispute and consequent industrial action. *(4)*

Total *(6)*

Chapter 43

Workforce planning, human resource objectives and strategy

Year 2

A Level students must know all of the content in this chapter.

This chapter is not applicable for AS students.

This chapter is concerned with the way in which a business plans how best to use its workforce. It is sometimes referred to as human resource planning. It is not just about the right number of people to employ and how the right staff are hired. It is more to do with ensuring the right people are employed at the right time. The right people are those who will fit in with the ethos of the business and will help the business to achieve its goals.

The role of workforce planning is now much more important, because the business world and the individual markets in which the business operates are constantly changing. Consequently, the human resource needs of a business will also change. The best businesses are those that can plan ahead and see what their needs will be as soon as possible, in order to gain the right staff at the right time.

Human resource objectives

Human resources are crucial to a business' success, and human resource management involves the setting of objectives in the same way that other functional areas of the business require them. Clear human resource objectives are necessary because 'the people element' underpins what every functional area in the business is trying to achieve. An oft-heard business quote is 'people are our most valuable asset' and it is obvious to see why – without the right people, properly trained and motivated, the work does not get done effectively and this will hinder progress towards the business' overall objectives. The sorts of issues that need to be planned with clear objectives in mind include recruitment, induction, ongoing training, pay rates, appraisal, changes in employment law and customer service.

Human resource objectives cannot be set in isolation; they need to be governed by the business' overall objectives. Thus the organisation's objectives are usually the starting point for a consideration of what the human resource objectives will need to be. Suppose a firm has the strategic objective of diversification into a new market and gaining a 10 per cent market share within three years. Assume also that this diversification will mean manufacturing a product that requires a new set of skills for employees. Will the objective be to successfully retrain existing employees, or recruit new ones by a certain date (i.e. to enable products to be made in good time for the launch of the marketing campaign)?

Without clear objectives for human resources being set the business' managers are likely to find themselves 'firefighting' problems resulting from a lack of employees with the right skills to carry out the work. At best this might mean increased overtime working or the use of agency staff and at worst the work might not get done at all causing problems in terms of reputation and possibly cash flow. Alternatively a failure to plan and set objectives for complying with a new piece of legislation (such as the entitlement to shared parental leave following the birth of a child) could mean a breach of the law and bad publicity. There is clearly both a financial and an opportunity cost to these sorts of issues.

All managers need to adopt a clear strategy for human resource management. Such an approach is important because the business environment is dynamic and a strategic approach takes account of, and plans for, changes in the internal and external environment of the business. It therefore enables the overall objectives of the organisation to be more easily achieved and for change to be more successfully implemented.

The human resource strategy

This is concerned with how a business forecasts its needs for the quantity and quality of human resources that are required to achieve the objectives of that business.

Meeting the needs of the business

It is well worth reminding yourself of the factors that affect the environment in which a business operates. These factors may affect the demand for labour in terms of quantity and quality.

To meet the needs of business, the workforce needs to be effective and efficient. There are only so many workers who will fit the needs of a particular business, and therefore ensuring the right staff are employed is vital to avoid a high turnover of staff as well as meeting consumers' needs. Furthermore, without an appropriate skill level and the correct number of employees, the business may not be as efficient or effective and this will have a detrimental effect upon its stakeholders, such as the shareholders and customers.

It is important to ensure there is a balance in the workforce in terms of the following factors.

Age

If all the workers are aged over 50, some of them may be planning to retire and there will be no one to replace them. Similarly, if the entire workforce were under 25, there would probably be a lack of experience and authority.

Innovation

While it is good to have long-standing and experienced members of staff, there might be a problem in that there are no new employees to bring enthusiasm, fresh ideas and innovation to the business.

Skills

In most businesses, there will be a need to have a range of skills available. For example, at the local garage, there will be a need for:

- a general manager to oversee all aspects of the business
- a workshop controller, to supervise the work of the mechanics
- trained mechanics, to fix and service the cars
- a receptionist to meet the customers and take bookings for work to be done on the vehicles
- accounts people to ensure bills for the garage are paid and charges for the work on the cars are paid
- car sales staff, to sell either new or second-hand cars
- cleaners
- a parts buyer, to ensure that the mechanics have the correct parts to fix cars.

All of the above will be essential for the smooth running of the business and for its stakeholders. Each of the above jobs requires different skills and therefore will need different training and working conditions to help the business achieve its objectives.

For example, the mechanic will need be fully qualified and will need a full set of working tools, whereas the receptionist will need to be computer literate and have a welcoming environment to make customers feel comfortable. Providing the right training and working conditions will help the retention rates of staff, and therefore help reduce labour turnover. Keeping the workforce contented will not only reduce the labour turnover rate, but also therefore make it easier for the business to forecast the demand for staff.

For a larger business, planning what staff are required may be considerably more complicated and therefore will need careful planning.

Human resource needs of a business

Balancing the human resource needs within the financial constraints of the business, and ensuring that the objectives of the business can be achieved, is not easy. There are several factors that affect human resource needs:

- Changing needs of the business: a change in sales trends may mean the business needs to increase the production of one product and decrease another. As a consequence there will be a need for more workers of one particular skill.
- Increased sales may mean there is a need for more staff overall.
- When staff leave, they have to be replaced. Staff may leave due to retirement, promotion, or being discontented with the job or the environment in which they have to work.
- Improved technology means that there is less need for human labour or the existing workforce have to be retrained to work with the new technology.
- Change in the method of production, moving from batch to flow (see **Chapter 62**). Again, this may mean that the workforce will need retraining or will be surplus to requirements.
- The level of budget may alter the number of employees that can be employed. If there are financial problems within the business and costs

have to be reduced, cutting the labour force is one possible method of achieving the necessary cuts.

- Unforeseen circumstances: natural disasters and terrorist activities have greatly affected the human resource needs of business. Flooding in a small part of Somerset in 2013 left some businesses without premises and consequently jobs were no longer available.
- The state of the economy will affect the demand for labour. If the economy is in a boom situation, there will be a high level of economic activity and therefore there will be a higher demand for labour.
- Changes in legislation which affect the ability of businesses to take on employees, whether it is in the form of financial constraints or incentives.

Ability of a business to meet its human resource needs

Unfortunately for business, forecasting the human resources needs is not straightforward. Sometimes, without real warning, circumstances change that alter the demand for workers (see above).

The following are some factors affecting the ability of a business to meet its human resource needs:

- Availability of potential workers: are there sufficient numbers available?
- Skills of the potential workers: are there sufficient numbers of workers with the right skills?
- Nature of the work required: if the job involves unsociable hours or is unpleasant, the number of potential workers will be restricted. However, if the job is of a high status or has additional benefits, it is more likely to attract a greater supply of interested people.
- Demand for workers from other businesses: this will affect the availability and the level of wages expected. If labour is scarce, then the general wage level will be higher.
- Location of the business: is the location attractive? If not, an insufficient number of workers will be willing to move to this area to gain employment.
- Cost of living in the locality of the business: the cost of housing is one reason why some businesses in the London area find it difficult to gain workers. To overcome this problem, some workers may choose to live some distance from the business; however, if this is to be a success, there is a need for the availability of a convenient form of transport. Or is working from home considered a viable option?
- Government legislation: this may make it harder or more expensive to take on workers. The increase in the national minimum wage may discourage a business from taking on additional staff due to the increased costs. EU regulations such as the working time directive, which limit the hours of work, may mean that additional workers are needed to complete the required tasks.

Businesses today have adopted alternative strategies to alleviate some of the responsibilities and problems of finding the right workers. The cost in terms of time and money are significant when trying to recruit labour. In addition, the cost of keeping labour is expensive. Not only do wages have to be paid, but also statutory working conditions have to be met. The rights of workers have been strengthened, making it harder to dismiss staff. It is for these reasons that many businesses consider alternatives to employing staff on a full-time basis.

Strategies adopted by business to meet their human resource needs

Outsourcing

A business normally has a number of employees who are employed on a permanent basis. However, usually in response to an upturn in business or for a one-off order, a business can subcontract work.

Outsourcing refers to the contracting jobs to external labour. Instead of a business having to hire its own labour, it will use another business to undertake a specific job.

This saves a business the difficulty of hiring staff, which may not be needed after a specific job or task has been completed. By outsourcing, the business will save money by not incurring additional costs of having permanent staff.

Staff can therefore be used as and when required. This is particularly important for businesses where trade is irregular.

In a competitive market, outsourcing is a way of reducing costs and has been undertaken by many UK businesses. Marks and Spencer's customer services is now run from India, as are several call centres.

Once the right staff have been recruited (see **Chapter 44**), it is important to ensure that they are looked after in an appropriate manner. If not they will leave or will not perform effectively, which could have repercussions upon the business.

Flexible working practices

With this need to look after the workforce, and to ensure the business operates in an efficient manner, businesses have expanded the use of the following practices.

Flexible working hours/practices (flexi-time)

More businesses are operating a flexible working time to gain the right staff. Many potential employees may prefer a choice of hours.

Numerous businesses operate a 'core' time, which may be between 10 a.m. and 3 p.m., when employees have to be present. Apart from the core time, there is flexibility, allowing the employees to work to suit their own particular lifestyles.

Many local authority employees work on a 'flexi-time' basis often having to work between stated hours but within those stated hours there is a degree of 'flexibility', provided the nominated number of hours are completed.

For example, employees may work between 8.30 a.m. and 7 p.m. and have to complete 37 hours a week with a minimum of 6 hours a day; which hours are worked within these parameters does not matter.

Although this system may be more expensive to administer and operate, as the place of work may need to be open for more hours, there are benefits.

The business may save some money by gaining or keeping good staff and therefore will not need to spend money on recruitment and training.

There may be further benefits for the economy as a whole if this system is adapted more widely as the 'rush hour' becomes more staggered.

Term-time working

This is simply where the working hours mirror term-time days. The employee will work as normal during term time, but will not work during the school holidays, which enables the employee to look after his or her child or children. The employee will still be classed as employed.

Structured time off in lieu

As part of some flexible working practices, firms may encourage structured time off in lieu, especially where there are peaks and troughs for how busy a business may be.

Employees may be asked to work longer hours during busy periods with the number of additional hours being recorded to enable the employee to take time off in compensation (in lieu) during less busy periods. There may be some limits on the number of hours that can be 'saved up' in this way.

Job sharing

A variety of schemes exist with some employees sharing jobs on a morning-afternoon basis, while others share on a day-to-day basis. Which system is operated usually depends upon the needs of the business and how much of a 'handover period' is required between those people sharing the role, to ensure continuity.

There are benefits to operating a job sharing scheme:

- Employees are able to work the hours or days that suit them and therefore a business can gain the staff it needs.
- If one of the job sharers is absent, the business still has some of the tasks covered by the other job sharer, who may even be able to take on the extra work if it is for a short period of time.

The downside is:

- There are additional administrative costs of employing two people instead of one.
- Careful planning may be required to ensure the job sharers take a similar approach to a given task so that there is consistency within the role.
- If the job sharers have managerial responsibilities, differing leadership styles may confuse staff under their supervision.

Remote working

This involves allowing the employees to work away from the business premises.

Remote working is now a lot easier due to the level of communications technology in place. Teleconferencing (a conference held over the phone) and video-conferencing allow effective communication without it being necessary for all employees to be present at the place of work.

The advantages are:

- Many businesses have found that the productivity of employees has increased, as there are fewer distractions and interruptions than at the place of work.
- Allowing employees to work at home saves valuable commuter time and allows the employee to choose when to work.
- A lower level of absenteeism has been recorded.

The disadvantages are:

- It is harder to check that employees are actually working.
- There is the initial set-up cost of providing the necessary technology.

Zero hours contracts

Zero hours contracts allow employers to hire staff with no guarantee of work. Staff only work when they are needed, which can be at short notice.

There has been much controversy over zero hours contracts, as they have been perceived by some to reduce the rights of employees, although in most cases this is not true, as the rights for zero-hours-contract employees are very similar to those of non-zero hour contracts, especially in terms of meeting the national minimum wage, holiday entitlement and agreement to work.

Sometimes zero hours contracts are referred to as 'on call work', because there are no guaranteed hours for the employees. Usually, employees are called for when they are needed and therefore do not have any security of employment.

There is no obligation on behalf of the employers to offer a set number of hours and the actual hours offered will normally reflect the demand for the goods or services being offered. Similarly there is no obligation for employees to accept the offer of work.

Many of the fast food and catering businesses use zero contract labour: McDonalds, Burger King, Subway, Wetherspoons, Domino's Pizza. Sports Direct are known to employ the vast majority of its staff on zero contracts.

The advantages are:

- It reduces the administrative costs of employing labour on a full-time basis.
- It is more cost efficient for employers as labour is only hired and paid when needed.
- Employees have units of labour readily available when required.
- It may well be cheaper than using agency staff.
- It is easier for employees to have breaks between jobs.
- Not having to accept offers of work allows employees greater flexibility.

The disadvantages are:

- There is no certainty of employment.
- There is no guarantee of job security for employees.
- There is no certainty of hours worked and therefore amount of total pay will vary.
- Employers cannot be certain offers of employment will be accepted.

Compressed hours

This is an attempt to provide an alternative working week in terms of the number of days per week actually worked by employees.

Assuming a 'normal' working week is usually 5 days, a compressed hours working week is often 'compressed' into 4 working days, albeit with the same number of hours per week.

For example, if a 'normal' working week is 5, 8-hour days, the compressed hours week would be 4 days of 10 hours per day.

The advantages are:

- Working one day less potentially reduces commuting costs for the employees.
- It may ease congestion on the roads.
- It allows employees greater flexibility.
- There are reduced costs of child care.
- It may enable employers to reduce costs.
- Staff morale may improve due to 'extra' day off; and therefore
- Productivity may increase.

The disadvantages are:

- It means a longer working day for employees.
- Productivity may fall as the working day is longer.
- A greater loss of production/service provision if staff have a day off.

Tips and techniques

Deciding which, if any, of the above advantages and disadvantages to use in your answer will depend upon the context of the case or question. It is therefore important to be selective in what you say.

Annualised hours

This is where employees work a total number of hours for the year as a whole, with a degree of flexibility as to how these hours are undertaken – either weekly or in shifts. Usually, a set number of hours are allocated per week and the residue of hours is worked on an employers' needs basis in order to meet demand.

Employees will be paid on the basis of the hours to be worked and therefore there will be less or no need at all for overtime pay as the residue or 'needs must' hours will have been included in the basic wage.

For example, if a 'normal' working week is 37 hours and there are 52 weeks per year, that means there are 1924 hours to be worked minus annual leave and bank holidays, which may mean a total of 9 weeks multiplied by 37 hours to be subtracted (333 hours), giving an annualised number of hours of 1591.

The employers will stipulate a set number of hours to be worked per week leaving a number of hours where the employee is 'on-call'. The wages will cover all of the annualised hours including the 'on-call' hours and therefore meaning the business can call upon the employees to come in for the 'on-call' hours in order to meet demand for the product or service offered.

The advantages are:

- It allows the employers to use the workforce when needed.
- There is no need for employers to pay expensive overtime rates, therefore reducing costs and thus helping the business to remain competitive.
- Allows employees flexibility.

The disadvantages are:

- Being 'on-call' may be restrictive for employees.
- There is some uncertainty when the employees may be called.
- The opportunity for employees to do overtime is usually lost.
- There is an additional administrative cost for employers to calculate and operate such a system.

Tips and techniques

You need to be prepared to be able to calculate annualised hours and /or compressed hour contracts. As always, it is very important to show your work.

Key terms

Workforce planning: The process used to plan the number and quality of employees that will be required, both in the short and long term.

Outsourcing: The usage of external labour to undertake a specific job or contract.

Further sources

www.cipd.co.uk/default.cipd
www.gov.uk
www.acas.org.uk

Your turn

Revision questions

1 Define workforce planning. *(2)*

2 State four factors that affect the human resource needs of a business. *(4)*

3 Explain two benefits of operating a job-sharing scheme. *(4)*

4 State four reasons why it might be beneficial to a business to have employees of differing ages *(4)*

5 Explain two reasons why a business may benefit from 'outsourcing'. *(4)*

6 Explain how 'compressed hours' may help to motivate employees. *(4)*

Total *(22)*

Case study

'V' festival at Weston Park Staffordshire 2013

This is an annual pop festival which takes place in Weston Park, Staffordshire.

Groups that appeared in 2013 included The Script with Danny O'Donoghue, Beyonce, Kings of Leon, Stereophonics, Emeli Sande and many more well-known acts. Staging such a massive festival involves a huge amount of people, all of whom have to be hired within a short period of time, yet in sufficient time to ensure their availability and thus ensuring the festival goes ahead without a hitch.

The numbers involved are very large and, consequently, organising and selecting the right quantity and quality of staff is paramount. Such a workforce plan takes careful consideration and management as so many variables are involved.

There will also be a need to decide whether to pay some of the staff who will be working at the festival zero hour contracts.

Firstly, there is the need to consider the tasks that will need to be undertaken in order for the appropriate amount of preparation to take place and then operate over the days of the festival. A list of the tasks should enable the right skills and jobs to be considered and from there the actual numbers to be hired, contracted or outsourced can be worked out. A consideration of the costs involved will be determined by the size of the budgets.

Even before the festival takes place a very large number of people will have been sourced. Booking the site and all the equipment necessary for an 'invasion' of thousands of festival fans involves a publicity manager who is responsible for marketing the festival. The passes for VIPs, the bands and security staff have to be organised and printed; tickets printed and sold via the internet which is manned by staff for several days; programmes printed once they have been written; and advertising space within the programmes sold.

The festival site needs the various stages to be constructed along with signs, toilets, showers, stalls, press tents, catering, barriers, hospitality areas, bars, tents and parking. In addition to this, the festival needs security, technical and administrative staff to ensure that it all runs smoothly.

Well over a thousand people are involved directly or indirectly, all of whom have to be thought of, accounted for, possibly trained and finally paid.

The V Festival

1 Analyse one factor that would affect the ability of the festival organisers to meet their human resource needs. *(4)*
2 Analyse one reason why the majority of staff employed for the festival will be hired regardless of the number of fans coming to watch the festival. *(4)*
3 Evaluate the use of zero hours contracts to pay a large proportion of the staff needed to organise and run the V festival. *(15)*

Total *(23)*

Chapter 44

Recruitment, selection and training

AS / Year 1 | Year 2

A Level students must know all of the content in this chapter.

AS students need to cover all of the content except:

- Training needs analysis (pages 307–308)

Recruitment

The recruitment process is vitally important to any business to ensure that staff levels are correct. Finding the right person for a particular job can be expensive in terms of time and money. Appointing someone and then discovering that he or she is the wrong person, or leaves quickly, make the process even more costly.

Job description

The first part of the process is to prepare a job description. This is usually produced by the human resources department or its equivalent, and sets out the job requirements.

JOB DESCRIPTION

POST: After School Care Assistant

REPORTS TO: Head of Preparatory Department

DUTIES AND RESPONSIBILITIES:

a. General: To operate an after school care service for pupils of the Preparatory Department as directed by the Head of the Department.

b. Detail: To keep a register of pupils remaining after school and to record the times they are collected;

To supervise, control and ensure the safety of pupils remaining after school;

To implement a planned programme of activities;

To collect, and serve a light snack and to clean up after service;

To prepare classrooms for activities and to ensure that they are left in a tidy condition;

To maintain a safe environment for the pupils.

Figure 44.1 A typical job description

Person specification

Once there is a job description, the business can start to look at the ideal characteristics of the person to undertake the job. This may include some or all of the following, depending on the job:

- qualifications
- previous experience
- ability to work with a team
- willingness to travel
- able to work under supervision or independently
- ability to use initiative
- flexibility.

Internal or external appointment

The recruiter needs to decide whether to recruit internally or externally. This decision will depend on the nature of the job and whether or not there are already suitable candidates within the business. Very often, internal candidates will be considered alongside external applicants.

Benefits of appointing an internal candidate

- Recruitment will take less time because the prospective candidate is already known to the business.
- There is no need to spend money on costly advertisements.
- There will be less need for induction training.
- The ways in which the business works will already be known to the candidate.
- There is less risk of being impressed by someone at interview who then turns out to be a poor appointment.
- The opportunity of promotion within a company may encourage good workers to stay rather than look for promotion elsewhere.

However, there is a risk that internal candidates who are not successful may react badly and sour the working relationship. It is also possible that an employee who previously worked well in a role, for example as part of a team, might fail to work well in a new position, for example in a managerial role.

Benefits of appointing an external candidate

- He or she is likely to bring new ideas and enthusiasm to the job.
- The field of applicants will be bigger.
- It might cause less resentment than choosing an internal candidate.

Advertising

When a business decides to advertise a job externally, there are a number of important factors to be taken into account.

The job advert must contain enough information to attract suitable applicants and deter unsuitable ones.

Certain vital information must be included, such as the title of the job and any required qualifications. Other information about the job can be put on a website or sent in the post.

The advert must be put in the right place to attract suitable applicants. For example, Chester Zoo would put an advert for a new director in the broadsheet daily papers such as *The Times* and *The Independent* or in the newspapers' jobsites; it would advertise for animal keepers in the periodicals aimed at employees who keep or look after exotic species; if it needed shop workers and ice-cream sellers for the summer months, the adverts would be placed in local newspapers. All of these adverts might also be placed on the Zoo's website.

Applications

Many businesses use application forms so that the process of comparison between applicants and choosing who to interview is made easier. In the initial stages, these forms might ask for basic information on experience and qualifications. There might then be a more complex form which asks for information about past experience that relates to the role. This might include extended questions about whether the candidate has worked well as part of a team or has had to make decisions under difficult circumstances. Most of these forms are now filled in online. The business might also ask for a letter of application from the candidate and a curriculum vitae (CV). The CV gives an overview in brief of an individual's experience, qualifications, job history and other interests.

In the first instance, the business will use the information from the application to draw up a list of candidates to be looked at more closely. Interviews might follow at this point. Some businesses carry out more selection before proceeding to face-to-face interview. Candidates might be asked to do a psychometric test, to fill out a further questionnaire, to complete an online multiple-choice test or to have a telephone interview. All of these things help to reduce the number or candidates for interview by assessing their suitability. Interviewing is a costly exercise in terms of managers' time and the business's money.

Interviews

As the next stage of the process, many large businesses perform a telephone interview to reduce costs. The candidates to be interviewed face-to-face will be selected after the telephone interview.

An interview is regarded as the most successful method of finding the right person for a job. However, some people feel that the process is flawed and that decisions are made on first impressions rather than on facts. For example, it is thought that some interviewers will decide whether a person is able to do the job in the first 60 seconds of an interview. The judgement will be based on punctuality, confidence, handshake, appearance and ability to make conversation in the initial stages of meeting.

The following factors are important for the business in the interview process:

- having the right number of people on the interview panel
- deciding beforehand what information is to be gathered
- making sure that the interviewee is put at ease and is not interrogated
- allowing adequate time for the interview to take place
- giving the interviewee the opportunity to ask questions.

Alongside interviews, businesses may also conduct other tasks to help them in the recruitment process. These may include:

- team tasks and activities
- presentations on a requested topic to the selection team
- personality tests
- references from previous employers or academic bodies
- a work task or work trial, e.g. teaching a class lesson for a prospective teacher.

At the end of the process, the business will hope to have a new employee who matches the initial job description, will adapt well to the workplace, and contribute positively to the success of the business.

Training

The need for training an employee begins as soon as they start to work for a business, and should then continue for the length of their employment. In recent years the need for ongoing training has become increasingly important for UK businesses. This is partly as a result of government incentives, initiatives and legislation, but also because businesses have experienced benefits from investing in training their employees. These benefits may include better motivation and performance (see discussion of Abraham Maslow in **Chapter 47** Motivation), and also give the business access to new markets; for example, meeting the government's ISO targets for quality and assurance is now a requirement for small businesses if they wish to become suppliers to large UK businesses. (See **Chapter 70**.)

Key term

ISO: an internationally accepted standard for quality. It ensures that businesses have effective processes and effective employees so that they can deliver an effective product.

Induction training

Starting a new job is a difficult time for any individual. Many employers find that this is the time at which labour turnover is at its highest. Perhaps there is something wrong with the recruitment process, or the induction process is so unsatisfactory that the employee feels uncomfortable in the job role or the work environment. Getting induction right is therefore crucial if the business wants its new recruits to stay. The cost of recruitment is high for any business, so money spent in ensuring that successful candidates stay in the job is well spent.

The factors that should be included in induction training are shown in Figure 44.2.

Figure 44.2 The induction process

It is possible for induction programmes to discourage new workers rather than making them enthusiastic about the job. This may happen if the induction bombards the employee with huge amounts of information about the business and its operation (see Figure 44.2). New workers are often most concerned about finding their way around the building, following correct procedure and avoiding making silly mistakes. They are not particularly interested in the disciplinary procedure and the history of the business. Some of the things they need to know will be learned over the first few weeks; others are better explained on the job by a line manager rather than as part of a series of endless presentations in the first few days.

Management need to think carefully about what needs to be in the programme to allay fears, explain systems and keep the introductory programme short. It is then possible to ensure that other information is acquired as the employee fits into the business.

Training methods

There are a variety of training methods that businesses can use to improve the performance of their employees. In choosing the method, employers need to think about the nature of the training to be given and the employees to be trained. What suits one situation and group of workers will not necessarily suit all.

On-the-job and off-the-job training

Training can either be at the place of employment or at a different location. In either case, the training can be delivered either by employees of the business, or by outside specialist training personnel.

On-the-job training

There are advantages to this type of training, including the following points:

- It may be easier to do a series of shorter training sessions where the worker is released for part of the day.
- It is likely to be much cheaper, especially if it is provided by the business's staff.
- It can be tailored to the specific requirements of the business.

However, there are disadvantages:

- It may be regarded as less valuable, especially if it is delivered by people who work within the business.
- It can be regarded as tedious, unimportant and a waste of time.

Off-the-job training

This type of training will probably cost more, but has the following advantages:

- For many workers this may be regarded as a perk, involving time away from work in pleasant surroundings.
- Being away from the workplace may encourage employees to think more seriously about training issues.
- It is an opportunity to spend time with colleagues in a different environment, which may change perceptions and break down barriers between managers and other workers.

However:

- It will be more expensive than on-the-job training.
- It may be regarded as a waste of time and money by employees.

Other training methods

There are many different ways in which training can be delivered to workers. Some of these will be through the involvement of the employer, but in other cases the individual may decide to invest time and money in their own training and development.

These are just a few methods of training:

1. Learning by watching and doing. This is sometimes called 'sitting next to Nellie'. You may have seen this type of training in operation at a supermarket checkout or in a bank. This type of training depends on the business having spare capacity so that an experienced member of staff can deliver the training.
2. Apprenticeships. These involve training that is both on-the-job and in college on a day-release system. It is a method that is used in skilled trades such as plumbing and car mechanics.
3. Distance and e-learning. Individuals take responsibility for their own work under the supervision of a mentor or tutor who will give feedback and assistance as required, in addition to marking assignments.
4. Courses. Businesses can use this method in a variety of ways. For example, the introduction of a new computer system will require training for all staff who use the system. Other courses may be used if it is felt that a particular group of workers is not working efficiently, or if the business feels that there are efficiency savings to be made through new work practices.
5. Academic training will be used in those jobs where it is appropriate. For example, trainee accountants will have to attend academic courses to gain the necessary qualifications to practise.
6. Vocational training is instruction in the practical skills needed for certain jobs. It is often part of an apprenticeship scheme. Trainee hairdressers will work in salons under supervision for part of the week and attend courses in a college for two or three days each week.

In addition to these methods, the government is now involved in a number of training initiatives, both for individuals and businesses. These include:

1. Investors in people. This involves developing skills in the workforce to meet government criteria in areas such as customer service. When a company achieves the target, it is given a display plaque to confirm the achievement.
2. The Skills Funding Agency is a government organisation that provides £4 billion of support for colleges, private trainers and employers.

Training needs analysis

By conducting a training needs analysis (TNA) a business ensures that its workers are given the skills that they need to do their job effectively. In doing such an analysis, the business will collect information from workers, customers, managers and suppliers, as well as observing the way in which jobs are performed in different areas. It is important that the whole workforce, including managers, is included in this exercise. There may be skill shortages in a particular area that have been overlooked in the past because no one has noticed the lack of training or there has been a failure in communication. TNA should help to resolve the problem by highlighting such problems in particular areas of the business.

This feedback will be collated and analysed, to make sure that training is appropriate and not a waste of money or time. The end result should be a better trained workforce, able to do its job more effectively.

The following factors ought to be considered as part of a TNA:

- The firm must first decide what it wants to achieve for the future, maybe in terms of sales, output, productivity or market share.
- From the results gained in the initial survey, decisions must be made about who is to be trained and how.
- It is vitally important at this stage to involve people who are to be trained in the process, so that they can have an input into the type of training they need. This will be particularly important when a new product or process is being introduced.
- Decisions must be made about how the training is to be delivered. Can some of it be done within the firm? How much should be done by external providers?
- External training providers need to be chosen carefully, to match the style of the business and the budget.
- The cost of a particular training solution needs to be considered before it is undertaken. Will the results be worth the expense?
- The number of people who need training is also an important factor. If it is only one or two people, it would probably be most cost-effective to send them on a course. If it is a large group, it may be better to deliver the course in house.

Evaluation of training

Once the training process has been completed, managers need to assess the work that has been done. Businesses often undertake costly training programmes without considering whether the exercise has delivered value for money, and without looking at what, if anything, has been achieved by way of improvement.

In some areas it will be easy to see the benefits of training. For example, the training for the introduction of a new computer system will have measurable results. It will be possible to measure the ease with which employees adapt to the new system, to look at problems that arise and address them. In a similar way, if a supermarket trains its staff in customer service, a survey among customers will demonstrate if the training has been successful.

In other areas it is more difficult to assess the results of training. This may be so for courses involving management training. If feedback is sought from the participants of the course, they will often not be able to see how they are putting its content into practice; they are more likely to comment on the delivery of the course than its success in helping them to do their job better.

Businesses also need to do a cost-benefit analysis on any training provided, to enable better decision making in this area in the future and avoid wasting money. Training at any level is expensive, and it is important that businesses ensure that money spent on training achieves positive benefits for the future.

Further sources

www.trainingzone.co.uk

Department for Business, Innovation and Skills: this government department contains information on all aspects of training, apprenticeships, grants and funding.

Your turn

Questions in red are for A Level students only.

Multiple-choice questions

1 One disadvantage of internal recruitment is:
- A It is more expensive than external recruitment.
- B It fails to bring new ideas into the business.
- C It is more time consuming.
- D There will be little information about the candidate. *(1)*

2 Off-the-job training:
- A Is cheaper than on-the-job training.
- B Is not usually appreciated by employees.
- C Can break down barriers between managers and workers.
- D Is easier to organise than on-the-job training. *(1)*

Revision questions

1 State four factors to be taken into account in a training needs analysis. *(4)*

2 State four elements of the recruitment process. *(4)*

Total *(8)*

Case study

Simon David Hairdressing

Simon opened his own hairdressing business in a Midlands town in 2011, in the depths of the recession. He had worked for a hairdressing chain in the town for many years and he had done his training with them, but decided that he wanted to have his own business.

At first all the work was done by Simon and an assistant whom he took on to work part time, but it quickly became clear that more staff were needed as business picked up rapidly. Recruiting employees of the right calibre successfully in the hairdressing sector is not always easy or straightforward, as Simon quickly discovered. He had set very high standards for the salon and expected his employees to work as hard and conscientiously as he did. Simon insisted on punctuality and good customer service as well as willingness from his staff to be adaptable in terms of hours they worked and to undergo training. Some of Simon's employees proved to be excellent in all these regards, but others could not meet his requirements.

Simon has discovered that one way to find good staff is to employ those who show initiative by coming into the salon with a CV that is well-presented and correctly written. In doing this, he can save money on advertising vacancies. All Simon's employees are given training, regardless of their previous experience and qualifications; it is important that every employee follows the same rules about health and safety, achieving customer satisfaction and giving good customer service. Some of this training is on-the-job, with Simon giving the training himself. Some of the specialist training in skills like hair extensions is given at courses in colleges and organisations by outside training providers.

As a result of good recruitment practices and training, Simon has created a very successful business in a relatively short time that now employs five people full-time with almost no labour turnover.

1 Analyse one method that Simon could use to recruit new workers. *(6)*

2 Analyse one benefit of using an induction scheme at the salon. *(6)*

3 Evaluate the advantages to Simon of using on-the-job training for his salon. *(15)*

Total *(27)*

Chapter 45

Appraisal and workforce performance

AS / Year 1 | Year 2

A Level students must know all of the content in this chapter.

AS students do not need to be able to explain the usefulness and effectiveness of appraisal.

An appraisal is an assessment of an employee's performance, and for this reason it is also known as 'performance management'. While it is clearly part of a manager's job to monitor employee performance in a general sense throughout the year, this is not usually regarded as 'appraisal'. An appraisal is usually a formal meeting between an employee and his or her line manager once a year, during which the employee is encouraged to reflect upon achievements, workload and development needs, and to agree targets to be achieved in the next year. The process should be a positive one, with any criticism being constructive rather than disparaging.

Until fairly recently, appraisals tended to be restricted to people in management posts, but it is now increasingly popular for them to be introduced for employees at all levels in a business. Responding to employee needs can help to give a competitive edge over rivals through increased motivation, productivity and commitment to the job.

Although there is no legal requirement for a business to have a system of appraisal, there are many potential benefits for a business in appraising its workforce. However, appraisals are often regarded with deep suspicion by employees who may view the process as 'spying' and showing a lack of trust in their ability to complete the job. It is therefore very important that any appraisal system is introduced and operated with as much co-operation from employees as is possible. Without this, it may be regarded by the workforce as irrelevant and a waste of time.

Key term

Appraisal: a formal assessment of an employee's performance.

Objectives and benefits of appraisal

Careful thought needs to be given to exactly what the process is designed to achieve before it is introduced, because this will affect how the process is designed, how it will operate and how it is perceived by employees. Will it be for reviewing performance? Will it be to identify training and development needs? Will it be linked to some sort of bonus or other reward? In practice, it may be all three.

Key term

Development needs: the requirements that an employee has in order to perform his or her job more effectively and/or gain the skills and abilities necessary for promotion.

The main purpose and benefit of appraisal is to identify an employee's strengths and weaknesses; although a better term to use would be 'development needs', as the word 'weakness' has negative overtones. A judgement can be formed about whether the employee is effective in his or her current post. If not, then the reason for this can be determined. Thus an appraisal can be used to gather information for human resource planning, and employee development needs can be linked to a programme of training in order to make the employee more effective. An employee's potential for promotion can be considered. The appraisal presents an opportunity for an employee to discuss his or her expectations of the future.

If these are linked to training and initiatives such as work shadowing, the employee is more likely to feel valued by the business. Such investment in career development is likely to be motivating as it is helping to meet self-esteem and achievement needs (see **Chapter 47**).

The employee's workload can also be considered. This is important because of the obvious link to morale and motivation. Appraisals can be used to see if the workload has changed over the past year. Is there too much work, or too little? Also, with employees now being able to sue for non-physical injuries such as stress, a discussion of workload with a formal record kept of the meeting could prove very significant if this ever occurs. There will also be a discussion of how work is actually performed, and it can therefore highlight any procedural issues, communication problems or other difficulties that are hindering efficiency.

Introducing appraisal

Appraisal should never be introduced for its own sake. It is not a stand-alone process; it should be clearly linked to human resource issues such as training and pay. Managers need training in order to carry out appraisals. Perhaps a production manager is perfectly competent with the technology his or her department has to use, but does not have good interpersonal skills. Such a person will need training in listening skills, making criticism constructive and giving praise when it is due. Unless line managers feel comfortable with the process and see that senior managers are committed to it, they may regard the process as a waste of time. This, in turn, will be 'picked up' by their subordinates.

Appraisal can be linked to an increase in pay or a bonus of some kind, based on the assessment of performance. If this is the case, the process must be transparent and judged objectively. If employees feel that there is a degree of favouritism when bonuses are awarded, they will become distrustful of the whole process. Apparent bias towards some people will not be conducive to high morale and teamwork. Employees must be clearly briefed on how the process will operate. There may be conflicts here as to whether the person conducting the appraisal is a 'judge' or a 'helper'.

Appraisals are an opportunity to discuss past performance and future goals

Tips and techniques

Students often assume that 'appraisal will motivate people'. Appraisal in itself is very unlikely to motivate employees. You need to mention that employees need to be able to perceive clear and direct benefits from the process for this to occur.

Creating effective appraisal systems

What will make appraisal ineffective?

1. A lack of commitment by senior staff. A proper system of appraisal can be expensive. Treating it as a cost to be minimised will not bring the desired results.
2. An inconsistent approach by line managers. If some managers are too negative in their assessments, employees appraised by them will rightly claim that they have been treated differently to others. This can lead to discontent, especially if the appraisal is linked to a reward.
3. Inadequate time allowed for the appraisal process. If managers give the impression that they are keen to be doing something else, this will be recognised by employees who will then regard the process as a waste of time.
4. A failure to respond to employee concerns and aspirations. If an employee acknowledges that he or she needs training in, for example, some

aspect of IT, then if the opportunity to attend a course that was promised at the appraisal never materialises, this will lead to a lack of confidence in the process, and also in the line manager.

5 Unrealistic targets being set. Employees may have unrealistic expectations of what can actually be achieved. Also, sometimes a line manager may persuade employees to accept targets that they do not really want. Neither of these is helpful to the process. A manager should ensure that the employee's targets, like the business's objectives, are 'SMART' (specific, measurable, agreed, realistic, and time-limited). There is no point in setting an employee up to fail.
6 The use of ambiguous language such as 'you have not done too badly; at least you've achieved some of your targets'. This sort of statement can leave an employee unsure of whether they are being praised for success or criticised for failure.

What will make appraisal effective?

1 Senior managers ensure that all managers are committed to the process, and that sufficient resources are available.
2 Consultation with employees (via their trade union if one exists) at the earliest opportunity on the objectives of the process and its procedure.
3 Ensuring that employees understand the system, how it will affect and benefit them.
4 Ensuring that line managers are adequately trained in the skills necessary to perform an effective appraisal, e.g. listening skills and 'SMART' target setting.

Key term

'SMART' target setting: a framework within which to set an employee's targets for the coming year. Targets should be Specific, Measurable, Agreed, Realistic and Time-limited. SMART targets are much more likely to be successful than ones worded in an ambiguous way.

Tips and techniques

Careful thought must be given to the business's culture when answering a question about appraisal. When answering a question about introducing (or changing) an appraisal system, it will be beneficial to develop a strategy building on the business's existing culture and 'people' strengths.

5 A willingness to modify the process if it is seen to be failing in reaching its stated objectives.
6 Allowing employees to comment on the outcome of their appraisal.

Appraisal process

There is no single process that will suit all organisations; different businesses must develop different appropriate models, although reference to ACAS (the Advisory, Conciliation and Arbitration Service) guidelines would be a sensible idea. There are, however, some common characteristics for most processes.

First of all it is usual for the employee to fill out a question-and-answer sheet relating to the targets that were agreed the previous year. The employee can comment on the extent to which he or she feels that they have been met. These targets and the employee's comments will then be reviewed by the line manager. An employee may be rated against the targets with statements such as 'fully met', 'partially met', or 'no progress towards target'. In the case of receiving the last rating, an employee should naturally be given the opportunity to offer an explanation; perhaps a key member of their staff who was crucial to the meeting of the target has been on long-term sick leave. In any event, the inability to meet a target should be approached by offering support to achieve it (if it is still appropriate) the following year, rather than a barrage of negative criticism.

That is not to say that a manager conducting the appraisal can only be 'nice', and an employee may have to be told that their performance has, in one or more areas, fallen short of the required standard. Even so, a constructive approach focusing on improvement and development is likely to prove more beneficial in terms of employee morale than condemnation.

Secondly, there is also likely to be a section for 'other achievements', and a section for the employee to comment on development needs for the future. The idea is for employees to have 'ownership' of their targets and career. Those who set unchallenging targets for themselves and show little interest in development can hardly complain that the business is ignoring them in terms of their career.

Finally, all sections are then discussed with the line manager and an overall judgement on the employee will then be made. A formal written record of the appraisal meeting and any forms completed will be kept. It is sensible, common practice for an employee to be given a copy.

In some businesses, certain types of employees have 'assessment sheets' that are completed monthly.

A sales assistant, for example, might be assessed on factors such as how smartly they are dressed, ability to work without supervision, the level of customer service provided, and so on. These sheets can be filled in fairly quickly and the employee graded by ticking a box which corresponds to a certain level of achievement. However, great care must be taken to avoid labelling the boxes to be ticked with words such as 'satisfactory', 'adequate' or even 'good', since such terms are ambiguous. A clear descriptor is necessary. If customer service is 'good', what does this actually mean? Words such as 'always pleasant and helpful' would be more useful.

These sheets are not really 'appraisals' in the true sense of the term, although the information recorded on them may be used at the appraisal interview and as part of the overall appraisal process.

As well as managerial assessment, there are other types of appraisal which can help evaluate the employee's contribution to a business:

Self-assessment

Self-reflection on performance can be useful, but there is an issue of how objective the person is likely to be when doing this. Are they supposed to judge themselves against others in their department, or against their own previous performance? There may be confusion between the two. Also, as ever with appraisal, the (self-assessment) questions need to be specific and focused; a question such as 'how do I think I performed last year?' is vague and therefore meaningless.

Sometimes, employees are encouraged to assess their performance using a simple 'tick sheet'. This sheet grades employees on certain aspects of their job.

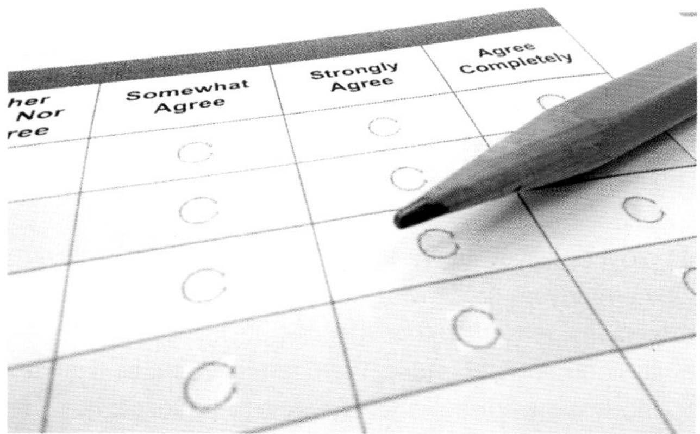

Employees can self-assess using a tick sheet

Another issue with any form of self-assessment is the likelihood of objectivity if a pay increase or a bonus depends (partly or wholly) on the self-assessment. It is now common for an appraisal system to have some degree of self-assessment within it. With carefully constructed questions that are standard for all employees to use, a self-assessment of some sort is often carried out by the employee in advance of the meeting with his or her line manager. This can then be used as a starting point for the whole process.

360 degree appraisal

A 360 degree appraisal is very different to the usual one-to-one appraisal process. It involves the appraisee receiving feedback from several people. The logic is that in large organisations an employee can contribute in a number of different ways; working with different people in different teams, on different projects. Therefore a broader 'picture' of the employee's contribution could be useful. This may therefore mean feedback from an employee's manager, subordinates, and peers. It will probably also involve a degree of self-evaluation. Feedback may also come from customers or other stakeholders in the business.

360 degree appraisals are useful for employee development since the feedback gives an insight into how others perceive them; it can be used to judge management style in terms of issues such as consultation and communication. The appraisee can then alter their behaviour and/or seek training to improve their skills in the light of the comments.

There can be a problem with this kind of appraisal insofar as those responding may not fully appreciate or understand the 'wider picture' of the manager's roles and responsibilities and may not appreciate why certain decisions affecting them have been taken. There is a concern that employees use the process to 'get their own back' if the appraisal comments are anonymous or, if they are not, that they make the comments artificially positive because they think there will be a benefit to themselves for doing so.

By their nature, 360 degree appraisals are complicated and time-consuming and are highly unlikely to be appropriate for all employees. The nature of the process means that there tends to be a focus on behaviour, rather than specific job requirements and the review of previously set targets.

This means that it can augment but not replace the one-to-one appraisal process.

Peer assessment

With the growth of team working in business, being assessed by work colleagues has become more commonplace. In theory it should work well because of the nature of the working relationship; peers have a very clear idea of exactly what needs to be done and how well someone is performing in that respect and how well they are contributing to the team. The questions that are asked need to be very specific to the role the appraisee is playing in the team; peers cannot just be offered the opportunity to make informal comments. In practice there is, once again, the issue of the peer appraisal being used to 'settle an old score' and peers deliberately commenting in a negative manner. Alternatively, all employees may agree to provide very positive comments on each other in the hope of gaining a pay rise. This, in turn, raises another issue; if the peer assessment is part of an appraisal process that could lead to increased pay, how much weight should the peer assessment carry compared to that of the line manager?

All of the methods of appraisal have their uses but it needs to be reiterated that careful thought needs to go into why a certain type of appraisal is being introduced and what the implications of it are likely to be. How will the information be used, and will the benefits outweigh the costs?

Other methods of evaluating workforce performance

Performance could also be measured by the number of units of output produced, which could then be related to the pay that an employee receives. What is more important than simply 'the number of units produced' is the productivity of an employee or employees. Productivity measures performance in terms of output relative to input (see **Chapter 64**).

A motivated and productive workforce will give a business an advantage in reaching its strategic objectives. However, there needs to be a way of evaluating just how satisfactory motivation and morale strategies actually are. A variety of simple techniques exist that enable a business to do this.

Quantitative data relating to workforce performance (e.g. employee absence and labour turnover) is useful for identifying problem areas in the business and also for planning purposes. For example, if the average annual labour turnover in a particular department of 50 employees is 10 per cent, the human resource department can plan ahead on the basis that five employees a year will have to be recruited if the department is to be fully staffed.

Tips and techniques

Putting a simple calculation into an A2 context is one way to help create an analytical answer and score higher marks.

Quantitative data on any business issue is subject to a number of limitations, and this is particularly true when applied to human resource issues. Some of these limitations are discussed at the end of this chapter. Nevertheless, the use of figures is an important and essential aspect of measuring employee performance.

Labour turnover

Labour turnover is concerned with measuring the number of employees who have left the business, and is usually calculated as an annual percentage by the following formula:

$$\text{Labour turnover} = \frac{\text{number of employees leaving during the year}}{\text{average number employed during the year}} \times 100$$

If the average number of employees in a business was 150 and, over the course of a year, 25 people leave, the rate of labour turnover would be calculated as follows:

$$25 \times \frac{100}{150}$$

$$= \frac{2500}{150}$$

$$= 16.7$$

The rate of labour turnover = 16.7%.

The higher the figure obtained, the more likely it is that motivation is low, otherwise why would so many employees leave? However, the figure does not explain why employees are leaving. It might be due to retirement or personal reasons rather than dissatisfaction and disillusionment with work. The figure is useful as a guide to motivation, but if managers want to evaluate the situation correctly, they will need to look behind the data to obtain an accurate picture of current occurrences. ACAS (see **Chapter 48**) provides a specimen 'analysis of labour turnover' form that a business can download and use – or modify – for this very purpose.

High labour turnover can be a symptom of low morale

Finally, with labour turnover, it should be remembered that while high rates are undesirable (because of the cost implications of recruitment and selection, disruption to work, the fact that new recruits are more likely to make mistakes, etc.) a workforce that has a zero rate of labour turnover is likely to become stale and resistant to change. This is especially true at management level; a certain level of labour turnover can therefore actually be desirable.

Key term

Labour turnover: a measure of the number of employees who have left the business (usually over the past year), relative to the number employed in that period. A high percentage is an indicator of poor morale and motivation.

Absenteeism

Absence from work imposes an extra cost on the business in the form of a replacement employee, or puts pressure and stress on existing staff who have to do extra work to cover for their absent colleague. However, a distinction must be made between different sorts of absence, and when analysing data on absence this must be acknowledged.

Long-term absence

This is where an employee is off work for a lengthy period, and is usually due to illness. A high number of absences due to illness or injury could be symptomatic of an unsafe and unhealthy working environment.

Short-term absence

This is a different situation, where an employee is absent from work for a day (or a few days) because of a minor ailment such as an upset stomach or a headache. It is this sort of absence that is referred to as 'absenteeism', and can be used as an indicator of the level of morale and motivation.

This is the most common type of absence. A certain amount of short-term sickness can be expected in any business, but where there is an upward trend overall or in a specific department, it is indicative of a problem.

A record of all absences and reasons for these should be kept by the business. This will be crucial if disciplinary action for recurring absence is ever taken against an employee. If a pattern of absenteeism starts to emerge with a particular individual or individuals (e.g. repeated absences on the same day of the week), this might be an indicator of a problem that should be tackled.

The formula to be used is similar to the one used for labour turnover. It could also be used with hours instead of days, and over any appropriate time period. Whichever is chosen, the calculation gives the rate for absenteeism which is also known as the lost time rate.

The calculation is useful for an overall picture of lost time in the business as a whole. It should also be undertaken for all areas of the business, because it can show up those departments with a particular absence problem.

The lost time rate generates an answer in the form of a percentage and is calculated as follows:

$$\frac{\text{Total days absent in the month} \times 100}{\text{Total available working days in the month}}$$

Consider the following:

- There are nine employees in a particular department.
- There are 23 available working days in the month.
- Eleven days are taken off work with the reason given as 'sickness'.

The lost time calculation is therefore:

$$\frac{(11 \times 100)}{(9 \times 23)}$$

$$= \frac{1100}{207}$$

$$= 5.31$$

The lost time rate = 5.3%

Key term

Absenteeism: employees are absent from work with minor medical ailments such as an upset stomach or a headache. Absenteeism can be a key indicator of low morale and motivation levels.

High absence rates need to be identified, analysed (is it one or two employees who are causing the high figures, or is it across the department?) and dealt with.

There is a distinction between 'authorised' and 'unauthorised' absence. The latter refers to the sort of short-term absences mentioned above; the former is where an employee asks for time off for a particular reason such as a medical appointment, to visit a relative who is ill, or to attend an important meeting at their child's school. This sort of absence can be hard to deal with because an employee cannot always have a medical appointment out of normal working hours. A business needs a clear and consistent policy on allowable absence (and whether employees will be paid for it). It cannot grant permission to one employee to be absent for a doctor's appointment during working hours and then refuse permission to another, without stirring up resentment. Once again, a record of these absences should be kept to see if a pattern emerges.

Lateness

Exactly the same principle can be applied to lateness. If there is a perception among managers that many employees are arriving late to work, this needs to be investigated and monitored properly. As in all matters relating to employee attendance, an individual record should be kept and the number of instances of lateness in a week or month can be recorded quite easily. ACAS provides sample forms to record this.

Consistent lateness can be a sign of dwindling motivation

In addition, a calculation could be done by a department or section to see if the lateness is a general or a localised problem.

In a particular section of a factory there are 20 employees. Suppose that last April there were 23 working days, and the total number of late arrivals in April was 58. The calculation would therefore be:

$$\frac{\text{Total number of late arrivals} \times 100}{\text{Total number of scheduled attendances}}$$

$$= \frac{(58 \times 100)}{(20 \times 23)}$$

$$= \frac{5800}{460}$$

The departmental lateness rate = 12.6%.

A high percentage is usually a good indicator of low motivation levels; a person who is motivated and who enjoys work is rarely late. The manager responsible for that area would need to examine the data to see whether the problem was being caused by a specific individual or individuals. Employees may be occasionally late for valid reasons, from childcare problems to traffic difficulties on the way to work. However, persistent lateness shows a disregard for taking the appropriate actions to arrive at work on time, that is, a lack of motivation.

Workforce productivity

An important indicator of workforce performance is how productive employees are. This is not just a measure of how much is produced; it is a measure of output relative to input. At its simplest, it is a measure of output per employee in a particular period of time.

Consider this example: 100 employees typically produce 1,000 units of output in one month. The business introduces some new technology that leads to 50 redundancies. The remaining 50 employees continue to produce 1,000 units per month. This is an improvement in productivity because output per employee has increased.

The formula is:

$$\frac{\text{Output (per week/month/year)}}{\text{Average number of employees}}$$

Using the example above, labour productivity (average output per employee) was initially:

$$\frac{1000}{100} = 10$$

After the change it has become:

$$\frac{1000}{50} = 20$$

Productivity has therefore increased.

Productivity is harder to measure in the tertiary sector, where there is no physical product produced.

Key term

Productivity: a measure of output per employee in a particular period of time. Productivity is a key indicator of employee performance.

Limitations to the use of quantitative data

There are a number of issues to bear in mind when using figures to assess employee performance, and it is important to highlight them.

Consider the following basic data relating to labour turnover in the four main departments of a business. The figures for the last 12 months are shown in Table 45.1. What do they indicate? On the face of it, an overall figure of 15 per cent for the business is not very impressive, and the accounts department, in particular, is a disaster in terms of motivation.

Table 45.1 Labour turnover for different departments

Department	Labour turnover (%)
Accounts	33
Marketing	5
Personnel	2
Production	20
Average for all departments	15

However, there are several points that can be made on the validity and use of these figures in forming a judgement on performance.

Averages can be misleading

The 15 per cent figure for the business as a whole is not representative of any of the figures for the individual departments. To use a single figure for the whole business would disguise the differences in the data and be misleading.

Not all departments employ the same number of people.

The figure for the accounts department has contributed significantly to the final 15 per cent. Assume that only six people work in that department. If one of them leaves, this will have a large impact on the departmental (and the overall business) figure. Two people have left, giving a figure of 33 per cent. This makes a key indicator of motivation in the business as a whole appear worse than it actually is. On the other hand, the production department has a lower percentage figure, but if that area of the business employs 100 people, then 20 of them have left; this is a significantly larger number of employees than the two from accounts.

A single figure in isolation is of limited use

The figure for production looks poor. However, if the figures for the previous three years were 27 per cent, 25 per cent and 22 per cent, the current 20 per cent looks rather different. It is still too high but there is a continued improvement. 'Headline' figures can certainly highlight a sudden change (for better or worse), but trends in the data are significant and need to be monitored.

Numbers do not explain the situation

Figures for employee performance cannot explain what is happening in the workplace. Assume in a particular business that labour turnover is 20 per cent, and the board of directors may rightly consider this unsatisfactory. However, having gathered the figures, their next job is to find out exactly why so many people are leaving. Some employees might have complained that they are poorly paid. However, a knee-jerk reaction to pay them more to solve the problem might be an expensive mistake. The true reason might be an unsafe working environment or poor management. Many businesses conduct 'exit interviews', or ask employees to fill out a questionnaire to discover the reason for leaving.

Potential benefits to employees of improving performance

The potential benefits for employees include:

- job security
- higher pay
- a bonus
- an improvement in conditions of service, e.g. an increased holiday entitlement
- an improvement in conditions of work, e.g. a subsidised canteen
- financial assistance for career development.

Further sources

www.acas.org.uk: the ACAS website. Practical guidance for businesses on how to introduce and operate a successful appraisal system.

www.cipd.co.uk: the online magazine for the Chartered Institute of Personnel and Development. Useful for information on appraisal. It also contains up-to-date articles about human resource issues of all kinds.

Your turn

Questions in red are for A Level candidates only.

Multiple-choice questions

1 If the average number of employees in a business was 90, and over the course of a year 25 people left the firm, the rate of labour turnover (to the nearest whole number) would be:
A 8%
B 18%
C 28%
D 38% *(1)*

2 In a particular section of a factory there are 15 employees. Suppose that last month there were 22 working days, and the total number of late arrivals in April was 44. The percentage of employees arriving late was (to the nearest whole number):
A 5%
B 9%
C 10%
D 13% *(1)*

3 Which of the following is not a limitation of using numerical data to assess employee performance across departments in a particular month?
A Data is distorted by absenteeism.
B A figure from a single month can be unrepresentative.
C Use of an average figure can be misleading.
D Departments vary in size. *(1)*

4 Which of the following best describes what is meant by 'productivity'?
A Total output
B Output per person
C Output per person in a particular period of time
D The value of output divided by the number of employees directly involved in the production process. *(1)*

Revision questions

1 Explain what is meant by 'appraisal'. *(2)*

2 Outline three factors that can help to ensure that an appraisal system is effective. *(6)*

3 Other than an appraisal process, state two other examples of ways to analyse employee performance. *(2)*

4 A business operates two shifts of 8 hours at its factory. The data for output and wastage rates are shown in the following table. In January a new bonus system based on output was introduced in order to improve productivity (average output per employee). Assume it is now March.

Taking into account the number of rejects, evaluate whether the introduction of the bonus system has been a success. *(9)*

Total *(19)*

	Shift A: 25 staff		Shift B: 25 staff	
	Total output	Number of rejects	Total output	Number of rejects
December	9,500	52	9,890	60
January	9,601	73	10,300	65
February	9,624	83	10,789	90
March	9,629	101	10,456	118

Case study

'Appraisals don't work'

In 2014 an online article in Personnel Today raised an interesting issue. Lucy Adams, the former Human Resource Director of the BBC, in a lecture, slammed the annual appraisal process that many businesses operate, claiming they don't work and instead strike fear into the hearts of employees. Ms Adams said that the assumption that appraisals increased employees' productivity and engagement was a 'myth'. She urged the audience that if their HR departments were putting them under pressure to complete appraisals to tell them: 'Why should I? They don't work.'

She cited neuroscientific research that shows how workers' brains respond to having their sense of status or certainty challenged, and how our reactions to feeling threatened kick-start the flight mechanism in our brains. She also referred to the fact that most managers and employees hate doing appraisals, and how relying on an annual feedback process made them less effective.

Adams said a better approach would be to focus on leadership capability, and to ensure that managers 'know the people on their team and what motivates them, enabling them to tailor their own reward framework to get the most out of them'.

Source: Adapted from Personnel Today. Website accessed 20 May 2014

This generated a wide variety of online comments such as:

- I've been saying this for years! The trouble is that the concept of the annual appraisal is so ingrained in most organisational culture that no-one – least of all HR – ever considers there might be a better way.
- Ms Adams' opinion has most likely been reached by experiencing an over-complicated, jargon-filled system. I can only imagine that the BBC appraisal process would be just that!
- Annual performance reviews are hated because (a) people are rating on the wrong items, (b) employees do not see objectivity, nor do they participate in defining and agreeing to expectations, and (c) most reviews don't include an evaluation of the manager's evaluation of employees.
- What's the story here? Asserting that appraisals are hard to get right and that conducting them in a way which motivates all, while discriminating high from low performers and identifying talented individuals for development is hardly hot news. Appraisals are here to stay despite anything Lucy Adams says. The challenges around conducting them effectively will remain the same.

The BBC has had problems with its appraisal system in the past. In 2013 the two unions at the BBC (The NUJ, National Union of Journalists and BECTU, the Broadcasting, Entertainment, Cinematograph and Theatre Union) reported problems from their members using the HR department's online appraisal form (which was subsequently scrapped). They also complained about the focus of appraisals being on paperwork rather than a quality conversation about performance and career development. Concerns were also expressed about 'inconsistent and sometimes unfair' judgements made by managers which led to dissatisfaction about pay progression.

1 Identify two likely objectives of the appraisal process at the BBC. *(2)*
2 Analyse two factors that could make an appraisal system ineffective. *(4)*
3 Analyse two possible benefits of appraisal to the BBC. *(4)*
4 Evaluate a strategy that could be used to try to ensure that future appraisals at the BBC are effective. *(15)*

Total *(25)*

Chapter 46

Functions of management and leadership

AS / Year 1

Both AS and A Level students must know all of the content in this chapter.

What do managers or leaders do?

What is the purpose of managers? Certain broadly defined functions can be identified, whichever section of a business they work in. These include:

- communicating
- controlling
- co-ordinating
- decision making
- evaluating progress
- leading
- motivating
- planning.

There is no particular significance in the order of these activities. It can be argued that all are equally important aspects of a manager's role. What is important is that the resources of the business (finance, employees and time) need to be managed with the aim of using them as efficiently as possible, in order to reach the business's objectives.

Many of these functions apply not only to a manager's specific department in isolation, but to others also. Planning one department's activities cannot be undertaken in a vacuum. For example, production managers need to know what to manufacture; marketing managers cannot try to sell products that the business cannot make, and so they need to know and understand production capabilities; new technology in any department cannot be installed without finance managers sanctioning and allocating the funds. Furthermore, communication and co-ordination between departments, once the business's strategic plan is underway, is crucial if the business's strategic objectives are to be reached.

There are, however, several other constraints which impinge upon any leader or manager. These include the:

- skills of the leader's ability to lead and or motivate
- ability to make decisions
- strength of the leader and therefore ability to delegate
- other departments/managers within the organisation
- structure of the organisation, whether centralised or decentralised
- nature of the market in which the business operates
- state of the economy (level of inflation, unemployment, growth balance of payments and strength of the pound)
- objectives of the business
- level of unionisation
- amount of competition within the market
- budget of the business and subsequently the department in which the manager/leader operates.

The success of management within a business may be judged in light of the ability to 'manage' within the constraints listed above. However, success may also be measured against:

- prescribed targets that may be stated within the annual report of the business
- individual targets set within an appraisal period
- level of profit the business achieves
- level of labour turnover within the manager's department.

Tips and techniques

A useful definition of management appeared in the *Observer* in 2007. Simon Caulkin wrote: 'Management is supposed to amplify effort by providing a creative framework for individual expression that benefits the team.' It is worth bearing this in mind when evaluating whether the actions of a manager are 'good' or 'bad'.

Similarly, Chris Nassetta, President and Chief Executive Officer, Hilton Worldwide, in an interview published in *The Times*, suggested that leadership meant:

'Setting the right strategy and building a culture that motivates and inspires people to do great things.'

The Times, 20 September 2014

Management/leadership style

There are essentially four styles of leadership/management. See Figure 46.1. The style that is chosen can have a dramatic impact upon employees and their motivation.

Lewin's style of leadership

In 1939 Lewin and his co-workers identified three styles of leadership decision making: the autocratic, the democratic and the laissez-faire.

Autocratic

Typical characteristics of an autocratic manager:

- sets the work and expects it to be performed precisely as directed
- does not involve employees in decision making
- very strict
- does not believe in employee autonomy
- believes in 'top down' communication and does not encourage employees to contribute
- believes in close supervision
- thinks that employees are solely motivated by money.

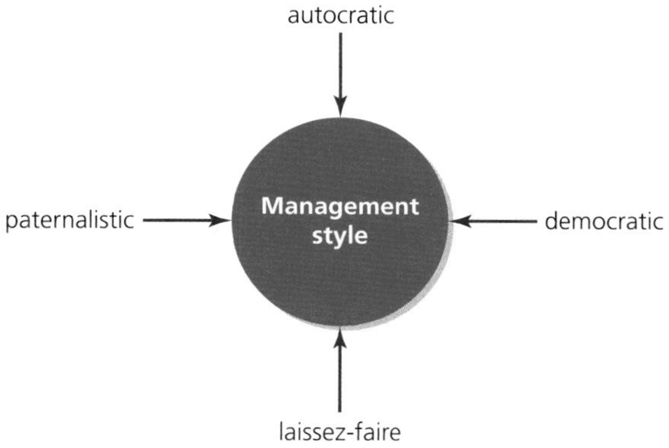

Figure 46.1 Different management styles

Democratic

A typical democratic manager:

- encourages employee input into decision making
- believes in employee autonomy
- encourages two-way communication
- allows employees to use their initiative
- believes that the motivation of employees is not simply financial.

Laissez-faire

Typical characteristics of a laissez-faire manager:

- is remote from employees
- provides very little direction for employees
- adopts a 'let them get on with it' approach
- often requires employees to set their own tasks and objectives.

Paternalistic

This is another style of leadership (not Lewin's). Typical characteristics of a paternalistic manager include:

- wanting the workforce to feel involved in decision making
- consulting employees
- persuading employees to accept his or her view, regardless of the employee's own views.

This style of management has traditionally been associated with Japanese companies.

Differences between management styles

Managers adopting these styles also tend to adopt a particular tone of voice and body language. Autocrats tend to be stern and abrupt, with an 'I'm the boss' manner. Democrats can be friendlier, willing to listen and often adopt a 'my door is always open' approach. Those who are laissez-faire may appear distant, with either a 'just get on with it' semi-autocratic manner or a dismissive 'I'm sure you can handle it on your own' type of comment, neither of which is very helpful. Paternalistic leaders often adopt a 'you see, the trouble with your approach is ...' manner, in order to persuade employees to think negatively about their own views. This 'mock consultation' will not be successful in the long run.

Autocratic managers are often found in businesses that are highly centralised, that is, all of the important decisions are taken by those at the top of the hierarchy, and strict company procedures are laid down for everyday operation. Democratic managers are more likely to be found in a decentralised business, where those at the top encourage creativity and autonomy at all levels.

There is a tendency to regard the democratic style as the 'right' one, but this is not necessarily the case. A good manager will vary style according to circumstance and will not remain permanently in one particular mode. For example, there may be an important deadline approaching which means that some aspects of an autocratic approach need to be adopted, for a time at least.

The democratic approach is certainly inclusive and should lead to better decisions being taken. However, it means that the process will take more time and this is not always available. Sometimes discussion continues without agreement being reached, and it will have to be cut short.

Finally, once a particular project is underway, a laissez-faire style may deliberately be chosen for a while, because a manager does not want to be seen to be constantly 'checking up' on subordinates (this could be perceived as a lack of trust which could demotivate them). This style can work well if employees are well-motivated and enjoy responsibility, but will be much less effective if this is not the case.

Key term

Centralisation: the amount of control exercised by senior executives over decision making. The business is highly centralised when middle managers and employees have little autonomy.

Tips and techniques

It is important to be able to identify the different sorts of situation where a particular management style will be appropriate. A good manager will vary style according to circumstance.

Theories of leadership styles

Theory X and Theory Y

Douglas McGregor's work is often misunderstood. It is sometimes presented as a theory of motivation, but strictly speaking this is not true. It is a theory of how managers view employees. The view adopted will affect how the manager believes employees should be treated and motivated. The theory states that there are two broad sets of assumptions about employees; these are known as Theory X and Theory Y.

Theory X

A theory X manager views employees as:

- inherently lazy, disliking work and responsibility
- lacking the will and ability to work unsupervised
- lacking initiative
- largely motivated by money.

A manager adopting such a view is likely to manage in an autocratic manner, offering little if any scope for employee input. Communication will be limited. The way in which work is carried out will take little account of job satisfaction, because it is assumed that the employee's driving force is money. Piecework will probably be the favoured method of payment and remuneration. This is the kind of leadership fostered by Frederick Taylor (see **Chapter 47**).

Theory Y

A theory Y manager regards employees as:

- enjoying their work (McGregor used the word 'natural') if the right conditions are created
- willing to accept responsibility and challenges
- creative and willing to contribute
- able to exercise self-discipline
- not just motivated by money.

A manager or leader adopting a theory Y view will see employees as valuable assets, rather than as a cost to be minimised. The style will be democratic, with employees encouraged to set their own goals and exercise self-control. Motivation comes from factors such as variety, challenge and self-development. Training needs will therefore be identified and employees encouraged to develop their skills. Such a style is more in keeping with Maslow and Herzberg (see **Chapter 47**).

The tendency is to think that theory Y must be right, since it is a much less pessimistic view of employees than theory X. Indeed, McGregor thought that such an approach was likely to be more effective. Nevertheless, there may be situations (particularly in low-skilled jobs with little opportunity for self-development and where labour turnover is high) in which a theory X approach may be adopted, with all that it implies for management and motivation. However, this view might become a self-fulfilling prophecy; autocratic treatment and poor motivation may bring the very response from employees that managers thought existed in the first place. Many of these issues are considered further in the next chapter.

Task and people needs

Another way of considering how managers manage is to consider task and people needs. A narrow view of management is that its function is to 'get the job done'. Such a view ignores the fact that achieving this effectively depends on people doing their jobs effectively. There is therefore something of a dilemma between 'task needs' and 'people needs'. A manager who has an over-riding desire to 'get the job done' will be task-orientated. A manager whose principle aim is to make employees contented and keep them in high spirits will be people-orientated. Most managers are a mixture of the two to varying degrees. Neither choice is 'right' or 'wrong', but it is possible for a manager to identify his or her leadership style and advise on skills to be developed in order to improve performance.

One of the best known ways to approach this was developed by Robert Blake and Jane Mouton in 1964. The grid (usually referred to as the Leadership Grid or 'Blake's grid') is very easy to understand and to apply. Along the horizontal axis are 'task needs'. 'People needs' are plotted on the vertical axis. By considering a manager's responses to a research questionnaire, his or her style of leadership can be established by where they are placed on the grid. Figure 46.2 indicates the five possibilities that can arise from the manager's actions and priorities.

Key terms

People needs: the needs of employees. A manager who concentrates on people needs will try to make employees contented and keep them in high spirits. This may be at the expense of getting the work done.

Task needs: the opposite of people needs. A manager who has an overriding desire to 'get the job done' will be orientated towards the task rather than employees' needs.

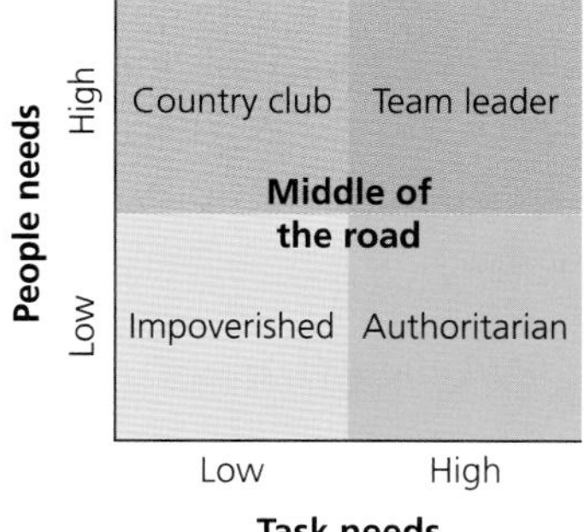

Figure 46.2 Blake and Mouton's Leadership grid

Blake and Mouton's grid was developed in the 1950s and concentrated on the trade-off between task and people needs which would then influence the likely style of leadership

Country club leadership

This manager is concerned about the well-being and feelings of his or her team of people, rather than completing the required tasks. While morale may be high, some employees may take advantage, and if deadlines are missed there may be repercussions on other areas of the business which depend on the completion of a task by a certain date.

Authoritarian leadership

An authoritarian manager will be concerned with the task rather than the employees. This manager believes that the needs of the employee must always take second place to completing the task. Leadership will be authoritarian and motivation very much a secondary consideration. A lack of attention to employees' needs can lead to resentment, a lack of commitment and other human resource problems.

Impoverished leadership

This manager will have a lack of concern for either task or people needs. He or she will be unable to devise procedures to ensure that work is completed to the required standard or on time, or to stimulate and motivate employees. This sort of leader is very ineffective at everything. Morale and productivity are both low and this leader's actions are therefore likely to affect other areas of the business negatively.

Team leadership

This manager will have a strong and equal regard for both employee and task needs. This is what a manager should aim for. These leaders believe that if employees are treated as genuine stakeholders, then their needs and the business's task needs will be in harmony. High levels of motivation will be accompanied by high productivity.

Middle-of-the-road leadership

By definition, a middle-of-the-road leader compromises between the two sets of needs. This implies that neither set of needs is truly met, and less than optimal outcomes for each are achieved. Such leaders may be indecisive and timid.

Once a person has identified his or her place on the grid, areas for leadership development can be identified, although the grid has to be used in context. Leadership styles have to be varied as the occasion demands. If a crucial contract needs to be fulfilled on time then a greater emphasis on task needs will be appropriate; whereas a country club approach may be adopted as the Christmas holiday period approaches.

Key term

Blake's grid: a method of identifying the actions, priorities and therefore leadership style of a manager. This is undertaken through an analysis of task and people needs.

The grid can, nevertheless, be a timely reminder to a leader of what they should be aspiring to, in order to avoid being stuck in one particular style.

Carlyle and Galton

Their 'trait theory' concentrates on the traits exhibited by successful leaders or, put into simple terms, the characteristics required of a leader. The original thoughts by Galton date back to the nineteenth century but were subsequently revived during the 1980s.

The original thoughts suggested that the characteristics of a good leader were attributes that such leaders had; they were not learnt.

Once these ideas were looked at in the 1980s, key characteristics of an effective leader were highlighted:

- motivational: the ability to motivate others
- integrity: showing an ethical approach
- self-confidence: being assured
- creative: new ideas
- intelligent: able to reason, and solve problems.

A more recent approach has been put forward by Zaccaro (2004 and 2007), whose model looks at leadership traits in more detail, listing around 15 key traits as opposed to the 5 listed by Carlyle and Galton. Zaccaro tries to suggest how significantly these traits relate to leadership. In other words, he attempts to indicate not only the likely traits of a leader but how important they are for an effective leader.

Zaccaro was concerned about the lack of consideration given to cognitive skills, motives and values of the leader, as well as social skills and the ability to solve problems. All of these were thought to be important traits of effective leaders.

Tannenbaum and Schmidt

Tannenbaum and Schmidt concentrate on the style of leadership (as do Blake and Mouton) and suggest that the style of leadership highlighted the degree of trade-off between the control exerted by the leader and how this affected the interaction between the leader and the employees. This theory is sometimes known as the 'contingency' approach. Figure 46.3 illustrates this trade-off quite clearly.

The continuum uses four styles, although a more detailed version offers seven styles.

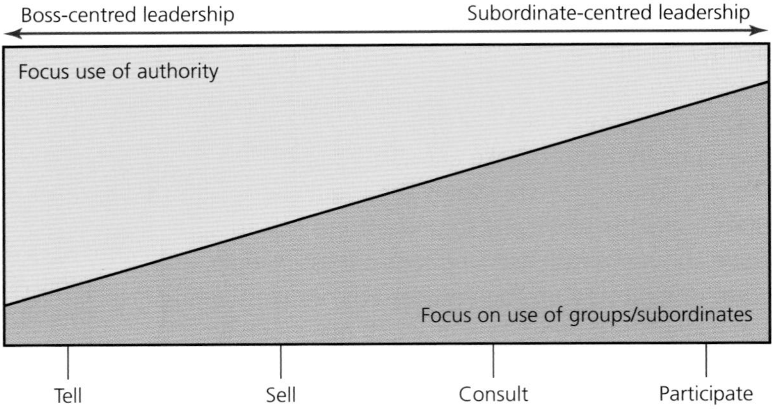

Figure 46.3 Tannenbaum and Schmidt's style of leadership

Tips and techniques

With reference to Figure 46.3, it is important to note that neither the leader nor the group has 100 per cent control.

Tell

This style is one in which the leader or manager just informs the employees of his or her decision and can be seen as an autocratic approach, as the focus is on the leader. The employees will be expected to comply. This approach does not give the employees an opportunity to be involved in the decision making process.

Sell

This is when a leader or manager makes a decision but attempts to 'sell' the decision to the employees. This style suggests that there is some consideration of the employees rather than just 'telling' them. A degree of persuasion is taking place. There is also the opportunity for feedback.

Consult

This style goes a step further than 'sell', as the leader will present his or her ideas to the employees and invite discussion and therefore offers a more collaborative approach. The leader will listen to the ideas of the employees and 'two-way' communication will be the norm, unlike 'tell'.

Participate

Finally, 'participate' shows that the focus is now on the employees and not the leader. Under this style of leadership, the leader or manager will ask the employees to make a decision, although usually within defined limits or boundaries. Nevertheless, the emphasis is on the employees and is similar to a more democratic style of leadership.

Adair

Adair's 'Action-centred leadership' highlights the three elements for all leadership situations, which are the:

1 achievement of the task
2 team or group involved in the task
3 individual members of the team or group involved in the task.

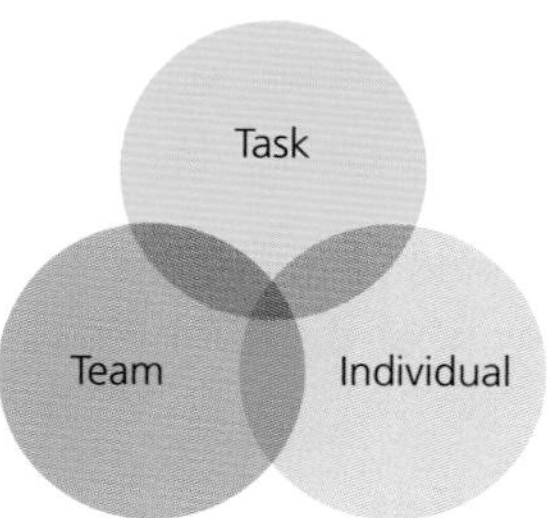

Figure 46.4 Adair's three circles

Adair suggests that the leader has to try and balance the needs of all three elements; a failure to consider all three elements is more likely to lead to failure.

However, there is an acknowledgement that the three elements can conflict with each other. Ensuring that the task is the key focus may be at the expense of the individuals who are in involved with the task. Alternatively, too much time spent on considering the welfare of the group or individuals may be to the detriment of completing the required task. Adair's theory is very similar to that of Blake and Mouton's Leadership grid.

Tips and techniques

Although there are several theorists and theories to consider, it is important that you are able to compare and contrast these in an evaluative manner. Similarly, it is a good technique to use a particular theory or theorist to justify a view you wish to impart.

When considering the usefulness of theories, it is important to consider:

- when the theory was written
- how much evidence is offered in support of the theory
- how practical the theory is for modern business.

Types of manager

There are different types of manager, both in terms of hierarchy and function.

Senior managers

These are at the top of an organisation, and are usually led by a Chief Executive Officer (CEO) who will work closely with the board of directors. Some businesses refer to their directors as senior managers. These managers are more concerned with long-term planning and strategy than day-to-day implementation of policy. Nevertheless, a particularly important function of senior managers is to ensure that their departments communicate with each another, so that the business runs smoothly from day to day. The different functional areas of a business have to work together: they cannot exist in isolation.

Middle managers

These managers will have more operational (i.e. day-to-day) control than senior executives, and are responsible to them for implementing their strategy. It is not considered good practice for a senior manager to interfere with the way in which middle managers choose to organise their departments.

Junior managers

This term can refer either to management trainees (destined for higher positions) and those in supervisory positions who have a degree of authority. Their work will involve some of the functions of a manager outlined above.

Line and staff managers

In terms of function, two types of managers exist: line managers and staff managers.

Line managers

Line managers have direct input into and responsibility for policy on the business's products. A line manager has 'line authority', that is, the authority and power to order subordinates in their department to perform appropriate tasks.

Staff managers

Staff managers exist to provide advice and support to the line managers; for example, the management information services department (which is essentially the numerical database of the firm) can provide all sorts of data for decision making and also design software support to the line managers. Staff support also includes personnel management, secretarial work and maintenance. Although there will still be a hierarchy within departments offering staff support, staff managers have no line authority over those whom they support. A high-ranking personnel manager has authority over his subordinates but cannot tell employees in the marketing department what to do.

Key terms

Line managers: managers who have a direct input into and responsibility for policy on the business's products.

Staff managers: managers whose function is to provide advice and support to the line managers.

Differences between a manager and a leader

'Leadership' is not the same as 'management', although they are linked. A really effective manager will almost certainly be a successful leader. Managers 'manage' via their organisational skills, whereas a leader is more inspirational. Some differences between the two are highlighted in Table 46.1.

Table 46.1 Differences between a manager and a leader

Characteristics of a manager	Characteristics of a leader
Obeyed by subordinates Minimises risk Prefers the status quo 'Steady state' Sets an example Tells employees to follow procedure Not very outgoing	Followed by subordinates Risk-taker Embraces change Creative Inspires others to behave in a certain way Encourages new ways of thinking Charismatic

Leaders still require managerial skills (e.g. maximising the use of people's talents and using time effectively) and have to be proficient in their job, but will be 'followed' rather than 'obeyed'. This is not because of their position in the hierarchy but because employees respect and trust them. Leaders are passionate about what they want to achieve and how they want to achieve it. A leader is usually more courageous than a manager, and will take greater risks. A leader will set an example and stimulate others to work towards his or her goals.

It is important to avoid stereotyping. None of the above means that managers are dull remote individuals, rarely moving from their office, pushing routine paperwork up and down the chain of command and generally stifling employees' creativity, while the dynamic leader speeds around motivating everyone with their charisma and enthusiasm!

Where management skills and leadership qualities are harmonised, the business will benefit hugely. However, a manager cannot just become a leader. It has been said that great leaders are born, not made, and there may be some truth in this. Leadership skills can certainly be learned, but unless a person is comfortable with the idea of adopting a leadership role, it will not be easy to put those skills into practice. It also has to be acknowledged that a dynamic, creative and charismatic leader can also become a loose cannon if he or she does not work within the framework of the business's deadlines and objectives.

Management of specialist departments within a business

A large business will have a number of different departments that perform specialist functions. It should not be assumed, however, that these are rigidly compartmentalised; all managers manage at least a few people, and so every manager has a degree of personnel responsibility even if they are not a personnel manager. Similarly, they have to set and adhere to budgets even if they are not finance managers. The departments are production, marketing, personnel and finance.

Production management

Production management involves more than just making the products. It is concerned with a variety of issues including production scheduling, purchasing, stock control, quality control and maintenance.

Marketing management

This position involves issues such as market research, the development of pricing policies, promotional campaigns and ensuring that the distribution of the product reaches the customers when they want it.

Personnel management

Personnel management is concerned with organising people. This encompasses issues such as recruitment, training, performance appraisal, offering advice on motivation, dismissal, and so on, to the line managers, ensuring that employee records are correct, wages and industrial relations.

Financial management

Finally, financial management is concerned with the housekeeping of the business accounts. All receipts and payments, however small, need to be recorded in order to ensure that the business is solvent and able to meet its overall financial objectives. It is also concerned with raising finance and the analysis of costs.

Other areas of management

The above are the four main functional areas within a business, but this does not mean that there are always only four departments. A business may for example have a research and development department ('R and D') where new products are developed and tested. It may have a management information services department for ICT support.

However many departments actually exist, the need for co-ordination and co-operation between the functions should be obvious. The production department must produce what marketing tells it to make, since this is how the customer is satisfied and repeat purchases are generated. However, this co-ordination cannot be done in isolation. The financial objectives of the business will have come partly from a consideration of the capabilities of the production department and the ability of marketing to sell the products. The finance department must ensure that even if products are being successfully produced and sold, the business is not overtrading; that is, ensuring that the cashflow is sufficient to support the growth. Personnel will have to ensure that the business has a manpower plan to make certain that all departments have the right people to achieve this.

Tips and techniques

When answering a question involving the four functional areas of a business, bear in mind that integration and co-operation between them is essential if the business is to operate successfully and meet its strategic objectives.

In a small business such as a sole trader, these functions still exist but will have to be performed by a single person, who may not be enthusiastic or effective at all of them. This sort of managerial specialisation results in managerial economies of scale.

Further sources

www.kevindecker.com/page.asp a website containing practical details on how to become a successful manager, and especially how to build a successful team.

www.nwlink.com/~donclark/leader/bm_model.html Blake's grid questionnaire.

www.mindtools.com

www.businessballs.com

personaldevelopmentguy.com

lindsay-sherwin.co.uk

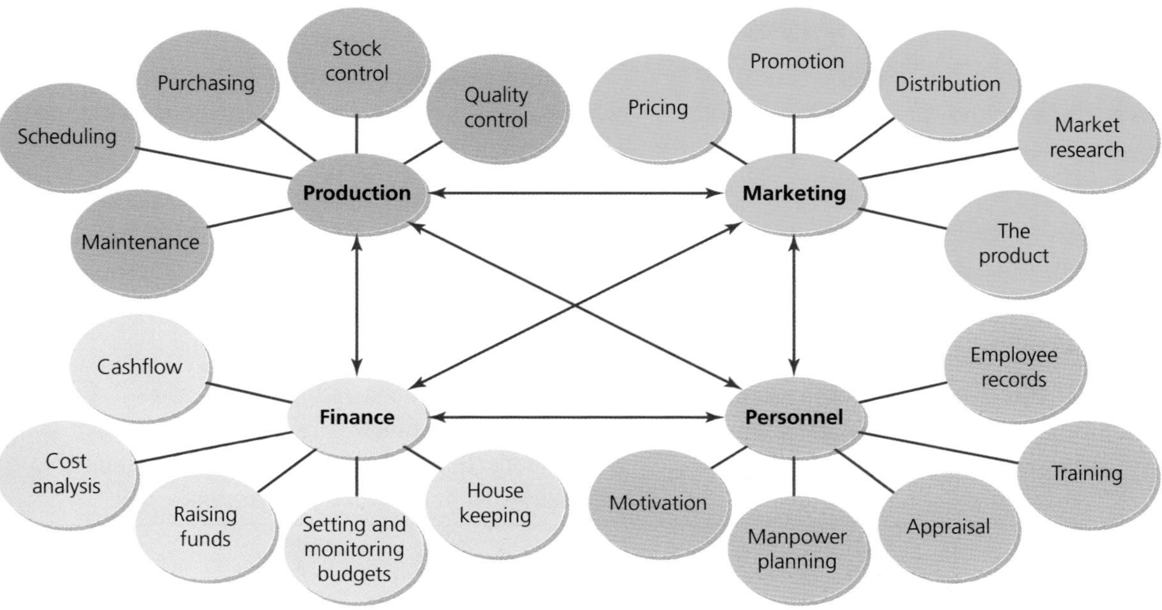

Figure 46.5 The four main departments in business and their most important functions

Your turn

Questions are suitable for all AS and A Level candidates.

Multiple-choice questions

1 According to Adair, all the following are part of his action-centred leadership except:
   A achievement of the task
   B team or group involved in the task
   C individual members of the team or group involved in the task
   D leader of the business. *(1)*

2 According to McGregor's Theory X, employees are not assumed to be:
   A inherently lazy, disliking work and responsibility
   B lacking the will and ability to work unsupervised
   C lacking initiative
   D not motivated by money. *(1)*

3 According to Carlyle and Galton, their theory relates to:
   A motivation of employees
   B leadership tasks
   C leadership traits
   D ability of employees. *(1)*

Revision questions

1 Define the term 'organisation by system'. *(2)*
2 Define the term 'line manager'. *(2)*
3 State four styles of leadership. *(4)*
4 Outline two differences between a manager and a leader. *(4)*
Total *(12)*

Individual or group task: Case study

Tesco management

Following a difficult year for Tesco, especially after the revelation of publishing 'misleading' profit trading results*, Tesco announced that its chairman, Sir Richard Broadbent, would be leaving (announced October 2014). He stated,

'The issues that have come to light over recent weeks are a matter of profound regret. We have acted quickly to clarify the financial performance of the company.'

Philip Clarke, the former chief executive of Tesco, stood down in July 2014. Eight executives were suspended after the overstated profits came to light. Shares in Tesco continued to fall in value, as did the level of its sales.

Earlier in the year Tesco announced that as part of its restructuring, it would be scrapping some of its 'team leader' roles. Tesco suggested that it wanted to reduce the number of traditional team leaders to reflect changing shopping habits.

Twelve stores, which included Corby, Kettering and Lincoln, were to be consulted, with redundancy packages being offered, or jobs with a lower paid role. Someone suggested that Tesco would not be able to function without the team leaders, as it is they who meet the consumers, not the line managers!

*An overstatement of profits to the value of £250 million was revealed in September 2014, which was followed by an announcement in October 2014 that the overstatement was actually £263 million.

1. Using your own research and any other information available, suggest to what extent the leadership of Tesco has failed. Use leadership theories to help justify your answer.

Chapter 47

Motivation

AS / Year 1 | Year 2

A Level students must know all of the content in this chapter.

AS students need to know everything in this chapter except goal-setting theory (pages 337–340).

If asked what they understand by 'motivation at work', some people might reply using phrases such as 'people working hard', 'employees believing that what they do makes a difference', or 'people wanting to do their best'. Certainly these sentiments form part of what defines a motivated employee. There are, however, sometimes misconceptions about what constitutes 'motivation'. Motivation arises from positive factors; when an employee is motivated, the motivation comes from within because the right conditions have been created and the employee wants to behave in a certain way. On the other hand, if an employee who does not care about his work is told that unless his conduct improves he will receive a formal warning, this may change his behaviour but it will not motivate him to do so.

Motivated people have a strong desire to act in a particular way and to achieve a certain result. A motivated employee is therefore one who wants to work hard, takes pride in his or her work and is committed to achieving the business's goals. This is not the same as 'morale'. The two are linked although there is a difference; morale can be defined as 'spirit' in the sense that if morale in a team (or indeed an individual) is high then team members are supportive of each other and there exists a spirit of confidence and purpose – which is likely to lead to increased motivation.

Key terms

Motivation: a strong desire to act in a particular way and to achieve a certain result.

Morale: 'spirit'; if morale in an individual, group or team is high then there exists a spirit of confidence and purpose and vice versa.

Why is motivation important to a business?

A business does not want motivated employees as an end in itself. Managers in a business may well feel it is ethically correct to make employees' lives as stimulating as possible at work, but ultimately a business wants its employees to be motivated so that they can be fully effective in helping the firm to meet its objectives. Although there are minimum standards of pay and safety at work laid down by the law, a business that wants highly motivated employees will have to exceed those standards. The benefits of a motivated workforce are:

- Employees who are motivated will be less prone to absenteeism and have lower rates of labour turnover which will help lower costs.
- Motivated employees will see themselves as true stakeholders rather than 'workers' and will be more productive.
- Motivated employees are more committed and more willing to 'go the extra mile' for the business.
- High levels of motivation in the workforce make change easier to implement.
- Motivated employees present a better image of the business to external bodies.

In short, motivated employees help to give a business a competitive advantage.

Motivation can arise from a wide variety of different factors which can broadly be divided into two areas:

1. Monetary methods: these assume that motivation will result from linking employee performance to pay in some way such as piecework, commission, profit sharing, share ownership, or a bonus.
2. Non-monetary methods: these assume that motivation results from factors other than financial incentives (although a fair rate of pay may still be important). These factors include being given work

that is interesting and challenging, working as part of a team, being given responsibility, and receiving praise from management for work successfully completed.

Much research has been conducted into how employee motivation is affected by these different factors.

Early research into employee motivation

Frederick Taylor (1856–1917): Scientific management

Taylor was an American writing in the early years of the twentieth century and is usually acknowledged as the first researcher in this area. His famous *Principles of Scientific Management* was published in 1911. Taylor was of the opinion that a scientific approach could be used to motivate employees whatever tasks they were performing. The scientific approach meant that the principles he believed in could be replicated and applied in most industrial settings.

Essentially the approach meant that jobs would be carefully observed to see exactly what tasks were being performed. They would then be broken down into simple tasks to ensure a high division of labour. Those who were best suited to each job would be recruited and then trained to perform the specialised task. They would be paid on a piece rate. The basic premise was that money was the key motivator. By using these principles a way could be found to use workers efficiently to increase productivity and link to their reward to their effort. This, Taylor claimed, would mean that the objectives of both managers and employees would be harmonised. The concept of money as the principal motivator for employees is still referred to as a Tayloristic approach.

Limitations of the theory

- The theory is in many ways a product of its creator and its time. Taylor was an engineer (not a psychologist) specifically interested in productive efficiency and not the psychological understanding of employee behaviour.
- At the time it was quite rare for the concept of job satisfaction to be uppermost in managers' minds. Employees might have wanted more than simply a day's work but were often grateful they had any work at all.
- Taylor's work was adopted by many businesses in the 1920s (notably at Henry Ford's car plants) but the approach, at least in the way that Taylor originally envisaged it, went out of favour as new theories of motivation based on psychological factors began to emerge.

Key term

Scientific management: the concept (originated by Frederick Taylor in the late nineteenth century) that a set of principles could be developed and applied by managers to motivate employees in most types of business. A central part of the theory is that employees are largely motivated by money.

Elton Mayo (1880–1949): Human relations management

Mayo was an American psychologist, whose most significant work was conducted in the 1920s and 1930s. Like Taylor, he was interested in improving employee productivity but he approached the issue from a different perspective; he felt that scientific management alone could not explain the behaviour, attitude and productivity of employees. Mayo is associated with the term 'Hawthorne effect'. This is because his most famous research was undertaken at the Hawthorne plant of the Western Electric Company in Chicago.

The initial research at the plant was concerned with altering the brightness of the lighting in a particular area of the firm. It was discovered that the productivity of employees nearly always rose when it was changed – although it later returned to normal. It was thought that the presence of the researchers was having an effect on productivity. The employees liked the fact that someone was taking an interest in them.

The second set of experiments involved a particular group of women who assembled telephone components as their work. Various changes were made to rest breaks and the length of the working day. Furthermore, the employees were allowed to choose who they wished to work with. They also had a supervisor who adopted a consultative attitude to the changes and who implemented some of the changes they suggested. The result was that the increase in breaks and the shortening of the day, coupled with being able to work in a group and being managed by a democratic supervisor, led to an increase in productivity.

Further research was conducted into group work and payment by results in the wiring room experiments. A group of male employees were observed soldering telephone equipment. It was discovered that being paid according to results on an individual basis did not always raise productivity. This was because the men were worried that if output rose by a large amount, the firm would reduce the rate they were being paid and that would mean having to work harder for the same pay.

Broadly speaking, it can be stated that the conclusions Mayo reached are that:

- Employees respond to changes in the working environment.
- A sense of recognition and consultation is important to employees.
- The workplace is a social system. Employees like to work in groups.
- Communication with management and group norms affect productivity.

Mayo's conclusions pointed to the fact that there was more to increasing productivity and motivation than the monetary method of motivation that Taylorism suggested. Psychological factors were also important as was teamwork, communication and an interest from management. These could bring quite significant results in terms of motivation.

Limitations of the theory

- It can be difficult to generalise what the Hawthorne effect actually is. Sometimes it is used to mean one of the above points and sometimes several.
- Several variables were often changed at the same time and so identifying the exact cause of a change in productivity is difficult.
- Mayo's work was conducted amongst employees at one plant in the first part of the twentieth century and therefore cannot be regarded as applicable to all employees anywhere in the twenty-first century.

Content and process theories of motivation

The research and the motivational theories that followed Taylor and Mayo can broadly be classified into two different areas: content theories and process theories. Content theories deal with the issue of 'what motivates employees?' and are therefore concerned with identifying a person's individual needs and then using motivation to fulfil those needs. Process theories deal with the 'process' of motivation itself and are concerned with the issue of 'how motivation occurs'.

Key terms

Content theories: deal with 'what motivates employees?' and are concerned with identifying a person's individual needs and then using motivation to fulfil those needs.

Process theories: deal with the process of motivation and are concerned with the issue of how motivation occurs.

Content theory

The three theorists that are most commonly associated with this type of theory are McClelland, Herzberg and Maslow.

Tips and techniques

Presenting the findings of the motivational theorists in a few words such as 'Taylor said people only work for money' is not the way to answer. Examiners are looking for much more depth and a clear understanding of how the work of the theorist could be used to justify a method of motivating the employees in the context of the specific business in the case study.

David McClelland (1917–1998): Three needs theory

David McClelland was a psychologist whose original work was in the 1960s. He developed a motivational model based on the proposition that people have three needs; achievement, affiliation and power. These needs exist regardless of gender, culture or race but can be changed by life experiences and shaped by cultural factors such as upbringing and parental expectations. He attempted to explain how these needs drive a person's motivation. If one of these needs is more dominant it will influence a person's behaviour in a particular way. He used what is known as a Thematic Apperception Test to measure these needs. The three needs are:

1 (N-Ach) The need for achievement – someone with this sort of need typically:

   A prefers challenging (but realistic) goals in order to feel a sense of achievement

B likes to work on a task or project in which the results are based on his or her effort, i.e. the individual enjoys, and seeks, personal responsibility
C likes to work with others driven by N-Ach
D likes to receive regular feedback on his or her work in order to assess progress towards the achievement of goals.

Therefore a person with a personality driven by achievement needs is motivated by accomplishment in the workplace, wants to help achieve the organisation's goals, and will actively seek promotion.

2 (N-Aff) The need for affiliation – someone with this sort of need typically:
A enjoys working as a part of a team because he or she likes to feel accepted and liked by others
B is people orientated rather than task orientated
C adheres to the culture of the workplace
D prefers a collaborative/co-operative approach to work.

Therefore, a person with a personality driven by affiliation needs is a team player, enjoys social interaction, and is unlikely to challenge the business's cultural norms when working and seeking a solution; this would make such an individual feel uncomfortable because of a concern about rejection.

3 (N-Pow) The need for power – someone with this sort of need typically:
A likes to influence, encourage or dominate others
B places a high value on his or her position in the business's hierarchy
C enjoys recognition and status
D likes to win.

Therefore a person with a personality driven by power needs is likely to be motivated by seeking a management or leadership position. This individual works best when he or she is in charge.

McClelland claimed that these categories of need are not mutually exclusive, but stated that individuals will develop a bias towards one of them. If the theory is accepted then it gives managers a clear idea of which sort of role in the business a potential employee is likely to be suited to. Alternatively, considered from another perspective, it indicates what sort of person should be employed to fulfil a particular organisational role.

If an employee's needs are correctly identified then that person can be managed and motivated appropriately. For example, an employee with N-Aff needs may work well when dealing with customers rather than being in a senior managerial position where difficult decisions that may upset employees and other stakeholders have to be taken. In contrast, high achievers may not work well in a team environment either because they become frustrated by the need for compromise, or because they assume that everyone in the team shares their own needs.

If an employee's motivation increases because the needs are met then they will become more effective and productive. McClelland observed that although one set of needs is likely to be dominant in an individual, they are not irrevocably unalterable. Needs can be 'shaped' by training; for example, an N-Ach employee in a management position could attend a training course to try to get him or her to empathise more with those with N-Aff needs and so manage them more effectively.

Limitations of the theory

- It cannot be assumed that just because an employee exhibits a particular need this means that the need can always be used to the benefit of the organisation. For example, an N-Aff employee is, according to the theory, going to be motivated by social interaction. However, this does not necessarily mean that the employee will always welcome such interaction. Perhaps the employee is repeatedly required to deal with the business's most 'awkward' customers, or maybe has to deal with a difficult disciplinary issue in his or her department; unless that employee is actually interested in that interaction he or she will not engage – and be motivated to perform – effectively. Employees will not always to be motivated by what their needs suggest that they will be.
- If motivation throughout a business is to occur, it is not as straightforward a matter as suggesting that an organisation should place a person with a particular set of needs in a particular role in the organisation. That person might be 'right' for the role in the sense that their needs technically match the role but their behaviour in achieving those needs may negatively affect the motivation of others. Those with strong and dominant N-Ach needs might make excessive demands on their subordinates and therefore demotivate them because they assume that they are driven by similar needs – whereas in practice they may not be.

Frederick Herzberg (1923–2000): The two-factor theory

Unlike Maslow's theory (see page 334), Herzberg's was constructed specifically for the workplace. The research was conducted in the 1950s. He was particularly interested in the factors that cause job satisfaction and job dissatisfaction. It was perhaps not surprising that he found that factors such as interesting work, responsibility, and the opportunity for self-development proved to be motivating for employees. However, what was interesting was that his research demonstrated that factors such as pay, pensions, working conditions and the relationship with the line manager did not result in job satisfaction. Herzberg called these 'hygiene' factors. They are also known as 'maintenance factors'.

This gave rise to his 'two-factor theory'.

The hygiene factors

These are similar to the lower levels of Maslow's hierarchy. In essence, employees are dissatisfied by a 'bad' working environment but are not motivated by a 'good' working environment. Hygiene factors do not motivate employees no matter how 'good' they are. This, however, does not mean that they are of no significance; Herzberg claimed that the absence of them causes job dissatisfaction and a negative attitude to the job. Thus improving these factors will improve the working environment generally and can lead to reduced discontentment and a reduction of the 'management don't care about us' attitude that employees often display.

The motivating factors

Hygiene factors are therefore important, but Herzberg claimed that the reduction of job dissatisfaction is not enough in itself to ensure motivation. If employees are to be motivated then certain other factors must be in place. These 'motivators' (which are similar to the higher levels of Maslow's hierarchy) relate to the job itself and not the working environment. They are factors such as responsibility, recognition, meaningful and rewarding work, and the opportunity for promotion. Jobs need to be designed with these in mind if motivation is to occur.

In conclusion, a business will need hygiene factors in place to prevent job dissatisfaction amongst employees but also a completely different set of factors (motivators) in place if it wants to motivate them. The theory has as its strengths that it demonstrates a straightforward approach to motivation and is relatively easy for managers to apply.

Tips and techniques

Remember; according to Herzberg, the presence of motivators will motivate but the presence of hygiene factors will not; they just prevent dissatisfaction. The two are not the same.

Herzberg's original research was conducted amongst white-collar employees (accountants and engineers) and has been criticised on the grounds that the conclusions may therefore not be applicable to all employees especially 'front line' blue-collar workers. Subsequent research by others has not been conclusive, but if Herzberg's findings are accepted then there are a number of practical issues for management.

There should be scope for job enlargement. This does not simply mean 'giving people more work' but redesigning and broadening the nature of a job. Employees should be encouraged and supported (e.g. via training) to take on new and more challenging tasks if they want to. Employees need greater autonomy at work and the chance to accept responsibility. Therefore, there is a need for job enrichment; the job itself needs to be interesting and enriching to the employee. This means that jobs need to be analysed and redesigned to allow personal growth. This enrichment could take the form of employees taking more responsibility for work being undertaken (i.e. getting rid of unnecessary supervision) and greater involvement in decision making. Where possible, employees should be able to complete a whole task not just a part of it.

There should also be job rotation, which allows greater variety in the tasks to be undertaken and should help prevent boredom. It will also enable employees to gain experience for promotion. This is not the same as job enrichment because it does not involve an increase in responsibility.

Another important issue was concerned with an obvious point that everyone involved in motivation should realise; people like to be praised for their efforts. Herzberg emphasised the importance of positive feedback to provide recognition and a sense of achievement.

Limitations of the theory

- The work could be considered a 'product of its time'; conducted in an area of the USA dominated by heavy industry rather than today's tertiary-based economy, amongst (what were probably – the data is not clear) white male accountants and engineers. It is therefore unlikely to be representative of 'a typical employee' of the twenty-first century.
- People have different personality traits: while one person (perhaps an executive on a very high salary who is also in line for a bonus) might consider pay a hygiene factor, another person (say a shop assistant working for the minimum wage) might regard pay as a highly motivating factor.
- Later researchers found that respondents stated that they received job satisfaction and dissatisfaction from both the motivating and hygiene factors.
- In practice, job enlargement, enrichment and rotation will be very time-consuming to plan and implement. Any proposed changes will need to be negotiated with employees – who otherwise may well see the process as an attempt just to give them more work.
- It is not always easy to enrich unskilled, repetitive jobs – although it could be argued that managers are paid, in part at least, to try to do so.

Key terms

Job enlargement: redesigning and broadening the nature of a job so that employees can take on new and more challenging tasks if they want to. It does not simply mean 'giving people more work'!

Job enrichment: making sure that a job is interesting and enriching to an employee; for example, through a greater variety of tasks, more responsibility, greater involvement, and so on.

Abraham Maslow (1908–1970): The hierarchy of needs

Maslow is famous for his work on human needs. Like Mayo he was a psychologist and in 1954 published his theory of the hierarchy of needs. Maslow had originally worked with animals and observed that some needs were fulfilled before others: for example, the need to satisfy thirst was met before the need to feed. Building on this observation with further research created his now-famous hierarchy of needs. Some of the work relating to the hierarchy is couched in quite complicated psychological jargon, but in terms of application to business it is essentially as follows.

Employees have a variety of needs at work that have to be satisfied and until the lower order needs are met, the higher ones cannot be. Once a person's needs are met at a particular level then he or she ceases to be motivated by them and will need to 'move up' to a higher level – unsatisfied needs are a motivating factor. On the other hand, if lower order needs are not satisfied then an employee will no longer be concerned about achieving higher-order (esteem and self-actualisation) needs.

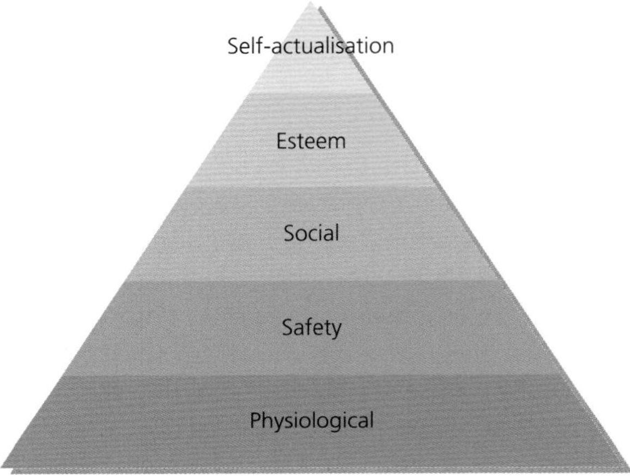

Figure 47.1 Maslow's hierarchy of needs

- Self-actualisation needs. Self-actualisation is hard to define precisely, but Maslow suggested that it was concerned with personal growth and the achievement of one's full potential as a human.
- The esteem needs. Humans look for self-esteem. They seek the respect of others, some recognition for effort as well as a degree of status.
- The love and belonging needs (usually called social needs). Humans as social animals do not like loneliness and isolation. They have a need for friendship and positive relationships with others.
- Safety and security needs. Once physiological needs are taken care of, humans seek security, stability and protection.
- Physiological needs. These include the need for shelter, water and food.

Although the theory was not designed specifically for business use, the significance of it in the business world is that if employees are to be motivated then managers must provide the conditions for needs to be met and employees to progress up the hierarchy.

Therefore:

- To meet physiological needs a business would have to pay a 'fair' wage for a 'fair' number of hours worked and allow appropriate breaks.
- To meet the security needs a business would have to ensure a high standard of health and safety, as well as ensuring that appropriate policies on issues such as bullying, discrimination and discipline are in place.
- To meet the social needs there should be an opportunity for social interaction with others; both employees via (say) teamwork and managers via a consultative, democratic approach.
- To meet esteem needs there should be the opportunity for leadership and promotion.
- To meet self-actualisation needs of employees, managers should try to identify what these needs are (via methods such as appraisal) and help to guide employees to appropriate goals and challenges. Training should be provided to help meet them.

There are some interesting issues here with lessons to be learned for motivation: the need for managers to be democratic and to actively help employees identify goals to be met at work; the fact that employees require the opportunity for social interaction at work for motivation to occur; and the fact that if lower order needs are not met (i.e. without an adequate wage earned in an environment free from health risks and victimisation) then the higher ones are likely to be meaningless.

Limitations of the theory

- The theory was not specifically designed for use in the business world. Furthermore, for a manager to try to identify each and every employee's needs to help them progress will be difficult, if not impossible, in practice.
- It is something of a generalisation. Do employees necessarily seek self-actualisation through work? It could be argued that once their lower order needs are met by an employer, employees may well seek self-actualisation through non-work activities such as sport, playing the guitar or painting.
- Are needs really hierarchical with an employee passing through them like levels in a console game? It could be argued that (given that humans are social animals) social needs are actually just as fundamental as security needs, indeed that security needs cannot be met without social interaction.

The content theories paved the way for the process-based theories that seek to explain the sort of mental processes employees go through when making a decision on how to behave.

Victor Vroom (1932 –): Expectancy theory

Vroom conducted his initial work on expectancy in the early 1960s. The theory suggests that individuals will decide to behave in a certain way because they are motivated to choose that particular behaviour instead of another type of behaviour, due to what they expect the result of their choice to be. Expectancy theory is about the mental processes an employee goes through when making a decision on a choice of action. The first two aspects of the theory are:

1. Expectancy: does the employee think that he or she is actually going to be able to achieve a target/complete a task? This view will be influenced by factors such as previous experience, support from others, and the availability of resources. If an employee feels that achieving a task is definitely possible then the expectancy is valued as 1. If he or she feels that the task definitely cannot be completed then expectancy is valued as 0. If the individual feels that the task is achievable then he or she will allot a subjective probability to it with a higher figure (such as 0.85) reflecting a more optimistic attitude than a lower figure (say of 0.35).
2. Valence: this refers to the value that an employee puts on the reward that is on offer. Valence can be between 0 and 1. If the completed task leads to an outcome that is highly desired by the employee, then valence will be near to 1. The higher the figure the employee allots, the more that person values the outcome.

Vroom said that the valence, expectancy and motivation are linked through a simple equation. Motivation or 'force' is the effort that an individual puts into a task:

Force = (Valence × Expectancy)

Consider two employees:

Employee 1 has been promised a bonus equal to one month's salary if a task is completed satisfactorily and on time. This person thinks this is a very desirable outcome and so allots a valence of 0.95 to it. However, the individual knows that he or she will have to complete the task with several others who they do not particularly like or work well with. Past experience of working with these people has been negative, with few tasks being completed on time. The expectancy figure allotted is therefore 0.2.

Force (Motivation) is therefore $0.95 \times 0.2 = 0.19$. The employee will not be very well motivated to complete the task.

Employee 2 is not as concerned with monetary reward as employee 1 but (unsurprisingly) still thinks a month's salary would be a desirable outcome and allots a valence of 0.6 to it. This person knows that the others working on the task are those who are pleasant to work with and are 'team players'. There is therefore a high probability that the task will be completed satisfactorily and on time. Accordingly, the expectancy figure allotted is 0.9.

Force (Motivation) is therefore $0.7 \times 0.9 = 0.63$. The employee will be more motivated to achieve the task than employee 1.

Vroom's research suggested that people have to believe that they will gain a reward and that the reward is desirable enough to warrant the positive behaviour (i.e. the motivation) to achieve it. Effort is not just linked to an outcome that is desired but is affected by the employee's assessment of the likelihood that it will occur.

The calculations above indicate that an employee will only act in a certain way if there is a fairly high expectation that their actions and behaviour will actually lead to the desired outcome. In this way, expectancy theory certainly accords with common sense in that if an individual has a perception that a reward is not worth having or/and that there is little chance of receiving it then one of the values allotted to expectancy or valence may well be 0. In turn, this means that the motivation to achieve the task is also 0; the employee simply does not bother to try.

There is another component to expectancy theory and that is instrumentality. This is basically the issue of 'will I get a reward for my actions at all?' A person will only perform in a particular way if he or she believes that their performance will lead to a desired outcome. Sometimes the calculation is used with instrumentality (I) in the formula as well as valence and expectancy i.e.

Motivation (Force) = I × (Valence × Expectancy)

This reflects the fact that if instrumentality is negative the whole calculation will be negative, that is, the employee will not be motivated to perform the task.

In short, Vroom's work postulates that when considering how much effort to expend, employees asks themselves 'Will I get a reward?' (instrumentality), 'How hard will the task be to achieve?' (expectancy) and 'Will it be worth it if I do achieve it?' (valence).

The implication of the theory is that making motivational factors available (such as a monetary reward) are, in themselves, not enough to ensure that sufficient 'Force' is expended and an individual behaves in the desired way. Viewed in this way, expectancy theory could therefore be seen as more realistic and useful than the theories of Herzberg or Maslow.

Another strength of the theory is therefore that managers using it, who can identify what their employees's needs are, have a mechanism for devising a predictive value which will enable an increase in the likelihood of an employee acting in the desired way.

If the theory is accepted then in terms of motivating employees, managers must ensure that:

- there is a positive relationship between effort and performance
- 'correct' performance will result in a desirable reward (i.e. the reward is perceived as 'worth having')
- the desire to gain the reward is strong enough to make the effort worthwhile
- jobs are designed and teams constructed of employees that encourage individual employees to 'want to achieve' and 'believe they can achieve'
- promises of rewards are fulfilled
- the targets set are achievable.

Limitations of the theory:

- One person's perception of effort and performance can be very different from another's – placing values on expectancy and valence is subjective.
- Trying to apply the theory in practice by identifying each employee's needs could be very difficult. Employees view rewards differently; what some regard as desirable others may not. Individualising rewards for each employee could be very time-consuming and might have a large opportunity cost in terms of a manager's time.
- The theory is not applicable to all organisations because reward is not always directly correlated with performance. Reward may be linked with effort or/and responsibility. For most employees in the public sector there is no monetary reward for

reaching a target and so the theory may not be useful in that context.

- If the theory is used by an organisation to reward employees in financial terms, the cost to the organisation of making the monetary rewards might be very high. Also the force that is expended will be affected by employees' perception of how consistent and fair the business's reward system is. It could of course be argued that these latter two points are not limitations of the theory per se.

Goal-setting theory

Peter Drucker (1909–2005): 'The father of modern management'

Drucker was a writer, lecturer and consultant for over 60 years. He published a number of books on management; the two best known of which are probably *The Practice of Management* and *The Effective Executive* where he identified the sort of skills necessary for managers to succeed in their role: time management, knowing how and where to apply talents, prioritising and planning, and making effective decisions. So wide and pervasive has been his influence that he has sometimes been called the 'father of management'. As far back as the 1950s his key beliefs had been stated:

The most important asset of any organisation is its employees who should be recognised as such and not treated as costs to be minimised. Drucker claimed that a manager's primary purpose is to enable people to perform. He wrote of the business as a community built on trust and respect for its employees. He coined the phrase 'knowledge worker' long before others appreciated how significant a commodity knowledge would be in a post-industrial society. Knowledge, unlike traditional skills, changes rapidly and so employees need not only formal education but ongoing training as well. The development of this idea was to be very persuasive in later years.

To try to do justice to Drucker's work in a few paragraphs is impossible but, in his view, some of the most important factors for managers if they want an effective and motivated workforce are to:

- decentralise and delayer the business as much as possible to allow organisational freedom for managers and employees to respond quickly to consumer demands
- take an interest in their employees and value their contribution to the organisation
- offer ongoing training to create and nurture 'knowledge workers'
- try to create a 'plant community' (i.e. community in the workplace) where individuals' social needs can be met
- keep a sense of perspective when it comes to reward. He was very critical that senior managers could reap huge rewards as a result of closing down plants and making thousands of employees redundant. He thought this was morally and socially unforgivable.

These straightforward ideas brought major benefits to American corporations in the post-Second World War period and they continue to hold their significance today. Many later researchers and theorists developed these ideas.

In the 1980s Drucker began to have grave doubts about the behaviour of many large US businesses and the executives who ran them. He claimed that the way businesses were being run was fundamentally wrong. Employees were expendable, and at board level self-interest ruled. High levels of executive pay particularly irked him and there was little sense of community in the workplace that he believed should exist. Thirty years after making his name as the person who laid down the ground rules for creating a successful business, he emerged as one of corporate America's most outspoken critics.

Drucker is particularly well-known for his concept of management by objectives (MBO), which was included in *The Practice of Managemen*t published in 1954. To begin with, the organisation's strategic goals are set by the senior managers and these are then 'cascaded' down the hierarchy. In some ways, Locke (see below) could be said to have built on this principle.

A lack of goals can in turn lead to a lack of job satisfaction with employees 'drifting' with no clear sense of direction or any understanding of how their work contributes to the achievement of the business's wider strategic objectives. If there is no recognition of this, then they will feel demotivated because they feel unimportant.

Therefore, at the heart of MBO is participative goal setting. Goals are set with the line manager so that each employee understands what is expected of him or her in terms of reaching the organisation's goals. They can then set personal goals to reflect this and these can be linked to their career aspirations. At a later date, there is a comparison of the employee's actual performance with the standards and goals set. If successful, they attain both their personal goals and the organisation's targets.

There are some distinct advantages to operating a system of MBO:

- Motivation: when employees are involved in the process of goal this can lead to greater job satisfaction and commitment to the business.
- Clarity of goals at all levels of the organisation: employees are not 'drifting'; they have a clear sense of direction.
- Improved communication and co-ordination: objectives should be regularly reviewed and superiors and subordinates can work together to solve problems.
- Managers can ensure that objectives of the subordinates are linked to the organisation's objectives: employees can understand the importance of their actions and how these play their part in reaching the overall fit with the goals of the organisation.
- The achievement of objectives can be linked to employee rewards: this could improve motivation.

Edwin Locke (1938 –)

Locke proposed his goal-setting theory in 1968 with the publication of *Toward a Theory of Task Motivation and Incentives*. Essentially, Locke stated that setting appropriate goals for employees can be a useful and powerful tool for motivation. Like Drucker he considered that employees like to have a goal, and if the goal is appropriate they will enjoy the process of working towards it and will be motivated to achieve it. Without a goal that recognises the employee's contribution to the business he or she may feel unimportant and therefore demotivated.

Locke worked with another researcher, Gary Latham, and they arrived at five principles that are important to goal-setting (and therefore motivational) success. If a manager wants to set effective goals then the principles should be followed. These are:

1. Clarity: vague goals are hard to measure and the employee will not have a clear idea of what is expected of him or her. This can lead to incorrect outcomes and employees feeling stressed because they are not sure if they are performing the right tasks. Specific goals lead to more effective performance and outcomes.
2. Challenge: goals need to be challenging. Locke found that 'do your best' type of goals were not effective – and were too vague anyway to be of use in motivating employees.
3. Feedback: is essential so that progress can be gauged and if necessary the goal can be altered. Encouragement, praise, constructive criticism and guidance are very important.
4. Commitment: employees have to understand and agree to 'have ownership' of the goals if they are to motivate.
5. Task complexity: employees must not feel 'out of their depth' in terms of what they are being asked to achieve. They also need the resources necessary to achieve it. This might be in terms of the time allowed to do it, an appropriate budget, or the ability to attend a training course.

Thus the two most important conclusions are:

1. Specific goals (such as 'My department will increase sales of product X by 10 per cent in the next 12 months') generate a much better level of performance than setting a non-specific goal (e.g., 'My department will aim to sell more in future').
2. With the correct approach to goal setting, goals that are harder to achieve are positively connected to performance; an employee will be more motivated to achieve them.

Drucker and Locke have both made an important contribution to motivation theory. Goal setting is now virtually universal in one form or another in business and forms an important part of human resource management. Goal setting has repeatedly been seen to be successful and failure is often due to a failure to follow the five principles.

Limitations of the theory of goal setting

- The mere 'setting of goals' will not motivate an employee – why should it? Employees have to understand the importance of the procedure and have ownership of their goals. Any reward for achieving the goals has to be perceived by employees as 'worth it' – see Vroom above.
- A manager who does not ensure that employee (and group) goals are aligned with those of the business as a whole will largely negate the whole point of the target setting. A senior manager's bonus may depend on his department increasing its level of profit by a certain amount and he may therefore 'encourage' his subordinates to set goals that help achieve this – at the expense of

their other tasks that are equally important to the business.

- Goal setting can mean that employees may feel that they have to concentrate on reaching the goal at all costs and in doing so fail to pay sufficient attention to other important aspects of their job – especially those that are not readily measurable. For example, a teacher who has set the target of improving the number of A grades may focus almost every lesson entirely on examination practice with little attempt to make the subject stimulating or enjoyable.
- Goal setting can be difficult for new and complex tasks where there is no guidance on how best to approach them.
- If goals are linked to a reward (particularly a monetary reward) then there may well be an understandable tendency to try to set a simple goal that is not appropriate for the employee or the organisation.
- Goal setting requires regular monitoring and feedback. This is time-consuming for managers and can sometimes be viewed negatively by employees, who see this as a process of 'checking up on them' rather than an opportunity for reflection on what has so far been achieved. Is the approach appropriate for positions at all levels of an organisation?
- Managers who are overly critical of progress towards goals and/or an inability to achieve them at all – rather than being supportive – will demotivate employees.
- Goal setting can encourage a narrow focus by employees; they concentrate on their own personal targets (especially if linked to a reward) or those of the department. They may not see 'the wider picture' and could fail to help people in other parts of the organisation because they do not see the relevance of others' work in the achievement of their goals.

In the latter part of the twentieth century a number of new approaches to management and motivation emerged. Among the most highly regarded writers is Tom Peters.

Tom Peters (1942–): In search of excellence

Tom Peters is usually considered a management 'guru' rather than 'a motivational theorist', but his work has clear implications for motivation. Peters was born in Baltimore USA and came to prominence in 1982 with the publication of *In Search of Excellence*, (co-authored by Robert Waterman). This book looked at how to improve corporate performance, and rapidly became a best seller. It dealt with how an organisation might try to gain a commitment to excellence from every person working there. This was followed by a string of other successful publications including *Thriving on Chaos* and *Crazy Times Call for Crazy Organizations*.

In Search of Excellence certainly stirred up current management thinking (Peters describes himself as 'a professional agitator') because he was very critical of the way that most large corporations in the USA were being run. His research found cautious executives who disliked change and who were obsessed with three things: numbers, bureaucracy and control. This obsession, he claimed, was a mistake because these did not lead a focus on the things that really mattered to business success – people, customers and action. On the twentieth anniversary of the publication of *In Search of Excellence* he stated:

> *I was scratching the Douglas McGregor itch. Doug was the guy who invented Theory X and Theory Y, which basically said that people are a really important part of business and that you can't motivate them by controlling and tyrannizing them. Everybody knew that what he said was true, and everybody continued to treat their workers like sh** and then kept asking why companies didn't perform better.*

Source: Fast Company, Issue 53, November 2001.

Many of Peters' basic premises are not in themselves new (and also not solely concerned with motivation) but the early 1980s were right for a restatement of some simple but important ideas. For example, Peters pointed out that problems are not likely to be solved quickly or effectively when a business is governed by bureaucratic policies, rigid organisation and multiple layers of hierarchy. Secondly, a business needs to focus on its customers and be run with the customers, rather than itself, in mind. Thirdly, if employees are to be motivated, they need to be valued and empowered at all levels of the firm. Taylorism (named after Frederick Taylor, see above), as a motivational tool, which was back in fashion in many corporations, was often misguided.

> *Taylor showed how he could increase productivity, reduce mistakes, and make even the dumbest ox of a man a dependable employee. Hardly an uplifting view of work or your employees.*

Source: Fast Company, Issue 53, November 2001.

Many of Peters' suggestions mirror the ideas of those who had preceded him. They include:

- acknowledging employee achievement and effort and also giving praise (giving employees a sense of recognition)
- involving employees in decisions (which gives employees a sense of belonging and self-worth)
- encouraging participation (giving employees a sense of involvement and responsibility)
- trying to offer continuous employment (giving employees a sense of security).

Limitations of Tom Peters' work

- Peters often makes a point by telling a story about a particular business issue, sometimes based on personal experience. He is a very charismatic speaker and the 'tales' he tells have a valid underlying point, but it has been suggested that turning these into a viable plan of action for managers has sometimes been neglected.
- Peters has been accused of inconsistency. For example, while *In Search of Excellence* championed large companies, by the time *Liberation Management* was published in 1992 'a smaller and more flexible organisation' was now the solution, according to him, with the emphasis on the individual rather than the corporation.

Tom Peters remains an influential figure and is ever ready to answer his critics. When *Thriving on Chaos* was published in 1987 each chapter ended with a list of action points for managers, and he argues that his ideas have altered because of the ever-changing nature of the business environment. In 2007 he was voted the Second Most Influential Leadership Professional by Gurus International, in an independent internet study.

Key term

Empowerment: allowing employees to make decisions about when and how a task is performed.

Which theory is right?

There cannot be a definitive answer to this question; what motivates some employees will not do so for others. The factors that motivate professionals may not be the same for those in jobs which require less skill. Some people may not want to seek fulfilment at work; they may do a perfectly good job but not be interested in any responsibility or self-development in a work-based context. That said, it cannot be claimed that this is going to be true across the whole of an organisation's workforce. Such a 'Theory X' attitude (see **Chapter 46**) is very dated.

It is nevertheless apparent that certain factors tend to come up time and again as 'motivators' whatever the nature of the employment; fair pay, managers taking a genuine interest in employees' work and development, allowing the business to meet employees' social needs, along with employees having some variety, autonomy and challenge in the work – to list just a few. There can be no 'right way' to motivate employees although clearly certain broad principles need to be followed.

Figure 47.2 Motivation can arise from a variety of different factors

These principles, however, cannot simply be treated as a 'tick list' that will guarantee a motivated workforce. In general, the factors affecting the chosen method(s) of motivation depend on:

- The culture of the business. A new manager arriving at a business which is run on autocratic lines will find it difficult to introduce employee involvement, job enrichment and empowerment. As with almost all successful initiatives, the support for this motivational route must come from the top.

- The nature of the workforce and (referring back to Douglas McGregor) the manager's expectations of it.
- A manager's people skills and leadership style. A person who is naturally at ease delegating, encouraging autonomy and discussing different points of view will find it easier to empower and motivate employees than a confirmed autocrat.
- The resources available. If the money for initiatives such as increasing pay, building a new canteen to facilitate social interaction, or sending people on training courses to improve skills (and therefore help facilitate promotion) is not actually forthcoming, all of the proclamations about 'valuing employees and their contribution to the organisation' will sound rather hollow.

It needs to be appreciated that the original research of many of the best-known theorists was 50 or more years ago. Since then others have built on their work and have added much to the literature of motivation and management. Changes in society, employees' expectations, the way organisations are managed, and the way research is conducted – using modern psychological questioning techniques – can make the original research look very dated, but this does not mean that the original conclusions were necessarily 'wrong'. Many of the basic principles underlying the motivation of employees are likely still to be true.

Tips and techniques

While it is important to know and understand the different motivation theories, simply quoting them will not access the highest levels of the mark scheme. You need to evaluate which one (or ones) will be most appropriate for the business in the case study. You can do this through considering the practical implications of implementing it. For example, who will initiate the strategic changes necessary? What timescale will be appropriate? What are the likely resource implications? This will be a more fruitful approach than just quoting the nature of the original research or saying 'they should use Maslow'.

Further sources

http://www.accel-team.com/motivation: a useful site that looks at motivation in theory and in practice. It deals with all of the major theorists.

http://ozgurzan.com/management/management-theories/theories-about-motivation: a site that combines information on the interrelated topics of management, leadership and motivation.

www.tompeterscompany.com: the website of Tom Peters. Information on what his management consultancy and training firm can offer to the modern business.

Your turn

Questions in red are for A Level candidates only.

Multiple-choice questions

1 Goal setting is typically associated with the work of:
   A Drucker and Locke
   B Maslow and Herzberg
   C Taylor and Vroom
   D Tom Peters *(1)*

2 According to Vroom, Force (motivation) is a function of:
   A Expectancy, valence and likelihood
   B Expectancy, reward and valence
   C Expectancy, reward and instrumentality
   D Expectancy, valance and instrumentality *(1)*

3 Making sure that a job is interesting and fulfilling would be an example of:
   A Job design
   B Job enlargement
   C Job enrichment
   D Job satisfaction *(1)*

4 According to McClelland, employees have three needs:
   A Achievement needs, affiliation needs and power needs
   B Basic needs, social needs and higher needs

C Empowerment needs, creative needs and psychological needs

D Financial needs, hygiene needs and motivational needs (1)

Revision questions

1 State the difference between 'motivation' and 'morale'. (2)

2 Explain the difference between content theories of motivation and process theories of motivation. (4)

3 Outline what is meant by the following terms:

A 'Taylorism' (3)

B 'Hierachy of needs' (3)

C 'Knowledge worker' (3)

D 'Hygiene factors' (3)

E 'Three needs theory' (3)

F 'Expectancy theory' (3)

G 'Excellence theory' (3)

Total (27)

Case study

Weightmans Solicitors: wellbeing is the key to keeping employees motivated

Free massages, office chiropody and a company fruit budget may sound frivolous, but it makes sound business sense to look after employee health and wellbeing. Healthy employees are happier and that impacts positively on motivation and labour turnover. Some companies offer health screening programmes as a way of discovering a problem that might otherwise lead to long-term sickness. Other services that may be on offer include physiotherapy, massage and flu vaccinations.

Free flu vaccinations are one health benefit offered by law firm Weightmans, which is a Limited Liability Partnership that operates in different locations across the UK. It offers a very wide range of legal services including Commercial law, Employment law and Maritime law.

The firm's employees also benefit from health and wellness initiatives such as office yoga and pilates classes and discounted gym memberships. Informed by feedback from its staff forum, the firm organises themed wellness activities covering areas such as heart health, cancer awareness and smoking cessation.

'Stress has been high on the agenda over the past 18 months,' says Sue Gould head of HR at Weightmans.

> We provide training on resilience, stress and wellbeing and we actively work to prevent stress. Where needed, we might arrange private therapy through our medical insurer or the Employee Assistance Programme. It's all about keeping people engaged with us. We've got to make sure they're happy and looking after themselves.

The Weightmans website states:

> We know you want to work for a firm where teamwork and respect matters. We know you value the type of commercial approach that leads to an enviable reputation. We know you demand clear decision making and a commitment to constant improvement. We know you want to work for a company that promotes equal opportunities and diversity. We know we deliver all this and more. But we don't expect you to take our word for it. Committed to reaching our full potential, we've worked hard to create a culture that motivates and supports all our employees to reach theirs.

1 Goal setting for employees is likely to occur in a firm of solicitors such as Weightmans.
   A Analyse one benefit to Weightmans of goal setting. *(4)*
   B Analyse one principle that will be important when an employee is being set a goal to achieve at Weightmans. *(4)*
2. Assume that an employee at Weightmans has been asked to undertake a particular legal case. The employee has a valence of 0.8 and an expectancy of 0.9. They have been promised a reward by their line manager if it is completed satisfactorily and there is no reason to doubt that promise. Calculate the force that will be expended in the task they have been asked to undertake. *(3)*
3 Evaluate the reasons why, as a business, Weightmans might choose to be actively concerned with its employees' wellbeing. *(9)*
4 Evaluate the methods that could be used to maintain a high level of motivation at Weightmans. *(15)*

Total *(35)*

Chapter 48

Employer/employee relations: trade unions and consultation

AS / Year 1

Both AS and A Level students must know all of the content in this chapter.

Change is a fact of business life, and positive employer–employee relations (the relationship between management and employees at national or local level) are a significant factor that will help facilitate this successful change. Employer/employee relations are also known as 'industrial relations' or 'employment relations'.

The process of change is easier in a climate where managers and employees work together with mutual trust and a willingness to compromise and co-operate. Consultation is an important part of the management of change and it is often conducted through a trade union. No manager can be truly effective in helping the business to meet its objectives if there is no consultation with the workforce.

Nature and recent history of trade unions

Many businesses have employees who are members of one or more trade unions. In order to achieve successful change, it is important for a business to communicate and negotiate with the union(s) involved.

A trade union is an organisation of employees that seeks to protect and improve the interests of its members. It does this by negotiating with employers on pay and conditions of work. Members of a union pay a subscription, usually every month. In return, as well as the union negotiating for better pay and conditions, members are entitled to all sorts of support, assistance and benefits. These include free legal advice on redundancy, harassment, dismissal and pensions, as well as special deals on non-work-related matters such as insurance, travel agency services and so on. Unions are built on a basic premise – 'unity is strength'; an organised group of workers acting together has a better chance of improving their working life than an individual acting on his or her own.

Key term

Trade union: an organisation of employees that seeks to protect and improve the interests of its members. It does this by negotiating with employers on pay and conditions of work.

At national level, unions have full-time salaried employees working at a permanent headquarters. The governing body is called the union executive. At local level (i.e. the workplace), the union representatives (sometimes called 'shop stewards') are elected from the workforce in that business. This person is by law allowed 'reasonable' time off work to take part in trade union activities.

'Unity is strength'

Unions in the UK enjoyed the most power in the 1970s. Many trade unions are affiliated to (i.e. are members of) the Trade Union Congress (TUC). This is an organisation that brings Britain's unions together to draw up common policies and lobby the government to implement policies that will benefit employees. In the 1970s the leaders of the most powerful unions in the TUC were so important that they were regularly invited for 'tea and talks' with the Prime Minister to discuss economic issues.

Key term

Trade Union Congress (TUC): an organisation that brings Britain's unions together to draw up common policies and lobby the government to implement policies that will benefit employees.

The coal miners' strike brought down the Conservative government of Prime Minister Ted Heath in 1974. However, this change of government did not mean that the unions were particularly sympathetic to the Labour government which came into power afterwards. This government was also to suffer at the hands of the unions during the so-called 'winter of discontent' of 1978. Union after union went on strike for higher pay with vast disruption to the public and businesses.

However, such attitudes and influence could not last; the unions' behaviour was not acceptable in a democracy. The incoming Conservative government in 1979 pledged to curb union power through legislation. It did so and union behaviour was severely constrained, especially over matters relating to strikes. A union now has to give notice of its intention to strike and offer its members a secret ballot regarding the decision to strike, otherwise it is breach of the law. This change in the legislation brought about a major change in employer/employee relations.

Trade unionism today

The UK has followed a similar path in terms of trade union membership to other European countries. Thirty years ago around half of the workforce was unionised; now it is around 27 per cent. Fewer than 6 million employees now belong to a union. There is a distinct difference between the level of unionisation in the public and private sectors. In the former it averages around 50 per cent and in the latter around 15 per cent. Younger, male manual workers are especially unlikely to join a union; the decline in the old 'heavy' industries, the rise of part-time working and self-employment have contributed to this, as has the growth of zero hours contracts.

Like many a product in decline, the majority of unions have rebranded themselves and no longer present an image of always being ready to start a conflict with management.

There is not always harmony and agreement between unions and management, as unions still exist to protect their members' rights; but most union leaders and indeed the TUC today are very different from their counterparts of the 1970s. The TUC now promotes a partnership which it defines as 'employers and trade unions working together to achieve common goals such as fairness and competitiveness'.

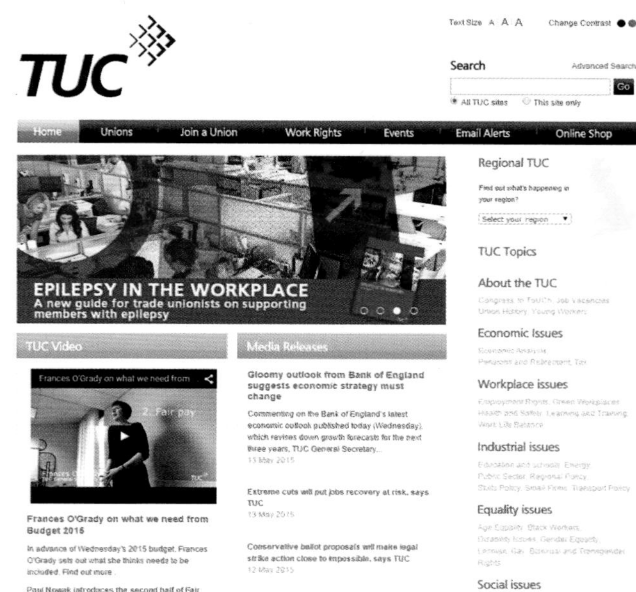

The TUC's website (www.tuc.org.uk) offers advice to union members and news of current campaigns

To help achieve this, it urges businesses to recognise unions. Employers that recognise a union will negotiate with it over members' pay and conditions. This negotiation is known as 'collective bargaining'. Union recognition may increase costs in the short run but result in benefits in the longer term. On the other hand, if both union representatives and managers are antagonistic towards one another, there may be very few benefits to either group whatever the timeframe.

Key term

Union recognition: employers who recognise a union agree to negotiate with it over members' pay and conditions.

One significant change from 'the old attitude' was that during the difficult years following the financial collapse in 2009, far from following the stereotypical 'we refuse to accept any job losses' stance, many union representatives were often conciliatory rather than aggressive; they recognised the fact that their business was struggling, wanted to ensure its survival. They helped to find ways to avoid redundancies by persuading members to reduce the number of hours worked in order to keep their jobs.

'No-strike' deals

Another change in trade union activity has been the use of the 'no strike deal'. This is where a union gives up the right to strike. Some unions are in favour of signing such an agreement on that the grounds that it might encourage a business to recognise a union when it would otherwise be hostile to the idea of doing so. Others are against it, saying that it undermines a very basic trade union principle.

Apart from recognition, a union signing any such deal would normally expect several benefits in return; for example, regular communication, a system of employee participation and consultation, a commitment from managers to agree to regular workforce training, and so on. Finally, it would seek an agreement to go to some form of arbitration in wage settlements if there is a dispute.

In the UK, the police and companies such as Nissan and Toyota are among those organisations to have such a deal in place. In 2014 following the privatisation of Royal Mail, the Communication Workers Union (CWU) signed up to measures designed to prevent local strikes, which have affected Royal Mail for years, in return for a five-year guarantee of job security, pensions and increased union involvement in the running of the business.

The advantages to managers seem to be self-evident; employees cannot withdraw their labour and so should be at work unless on holiday or ill. However, even if employees cannot strike, this in itself cannot guarantee good employer/employee relations; employee discontent could easily manifest itself in some other way such as, for example, through a work to rule, absenteeism or poor timekeeping.

Key term

Work to rule: employees do exactly what is stated in their contract and no more; there is no 'goodwill' towards the employer.

Confederation of British Industry

The counterpart of the TUC is the Confederation of British Industry (CBI), the employers' organisation. The CBI provides information to its members and lobbies the government on policy issues that directly affect business. Relations between the TUC and the CBI can still become rather strained but are usually much more friendly and constructive than they were in the 1970s.

Employee participation

Employee participation is also known as 'industrial democracy'. If it is accepted that consultation with employees is necessary for effective change management, several questions arise.

1. When will any consultation take place and who with?
2. How many employees will be involved?
3. From which sections of the factory/office will they be drawn?
4. How will they be chosen?
5. When will the meetings be held?
6. Who will 'cover' for the employees while they are being consulted?
7. Also, if the business operates a bonus scheme, how will their bonus be affected by 'absence' due to being involved in the consultation process?

One obvious way for employee participation to occur would be with the union representatives. If the union is recognised and the collective bargaining process already established, the arrangements for the timing of the meetings, the pay issues and the personnel involved may already be established. The scope of meetings would be extended beyond simply 'bargaining' and would involve consultation and participation in decision making.

If there is no trade union then managers may want to consider recognising one. Indeed, as so much rests on the sincerity of the consultation process when implementing change, it would be difficult for managers to claim to be truly interested in consultation and then refuse to accept a union's existence!

Key term

Employee participation: Employees have the ability to participate in the decision making process at work.

Benefits to a business of employee participation

Participation indicates a willingness to engage in discussions with employees and treat them as stakeholders. This can mean:

- Increased levels of motivation: If employees feel that their view counts, they may become more motivated. This may cause productivity to rise. It can also lead to a greater acceptance of decisions, since employees have been part of the decision making process and understand what the business is trying to achieve.
- Better communication: Participation should mean better communication between managers and employees. Even if the business has a clear set of objectives and a strategy to achieve them, this cannot guarantee success. The commitment of employees will play a major part in whether the strategy succeeds or fails. Participation can improve trust, lead to agreed goals and improve that commitment.
- Improved quality of decision making: Managers do not and cannot 'know it all'. Employees often complain that senior managers have little idea of what goes on at 'the sharp end'. They know from direct experience where the real problems lie and whether these are technical, financial or procedural. Such information would be very useful to managers, especially when planning for change. Therefore management decision making on issues such as training is improved.
- Complying with the law: Consultation is now a legal requirement for many issues (e.g. redundancy) and for certain types of business. Non-compliance would be a breach of the law and would be likely to attract bad publicity. This may affect the business's ability to recruit.

The factors above can impact positively on productivity and costs and so, if these benefits actually do occur, they will assist the business in reaching its objectives. The strategic benefits of participation could therefore include:

- reduced labour turnover and therefore reduced recruitment costs
- fewer days lost through work-related injuries and illnesses, thus minimising lost output, fines and compensation payouts
- the ability to manage change more effectively, thus giving the business a competitive advantage in a changing environment.

Other than extending the scope of collective bargaining, there are other ways of allowing employee participation.

Quality circles

These are regular short meetings of a group of employees during working hours. The objective is to discuss and resolve work-related problems. Through quality circles, managers can gain a much greater awareness of employees' problems and concerns.

Works councils

A works council is a formal meeting of managers and employees in a particular factory (or the business as a whole) to discuss pay and working conditions or grievances, and negotiate on issues such as changes in working practices.

The works council model (also known as a consultative committee) for participation and consultation has existed among some firms in the UK for many years, and in 1994 it became a legal requirement from an EU Directive. It applies to any company with 1,000 or more employees, including at least 150 employees in two or more EU member states. European Works Councils (EWCs) give employees the right to information and consultation on their company's decisions.

Consultation was defined as 'the exchange of views and establishment of dialogue between employees' representatives and management'. It was hoped that EWCs would deal with a large range of issues (such as the business's impact on the community within which it operates, and the wider environment) but this was not always the case and so the Directive was amended in 2009.

It strengthened the role and rights of EWCs in a number of areas. It:

- more clearly defines the information and consultation rights of EWCs
- gives a greater role to trade unions
- entitles EWC members to training without loss of pay.

Although by law only these multinationals are required to have a works council, any business not covered by the criteria could still adopt the model.

Key term

Works council: a formal meeting of managers and employee representatives to discuss pay and working conditions and to negotiate on issues such as changes in working practices. There is a legal requirement for large multinational companies operating in the EU to set up a European Works Council.

Employees as shareholders

The owners of a company's ordinary shares are entitled to vote at the Annual General Meeting on the basis of one vote per share. If employees are encouraged to buy shares in their company, or are given them as a bonus or a reward for long service, it could be argued that this ability to vote is a form of participation.

However, the meeting is by definition annual, and so the opportunity to participate is restricted. Furthermore, if employees own a modest number of shares (such as 500) and there are millions of other shares, they may feel that their 'voice', even if joined by several hundred other employees, will not be heard since they can easily be outvoted.

This is not to say that employees owning shares in the company for which they work is not valuable. It may assist with motivation (see **Chapter 47**) but, as a method of participation in decision making, its value is rather limited.

Tips and techniques

If you think that employee participation would be beneficial to a business, you need to think carefully about the nature of the business before reaching any judgement on the form it should take. What is the culture of the business like? What about size? Is the business small with no formal employee representation? Or is it a large multinational with recognised unions? What resources are available for the consultation process? These sorts of issues will be crucial to your analysis and recommendations.

Consultation in action

It would be naïve to assume that if a consultation process such as one of the above exists it will automatically lead to harmonious employer/employee relations. Much will depend on:

- Whether or not the consultation is genuine, i.e. employees' views are actually listened to as part of the culture of the business. The Advisory, Conciliation and Arbitration Service (ACAS) website states: 'Making a pretence of consulting on issues that have already been decided is unproductive and engenders suspicion and mistrust about the process among staff'.
- If the process of consultation is driven from 'the top': if junior managers see that senior managers are not really interested or concerned with genuine consultation, those junior managers will not devote much time and effort to it either.
- Employees accepting that their views will not always be accepted and acted upon. There may be very good reasons for managers not doing so. They also have to accept that they will be involved in decisions that have previously been 'management territory'. Some of these decisions will be difficult, especially in matters such as redundancy.
- Whether either side tries to score points off the other, and in a 'workers versus management' confrontation.

Costs to a business of recognising a union

Recognising a union might be a logical way to start the process of employee participation. However, union representatives will press for better wages and conditions for their members, and decision making in the business will be slower, but it is to be hoped that better decisions (i.e. ones which have a measure of agreement and support from all parties) will be made. There will have to be a trade-off between the need to reach a consensus and the speed with which some business decisions are made. This is likely to increase costs and reduce the business's profits, at least in the short term. This could mean a reduction in the benefits that other stakeholders in the firm gain such as a fall in dividends for shareholders, a rise in price for customers, or worse terms being imposed on a supplier. Only if the gains to the employees result in greater productivity and profitability in the long term will recognition be beneficial to all stakeholders.

There is, however, no substitute for good employer/employee relations if managers want to have a productive, committed workforce that will accept change readily. In addition, there are certain principles that will be useful when unions and managers are negotiating and/or bargaining:

- Meetings should be at a convenient time to both parties.
- The personnel attending the meeting should be agreed in advance.
- Both parties should be allowed to submit agenda items for discussion – along with some information/data/figures concerning their current bargaining position.
- The chairman of the meeting must ensure that all agenda items are raised and that no one party dominates the meeting.
- A written statement at the end of the meeting on what (if anything) has been agreed is good practice.

Both parties should be prepared to compromise. Perhaps a union wants a 5 per cent rise in pay and management offers 3 per cent. They could both settle for 4 per cent. Where the bargaining is over changes in working practices rather than pay rises, it will be best for each side to set out clearly its objectives in an open manner in order to identify some common ground and so move forward more quickly.

Industrial action

Instead of negotiation and bargaining there is another way in which the union might affect the achievement of a business's objectives. 'Industrial action' refers to the measures that can be taken by a union to put pressure on management over a decision that has been made or is about to be made. Managers are aware that those workers in a union are better placed to do this than an individual employee would be. Failure to resolve a dispute could therefore result in the following:

Strike action

This will severely disrupt the fulfilment of the business's contracts with customers, and, as such, is a powerful weapon. However, employees who take strike action face financial consequences. As they are not working they are in breach of their contract, although if the strike is legal (see **Chapter 49**) they cannot be dismissed for this. Naturally, they will not receive any pay and they are not entitled to any social security benefits while on strike. Any pension contributions due to be made by the employer will not be made for the period on strike.

Work to rule

This can be very effective since employees working to rule are not acting illegally, but are simply doing exactly what is stipulated in their contract of employment; they will start and stop work at exactly the stated time with no 'goodwill' (i.e. a few minutes extra) worked at all.

Refusal to work overtime

If overtime is a normal part of completing the work, a refusal to work any hours in excess of those in the contract can be quite effective, as it can impact on the business's ability to meet customer requirements.

Key term

Industrial action: the measures that a union can take to put pressure on management in a dispute in order to make them change their mind about a decision.

ACAS

The main way to avoid conflict between management and employees is for unions and managers to follow ACAS guidelines. ACAS stands for Advisory, Conciliation and Arbitration Service. It gives advice on industrial relations to employees and managers, offers them a service of conciliation (i.e. mediation – trying to reconcile two different positions and persuade one party to see the other's view), and finally (if both parties agree) it will provide arbitration; an independent ACAS assessor will decide between two conflicting claims who is right.

ACAS is funded by the government, which ensures that it is independent. Its website states:

> *Our aim is to improve organisations and working life through better employment relations. We provide up-to-date information, independent advice, and high quality training. We work with employers and employees to solve organisations' problems and disputes and improve performance.*

ACAS can provide guidelines for those managers who want to set up an effective system of industrial relations with employees (with or without a union).

The website has up-to-date, accessible information and impartial guidelines covering every aspect of workplace life; from appraisal to age discrimination, from recruitment to redundancy.

ACAS also has codes of practice in key areas of industrial relations, for example on dealing with dismissal. These give authoritative advice to which employment tribunals refer. There is a 'helpline' which gives access to an advisor for immediate guidance.

Advice

ACAS is, however, not a kind of emergency service that can be contacted and expected to solve the problem in a matter of hours. Their regional offices are not drop-in centres for angry employees and managers. The first step is for either the employee(s) or employer to call the ACAS helpline, where they can speak to someone who can give general advice and refer the party to the relevant guidelines. The information in the guidelines can then be presented to the other party. This may help to resolve the dispute since advice has been offered by the organisation best placed to do so.

Key term

ACAS: the Advisory, Conciliation and Arbitration Service. It gives impartial advice and guidance on how to improve employer/employee relations.

Mediation

If this does not succeed, ACAS offers mediation, which is a way of sorting out disagreements or disputes without having to go to court. A member of ACAS will work with those in disagreement to help them sort out their problems. Initially, this will be carried out by phone and by considering any relevant documentation. Later on, the mediator will bring both parties together in a meeting and, once in possession of all the facts and opinions, will seek to persuade them to reach an agreement that will sort out their problems and be agreeable to both. The emphasis is on the two sides reaching a settlement by themselves but, if both sides ask, the mediator can recommend a way forward (this is not legally binding on either side, however). The ACAS website states:

> *[T]he aim is to maintain the employment relationship if at all possible and so mediation is about the future, not the past and who was right or wrong.*

This process has to be voluntary; if a union suggests mediation but the employer does not want to participate, that is the end of the matter. Both parties must willingly have ACAS involvement. If not, the dispute will then either end or escalate – possibly to a tribunal. Both of these will result in bad feeling and therefore have a detrimental effect on the business.

Arbitration

If mediation fails, then that is the end of the matter unless both parties wish ACAS to arbitrate. Arbitration is final and binding, and is usually only available for serious matters such as unfair dismissal or flexible working disputes. Arbitration is a judgement as to which party is in the wrong and, as such, is distinct from mediation. It is sometimes called 'pendulum arbitration' because there must be a distinct judgement; the arbitrator cannot find both parties right or wrong. Those who agree to arbitration need to understand that it is an alternative to going to an industrial tribunal (a special court for hearing matters of employment law) and so if the judgement goes against them, they cannot go back to court.

Hearings usually last less than a day, and the arbitrator will base their judgements and any awards made on the same criteria as a tribunal. In a typical year, three out of four cases referred to an employment tribunal never arrive there, and this is largely because of ACAS's help.

If employees and managers want to work in harmony and avoid disputes, they should try to abide by the ACAS guidelines and codes. The ACAS helpline (and guidance from the website) is free, as is conciliation which is often conducted over the telephone. ACAS do however charge for mediation and training services.

Further sources

www.acas.org.uk: the ACAS website. The mother-lode of employer/employee relations information in the UK. Very informative and extremely easy to navigate. It includes clips that can be watched to illustrate the issues.

www.gov.uk/government/organisations/department-for-business-innovation-skills: The Department for Business Innovation and Skills provides information on government policy and assistance available for businesses on these matters.

www.cbi.org.uk: the Confederation of British Industry. The CBI is 'the employers' organisation' ('the voice of business'). It provides information to its members and lobbies the government on policy issues that directly affect business. Useful for up-to-date responses to government policy and trade union proposals.

www.tuc.org.uk: the TUC's website. Lots of up-to-date information on the TUC itself, an employee's rights at work, labour law, the economy, etc.

www.unitetheunion.org: Unite is the largest trade union in the UK. Its website is very comprehensive and offers news of its current campaigns and its benefits for members.

Your turn

Questions are suitable for all AS and A Level candidates.

Multiple-choice questions

1 The basic premise of trade unionism is:
   - A 'Fight for the right to work'
   - B 'Power to the people'
   - C 'Unity is strength'
   - D 'Workers of the word unite' *(1)*

2 'ACAS' stands for:
   - A Advisory, Conciliation and Action Service
   - B Advisory, Complaints and Arbitration Service
   - C Advisory, Conciliation and Arbitration Service
   - D Allied, Conciliation and Arbitration Service *(1)*

3 A large plc wants to introduce a system of employee participation. Which of the following is least likely to be an effective method of participation?
   - A Establishing a works council
   - B Giving employees a small allocation of company shares
   - C Recognising and bargaining with the employees' trade union
   - D The use of quality circles *(1)*

4 Which of the following is not a form of industrial action?
   - A A 'go slow'
   - B A lockout
   - C An overtime ban
   - D A work to rule *(1)*

Revision questions

1 State what is meant by 'employer/employee relations'. *(1)*

2 Outline two possible benefits to a business of good employer/employee relations. *(4)*

3 Outline two costs of poor employer/employee relations on a business. *(4)*

4 Outline two likely reasons for a dispute between employees and management. *(4)*

5 Explain what is meant by 'industrial action'. *(2)*

6 Outline two examples of industrial action that employees might take. *(4)*

7 Outline two functions of ACAS. *(4)*

Total *(23)*

Chapter 49

Employer/employee relations: employment law

AS / Year 1 | Year 2

A Level students must know all of the content in this chapter.

AS students need to cover all of the content except:
- Employment tribunals (page 358)

All businesses have to keep up with changes in employees' rights. The reason why a business needs to be aware of changes in employment law issues is put very well on the hrzone website:

> *Human resource management is bound by a fast-paced legislative environment, sensitive to external events and political pressures. Employment law exists around all aspects of the HR function; staying up-to-date and making this felt throughout the business allows leaders and employees to perform their jobs confidently. It also establishes faith in senior leadership and the company's ethics, with the associated engagement and productivity benefits. Knowing the law and knowing its practical effect on the business are two different things; HR decision-makers must have a comprehensive knowledge of both.*
>
> Source: www.hrzone.com/employment-law

Employment law

Tips and techniques

You need to have a working knowledge and understanding of employment law, but it is also very important to be able to recognise the implications of the legislation to the business that features in the examination question. This approach will help to score higher marks.

Going to court to settle a dispute between an employee and an employer creates a winner and a loser. This does not make for harmonious employer–employee relations once the case is concluded. For this reason, the government funds ACAS, the independent organisation dedicated to improving employer–employee relations (see **Chapter 48**).

There are a very large number of laws governing the treatment of employees. It is no defence in law for employers to claim ignorance of a particular piece of legislation, or that they thought that the Act did not apply to them. It is essential for a business to keep up to date with any new legislation, and indeed changes to existing laws if they want good relations with employees and to avoid prosecution.

Employment law can be broadly divided into three sections:

1 Laws relating to the recruitment process
2 Laws relating to employees in the workplace
3 Laws relating to the termination of employment.

A common legal theme running through all of these three areas is the prevention of discrimination. Discrimination occurs when an employer treats a person less favourably than another employee without any justification.

Discrimination is illegal, and over the years a number of pieces of legislation have been passed to help prevent it such as the Equal Pay Act (1970), the Sex Discrimination Act (1975), the Race Discrimination Act (1976) and the Disability Discrimination Act (1995).

The Equality Act of 2010 was an important milestone in this process because it replaced all the previous anti-discrimination laws with a single Act, making the law easier to understand and apply. The Equality Act protects people at work from discrimination and its principles apply to the wider society as well (for example, how a firm treats disabled customers). Basically the Act sets out the different ways in which it is unlawful to treat someone. It is against the law to discriminate against anyone because of:

- age
- being married or in a civil partnership
- being pregnant or having a child
- disability
- race, including colour, ethnic or national origin
- religion
- sex
- sexual orientation.

In the Act these are referred to as 'protected characteristics'. The Act protects employees against discrimination in a wide variety of circumstances, for example:

- recruitment
- promotion
- employment terms and conditions
- pay and benefits
- training
- redundancy.

Law relating to recruitment

It should be clear from the above that any advertisement for a post must not state, or even imply, that the business will discriminate against a potential employee. Care has to be taken with questions at the interview. An interviewer must not ask someone about any of the protected characteristics.

There are some exceptions to the Act, for example, in a nursing home where a carer is required for females needing help with dressing or bathing. This firm could advertise for a female attendant without contravening the Act. Also, in some jobs 'full mobility' is required such as the police force or fire service.

The Act makes clear that a business should make 'reasonable adjustments' to help those job applicants who have disabilities by, for example, making application forms available in Braille and allowing extra time for certain types of aptitude test.

The Act also applies in terms of access to facilities and services. The 'reasonable adjustments' also apply to the way in which a business's products and services are delivered so that disabled people can use them. The adjustments can be physical, for example changes to the actual building such as ramps and handrails, or procedural, such as always having a member of staff available to help a disabled person.

The implications of the Equality Act for a business regarding access to facilities and services are as follows:

- There needs to be a clear policy on how services are to be provided to disabled people.
- This policy needs to be clearly communicated to all staff.
- The policy needs to be reviewed and monitored. The Act makes it clear that it is not a 'one-off' but a continuing duty on a business.

Law relating to employees at work

A contract of employment is an agreement between a business and an employee, under which each of them has certain obligations. ACAS states that:

- As soon as someone accepts a job, a contract comes into existence.
- Starting work proves that the employee has accepted the terms and conditions offered.
- A contract does not need to be in writing; it could be oral or implied, although a written contract is better.

The implied terms of a contract are those that are so obvious they do not need to be explicitly agreed; for example, duties on employers to pay wages and take reasonable care of employees. In return, employees must 'render service' (work properly) and obey lawful and reasonable instructions.

Most employees are legally entitled to a 'Written Statement of Employment'.

This is a document setting out the main aspects of a person's employment. The sort of information in a statement would be: the hours of work (including overtime or shift work), pay, sickness entitlement, pension scheme details and the period of notice required. It is not in itself a contract, although it will cover most of the particulars in the contract.

The existence of a contract and the written statement of employment mean that both the business and the employee are clear about their rights and responsibilities.

The Health and Safety at Work Act 1974 (HSWA)

As well as duties at work, there is a vast amount of law relating to employee rights. One of the most important is the right to a healthy and safe working environment. An employee's health, safety and welfare at work are protected by law. The 1974 Act was a very important piece of legislation, which has since been amended and extended to take account of new issues and hazards such as repetitive strain injury or possible damage to the eyes from working at computer screens. Furthermore, since 1993 all employers have been required to make estimates of workplace health and safety risks and to take the steps to manage and minimise them.

Not only do businesses have 'a duty to take reasonable care' of employees, but criminal law lays down minimum safety requirements. There is a positive obligation to create a safe and healthy working environment; breaches of the law can lead to criminal prosecution as well as civil proceedings for compensation.

The provisions of this Act relate to:

- the place of work
- the system of work
- the working environment
- any machinery used
- the use and storage of substances
- employees.

The implications are that a business must:

- ensure that the building is safe: entry to it and exit from it must be safe
- co-ordinate the whole system of work so that it is safe
- ensure that the temperature in the working environment is within certain limits; the atmosphere must be safe to breathe, the floors must be safe to walk on, etc.
- fit guards onto machinery to prevent accidents; employees must be provided with the correct safety equipment (and clothing), and trained to use it
- provide training in any hazards associated with the work, e.g. the lifting of loads and the handling of substances; a business that failed to provide any training 'because it was common sense for an employee not to lift a heavy load' would not have a legal defence if the employee became injured
- have a written safety policy which states who is responsible for safety issues; this policy must be clearly communicated to employees.

The HSWA also places a duty on employees to comply with the legal provisions regarding health and safety. All employees must:

- take reasonable care of their own health and safety and of others who could be affected by their actions
- comply with lawful instructions relating to safety matters; an employee who was trained and told to use lifting equipment could not try to sue the business for an injury to his back if he ignored the instructions
- not interfere or misuse anything provided for health and safety purposes; e.g. letting off a fire extinguisher for malicious purposes or 'in fun' is a serious matter, for which an employee can be summarily dismissed (i.e. dismissed 'on the spot').

The Act says that a business must comply 'so far as is reasonably practicable'. A business may dispute that it can comply with every single part of the Act, saying that the expense is not reasonably practicable. If an accident occurred and the business was prosecuted then the court would decide whether it was reasonably practicable or not.

The law requires employees to comply with safety rules

There are two other organisations that operate in conjunction with the law:

Health and Safety Commission (HSC)

The organisation responsible for health and safety in the UK is the Health and Safety Commission. The HSC's role is to protect people's health and safety by ensuring that risk in the workplace is properly controlled, to conduct research, promote training and provide an information service on health and safety issues.

Health and Safety Executive (HSE)

The Health and Safety Executive and local government are the enforcing authorities that work in support of the Commission. The HSE is responsible to the HSC for the regulation of risks to health and safety in organisations such as nuclear installations, factories, farms, hospitals and schools, gas and oil installations, and the movement of dangerous goods and substances. Local authorities are responsible to HSC for enforcement in offices, shops and other parts of the services sector.

If an employee feels that there is a health and safety issue, he or she should first discuss it with his or her manager, possibly involving their trade union or safety representative if one exists. If the issue is not resolved, the HSE can be contacted for advice on the law. The HSE has the power to ensure that the law is complied with, and if a breach of the Act is serious enough or there is repeated disregard for it, the HSE can close a business down. Needless to say, this is very much a last resort.

Equal pay and equality policies

The 2010 Equality Act reasserted that women and men are entitled to be paid equal amounts for work of equal value. The same reasoning applies to the provision of any benefits such as private health care or a company car.

ACAS strongly suggest that all businesses have an equality policy to ensure fair and consistent treatment of all employees – and not just over pay. Managers should ensure that all employees are aware of this policy and its implications; that is, it is unlawful for someone to be discriminated, bullied or harassed on the grounds of sex, race, sexual orientation, and so on, and that disciplinary action will follow if they engage in any such behaviour. Employees should know about the business's procedures and whom to approach if they think they are not being treated in accordance with the policy. ACAS stresses that the policy needs to be reviewed and monitored constantly. The Equality Act makes it clear that this is a continuing duty on a business.

Key term

Equality policy: a policy to ensure fair and consistent treatment of all employees so that they are not discriminated against, bullied or harassed on the grounds of sex, race, sexual orientation, and so on. Managers should ensure that all employees are aware of this policy and its implications.

The Minimum Wage Act 1999

This Act lays down the minimum level of pay to which employees aged 18 years and over in the UK are entitled. It does not matter if an employee is in part-time or full-time employment.

If employees are paid on a piece rate (a certain amount for each item produced), the business has to ensure that the system of work enables enough items to be made for the employee to earn at least the minimum wage. The idea is not only to guarantee a certain level of wages but to ensure a 'level playing field'; that is, all businesses compete on the basis of quality of products, efficiency and customer service rather than low wages. Employers who treat and pay their employees well cannot now be undercut by others whose low prices are based on low rates of pay. The minimum wage is increased every year.

Maternity/paternity provision: the Work and Families Act 2006

Maternity leave was already a legal right and this Act enshrined the right to paternity leave in law. The Act also introduced rights to paid leave for parents adopting children, and the right for parents of young children to apply to work flexibly. These rights aim to give parents greater opportunities to balance work and family life.

In 2015 employees became legally entitled to new maternity and paternity rights – 'shared parental leave'. The objective is to encourage firms recruiting women of child-bearing age. Fathers will also get a new right to unpaid leave to attend up to two antenatal appointments. Parents will be able to share 12 months of leave after the birth of a child. A couple will have to give their employers an indication of how they intend to share their leave eight weeks before it starts.

Nick Clegg, the Deputy Prime Minister at the time, said that employers will benefit from a more motivated workforce as a result. This could be true, but it is likely to cause administrative issues for a firm that will want to plan ahead for 'who is off work and when' and will need to keep a clear record of this. These administrative issues will particularly affect a smaller business. There have been complaints that although large businesses might be able to cope with the cost and managing the absences, smaller businesses may not be able to do so very easily.

The Data Protection Act 1984 (updated 1988 and 2003)

Even if a business is complying with the law in all of the above matters, it may still fall foul of the law if it fails to keep its employee records properly.

Any business will need to keep all sorts of employment-related records on its employees, but it is not allowed to disclose this information to other individuals within the business or another organisation. The Act is designed to prevent harm resulting from the misuse of any data that is held. Information about an employee's sickness or disciplinary record for example could easily be misused – particularly if the information (e.g. about a criminal conviction that is now 'spent') had become outdated. The Act tries to balance the need for a business to process essential information with the individual's right to privacy.

The Act was updated in 1988 and again in 2003. The law now covers all systems of data storage whether 'paper-based' or electronic. It also now applies to any data on the business's customers.

All users of personal data must register with the Data Protection Registrar. A business making this registration must detail the nature of the data and the purposes for which it is held, as well as a list of the parties to whom the data may be made available. It is a criminal offence to hold unregistered data, and breaches of the following principles can also lead to prosecution:

- Data must only be kept for the specified purposes.
- Individuals are entitled to reasonable access to any data relating to them.
- Data can only be passed to a third party with the consent of the individual concerned.

There are several implications of this Act for a business:

- There is a clear legal obligation to protect the security of any data on an employee.
- In the past, much of the data held by a business used to be kept in filing cabinets that were only accessible by senior members of staff. When data is on a computer it could potentially be viewed, altered and passed on easily (often without leaving a clearly identifiable trace), and so it is important that safeguards are in place.
- There are training implications on the management and security of data and therefore a cost implication because of this.

Social media

In recent years the actions of employees in the social media has received attention. Employees need to be made aware that, for example, if they send any tweets 'that could be viewed as acting in the course of their employment' that criticise a competitor, this could lead to legal action against the business for defamation. Whether an employee was actually 'acting in the course of their employment' and 'how badly another firm has been defamed' are legal matters that could potentially cost a huge amount in legal fees. There needs to be a clear policy in place in relation to how employees conduct themselves in the social media.

'Whistle blowing'

If an employee has evidence, or 'reasonably believes', that malpractice in an organisation is occurring (and it is in the public interest that it should be disclosed) he or she can bring it to the attention of someone in authority at the business without fear of retribution. This is known as 'whistle blowing', although officially it is known as 'making a disclosure in the public interest'.

In essence, an employee will be eligible for protection against dismissal or victimisation if they honestly think what they are reporting is true and they think they are telling the right person about any of the following (either that it is happening, has taken place, or is likely to happen in the future):

- someone's health and safety is in danger
- damage to the environment
- a criminal offence
- the company is not obeying the law (e.g. not insuring its vehicles)
- someone is covering up these sorts of wrongdoing.

Grievances

A grievance exists when an employee has a concern, complaint or problem. It may, for example, relate to their terms and conditions, discrimination, bullying, or the relationship with a colleague or a manager. Grievances are always best dealt with at an early stage, informally, with the employee's immediate line manager – perhaps by 'a quiet word' with those involved. However, by law all employers must have a written grievance procedure to be followed formally if the grievance cannot be resolved informally. Employees need to be made aware of this. The procedure should indicate:

- whom to contact in the first instance
- a statement that if the matter cannot be resolved informally, there will be a meeting called a formal grievance hearing; the statement should also indicate that an employee can be accompanied in a meeting by a union representative or a colleague if they wish

- how the employee can appeal against a decision
- the time limits for each stage of the procedure.

A grievance procedure is important because grievances can escalate and become very unpleasant. This will affect productivity and morale. If managers are not seen to deal with a grievance quickly and impartially it can impact negatively on employer–employee relations.

European Union (EU) laws

Finally, it needs to be recognised that some laws affecting UK businesses have come from the EU. The EU's Social Charter is a charter of rights for employees concerning areas such as working conditions, wages and consultation of the workforce. UK businesses have to adhere to these EU laws just as if they had originated from the UK Parliament. There are two types of EU law:

1. Regulations: these must be adopted and applied in a certain way.
2. Directives: these must also be applied as law, but it is up to the individual member country to decide how to implement them.

Working Time Directive

This EU Directive is an example of law coming from the EU. It became part of UK law in 1998 (and updated in 2003 to cover a wider range of employees such as junior doctors). It states that a business must not allow an employee to work more than 48 hours per week on average. The Directive is partly aimed at reducing the UK's culture of long working hours. There are also provisions relating to an employee's entitlement to rest breaks and the pattern of shifts that can be worked. An employee can sign away their legal rights to these if they wish, but if a business dismissed a person for a refusal to do so, this would constitute unfair dismissal. Some employees (such as the police) are exempt from the Directive.

Key term

EU Regulations and Directives: legislation emanating from the European Parliament. Regulations have to be adopted and applied in a certain way, whereas it is up to the individual member country to decide how to implement a Directive.

Law relating to termination of employment

This is potentially a very difficult area of employment law, and businesses have to be careful to avoid legal complications when terminating employment. Termination could occur through redundancy or dismissal. It is important to be clear about the difference.

Redundancy

An employee is not made redundant because he or she has done anything wrong. Redundancy arises from a situation where the job that used to be performed no longer exists and so the employee is surplus to requirements. This might arise because a particular job is mechanised or where a section or all of a factory or office is closed down. Employees who are made redundant are entitled by law to a redundancy payment, which varies according to how long they have worked for the business. It is of course open to a business to pay them more than this.

The ACAS guidelines for selecting employees for redundancy state that a business:

> *... should be using objective criteria wherever possible, precisely defined and capable of being applied in an independent way. This is to ensure that employees are not selected unfairly. The chosen criteria (e.g. skills, experience, standard of work) should be consistently applied. There should also be an appeals procedure.*
>
> Source: ACAS website.

A business might ask its workforce for 'voluntary redundancies', that is, employees can put themselves forward to leave. Sometimes a monetary incentive in excess of the statutory amount to be paid is offered. To qualify, an employee must have two years of continuous service with the business. The amount is based on a certain multiple of weekly pay and the number of years' service. Where employees take voluntary redundancy (or early retirement) this can avoid conflict since it reduces the number of compulsory redundancies.

Key term

Unfair dismissal: where an employee is dismissed without a valid reason or the employer fails to follow the proper procedures.

Dismissal

There are different types of dismissal but the one most commonly brought before an employment tribunal is unfair dismissal. A dismissal has to be justified and must be fair if it is to be legal. Employees who have been employed for a minimum of one year have the right not to be unfairly dismissed. Summary (i.e. 'on the spot') dismissal is only 'fair' in two instances:

- gross misconduct, e.g. an employee physically assaulting a customer
- gross negligence (a reckless or wilful disregard for the safety of others), e.g. a manager at a theme park allows a ride to remain open when he knows that a safety fault exists.

Other types of dismissal that can be justified as fair are:

- repeated poor conduct such as lateness or failing to comply with reasonable requests (to perform tasks) from a manager
- incapacity, e.g. being too ill to work at all or taking time off work when genuinely ill on a regular basis
- capability: repeated inability to do the work required, or a major incident such as losing the business a very valuable customer
- redundancy: if the employee's job no longer exists and there is no work to do
- 'some other substantial reason': a tribunal would look at each case on an individual basis.

If one of these is the reason for the dismissal, then it will normally be fair as long as the employer has acted 'reasonably'. This means that the employer has not summarily dismissed the employee but has followed appropriate disciplinary procedures.

For any disciplinary related dismissal, the employer should follow the ACAS guidelines. A failure to follow the ACAS guidelines does not automatically mean that the dismissal was wrong, but it will weaken the employer's case at the tribunal. Summary dismissal is not appropriate in the overwhelming majority of cases. The guidelines state that there are certain stages to be followed if the dismissal is to be fair and legal:

- The manager should give at least one verbal warning to the employee.
- This should be followed by at least one written warning.
- There should then be a final written warning. By law an employee has to receive all allegations in writing, and attend a formal meeting to discuss the issues. It would be normal practice to allow a trade union representative or a friend to accompany an employee in to such a meeting.
- There also has to be an appeals process. It must be made clear to the employee how to appeal and to whom.

There are two other types of dismissal: wrongful dismissal and constructive dismissal. Either of these can proceed to a tribunal, although constructive dismissal can sometimes be hard to prove.

Wrongful dismissal

This occurs where there has been a breach of the employment contract. What is 'wrongful' will therefore vary according to the terms of the individual contract. For example, an employee who is entitled to eight weeks' notice of termination of employment but is only given four weeks' notice would be wrongfully dismissed.

Constructive dismissal

This happens when the behaviour of a manager or managers forces an employee to leave the job. This could result for example from bullying, or changing the conditions of employment without consent; for example, forcing the employee to work at weekends when their contract states 'Monday to Friday'.

Employment tribunals

Alleged breaches of employment law are heard in an employment tribunal. A tribunal is a special sort of court which deals with employees' claims for matters such as unfair dismissal, discrimination or victimisation by their employer. Employment tribunal hearings usually take place before a legally qualified chairman and two 'ordinary' members, one nominated by the employer and one by the employee.

A tribunal is less formal than a criminal court, and almost all hearings are open to the public. A very large number of cases are settled before they ever reach the tribunal. Since 2014 anyone intending to make a claim at an employment tribunal has to notify ACAS first. This is in order to try and stop the matter escalating in an acrimonious and possibly expensive manner. ACAS will work impartially with both sides to try to settle the issue. This is known as Early Conciliation.

If the tribunal rules in favour of the employee, it will order the business to make a payment to the employee to compensate for what has occurred. There are 'caps' (i.e. limits) on what can be awarded, except in cases of discrimination when it is unlimited.

Key terms

Employment tribunal: a special sort of court dealing only with employment law; for example, an employee's claim for unfair dismissal, discrimination or victimisation by their employer.

Termination of employment: an employee's contract of employment is ended due to redundancy (the job no longer exists) or dismissal (the job ends due to poor conduct, incapacity, etc.).

Rights of part-time employees

Part-time employees now have the same statutory employment rights as other employees. Until 1999, part-time employees had to work for three years continuously for the same business before they were entitled to any employment protection; as opposed to full-time employees who only had to work for 12 months. This meant that part-time staff were easier to discriminate against in matters such as pay, holiday entitlement and redundancy rights. The adoption of the EU Directive on part-time rights at work now means that part-time employees who have been employed for a year are entitled to exactly the same legal rights as those in full-time employment.

Trade unions and the law

Trade unions are bound by the law just as businesses are. The Employment Acts of the 1980s represented a major change in the way in which unions could operate. Until then, a union representative at a plant could call a 'mass meeting' at a few minutes' notice and decide on a show of raised hands whether or not to call a strike. There were no secret ballots. These 'wildcat' strikes were very disruptive to businesses. Also, unions could legally have large numbers of members picketing (i.e. blocking) the entrance to the place of work which prevented goods entering or leaving. Until the 1980s it was also legal for one union to strike 'in sympathy' with another. This meant that the coal miners might themselves go on strike 'in sympathy' with the railway workers' pay claim, even though this pay dispute was nothing to do with them.

The changes to the law were effective:

1 A union must now ensure that all members can vote in secret if it wants to call a strike

   Union members can no longer be intimidated into voting for a strike at a public meeting held on the spur of the moment. The union must send the ballot papers to its members by post and must not interfere with the balloting process. Majority support must be obtained in response to a clearly asked question on the voting paper, which asks if members are prepared to take part in (or continue with) strike action. Secret ballots also apply to other union matters such as the election of executive members.

2 'Sympathetic' strikes and sympathetic picketing are against the law

   The legal status of a union has changed. A union can now be fined in a criminal court for calling a strike without a ballot, and it can also be sued for damages in a civil court by a business if that business loses out as a result of the illegal action. If the miners' union now took sympathetic strike action on behalf of another union, it could be sued for damages.

3 Picketing is legal but must be 'peaceful'

   The police can restrict the number of pickets if they think it is necessary to prevent a breach of the peace.

The Employment Acts were labelled 'anti-union' by some groups, while others merely saw them as a necessary step to redress the balance between employers and employees. There have been further pieces of legislation since the 1980s which have continued the process of reforming the rights of businesses, employees and their unions. Some of this has weakened union power and some has strengthened it.

The Trade Union Reform and Employment Act 1993 introduced new procedures which a union must follow before industrial action can lawfully be called, including giving advance notice to the business. This weakened union power. Other legislation has strengthened it. An Act passed the previous year in 1992, The Trade Union and Labour Relations (Consolidation) Act, forbids an employer from refusing to employ someone or treating them unfairly because of trade union membership or participation in trade union activities – or conversely because they refuse to join a trade union. Also if a business employs more than 20 people and has a union then that union has a right to be 'recognised', that is, the firm acknowledges its existence and negotiates with it. If the business refuses to recognise it then the union involved may apply to the courts for legal recognition under the Employment Relations Act 1999. To achieve statutory recognition, the union has to demonstrate that more than 50 per cent of the workers in the business are members of the union.

Further sources

www.adviceguide.org.uk/wales/work_w/work_rights_at_work: a straightforward guide to your rights at work.

www.acas.org.uk/index: guidelines on employer–employee relations and information updates on coming changes in employment law.

www.gov.uk/equality-act-2010-guidance: a guide to the rights of employees and the responsibilities of an employer in matters relating to equality.

www.gov.uk/data-protection/the-data-protection-act: the requirements of the Act, How to find out what data an organisation holds on you and how to make a complaint.

Your turn

Questions in red are for A Level candidates only.

Multiple-choice questions

1 Which of the following statements best describes an employment tribunal?
- A a special sort of court dealing only with employment law
- B the place where employers are fined for a breach of employment law
- C a court that considers cases of employee discrimination
- D a court that rules on breaches of an employee's conditions of work and service *(1)*

2 Which of the following would not be grounds for a summary dismissal?
- A being drunk at work
- B deliberate breach of a health and safety provision
- C rudeness to a customer
- D starting a fight with another employee. *(1)*

3 Which of the following would not be found in a contract of employment?
- A the rate of pay
- B sickness entitlement
- C promotion opportunities
- D pension arrangements. *(1)*

4 EU Regulations from the European Parliament:
- A are temporary measures which exist until the full EU Directive is published
- B are voluntary
- C can be varied by an individual member state's parliament
- D have to be applied in a prescribed way. *(1)*

Revision questions

1 Outline two effects of the Equality Act 2010 on a business. *(4)*

2 State two reasons why a business should have an equality policy. *(2)*

3 State two ways by which a business could make its employees aware of an equality policy. *(2)*

4 What is meant by the term 'a contract of employment'. *(2)*

5 Identify two issues that are likely to be included in a contract of employment. *(2)*

6 Explain what is meant by the term 'dismissal' *(2)*

7 Explain what is meant by the term 'redundancy'. *(2)*

8 State what is meant by the term 'unfair dismissal'. *(1)*

9 State what is meant by the term 'wrongful dismissal'. *(1)*

10 Explain the purpose of an employment tribunal. *(1)*

11 Outline two ways in which the Employment Acts of the 1980s weakened trade unions. *(4)*

Total *(23)*

Case study

Grangemouth – Back to the 70s?

For a while in the autumn of 2013 it seemed as if the industrial relations typical of the 1970s were back. The dispute at the Grangemouth oil refinery in Scotland had all the hallmarks of a classic 'union versus management' dispute. The owner of the plant, Ineos, is the largest private company in the UK and the union taking the industrial action, Unite, is the largest trade union.

Management at the plant had for some time been trying to make the cost reductions it claimed were necessary to keep the plant open. It claimed the plant was losing £10 million a month. This cost-cutting was fiercely resisted by the union. There was a huge amount of bad feeling, with one Ineos executive having to call the police after demonstrators surrounded his house, leaving him fearful for his family; to which the union retorted 'bad employers should have nowhere to hide'. For their part, the union claimed that management had adopted bullying tactics by imposing cost cutting, rather than negotiating properly, and then shutting the plant down when it threatened a strike in response, as it was legally entitled to do. Both the union and Ineos agreed to meet with members of ACAS in mid-October.

The dispute ended fairly soon after the shutdown. It seemed as if, with unemployment high in that part of Scotland and little prospect of a similar job, many employees had little appetite for any prolonged industrial action. If the petrochemical plant had shut it would have cost 800 jobs. When the dispute ended Ineos announced that, following the union's agreement to its demands, it would now be investing £300 million at Grangemouth.

The dispute was ill-tempered, but was it a return to the 1970s and early 80s? No, it was not. The media certainly showed some angry and bitter people but not any images of mounted police charging rows of pickets. Most telling, however, was the way the dispute concluded. The union accepted a no-strike deal, a three-year pay freeze, a change to the employees' pension arrangements, as well as a change to the consultation procedure between itself and the management. In the 1970s, managers would never have believed this could be possible. Some newspapers used the phrase 'union humiliation' and perhaps it was. Others said the union had 'taken a responsible attitude'. There are always two sides to every industrial dispute and its resolution.

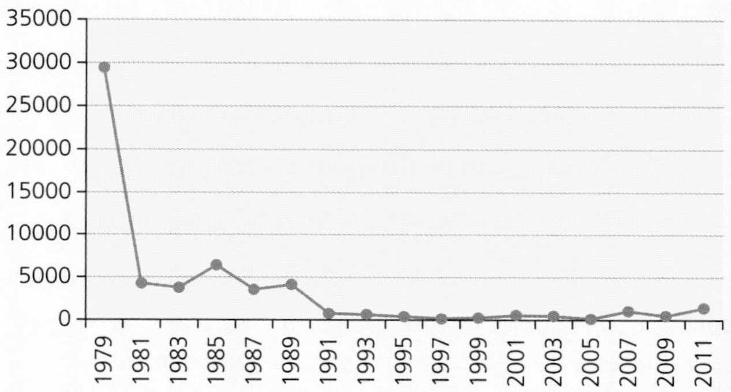

Figure 49.1 Working days lost (thousands) in the UK to industrial disputes.

Source: ONS.

1a State what is meant by 'a trade union'. *(2)*

1b Analyse one cost to Ineos of recognising the trade union Unite. *(6)*

2a Refer to Figure 49.1. Calculate the percentage fall in the number of disputes between 1979 and 1989. *(4)*

2b Explain two costs to Ineos of the dispute with Unite. *(4)*

3 Evaluate the contribution that ACAS might be able to make in solving the Grangemouth dispute. *(15)*

4 Evaluate the impact of Ineos complying with employment legislation at the Grangemouth refinery. *(15)*

Total *(46)*

Chapter 50

Marketing within a business environment

AS / Year 1 | Year 2

A Level students must know all of the content in this chapter.

AS students only need to cover:

- Marketing resources including SWOT analysis (starting on pages 366–367)

Marketing objectives

In any business it is important to take into account the situation within the market, the needs of the consumer and the action of competitors. Setting market objectives is vital to ensure that all of these factors are taken into account in the application of the marketing mix. For example, a business such as Unilever might want to introduce a new range of skin products. Before doing this, it will need to identify its target market and undertake some initial market research to investigate it. The business will want to set out its objectives for any marketing activity at this point.

These objectives may be:

- a certain level of sales
- to increase market share
- to reach a particular segment of the population.

This analysis of the market should help Unilever in the production of the product range and its subsequent marketing to consumers. Knowledge of the market, the consumer and the competition will help to show the best ways to price and promote the product when it is launched.

Setting objectives

This will involve asking and answering a series of questions about the present and the future of the business. One of the main uses of setting objectives is to help employees identify the marketing strategy for the business. The plan will help to explain necessary actions, set a budget and identify goals that are to be met. In small firms, the marketing plan may often be a series of discussions among the staff; in larger businesses the marketing plan will need to be a more formal document that can be viewed by all concerned.

The marketing plan will need to answer these questions:

1. Where are we now?
2. Where do we want to be?
3. How will we get there?

Where are we now?

This is sometimes called a marketing audit. To answer this question the business will need to look at the internal and external factors that affect it. This will involve doing a SWOT analysis (see below). The strengths and weaknesses are internal factors that are within the business control; the opportunities and threats are external factors that are likely to be outside the business's control. There are economic, social, political and technological factors, as well as the actions of competitors. This audit will analyse the product portfolio in the current business climate, ensuring that the business matches its product range to the needs of the consumer.

Where do we want to be?

The answer to this question will involve setting objectives for the future. This might be a strategic objective for the whole business, such as growth or diversification, or it could be a marketing objective, such as increasing market share or becoming market leader.

How will we get there?

To answer this question, a strategy for the future of the business needs to be developed. For example, the business could set itself an objective of becoming market leader. This will then require the use of the marketing mix (see **Chapter 54**) to formulate a strategy by which this might be achieved within a particular timeframe.

Advantages and disadvantages of setting objectives

Advantages

1 The exercise of setting marketing objectives helps the business to identify what it hopes to achieve through any spending on marketing. Marketing planning and marketing are both costly exercises. Too often a business will spend money in these areas without having a clear idea of what it hopes to achieve.
2 Setting clear marketing objectives as a result of planning is a good way of motivating workers and setting targets for goals like market share, market growth or market leadership.
3 Marketing planning helps the business to rank projects so that money can be targeted and used where it will be most effective in improving performance from marketing spending.
4 A marketing plan should make it possible for the business to assess performance against expectations. Businesses can often undertake promotional campaigns with no clear idea of a result in terms of improved sales, for example. Marketing planning, if used correctly, should help to avoid this.

Disadvantages

1 Marketing planning may look at every aspect of marketing, except the consumer. Businesses need to remember that the consumer is vital to success in any plan.
2 Marketing departments need to ensure that their plans include other departments in the firm. There is no point in having a promotional drive to increase sales if the production department has not been involved in the planning. Marketing departments cannot operate in isolation.
3 The marketing objectives need to be specific, clear and focused rather than vague or wide-ranging. The objectives should involve a limited number of goals and concentrate on specific targets.
4 The objectives must also take the external situation into account. A business selling luxury holidays is unlikely to achieve a large growth in sales from a new promotion at a time of economic recession.

Tips and techniques

It is important to remember that the market and the economy change very rapidly. Businesses need to be prepared to adapt policies to changes in the market. The most successful firms are those that identify and predict changes and are prepared to adapt their policies to the changes.

Assessing success

Once the objectives have been formulated, and marketing strategy has been put into operation, the business needs to measure its success. Marketing work is completed in order to achieve a goal such as increasing sales; it is important for the business to evaluate its success in achieving the goal. For example, a business might undertake an advertising campaign in order to launch a new product with a view to taking 5 per cent of the market within six months of the launch. Throughout the six months the business should monitor the situation to see if the target is likely to be achieved. If sales are slower than expected, it may be possible to switch the advertising to a different media or time so that it is more effective in increasing demand.

Tips and techniques

A marketing strategy is the use of some or all of the four Ps (Product, Price, Place and Promotion, see **Chapters 54–57**) to achieve a final objective. It is a good idea to always start with the 4 Ps when suggesting a marketing strategy.

The business can use any of the following measures to assess the success of putting a marketing plan into operation.

Sales

The business can look at the increase in sales generated by implementing the marketing plan. So, for example, a business might wish to achieve a particular rate of return on the amount spent on an advertising campaign. This type of analysis is probably the most commonly used. However, it is important to look at sales in the context of the wider picture of the total market, and whether the total market is rising or falling. Viking River Cruises spend large amounts on sponsorship of television dramas. They will want to be sure that this expense is justified by increased sales and recognition of the name.

Key term

Market share: the proportion or percentage of total sales within the market in question that is controlled by the business.

Market share

For some businesses, the market share they control is as important as the level of sales. These businesses will monitor the effect of the marketing campaign on their share of the market. This may be the case for supermarkets, which are interested in their share of the market compared with competitors. Aldi and Lidl have had to use different sorts of marketing to achieve brand recognition as they have expanded in the UK.

Number of enquiries/hits

Internet and mail-order businesses will be particularly interested in the number of enquiries generated by a marketing campaign. For example, following a new advertising campaign, a car insurance company will be able to monitor success by looking at the number of requests for quotes that it receives.

Satisfaction surveys

These will involve sampling a selection of customers to see if they are happy with the good or service. Satisfaction surveys are frequently undertaken by banks, building societies and travel firms. They can be done by telephone or post but, increasingly they are being done on the internet when the customer logs on to the site of the business.

Marketing strategy

Strategic planning is a vital element of the marketing process. To be able to develop and use a marketing strategy effectively, the business must have an in-depth knowledge of its market, its competition and its consumers. The process of market planning is the first part in the process of formulating a marketing strategy. The business will need to prepare a review of its current internal and external performance using a SWOT analysis (see **page 366**). Alongside this the business will need to look at the budget that is available and the productive capacity. Marketing cannot be carried out in isolation from the production and financial departments of the business.

Once all these things have been done, the business will then be ready to put a marketing strategy in place, taking account of the following factors:

Tips and techniques

Always make sure that your suggested strategy is appropriate for the size and nature of the business that you are considering.

1. Business objectives: If the business wants to increase market share, it will need to look closely at the needs of the consumer and the actions of competitors.
2. Size of the business: Small businesses may find it difficult to market aggressively, particularly if they face competition from large businesses with more money in their marketing budgets.
3. Nature of the market: Businesses in markets like mobile phones and games consoles, such as Apple and Samsung, will need to change their strategy frequently to take account of new products and to respond to threats from competitors and the rapid changes in technology in the sector.
4. Management changes: New management in a business will often mean new ideas about marketing. New managers will usually be more willing to take risks in an effort to show that their appointment has been successful for the business.

Competitive strategies

The twenty-first century has seen a huge increase in the level of competition faced by businesses of all sizes. Much of this is as a result of the globalisation of world trade. Today, most businesses compete in markets with producers from all over the world, so it is vitally important for each business to develop a marketing strategy that takes account of these competitors.

Key term

Globalisation: the integration of the countries of the world through trade, ideas and culture.

In these circumstances, the first thing that the business needs to do is to identify the competition and investigate all aspects of competing businesses. It will usually be easy to identify competitors in the same line of business, but many businesses face competition from outside their own specific segment of the market. For example, a theme park like Alton Towers might be in competition for its visitors with a stately home like Chatsworth House or Warwick Castle, an attraction like Chester Zoo or even a visit to a shopping mall. All of these businesses are in the leisure market, trying to attract the same consumers.

Once the competition is identified, it is then necessary to look at all aspects of the way such a business is operating. For example:

1 How does it market itself?
2 Who are its customers?
3 What are its strengths and weaknesses?
4 What are its objectives for the future?
5 How well is it placed to succeed compared with us?

Having investigated the competition, a business can then start to develop strategies for competing within the market. This strategy may be confined to one product or range within the business; it may be a range of strategies for different parts of the business; it may also be directed to increasing profit or market share, or to allowing the business to grow.

Market-leader strategies

The majority of markets have one dominant business that has control over the largest share of the market. Market leaders use a variety of strategies to retain that position and improve on it in the long term. They may try to improve their market share by the use of aggressive marketing, or they may try to achieve market growth and at the same time improve their market share. Tesco is an example of a business that has used all these tactics to achieve and maintain its market dominance. For example, Tesco has moved into many new areas of activity, like banking and insurance; at the same time, it has tried to ensure that it has at least one retail outlet in every postcode area of the UK to give it as wide a market coverage as possible.

Market-challenger strategies

In this situation, a business with a smaller market share may try to attack the dominance of the market leader. In order to be able to do this, the business will need a substantial marketing budget at its disposal. The attack may be made directly by trying to take market share through the use of promotion. More commonly, however, the challenge will be made in an area where the dominant firm is relatively weak.

Market-follower strategies

Market leaders will normally respond to 'market challenger' strategies with some form of retaliatory action. For example, if one supermarket starts a cut-price campaign, others are likely to follow and the market leader will be well-placed to cut prices most aggressively to win the price war. In many ways this is a 'no-win' situation. All that happens is that profit for all competitors is reduced. As a consequence, many businesses are happy to follow the market leader in whatever actions it takes. For example, the market follower may introduce new products or services to match those of the market leader.

Niche market strategies

Niche markets are small corners of a bigger market where businesses may choose to specialise. The market segments are usually quite small and customers have very specific demands. The Morgan car company operates in a niche market, selling handmade touring sports cars.

The sports car market is a niche market

Differentiation

Companies in many areas of the economy will try to differentiate their product from that of their competitors, to try to attract business. For example, the National Westminster Bank (NatWest) uses advertising to inform consumers that it operates a 24-hour call centre within the UK and that many of its branches are open on Saturday mornings. This sets it apart from its main competitors.

Low cost strategies

Some large firms may try to maintain their dominance in the market through their ability to buy in bulk from suppliers at low cost per unit. This reduces their production costs, making it possible for them to pass these savings on to the consumer in terms of lower prices. Smaller businesses will be unable to match these prices because they will not have the power to command such low prices from their suppliers. For example, Tesco buys electrical goods in such a large volume from suppliers that it is able to offer the consumer huge discounts.

Market growth policies

If the firm wants to use its objectives and a marketing strategy to achieve growth in its markets, there are four options open to it. These are market penetration, product development, market development and diversification. The use of the marketing mix in these situations is explained by Ansoff's Matrix (see **Chapter 11**).

Once the business has decided on its marketing strategy, its performance needs to be monitored and reviewed at regular intervals. The market situation will be changing constantly; businesses cannot afford to set policies in place and then leave them to run; nor should marketing strategies be left to operate without ongoing assessment of their effectiveness. Unfortunately, the market is subject to constant change, some of which can be anticipated and some which cannot. Marketing strategies will always be operating in a climate of uncertainty. Businesses must be prepared to change or adapt their objectives in the light of changes in the market. It might be that a new competitor enters the market or that the economy takes a downturn. Objectives must always be realistic and attainable if they are to be of any use to the business.

Marketing resources

In order to market a product or service the business will need the following resources:

- marketing budget
- marketing department or, for a small firm, someone with responsibility for the marketing function
- knowledge of the market in which the business operates, usually obtained through some form of market research
- set of objectives to be achieved through marketing set out in a marketing plan or strategy.

In setting out a marketing strategy, one of the most important requirements is that the business should be realistic, particularly with regard to the amount of money it spends. Small firms will only usually be able to market through the use of local advertising; flyers, local media and publicity are the most likely methods of promotion. Only large businesses can afford to run large marketing departments and make use of national and international media for promotion. Small firms may be able to adjust their good or service to meet the demands of their market, but they are likely to have less pricing flexibility than larger businesses.

Tips and techniques

Make sure that any strategy you suggest is possible and feasible in relation to the size of the business.

SWOT analysis

Key term

SWOT analysis: involves looking at the strengths, weaknesses, opportunities and threats for a business.

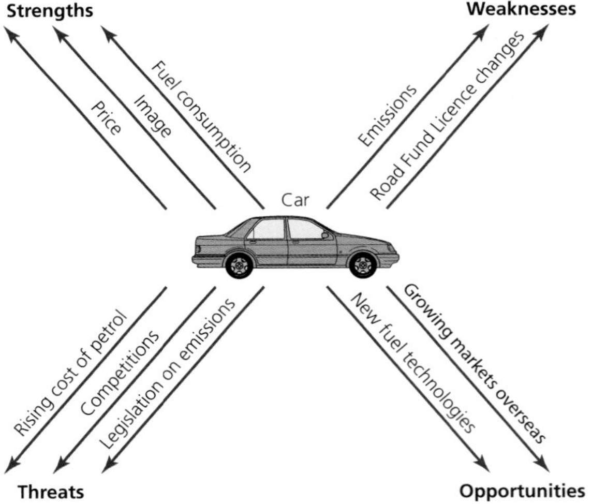

Figure 50.2 SWOT analysis of a car

Any business making a decision about its future strategy needs to consider the business situation, both internally and externally. A SWOT analysis can help the business to look objectively at its competitive situation and to decide on the best strategy for the future. SWOT stands for:

- Strengths
- Weaknesses
- Opportunities
- Threats.

The strengths and weaknesses of the business are internal factors, whereas the opportunities and threats will be part of the external market in which the business is trading. For example, for a large business like Unilever, one of its main strengths is likely to be the well-known brand names it produces such as Persil and Comfort. A possible weakness may be that the customer starts to view these brands as old and out of date if Unilever does not continually relaunch the products in different packaging or with new properties. Opportunities for a global company like Unilever will lie in the newly developing areas of the world economy. The threat of competition in this oligopolistic market (see **Chapter 13**) is very high, and is likely to influence much of the company's strategic planning.

Uses of SWOT analysis

A SWOT analysis can be carried out by an individual department within a business or by a business as a whole. For example, a marketing department might assess the current market conditions and the quality of its current marketing strategies. These can then be considered in relation to the future. What might happen? How might the competition react? What is happening in the wider market?

The whole analysis can be used as a forward-looking tool. The managers can consider how effective the business is in respect of the environment in which it operates, and adjust their strategies and tactics as appropriate (see **Chapter 7**).

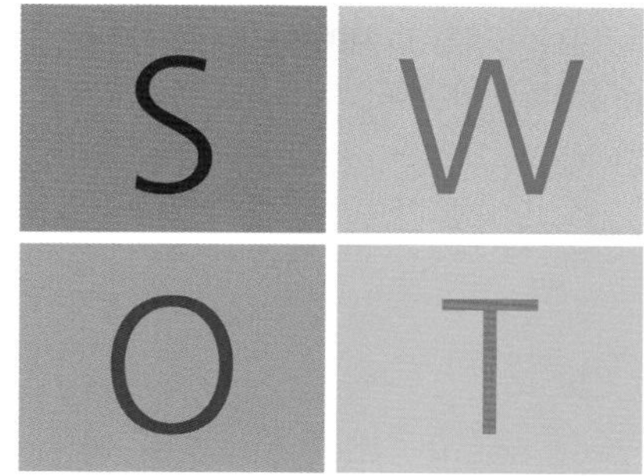

Figure 50.3 SWOT grid

Any business beginning a strategic planning process for the future will probably begin by completing a SWOT analysis. The analysis will be a useful beginning to discussion and planning, and will help the business to identify the best way to proceed for future success, but it will need to be used in conjunction with other methods of forecasting and formulating strategies, not as an exercise in itself.

Further sources

www.marketingsegmentation.co.uk
www.marketingweek.co.uk
www.marketingdonut.co.uk

Your turn

Questions in red are for A Level candidates only.

Multiple-choice questions

1 A business allocates 2.5% of its turnover of £3 million to the marketing budget. How much is the marketing budget?

A £7,500
B £50,000
C £75,000
D £5000 *(1 mark)*

2 A business anticipates that it will increase its sales from 6,000 units a week to 6,500 units a week as a result of its new marketing strategy. What is the percentage increase in sales?

A 8.3%
B 12%
C 0.8%
D 1.2% *(1 mark)*

3 Which of these elements of a SWOT analysis are internal to the firm?

A strengths and threats
B weaknesses and opportunities
C strengths and weaknesses
D opportunities and threats *(1 mark)*

Revision questions

1 Explain the meaning of a niche market. *(2)*

2 State two ways a business can measure the success of a marketing initiative. *(2)*

3 Explain is the difference between 'market share' and 'market growth'? *(4)*

4 Define the term 'globalisation'. *(2)*

Total *(10)*

Case study

Bespoke Beauty Clinic

Karen and Paul Bowen opened their business, Bespoke Beauty Clinic, in the West Midlands in 2007. In 2010, during the UK recession, they made the decision to expand the business and move to bigger premises. At that point, Karen was responsible for the beauty treatment in the business and Paul was responsible for the day-to-day management.

From the outset, the decision had been made to operate at the top end of the market. Although Bespoke offers manicures and tanning, the bulk of its business comes from treatments like facials, peels, radio frequency treatments and electronic lifting treatments. Karen's training and experience are in these areas of beauty therapy. The business has grown rapidly in the past four years, taking on four therapists, allowing Karen to concentrate more on promoting the business in the local area. For the past three years the salon has won a national award as one of the ten 'most inspirational salons in the country'.

Karen and Paul had to think very carefully about how to market their business, especially as they were located in an area where they were unlikely to benefit from passing trade; therefore word-of-mouth recommendation was going to be important. However, they had to think of other ways to make themselves known. The business's marketing budget was not large and the local economy was suffering from high rates of unemployment.

Karen used her expertise to write articles for local magazines, like *Staffordshire Life*, which have their circulation among people who are likely to spend money on beauty treatments. A decision was also made to spend a large proportion of the budget on advertising on local independent radio. As a result of advertising on Signal Radio, Karen was given a slot on the radio company's breakfast show to talk about treatments that are available, while giving her business publicity. She is often invited in to contribute to the breakfast show at the radio station. The coverage achieved by Signal Radio in the local area is 304,000 listeners from a population of 794,000, which has helped considerably in the rapid expansion of the business.

1 Analyse two factors that Karen and Paul had to take into account when setting the marketing budget. *(4)*

2 The total population of Signal Radio's coverage area is 794,000 and it is listened to by 304,000 people. Calculate Signal's market share. *(2)*

3 Evaluate the benefits to Bespoke Beauty of the type of marketing strategy it uses. *(15)*

Total *(21)*

Chapter 51

Identifying customer needs: Market research

AS / Year 1

Both AS and A Level students must know all of the content in this chapter.

Market research

Keeping up with the pace of change, not only in the general economy, but also within any given market, requires a constant updating of the information that a business collects.

Most businesses want to ensure that they are well informed on what is happening in the market for their particular products or services. In addition, they want to know about anything that may affect their particular markets, both at the present time and in the future. In order to achieve this, market research is essential.

Market research is a systematic, objective collection and analysis of data about a particular target market. It always involves some form of data collection, whether primary or secondary (see below). Market research concentrates on recognising a consumer need and exploring how best to satisfy that need.

The purpose of any market research project is to achieve an increased understanding of the subject matter. With markets throughout the world becoming increasingly more competitive and complex, market research is now essential for most organisations, large or small. Knowing the market may help a business keep in touch with market trends and therefore avoid being left behind by competitors.

Market research is undertaken in order to:

- describe the market
- explain the market
- predict changes in the market
- investigate the reaction of consumers in the future.

Describing the market

The business must be able to identify the customers or consumers. This information can be used to ensure that customers are targeted in an appropriate manner. If the market is for young female clothes, then advertising can be positioned carefully in order to reach the target market.

Identifying trends within the market is also vital. If sales are declining, it may be appropriate to increase the marketing budget to counter the fall in sales. Alternatively, sales may be in permanent decline and therefore an alternative product may be required. The business may be advised not to join a market with a declining trend; equally, if there is an upward trend, the business may be well advised to join the market. Regardless of which strategy is adopted, knowing the trends is essential.

The market also refers to the actual market share. Information about the percentage of the market which a business holds is valuable, as it can help a business to decide what it ought to do next. The business can attempt to increase or maintain its market share.

Explaining the market

The business must understand why changes in the market have taken place and, more importantly, why one particular business has increased or decreased its market share.

It is also important to identify the reasons for the success or failure of a change in the marketing strategy of a business. Did the recent changes in prices or sales promotion work? Did the consumers see the adverts on the television? Market research can answer such questions. In the magazine *Marketing*, a weekly analysis is made of consumers' ability to recall particular adverts.

Market research makes it possible to find out why consumers prefer to purchase one brand as opposed to another. Lego has recently introduced a new range of models aimed at girls after research showed that girls often showed little interest in traditional Lego models. The result has been a rapid increase in sales worldwide.

Businesses need to know whether there are differences in consumer reactions on a regional basis:

- The Loyalty Management Group (which operates the Nectar card) has an online research tool for some of its clients such as Sainsbury's, Nestle and Unilever.
- Boots the Chemist holds a vast amount of data about its customers through its very successful loyalty card. It is particularly important to know the customer's age and gender, but they also have a special scheme for the mothers of babies and young children. This allows them to target different sectors of the market with special offers and vouchers.

Predicting the market

Knowing how consumers will react to changes in the prices of products provides a valuable insight which can then be exploited. Supermarkets, in particular, will benefit from this information. Reducing the prices of certain key products and promoting this may draw customers into the store and then encourage customer loyalty for the future.

Research can be used to highlight the consequences of introducing a new model. After launching the new, partly electric Range Rover in 2013, the business would have wanted to know how it was regarded by potential customers and whether they thought that the £100,000 price tag made it a good buy.

If competitors introduce new products or reduce prices, research is helpful in gauging the reaction of its existing customers. Have they been tempted to switch to the competitors' brand, will they do so in the future and, if so, why?

Being aware of changes in lifestyles is also significantly important. Marketing departments in many businesses have taken notice of the trend for a healthier lifestyle, and have responded to a market in which consumers are aware of the latest health issues surrounding sugar, salt, e-numbers, chocolate, wine, low-fat foods and the need for exercise.

Market research process

In order to conduct market research, businesses may decide to undertake the project themselves (perhaps by using a marketing research department) or they may choose to hire a market research agency or consultancy. Regardless of which approach is taken, it is crucial to define the research objectives before undertaking any research project, listing what the business needs to find out.

Once the objectives of the research have been established, the researchers can use many types of research techniques and methodologies to find the required information. The research collected will either be quantitative or qualitative information. Which type of information is used and what order it is collected (if both are used) depends on the research objectives. It is generally accepted that results are most useful when the two methods are combined.

Quantitative research

This type of research is regarded as being objective as it involves the collection of facts. It concentrates on what consumers actually purchase or use, such as how many consumers eat cereals.

Quantitative research concentrates on numerical data. It requires significant attention to the measurement of market trends and often involves statistical analysis. For example, a hotel might collect data on the number of people taking holidays in the area in which the hotel is located. This will provide quantitative information that can be analysed statistically.

The main rule with quantitative research is that every respondent is asked the same series of questions. The approach is very structured and normally involves large numbers of interviews, questionnaires, or simply looking at records.

Quantitative research is often used initially to establish the trends within a particular market. Undertaking this type of research can help the business to decide whether it is worthwhile continuing with a more detailed level of research, which may involve qualitative research.

Often quantitative research will be seen as secondary research. Market research surveys are a popular method of collecting quantitative data. These quantitative surveys can be conducted face to face (in-street or in-home), by using post, telephone, email or the internet, or using past records and journals. The questionnaire is one of the more common methods for collecting data from a survey, but it is only one of a wide-ranging set of tools.

Tips and techniques

Use primary research where opinions are sought and secondary data that concentrates on numbers and trends.

Qualitative research

This type of research is often regarded as being subjective because opinions are sought. Qualitative research provides an understanding of how or why things are as they are. For example, a market researcher may stop a consumer who has purchased a particular type of bread and ask him or her why that type of bread was chosen. Unlike quantitative research there is no fixed set of questions, but instead a topic guide (or discussion guide) is used to explore various issues in more depth. The discussion between the interviewer (or moderator) and the respondent is largely determined by the respondent's own thoughts and feelings.

As with quantitative techniques, there are also various types of qualitative methodologies. Research of this sort is mostly conducted face to face, and one of the best-known techniques is market research group discussions (or focus groups). These are usually made up of six to eight targeted respondents; a research moderator whose role is to ask the required questions, draw out answers, and encourage discussion; an observation area usually behind one-way mirrors; and video and/or audio taping facilities.

Qualitative research often involves primary research, which concentrates on the opinions of consumers. Secondary research will inform a business about the numbers within a market for a product, whereas primary research starts to establish why products are bought.

Tips and techniques

Businesses will usually want to use both types of research methods, rather than one or the other. The quantitative research will give more factual information, but opinions and ideas from qualitative research can bring in new ideas.

Conducting the research

Primary (field research)

Primary research can be carried out in a number of ways, such as interviews, questionnaires, observation, consumer panels and focus groups. Marketing plans will consider the most appropriate way in which to collect the information required. Deciding which method to use will depend upon a variety of factors:

- cost and budget constraints
- marketing objectives
- information required
- information already available
- number of persons to be questioned
- location of respondents.

Interviews

Interviews allow for a great amount of detail to be extracted from the consumer, whose opinions can be clarified immediately. However, it is a time-consuming and therefore expensive method of research. Interviewers need to be well trained to ensure that questions are asked without bias and that the responses are recorded appropriately.

Today, many interviews take place using CAPI (computer assisted personal interviewing.) Interviews are conducted face to face and the replies recorded onto a laptop computer. Once a reply has been recorded, the next question automatically pops up on the screen. This ensures a consistent approach where all respondents are asked the same questions in the same order.

In addition, CATI (computer assisted telephone interviewing) and CAWI (computer assisted web interviewing) are used.

Surveys/questionnaires

One of the most widely used methods of collecting research material is the questionnaire. It is a quick and economical method of gaining the opinions of consumers and potential consumers. If the questionnaires need to be posted, the usual procedure is to enclose a business reply card. The more replies gained, the more reliable is the information.

Example of a questionnaire

Effective questionnaires are brief to ensure that potential respondents are not put off answering due to the amount of time that would be taken to complete them. Many effective questionnaires offer incentives to encourage respondents.

Observation

Watching consumers and users of products can offer a good insight for the researchers. In situations where interviewing and using questionnaires may prove to be difficult, observation is a viable alternative. For example, when testing how young children play with particular toys, it is not always possible to ask them, and therefore observation provides the necessary information.

Consumer panels

Testing products is often done by the use of consumer panels. Such panels frequently test washing powders and liquids. Samples of new products are sent to panel members who fill in forms to gauge their responses to the products.

Similarly, perfume and aftershave products are often tested in this manner.

Focus groups

These usually consist of about eight to ten people who are offered various stimuli and their responses gauged and recorded.

Sometimes Monadic rating is used: the respondent is asked to rate a product on a scale, but without comparisons to another product.

Trial marketing

This is a system of 'testing the water' before going ahead with a full launch of a product. Businesses may trial their product in a retail outlet like a supermarket, or they might try to find a representative group of consumers. For example, when launching a newly packaged drink aimed at young children, Marks and Spencer trialled it with the pupils in a local school. The most effective area to use trial marketing is in the digital sector. The trial can be done at almost zero cost over the internet and results can be fed back instantly. For example, the BBC can allow downloads of new apps to a target market and gain insight quickly on how they will be received by potential customers.

Secondary (desk research)

This is data that already exists. There are two main sources: internal and external sources.

Internal sources

Internal sources include:

1. Sales data/figures: assuming that the information recorded is accurate, trends can be established to help in the decision making process for future marketing and production schedules.
2. Previous survey results: although these can be used as a basis for comparison, the reliability of such data is questionable. This will depend upon the nature of the product and its market. For some goods that change rapidly in terms of technology, data for sales of an old model may not be very useful.
3. Customer information: (often collected from loyalty card details) knowing who buys what, when and where can be invaluable data. When planning at whom or where to target a particular sales promotion, or deciding which advertising media to use, knowing the details of its consumers allows a business to be more effective in its marketing spend.
4. Company reports: the business may have undertaken its own marketing reports and summaries of past performances. There may be occasions when such information is useful.

External sources

External sources include:

1 Market research companies: although the collection and collation of secondary data may be expensive, it can be good value for money, especially to the smaller businesses that cannot afford to generate their own research. Mintel is one of the largest market research businesses. Other market research companies such as TNS, Mori, Millard Brown and Nielson all provide research material for a wide range of clients.
2 The internet: the internet now plays a much larger role in providing secondary data. Market research businesses have their own websites and some reports are available online for a fee. Small firms can access information more cheaply than hiring a market research company to do the research for them.
3 Trade publications: reading trade publications (such as *Marketing*, *The Grocer*) is a cheap method of keeping up to date on any particular market. Information is available not only on the latest developments, but also on competing businesses. Because such journals tend to specialise in a particular market, the information is easier to extract than from a more general business magazine.
4 Newspapers and magazines: some newspapers carry particular features on certain sectors of industry that may provide valuable secondary information. *The Times*, *Guardian* and the *Daily Telegraph*, along with the Sunday press, carry such features.
   The Economist, *Business Today*, *Marketing* and *Marketing Weekly* all provide useful material on a wide range of topics.
   Marketing, a weekly trade journal, often includes features on various markets. Although such research is often conducted by market research companies, the collation of their findings into one article makes the information more accessible and convenient.
5 Competitors: see the section on trade journals above. In addition, it is of course possible to purchase competitors' products and see exactly what is being offered. It is clear that when Ford first introduced ABS braking systems, other car manufacturers were quick to follow suit. This was also the case with the Dyson vacuum cleaner; other manufacturers were quick to introduce their own versions, without breaking any patent laws, as soon as they were legally entitled.
6 Government statistics and reports: government statistics are available in abundance. Each government department has its own website and issues documents and statistics regularly.

Tips and techniques

Primary research is very expensive and may not be possible for smaller firms. Its main benefits are that it is specific to the particular business and more up to date.

Summary

It is important to understand that market research is not an exact science. Bias is often a problem and may influence the answers gained from respondents. To gain a reliable response, the number of respondents is important. However, the cost of collecting the data also must be considered. Consequently, market research is often a trade-off between accuracy and reliability on the one hand, and cost-effectiveness on the other.

To add to the dilemma facing those who collect data, the time factor is crucial. Collecting sufficient information may contradict the need to have up-to-date information. Time spent collecting information may improve its reliability in terms of asking a sufficient number of people, but the information may quickly become out of date.

Further sources

www.mrs.org.uk
www.gov.uk/market-research
www.marketingdonut.co.uk

Your turn

Questions are suitable for all AS and A Level candidates.

Multiple-choice questions

1 An example of field research is:
   A looking at the Yellow Pages
   B completing a survey
   C using company reports
   D using other business's data. *(1)*

2 One of the problems with completing primary research is:
   A It might be out of date.
   B It is not appropriate to the particular firm.
   C It is cheap to do.
   D It is expensive to do. *(1)*

Revision questions

1 Explain the difference between quantitative and qualitative market. *(4)*

2 State two benefits for a business of using primary market research rather than secondary research. *(2)*

3 State two sources or secondary market research. *(2)*

Total *(8)*

Case study

Ryanair

Ryanair recently undertook market research after being voted the worst of the top 100 UK companies for customer service by *Which?* magazine. The purpose of the research was to:

- understand the needs of Ryanair customers
- establish how Ryanair could expand its routes to meet customer needs
- find out whether an advertising campaign could improve the Ryanair image
- find out why some people chose not to use Ryanair
- find out what was right and wrong with the booking process
- find out what the public's perception of Ryanair was and whether the company's reputation put off potential customers.

Despite having one of the best records in the industry for reliability and punctuality, the research showed why customers had such a poor view of Ryanair. The research highlighted customer dissatisfaction with the:

- aggressive and confrontational style of the CEO, Michael O'Leary
- complicated booking system, with numerous 'add-ons' to the initial price shown on the website
- scramble for unallocated seats on the planes
- relentless on-board selling
- arguments at the gates about luggage dimensions.

As a result of this research, Ryanair has made a number of changes to its marketing strategy. These include revamping the website to reduce the number of procedures before completion and a move out of the limelight for Michael O'Leary. Ryanair launched its new website in spring 2014, together with extensive advertising that stressed the way in which the business had changed its strategy.

1 State two methods that Ryanair could use to collect primary data from its customers. *(2)*

2 On the announcement of the new strategy, Ryanair shares rose 2 per cent to 6.30 euros. Calculate the share price before the announcement. *(2)*

3 Analyse one reason for Ryanair's decision to change its image. *(4)*

4 Evaluate the usefulness of the market research techniques that Ryanair can use to collect information about its customers and market. *(20)*

Total *(28)*

Chapter 52

Identifying customer needs: market research analysis

AS / Year 1 | Year 2

A Level students must know all of the content in this chapter.

AS students need to cover all of the content except:

- Normal distribution (page 377)
- Standard deviation (page 377)

Once the initial market research plan on how the information is to be collected is in place, consideration needs to be given to the sampling techniques employed.

Insufficient data will not be reliable, and therefore any analysis will be flawed.

In order to improve the likelihood of gaining reliable data, there are several sampling techniques that can be applied.

Sampling methods

For most surveys, access to the entire population is almost impossible. However, the results from a survey with a carefully selected sample should closely resemble results that would have been obtained had the whole population provided the data.

Sampling, therefore, is a very important part of the market research process. If you have undertaken a survey using an appropriate sampling technique, you can be confident that your results will be 'generalised' to the population in question. If the sample were biased in any way such as, for example, if the selection technique gave older people more of a chance of selection than younger people, it would be inadvisable to make generalisations from the findings.

There are essentially two types of sampling: probability and non-probability sampling.

Key term

Population: in sampling, the term population usually refers to the total group included in the sample; for example, all the pupils in a school to do a survey on school meals.

Probability sampling methods

Probability or random sampling gives all members of the population a known chance of being selected for inclusion in the sample. This does not depend upon previous events in the selection process. In other words, the selection of individuals does not affect the chance of anyone else in the population being selected.

Many statistical techniques assume that a sample was selected on a random basis. There are four basic types of random sampling techniques.

Simple random sampling

This is the ideal choice as it is a 'perfect' random method. Using this method, individuals are randomly selected from a list of the population, and every single individual has an equal chance of selection.

This method is ideal, but if it cannot be adopted, one of the following alternatives may be chosen.

Systematic sampling

Systematic sampling is a frequently used variant of simple random sampling. When performing systematic sampling, every 'nth' element from the list is selected (this is referred to as the sample interval) from a randomly selected starting point. For example, if we have a listed population of 6,000 members and wish to draw a sample of 200, we would select every thirtieth (6,000 divided by 200) person from the list. In practice, we would randomly select a number between 1 and 30 to act as our starting point.

A potential problem with this method of sampling concerns the arrangement of elements in the list. If the list is arranged in any kind of order such as, for example, if every thirtieth house is smaller than the others from which the sample is being recruited, there is a possibility that the sample produced could be seriously biased.

Quota sampling

Quota sampling involves splitting the population into sub-groups according to their distribution in the population. For example, if 52 per cent of a given population is male and 48 per cent is female, the samples that are questioned will be in this proportion. Quota sampling is a non-random form of sampling that may be influenced by the perceptions of the interviewer.

Convenience sampling

Convenience sampling involves using those people who come to hand most easily to be questioned. For example, in a house-to house survey the interviewer may only use the sample of people who happen to be at home at a particular time of day. Similarly, if a questionnaire is completed in a shopping centre on a weekday, it will only be targeting those who do not work, are on holiday or work in the vicinity. For these reasons convenience samples will be distorted.

Stratified sampling

Stratified sampling is a variant on simple random and systematic methods, and is used when there are a number of distinct subgroups, within each of which it is required that there is full representation. A stratified sample is constructed by classifying the population in sub-populations (or strata), based on some well-known characteristics of the population, such as age, gender or socio-economic status. The selection of elements is then made separately from within each stratum, usually by random or systematic sampling methods.

Stratified sampling methods also come in two types – proportionate and disproportionate.

1. Proportionate sampling: In proportionate sampling, the strata sample sizes are in proportion to the strata population sizes. For example, if the first stratum is made up of males, then as there are around 50 per cent of males in the UK population, the male strata will need to represent around 50 per cent of the total sample.
2. Disproportionate sampling: In disproportionate methods, the strata are not sampled according to the population sizes, but higher proportions are selected from some groups and not others.

Cluster or multi-stage sampling

Cluster sampling is a practical and frequently used random sampling method. It is particularly useful in situations for which no list of the elements within a population is available and therefore the elements cannot be selected directly. As this form of sampling is conducted by randomly selecting subgroups of the population, possibly in several stages, it should produce results equivalent to a simple random sample.

Reasons for errors

Regardless of the sampling technique used, errors occur for a variety of reasons.

Non-sampling errors

A respondent (person being interviewed) may give what he or she thinks should be said. This is often a politically or socially correct answer, rather than an honest answer that reflects what the respondent really thinks.

1. There are occasions when respondents give an answer that they think will please the interviewer.
2. Sometimes if the respondent is in a hurry, they may give the first answer that comes into their head.
3. Infrequently, there are occasions when a deliberate false answer is given. This sometimes occurs when respondents are asked how they voted. Voting is considered a private matter and therefore some people will not say how they actually voted.

All of the above may be classed as non-sampling errors and need to be noted when analysing research results.

Sampling errors

A sampling error is the difference between the mean value of the sample and the actual or true mean value of the population. (See below the calculation for arriving at the mean value.) If the mean value of a sample is 25 and the actual mean of the population is 26, the sampling error is 1.

Normally as the sample size increases, the sampling error falls.

Mean or average value

When research is undertaken, those responsible for its interpretation need to be aware of the significance of the data and its reliability. Ensuring that the data is used properly will depend upon how it is interpreted. Therefore it is important to find the average or mean for a selection of data. This average or mean is also referred to as the central tendency.

To calculate the mean, the aggregate of all the results is divided by the number of results.

For example: add together 6, 7, 8, 9, 11, 14, 15 = 70, divide by 7 = 10

Normal distribution

When looking at the results of any research, the data can be considered in terms of how it is distributed. A normal distribution is bell-shaped (see Figure 52.1).

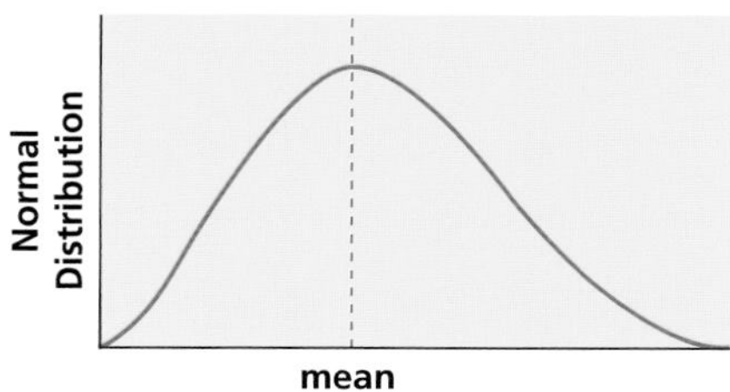

Figure 52.1 Normal distribution

To consider the distribution of the data still further, it can be compared to the mean (average).

Standard deviation

This is a measure of how spread out your data is, compared to the mean.

The standard deviation measures how far from the mean any finding, observation or response is, and can therefore be used to assess whether the result is roughly in line, more than, or less than the average or mean.

It is important to realise that the closer the results are to the mean, the narrower the spread of data is; a large standard deviation suggests there is a wider spread around the mean.

Calculation of the standard deviation:

For example: a market research survey collected the following data:

32, 34, 35, 35, 37, 37, 37, 38, 39

First, it is necessary to calculate the mean or average (aggregate of results divided by number of results).

32 + 34 + 35 + 35 + 37 + 37 + 37 + 38 + 39 =

$\frac{324}{9} = 36$

To find out how far each value deviates from the mean, each number is compared to the mean of 36. If less than the mean, it will be a minus number and if more than the mean, it will be a positive number. See Table 52.1.

Therefore 32 = −4, 34 = −2 and so on:

Table 52.1

Data result	32	34	35	35	37	37	37	38	39
Amount of deviation for the mean	−4	−2	−1	−1	+1	+1	+1	+2	+3

The next step is to ensure that all the numbers are positive, and therefore each number is squared. See Table 52.2

Tips and techniques

Squaring the numbers is part of a formula to gain an end result which can be used and judged for its reliability. You do not need to know why the numbers are squared; if you clearly state how you gained your figures that will suffice.

Table 52.2

Data result	32	34	35	35	37	37	37	38	39
Amount of deviation for the mean	−4	−2	−1	−1	+1	+1	+1	+2	+3
Square the deviation	16	4	1	1	1	1	1	4	9

Once the square of the deviations has been calculated, these numbers are then added and divided by the number of units of data (9).

16 + 4 + 1 + 1 + 1 + 1 + 1 + 4 + 9 = 38

$\frac{38}{9} = 4.22$ (the variance)

The square root of this number is calculated = 2.055.

This number represents the standard deviation; 2.055 is a small standard deviation, and therefore the spread around the mean is small.

The actual formula to find the standard deviation is given in the box below.

Marketing

Standard deviation = $\sqrt{\frac{\Sigma(x-y)^2}{n}}$

x = each piece (unit) of date (the result)

y = the mean

n = the total number of pieces/units of data/result

x = 32, 34, 35, 35, *etc.*

mean = $\frac{\text{total of pieces of data}}{\text{number of pieces of data}} \frac{(324)}{(9)} = 36$

$(x - y) = 32 - 36 = -4$

The standard deviation shows how far away from the mean any results may be. Using a normal distribution curve, the standard deviation can be shown and the corresponding percentages of the distribution of the data.

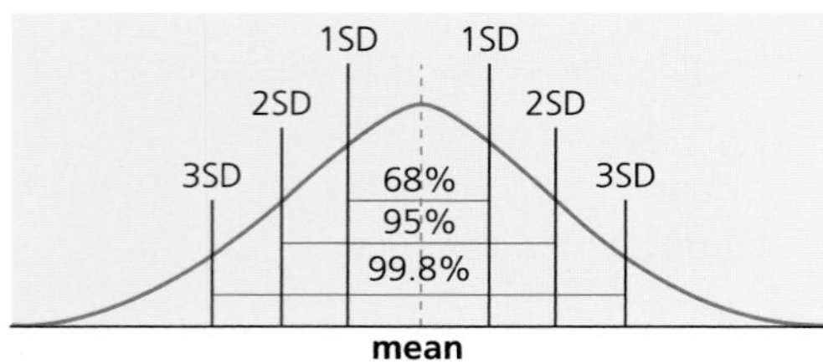

Figure 52.2 Normal distribution and standard deviation

Figure 52.2 shows that one standard deviation away from the mean will cover 65 per cent of the data, two standard deviations from the mean will cover 95 per cent of the data and three standard deviations for the mean will cover 99.8 per cent of the data.

Scatter graphs

An alternative method for analysing data is to plot the relationship between two variables to see if there is any correlation. Correlation is a term used to show how closely two factors or variables are linked to each other.

A scatter graph could look at the link between the amount of rainfall and flooding. For business studies, it could be used to look at the relationship (if any) between the level of expenditure on marketing and the level of consumption of a product. By plotting the figures onto a graph, it is possible to see if there is any correlation, once a line of best fit has been drawn.

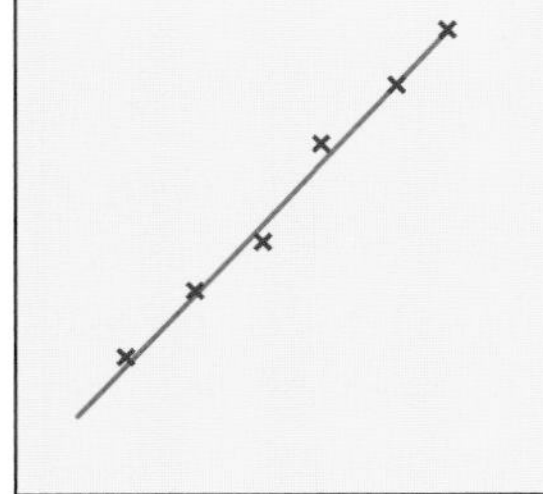

Figure 52.3 There is a strong correlation between the two variables

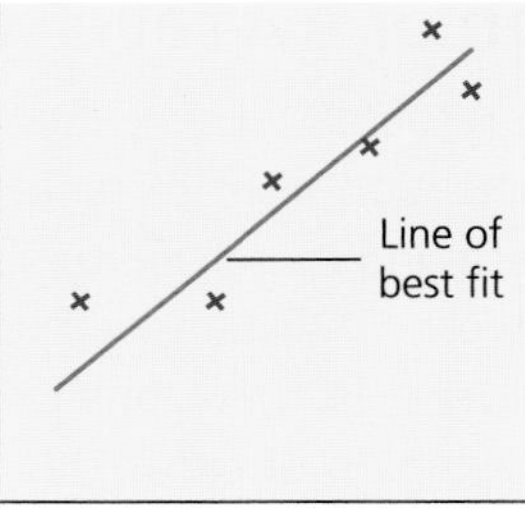

Figure 52.4 There is a weak correlation between the two variables

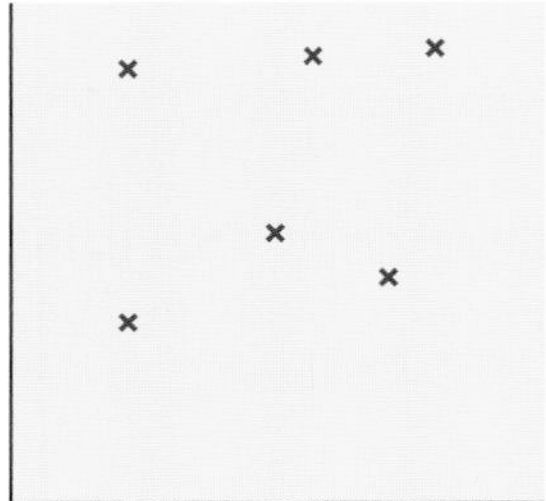

Figure 52.5 There is no correlation between the two variables

Although the graph may show a strong correlation, it does not prove that there is a definite link in terms of cause and effect. It is plotting just two variables and, of course, there may be other variables that explain what appears to be a strong correlation.

Graphs can also be used to predict the likely trends that are based on previous data.

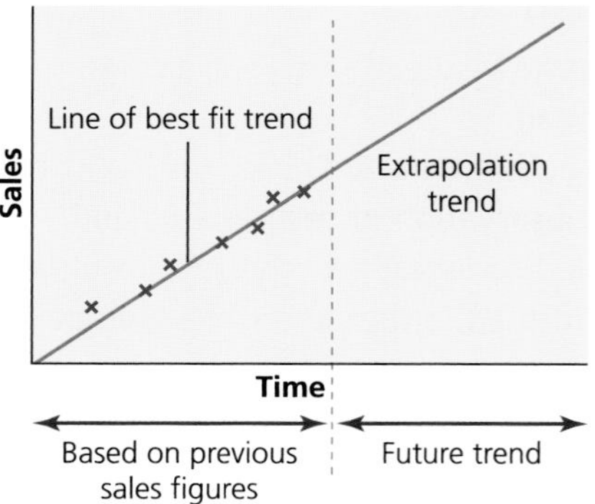

Figure 52.6 Extrapolating to predict future trends

Once the figures (e.g. sales figures) have been plotted, it is possible to continue the line. The data is extrapolated (continuing the line of best fit), and a future trend can be seen.

It is, however, dangerous to assume that this is an inevitable trend; once again, there are many factors that may affect the sales of products in the future. Nevertheless, this information is of some value and may help the other functions within the business to be able to respond accordingly.

Market segmentation

Once a business has used market research to find out about its customer base, it can begin to split its market into different groups with different characteristics and needs. This process is called market segmentation. Knowledge of different groups within a potential customer base can help the business to target those consumers by a variety of methods. For example:

- differentiated products
- special offers
- targeted advertising
- the range of goods stocked.

An example of the use of market segmentation is that Marks & Spencer stock different ranges of clothes in its smaller stores to reflect the age and employment characteristics of its customers. In its store in the City of London, most of the clothes are smart suits and accessories for both men and women; in a seaside resort like Llandudno, a section of the clothes are aimed at the older age group who are likely to visit the town on day trips and coach tours.

The market can be segmented in many different ways. A business may use different types of market segmentation in different situations.

Types of market segmentation

Age

This is one of the most obvious methods of segmentation, separating the potential market into different groups that can be targeted by a particular range of the business's goods or services. The age distribution of the UK population has changed dramatically over the past century. For the first time in the UK's history, in 2008 there were more retired people in the UK population than children under the age of 16. This means that there is a growing market aimed at the older sector of the population. Holiday companies like Kuoni and Viking River Cruises now target pensioners who have plenty of time and high levels of disposable income with holidays such as educational, historic cruises or guided holidays to long-haul destinations like New Zealand.

Geography

This involves splitting the population according to the area in which they live within the UK, within the EU or within the world economy. In some markets there are significant regional differences in the characteristics of consumers. Segmenting the market makes it possible for a business to target these regional markets more effectively. For example, the sales of alcoholic drinks through off-licences and supermarkets vary from region to region. In areas where there is a large proportion of elderly people there will usually be higher than average sales of sherries, ports and spirits.

Gender

Many products are aimed either at men or women. A business may produce or adapt its products to ensure that they can be marketed effectively to one or other of the sexes. For example, Gillette, the shaving equipment manufacturer, produces a range of shaving equipment aimed specifically at female users, which is different from their range of razors for men.

Social class

Several different systems are used to define social class. An example of one such system is given in the box below.

Social class groupings A–E

A Upper class/upper-middle class – professional, higher managerial (e.g. company directors, lawyers, accountants)

B Middle class – other professional, middle management, senior administrative (e.g. teachers, nurses)

C1 Lower-middle class – junior management, skilled non-manual workers (e.g. police, clerical staff)

C2 Skilled working class – trained (trade) skilled workers (e.g. technicians, plumbers, electricians)

D Working class – unskilled manual workers, semi-skilled workers (e.g. labourers, farm workers)

E Unskilled/unemployed – those on state benefit (e.g. pensioners, unemployed)

Residence

The ACORN (A Classification of Residential Neighbourhoods) system of classification allows businesses to target people living in a particular type of accommodation. This system categorises different types of housing such as flats, terraced housing, large detached housing, and so on. This system might be used by an independent school that wanted to send a mailshot to parents who are likely to consider private schooling for their children.

Type of housing	UK population (%)
A. Agricultural areas	3
B. Modern family housing, higher incomes	18
C. Older housing of intermediate status	17
D. Poor quality older terraced housing	4
E. Better-off council estates	13
F. Less well-off council estates	9
G. Poorest council estates	7
H. Multi-racial areas	4
I. High status non-family areas	4
J. Affluent suburban housing	16
K. Better-off retirement areas	4
U. Unclassified	1

Table 52.3 Classification of housing

Religion or ethnic grouping

Some firms may produce ranges of products for specific ethnic or religious groups in societies. Food manufacturers, for example, may produce ranges of ingredients for Indian or Chinese customers, although there will obviously be others outside those groups who will also buy these products. Similarly, specialist butchers (such as halal) provide for the requirements of certain groups in the type of meat they sell.

Disadvantages of market segmentation

Although there are obvious advantages for a business in segmenting the market, it is also important for a business to ensure that it is not excluding other customers by taking segmentation too far. Increasingly, consumers are prepared to move over boundaries in their purchasing patterns, and it is becoming increasingly difficult to categorise consumers and their behaviour. Too much segmentation may mean that potential sales are lost.

Market share

Market share is the proportion of the total market that a particular firm has achieved. The market share can be measured in different ways; the main methods are by sales volume or by sales value. In some cases, however, a business may look at the number of customers it has, or the number of retail outlets. A high street bank may be interested in the number of customer accounts it holds, or in the number of branches it has in comparison to its competitors.

Measuring market share by sales volume or sales value may give different results. It is useful and valuable to compare these values and to account for any differences.

The formula for calculating market share is:

$$\text{Market share} = \frac{\text{sales value or volume for the individual business}}{\text{sales value or volume for the whole market}} \times 100$$

For example, if a local bakery sells £2,000 of bread each week in a small town and the total bread sales in the town are £10,000, its market share will be as follows:

$$\text{Market share} = \frac{2{,}000}{10{,}000} \times 100$$

$$= 20\%$$

The calculation of market share allows a business to assess its success, both in comparison with its competitors and with past performance. Increasing market share may also be used as a target or objective for the business in the future. Businesses like the major supermarkets are often as concerned with their share of the market as they are with profitability

To be able to use the calculation of market share in a sensible way, the business needs to be able to identify accurately which market it is in, and who and what is its competition. A business like Boots the Chemist is selling in a number of different markets such as pharmaceuticals, beauty products, small electrical goods and baby products. Market share calculations need to take each of these markets separately because it is unlikely that there is a similar business among Boots' competitors, selling exactly the same range of goods, with which it could make comparisons.

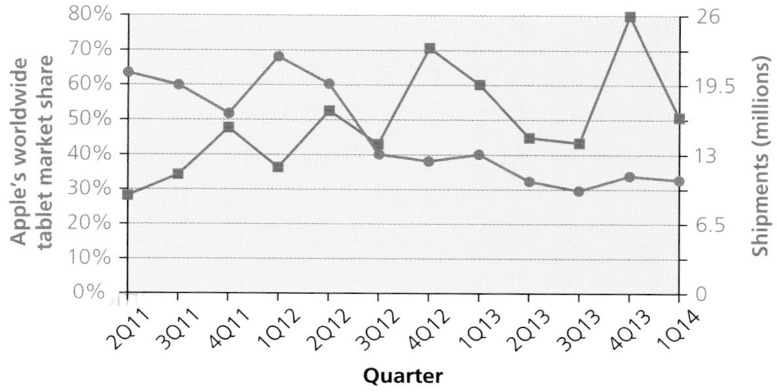

Figure 52.7 Apple's market share first quarter 2014
Apple maintained its lead in the worldwide tablet, shipping 16.4 million units in the last quarter of 2013. That's down from 26.0 million units in the previous quarter and well below its total of 19.5 million units in the first quarter of 2013. Despite the contraction, the company saw its share of the market slip only modestly to 32.5%, down from the previous quarter's share of 33.2%. Samsung once again grew its worldwide share, increasing from 17.2% one quarter to 22.3% the next. Samsung continues to work aggressively with carriers to drive tablet shipments through attractively priced smartphone bundles. Rounding out the top five were ASUS (5%), Lenovo (4.1%), and Amazon (1.9%).
Source: Macrumores.com.

Market growth

As well as knowing about their share of the market, businesses also need to know what is happening to the market in terms of its overall size. Market growth and its impact on the sales of a business can have a dramatic impact on the success of the firm.

If a business knows that the market it is in is growing, it would hope to maintain or increase its share of the market. Businesses will always want to target markets where sales are growing if possible. Market growth may be affected by any of the following factors:

1 The nature of the product. Products such as mobile phones and games consoles face volatile markets that have periods of rapid growth in sales when a new product is launched.
2 Changes in fashion and tastes. The market for women's clothes changes very rapidly through the seasons.
3 Population changes. Changes in birth and death rates or in immigration can cause the market to grow rapidly. For example, recent increases in the birth rate in the UK increased the market for baby-related products.
4 Standard of living. Increases in income and employment usually mean that people have more disposable income. The result may be an increase in the market for DIY products and home improvements.

Market growth can also be calculated, either using value or volume figures. For example, if the market for baby clothes increases from £2 million to £2.5 million, the market growth is calculated as follows:

$$\text{Market growth} = \frac{\text{Increase (or decrease) in total sales by value or volume}}{\text{Original sales value or volume}} \times 100$$

$$= \frac{(2.5 - 2)}{2} \times 100$$

$$= 25\%$$

Factors affecting buyer behaviour

When looking at its share of the market and its performance in a growing market, a business will want to understand the way in which buyers behave. Marketing departments and analysts now spend large amounts of time and money trying to assess and predict buyer behaviour; sometimes they will be successful in doing this, but sometimes buyers will behave in ways that seem unpredictable and irrational. The following factors are likely to be the most important in influencing buyer behaviour:

1 Income, standard of living and employment. In general as the state of these economic factors improves, customers are likely to increase their spending in most areas. The exception may be items such as economy brands from supermarkets, which usually experience higher sales when economic times are difficult.
2 Consumer confidence. Sometimes, even when the economy is doing well, consumers may lack confidence about the future. This will reduce spending, particularly on non-necessities.
3 Advertising or publicity campaigns can have an impact on buyer behaviour. Similarly, bad publicity for business will put buyers off. The discovery of the use of horsemeat in burgers and other meat products by supermarkets like Tesco in 2012 caused huge damage to the sales of the supermarkets involved, not just in meat products, but across their whole product ranges.
4 Supermarkets make sure that the layout of their shops encourages the consumer to spend more and to take their time wandering around the store. Common purchases such as bread, milk and tea are usually positioned in different parts of the store to encourage consumers to walk along all the aisles.
5 Many consumers (particularly young people) are very influenced by fashion trends, media coverage and celebrities. They may feel that they need the latest 'must-have' handbag or pair of trainers.

In all of the above, it is important for the business to have an awareness of the market in which it is operating, and a thorough knowledge of its customer base. It will usually find this information through the use of market research.

Further sources

www.mathsisfun.com Straightforward to get to grips with mathematical concepts
www.wisegeek.org Clear answers for common questions

Your turn

Questions are suitable for all AS and A Level candidates.

Multiple-choice questions

1 After undertaking some market research a local bakery finds that it has a 40 per cent share of the bread sales in the immediate vicinity. If its annual sales of bread are £30,000 of the total local market, what is the value of the total market bread sales?
   A £12,000
   B £60,000
   C £75,000
   D £40,000 *(1)*

2 If a market with an annual turnover of £20 million is expected to grow by 20 per cent this year and a business hopes to gain 3 per cent of this market growth, by how much will its sales increase?
   A £0.12 million
   B £0.6 million
   C £0.13 million
   D £3 million *(1)*

3 Which of the following best describes random sampling?
   A Every 'nth' person from the population is chosen.
   B The population is split into groups and a given number of people are chosen from each group.
   C A given proportion of each strata in the population is used.
   D Every member of the population has an equal chance of being chosen *(1)*

Revision questions

After 1 to 3 weeks of using L'Oreal-Elvive Triple Resist for men hair shampoo, 78 per cent of 119 men said their hair felt stronger.

Source: as advertised on TV, 1 September 2013.

1 To the nearest whole number, how many men in the L'Oreal-Elvive sample said their hair felt stronger? *(2)*
2 Evaluate the usefulness of the market research data obtained by L'Oreal-Elvive. *(9)*
Total *(11)*

Case study

Poundland

The discount store, Poundland, has been very successful in growing its market share during the recession as might be expected. It continues to open new stores in the UK and Ireland and its profits continue to rise year-on-year.

It would appear, however, that not all this growth in Poundland's market share has come from customers who have had to economise. Poundland has grown its market into socio-economic groups B and C who are interested in buying basic household items, like laundry products, bleach and soaps. These customers continue to do their main shopping in stores like Sainsbury's and Waitrose, but often shop for bargains at Poundland.

When Poundland opened its first store it managed to sell its products cheaply by buying end-of-line or surplus production/stock from manufacturers. That is no longer the case. Poundland is so successful in its market that it can now negotiate special prices for non-standard sizes of items such as milk and bread that can be sold for £1. The business has built up a reputation for prompt payment to its suppliers, which makes them happy to accommodate Poundland's specific demands.

However, despite its success, Poundland, like similar discount stores, has found it difficult to achieve a greater market share, especially at a time when the grocery market overall has been fairly stagnant. It is also anticipated by commentators that the outlook for increased market share is uncertain. Inflation will make it difficult to maintain the 'pound' store concept in the long run.

1 In the last 18 months, Poundland has added 70 new stores, bringing its total to 460 stores. Calculate the percentage increase in the number of its outlets. *(2)*
2 State two other marketing methods that could be used to increase Poundland's growth. *(2)*
3 Analyse one problem faced by Poundland for achieving increased market share. *(4)*
4 Evaluate the problems that Poundland is likely to face in the future in maintaining its market share amongst higher income earners. *(15)*
Total *(23)*

Chapter 53

Customers and consumers and anticipating consumer needs

AS / Year 1 | Year 2

A Level students must know all of the content in this chapter.

AS students need to cover all of the content except:
- Marketing models (pages 384–386)
- The importance of customer service (page 387)
- Service marketing (pages 387–388)

It is important for businesses to take account of customer behaviour when marketing. In most situations, customers will plan their shopping; this is particularly true of supermarket shopping where customers will buy similar baskets of food each week or month. Supermarket home deliveries take account of this fact by giving the customer a regular shopping list when they are placing an order so that they can choose items from it.

Most customers will also make impulse purchases in addition to regular items or planned purchases. Businesses can use ploys to encourage these impulse purchases; for example, by placing items at the entrance to the shop, or using pop-up screens on the computer.

Niche marketing

Niche marketing is essentially about targeting a business's marketing efforts to a specific market segment. The alternative to niche marketing is mass marketing. In mass marketing, a business attempts to reach the entire market with a single product idea, such as Coca-Cola.

Niche marketing is an option for firms in markets where segmentation allows them to break down a large market into smaller, characteristic groups that can be targeted separately. Niche marketing has the main advantage of there being fewer competitors. Unless another firm has decided to target the same niche, it may be possible to exploit economies of scale in that small market.

The main disadvantage of selling to a niche market is related to size. Smaller markets often have less potential to make a large profit. Another issue could be overreliance on a single, small market. If this market changes and demand falls, it could be bad for the business. Another problem is that success in a niche market encourages others to enter it. This can limit the company's success in the future.

Examples of firms currently operating in niche markets are Rolls-Royce in the luxury car market and Equestrian Tourism, which provides equestrian holidays.

Key terms

Niche marketing: targeting a clear and identifiable segment of the market.

Mass marketing: selling into a market containing many products that are similar.

Marketing models

Promotion is an important part of the marketing mix and a feature that has increased in prominence as the impact of the media has grown in modern society. The object of promotion is to persuade the consumer to buy the goods or services of an individual business. Its other purpose is to inform the individual so that they can make a rational choice.

When promotion is successful, it will increase demand and encourage brand loyalty. This is made by altering the elasticity of demand through the use of advertising. For example, a large number of people will always buy the same bar of chocolate, whatever its price. Kit Kat has a high brand loyalty, meaning that for some consumers it will always be the chocolate bar they purchase. This means that its elasticity of demand is low and that a change in price is likely to result in a proportionately smaller change in demand. In using promotion, Nestle want to attract new customers, but they also want the advertising to make its existing customers loyal to the brand.

DAGMAR

DAGMAR is a model aimed at promotion. One of the purposes of promotion is to help the consumer to become aware of the characteristics of the good or service, and to stress the ways in which it differs from competing products in the market. The acronym DAGMAR stands for:

- Defining
- Advertising
- Goals
- Measuring
- Advertising
- Results.

In using DAGMAR, therefore, the business should be able to formulate a strategy for any new promotional campaign. In the first instance, the business should make decisions about what is to be achieved through the promotion in terms of customer awareness, explanation of the product and image. Having done this, the business then needs to measure the success in terms of some previously agreed criterion. This may be increased sales or market share. For example, a business like Muller Yoghurts may have an advertising campaign to launch a new range of chilled desserts on to the market. The promotion will need to differentiate the range from competitors and stress any special features. In launching the product, Muller will have set itself targets for sales over a period of time, and it will collect data from the supermarkets and other outlets to be able to monitor the success of the advertising campaign.

AIDA

AIDA is also a promotional model applied specifically to advertising. The application of AIDA will help a business to judge whether an advertisement is likely to succeed.

1. Attention: the first thing that an advertisement needs to do is to grab the attention of the prospective customer. For example, some producers may use a particular jingle or music throughout all their advertisements so that consumers begin to associate its use with the product.
2. Interest: having caught the attention in the first instance, the advertisement must retain the customer's attention so that the information about the product and its qualities can be delivered. The hope then is that once consumers have listened to the advertisement, they will want to purchase the product.
3. Desire: the result of all this must be a desire on the part of the consumer to buy the product, resulting in demand for the good or service.
4. Action: this desire must then lead the consumer to act and actually purchase the product.

If the AIDA cycle is broken at any point, the advertisement will not result in a successful purchase. There are a number of ways in which this might happen.

The consumer may watch the advertisement and be interested in the product but have no desire to buy. This can happen with advertisements that are artistically excellent and interesting or amusing to watch, regardless of whether the individual might buy the product or not. Guinness advertisements often win awards and are impressive to watch, although a large proportion of those who watch and admire the advertisements are unlikely to be interested in buying the product.

The consumer may be unable to act on the desire to buy because of lack of availability of the product. For example, it is sometimes the case at Christmas that advertisements for toys or new electronic games are followed by shortages of supplies. The advertisement may be successful in encouraging a desire to buy, but the action will not be possible.

The consumer may go through each stage up to the point of action and then be attracted to a competing product, or be discouraged from purchase by the price.

Awareness Trial Repurchase (ATR) marketing model

This model is useful for a business because it goes through the steps that a consumer will follow, from early decision making on what to buy, all the way to actual purchase.

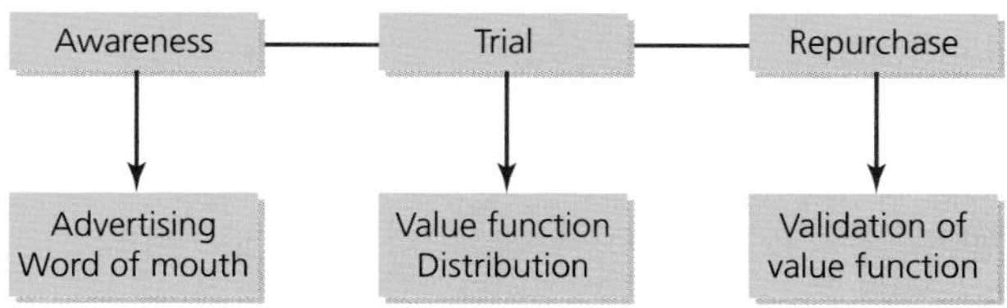

In general, a potential consumer will find out about a new product through advertising or by hearing about the product from other consumers. This is the awareness stage.

The consumer will then try to find out if the attributes of the product match the requirements that they have for the product. This is the trial stage of the process. If the product does not match up in terms of price and performance, or if the consumer experiences difficulty in finding it, the process will end at this point.

Having bought the product, the consumer may find that it does not meet expectations in any one of a number of ways: too expensive; poor performance; poor value for money. If this is the case, repurchase is unlikely. With the purchase of expensive items, like cars, customers are likely to be contacted after the purchase to check that they are happy with the product. This is likely to help in preventing problems before the consumer can give poor word-of-mouth reports.

The model uses aspects of the marketing mix at different stages. For example, advertising and awareness are important at the outset; distribution and the value aspect are important at the trial stage; customer service and the perceived value of the product are important at the repurchase stage.

SWOT analysis

Any business making a decision about its future strategy needs to consider the business situation both internally and externally. A SWOT analysis can help with this. For full details of SWOT analysis see **Chapter 50**.

Market and product orientation

Key terms

Market (or customer) orientation: gets the right product.

Product orientation: gets the product right.

Market (or customer) orientation means that the business is trying to ensure that it targets each of its products to the appropriate market sector. If a business is market orientated it will put satisfying the needs of the customer first. Market research is consequently vital for this type of business. This is the most common type of business organisation to be found in the UK economy.

Product orientated businesses are concerned, first and foremost, with the product and its specification. This type of business is most often found in technology companies, such as mobile phone production, where it is important to make sure that the product is as up to date as possible. Market research is still important when it comes to the product's final specification and design, but in the first instance the business will need to ensure that the product has cutting-edge technology and that it can compete successfully with competitors' products. Apple and Samsung are always in competition with each other to try to give their mobile phones better and different features from the competition.

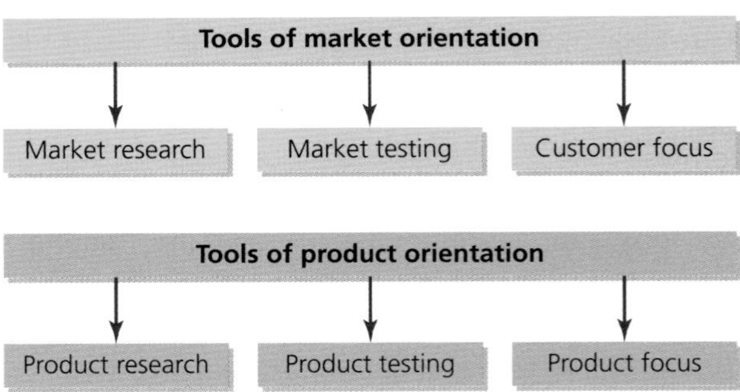

Figure 53.2 Tools of market and product orientation

Services

The economy can be split into sectors: producing industries and service producing industries. The service producing sectors include the following:

- the retail trade
- wholesaling
- information and culture
- transport
- information technology
- education
- health
- hotel and catering
- finance and insurance
- property services.

In each of these sectors, the business has to 'produce' a service in the same way that goods are produced in manufacturing. The business has to investigate its potential market; make decisions about the nature of the service; decide whether to be in a niche or mass market; use marketing to complete the process of providing the service to the consumer.

Importance of customer service

Customer service is important in all sectors of the economy, but the personal contact that is part of providing a service makes it vitally important in this sector. In recent years, businesses have had to do much more than give customers the goods and services they want to purchase; customer service has become an increasingly important part of the buying experience. Businesses in the service sector that fail to take into account this important requirement are unlikely to achieve the same level of success. Customers who receive poor customer service are likely to pass on the experience to friends and colleagues so that a poor reputation can be gained very quickly.

A business such as the John Lewis Partnership has built its reputation on the quality of its care for the customer, Conversely, in a 2013 survey of its potential customers, Ryanair found that its poor service to customers in a number of areas was limiting its ability to achieve the growth in customers it had hoped for. Customers did not complain about prices, punctuality and routes available, but did complain about surly staff, a complicated website for bookings and the constant selling of items during flights. As a result of this research, Ryanair has completely changed its approach to customer service. The Ryanair website has been changed to make pricing clearer; there is less aggressive selling on flights and a more tolerant attitude to baggage allowances.

It is vitally important that a business in the service sector invests money into staff training. This training needs to be provided throughout the entire workforce of a business, regardless of the level of each person's contact with customers. For a supermarket such as Waitrose, it seems obvious that checkout staff should receive customer service training, but other employees might come into contact with the customer even though it is not part of their role: the bakery operative might be stopped with a question while filling shelves; the cleaner will be on the shop floor on occasions clearing a spillage. These workers need to know how to respond to customers even though they may not know the answers to their questions. Similarly, anyone who might have to take a customer phone call should be provided with the training to deal with the situation. An irate customer in any situation needs to be dealt with carefully if the situation is not going to escalate into a serious complaint.

Service marketing

Marketing a service will differ from marketing a product mainly because there is no tangible product for the customer to touch, feel or view. For this reason the marketing of services will in some ways usually have to be different from that of products. At the same time, many of the factors that will apply to marketing products will also be the same as those for services. The advertising of services like insurance, tourism and banking is undertaken in same ways and through the same media as that for supermarkets, cars and chocolate bars.

The ways in which service marketing is likely to be different from product marketing, particularly for small service-sector businesses, are as follows.

- The quality of the service is of vital importance in the service sector. Good service will result in good customer feedback, repeat purchases and high-quality word-of-mouth reviews. This is often the best method of promotion in the service sector.
- It is important to try to use satisfied customers to promote your service. This can be done by using their accreditation in advertising literature, but it can also be done increasingly using social media like Twitter or Facebook to circulate these comments, accreditations and recommendations. Satisfied customers can be asked to promote your business to others by word-of-mouth or by the use of advertising boards outside a property. Many builders and window replacement firms use this method.
- Service providers also benefit from promotion through publicity. This might be sponsorship of a local school or football team or using staff to fundraise for a charity like a local hospice. Estate agents in some areas allow schools to use their sale boards to advertise events like school fetes.
- Service providers need to ensure that all their employees are honest, reliable and trustworthy, especially if they are working in people's homes. People using decorators, plumbers and other contractors will want to know that it is safe to have these workers in their homes. The business must ensure that all of its employees meet these standards if its reputation is to be maintained.
- It is also important to use every method possible to promote the business and to have a consistent and well-prepared advertising campaign. This campaign must be updated regularly and take account of

new methods of promotion if it is to continue to attract new business. Obviously the method must be within the financial means of the business, but there are many affordable methods available – these include flyers, business cards, social media, email circulation, sponsorship, 'news' articles in local free publications.

People, process and physical evidence in services

1 Process: attention to this helps companies to focus on improving performance so that customer needs are met in the provision of the service.
2 People: the personal input in the buying process is vitally important in the delivery of a service. The customer will remember the attentive waiter, or the holiday rep who listens to their problems; this will enhance the name of the business in the eyes of the consumer and is likely to lead to repeat business or new business through recommendation.
3 Physical evidence: the space that surrounds the delivery of a service is important. Customers will respond to the ambience and environment when the service is delivered. Businesses need to consider factors such as branding, signage, packaging, furniture and uniforms at the point of sale, all of which will add to or detract from the consumer experience.

Difference between customers and consumers

Businesses in some sectors also need to be aware of the difference between the customers they sell to and the consumers of their goods and services. In many sectors customers and consumers are the same people, but this is not always the case. Most products aimed at babies and young children will have adults as customers and the children as consumers. In these sectors, therefore, businesses need to be aware of this fact; the product will need to meet the needs of the children in the design of the goods or services, but they will also need to ensure that they attract adults – mainly parents and grandparents – as potential customers.

Business-to-business marketing

Most of the methods explained in this chapter are those used by businesses to market their products to consumers. If a business sells its products to other businesses it may be more limited in the types of marketing it can use. Use of the media may be restricted to trade magazines or specialist publications. Business-to-business marketing is most likely to use personal selling with sales staff making personal approaches to personnel in other businesses either through telephone, email or personal calls.

Further sources

www.marketing.about.com a website that gives many practical examples of marketing

Your turn

Questions in red are for A Level candidates only.

Multiple-choice questions

1 Which two elements of a SWOT analysis are internal to the firm?
  A strengths and weaknesses
  B strengths and opportunities
  C opportunities and threats
  D threats and weaknesses *(1)*

2 A business decides to calculate the effectiveness of an advertising campaign. Sales have increased by 5 per cent. If the original sales were £300,000, what are the new sales?
  A £450,000
  B £330,000
  C £315,000
  D £305,000 *(1)*

Revision questions

1 Explain the meaning of the acronym DAGMAR represent? *(4)*

2 Explain how the marketing model AIDA is used. *(4)*

3 Explain the difference between a customer and a consumer. *(2)*

4 State three reasons why customer service is important for a business. *(3)*

Total *(13)*

Case study

ASOS

The online clothing firm ASOS started life as 'As seen on screen' in 2000, selling items of clothing that had been seen in magazines, newspapers, on TV and in other media. Its market is made up of young people who are interested in clothes and fashion and want to be wearing up-to-date designs that are available at reasonable prices. ASOS reproduces clothes seen in the media very rapidly and at low cost, selling them at affordable prices.

From 2005 to the present day ASOS has managed to double its revenue every year, at a time when many other clothing firms have experienced difficult trading situations. Its revenue has increased from 13.5 million in 2005 to £553 million in 2012. It now has 1.4 million users in the UK, Australia and the USA.

All of this has been achieved while spending almost nothing on marketing. ASOS does not advertise in the media like other clothing businesses such as Next, John Lewis, Marks and Spencer. Instead it uses social media sites to make customers aware of its products. ASOS uses all social media sites, but its Facebook site is the one that attracts most attention from customers. Each day, new items are posted on the site as they come into stock. Customers can then ask questions, post comments and they are also able to find information from those who have already purchased the product about the fit, colour and quality. This gives the customer immediate feedback and up-to-date information and access to products.

1 Calculate the percentage increase in ASOS's revenue from 2005 to 2012. *(2)*

2 Analyse two methods other than those used in the case study that ASOS could have used to advertise its products. *(4)*

3 Analyse the ways in which ASOS could use Ansoff's Matrix if it wishes to increase its market in the UK. *(4)*

4 Evaluate the advantages for ASOS of the marketing method it has adopted. *(12)*

Total *(22)*

Chapter 54

Product

AS / Year 1 | Year 2

A Level students must know all of the content in this chapter.

AS students need to cover all of the content except:

- Value analysis (page 391)
- Extension strategies (pages 392–393)
- Selecting the appropriate product mix (page 395)

Marketing mix

When making marketing decisions, a firm will have to consider what is often referred to as the 4 Ps: product, price place and promotion. A combination of all these things will help a business to formulate a marketing strategy. The following chapters will discuss each of the elements of the marketing mix in detail. The marketing mix chosen will depend on the results that the business wishes to achieve and the type of market it is in. For example, if the business is changing the style of its product it will need to use the product and promotion aspects of the marketing mix. The business will also need to consider its market; if it is targeting a global market different strategies will be more appropriate than if the business is targeting a local market.

Tips and techniques

If you are asked to give a marketing strategy for a business, you should use the elements of the marketing mix. It may not be necessary to include all of them, but you should try to use at least two.

Differentiation

Making the product distinctive is a marketing task which is very important to the success or failure of the product. Finding a unique selling point (USP) helps the product to stand out. If the product is one of many in a highly competitive market, any form of uniqueness will be valuable.

Choosing the correct type of differentiation:

1. Branding is one way of establishing distinctness. A logo or distinct way of writing the name helps to make a brand recognisable.
2. Branding may help consumers to recognise a product, but if the product is poor, any distinctive branding will be wasted.
3. Producing the 'right' type of product ought to be based on effective research. A market-orientated approach is more likely to lead to a successful product.

In a mass market, any form of differentiation will help to make the product distinctive when compared to the rest of the market. Even the best-established brands occasionally need to relaunch or reposition their brands to help maintain their market share.

Heinz rebranded in 2008, moving away from Heinz Baked Beans to Heinz Beans, to link with its slogan of 'Beanz Meanz Heinz'. The product positioning uses an established brand name and an association with quality; if you are thinking about beans, it must be Heinz beans. Special K has moved away from being just a breakfast cereal to part of a personalised diet plan programme.

Wherever a product is positioned, it aims to increase revenues, either directly as a result of higher sales of a specific product in a specific position within the market, or indirectly by being in the market and therefore enhancing the recognition of the brand name without increasing revenues.

Unique selling point (USP)

A business can increase its market growth and share is by finding a good or service that has a unique selling point, something that makes the business stand out against competitors. For example, John Lewis has always marketed itself as 'never knowingly undersold' and has built up a reputation for excellent customer service. Moorcroft Pottery has achieved its success from the use of the tubelining process, colourful glazes and distinctive design in producing vases and other items. Its products command high prices around the world.

Value analysis

Using value analysis to consider the nature of the product enables the business to assess its priorities. Value analysis helps to focus the manufacturer's mind on the main characteristics of the product (see **Chapter 61**).

It is important to achieve the right balance between:

- the function of the product
- the aesthetics of the product, and
- the economic cost of the product.

The purpose of the product dictates whether the shape and colour are more important than the functional qualities. An iPod needs to have the functional qualities to meet the expectations of the consumers in terms of its ability to 'play' music. However, it needs to look good and therefore the aesthetics are also important.

The economic cost is less important if the first two are of a high standard. The cost's significance will depend on the competitiveness of the market. Producing a product at a low economic cost will ensure a profit for the business. It would be of little value to produce a well-designed product that performs its function extremely well, but a loss is made.

For other goods, the most important aspect will be the aesthetics. The look of a fashion dress is essential; alternatively, the aesthetics of a plastic cup is of little importance when compared to the cost and its functional qualities.

Product life cycle

Regardless of the value analysis mix, all products progress through a life cycle. They are launched, hopefully increase in popularity, and eventually are replaced by new improved products or naturally decline.

The soft drink Coca-Cola has been sold since Dr John Pemberton invented it in 1886, and it is still selling well. However, some of the differently flavoured Coca-Cola drinks have not lasted for very long.

There are four stages to the product life cycle:

1 introduction/development stage
2 growth stage
3 maturity/saturation stage
4 decline stage.

Each stage of the product life cycle requires a different marketing mix.

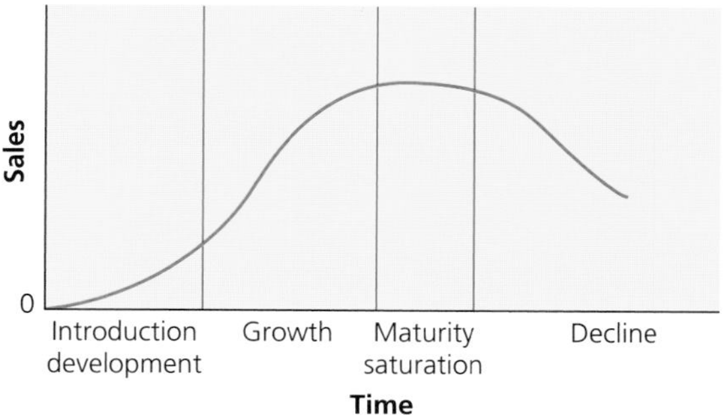

Figure 54.1 A product life cycle

Introduction/development stage

During this stage, the research and development will have been undertaken to discover what the consumer needs. The launch of the product will take place either in one particular region of the country or nationally. Initial sales may be slow until the consumer has tried the product and any marketing activity has had time to build interest. There is often reluctance on behalf of consumers to try anything new or change from the brand they are used to. It is at this stage of the life cycle that a product may fail.

At the development and introduction stages the business will need to take account of all the following factors in its marketing mix:

- Sufficient market research to ensure the product meets its consumers' needs.
- Depending on the nature of the product, the pricing will include introductory offers to encourage consumers to try the product.
- Occasionally, research costs are very high and therefore the price of the product will initially be high until sales increase.
- The advertising will be informative to increase consumer awareness.
- Distribution channels will be low, though increasing sales outlets will be a priority.

Tips and techniques

The marketing mix ideas are only suggestions, because every product may need a distinct marketing strategy for its mix. Nevertheless, this is an attempt to emphasise that the mix will change in line with the stage of the life cycle.

Growth stage

Once consumers are fully aware of the new product, sales are likely to grow more quickly. Word-of-mouth and continued promotion may enhance sales still further. If products can reach this stage and achieve growth, the product is more likely to be a success. The rate of growth in sales will depend upon the nature of the product and the amount of alternatives (competition) in the market.

Marketing mix

- Modifications may be made after initial feedback from market research.
- If in a competitive market, pricing will have to reflect the market price unless a highly distinctive edge allows for a premium price.
- Informative advertising may continue but a move to competitive and persuasive styles is likely.
- Distribution is now much wider and therefore additional channels may be required.

Maturity/saturation stage

If this stage can be reached, it is likely that the product will be profitable. Depending upon the nature of the product and the level of development costs, by this stage all such costs should have been covered. Maintaining the product in this stage of the life cycle becomes the next issue. Sales are likely to flatten out, the nature of any marketing will have changed and competition from newer products becomes a concern.

Saturation implies that all the consumers who wanted to purchase the product have now done so and, therefore, any additional sales will be difficult. The Mars Bar is still in its maturity stage, as is the Kit Kat and Cadbury's Dairy Milk bar. Hovis bread has managed to remain in the maturity stage by promoting itself as a traditional loaf. These products are the exceptions!

The marketing of products in the maturity stage is concentrated on keeping sales constant and avoiding sales falling. The promotion often reminds consumers of the existence of the product. There are several ways in which the business can encourage consumers to continue buying its product in the maturity stage. The strategies used are called extension strategies (see below).

Marketing mix

- The product is established although there may be slight variations to maintain sales.
- Depending upon the actual product, pricing will reflect the amount of competition in the market. However, price reductions may be used as extension strategies (see below).
- With an established product, any advertising will be used just to remind consumers of its existence. Such advertising will increase if newer products enter the market. Similarly, advertising and sales promotions could be used as extension strategies.
- There is the possibility of seeking new markets for the product and therefore establishing new outlets in which it can be made available.

Decline stage

Sales are now falling. Consumers may have lost interest in the product as newer and better alternatives enter the market. Sales may be so low that there is no reason to continue to make the product available.

In this stage a business has to decide if it wants to offer the product at heavily discounted prices to boost sales, or simply allow sales to decline. Much will depend upon whether the business has a replacement product that is soon to be launched into the market. The business does not want consumers to think that its product is outdated and may therefore allow sales to decline, ready for an improved version!

Marketing mix

- There is little point in spending money on a product in decline.
- Prices may be drastically reduced in order to sell off any stock that is left before the new model/ product is launched.
- Sales promotions may be heavily used to help sell off final stock.

Extension strategies

In order to maintain sales, extension strategies are used. Within the car industry, extension strategies are commonplace. They are often used to help sell a model that will soon be replaced. Consumers may be aware of the new model that is soon to be launched, and are therefore reluctant to purchase an old model. However, the manufacturer is able to sell the old model by offering 'special editions'. Incurring only low additional costs, a model can be temporally revived with this technique. A special edition colour or design may be added.

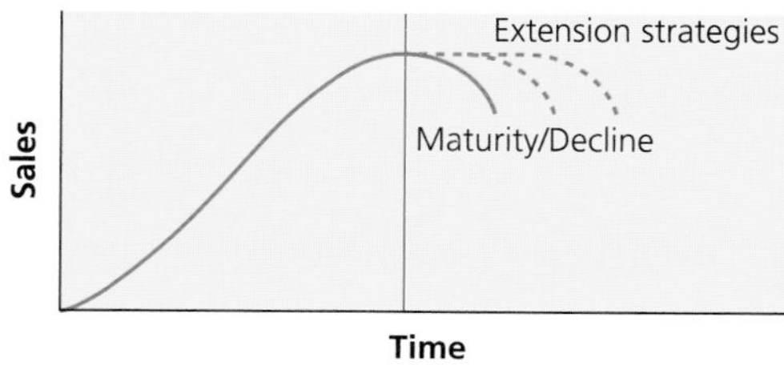

Figure 54.2 Extension strategies

Figure 54.2 shows how an extension strategy extends the life of the product but does not actually prevent the inevitable decline stage.

Product life cycle variations

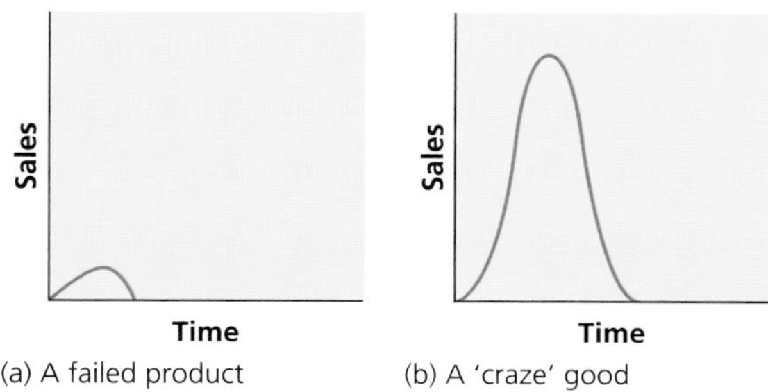

(a) A failed product (b) A 'craze' good

Figure 54.3 Product life cycle variation

The length and 'shape' of the product life cycle may vary considerably. Figure 54.3 shows two completely different life cycles. Figure 54.3a represents a failed product: sales are minimal and the life of the product is very short. In Figure 54.3b, the life of the product is short: sales quickly rise, but just as quickly fall. This is typical of a craze product. Its popularity is intense for a very short period of time before it quickly 'dies' as the next craze enters the market. Examples of craze products include merchandise associated with successful film, or a toy such as a product related to the Disney film, *Frozen*.

Cash inflows and outflows

Although the product life cycle clearly shows the level of sales over time, it does not show what is happening to the level of cash inflows and outflows. Figure 54.4 shows these cashflows for each stage of the life cycle.

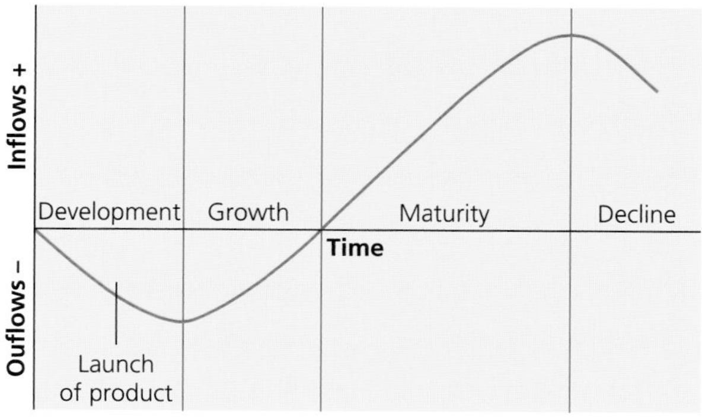

Figure 54.4 Product life cycle cash inflows and outflows

It is worth noting that for all of the first stage of the product life cycle, there is a negative cashflow for this product. The cost of the research and development, the cost of marketing the launch and subsequent promotion, means that more money is going out of the business than is coming in. Even when sales revenue starts to flow in, it may be some considerable time before there is a positive cashflow for this product.

The pricing strategy for the product will affect how quickly the cashflow becomes positive. The problem facing the business is what price to charge for the product. It may decide to set its price at a low level in an attempt to attract consumers. However, by charging a lower price, more sales will be needed before the initial costs are covered. Similarly, if a high price is set, sales may be harder to achieve but if achieved, the initial costs will be covered more quickly. There is no 'right' approach to this and the business will need to be mindful of the type of product and the market in which it is to be sold.

Once the cashflow is positive, the product may have moved into the maturity stage, although there is no set time when this occurs.

Any additional marketing expenditure will have to be considered in terms of its costs set against any likely increased revenue from additional sales.

Product positioning and the product portfolio

Product positioning

Selling the 'right' product in the 'right' segment of the market is a decision that a business will have to take. It is sometimes helpful to undertake research to ascertain what other products are in the market, and where each of them is positioned. Once the information has been collected it can be plotted to show the positioning. This can be done for the whole market, or a business can do this for its own product portfolio. Figure 54.5 shows a typical product-positioning chart.

Product positioning can be achieved by:

1 the price in relation to that of competitors in the market
2 having a beneficial quality, such as durability, when compared to others in the market, or by being a niche product
3 satisfying a small segment of the market
4 being something completely different, such as the Dyson vacuum cleaner when it first entered the market.

Wherever a product is positioned, it aims to increase revenues, either directly (as a result of higher sales of a specific product in a specific position within the market), or indirectly (by being in the market and therefore enhancing the recognition of the brand name without increasing revenues).

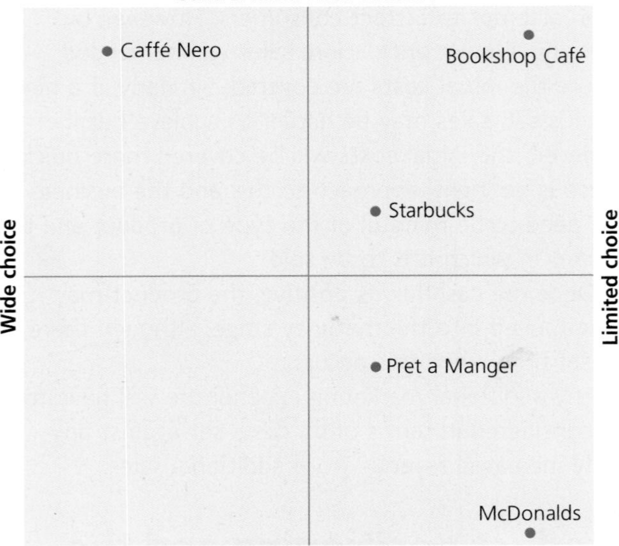

Figure 54.5 Fast food outlets product positioning map

Tips and techniques

There is no correct way in which to plot the products within a given market. What is used to mark the axis and help distinguish the various products is often arbitrary.

Product portfolio

Having considered one product, it is important to realise that many businesses produce a range of products. This collection of products is often referred to as the product portfolio. Deciding what products ought to be in a portfolio will depend upon a variety of factors.

The information on a product positioning chart such as Figure 54.5 can be used to help a business to decide if it wants to produce a product that will fill a gap in the market. However, the business needs to be careful because there may be a very good reason for the existence of that gap in the market; it may simply be that there is no demand for that type of product. The product positioning chart can be used to see where the majority of the products are positioned. A business may then decide that it too should launch a product in a sector that all the others are concentrated in, even though it will mean entering a highly competitive sector of the market.

The product positioning chart can also help a business to see any obvious gaps in its own product portfolio. Many car manufacturers have a range of cars in their portfolio, each model ensuring that the name of the manufacturer is represented in most segments of the market. For example, Ford produces a wide range of cars, ranging from the Ford Ka, Ford Focus, Ford Galaxy to the Ford Transit Van. Each model is designed to satisfy a demand in the market, whether it is for a small family saloon car (the Fiesta), a people carrier (Ford Galaxy) or the 4x4 market (Ford Kuga). Ford has a very comprehensive product portfolio, with a model for almost every single type of car and commercial vehicle.

Boston Matrix

Another tool that a business can use when deciding what products to produce is the Boston Matrix. This is a different way of categorising the products within the portfolio of a business. This matrix considers products in terms of their market share and potential for market growth.

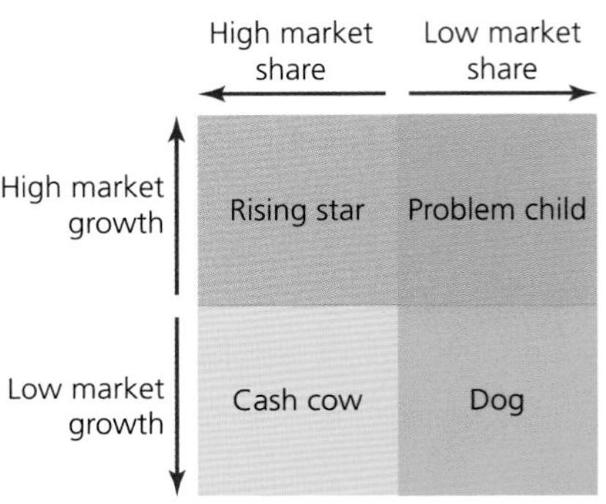

Figure 54.6 Boston Matrix

Figure 54.6 shows the four categories of products.

1 Star
2 Cash cow
3 Problem child
4 Dog.

Star

This is the category where the product has a high market share and it is in a market which has potential to grow. (It is sometimes referred to as a rising star.) Although this may appear the best category to be in, this is slightly misleading. In order to gain and maintain a high market share, the business may have had to advertise heavily in order to establish itself fully, and maintain a high advertising spend. Such products have the potential to be future cash cows.

Cash cow

The cash cow is the category that ensures high revenues. It is an established product that has a high share of the market. Although the market has low growth, the product generates large amounts of cash. The cash cow is normally a mature product that does not need heavy marketing expenditure, and therefore sales revenues are profitable. The fact that it is sold in large quantities allows for low unit cost and therefore high profits. The large profits gained from cash cow products can be used to support problem child products, which do need the investment.

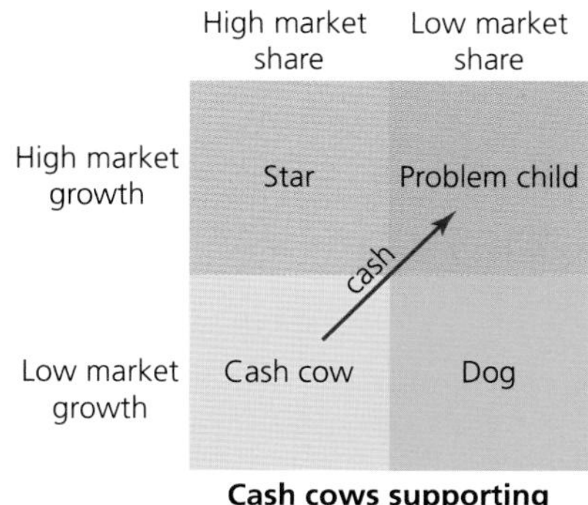

Figure 54.7 Boston Matrix: a marketing strategy to support the product portfolio

Problem child (or question marks)

The problem child has a low market share within a market that is rapidly growing. The aim is for a problem child to become a star or a cash cow. In order for this to be achieved, the business will need to invest heavily to help increase the market share of the product. A problem child product is normally a new product that has yet to establish itself in the market, and consequently is not profitable yet. Investment in marketing is needed in order to raise the profile of the product within the expanding market.

Dog

Dogs have a low market share and low market growth; consequently they have no real future. Unless the dog is a vital addition to the range of products offered by the business, it ought to be dropped as quickly as possible.

Advantages of using the Boston Matrix

By looking at its range of products within the Boston Matrix, a business can see if it has a balanced portfolio, and whether it has sufficient cash cows to feed the problem child. A business does not need dogs, but does need cash cows in order to convert problem child products into stars or cash cows. Too many stars may be a drain on financial resources, as they require large funds to maintain their position in the growth market.

Selecting the appropriate product mix

Businesses will vary in the content of their product mix; some businesses may only produce one product and sell it very successfully; others may have a range of products, often at different stages of the product life cycle.

A firm like Cadbury's sells a complete range of chocolate products. Dairy Milk bars will be regarded as cash cows; they have changed little over time and still sell well. Other products may be tried and either prove successful with the public, or flop on launch. A recent success for Cadbury's has been the range of mini-bites of Twirls and Flakes. These bags of mini-bites are popular with the public and have a high profit margin.

Service marketing

Unlike the manufacturing sector, the service sector does not have a tangible product. If a customer is buying a new car, they can look at the model in the show room, sit in it and take it for a test drive before making the decision to buy. This is not possible with a product like a holiday, a theatre ticket or house insurance. In these cases the customer may be taking the business on trust. For this reason reputation, customer recommendation and word-of-mouth reports are likely to be very important in the service sector. The restaurant sector is a particularly good example of the importance of good customer feedback. Diners who have been to a pub or restaurant are likely to talk about it in the following days to family, friends and work colleagues. Good reviews will significantly increase business, whereas poor reviews will be quickly passed on to others. For this reason, it is of utmost importance that the product is of the highest quality in the service sector.

Further sources

www.ford.co.uk The website for the car manufacturer, clearly showing its product mix

www.dyson.co.uk As above but showing Dyson's product mix

www.productlifecyclestages.com Clear examples of stages of the product lifecycle

Your turn

Questions in red are for A Level candidates only.

Multiple-choice questions

1 Product positioning refers to:
A where the product is sold
B where the product is placed in the shop or supermarket
C which sector has most sales
D selling the 'right' product at an appropriate sector *(1)*

2 Which of the following is not a stage of the product life cycle?
A maturity
B recession
C growth
D saturation. *(1)*

3 In the Boston Matrix, a cash cow has a:
A small market share in a slow-growing market
B large market share in a fast-growing market
C large market share in a slow-growing market
D small market share in a fast-growing market. *(1)*

Revision questions

1 Explain what is meant by 'marketing mix'. *(2)*

2 Explain two reasons why a business might find the early stages of the product life cycle difficult to survive. *(4)*

3 What is the definition of a 'problem child' in the Boston Matrix? *(2)*

4 State two examples of an extension strategy for a well-known business, other than those given in this chapter. *(4)*

5 Draw a product positioning map for at least eight different existing chocolates and chocolate bars using cheaper and luxury on one axis and widely available and limited outlets on the other. *(8)*

Total *(20)*

Case study

Dyson vacuum cleaners

Dyson vacuum cleaners can be used to show the different phases of the product life cycle.

For James Dyson, the development stage of the bagless vacuum cleaner was lengthy as he struggled to find financial backing for his idea.

When the product was first produced it was very expensive compared with other traditional vacuum cleaners and, indeed, its price remains higher than most of its competitors even now.

Dyson has since used extension strategies to good effect to ensure that sales and market share are maintained. Sometimes the extension strategy might be something fairly easy to introduce, like a change in the look and outer design of the product. Other extension strategies have included new products like a small, lightweight cleaner designed for smaller homes and flats or major improvements to the mechanism of the vacuum cleaners. Dyson recently introduced a cordless vacuum cleaner to its range which has proved to be very popular. Essentially though, the product remains the same as the original with its bagless cleaning system. However, James Dyson understands that investment in research and development is essential to extend the life and success of his product. In 2011, Dyson invested 36 per cent of its profits, £70.3 million, into research and development.

1 Calculate Dyson's total profit for 2011? *(2)*

2 Analyse one reason why the bagless vacuum cleaner is a unique selling point for Dyson. *(4)*

3 Evaluate the reasons for Dyson's success in its market. *(9)*

Total *(15)*

Chapter 55

Price

AS / Year 1

Both AS and A Level students must know all of the content in this chapter.

However, AS students will not be asked to evaluate the usefulness of the three elasticities, where as A Level students may be examined on this.

The price of a product or service indicates both its value and its quality. A consumer can use the price of a product to make a comparison with other goods and services.

The price that a business fixes for its products will determine the level of revenue that is earned. The price must also fit with the rest of the marketing mix that is implemented by the business, as the image of a product is influenced by its price. A product that has a high price ought not to be sold at discount shops or local markets, as this would not be compatible with its image. The pricing mix must take into account the costs of the business, the prices charged by competitors, the willingness of consumers to pay and the business's objectives.

Pricing can be viewed from different perspectives. Within the business, different departments and stakeholders will have differing views on the ideal price of a good or service:

- The finance department may want a price that yields a high profit.
- The marketing department will want a price that helps to gain a foothold in the market, especially if it is a competitive market.
- The consumers will want value for money, and therefore usually a lower price.
- Shareholders will want a return on their investment.

All these stakeholders have some input on the eventual price of a product.

Factors affecting price

There is also a wide range of factors that affect the price charged for a good or service:

- objectives of the business, and its objectives for the given product or service
- consumers, their income and tastes
- cost of producing the good
- level of demand within the market
- level of competition within the market
- actual nature of the product or service
- its stage in the product life cycle
- rest of the marketing mix
- scale of production
- economic environment (boom or recession)
- value of the pound (exchange rates)
- legislation
- weather conditions.

Market forces and price

Aside from the points listed above, it is also thought that market forces normally determine the price of any good or service. Market forces consist of demand and supply.

As prices rise, the demand for goods and services fall because consumers can no longer afford to pay for the goods. On the other hand, suppliers are usually willing to supply more goods if prices are rising. The actual price that is charged for a good or service is a combination of the forces of demand and supply.

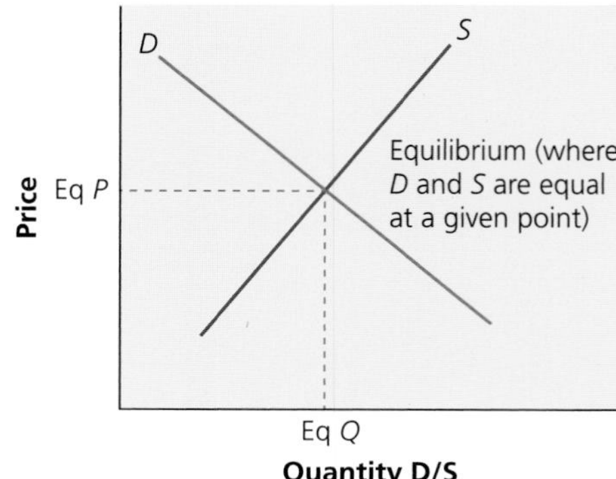

Figure 55.1 Demand and supply (price determinants)

The point that demand and supply intersect represents the equilibrium price. However, it is not easy for a business to know what this particular price is. There may be a certain amount of guessing or an attempt to gauge the right price by using market research. With so many factors affecting the setting of the price, it is not a straightforward process. For example, setting the price of petrol during 2013 and 2014 was not easy. The petrol companies had to consider:

- the cost of a barrel of oil
- the level of tax (excise duty and VAT on the product)
- what the competitors were charging
- the objectives of the business
- the area in which the petrol was sold
- what was happening in the economy.

Price elasticity

Elasticity measures the response of demand to a change in price (price elasticity of demand) or income (income elasticity of demand).

Price elasticity of demand (PED)

Whenever the price of a good or service is changed, the level of demand will also change. How much it will change will depend upon a number of factors:

- the nature of the product (whether it is a necessity or a luxury good)
- the level of the price change
- the income of the consumer
- the number of previous price increases
- how high the product is on a consumer's preference scale
- whether the purchase can be postponed.

A business will want to know the likely consequences if it decides to change the price of its product or service. As a consequence, the business will have to consider all of the listed factors above in an attempt to assess what will happen to the demand.

The combination of the above factors determines by how much demand changes. Looking at the characteristics of the product and the consumer will help to decide the likely elasticity of the product or service.

Table 55.1 Characteristics of elastic and inelastic demand

Elastic demand	Inelastic demand
Large price increase	Small price increase
Large proportion of consumer's income	Small proportion of consumer's income
Purchase can be postponed	Purchase cannot be postponed
Large number of substitutes	Very few, if any, substitutes
Low on preference list	High on preference list
Low level of consumer income	High level of consumer income
Luxury good	Necessity

The rate of change is referred to as the elasticity of the product.

Apart from using the characteristics of the product and the consumer to judge the elasticity, it is possible to calculate a value for both price and income elasticity.

Once the elasticity is established, it is easier to gauge the likely consequences of any changes in the prices charged.

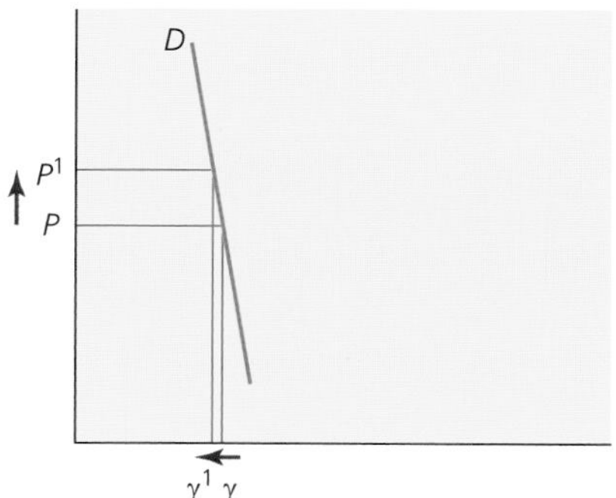

Revenue rising
10% increase in price – 2% fall in demand

Figure 55.2 Inelastic demand

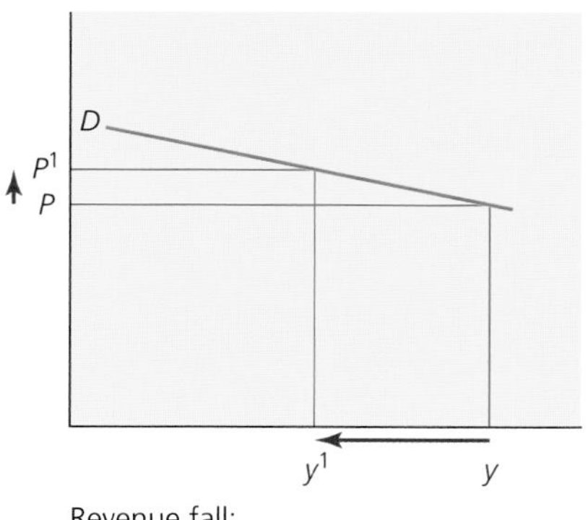

Revenue fall;
10% increase in price – 30% fall in demand

Figure 55.3 Elastic demand

A business is able to see that if it increased its prices for a price inelastic product by 10 per cent, demand will not fall very much (2 per cent); consequently, the revenue will actually increase. However, an increase in the price of a price elastic product of 10 per cent will lead to a greater fall in demand (30 per cent) and a fall in revenue.

Whether the marketing department will consider a loss in revenue acceptable will depend upon the reasons for the increase in price.

The marketing department will want to know the likely price elasticity of demand to help decide whether to increase or decrease its prices. An inelastic product can withstand price increases, as demand will not change by very much. However, if the product is more price sensitive (elastic), even small changes in the price could affect demand significantly.

The price elasticity of demand (PED) measures the response of demand to a change in price.

The formula for determining PED is:

$$\frac{\text{Percentage change in demand}}{\text{Percentage change in price}}$$

Tips and techniques

As always, remember to state the formula, as you will be rewarded for showing your working. For A2 modules, to gain level 3 (analysis), it is important that you are able to comment on the significance of the answer in the context of the business and its products.

Income elasticity of demand

This measures the response of demand to a change in income.

Usually, when consumer income increases, the level of demand increases as consumers have more spending power. What the extra income is spent on depends upon a wide range of factors.

The key characteristics that will help to determine the level of income elasticity of demand are shown in Table 55.2.

Table 55.2 Income elasticity of demand

Elastic demand	Inelastic demand
Inferior goods	
Luxury goods	Necessities
Large increase in income	Small increase in income
Consumer's income is low	Consumer's income is high

The formula for determining income elasticity of demand is:

$$\frac{\text{Percentage change in demand}}{\text{Percentage change in income}}$$

Tips and techniques

One of the major limitations of using the formula to gauge the elasticity is that it assumes you know the price or income changes and what happens to demand. This is highly unlikely when bringing out a new product. It is also unlikely that the use of previous changes in prices or incomes and demand will guarantee the same response.

Cross elasticity of demand

Cross elasticity of demand shows how a change in the price of one good will affect the demand for another.

The formula for calculating cross elasticity of demand is:

$$\frac{\text{Percentage change in the demand for A}}{\text{Percentage change in the price of B}}$$

It is used to show the connection, or lack of connection, between two commodities. If the goods are substitutes for one another, there will be a high cross elasticity of demand. For example, a rise in the price of beef will increase the demand for other meats, such as chicken. If the price of one good goes up, the demand for the substitute will also go up. If the goods are complements to one another there will also be a high cross elasticity of demand, but this time when the price of one good goes up (or down) the demand for the complement will also go up (or down). For example, if the price of tablet computers goes down, the demand for them will rise, but so will the demand for accessories, like cases, even though their prices have not changed. Where cross elasticity of demand is very low it means there is little or no connection between the two commodities. For example, a rise in the price of strawberries will have little effect on the demand for cars.

Pricing strategies/methods

As we have seen above, deciding on the prices for the goods and services is not straightforward. However, the overall objectives of the business are crucial. Once it has decided what it wants to achieve for the business as a whole and for any individual product, the business can then decide which pricing strategy or strategies to use.

Tips and techniques

When answering a question on pricing, it is worth remembering that there is no right strategy. It is important to use the information given in the case study, as it will probably help you to eliminate several options as being inappropriate for the specific business.

Skimming

Skimming describes the process in which the business sets a high price for its goods or services in an attempt to gain profits quickly.

This pricing strategy is used for products that have a short life cycle because it is necessary to gain maximum benefits while possible. If other businesses note the high returns made by a specific business, they may also enter the market, which forces the price of the goods down. In summary, skimming starts with a high price which it may eventually have to reduce.

Penetration pricing

This is a strategy that is used to help establish a new product in the market and subsequently gain a share of the market. To establish itself in the market, the business sets a low price initially, hoping to attract consumers. The product may also be heavily advertised, highlighting the introductory low price. Once a reasonable share of the market has been achieved or loyal consumers gained, the price may be increased. The level and rate of price increases will depend upon the desired price level when compared with the introductory price.

Premium pricing or prestige pricing

A high price is set for a product or service in an attempt to create an image and indicate a high level of quality. Initially, BMW took this approach in terms of its pricing. Stella Artois has tried to position itself as a premium product by selling its lager at a higher price. However, as competition has increased, it has reduced its prices, using various promotional pricing campaigns.

Psychological pricing

This involves setting a price that sounds less than it really is. Charging 99 pence sounds substantially cheaper than one pound; similarly, charging £9.99 sounds much less than £10.

It is a practice that is used by many retailers and manufacturers:

- The clothing industry prices the majority of its clothes using this strategy; e.g. £10.99, £29.99. £69.99.
- The car industry prefers to price models at a pound below its ideal price, e.g. £6,999 rather than £7,000.
- The selling price for a house may be £199,950 rather than £200,000.

The difference in the actual price is minute but if it appears less, it may encourage consumers to purchase.

Psychological pricing is often used by the sellers of petrol, where the price per litre may be expressed as 99.9p or £1.09p. The difference of 0.1p is meaningless in terms of expenditure, and yet consumers will refer to the price as 99p and not almost £1. For this reason, it is a worthwhile practice.

Loss leaders

This pricing strategy is often used in order to entice consumers into a particular retail outlet. It is heavily used by supermarkets, which usually reduce the price of essential products such as sugar, milk, soups, beans and bread to below cost.

Careful consideration is given to the placement within the shop of the loss leader so that once consumers are enticed into the shop, they will have to pass a wide range of products that it is hoped they will purchase, often on impulse. These sales will more than compensate for the losses made on the loss leaders.

Competition-based price

There are occasions when a business will set the price of its goods below those of its competitors with the intention of gaining additional sales and 'beating' its competitors. This is a short-term pricing policy to gain additional sales until the competition respond. Predatory pricing (see below) is a similar pricing policy but on a more drastic level.

Predatory pricing (destroyer pricing)

Whichever name is used, the Competition and Markets Authority often sees this type of pricing as anti-competitive. Predatory pricing is used when an established business responds to a new business entering the market by reducing its prices (often even to incur a loss in the short term). With such low prices, the new entrant will find it impossible or very difficult to compete, and even if it did try to match the prices of the established business, it would also incur a loss it cannot afford. As a new entrant into the market, it would not be able to make cost savings due to a lack of economies of scale (still selling in small quantities) and may therefore find it impossible to sustain such low prices. The established business is then able to 'force' the new entrant out of the market.

This type of pricing is occasionally attempted with established rivals, but such price wars are often only short-lived or used as a form of promotional campaign.

Market-based pricing (going-rate pricing)

For products that are very similar, or even identical (homogeneous), a business will take its price for the product from the market. Milk and petrol are classic examples. Oil companies tend to follow each other when prices fluctuate, due to the changing price of a barrel of oil. In 2008, when a barrel of oil reached over \$140, the price of a litre of petrol rose to 125p. However, as the barrel of oil price fell to below \$60, petrol prices fell to 95p a litre and all petrol stations were charging very similar prices.

Promotional pricing

There are several forms of promotional pricing.

- BOGOF (buy one get one free)
- price reductions (10% off)
- '3 for 2' offers, as used extensively at Boots the Chemist
- loss leaders (see above).

These can be used at any stage of the product life cycle, and are useful strategies to maintain a high level of sales.

Cost plus

This is a way of actually setting the price to be charged to the consumer. The costs refer to the expenses of producing the product, namely the materials, labour and other costs such as marketing. In order to ensure that a profit is made, costs must be less than the selling price. The process of finding this price involves calculating the actual costs for the product and then adding an amount or percentage to the costs. For example:

A restaurant has costs of £4 for a steak meal and decides to add a mark-up of 300 per cent.

The price will therefore be:

costs of £4 + 300% (£12) = £16

There is often some confusion between mark-up and margin. The mark-up is when an amount (usually a percentage) is added to the total costs to gain the selling price. The margin (or profit margin) is the level of profit expressed as a percentage of the selling price.

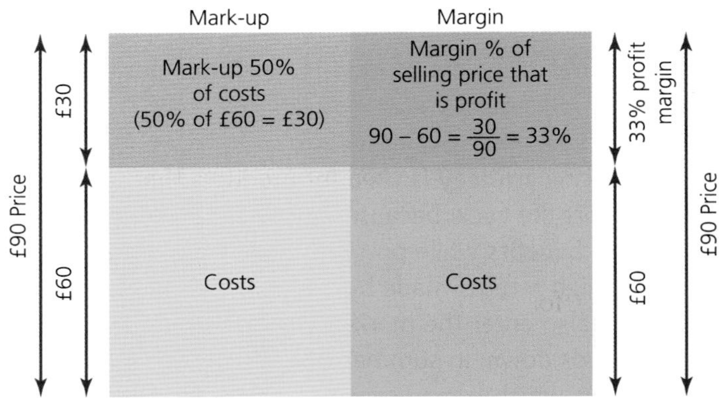

Figure 55.4 Mark-up and margin

In Figure 55.4, the mark-up is simply a percentage (50%) of the costs that is added to the costs, to give a price of £90.

The margin is calculated as a percentage of the selling price, therefore is:

£90 – costs (£60) = £30

$\frac{£30}{£90} = 33\%$

Contribution or marginal cost pricing

Contribution or marginal costing is a method whereby fixed costs or overheads are ignored and the business considers only the variable costs of production (see **Chapter 27**). Contribution is the selling price of a product minus the variable cost of producing it. This can be calculated as a total across all production, or the contribution made by each extra unit produced. Once the variable cost has been covered, anything left over can be used as a contribution towards fixed costs.

Contribution per unit (cpu) = price – variable cost per unit

Total contribution = sales × cpu

It is important that contribution is not confused with profit. Output making a positive contribution may increase profits, but this is not necessarily the case. Businesses are most likely to consider contribution costing when they are considering accepting an order that will not increase their overheads (see **Chapter 27**).

For example, an airline like British Airways may consider filling the last few seats on a plane by costing them to cover the extra variable cost or marginal cost of carrying that passenger. These marginal costs will be the cost of food, the extra fuel to carry an extra passenger and the costs of the ticket itself. All the other costs like the crew, the fuel and services and parking slots at the airports will already have been paid. Any extra income can then be used to contribute towards the overheads of the business. Therefore, British Airways will be happy if the price it achieves for the last few seats gives a positive contribution.

Price discrimination

Price discrimination occurs when different prices are charged for the same product or service within different markets. Price discrimination is operated in several forms.

Area

A different price is charged for the same product in different parts of the world or country. For example, businesses will charge in export markets according to the competition they face.

Time

A different price is charged for the same product or service at different times of the day. Prices for train tickets or rates for the telephone, gas and electricity vary according to the time of day. These are usually denoted by the terms 'peak charges' and 'off-peak charges'. The ability to charge different prices at different times of the day is related to the elasticity of the products or services. If a businessperson needs to be in London for a meeting at 9 a.m., it will mean catching an early train. The train company knows that such travel is essential (inelastic) and therefore is able to charge a much higher price.

Reductions for railcards, buses and admission to various entertainment complexes are available to people over the age of 60. Similarly, lower prices are charged for children of varying ages, depending upon the service being used.

Tips and techniques

This chapter concentrates on the strategies for pricing, and not how to actually calculate prices. The methods for calculating prices are to be found in other chapters as stated: absorption, marginal costing (contribution), cost-based or full cost, standard pricing (see **Chapter 27**).

Examination questions tend to ask about strategies; in other words what it is hoped to achieve and therefore how to price the products, or how to calculate actual prices.

Service marketing

Price is a significant marketing tool in both product and service marketing and the same rules are likely to apply in all cases. For example, when booking a flight, in some cases the customer might be looking for the cheapest product. This will mean the consumer only considers budget airlines. In other cases the consumer might be looking for the best value for money. This might mean using one of the national carriers, like British Airways, if the passenger wants to take a large amount of luggage, travel at a more convenient time or be provided with free refreshments on the plane. In other situations passengers may not be interested in the price at all and may simply be looking for a luxury flight. Service providers need to consider price in relation to the service they are providing and the type of consumer they wish to attract.

Further sources

www.marketingteacher.com Free marketing resources

Your turn

Questions are suitable for all AS and A Level candidates.

Multiple-choice questions

1 If the price of a product rises from £8 to £10, the demand falls from 20,000 to 16,000 units a week. What is the price elasticity of demand?

A 1.25
B 1
C 0.8
D 1.5 *(1)*

2 If the demand for one product falls when the price of another rises, these goods are:

A Substitutes
B Not connected
C Complements
D Inferior goods *(1)*

3 Which characteristic would you expect of a good that has low income elasticity of demand?
   A Luxury good
   B Necessity
   C Many substitutes
   D High value good (1)

Revision questions

1 State the formula for price elasticity of demand. (2)
2 State two examples of promotional pricing. (2)
3 Explain price discrimination. (2)
4 Explain the 'predatory pricing' term. (2)
5 If incomes increase by 10 per cent and demand for a given product increases from 120 to 150, calculate the income elasticity of demand. (3)
6 If a product has costs of £120 and a mark-up of 15 per cent, calculate the selling price. (3)

Total (14)

Case study

MacQuarrie Infrastructure Group (MIG)

Operating toll roads

The Midlands Expressway was opened in 2003 in an attempt to ease congestion on the M6 motorway around Birmingham. At present the road runs at a third of its capacity of 100,000 vehicles a day.

When the road was first opened the charge for a journey by car was £2; by 2014 it was £5.50 at peak times. MIG maintain that the reason for the price increases over the intervening period is the fall in the number of toll-road users. Most people would argue with the logic of this, saying that raising price will reduce demand, but MIG is more interested in maximising the revenue that it is earning from the toll road. In this situation price elasticity of demand is the important factor.

In general, the price elasticity of demand for toll roads and bridges is around 0.2, but if there is an alternative route, as is the case with the M6, the elasticity may be as high as 0.8. This means, therefore, that the demand is inelastic and that a higher price will lead to an increase in total revenue. If MIG are sure that demand is inelastic they can raise the price to increase revenue and try to maintain operating costs at a stable level. This will then lead to an increase in profits.

For the future, however, MIG will need to proceed with caution in raising its prices further. Price elasticity does not remain constant; it tends to rise as prices rise. At some point, the elasticity for the toll may become elastic and then a further rise in price will lead to a fall in revenue.

1 The price of a journey rises from £5.50 to £6 and the demand falls from 32,000 to 30,000. Calculate the price elasticity of demand? (4)
2 Calculate the total revenue at £5.50 and £6. (2)
3 Analyse two factors that will affect the demand for the Midlands Expressway. (4)
4 Many toll users and local residents argue for a reduction in price to encourage increased use of the toll. Evaluate the arguments for doing this. (9)

Total (19)

Chapter 56

Place

AS / Year 1

Both AS and A Level students must know all of the content in this chapter.

The third 'P' of the four Ps in the marketing mix is 'place'. This refers to the methods by which the business delivers its goods or service to the right place at the right time.

The place or distribution mix means getting the right method of distribution for the product in the most cost-effective manner.

Tips and techniques

It is important to remember that 'place' refers to distribution and not the location of the business. Under exam conditions, candidates often write about the wrong concept for this part of the marketing mix.

Channels of distribution

This is the method by which the good travels from the producer to the consumer. The main five channels of distribution are shown in Figure 56.1. Some of the channels of distribution involve the use of intermediaries: these are wholesalers, retailers and agents.

Wholesalers

The job of wholesalers in the distribution chain is to 'break bulk'. This means that wholesalers buy from manufacturers in large volume, and then break down what they buy into smaller units. This is particularly important for businesses such as corner shops or public houses, whose owners may wish to buy in small volume and require mixed lots. For example, if a small shopkeeper was buying from a yoghurt producer directly, he might have to take large volume packs of the same yoghurt. The wholesaler will receive the larger packs in a variety of flavours and types, and put together a selection of mixed packs to be sold to a number of similar small businesses.

- Wholesalers are able to use specialist knowledge of their part of the distribution network to benefit producers and retailers.
- They move goods around the country using their own network, reducing costs and valuable time for other businesses.
- They have purpose-built warehouses and storage facilities for the range of products they supply.
- The manufacturer and retailer are able to concentrate their efforts on the areas in which they specialise.
- They offer choice to the retailer.

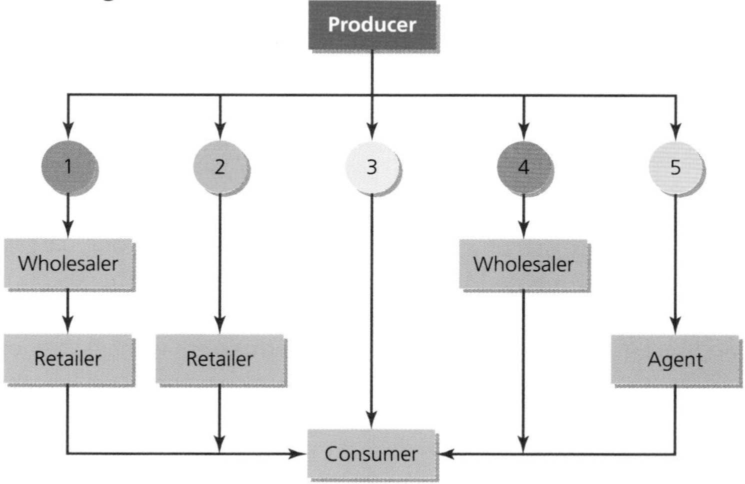

Figure 56.1 Channels of distribution

Retailers

Retailers are responsible for the final part of the distribution chain: selling the final product to the consumer. Retailers vary from the tiny shop in a rural village, to huge businesses like Tesco and Marks & Spencer; in-between these two extremes lie chain stores (e.g. Next and PC World), department stores (e.g. John Lewis and House of Fraser), and voluntary retail chains such as Spar. Increasingly, in recent years, large retailers such as Sainsbury's and Argos have begun to use regional distribution centres. These centres are sited near motorway links (for example, the M6/M1 junction), to make distribution quicker, cheaper and more effective.

Agents

Agents work in several sectors of the distribution network. Their role is to negotiate between buyers and sellers. In doing this, they will never have control of the good or service they are selling. They are usually paid on a commission basis, and often work in such sectors as travel and ticket sales. When you buy a holiday in a travel agency, the agent is acting on behalf of the travel business or airline. If the sale is completed, the travel business will pay the agent a percentage of the sale as commission.

In some countries (e.g. Japan), it is necessary for exporters to sell their goods through an agent, rather than directly to the retailer or customer. For businesses about to break into a new market, this process can be very useful as the agent will have specialist knowledge of the market, the law and customs, and will often speak the language. All this is helpful to prospective exporters moving into a new market.

Changes in distribution

In the past, the most common channel of distribution in the retail trade was the first one shown in Figure 56.1. Most large retailers such as supermarkets, department stores and chains, bought from wholesalers who held stock that they had purchased from producers. The growth of the supermarket sector, in particular, has led to the increasing use of channel two. As the supermarkets grew, they realised that they would be able to reduce their costs if they bought direct from the producer. In addition, as they grew, the size of their orders made it possible for them to negotiate huge discounts that could be passed on to the consumer.

Channel 3, where the producer sells direct to the customer, has also become much more popular with the growth of mail order and internet sales. This channel of distribution, called direct marketing, has benefits both for the producer and the consumer. For the producer, it cuts out the middleman and gives all the profit from the sale directly to the seller. For the consumer, it means that there is no need to visit a retail outlet; goods can be bought at home and delivered to home. As the cost of driving rises and congestion on the roads worsens, this is an important advantage for the customer.

The fourth channel in Figure 56.1 involves the public buying direct from a wholesaler. This channel is most commonly used by groups such as sports associations or scout groups, where food is being bought for catering purposes. The purchaser often needs a special card to be able to buy from the wholesaler to show that they belong to such a group. In some cases, warehouses may sell directly to the public to clear surplus stock.

Channel 5 in Figure 56.1, together with any channel using an agent, is used in very specific cases like that of a travel agent or estate agent. Some businesses (e.g. Avon and catalogue companies) use agents to sell their products direct to the consumer. The agent will usually have a catalogue to display the range of goods and place customer orders with the producer. Avon representatives are paid commission by Avon on any goods that they sells.

Reasons for changes in distribution channels

In the past 20 years, the retail sector has probably experienced more changes than any other sector of the economy. In order to meet the new needs of this sector, it has been necessary to change distribution methods.

The size of supermarkets has risen sharply, as has the number of outlets they have. Tesco is now represented in almost every postcode area of the UK. This means that Tesco has strong bargaining power with producers and can make demands on them, in terms of price and delivery. Seven-day and 24-hour opening means that supermarkets want deliveries throughout the week to ensure that their shelves are full.

Many retail businesses have now moved to out-of-town retail parks, like Westfield. This makes physical distribution easier. Instead of having to deliver to congested town and city centres, where the road network is often poor, deliveries can be made to retail parks that are served by good road systems.

At one time, supermarkets only sold food items. They now sell clothing, electrical goods and services like banking and insurance. This has put the major supermarkets into competition with many other areas of the economy, where their size and power is a considerable threat to smaller businesses.

The retail sector is increasingly customer-orientated, and a great deal of time and effort is spent improving the shopping experience and giving customers what they want. Customer service in all areas of retailing, whatever the distribution channel, is more important now than it has ever been. Customers are often aware of the law and their rights as a consequence of television programmes like 'Watchdog', and they will take action if they feel that their rights are being abused. Getting the delivery system right is an important part of achieving customer satisfaction.

Online and digital distribution

Improvements in telecommunications have meant that customers can contact producers directly or through call centres to place orders. This is often a more convenient way of shopping for busy people. Deliveries will then be made direct to the customer, either by post or courier service. The use of courier businesses as a means of physical distribution has grown alongside mail order and internet sales.

The growth of the internet and broadband access has made buying online one of the biggest changes in retail sales in recent years. Even traditional retailers, like Marks & Spencer and John Lewis now achieve a major part of their business through online sales and the use of click and collect services.

New technology has meant that, in some sectors of the economy, traditional methods of distribution have changed completely. The use of electronic methods to deliver written word and music to consumers are the areas where the main changes have taken place.

- The introduction of electronic readers, like the Kindle, means that the market for electronic books has grown rapidly in recent years. In 2013, the size of this market was 12 per cent of total books sold, but this figure is expected to more than double by 2018 (Statista.com). However, there are some signs that the market is beginning to slow down and level out in terms of growth, possibly because there will always be those who prefer to read a print rather than digital book.
- Many students in schools and colleges are now given access to textbooks in electronic form rather than as printed text.
- The BBC's news website is one of the most widely used internet sites in the UK. The purchase of printed newspapers is in decline and the use of websites like the Daily Mail and the Guardian is growing rapidly. In a similar way, specialist magazines are increasingly being produced in a digital format.
- The purchase of CDs has declined very rapidly with most consumers now buying music as a download to a smartphone or notebook. Music charts have had to use downloads in their statistics to reflect this change in distribution.
- The traditional watching of television has also changed. Families are now likely to be watching TV programmes on laptops, smartphones and notepads using an on-demand service like BBC iPlayer or Netflix. They will also be buying films from businesses like iTunes to watch on devices rather than purchasing DVDs to watch on a television. Access to films and television programmes in this form continues to grow rapidly.
- Many businesses now send out tickets in email rather than printed form. This is the case for theatres, cinemas, rail companies and airlines.

Physical distribution

This refers to the physical method of distribution which a business uses. For the UK economy, road transport is the most common method of moving goods from one place to another. Road transport of goods began to replace rail transport in the second half of the twentieth century. However, environmental concerns together with the high price of oil have encouraged businesses to look again at the viability of rail and canal transport.

Air transport is also more widely used now. This is obviously an important method of physical distribution for firms that have export markets. It is also important in situations where it is necessary to deliver a perishable product to its market in as fresh a condition as possible. Fresh flowers and vegetables such as mange-tout peas and asparagus are air-freighted into the UK from Kenya and South America on a daily basis.

Sea–shipping containers ready for export

The means of physical distribution selected will depend on the following factors:

- the need for freshness for perishable items (e.g. fish)
- the price which the consumer is prepared to pay for fresh rather than frozen produce
- the bulkiness of the product
- the need to make regular deliveries (e.g. to a 24-hour supermarket)
- the price of the product (low value products need cheaper distribution systems)
- the size of the product: heavy or awkward items such as bricks or trampolines would usually be moved by road or rail
- the nature of the consumer: if Amazon is delivering books to an internet shopper, the postal service will be used; larger orders to commercial customers are likely to be sent by road
- the method of production: using just-in-time (JIT) production and stock control has meant that businesses have looked for suppliers that can meet their needs efficiently. If a manufacturer of washing machines is using JIT production, they will need to be confident that their suppliers will ensure that they always have the components to maintain production
- the sunk, unrecoverable cost of the capital investment in equipment: e.g. docks in the UK are largely equipped with machines for lifting containers from lorries. This means that it would be very difficult for an exporting business to distribute its products through the docks by rail.

Service marketing

Digital technology is increasingly being used to distribute services. Businesses like airlines, theatres, cinemas, music producers and banks are increasingly using the internet to distribute the services that they provide. At the same time, there will always be those who choose not to use the digital method and prefer personal service. For that reason, service sector businesses like banks and travel agents still have a presence on most high streets, but in much smaller numbers than used to be the case.

Further sources

www.marketingdonut.co.uk Marketing resources for a business

www.marketingmo.com Step-by-step plans for an effective marketing campaign

Your turn

Questions are suitable for all AS and A Level candidates.

Multiple-choice questions

1 The definition of a wholesaler is:

A a large seller of goods

B an organisation that stores goods for other businesses

C an organisation that breaks bulk

D an organisation that sells direct. *(1)*

2 All the following have been major changes in distribution in recent years except:

A the decline in small retail outlets

B increased specialisation by major supermarkets

C direct selling to consumers by manufacturers

D a rapid rise in internet and mail order sales. *(1)*

3 The term 'place' in the 4Ps of the marketing mix refers to:
A where the product is sold
B where the product is made
C how the product is sold
D how the product is distributed. *(1)*

Revision questions

1 Explain what is meant by the term 'agent' in terms of distribution. *(2)*
2 State two reasons for changes in the most commonly used channels of distribution in recent years. *(2)*
3 Explain what is meant by 'physical distribution' and give two examples of it in practice. *(4)*
Total *(8)*

Case study

Hermes

For most consumers, buying online has now become the quick and easy way to shop. The problems begin, however, when it comes to taking delivery of those goods. Many people are out at work when deliveries are made and others do not want to be tied to the house for hours while they wait for a delivery to turn up.

The logistics firm, Hermes, is the largest parcel delivery firm in the UK, delivering 190 million parcels a year. It has contracts with major retailers such as Next, AOS, John Lewis and Tesco. Some of its customers, like Next, demand a next-day delivery to households, together with the option of collecting items for return. Hermes has built up a reputation for reliability and flexibility in its field, being willing to leave parcels with neighbours, or in a designated safe place.

Hermes has also introduced a large number of local pick-up points, mainly in convenience shops, local stores and off-licences. Customers can designate the shop as their collection point and can collect the parcel at a time convenient to them. For the shops there are two benefits; the commission per parcel that they get from Hermes and the chance that the customer collecting the parcel will also buy something in the store. For Hermes it means that there are fewer undelivered parcels and that there are fewer 'drops' on the delivery round.

Hermes and other courier firms are now looking into expanding this service further. One possibility is the use of texts to find out where the customer will be at a particular time and then deliver direct – to the gym, the hairdressers or a local coffee shop. These measures will not only result in more satisfied customers, but will also cut down on the time and staff that courier firms have to use when trying to deliver parcels to unoccupied addresses.

1 Analyse one reason the changes in channels of distribution in recent years have increased business for Hermes. *(4)*
2 Explain one way in which internet shopping creates problems for retailers. *(2)*
3 Evaluate the impact on the local stores from being involved in the distribution process with Hermes. *(9)*
4 Evaluate the extent to which the growth of internet shopping is likely to affect Hermes in the future. *(20)*
Total *(35)*

Chapter 57

Promotion

AS / Year 1 | Year 2

A Level students must know all of the content in this chapter.

AS students need to cover all of the content except:

- Drip marketing (page 413)
- Viral marketing (page 414)
- Advertising elasticity of demand (page 414)

What is promotion?

Promotion is a collection of techniques used to inform and persuade potential consumers to buy a product or service that meets their needs. It is an integral part of the marketing process. A promotion mix is a combination of promotional methods that best suits the firm, its budget and the product or service it is selling.

The purpose of promotion is to:

- inform consumers or raise awareness
- increase sales
- encourage brand loyalty
- enhance the reputation/image of the business.

Promotion strategies

Promotion includes various marketing tools such as advertising and sales promotion.

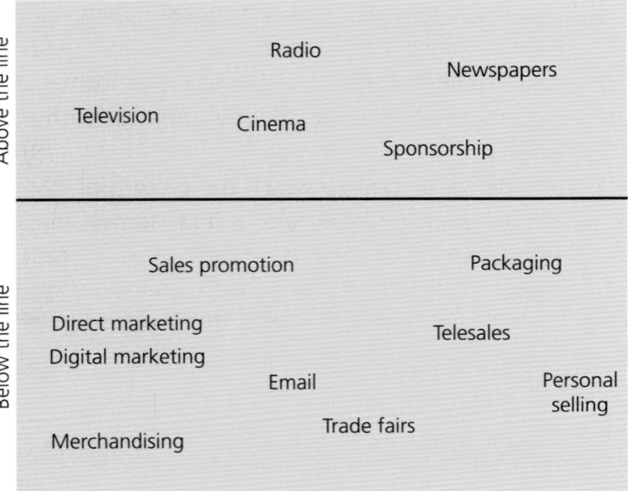

Figure 57.1 'Above the line' and 'below the line' promotion

'Above the line' promotion

'Above the line' promotion uses media where there is no direct contact with the potential consumer. The business has no control over the media involved. The media used is often referred to a mass media.

'Below the line' promotion

'Below the line' promotion uses the type of media where the business can directly contact the potential consumer. It can also have some influence and control of the media used.

Television

Television remains a powerful media for promoting a product. The visual aspect of an advert is easier to remember than the spoken or written word. This is a very expensive form of promotion for a business, especially for an advertisement that is shown in the interval of a popular programme.

Commercial radio

Radio advertising is common, especially for local radio stations. In the Midlands, BRMB and Beacon are examples that concentrate on providing an advertising media for local businesses. There are also adverts for national chains, but these are less frequent.

Magazines

Although there are many specialist magazines that can target consumers, it is still an 'above the line' media because there is no direct contact with the selected consumer.

Customer publications (magazines)

This media is not to be confused with ordinary magazines, which are classified as 'above the line' media. Because customer magazines are specifically targeted and deal direct with the customer, they are classed as 'below the line' media.

There is a growing trend for businesses to strengthen the recognition of their brands by publishing their own magazine. According to ABC, seven out of the top ten magazines by circulation are customer publications.

The agency Seven Squared publishes customer magazines for British Airways, Marks & Spencer, Coutts, Waterstones and Sainsbury's.

In-flight magazines are a type of trade magazine

Many businesses now produce trade magazines that are seen by a very large leadership. This might be an inflight magazine produced by an airline or one sent out by a bank or supermarket to its customers. Businesses are spending increasing amounts of money on such magazines. It is suggested by Millard Brown/APA that brand sales increase by about 8 per cent as a result of people reading a customer magazine.

Digital magazines

Taking advantage of consumers' greater usage of the computer as a source of information, businesses have grasped the opportunity to promote their products via the digital media.

Some customer magazines have now transferred into digital format. Ford has used this format to target specific segments of the market. It has also been used to claim that such a media is meeting its environmental promises by reducing the need to print on paper and using less fuel, as no distribution is required. This type of media is able to use the written word, pictures, video clips and flash imagery in an attempt to engage its targeted audience.

The success of Heineken with its Balloon Facebook campaign came mainly from the fact that it involved the public and made them laugh. MAC Cosmetics have established themselves at the forefront of digital marketing, using an interactive video in a recent campaign.

Cinema

Cinemas have experienced an increase in audiences over recent years, and consequently have become more popular as a media for adverts. The cinema has the advantage of appealing to both national and local advertisers, and is considerably cheaper than television advertising rates.

Newspapers

Newspapers are both national and local, and therefore appeal to a wide range of advertisers. The type of adverts that can be placed in newspapers varies considerably, from a full-page colour advert to a classified advert, depending upon the needs and budget of the advertiser. Because there is such a wide range of newspapers, it is possible to target a particular segment of the market.

Billboards, posters and video/plasma screens

These are static adverts and therefore only able to target a limited audience; nevertheless, they are a cheap and effective form of advertising. With a limited amount of space to put across the message, this form of advertising needs to be eye-catching and visual. The location of their placement is crucial if a sufficient number of people is to see them. The benefit of such adverts is that they can be used on a national basis or a local basis, even down to advertising the local village jumble sale.

Sponsorship

Some people would argue that sponsorship became popular when it was no longer possible to advertise cigarettes on television, and that sponsoring televised sporting events was a way around the law for the tobacco companies. However, sponsorship is an effective media to increase product awareness. Businesses are quick to have their name or brand name associated with a particular sporting or cultural activity.

The Emirates airline, one of the fastest growing airlines in the world, has spent significant amounts of money on sponsoring cricket, and the England football team is sponsored by Nationwide to help raise its profile. Local businesses help local sports teams in an attempt to establish their brands or names. Some people consider sponsorship at local level as an ethical gesture, by helping others as well as themselves. Grand Prix motor racing relies on sponsorship; you only have to look at the Formula 1 cars and the clothing worn by the racing drivers.

Key term

Publicity: any form of free promotion for the business. It could be a picture of a sponsored boys' football team in the local paper, or it may be negative publicity on a consumer affairs programme about a product fault.

Companies are using sponsorship to enhance their brand awareness by association with a particular sport or sports stars. Usain Bolt signed several lucrative sponsorship deals after the London Olympics.

Direct mail

Direct mail or the usage of mailshots is often referred to as 'junk mail' – much of what is received through the post has not been requested and is therefore placed straight in the bin. Its effectiveness is therefore in doubt but, nevertheless, there is a place for this method if targets are carefully selected.

The economic downturn in 2008 and the increase in environmental lobbies have since led to a fall in the amount of money spent on direct mailing. It has, however, encouraged businesses to spend their money efficiently and target consumers more carefully. Direct mail has also suffered from alternative direct channels such as email, which is significantly cheaper. As broadband becomes more widespread in the UK, direct mail will be used less and less. According to the experts, direct mail is now most effective when targeted at existing customers rather than potential or 'cold target' customers. The latter regard direct mail as junk mail, much of which is thrown away unopened and is therefore ineffective.

Electronic adverts

As usage of the internet continues to grow, so does the number of 'pop-up' adverts and side bar links. Such adverts appear with annoying regularity on certain websites. Nevertheless, it is a media that continues to grow in popularity.

Social media and internet promotion

Many businesses have looked for more cost-effective ways to advertise or have stopped advertising in the media altogether. Some of these firms have turned instead to social networking sites as a more effective and much cheaper method of getting their message across. Others have used the internet to place adverts, sometimes on news sites and search engine sites and at other times as pop-ups. For the business, this gives the advantage of a low-cost form of promotion.

The use of social media also makes it possible for companies such as ASOS to target particular groups, like young fashion-conscious people. Social media can also be used to involve them in blogs and discussions about the latest trends. This allows the customers to feel involved and valued, and it allows the retailer to see how well products are being received. The result is that the information they gather on the consumer is immediate and up to date for the consumer; something that is very important in fashion retailing.

Sales promotion

Sales promotion is an incentive at the point of sale (at the retail outlet). The types of sales promotion used include:

- BOGOF (buy one get one free): consumers are always interested in something that looks like a bargain.
- Win a competition: often the competition will encourage more than one purchase.
- 10% more: often used for food and drink products, where adding to the normal quantity is practically possible. This is often used for things like jars of coffee.
- Buy 3 pay for 2: a favoured strategy of Boots the Chemist chain.
- Donations to charity: an ethical approach to sales promotion. The business hopes that the consumer will be pleased that they have indirectly helped donate something to charity by buying the product.
- Some schemes have vouchers to collect, to encourage brand loyalty.
- Loyalty points: many of the hotel chains offer points as a reward for staying at their hotels. Once sufficient points have been gained, it is possible to exchange them for a free night at one of the

hotels within a chain. This type of sales promotion encourages brand loyalty. Holiday Inn offers a free one-night stay after a specific number have been paid for. Other examples of loyalty points include Nectar points at Sainsbury's or Tesco Clubcard points.

- Credit: for expensive items such as cars, furniture and kitchens, offering credit facilities with low-interest payments or even free credit at 0% finance are huge incentives to consumers to purchase. Sofa and kitchen firms use this type of promotion.
- Buy now pay later: in an attempt to encourage impulse buying, offering a consumer the opportunity to take a product away but not have to pay for it for a period of time, is another huge incentive to buy. Examples include DFS and Sofa World.
- Most supermarkets put the special offers at the end of an aisle or near the tills, where customers are more likely to make impulse purchases.

Merchandising or branding

Merchandising or branding is any action that encourages the consumer to purchase goods; it includes presentation, packaging, the range of goods available, pricing and discounting.

Packaging

Packaging still has a large role to play in the promotion of products; it helps define the brand. Not only does it protect and preserve the product, it can advertise and promote the product by the careful display of the brand name or its selling features. The packaging can enhance the display of the product on the shelves and can add value to entice the customer to purchase. Packaging also allows a business to offer its sales promotions such as multi-packs.

Public relations

The image of the product or service and its reputation can be a sales asset, and therefore it is important to maintain this positive image. Public relations plays a vital role in either strengthening the image of the business by issuing a press release or defending/repairing an image if the business has to deal with a problem. For example, if a company has to recall a product due to a fault, the customers' image of the product may be damaged and therefore the public relations department will work hard to counter any adverse publicity. In 2013, Tesco and Asda suffered a loss of reputation when some of their meat products, including burgers, were found to contain horsemeat. (The public relations departments worked to restore the image of the businesses.) Similarly, the brand image of Toyota cars has suffered from a number of recalls for safety problems.

Personal selling and telesales

Personal selling or direct selling occurs when there is a direct link or communication between the salesperson and the customer. Sales assistants can encourage a sale by 'persuading' customers to buy. Personal selling can be achieved not only through face-to-face contact (often done door-to-door) but via a phone (telesales.) This can be seen as an intrusion, however, as the customer has not asked the salesperson to phone them and therefore may resent the call.

Trade fairs

Trade fairs and exhibitions are a popular method of encouraging interested parties (businesses and consumers) to visit a wide selection of fairs and exhibitions. The Car Show, The Clothes Show and the Good Food Show are good examples of trade fairs. At the business stands, customers will be able to meet staff, who can achieve face-to-face sales of products.

Drip marketing

Drip marketing is a strategy employed by businesses where information is sent in bit by bit over time to the consumer using a particular medium. This medium is usually email, because this can be done at low cost by the business. It is also possible to use drip marketing using post or social media. The latter is becoming increasingly popular particularly amongst young people. ASOS the online fashion company has used drip marketing successfully using Facebook (see case study) to keep its customers up to date with new styles and garments as they come on to the market.

Viral marketing

Viral marketing is sometimes referred to as marketing buzz. It is the use of social networking sites to increase brand awareness and is so-called because the advert will spread through the site like a computer virus in the form of video clips, pop-ups, flash games or images. Again, its use is particularly popular in markets where the customer base is young. Burger King has used viral marketing on a number of occasions in recent years to launch special campaigns and increase brand awareness.

Advertising elasticity of demand

Advertising elasticity of demand shows the extent to which spending on advertising will affect sales. The formula for calculating it is

$$\frac{\text{Percentage change in demand}}{\text{Percentage change in advertising spending}}$$

The business will hope that the result is positive and large – that an increase in advertising spending will result in a much larger increase in demand. However, this may not always be the case. Using this calculation will help a business to see how effectively it is using its advertising budget.

For example, if a business increases its advertising spending by 5 per cent and this results in a 6 per cent increase in sales, the advertising elasticity of demand is:

$$\frac{6}{5} = 1.2$$

meaning that demand is elastic in relation to advertising spending.

Selecting appropriate promotional method(s)

Choosing which type of sales promotion to use will depend upon the type of product or service. In addition, the business and its budget will also affect which sale promotions are selected.

However, the most important issue is the consumer. The type of sales promotion must be something that will actually appeal to the consumer. It must also fit with the rest of the marketing mix and help achieve the marketing strategy of the business. The important factors affecting the method of promotion are:

- the business, its size, location and its budget
- the actual product or service to be promoted
- the customer
- the marketing strategy to be used (the marketing mix)
- external factors (legislation, economy and technology)
- time factor
- the product's stage in its life cycle.

Tips and techniques

Selecting the most appropriate promotion must be done in the context of the case information, taking careful note of the bullet points shown here. Be careful to select a method that can be afforded by the business in question. Many small firms have little or no advertising budget.

Service marketing

In many cases promotion in the service sector will be identical to that in the product sector. For smaller businesses, however, methods of promotion like word-of-mouth and recommendation are likely to be more important than advertising above the line. Small businesses may also be restricted by the amount of money available for promotion. For this reason new promotional methods using the internet are likely to be attractive. This may include email campaigns or the use of social media sites, which are relatively cheap to use but allow the business to target the campaign and to reach a large number of potential customers at a low cost. Some businesses, like estate agents, use traditional methods of promotion, like newspapers and magazines, but they also have websites of their own and use national websites, like Rightmove, to advertise properties.

Further sources

www.smallbusiness.chron.com
www.forbes.com
www.businesscasestudies.co.uk
www.urbanriver.com

Your turn

Questions in red are for A Level candidates only.

Multiple-choice questions

1 If a firm increases its advertising spending from £16,000 to £20,000 and finds that demand increases by 10 per cent, what is the advertising elasticity of demand?

A 2.5
B 2
C 0.5
D 0.4 *(1)*

2 Which of these are ALL below-the-line advertising methods?

A TV, email, newspapers
B Sales promotion, radio, personal selling
C Direct marketing, trade fairs, packaging
D Sponsorship, cinema, digital. *(1)*

Revision questions

1 Explain the difference between above-the-line and below-the-line marketing. *(4)*

2 State two ways in which promotional methods have changed in recent years. *(2)*

Total *(6)*

Case study

The Dove advertising campaign

The Dove range of beauty products and soaps is produced by the multinational company Unilever. In 2004, Unilever began a new marketing campaign called 'Real Beauty' that used ordinary people instead of models in its advertising campaigns. Initially, the campaign was used in magazines and on billboards, but over the years the range of marketing media used has increased to include TV, radio and cinema adverts.

The fact that the campaign was so different from anything that had been used by other competitors resulted in a large amount of publicity for Dove products in the press and on TV, together with discussion amongst potential users who appreciated the use of real people to market products.

The Dove brand started with soap products in 2001, but by 2014 it included a huge range of different products for men and women. The advertising methods have also moved on, although the company still uses real people wherever possible. Dove has used advertising clips on YouTube and it has pioneered one-on-one email marketing. The latter allows customers to have a personal online conversation about things like skin problems and the relative merits of products in the Dove range. As well as being appreciated by existing and potential customers, these conversations allow Unilever to collect valuable marketing information about its customer base.

The success of the decision to move away from models and airbrushing is that the name 'Dove' is now synonymous with products that are aimed at ordinary people with a wide range of needs.

1 Explain what is meant by 'publicity'. *(2)*
2 State two types of above-the-line advertising used by Dove products. *(2)*
3 Analyse one advantage for the Dove campaign from using real people in its adverts. *(4)*
4 The name Dove is now associated with 'real people'. To what extent does this limit Unilever in its future advertising campaigns for Dove products? *(12)*

Total *(20)*

Chapter 58

External influences on marketing

Year 2

A Level students must know all of the content in this chapter.

This chapter is not applicable for AS students.

Marketing and the law

Over the past 50 years, there has been a rapid increase in the amount of protection given to consumers by the law. As the business world has become increasingly competitive, successive governments have recognised that consumers sometimes need to be protected from the actions of businesses. The following factors have contributed to this situation:

- monopoly control of the industry
- health and safety concerns
- new products and services
- the growth of internet and mail-order buying
- the globalisation of markets.

Laws governing consumer protection

Sale of Goods Act (2012 and 1979)

This was an important Act when it was introduced in 1979, and remains important today. The Act was amended in 2012. The main change in this amendment was to state that, if a fault was found within the first six months of the life of a product, it would be assumed in law that the fault existed at the point of purchase. The original rules of the 1979 Act would then apply.

Under the Sale of Goods Act, all goods must be:

- of 'satisfactory quality' (i.e. the product must not be damaged or defective)
- 'as described' – this applies not only to advertisements but also to any explanations given by a shop assistant
- 'fit for the purpose for which they were intended'.

If any of these conditions is not met, a business must provide consumers with a replacement or their money back. A business cannot avoid the law by saying that it has a policy not to accept returned goods. The Act also imposes a duty on businesses to ensure that their products are safe to use.

In addition to these civil laws, there are a number of criminal laws.

Consumer Protection from Unfair Trading Regulations (CPRs) (2008) and Trade Descriptions Act (1968)

A consumer cannot be expected to understand everything about a product. The purpose of this Act is to prevent consumers from being intentionally misled when they buy goods. The 1968 Act states that any description of the goods on sale must not be false or misleading. The Act refers to all types of description – sign, advertisement or verbal.

The new legislation introduced in the 2008 Regulations replaced the original Act, but went much further in the rules it imposed on sellers. CPRs provides protection for consumers from unfair or misleading practices. The legislation has three main sections.

1 a ban on unfair practices
2 a ban on misleading or aggressive practices
3 a blacklist of unfair practices.

The legislation is intended to stop the following types of activity by businesses:

- claiming an item is 'free' when that is not the case
- aggressive doorstep selling
- a salesperson refusing to 'take no for an answer'
- persistent cold calling.
- time-limited offers that are not limited at all.

Weights and Measures Act (1985)

It is an offence to give 'short measures' or an incorrect indication of the amount of a product on sale. If a product is labelled as containing 1 litre, that is what it should contain.

Unsolicited Goods Act (1971)

It is illegal to demand payment for services that have not been ordered. If a publishing business delivers a quantity of books that have not been ordered to someone's house, and then demands payment for them, the business is breaking the law.

The Trading Standards Authority is a public body that investigates breaches of consumer laws. It also assists consumers in taking a business to court if the business refuses to comply with its legal obligations.

EU laws

Some laws affecting UK businesses originate in the European Union (EU). Many of these come from the EU's Social Charter, which is a charter of rights for employees concerning areas such as working conditions, wages and consultation of the workforce. UK businesses have to adhere to these EU laws just as if they had originated from the UK parliament. There are two types of EU law:

1 Regulations, which have to be adopted and applied in a certain way.
2 Directives, which must also be applied as law, but the individual member country can decide how to implement them.

Working Time Directive

The Working Time Directive is an example of EU legislation. It became law in the UK in 1998, and states that a business must not allow an employee to work more than 48 hours per week on average. The directive is partly aimed at reducing the UK's culture of long working hours. There are also provisions relating to an employee's entitlement to rest breaks and the pattern of shifts that can be worked. Employees can sign away their legal rights to these if they wish, but if a business dismisses a person for refusing to do so, this constitutes unfair dismissal. Some employees (such as the police) are exempt from the directive.

Effects of increased legislation on businesses

Changes in legislation and increased consumer protection affect businesses in a variety of ways.

The need to ensure health and safety concerns are addressed at every stage of production and beyond, and imposes costs on businesses. For example, a business that manufactures toys must be aware of the paint finishes and components that are used in production, even if these toys are made abroad. Lead in paint, or easily detachable components that can be swallowed by a child are prohibited. Not only will the business run the risk of prosecution by ignoring these rules, it may also cause widespread bad publicity for the business.

Increasingly, businesses need to become market-orientated rather than product-orientated. They need to ensure that they are producing goods and services that the consumer wants to buy. This involves extra costs in undertaking market research before new products are introduced, and follow-up research when they reach the market.

Customer service is an increasingly important part of the operation of businesses, particularly in the service sector. Businesses need to have staff that can deal with customer complaints and questions in a sympathetic and calm manner, and are then empowered to deal with the problems. The department store John Lewis has built up a reputation for dealing promptly with customer complaints without the need to refer the problem to senior managers. This results in customer satisfaction and confidence in the business.

What happens if a business breaks the law?

For alleged breaches of criminal law, the business will be prosecuted in the criminal courts, either a magistrates' court for minor offences or the Crown Court, where the penalties are more severe, for serious offences. If a business is found guilty, it can be fined and/or those responsible for the breach may be imprisoned. Any alleged breach of the civil law will be heard in the County Court, where the business can be sued for damages.

If a business fails or refuses to pay damages or compensation, the business or person that is owed the money can apply to the County Court for payment to be enforced. County Court judgments against a business can generate bad publicity and the hearing will be expensive. Furthermore, an adverse County Court judgment can affect a business's ability to obtain credit.

Competition and Markets Authority

The Competition and Markets Authority (CMA) is a government department responsible for making markets work well for consumers and to protect them from unfair trading. The CMA investigates situations where businesses are operating unlawfully in any area of UK trade.

In 2008 a new piece of legislation was introduced called the Unfair Trading Regulations 2008.

Office of Fair Trading: Consumer Protection from Unfair Trading Regulations 2008

The Consumer Protection from Unfair Trading Regulations 2008 came into force on 26 May 2008. They implement the Unfair Commercial Practices Directives (UCPD) in the UK, and replace several pieces of consumer protection legislation that were in force prior to 26 May 2008. The Regulations introduce a general duty not to trade unfairly and to seek to ensure that traders act honestly and fairly towards their customers. They apply primarily to business to consumer practices (but elements of business-to-business practices are also covered where they affect, or are likely to affect, consumers).

The vast majority of UK businesses are fair dealing and should not have needed to change their business practices to comply with regulations, which aim to tackle those businesses who don't always treat their customers well.

The new Regulations cover unfair trading in many areas which include:

- giving incorrect pricing and product information to mislead the consumer; for example, falsely claiming that a product can cure illness
- using promotional information that misleads; for example, packaging shampoo so that it resembles that of a well-known competitor
- aggressive sales practices that put the consumer under undue pressure; for example, pressurising an elderly or confused person to sign a contract immediately for roof repairs
- falsely claiming accreditation; for example, claiming to have signed up to an industry code of conduct when this is not true.

Trading Standards

The Trading Standards Organisation offers advice both to businesses and consumers on the application of the laws for buying and selling. Its work covers retail sales and internet buying and selling. If a consumer has a problem with a retailer, Trading Standards will investigate the issue for them and discuss the legal situation with the business concerned. For example, suppose a consumer purchases a handbag which falls apart after two weeks. This situation will be covered by the Sale of Goods Act because the bag was 'not fit for purpose'. In these circumstances the consumer is entitled to his or her money back. If the retailer refuses to do this, the consumer can take the issue to the local Trading Standards Office. An officer will be appointed to take up the case and investigate on behalf of the consumer.

Advertising

The use of advertising in the UK is under the control of the Advertising Standards Authority (ASA).

About the ASA: what we do

The Advertising Standards Authority regulates the contents of advertising, sales promotions and direct marketing in the UK.

We make sure standards are kept by applying the advertising standards codes.

We can stop misleading, harmful or offensive advertising. We can ensure sales promotions are run fairly. We can help reduce unwanted commercial mail – either sent through the post, by email or by text message – and we can resolve problems with mail order purchases.

Anyone who is unhappy with an advertisement can make a complaint to the ASA who will then investigate the situation. The ASA has codes of conduct for advertising on television, radio and all other areas. In general, the ASA works on the understanding that advertising should not mislead, cause harm or offend. In addition, there is a separate set of rules for advertising products such as alcoholic drinks, children's items and gambling. The advertising of cigarettes and tobacco is now prohibited in the UK.

For example, in a recent case that was investigated by the ASA, the retail store Halfords was prohibited from running a series of advertisements because the ASA felt that customers had been misled about some of the price reductions they were offering, and also because the advertisement seemed to suggest that bicycle safety checks were only available through them.

After a judgment has been made, most businesses agree to follow ASA recommendations by changing or removing advertisements. Those who ignore the rulings will be reported to the Office of Fair Trading who will take up the issue.

Data protection

The Data Protection Act 1998 was introduced to protect individuals where information about them was held by any business or organisation. Businesses or organisations that hold any information about customers or employees are bound by this legislation. For example, a bank or building society must ensure that customer information is held securely.

The Act works in two ways. Firstly, anyone who processes personal information must ensure that the information is:

- fairly and lawfully processed
- processed for limited purposes
- relevant and not excessive
- accurate and up to date
- not kept longer than is necessary
- processed in line with the individual's rights
- secure
- not transferred to other countries without adequate protection.

The second part of the Act covers the rights of the individual to know what information is being held about them by any organisation.

Government's regulatory bodies

As part of the privatisation in the 1980s and 1990s, the Government set up a number of regulatory bodies to oversee the operation of the previously nationalised utilities such as water, gas and telecommunications. Most of these companies had been in monopoly or near-monopoly markets previously and the regulatory bodies were put in place to ensure that they did not abuse this situation in the private sector. The main regulatory bodies are Ofgem (electricity), Ofwat (water) and Ofcom (tele-communications). They are able to act if the actions of the businesses they oversee are taking advantage of their situation to the disadvantage of the consumer. For example, the regulatory bodies have had the power to control price increases and, in the telecommunications industry, they have taken action to stop nuisance calls and to make it easier for customers to switch provider.

International marketing

Recent years have witnessed the increasing globalisation of trade and a growth in the number of businesses that now trade across international boundaries. In the past, only the largest and most successful businesses were willing to consider selling overseas; today, overseas markets, particularly in the emerging and developing countries, are seen as markets that can be targeted by businesses of any size. The growth of electronic communication and improved transport has made trading much quicker and easier. It is now possible to make contact within seconds with anyone who has internet access, regardless of where they are in the world.

For UK businesses, the fact that trade is opening up in the European Union and the expansion of membership (with the entry of Eastern European countries) means that this is a market that cannot be ignored.

Within the EU there are no tariffs or trading barriers, so, in this respect, selling in Warsaw or Paris is the same as selling in Edinburgh, Cardiff or Newcastle. This gives businesses the opportunity to access huge markets throughout the EU. There are, however, marketing issues that businesses need to consider before trading in other countries.

Reasons for international marketing

Population and the size of the market

For some businesses, the attraction of selling overseas is the access to a large market when compared to the UK market. Larger sales mean increased economies of scale for the business. A business such as Nestle sells its product range throughout Europe and beyond, achieving economies of scale in marketing and management. Multinational firms like Nestle can employ specialist sales staff and negotiate preferential distribution and advertising rates for its products.

Economic cycles

If a business is active in a number of different markets, it will have the opportunity to spread the risks of trading. If one market is moving into recession, it is likely that there will be other markets where trading prospects will be more promising.

Consumer law

In advanced economies, businesses have to be careful to adhere to trading laws. In the developing world, the rules are often much less rigorous. For example, tobacco firms have found that their sales have been badly affected by public smoking bans and advertising restrictions in many Western European countries. The trading conditions in Eastern Europe are not subject to these rules and regulations, and the opportunities for sales and profit are therefore much greater.

Differences in marketing overseas

Although moving into international markets may seem to be attractive to a business, there are also problems and pitfalls that businesses need to be careful to avoid. Moving into new overseas markets can only be done through the use of careful planning and a thorough awareness of trading and other conditions in the overseas market.

Even within the EU there are different rules for business and trading behaviour. Businesses moving into overseas markets need to make themselves aware of the laws of those countries so that they do not run into problems. Examples of these differences would be those laws applying to the labelling of cigarettes with health warnings, or the rules applying to the safety of toys.

HSBC often uses advertisements to explain some of the many cultural differences between countries. These differences can lead to misunderstanding, at best, or hostility, at worst, if a business gets it wrong. For example, colours have different significance in other cultures; this can have an impact when businesses make decisions about packaging.

Businesses need to be aware of the political climate in other countries. In the West we are used to democratic political systems and the freedom of individuals to speak. Western European businesses operate relatively independently of control and government intervention. These circumstances are often different in other countries. For example, the advertising of alcohol is very strictly controlled or prohibited in some countries in the Middle East and Asia.

Religious and cultural differences also need to be considered. There may be particular implications for advertising, where it can be very easy to give offence in a country that has a strong religious background. The role of women in society may also be different. This factor must therefore be considered in advertisements and in the range of products being sold.

In some countries, even in Europe, a payment that would be regarded as a bribe in the UK can be expected before a deal is achieved. In some instances, this payment might have to be made to a government official. Businesses may find that they have to overcome their resistance to this sort of business practice if they are to succeed.

It may be necessary to take advice from within a country about ways to appeal to the market, particularly if there are large cultural differences from the domestic market. Very often, a business moving into a new country will use an agent to help ensure that all the important issues of marketing in the new country are appreciated and addressed.

Language difficulties can also present problems. Translations need to be made by someone who speaks the language fluently. It is always better to use a resident who is not only fluent, but aware of current language usage and styles of speaking. The use of names for products its also an important consideration. A word that is acceptable in one country could be offensive in another.

Differences between markets

The following factors need to be considered before moving into a market in another country. These factors should be investigated thoroughly before anything else is done, through the use of market research. Knowledge of all aspects of the market is essential if a venture into an international market is going to be successful. This research may be costly, but it is likely to alert the business to any possible problems and it may result in substantial savings in the long term. In some cases, the result of market research may be to persuade the business not to proceed.

Political factors

- Is the country politically stable?
- Are the trade unions active? Is there industrial unrest? Will these issues cause problems?
- Is it necessary to offer bribes to government officials or others? If this is the case, the business needs to think about whether it is prepared to be involved in bribery to attract business.

Economic factors

- Is there buoyant demand in the market?
- Is it a free market economy or is it centrally planned?
- Is the economy growing?
- What is the age distribution of the population?
- Is the population growing?
- What is the level and distribution of income in the population?

Legal factors

- How much legislation is there affecting business and trade?
- What are the laws on advertising?
- Do the courts operate freely and fairly?

Cultural factors

- What are the religious and cultural influences in the country?
- What is the attitude to women in society?
- How do people spend their leisure time?

Will the business be able to advertise its product freely?

A move into an overseas market, however familiar a country may seem, is something that needs to be investigated carefully. Businesses must proceed cautiously and use local advisers wherever possible. The alternative may be a costly mistake that ends in failure.

Further sources

www.bbc.co.uk/consumer Up-to-date advice on a variety of consumer issues

www.gov.uk/government/organisations/competition-and-markets-authority The regulatory body responsible for ensuring competitive behaviour and consumer protection

Your turn

Multiple-choice questions

1 Which of the following is not a disadvantage of monopoly?

A It allows firms to gain economies of scale.
B It can raise prices.
C It restricts the consumer's choice.
D It means that there is duplication of services. *(1)*

2 A business sells 20 per cent of its production in export markets. If the firm's total revenue is £3.5 million, what are its export earnings from sales.

A £350,000
B £700,0000
C £700,000
D £350,000 *(1)*

Revision questions

1 State three requirements a business has to meet for its products under the Sale of Goods Act? *(3)*

2 State two functions of the Advertising Standards Agency? *(2)*

3 Explain two examples of a restrictive practice. *(4)*

Total *(9)*

Case study

JCB

At the beginning of the recession in 2008, JCB, the manufacturer of heavy earth-moving equipment, was facing a very difficult trading situation. By 2009, its sales were down 75 per cent year-on-year and the business was forced to reduce its staffing considerably, with workers voting to work a shorter working week rather than face redundancy.

In the following years, JCB has turned round the situation completely, announcing its highest-ever profits of £365 million in 2013. This has been achieved largely as a result of an expansion into export markets. Only 2.5 per cent of the world's construction is undertaken in the UK. Recognising this, JCB has actively sought out new markets, especially in the so-called BRIC economies – Brazil, Russia, India and China – and the business now exports 75 per cent of its output. It has recently built a £365 million factory in Brazil, seen its trade double in Africa, increase by 12 per cent in the Middle East and it is in the process of building a new factory in India. Brazil has become a particularly important market for JCB because of all the construction involved in hosting the 2014 World Cup and the 2016 Olympic Games.

Chief Corporate Development Officer David Bell has outlined some of the problems faced when moving into new markets, even if doing so with a product that has a unique selling point, such as a JCB digger. He explained that, when choosing a new market, it is important to take account of its size, the product requirements for the market, the barriers to entry and the extra work involved in selling in that market. His advice is that businesses should not try to do too much too quickly; they should move in at first with their best-selling product – but only if there is space in the market. Bell also stresses the importance of obtaining local knowledge, which he regards as critical. He stresses that there is no substitute for expertise and knowledge obtained locally; the background of local people can help in removing barriers to entry more effectively than anything else.

1 Explain what is meant by a 'unique selling point' for JCB. *(2)*

2 Analyse two difficulties that are likely to be faced when selling in any of the BRIC countries. *(6)*

3 Analyse two benefits for JCB of building factories in its export markets rather than producing in the UK and then exporting the goods. *(6)*

4 To what extent may JCB's export performance help reduce the effects of any possible recession? *(12)*

Total *(26)*

Chapter 59

Operations management objectives and external influences

Year 2

A Level students must know all of the content in this chapter.

This chapter is not applicable for AS students.

As with other areas of a business the objectives for operations management must fit with the overall objectives of the business. The objectives will provide a sense of direction, they may provide a motivational incentive to the employees involved and the objectives may also help operations management to control its operations. The key factor for having objectives is to help achieve the overall goals of the business.

For operations management many of the actual objectives may be productive targets in order to meet demand and any long-term goal of the business.

The objectives may also refer to the level of quality or the level of the rejection rates. (See **Chapter 68**.) It is also likely that the objectives will refer to the level of productivity. (See **Chapter 64**.)

The need for clear objectives (see SMART objectives on page 33) will help employees know exactly what is required of them; effective communication is essential. (See **Chapter 42**.)

How useful the objectives are to the business will depend upon how realistic they are within the context of the business and the business environment. Without sufficient employees or the right machinery some targets may be unrealistic, and may consequently not be motivational. (See Vroom on **page 335**.)

Tips and techniques

It is essential when evaluating objectives for operations management that the context of the business is clearly used.

When setting operations management objectives it is important to note the following.

- The legal status and size of the business – the level of profit that is set for a public limited company may be substantially different from that of a sole trader.
- The other objectives of the business – whether it is a production target or a target to launch new products – will all have a financial implication for the business. In almost all instances a budget will have been set: one that ought to 'fit' with any financial objectives.
- The state of the economy – a growing economy, as was the case in 2014/15, will make it easier to achieve targets or objectives than if the economy is in recession.
- The level of competition within the market in which the business operates – a highly competitive market may mean that prices have to be lower in order to compete and consequently profit margins may be lower, which in turn will affect the ability of a business to achieve its production target.
- The government of the day – the government may be encouraging or discouraging business as part of its political agenda. The level of taxation imposed upon businesses will impinge upon the ability to achieve any operational target set, or even the size of the target in the first place.
- The work of the Monetary Policy Committee (MPC) – the MPC sets the level of interest rates that govern the economy. In turn this rate will affect a business in terms of borrowing money, and therefore its ability to purchase new capital goods needed to enhance productivity.
- Legislation may also affect the production targets set or the ability of a business to meet its productive targets/objectives.

It is therefore essential that a business is able to see the value of having operations management objectives, having noted what impact the important factors listed above have on a business.

Overall, having operational management objectives allows a business to be able to manage its productive capacity and output in the context of the objectives of the business as a whole.

Tips and techniques

It is essential that any discussions of objectives for operational management are considered in the context of all the other areas of the business; for example, the marketing, financial and HRM objectives. This is essential as any business needs to be able to operate in unison and not in isolation.

Operations management strategy

A business may wish to achieve its aims and goals in the long run, and therefore operations management may have a role to play. There may be a desire to reduce costs in order to be able to compete in a highly competitive market. Consequently the level of production and the level of productivity will be essential in helping to reduce costs (by reducing the unit costs via economies of scale, for example). If the costs can be reduced then it is more likely sales will increase, therefore aiding in the achievement of the goals of the business.

Ensuring the quality of products is high is essential to the good reputation of the business, and thus helps the marketing and HRM departments – not forgetting a positive effect on finances as sales and reputation grow.

The actual budget allocated will of course be a major constraint on how operations management set and implement a strategy.

External factors on operations management

The following may have an influence upon the workings of the operational management area of a business.

Social factors

Cultural factors in terms of:

- Changing tastes that may affect the demand for certain goods and thus affect what the business is prepared to produce.
- Holidays aboard cruise liners have grown significantly as the illusion that cruise holidays were only for the over-60s has been well and truly shattered.
- Religious changes – as the United Kingdom has moved into being seen as a multi-cultural society, there have been several changes in purchasing habits: what types of food and desired consumables are consumed. This has meant that businesses have responded in terms of what they produce and in some cases how food may be prepared.

Ethical factors

- As ethical issues take a higher priority within society, businesses have also taken on board the need to consider such issues.
- How a product is produced may alter as sustainability becomes more important and may also be used as part of the marketing of a business.
- The need to consider the level of waste is often viewed as an ethical issue, as the planet's resources continue to diminish. Consequently more research is undertaken by businesses to consider if the production process can be altered to save energy, resources and time.
- Changing the resources used has become significant within the car manufacturing industry, where there is a substantial growth in the use of standardised components for a range of car models. This saves on resources and of course helps to reduce costs.
- Labelling on packaging, although it may be governed by legislation, also has ethical influences as manufacturers wish to be seen as operating in an ethical manner.

Environmental factors

- A healthy regard for the planet and its resources has seen a growth in the level of concern and awareness of environmental issues. Similarly, businesses are conscious of being able to promote environmental awareness of how products are produced.
- The use of sustainable resources in the production process will enhance the credibility of the business, and may in many instances enhance its sales as discerning consumers often favour such products. Book publishers will state their policy on paper usage; for instance, look at the second page of this book. The publisher, Hachette, highlights its use of sustainable paper above the copyright details.

Legal factors

- The level and specific nature of legislation may well impinge upon the operations management of a business.
- Complying with the law is essential, as not doing so may damage the reputation of the business and subsequently the goodwill of the business (non-tangible asset).
- Legislation can affect the productive process within a business, such as health and safety issues, which in turn may have a cost implication and impact how the productive process takes place.

Economic factors

- The state of the economy, in terms of the level of inflation, will affect the costs of production.
- The level of unemployment will affect the availability of labour required in order to produce goods and services.
- The cost of labour – when there is full employment, the wage level increases and therefore the cost of labour increases, which in turn may encourage businesses to seriously consider using machines instead of labour (capital substitution).
- The level of growth within the economy – when the economy is growing as reported in March 2015, with a growth of 2.6 per cent (this being one of the highest levels of growth in the Western world), businesses feel more confident to invest in both capital equipment and labour in order to meet the growing level of demand within the economy.

  Consequently businesses will want to ensure that the productive capacity will be sufficient to meet that growing demand.

The value of the pound may also affect the operations management of a business if the business is an exporter. A strong pound will make it harder to sell abroad and therefore there may need to be serious consideration as to how the business can lower its costs, or it may have to settle for a lower profit margin. Similarly, if the business imports components with a strong pound these components will be cheaper and therefore the business can sell more, by passing on the reduction in costs through lowering its prices and thus increasing revenues. Alternatively, the business may decide to keep prices constant and thereby increase its profit margins.

Political factors

- The nature of the actual government in power will affect the operations management of many businesses. In the pre-election campaign of 2015 the leader of the Labour Party stated he wanted to freeze energy prices for 18 months. Such a move, whether sensible of not, may have influenced the energy companies to increase their prices at an earlier time. As it happened, prices were lowered as the price of oil fell significantly during the latter part of 2014 and into 2015.
- The concern as to whether a particular political party would increase the minimum wage would affect businesses as they try to ensure they can budget for the coming year in an accurate manner and at the same time ensure that the additional costs can either be passed on to the consumer or absorbed, often depending upon the price elasticity of the product.
- There are also political factors to be aware of from within the EU. In 2014 it was announced that hairdryers could only be of a certain power as an environmental issue was identified. The manufacturers of hairdryers may well be considering the consequences for their own particular product range and what changes they may or may not need to make. If changes to their range were necessary to comply with the new EU regulation, if implemented, there could be a need for further research and development to produce a compliant hairdryer, with consideration of any new product line and new sources for the power units. All such considerations would take time and have cost implications.

Technological factors

- Technology is ever changing and consequently the operations management area of a business must keep pace with such changes in order to remain competitive.
- Rapid technological advances within the mobile phone industry is a classic example of technology impinging upon the operations management of a business. More money is being spent on research and development in order to either remain competitive or, in some instances, be viewed as the market leader in terms of new technology. The amount of new 'apps' continues at a pace as businesses realise the advantages of such apps, such as convenience. Being able to buy theatre tickets via

theatre apps is highly convenient, as is being able to download your boarding pass onto a mobile phone.

- Material technology has shown significant progress in recent years, allowing for the rise of battery operated cars, due to lighter batteries.
- Technology for automatic parking has grown, as has the ever-improving technology for self-steering cars, where the 'driver' has nothing to do because the car is operated in a similar way to an automatic pilot.
- Technological advances in solar energy have allowed businesses to cut their energy bills significantly, allowing operations managers to possibly spend the energy-saving expenses on further technological advances.

International factors

As the pace of globalisation increases, operations managers need to be aware that markets are growing, as is the degree of competition. Globalisation offers potential customers more choice and consequently those working in operations management need to be mindful of keeping up to date with the competition, or ensure there is a 'USP' that will appeal to the wider market. The wider market may, however, give rise to the need to vary products according to specific international tastes, cultures or religious beliefs.

In order to evaluate the factors that affect operations management within the external environment, the nature of the business itself is critical. Not all of the factors mentioned above will be relevant to every business.

Tips and techniques

For any evaluative point with regards to external factors, it is vital that consideration is given to the type of business, its markets, the product involved and any particular objective that is vital to the well-being of the business.

Your turn

1 When the economy is nearing full employment the cost of labour will:

A Fall, as demand for labour is higher
B Rise, as supply of labour is scarcer
C Rise, as labour is more available
D Fall, as wages may be above the minimum wage. *(1)*

2 If the value of the pound increases, the cost of importing raw material for the production of goods within the UK will:

A Fall, as imports will be cheaper
B Fall, as imports will be more expensive
C Rise, as raw materials are inelastic
D Rise, as the raw materials are necessities. *(1)*

3 The environmental factors affect operations management and affect ONLY:

A Batch production
B Flow production
C Lean production
D Job production. *(1)*

Chapter 60

Added value

AS / Year 1

Both AS and A Level students must know all of the content in this chapter.

Adding value is a vital concept within the business world. It involves businesses charging consumers a price for a good or service that is higher than the cost of producing the good or service. Any additional feature that may be added to a product, which then allows the product to be sold at a price above the cost of the additional features, is also adding value and allowing a profit to be made.

Key term

Adding value: the difference between the actual price charged for a product or service and the actual cost of all the components and assembly of the product or service.

For example:
Selling price = £20
Cost of inputs = £12
Value added = selling price – cost of inputs = £8.

Tips and techniques

It is usually worthwhile including a simple numerical example to enhance any definition/explanation of value added you may offer.

- A business is concerned with adding value in order to make a profit, while ensuring there is a demand for the product or service. Taking a piece of wood, cutting it, shaping it and then painting it are all adding value to the original piece of wood, providing the price covers the cost of adding value via the processes of cutting, shaping and painting.
- An alarm clock can have value added to it by highlighting the 'additional' features of a snooze button, but marketed as 'allowing you that extra five minutes in bed without the fear of going back to sleep and not getting up on time'.
- Further additional features could be marketed as 'use the bright and easy-to-see figures on the clock to help you see the time when you are bleary eyed'.
- Consumers are likely to be prepared to pay more for such additional features; assuming the additional costs are less than the additional price that may now be charged, at which point additional profits will be made.
- For example, if the costs of providing additional features on the alarm clock are £2 and the increase in the price that can now be charged is £3 then the value added has led to a higher level of profit.
- Similarly, value may be added to a product by gaining a distinct brand image and therefore making the product appear more valuable, which in turn allows a higher price to be charged.
- Certain products are perceived as being 'better' because of the association of quality associated with a particular brand name. The premium price of Dyson vacuum cleaners is tolerated because the Dyson brand is known for its high quality.
- Offering a high standard of customer service may also allow a retailer to add value; for example, John Lewis.
- A delivery service is another common way to add value. There are often limits on the distance to deliver goods; otherwise, the cost of delivery may become higher than the additional price charged.
- Looking at supermarkets, Waitrose is perceived as a high-quality supermarket and consequently its prices tend to be higher, but because of the high-quality brands stocked and the level of service within its stores, consumers are happy to pay a higher price for their groceries.
- Ford motor cars spend a lot of time and effort offering a range of models for its cars. The Ford Fiesta comes in a wide range of models, from a basic model to the top of the range model, the Titanium. The car is the same but additional features have been put in, or on,

the car to enhance its price. Such additions increase the price significantly without increasing the costs at anywhere near the same level, and hence value is added.

- Value can be added to a house by building extra features, so that the house may be sold on for more than it was bought. Adding a conservatory, fitting stainless steel light switches, laying down a lawn, fitting extra plug points or fitted wardrobes, are all examples of features that enable a seller to increase the price.

Usefulness of added value

The main advantages for a business of adding value are:

- being able to charge a higher price and therefore
- a higher level of profit
- the higher price may enhance the image of the product or service
- it may enable the business to target its chosen market more easily
- it may offer the opportunity to make the product more distinctive and, in turn, establish a unique selling point (USP).

Stakeholders benefits are:

- Although the price of the good or service may be higher, consumers benefit from a more unique product.
- Consumers may gain additional service.
- Consumers may feel additional features are of good value for money.
- Consumers will be able to recognise the brand name and associate the brand with quality.
- If adding value leads to increased sales, suppliers will be able to supply more and therefore have the opportunity to increase profits.
- Shareholders may benefit as profits increase, therefore dividends may increase also.

However there are some disadvantages:

- It is not guaranteed that the cost of adding value can be recouped by increasing the price.
- The increase in price needed to gain from adding value may restrict sales and therefore sales revenue.
- The amount of competition may make it harder to increase the price in order to recoup the cost of adding value.
- The elasticity (price, income and advertising elasticities) may make any required price increase difficult to be accepted within the market.

Tips and techniques

Try to ensure you are able to clearly explain the benefits of value added.

Your turn

Questions are suitable for all AS and A Level candidates.

Multiple-choice questions

1 If a business has added value it means that:
  A it is in a competitive market
  B its costs will rise by more than the price rises for the additional components
  C the price will increase more than the costs of the additional components
  D profits will fall. *(1)*

2 A manufacturer of bread may add value by all of the factors given below except:
  A offering a delivery service
  B offering a distinctly branded bread
  C increasing the price
  D baking bread to the customers' requests. *(1)*

Revision questions

1 State two reasons why it may be difficult to add value to a given product or service. *(2)*
2 Suggest how you would add value to an umbrella or a mobile phone. * *(4)*
Total *(6)*

*For this question, a group discussion could be undertaken for a range of products or services.

Case study

Sweetart

Sweetart is owned and run by Heather Sweet who produces incredible cakes for weddings and all special occasions such as birthdays, anniversaries and corporate events. Heather became famous when she was invited to appear on the BBC's *Ready Steady Cook* programme. Apart from making bespoke cakes, Heather also produces sugar and ceramic sculptures.

Sweetart provided the wedding cake for singer Gareth Gates, which consisted of a 5-tiered cake with a variety of sponges including white chocolate champagne truffle, carrot with lemon and chocolate with Baileys.

There appears to be nothing she is not prepared to try and produce in order to satisfy her clients. Such is her popularity, there may be as much as three months' notice required, especially if the request is complicated.

For wedding cake orders, Heather offers clients a 'tasting session' to ensure they are satisfied; this additional service enables Heather to charge more for the final product, which, given her feedback from satisfied customers, is excellent. Some of the sculptures can be as high as a metre though the majority are around 30 cm.

There are no restrictions on what Heather is able to sculpt in sugar and the range of cakes appears to have no boundaries at all; consequently clients are able to have a totally unique cake whatever the occasion.

One of the marketing pamphlets states:

'Looking for a wedding cake that's royal iced, very conventional or an exact copy of your friend's cake, guaranteed not to surprise Granny? Sorry, you're looking in the wrong place'

Cakes can be delivered and are charged according to when they are required and where the destination is.

1 Explain two ways Sweetart is able to offer added value. *(4)*
2 Analyse one advantage to Sweetart of being able to add value. *(6)*
Total *(10)*

Source: sweetart.co.uk

Chapter 61

Innovation, research and development

Year 2

A Level students must know all of the content in this chapter.

This chapter is not applicable for AS students.

What is innovation?

Innovation is the introduction of a new idea, or method of production or new equipment into the production process. It is a new and better idea that should result in an increase in productivity that occurs to meet a market need. It will often arise as a result of research and development by the business, but it could also come at the suggestion of an employee, or as a result of solving problems in the production process.

Product innovation is the introduction of a new and usually better product to the market; process innovation is the introduction of a new production process that either improves productivity and lowers costs or produces improvements to the original product, or produces a completely new product.

What is research and development?

Research and development is essential for many businesses, particularly those in a highly competitive or technological market. Keeping up with or being ahead of the competition is vital if a business is to survive. Any business involved with mobile phones, cameras, airplanes or medical drugs will spend significant sums of money on research and development, in an attempt to beat the competition within the market.

The importance of research and development has grown for many businesses as a consequence of increasing globalisation. Many markets are truly international and therefore open to other competitors, often with a significant advantage in terms of cheap labour costs (this is true of some of the Eastern bloc economies and China). One obvious way to remain competitive in such a global market is to ensure that sufficient amounts of money are spent on research and development in order to gain in terms of technological advancement.

In simplistic terms, research and development is a process that enables the creation of new or improved products to meet the needs of its consumers. Research and development:

- is necessary to launch new products successfully, to ensure that they meet customers' needs
- examines how to improve the production process and its efficiency
- explores alternative materials to produce the goods
- aims to reduce the amount of waste generated in the production process.

These actions will help a business to maintain or gain a competitive advantage. Innovation can allow the business to charge a premium price as a reward for its high costs.

Research and development problems

Cost

Research and development can be very expensive. The cost depends upon the nature of the product. Pharmaceutical companies may spend millions of pounds on research.

Risk

There is no guarantee of success, as research does not necessarily yield effective results. Consequently, the money spent will be a cost without any revenue to cover such costs. This often explains the high prices of certain products such as new cancer drugs or sophisticated technological products.

Copying from other businesses

Even if the research and development is successful, there is a danger of other companies copying any new initiatives. Although such research can be protected by patents, they do not last forever. Furthermore, companies that copy products will not have incurred the same research and development costs, and could therefore charge less for their product.

Limited protection of new ideas

Patents do not cover all aspects of new products. Also, nothing can prevent a copy being made if no patents have been applied for. There are additional problems of ensuring that companies do not copy, as it can be time-consuming and expensive to prove that a copy has been made.

Coping with such rapid changes in technology

For certain industries, the rate of change is significant. The mobile phone industry is a good example. The technological rate of progress is so fast that without research and development, a business could fall out of the market very quickly if it failed to keep pace with the level of changes being made.

Constant changes may annoy consumers

Again, the mobile phone provides a good example. Although some consumers crave for the latest model, others are happy with the type and model they have, and become annoyed if their next phone operates in a totally different way.

It may also be annoying to the consumer if replacement parts for old models are no longer available. In this case, consumers may feel they are being forced to update their mobile phones unnecessarily.

Unemployment

Constant improvements because of research and development have meant in many cases a shift from labour-intensive processes to capital-intensive processes. This can have a significant effect on the level of employment, to which trade unions object.

Technological changes

Technological advancement in communications as a result of research and development has led to many changes in the working practices of employees. The workplace has been altered by hot-desking, and video- and telephone-conferencing, and more people are now able to work from home. Although this may have several advantages for both the employer (costs) and the employee (convenience and costs), there are disadvantages in terms of isolation and in the lack of team-building.

Process for research and development

Some businesses spend a huge amount of money on research and development. The chemical and metals company Johnson Matthey announced in 2013 that it had increased its research and development spending by 12 per cent to £153 million for 2013–14. Before a product is produced, great care is given to several key aspects.

Market research

The business needs to ensure that the product will be something which the consumer will want to buy. It is essential to undertake market research to ensure that a market-orientated approach is adopted. There are very few types of product which are product-orientated, where market research is not undertaken.

Key term

Product orientation: this means that a business concentrates its activities on improving the quality or efficiency of the product.

Research into market trends is important. Fashions and consumer lifestyles change, and it is essential for a business to be aware of such trends. If the business is a pioneer, it may wish to try to influence or even set such trends. How easy this is to achieve will depend on many factors, including the size of the business, its financial status and the skill of the research and development department.

Research may also take place within the business to assess its capability to produce any new product. This will involve a consideration of the resources required to make the new product, both in terms of capital equipment and the materials to be used.

Brainstorming

Whether this takes place before or after any initial research will vary, according to the type of business and the products involved. However, morphological studies can generate ideas very quickly.

Key term

Morphological study: a method that generates a lot of ideas very quickly and therefore more cheaply.

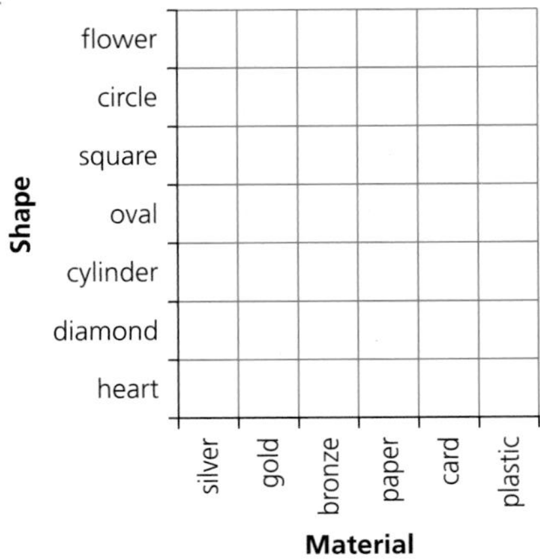

Figure 61.1 Morphological study for decoration design, using two axes/grids

Figure 61.1 shows simply how morphological studies can be used so that an idea can quickly be developed with a wide range of alternatives. In this example, the matrix shown has only two axes or grids. One represents the shape of the decoration, and the other the material to be used. If additional axes or grids are added, the number of ideas or options generated is even greater.

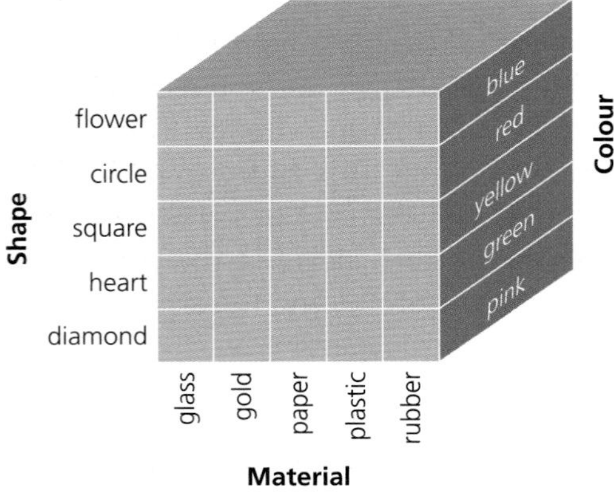

Figure 61.2 Morphological study for decorations, with additional grid

When designers are developing a new product, consideration will be given to three key aspects. This involves the process of value analysis.

Value analysis

There are three aspects to value analysis:

1. function
2. cost
3. aesthetics.

Function

The nature of the product will determine its task. It is essential that a lawnmower is capable of cutting the grass, as this is its main function. A kettle needs to boil water, a mobile phone needs to be capable of making and receiving calls and texts, and a car needs to be able to move and carry people. For many products the functional aspect is taken for granted by the consumer, but at the research and development stage, this is of paramount importance, simply because if it does not fulfil its function, the item will be useless.

Cost

The significance of the cost will vary depending on the nature of the product and the market in which it is to be sold. Nevertheless, keeping down costs for any product allows the business to be competitive and/or more profitable. It can also improve how the product is perceived; being good value for money may be attractive to the customer.

It is often a challenge to guarantee the functional element of the product without incurring high costs. Different materials can be considered to reduce cost, ensuring that they do not reduce the functional ability of the product.

Aesthetics

This is where the looks of the product become important. For some goods, the look is of little or no consequence. The water bottle for spraying a car windscreen is hidden under the bonnet of the car; therefore its appearance is not important. However, the shape and style of the car as a whole is important, as this influences many potential consumers.

Clothes are a strong example of when the aesthetics of the product are a top priority. Ensuring that the product (and its packaging) appears attractive is vital for many goods.

Balancing the three aspects of value analysis

The difficulty for the research and design department is how to balance the three aspects of the value analysis. All three aspects should be covered, but the nature of the product will determine which aspect is prioritised.

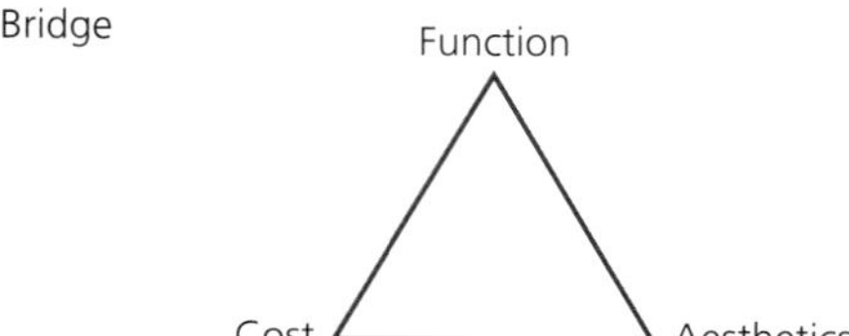

Figure 61.3 Function is the most important aspect

Figure 61.3 shows that, in its simplest form, the triangle can be used to prioritise the three aspects.

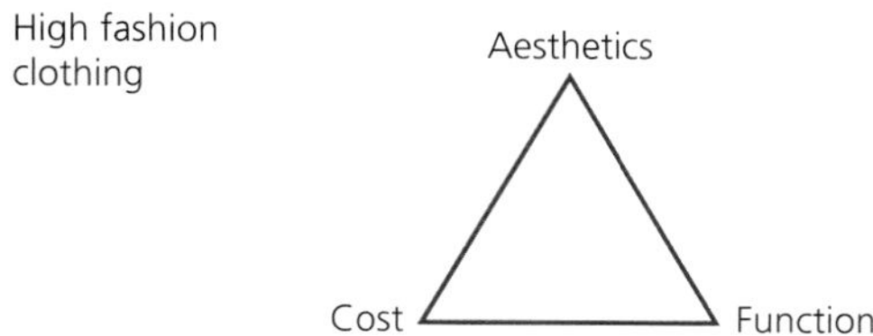

Figure 61.4 Aesthetics is the main aspect

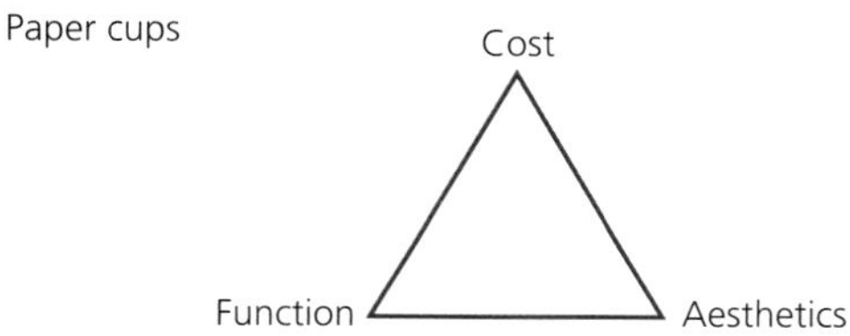

Figure 61.5 Costs are important for this product

For the products shown in Figure 61.3, 61.4 and 61.5, a different aspect of value analysis takes priority. In Figure 61.3, the product is a bridge, which must be able to support the weight of the vehicles that are using it to cross the river (function). Regardless of its costs and aesthetics, if it does not withstand the loads upon it, it will cease to function.

However, in Figure 61.4 the main priority switches to the aesthetics, as the look of the product (a handbag) is highly significant. In Figure 61.5, the product is paper cups. In a highly competitive mass-market and being a low value product, the main priority is to produce the product at its lowest costs. The functional qualities are not completely ignored, but cost is a high priority.

There are some products for which it is hard to suggest which aspect of the value analysis triangle takes priority. Using a car as an example, the price and therefore its costs are very important, especially as most cars are sold in a highly competitive market. However, the various components of the car will have different priorities attached to them regarding costs, function and aesthetics. The engine has to function, with costs being a consideration, but aesthetics as a low priority. The overall shape of the car must consider aesthetics, be conscious of costs and also emphasise function, particularly with aerodynamics affecting its performance and petrol consumption. Finally, hub caps covering the wheels are an aesthetic touch, with some cost consideration but few functional qualities.

The above example shows that the research and development process is not straightforward, and the complexity will vary according to the product. Cutting costs may affect the quality and the reliability of its functional qualities. Spending too much on either functional aspects or the aesthetics may affect the ability of the marketing department to sell the product.

Factors affecting research and development

Level of competition in the market

If the product in question is in a highly competitive market, it is more likely that research and development expenditure will be higher. A competitive advantage may be gained, but any additional research and development expenditure may affect the costs of the business. Increases in costs may affect the level of pricing (and therefore the product's competitiveness) and also the profit margins, which may already be tight in a competitive market.

International markets can be highly competitive, in which case additional research and development could be essential to attract the customer faced with so much choice.

Product

The more sophisticated the product in terms of technology, the more likely that research and development will be needed to keep up with technological developments.

The pace of technological development within the telecommunications industry is very fast. Research and development expenditure within the pharmaceutical industry, particularly for cancer drugs, has grown immensely.

External environment

Following the vast increase in the cost of oil in 2008 (nearly $150 per barrel), the car industry responded with further research and development into better fuel consumption. There was also additional research and development expenditure to lower carbon emissions, following the government's decision to introduce a progressive road fund licence tax based on emissions.

State of the economy

When the economy is in recession, it is more likely that businesses will undertake cutbacks. One such cutback is research and development expenditure.

Responding to a particular problem

Coca-Cola bottle suppliers were faced with the problem of distributing large bottles to be filled at different plants. They quickly worked on the problem to reduce costs, as distributing empty one and two litre bottles was expensive.

Further sources

www.matthey.com
www.renishaw.com

Your turn

Multiple-choice questions

1 If Johnson Matthey has increased its spending on Research and Development (R and D) by 12 per cent to £153 million, what was its R and D spending before the increase?
A £136.6 million
B £134.6 million
C £127.5 million
D £140 million *(1)*

2 The main reason for lack of spending on Research and Development by businesses is:
A knowing what areas to research
B the cost
C lack of interest
D lack of suitable workers. *(1)*

Revision questions

1 State four reasons why Research and Development is important for technology businesses. *(4)*

2 State four reasons why small businesses may find Research and Development difficult to undertake. *(4)*

3 Identify three questions that would be valid to ask in the process of value analysis. *(3)*

4 Explain what is meant by a 'morphological study'. *(3)*

Total *(14)*

Case study

Renishaw

Renishaw is a global company, specialising in measurement, motion control, spectroscopy and precision machinery. To maintain its position at the forefront of its markets the business invests 18 per cent of its sales turnover each year in Research and Development.

The company has always had to be involved in Research and Development of new and existing products because of the nature of the markets in which it operates. An example of taking the long-term view for the business was the development of Raman Spectroscopy technology. This technology identifies the composition of materials and has uses in many industrial processes. Working with Leeds University, the company struggled for a long time to get the technology through from the laboratory to becoming a viable product that was commercially successful. However, its perseverance paid off because during the recession this was the only one of the business's products that continued to achieve growth.

The company is, at present, the only UK manufacturer of a metal-based machine

that prints metal parts. It is in the process of developing the world's first 3D printed metal bike frame alongside Empire Cycles, the manufacturer. The frame is stronger and 33 per cent lighter than other equivalent bike frames with greater corrosion resistance. In addition, the system allows design improvements right up to the point of manufacture and also gives the consumer the opportunity to customise the bike. By working effectively with research departments and manufacturers, Renishaw is able to keep its business at the head of the field.

1 Analyse the two benefits for Renishaws that arise from working directly with a manufacturer. *(6)*
2 Evaluate the reasons why Renishaws continued to invest heavily in research and development, despite the recession. *(12)*

Total *(18)*

Chapter 62

Methods of production

AS / Year 1

Both AS and A Level students must know all of the content in this chapter.

Types of production

There are three main methods of production: job, batch and flow. In addition, cell production is a variant of flow production.

Job production

Job production often involves producing a single item or product. Various terms are attributed to job production, such as bespoke, unique, tailor-made and one-off. Job production is usually concerned with satisfying a consumer's specific needs, and can also refer to the production being undertaken by one employee who completes the whole task. This type of production is often undertaken by small, local businesses. For example, a customer chooses flowers for a wedding, which will be ordered and arranged in the chosen colours and requested arrangements. Similarly, a football team may order a logo for its shirts in a distinct design with specific colours. A person may want a garden makeover to meet certain requirements and with a particular layout. Each of these jobs is unique, specifically requested and produced to satisfy that individual customer.

The size of job production can vary, depending on what is being produced. A business producing crisps may order a machine that packages them. This machine will be made to meet the specific demands of the crisp manufacturer and be unique, made to order.

Job production tends to be labour-intensive, as the number of goods produced would not make it worthwhile investing in an automotive process.

The costs of setting up a job production process are significantly less than batch or flow. The process is more expensive in terms of labour costs and the cost of materials, as there are few opportunities to gain from bulk-buying economies of scale.

Costs are, however, lower in terms of stock held. For job production, there will be little work-in-progress, and materials need only to be bought for a particular job.

Some job production projects can be very large but still a single product, for example a luxury hotel.

An example of job production of a large product is the construction of the magnet railway system being built in Dubai, United Arab Emirates. This is a massive project but is a one-off job, meeting the specific requirements of the Dubai government.

Benefits of job production

- It can meet customer needs exactly.
- The quality of work is usually high as only one item is being produced, and so work is concentrated on a single unit.
- It is easier to motivate workers involved in the production process, as they will build the product from start to finish in many instances and so feel involved and committed.
- There is flexibility to produce whatever is required.
- It is easier to add value due to the highly specialist work that is undertaken.
- Little stock is tied up.

Limitations of job production

- There are usually no opportunities for benefiting from economies of scale.
- There are higher costs of production.
- Labour is more likely to be skilled, therefore harder to find and more expensive to employ and train.
- In most instances, it will be a slower process.
- It is difficult to gauge the costs for the job, as in many instances it will not have been done before. Jobs tend to be costed on an hourly rate for labour with additional costs for the materials used and the hire or purchase of any specialist equipment.

Batch production

Batch production is used when there is a set procedure and stages that the production process needs to go through in order to create a product. One process has to be completed before the next stage of the production process can be started.

Every batch of goods goes through every stage of the process together. The process is then repeated, when the next batch goes through exactly the same processes. As each stage of the production process is the same, different products can be produced using the same process. A batch quantity will vary according to the nature of the product and how it is made. There can be some variations within each batch process to suit specific orders, as long as the actual process remains the same.

For example, to make bread the raw materials need to be mixed, then put into an oven and finally wrapped (packaged) or left unwrapped. However, at each stage, every batch of bread being produced can be different because different ingredients can be used in the first process; for example, to make white bread, brown bread, wholemeal bread, and so on.

Pottery manufacture is another good example of batch production. A batch of the raw materials are mixed in the first stage of the production process; then the batch will be moulded into the required shape (mugs); the moulded shapes will then be heated and once cooled finally painted to a specified design. The next batch of raw material will be moulded into different shapes (cups) and will then follow exactly the same process.

Whether a particular batch process is done by hand or machine is not important.

Benefits of batch production

- The system is able to produce in larger quantities than job production.
- There may be some economies of scale, depending upon batch sizes.
- Batch production is generally faster than job production due to the larger number of products produced.
- As greater quantities of goods are produced, the unit costs should be lower, benefiting from some economies of scale.
- There is more flexibility than flow production (see below) to meet the needs of the consumer.

Limitations of batch production

- There may be a time delay between batches which means that nothing is being produced (downtime).
- When batches of parts are produced with presses (dies), that is, the machine that shapes a particular part, for example, of a car, the changeover to a different press can take several hours, during which time nothing happens for that process (downtime).
- The increased downtime between batches reduces the level of output when compared to flow production.
- As the level of production is higher, more stock needs to be held, adding to the cash outflows of the business.
- Storage space for products waiting to go into the next batch process may be needed. This space could have been used for productive purposes.
- The amount of variation will not be as great as it is for job production.
- There is less variety of work and a lower level of skill required; therefore the tasks may not be as motivating as with job production. This, in turn, may affect the morale and subsequently the productivity of the workforce.

Flow production

Flow production provides a continuous process, utilising a conveyor-belt approach, whereby the product is assembled on a production line with employees undertaking specific repetitive tasks for each stage of the individual processes.

The manufacture of cars is a good example, although there are lots of products that are assembled in this manner. Most 'white goods' (e.g. washing machines) are assembled using a flow system.

Flow production is used in order to produce vast quantities of a standardised product. The division of labour enables employees to concentrate on one particular task in the production process and therefore they are able to increase the level of productivity (see **Chapter 64**).

Due to the large numbers that are produced, the level of capital equipment used in the production process is very high. Flow production is often automated. This is an example of a capital-intensive factory (a greater reliance on machines rather than labour).

Automated production

Benefits of flow production

- The business is able to gain the benefits from economies of scale and therefore reduce the unit cost of production.
- Due to the large-scale production, the business can benefit from the division of labour (see also **Chapter 64**) and therefore reduce costs still further.
- The business can produce a standardised product in very large numbers much more quickly than the other methods of production.
- Unlike batch production, because the process of flow production is continuous, there is little downtime and therefore production levels are optimised.
- It enables a business to remain competitive due to low unit costs and large scale production, to enable demand to be met.
- It will offer more opportunities for the division of labour (specialisation) where labour can concentrate on specific tasks and therefore enhance the productivity for the business.

Limitations of flow production

- The initial set-up costs are very high because of the cost of the automated systems.
- It takes a considerable amount of planning to organise the flow system and timings to ensure that all components and sub-assembly are completed in the right order at the right time to keep the line moving at all times.
- It lacks the flexibility to produce a wide range of products.
- If the line stops for any reason, the whole production process is stopped, unlike batch production, where another stage of the production process could continue.
- Any significant fall in demand will make the process uneconomical. (This happened during the recession that started in 2008, causing several car plants to reduce their production levels, or even close down.)
- Given the repetitive nature of the production tasks, the employees are less likely to be motivated, which may affect productivity, absenteeism and labour turnover levels. All of these have a negative effect on costs.
- There will be large amounts of stock in terms of work-in-progress.
- There will be a greater reliance on suppliers to deliver on time (possibly on a just-in-time basis). (See **Chapter 68**.)
- The lead time in setting up a 'flow' production method may be substantial.
- Any change in the products to be produced may involve a considerable amount of 'down-time' as machines need to be changed.

Cell production

The definition of cell production varies considerably. Some people define it as a production system that has employees working in teams, who are responsible for the whole of the production process for a given product. Within the factory, there will be a number of such teams operating in the same manner. This complete cell production process is expensive to set

up, as the tooling for the process has to be duplicated depending upon the number of teams involved.
The Volvo Kalmar plant in Sweden operated a cell production process with considerable success, especially as this method gave the employees the satisfaction of producing a whole car or a significant part of it, from start to finish. The alternative, flow production, for manufacturing cars means that employees are normally only involved in one small part of the production process, and it is therefore considered harder to achieve any sense of pride in the finished product, unlike the members of the cell teams.

The layout of a cell production plant is often U-shaped to enable the process to be contained within a given area in which a team operates. Canon, the camera manufacturer, has used this approach with considerable success.

A reduced version of cell production operates when a team is responsible for a section of the production process or collection of workstations within the productive process. This is a diluted form of cell production, with the intention of trying to empower the workforce and encourage them to take more responsibility for the work they do and consequently gain more pride and a sense of achievement (see Mayo's theories of motivation, **Chapter 47**).

Benefits of cell production

- There are improved working conditions because the employees operate in a team and are therefore responsible for their particular cell. This provides a greater degree of motivation and reduces boredom and absenteeism.
- As the employees are responsible for the work within their own cell, there is an incentive to ensure that the quality of the work is high. This reduces the amount of waste and therefore reduces costs.
- It encourages a sense of responsibility and pride in the work (see Herzberg's theories, **Chapter 47**).
- There are opportunities for job rotation (see Herzberg's theories) within the team.
- It allows the employees to set their own pace of work. As long as the tasks are completed within a specified time, the team can organise and decide the pace of work at any stage of the day to suit themselves. Products can be stockpiled following a period of a high work rate, and used when they decide to have a period of a slower work rate.

Businesses are constantly looking for ways to increase the standard of their products and improve the productivity, in order to gain even the smallest competitive advantage. In 2007, Volvo spent millions on a new automated multi-task cell at its aero plant in Trollhattan, Sweden. The cell, one of the world's most advanced, undertakes several tasks within a confined space in a fully automated manner. This is an unusual example of a production method that is both cell and flow production.

Division of labour (specialisation)

This occurs when a job or task is broken down (divided) into separate tasks. This will make the task easier to perform and therefore quicker and cheaper to train an operative to perform the specific task.

Once the task has been learnt, the operative ought to be able to perform the task more quickly and therefore increase the productivity rate and thus increase output while lowering the unit cost and consequently improve the profit margin.

The downside to dividing a job into tasks is that the tasks may well become repetitive and therefore boring. The opportunity to find the repetitive task motivational is minimal and may therefore lead to errors and/or a higher rate of labour turnover.

The employees may also 'lose out' if the tasks are so small and specific that they can be automated and therefore create redundancies. However, the business and its shareholders may benefit if automation of some of these tasks helps to reduce unit costs still further.

Introducing division of labour into a business is usually as a method of reducing costs and being able to increase production. Both of these reasons are linked to the desire to remain competitive within a given market.

Impact of division of labour on the stakeholders of the business

- Shareholders may benefit from increased efficiency and productivity, which lead to an increase in profits and therefore dividends.
- Suppliers may benefit from supplying more components to the business (though the suppliers may also be squeezed for lower prices).
- Employees may be bored or demotivated, due to the repetitive work.
- Customers may be able to buy the product at a reduced price (depending on the elasticity) due to the increased efficiency and productivity.

- Management may be rewarded with bonus payments as production increases (as may the employees).
- HR department may find an increased workload countering the demotivated workforce.

Changing the method of production

One of the main dilemmas facing a business when thinking about changing the method of production is whether it is right to do so, and deciding when is the best time to change.

Changing from batch to flow may increase efficiency, but the initial outlay is very expensive. Buying all the machines in order to operate flow production may be too expensive for some businesses. Furthermore, while the changeover is taking place, there will inevitably be a loss of production.

A very small business that operates in a niche market, satisfying its customers' specific needs, may not want to switch to batch production and risk being unable to satisfy its customers so easily.

It is possible to switch from batch and flow to cell production, though much will depend upon the skill of the workforce and their ability to change the manner in which they work. It will also depend upon the quantity of products that are produced. Although cell production may be better in terms of job satisfaction for the employees, the ability to produce products as quickly is in doubt.

The decision to change will depend on the:

- nature of the products involved
- actual cost of the machinery
- financial situation of the business (budget)
- significance/importance of its customers, in terms of meeting their specific needs
- degree of competition in the market in which the business operates
- views of the stakeholders of the business
- objectives of the business
- practical ability to change: sufficient room within the factory
- support of the workforce
- cost of any possible redundancies
- need to produce a standardised product (reducing the degree of variation)
- availability of the required technology.

Tips and techniques

It is possible to consider the points listed above as reasons why there may need to be a change in the method of production.

Tips and techniques

Questions that relate to the different types of production and possible changes need to be answered in the context of the case material. This will avoid a generic answer that will not gain many marks. Think about the finances and other resources of the business, its objectives and the likely demand for the products.

Table 62.1 Methods of production

Characteristics of the production process	Job	Batch	Flow
Quantity produced	Often one	More than one and increasing in number	Increasing in number – very large quantities
Variety of product	Each one is unique	Some variation for each batch produced	Standardised product but with some variation, often in colour
Capital required	Can be high because a one-off product	More capital outlay due to size of production	Large capital outlay for convey system and automated processes
Skill of labour	Often highly skilled because each product is unique, therefore skill needs to be adaptable	A particular part of the batch process might require a level of skill	Less skilled as jobs are more likely to be repetitive
Organisation type	Organic		Mechanistic as size increases

Impact of choosing a specific method of production

Using Table 61.1 will allow the decision-makers to consider the various variables involved. The desire to expand may well necessitate a change in the method of production to accommodate a larger scale of production.

However, certain stakeholders may view this with concern. For example, a move towards mass production may require a greater usage of capital equipment and consequently less units of labour (Capital substitution). All of the factors/variables listed in Table 61.1 will need to be considered so the desired outcome can be achieved while noting the likely opportunity costs.

Further sources

www.themanufacturer.com
www.businessweek.com
www.sweetart.co.uk

Your turn

Questions are suitable for all AS and A Level candidates.

Multiple-choice questions

1 A factory produces 12,000 units a week. If the division of labour increases the weekly production by 15 per cent, the new level of units produced would be:
A 1,500 C 3,000
B 1,800 D 2,700 *(1)*

2 Which of the following is not a method of production?
A batch production
B flow production
C lean production
D job production *(1)*

3 Job-production characteristics include all of the following except:
A tends to produce low numbers
B skilled labour used
C produces a standardised product
D each product is usually unique *(1)*

Revision questions

1 State three characteristics of job production. *(3)*
2 Explain two likely costs of setting up a flow production process. *(4)*
3 Analyse two likely impacts on the employees of operating cell production. *(4)*
4 Explain two reasons how a wide range of products could be produced using batch production. *(4)*
5 State three products that are likely to be produced using:
A job production *(3)*
B batch production. *(3)*
Total *(21)*

Case study

Sweetart cakes for all occasions

Heather Higgins has operated her bespoke cake business for several years. It is based in Staffordshire, but is known across the country. She has specialised in designing and making cakes for all occasions. Her cakes are bought for weddings, birthdays and other special occasions. Not only does she produce cakes, but also sugar sculptures are available and can be produced to match customer requests or selected from a vast range of designs available in albums.

There are tasting sessions for weddings customers so that they may choose the type of cake and the filling. Fruitcakes, sponge cakes and cakes containing champagne are all available and produced to exacting standards.

Her website states that she can design humorous sculptures, which are influenced by puppets, gothic art and doll artists in America. She explains, 'I have no desire to illustrate from life, I much prefer to use my imagination so there are no rules!'

Such is the standard and uniqueness of her work that she has won national and international awards. Heather designs and crafts each sculpture by hand to each client's unique specification, no matter how outlandish the idea.

Sweetart cakes

1 Explain why Heather's business is most likely to use job production. *(4)*
2 Analyse the benefits of job production for a stakeholder of Sweetart. *(6)*
3 Evaluate whether the business should change the production process from job to batch in order to meet increased demand for Heather's cakes and sculptures. *(15)*

Total *(25)*

Chapter 63

Project management

Year 2

A Level students must know all of the content in this chapter.

This chapter is not applicable for AS students.

Project management is a process which involves planning and organising activities using resources to help achieve the objectives of the business.

Project management can also be viewed as the application of techniques and skills in order to complete a given project in an efficient manner.

Project management can be divided into several processes:

- planning
- executing
- monitoring
- completing.

Project management uses a range of techniques in order to plan, execute, monitor and complete.

Critical path analysis

Critical path analysis (CPA) is the process that allows for the overall time of a project to be calculated, and to allow a diagrammatic network to be drawn which shows when activities should start and finish.

It also allows planners to see which activities can be undertaken simultaneously. Once the network is drawn, it allows the business to monitor the progress of the project.

The building of Terminal 5 at Heathrow took years to complete. Nevertheless, much of the work went into the planning stage, before a brick was laid. Each activity that was necessary to be undertaken in order for the terminal to be finished, would have been allocated a period of time in which to be completed. Certain activities would have been examined to determine the order in which they were to be tackled, and if certain activities could be undertaken at the same time.

Tips and techniques

Critical path analysis is sometimes known as network analysis.

There is also another version which is called PERT (Programme evaluation and review technique).

A node and an activity

In CPA, there are certain types of symbol that are drawn to show activities and timings.

Figure 63.1 A node

A node represents:

- the start of an activity
- the end of an activity
- both the start and end of an activity.

Figure 63.2 An activity

An activity represents a task that is actually undertaken; for example, laying foundations, building walls, assembly of roof trusses (supports), tiling roof, installing electrics. For simplicity and convenience, each activity is given a letter; see Figure 63.2.

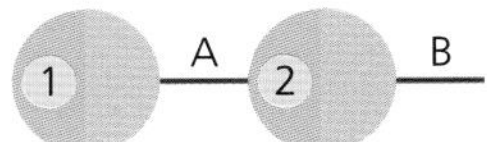

Figure 63.3

In Figure 63.3, A starts and is followed by activity B. This means that B cannot start until activity A has been completed. Consequently, the path diagram helps the user to see which activities are dependent upon which other activities.

The network is also able to show which activities can take place simultaneously.

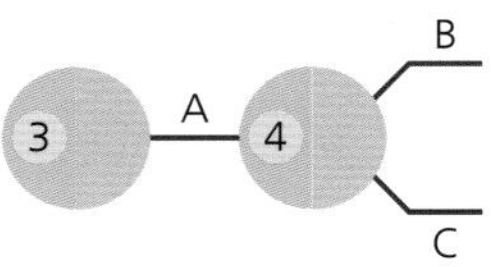

Figure 63.4

In Figure 63.4, activities B and C cannot start until A is finished, but can take place simultaneously. To show this, B and C are drawn in parallel.

Where two activities have to be completed before another activity can start, as in Figure 63.5, the node will have two activities joining before the start of another activity. For example, G cannot start until both E and F have been completed.

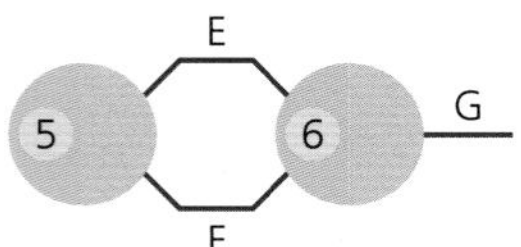

Figure 63.5

In Figure 63.5, node 5 represents the end of an activity and the start of activities E and F. Node 6 represents the end of activities E and F AND the start of activity G.

It may also be the case that two activities cannot start until other activities are completed. The approach is exactly the same. Activities are drawn parallel and both have to be completed before the others can start. In Figure 63.6, activities S and T have to be completed before both V and W can start.

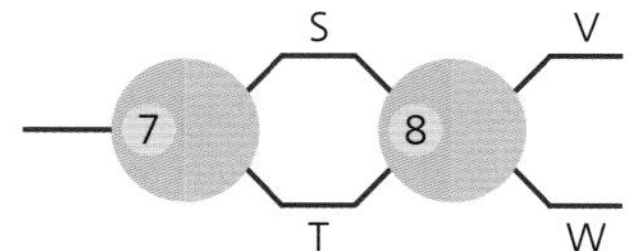

Figure 63.6

In Figure 63.6, node 7 represents the end of a previous activity and the start of both S and T. Node 8 represents the end of activities S and T AND the start of activities V and W.

At this stage, the nodes and activities have been drawn to represent the order of events (activities). In addition, it is now clear as to which activities have to be completed before other activities may start.

However, what has not been included is the actual amount of time that each activity takes. Introducing a time element is essential if the activities are to be in the right order, and for a time for the overall project to be calculated.

To help keep the diagrams (networks) simple, the nodes and the activities are used to show the length of time involved and other essential information, such as earliest starting times and latest finishing times (see below).

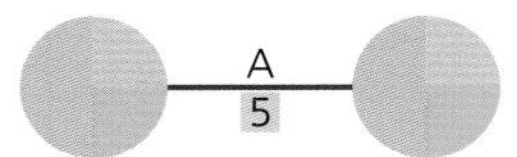

Figure 63.7

In Figure 63.7 the length of the activity is usually posted under the activity line.

Earliest starting time

To calculate the earliest starting time (EST), add the length of the previous activity and put the answer in the next node (see Figure 63.8).

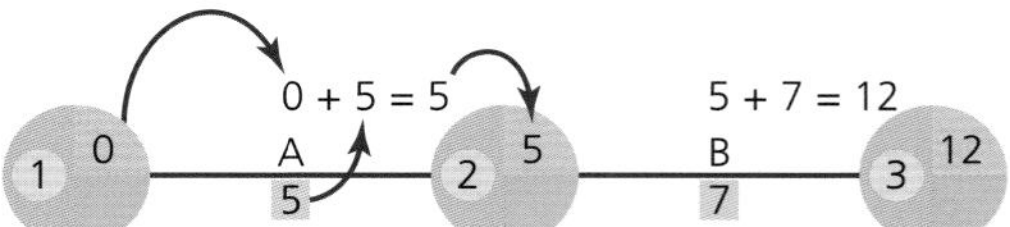

KEY:

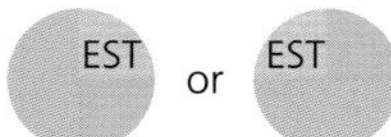

Figure 63.8

In Figure 63.8, the activity takes five days. To calculate the EST for activity B, simply add the EST for the previous activity to the length of the activity. There is nothing before A, therefore 0 and A takes 5 days:

0 + 5 = 5

The answer is then placed in the node at the start of B.

Tips and techniques

Where the EST is placed within the node may vary. It is therefore important to ensure that whenever you draw a network, you always include a key (see Figure 63.8). There is no right way, though most favour the first example.

Calculating the EST for the next activity, C:

EST of previous activity (5) + length of activity (7) = 12

Therefore, 12 is placed in the node at the start of the next activity.

If there is more than one activity going into another activity as in Figure 63.9, then it is important to realise that the highest number of days needs to be taken, as the next activity cannot start until BOTH activities are complete.

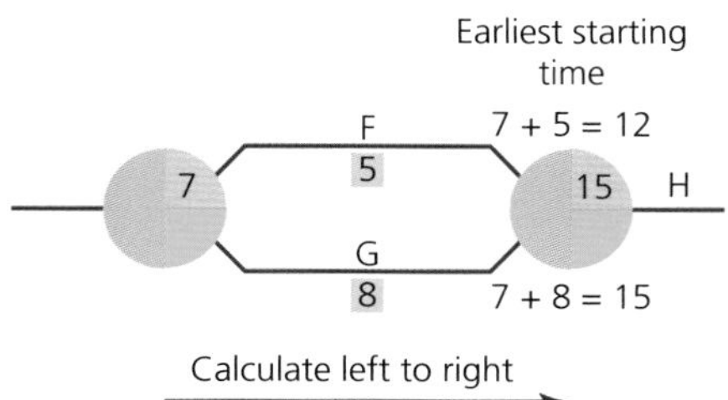

Figure 63.9

In Figure 63.9 both F and G need to be finished before H can start. The earliest starting time for H needs to be the HIGHEST figure.

EST of previous activity (F = 7) + length of activity (G = 5) = 12

Or, EST of previous activity (7) + length of activity (G = 8) = 15

Therefore the EST for H = 15. This is because H cannot start until both F and G are complete, and G will take longer to complete.

At the end of the activities, the last EST is also the overall duration of the project as a whole (see Figure 63.10).

Figure 63.10

In Figure 63.10 the last activity is Z and its EST is 22 days. As there are no more activities in the project, 22 days is the total length of the project.

Tips and techniques

It is wise to write out 'the total length of the project is 22 days', rather than leaving it up to the examiner to see your answer in the network.

Latest finishing time

The latest finishing time (LFT) refers to the latest time in which an activity can be completed without causing a delay to the next activity.

To calculate the latest finishing time (LFT) you need to work from right to left. Calculations are started from the end of the project. The starting point is at the end of the project, so that in Figure 63.10, if the EST in the last node is 22 days, the LFT will also be 22 days.

To calculate the LFT:

LFT at the end of an activity minus the duration of the activity

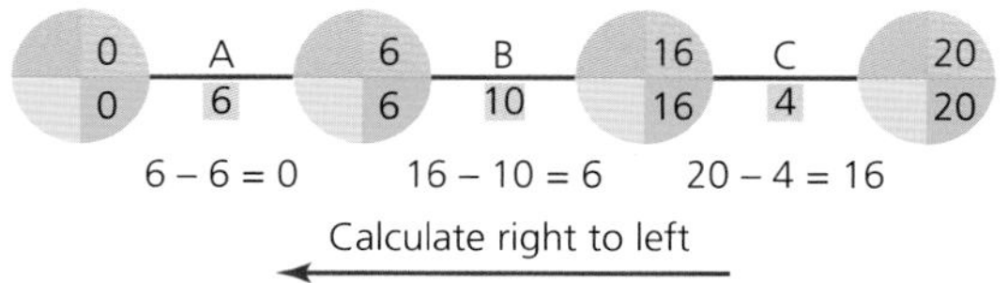

Figure 63.11

In Figure 63.11, to calculate the LFT for activity B:

LFT at the end of the activity (20) – length of activity B (4) = 16

Therefore 16 is placed in the node at the end of activity B.

Similarly, to calculate the LFT for activity A:

LFT at end of B (16) – length of activity (10) = 6, which is placed in the node at the end of activity A.

Tips and techniques

The very first node at the start of the project should always have a LFT and EST of 0. If you do not have this then you have made a mistake.

Whenever there is more than one activity going into a node from right to left, the LOWER number is taken.

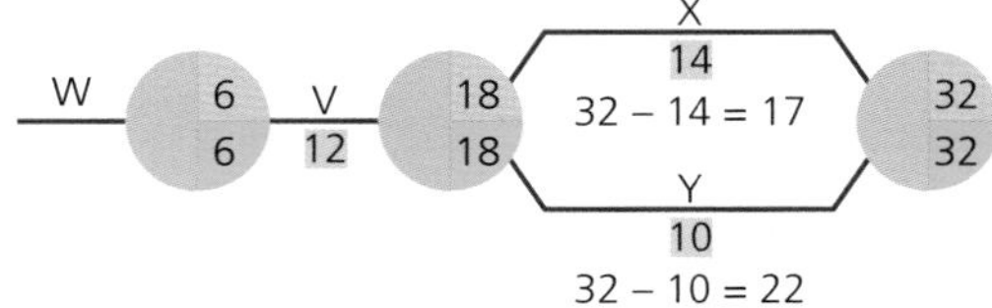

Figure 63.12

In Figure 63.12 activities X and Y 'feed' into activity V. To calculate the LFT for V:

LFT of X = LFT at end of X – length of activity X = 32 – 14 = 18

LFT of Y = LFT at end of Y – length of activity Y = 32 – 10 = 22

Taking the lower figure means that the LFT for V = 18 and the LFT for W:

LFT of V = 18 – 12 = 6.

Finally, a whole network may look like the one shown in Figure 63.13.

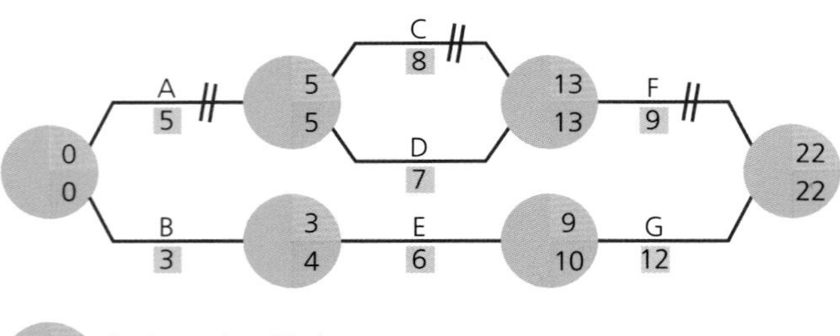

Figure 63.13

Critical path

The critical path is where, in a given node, the EST and the LFT are the same. Looking at Figure 63.13, the critical path is A, C and F. For these activities the EST and the LFT are equal.

This means that for these activities, any delay will affect the length of the whole project and is therefore a serious issue.

The route of the critical path is marked with parallel lines on the activity.

Tips and techniques

It is also worth remembering that adding the duration of each activity on the critical path ought to be the length of the overall project. This is another check which you can use to ensure that you have worked out the ESTs and LFTs correctly.

You are encouraged to write out the critical path as well as marking it on the diagram.

Dummy activity

A dummy activity is one that has no significant time but is an essential link between other activities. Because it has no real time factor, it is marked with a dotted line (see Figure 63.14).

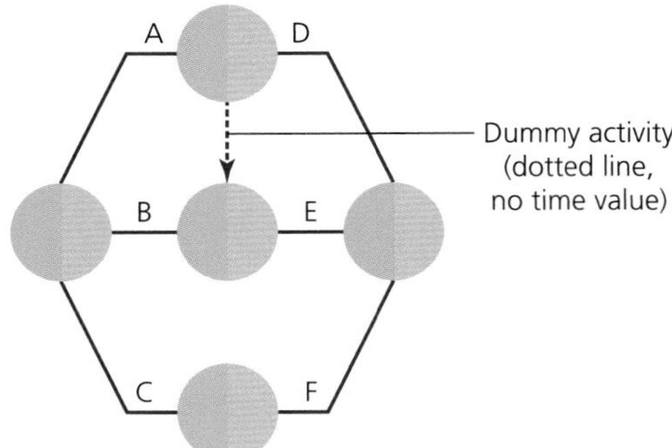

E is dependant upon A and B finishing

Figure 63.14 Dummy activity

Tips and techniques

Questions may ask students to draw up a network from the information provided (see the sample question below). Although this is probably too long to be set as an examination question, it is nevertheless a good test of your ability to draw networks. It is more likely that the network diagram will be given to you and that you will be asked to calculate the ESTs and LFTs in order to calculate the total length of the project. In addition, calculating the floats is a common question. This example is set in the 'Your Turn' section at the end of the chapter.

Example

Buzzboards are thinking about producing their own surfboards, and have attempted to work out the activities that have to be undertaken in order to produce the boards. Construct a network and calculate the length of the project, given the information below.

Table 63.1 Construct a network

Activity	Duration of activity	Previous activity
A	5	–
B	8	–
C	10	–
D	10	A
E	9	B
F	6	B
G	12	B
H	2	D and E
J	9	H and K
K	5	F and G
L	3	J

Floats

A float shows how much time an activity may overrun (be delayed) before it has an effect on either the next activity, or the project as a whole. There are two types of float: a total float and a free float.

Total float

A total float represents the longest time which any activity's start may be delayed without affecting the length of the project as a whole. This is the most serious type of delay, as a delay in the overall finishing time of the project may mean that additional costs are incurred, or a penalty fee may need to be paid to the customer. Penalty clauses are common in the construction industry. Total float is concerned with the total path of the project, and is calculated:

LFT of the activity – duration of activity – EST of the activity

For example: using Figure 63.13, calculate the total float for activity D:

LFT of D = (13) – duration of D (7) – EST of D (5) = 1

This means that the start of activity D can be delayed by one day without affecting the overall length of the project of 22 days.

If the float was more than 1 in this example, the overall length of the project would be affected.

The total float for activity C:

LFT (13) – duration (8) – EST (5) = 0

This means that there is no room for any delay: any delay in the start of C would delay the whole project.

Free float

The free float refers to the effect upon the next activity and not the project as a whole; consequently, any such delays are not as serious.

The free float is calculated as shown:

EST of the next activity – duration of the activity – EST at the start of the activity

Using Figure 63.13, the free float for G =

EST at end (22) – duration (12) – EST at start (9) = 1

This means that the start of G can be delayed by one day before it will affect the start of the next activity, assuming there is one.

Tips and techniques

It is worth remembering that the total float is always larger or equal to the free float, otherwise you have made a mistake with your calculations.

Using the network

By calculating the floats and having knowledge of the ESTs and LFTs, critical path analysis can help to resolve problems related to delays. Where the total float for an activity is 1 or more, any delay at the start of the activity will not delay the overall length of the project. However, if the total float is 0, this means that any delay will lead to a delay in the project as a whole.

If the figure is 1 or more for free floats, this means that any delay in the start of the activity will not affect the start of the next activity, unless the delay is greater than the value of the free float. If the free float is 0, a delay at the start of the activity will cause a delay at the start of the next activity but NOT the overall project.

Knowing the float times may allow management to switch resources away from activities with a positive float to the critical activities, in order to resolve any delays.

Tips and techniques

Apart from the values of the floats, it is still important to consider the context of the question. Knowing not only the length of the delay, but also the cause of the delay may be of significance.

Gantt charts

The precursor to Gantt charts was created by Karol Adamiecks in 1896, although Henry Gantt designed his version at the time of the First World War. A Gantt chart is a graphical representation of the order and duration of given tasks within a project. It is a simple and useful tool for planning and monitoring progress of a project. It can be used to calculate how long a project will take, and which activities are dependent upon other activities. It also shows which activities should be completed at any given time within the duration of the project.

In other words, it is similar to a critical path or network diagram.

However, it can also be used to show simply how particular resources such as labour can be assigned to a given activity.

Because it is a simplistic version, it is less valuable for more complicated and lengthier projects.

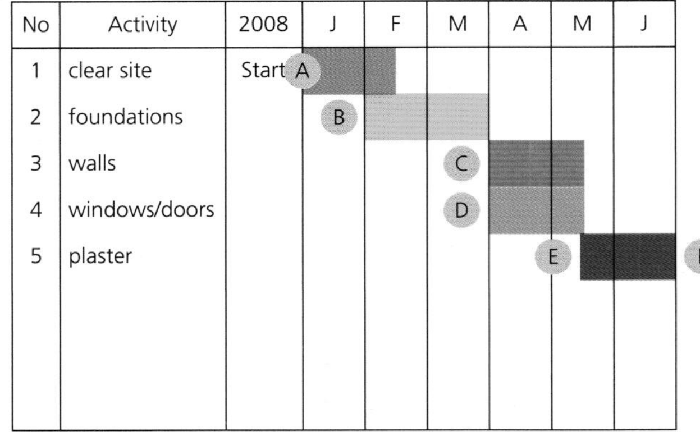

Figure 63.15 Gantt chart

The nature of the activity within the project is written on the left, and the duration of the activities is usually presented along the horizontal axis. The timescale should be included to allow for progress to be monitored and for a visual version of which activities are dependent upon which.

- A represents the start of the project, at the beginning of January.
- B represents the foundations which start at the beginning of February. Note that the foundations can start before the end of the first activity.
- C and D (the walls and windows) start when the foundations are complete at the end of March and the beginning of April.
- E plastering starts when the windows, doors and walls (C and D) are complete.
- F is the end of the project which is due to finish at the end of June.

By displaying the activities in this simplistic manner, it is easy to compare what is actually happening with what ought to be happening. It is, of course, not able to show so easily which activities are critical, and is therefore limited in its usage.

However, it is useful in solving some resource problems related to specific activities. See Figure 63.16 for a simple network diagram.

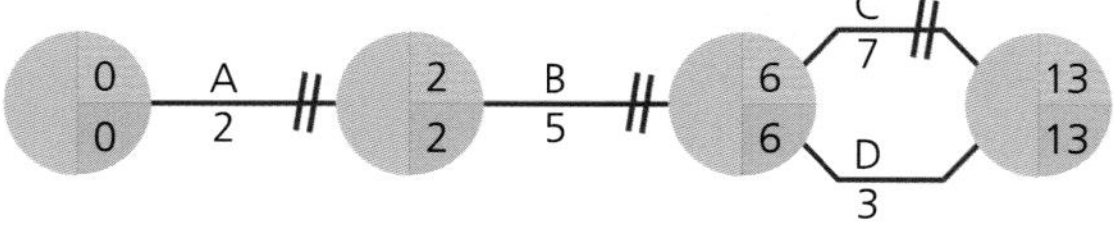

Figure 63.16 A simple network diagram

This network can be shown in a Gantt chart (see Figure 63.17).

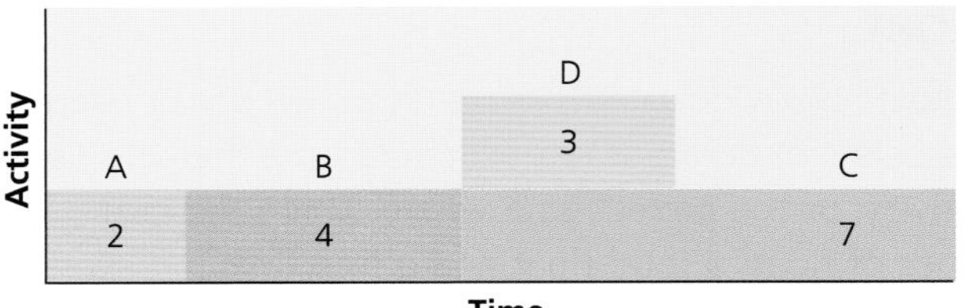

Figure 63.17 A Gantt chart

Activity	Number of employees required
A	10
B	8
C	18
D	8

Table 63.2 Figures for use in a Gantt chart

However, if the units of labour are now added to the chart, it is clear who is doing what: see Figure 63.18.

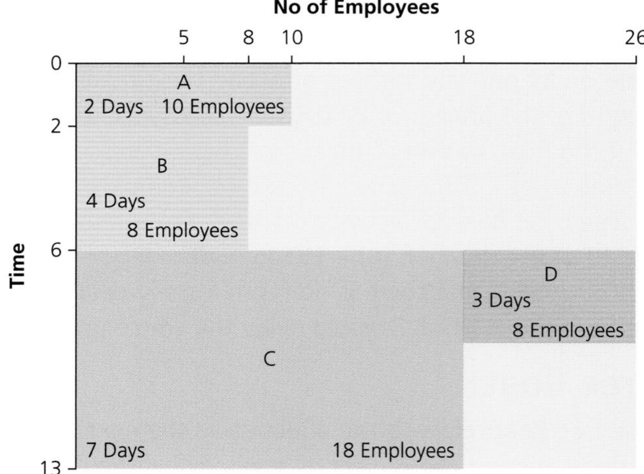

Figure 63.18

Activities C and D take place at the same time, so there could be a shortage of labour to complete these activities. In other words, the number of workers required could be greater than the number of workers available. By drawing a Gantt chart, this could be displayed and resolved.

Tips and techniques

To draw the Gantt chart with an allocation of the resource labour, the time axis can be changed to the vertical axis, and the horizontal axis used to display the time.

Limitations and benefits of critical path analysis

Benefits

- CPA is a simplistic visual form of communication to show the order and timing of activities.
- It offers a simple method to calculate the shortest time in which to complete the project.
- It gives a method to identify the activities which are critical.
- Knowing the EST allows for supplies to be delivered just-in-time (JIT).
- It helps a business to see when finance (cash) will be needed to ensure that supplies are ready for any given activity.
- CPA allows management to see the consequences of potential delays.

Limitations

- The value of CPA depends upon the accuracy of the activity times.
- Knowing that some activities are critical may encourage a reduction in quality in order to complete the activity on time.
- CPA only considers the timings of activities, but does not consider any of the cost implications.

Limitations and benefits of the Gantt chart

Benefits

- It is a simplistic visual representation of a project.
- It is easy to use for monitoring progress of a project.
- You can see at a glance what activity should be taking place at any given moment in time.
- It shows both time and a resource allocation, such as labour.

Limitations

- It cannot allow the user to see which activities are critical.
- It does not allow the user to see at a glance the ESTs and LFTs.
- The calculation of floats, although possible, is not straightforward.

PERT

This is another statistical tool that is used within project management.

This is very similar to critical path analysis but is more pessimistic in the approach to the time taken to complete various tasks within a project.

There is a need to estimate the shortest (optimistic) time and the longest time to complete a given task (pessimistic).

Then by applying the formula:

Estimated duration of a project is =

$$\frac{\text{Optimistic time} + 4 \times \text{likely time} + \text{pessimistic time}}{6}$$

By applying the formula it is more likely to gain a realistic time for a given project rather than as is often the case an optimistic time due to the fact that when a business is tendering for a job it may decide to be optimistic so time is lower and therefore the business may be more likely to win the contract.

However, deciding on the pessimistic, optimistic and likely times is still, to some degree, guesswork.

Advantages

- More realistic given the pessimistic view
- Simple formula to apply
- Able to see the critical path within a set of activities
- A lot of data can be visually represented to aid decision making.

Disadvantages

- Gauging the optimistic times is guesswork unless project been done before
- Gauging pessimistic times is guesswork
- Complicated to use.

Further sources

www.pmi.org

Your turn

Multiple-choice questions

1 The time allocation for a dummy activity is:
A 1
B the same as the float time for an activity
C 0
D the same as the LFT for an activity. *(1)*

2 A total float represents the longest time which any activity's start may be delayed without affecting the:
A next activity
B project as a whole
C amount of free float
D cost of completing next activity. *(1)*

Revision questions

1 State two reasons for using critical path analysis. *(2)*
2 Explain two differences between total float and free float. *(4)*
3A Using the information in Table 63.3 and Figure 63.19, calculate the ESTs, LFTs and the length of the project. *(5)*
3B Calculate the total and free floats for each activity B, C and E. *(3)*
4 If there was a delay of two days for each of the activities B, D and E, analyse the likely consequences. *(6)*
5 If the optimistic time = 25, the pessimistic time = 30 and the likely time is 28; using the PERT formula, calculate the expected duration of the activity. *(2)*
Total *(22)*

Table 63.3 Data for questions

Activity	Duration of activity	Previous activity
A	5	–
B	8	–
C	10	–
D	10	A
E	9	B
F	6	B
G	12	B
H	2	D and E
J	9	H and K
K	5	F and G
L	3	J

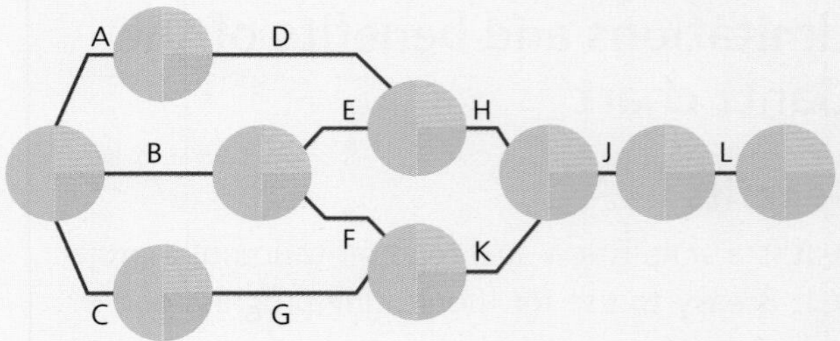

Key:

Figure 63.19

Case study

WMG Academy Coventry

The builders of the new academy which opened for students in September 2014 used a Gantt chart (see Figure 63.20 below).

1 Evaluate the usefulness of the simplified Gantt chart (Figure 63.20) to the builders of the WMG Academy. *(9)*

Line	Name	Start	Duration
34	**Roof**	**10/02/2014**	**24w 1d**
35	Edge protection	10/02/2014	1w
36	Parapet	17/02/2014	6w
37	Rooflights	10/03/2014	6w 3d
38	Insulation & single ply	17/03/2014	7w 3d
39	Walkways	28/04/2014	3w 4d
40	Detailing & capping	12/05/2014	3w 4d
41	Heat recovery plant	27/05/2014	4w 4d
42	PV array	16/06/2014	4w
43	Man safe system	14/07/2014	2w
44	Strip edge protection	28/07/2014	1w
45	**Envelope**	**20/01/2014**	**18w 1d**
46	FF SFS	20/01/2014	6w
47	FF Windows	10/02/2014	5w
48	SF SFS	10/02/2014	6w
49	SF Windows	03/03/2014	5w
50	GF SFS	17/02/2014	6w
51	GF Windows	10/03/2014	5w
52	Brickwork	03/03/2014	9w 2d
53	Entrance lobby	14/04/2014	6w 1d
54	**Internal Works**	**27/01/2014**	**30w**
55	**First Floor**	**03/02/2014**	**23w 1d**
56	Internal blockwork	03/02/2014	5w
57	1st side partition walls	10/02/2014	6w
58	1st Fix M&E	17/02/2014	6w
59	1st Fix Carpentry	17/02/2014	6w
60	2nd side board walls	03/03/2014	6w
61	Plaster & skim	10/03/2014	5w 4d
62	Mist coat	17/03/2014	5w 3d
63	2nd Fix M&E inc classroom lights	24/03/2014	5w 3d
64	2nd Fix carpentry	24/03/2014	5w 3d
65	Fixed FF&E	07/04/2014	5w 2d
66	Final Fix M&E	22/04/2014	5w 2d
67	Final Fix Carpentry	22/04/2014	5w 2d
68	Final decorations	06/05/2014	5w 3d
69	Floor finishes	19/05/2014	5w 4d
70	FF&E inc lockers	02/06/2014	5w
71	Test & Commission	06/05/2014	10w 3d
72	Snag & clean	02/06/2014	7w

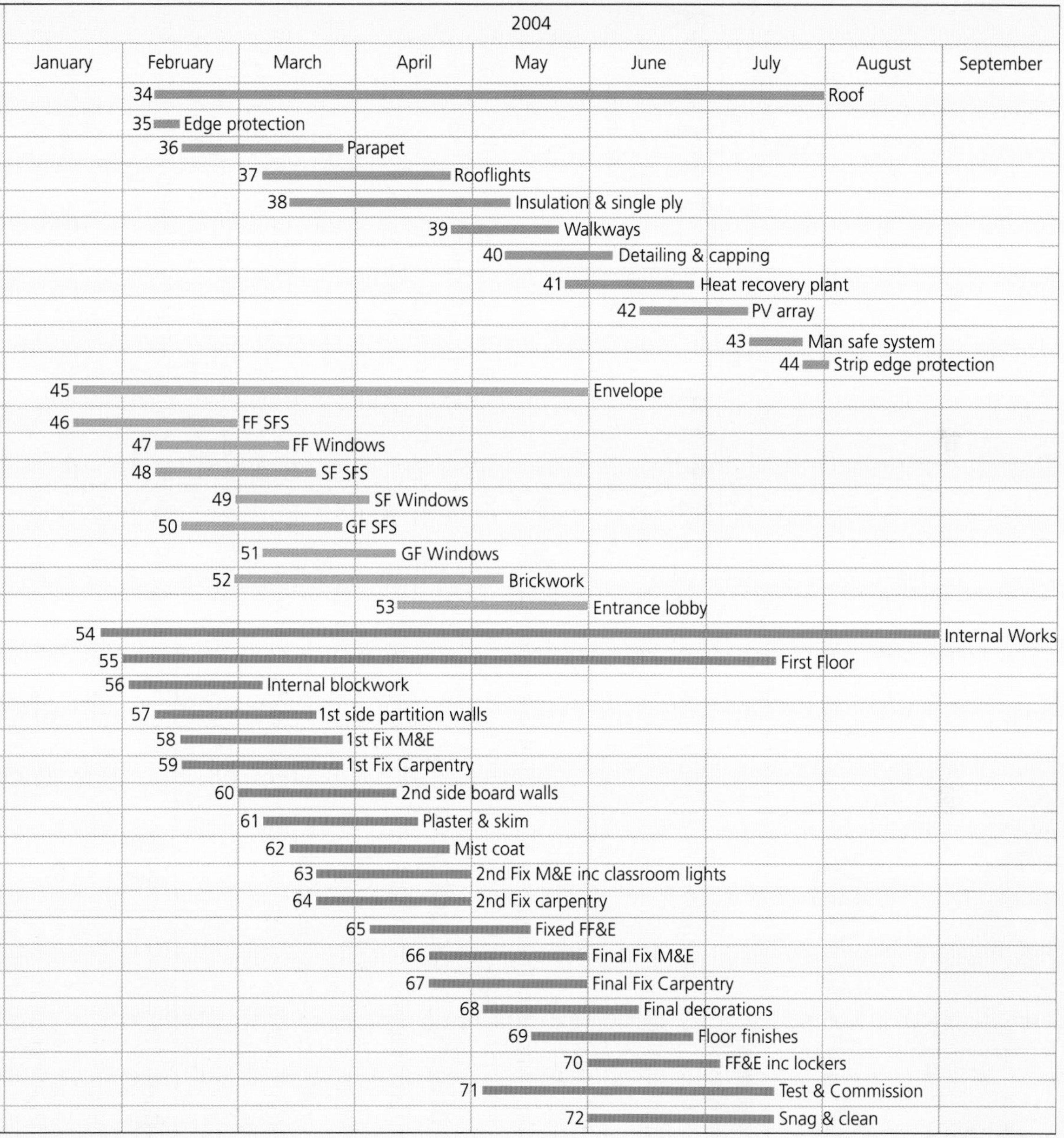

Figure 63.20

Chapter 64

Productivity

AS / Year 1

Both AS and A Level students must know all of the content in this chapter.

Productivity considers the relationship between inputs and outputs. The greater the output in relation to the input, the higher is the level of productivity.

Calculating productivity

In its most simplistic form,

$$\text{Productivity} = \frac{\text{output}}{\text{input}}$$

This ratio measures the efficiency of a business in its ability to convert inputs (resources) into output (manufactured products).

Example 1 (Business A)	Example 2 (Business B)
Output 30	Output 25
Productivity = 30 units (Input) 3 labourers = 10 per unit of labour	Productivity = 25 units (Input) 2 labourers = 12.5 per unit of labour

Figure 64.1

In Figure 64.1, the number of employees in business B is fewer than in Business A. Although they do not produce as many goods as business A, their productivity is higher. Each unit of labour in business B produces 12.5 goods, compared with business A where each unit of labour produces 10 goods.

Alternatively, by introducing the specialisation of labour (division of labour), their output should in theory be higher, although it may mean an increase in the number of workers required. A higher level of output per worker suggests a higher rate of productivity (see Figure 64.2).

Business C	Business D
Before division of labour	After division of labour
Output 100	Output 200
Ratio 1 labour produces 20 goods	Ratio 1 labour produces 25 goods

Figure 64.2

In Figure 64.2, business C has five units of labour producing 100 goods. After division of labour is introduced, the number of units of labour actually increases but the output increases to 200 goods. The input to output ratio for business is 20 goods per unit of labour, whereas the input to output ratio for business D is 25 goods per unit of labour. The productivity rate is therefore higher in business D, where the division of labour operates.

Productivity is the output per unit of input; it can be applied to any factor of production (land, labour, capital, enterprise), but it is most normally applied to labour.

Measures of productivity can be calculated in other ways:

1 $\dfrac{\text{Number of goods produced}}{\text{Average number of employees}}$

2 $\dfrac{\text{Output}}{\text{Number of employees and machines}}$

3 $\dfrac{\text{Sales revenue}}{\text{Number or value of machines (non-current assets)}}$

4 $\dfrac{\text{Sales revenue}}{\text{Wage bill or number of employees}}$

Productivity in a business can be improved in a number of ways:

- by using fewer inputs to achieve the same level of output.
- by an increased output using the same number of inputs.

However, there are many individual ways to increase productivity that may be of value to a business.

- Monitoring employees. It is important to set targets for employees, but it is also vital that managers follow up on these targets. Setting the target in itself is not enough. See **Chapter 45**.
- Avoiding micro-management of employees. If employees feel that they are being watched and constantly criticised, they will soon begin to feel demotivated and demoralised.
- Setting realistic targets. Targets must be achievable if they are to encourage the workforce to increase productivity (see Vroom, motivation, **Chapter 47**).
- Investing in machinery and technology. It is important that workers are given the best tools and equipment for the job (see Herzberg, **Chapter 47**). Investment in new technology, if undertaken with training, is often the best way for a business to improve its productivity. See **Chapter 44**.
- By ensuring that jobs are rewarding and meaningful. Job rotation, team working and job sharing will keep workers engaged in their work and should improve productivity. See **Chapter 43**.
- By making work enjoyable. This may sound unrealistic to some people. There are now, however, fewer routine production line jobs in modern industry. Most employees spend a large part of their week at work. If this work is made more enjoyable it is more likely to be productive.
- By avoiding spending too much time talking and too little time 'doing'; for example, by having too many meetings and not concentrating on producing the products.
- Encouraging a team spirit. If people are working as part of a team, they will usually feel a responsibility not to let others down (Mayo and Herzberg, see **Chapter 47**). They can also often discuss problems and find improved ways of doing jobs.
- Offering training to ensure employees are able to be more productive.
- Ensuring the factory layout is ergonomic (see Lean production, **Chapter 68**).
- Introducing division of labour.
- By offering profit-sharing incentives; employees may well increase their productivity if there is a direct correlation between effort and reward.
- Introducing suggestion box schemes. Many businesses encourage ideas to improve the product and how it is produced, which may increase productivity.

Tips and techniques

Always show the formula you are using and show your working.

Importance of productivity to the business and its stakeholders

Productivity will enable a business to save money in terms of costs

Table 64.1 Prodoctivity rates and labour costs

Average wage rate per employee (per month)	Productivity rate per employee	Labour cost per car
£2,500	10	£25
£2,850	15	£19

Table 64.1 suggests the savings as a result of increased productivity can be significant.

1. In this example, it is clear that the increase in productivity leads to a large fall in the labour costs for each car produced. This provides the car manufacturer with the opportunity to either reduce its selling price in the hope of gaining a competitive advantage, or allow the business to increase its profits as costs have fallen. Either of these possible savings will please the shareholders of the business and, if competitive prices are selected, sales may increase which may enhance job security for the employees.
2. An increase in productivity may also allow the products to be produced more quickly, which may shorten the delivery time and also become a competitive advantage as customers do not have to wait too long.
3. It may help the business to be competitive in the international market (see 1 and 2).
4. The business may be able to manage with fewer units of labour while producing the same number of goods, and subsequently reduce costs, the number of employees to be trained and supervised, thereby further reducing costs, to the benefit of shareholders.
5. However, if the number of units of labour are reduced this may lead to job insecurity for employees and make management's task harder if the employees become discontented.
6. An increase in productivity may allow the business to pay off debts as costs have fallen, and therefore creditors of the business will be pleased.

7 Improved productivity often encourages investment either by the business itself, or by interested investors. This investment provides another further opportunity for the stakeholders of the business in terms of profits and being able to compete in the globalised markets.
8 Productivity is a measure of performance and can therefore be used to monitor the efficiency of a business, thus allowing management to see if targets and objectives are on course.

Tips and techniques

It is important to note if there is a specific stakeholder to which your points can refer when evaluating the importance of productivity.

Further sources

www.rolls-royce.com: statement with regards to efficiency, productivity and cost cutting (November 2014)
www.cranfield.ac.uk: for information on UK manufacturing productivity
www.gov.uk foodchainanalysis-productivity-statsnotice-31july14.pdf
reportlinker.com: detailed food market reports in the UK 2014

Your turn

Questions are suitable for all AS and A Level candidates.

Multiple-choice questions

1 Given the units of labour of 120 and output of 4,200 the productivity of labour is:
A 28 units per unit of labour
B 2.8 units per unit of labour
C 35 units per unit of labour
D 3.5 units per unit of labour. *(1)*

2 If sales revenue increased by 5 per cent from £150 million and the number of machines increased from 9 to 10:
A productivity fell by 4.6
B productivity increased by 15
C productivity increased by 0.4
D productivity fell by 0.91. *(1)*

Revision questions

1 Explain, using a numercial example, how an increase in productivity may reduce the unit costs of a business. *(4)*

2 State the formula for calculating productivity in its simplest form. *(1)*
Total *(5)*

Case study

According to figures released by the government (Department for Environment Food and Rural Affairs), as of 31 July 2014 food and drink manufacturing has had the largest long-term gain in productivity in the food chain with labour volume dropping by 26 per cent since 2000.

For the total factor productivity of the food sector, given 2000 as a base year, the index number for 2012 was 105.

1 Explain how a drop in labour volume has increased productivity. *(2)*
2 Using the figures given, state the percentage change in the productivity for the food sector. *(1)*
3 Explain two likely reasons for the percentage change in productivity. *(4)*
Total *(7)*

Chapter 65

Economies and diseconomies of scale

AS / Year 1

Both AS and A Level students must know all of the content in this chapter.

The size of an organisation or part of an organisation can have a crucial impact on overall efficiency. Firms wanting to increase their productive efficiency try to reduce the cost of each item they produce. This chapter considers the internal and external factors that influence firms in trying to operate at their best level of production. It looks at the factors that encourage firms to increase their scale of production (economies of scale) and the reasons why firms might choose to operate at over and under full capacity. Economies of scale are benefits that arise as the firm grows that result in a lower cost per unit of output; diseconomies of scale arise when the cost per unit of output rises as the firm grows.

Why do businesses grow?

Firms have an almost natural wish to grow. It is quite common for a firm to change from being a sole trader to a partnership to a limited company (private or public). This growth occurs as part of a natural progression. As the objectives of firms change, the desire to achieve greater profits encourages growth.

While there may be good reasons why a firm may choose to stay small, there are a number of benefits to growth. Firms will grow to achieve:

- Greater profits: larger firms are able to increase sales and this can often lead to higher profits.
- Increased market share: this increases the relative and actual power of firms, which are then able to have a greater say in determining prices, achieving higher profit margins as a result. This may also give the business more control when it comes to negotiating with suppliers.
- Higher chances of survival: larger firms generally find it easier to survive. Firms often merge to increase their power and achieve longer lives for them both. Larger firms are also more likely to find it easier to borrow money.
- Cost reductions: larger firms tend to be more efficient, as they are able to make better use of the resources they have available. They gain the benefits of economies of scale through being able to utilise factors of production more efficiently.

Types of growth

Organisations can grow in a number of ways, but they tend to fit into one of two categories.

1. Internal (organic) growth is where a firm grows naturally over time. It does this simply by increasing in size to satisfy increases in demand. Many organisations have started small and have increased in size as the popularity of what they provide has increased. Even Microsoft started as a small organisation and achieved growth by essentially doing more of the same.
2. External growth is where a firm is able to grow quickly by merging with, or taking over, another business, often a local or national competitor. External growth works well if firms can finance this expansion in an economical way. However, some firms find it difficult to manage this kind of sudden growth.

Key terms

Internal growth: natural growth of a firm achieved by increased production and sales.
External growth: growth achieved by takeover and merger.
Capacity: the maximum that a firm can produce in a given period with the available resources.
Capacity utilisation: the percentage of total capacity that is actually being achieved in a given period.

Economies and diseconomies of scale

The theory of economies of scale relates to the benefits that firms can gain by increasing the scale of production. In simple terms, the theory suggests that as the scale of production increases, the average or unit costs of production fall. It is crucial that the definition is stated carefully. Missing out the word 'unit' in the definition completely changes the meaning and makes it incorrect.

The benefits of economies of scale can be explained in a number of ways. It is normal to distinguish between internal and external economies of scale.

Key term

Economies of scale: a reduction in unit costs achieved as the scale of production increases.

Internal economies of scale

Internal economies of scale are achieved as a result of a firm growing internally. There are many examples:

- Purchasing economies. These are gained as a benefit of being able to purchase raw materials and other supplies in larger quantities. The larger the firm, the greater the likely discount that can be achieved. In recent years there have been numerous complaints from dairy farmers about the amount that they receive for each pint of milk they sell. Large supermarkets are able to demand large discounts from the milk processors.
- Financial economies. Larger firms are able to negotiate cheaper loans and are more likely to get a loan in the first place because lending institutions are likely to experience a lower level of risk with them. These businesses have more assets to act as security, especially now that banks are more reluctant to lend.
- Managerial economies. Larger firms are able to employ specialist managers. This allows the firms to operate more effectively. Each of these managers can carry out his or her role in an efficient way.
- Technical economies. As a firm gets bigger, it can gain the benefit of buying more effective capital equipment. Smaller firms are unable to invest in the same way. For example, a distribution firm can buy a bigger lorry which would still only need one driver.

- Marketing economies. Larger firms can benefit from being able to use more effective methods of marketing. Above-the-line methods (see **Chapter 57**) such as television advertising are only available to larger firms.
- Risk-bearing economies. Small firms tend to concentrate on a limited range of products, while larger firms can spread the risk by diversifying into different products. They may even expand by taking over their suppliers. This allows the firms to reduce their costs.

External economies of scale

External economies of scale are achieved by a firm as a result of growth in the industry in which it operates. Many of these advantages occur if the firm is located close to other competing firms. Examples include the following:

- Concentration economies. Firms benefit as an industry grows in a specific region because skilled labour tends to move to that area. Local training colleges run specialist courses and suppliers to that industry tend to locate nearby. All these factors reduce costs and make the use of just-in-time systems more achievable.
- Information economies. Firms can benefit as information services are set up for the benefit of the industry. This could be access to data or market research information that has been collected for whole industries, making it cheaper for individual firms to access information. The internet has provided firms with many advantages of this kind.

Tips and techniques

Remember to define economies of scale carefully. Unit costs, not just costs, fall as a result of increased size.

Diseconomies of scale

Economies of scale suggest that unit costs fall as the scale of production increases. However, beyond a certain level of output it becomes less likely that further cost savings can be achieved. A point is eventually reached where unit costs start to rise. Diseconomies of scale occur for a number of reasons:

Key term

Diseconomies of scale: an increase in unit costs as a result of an increased scale of production.

- Communication problems. As a firm increases in size, it becomes more difficult to communicate in an effective way. The increased number of staff makes decision making more complex. The organisational structure of the firm develops increased levels of hierarchy and communication slows down.
- Problems in managing the production process. Large-scale production can be difficult to manage. Storage costs may increase and, as the firm reaches full capacity, there is a need for physical growth, which can involve additional fixed costs.
- Reduction in morale. Workers tend to lose their sense of belonging to the organisation as the firm gets bigger. As workers feel less important, they will be less inclined to push themselves and work hard. Labour turnover and absentee rates will increase, and therefore costs will rise. The firm may need to add an extra layer into its organisation. See **Chapter 41** for 'Span of control'.

Costs and benefits of diseconomies of scale

- As a business gets closer to full capacity it may be forced to pay overtime to meet further orders and therefore unit costs may rise, reducing margins.
- As full capacity is reached, machines may be working for longer and so reducing the time to maintain them, which in turn may lead to breakdowns.
- Diseconomies of scale must be monitored carefully. Larger firms need to review the impact on costs when they take the decision to increase the overall size of the firm.

Tips and techniques

Consider carefully the actual situation presented to you in a case study or data-response question. A firm will have specific issues that may more easily allow it to operate at either over, or under the full capacity position.

Further sources

www.growthbusiness.co.uk
www.entrepreneur.com

Your turn

Questions are suitable for all AS and A Level candidates.

Multiple-choice questions

1 As a firm grows and achieves economies of scale its unit costs will:
A rise
B fall
C stay the same
D rise and then fall. *(1)*

Revision questions

1 State the difference between internal and external growth. *(2)*
2 Define the term 'economies of scale'. *(2)*
3 Analyse two economies of scale that a hotel may gain by taking over another hotel. *(4)*
Total *(8)*

Case study

Procter and Gamble

Procter and Gamble (P & G) is one of the world's largest businesses. It has 20 brands that are worth more than a million dollars and more than 20 half-million dollar brands. It has 4 million customers and sells in 180 countries; it spends more on marketing than any other corporation.

P & G is an excellent example of the benefits of economies of scale in many areas of its operations. In recent years, the business has streamlined its brands to increase its level of efficiency by achieving cost reductions in production, buying and selling.

The business has also co-ordinated its channels of distribution, so that it is able to respond efficiently and effectively to the needs of its customers.

P & G has always made research and development an important part of its business, appreciating that it is operating in a market that is oligopolistic in most countries and that it therefore needs to be aware of its competitors. The fight to maintain market share and introduce new and different products is always prevalent in oligopoly.

In recent years, P & G has also acquired other well-known brands such as Clairol, Gillette and Wella. These acquisitions fulfil several functions. They:

- reduce competition in the market from smaller businesses
- increase P & G's market share
- increase economies of scale in marketing and distribution.

P & G has also rationalised its product range to make distribution more efficient. It now produces in three divisions: global beauty care, baby and family care, and household. This means that marketing and sales staff can be targeted more effectively and also that specialised production units can be set up for each of the divisions.

For large businesses like P & G, the benefits from economies of scale can be enormous throughout the firm, but they will only be achieved if the business is well organised and efficient.

1 Analyse two examples of economies of scale at P & G. *(4)*
2 Analyse two economies of scale that P & G might achieve through improving its channels of distribution. *(4)*
3 Analyse the diseconomies of scale that P & G might suffer from. *(4)*
4 Evaluate the benefits that are likely to arise from P & G acquiring new brands through take-overs. *(20)*

Total *(32)*

Chapter 66

Capacity utilisation and management

AS / Year 1 | Year 2

A Level students must know all of the content in this chapter.

AS students need to cover all of the content except:

- Calculating capacity utilisation (pages 459–460)

Capacity utilisation

Using the resources of the business in an effective and efficient manner is part of the key to a successful business. Most resources used are scarce and therefore costly; any way in which such resources can be used to the maximum will be of benefit.

It is also important to note that the capacity of a business needs to be measured with care. A factory may have 10 machines all capable of producing 20 items; however, in reality, the 'effective' capacity, that which is actually available, fit for use, may well be less.

Capacity management

Capacity management is concerned with the usage of the resources of a business. The factory space, the amount of machines available, the amount of raw materials at the disposal of the business, the IT capacity within a business and the amount of labour available, all have to be managed in order to produce the goods required at any given time. However, in its broadest sense capacity management is concerned with how the capacity of a business is managed. This includes:

- the analysis of performance and the effect on capacity of introducing new products
- performance fine tuning in an attempt to gain the most effective and efficient usage of the present capacity
- capacity planning to aid the development of a strategy for the business
- monitoring the capacity of the IT server within a business.

Calculating capacity utilisation

Knowing the level of capacity utilisation is important to a business because it affects the covering of its fixed costs. If a business has fixed costs (non-current) of £10,000, a maximum of 1,000 units of production, and is operating at 50 per cent of its capacity, it only has the 50 per cent of its productive capacity to cover all its fixed costs (there is a smaller level of production to cover all the costs). However, if the business operates at 100 per cent capacity, its maximum, therefore, is twice the output to cover the same level of fixed costs, consequently the average fixed cost would be considerably lower, allowing the business to either lower its prices, or increase its profits. Using the figures:

Fixed costs of

$$\frac{£10{,}000}{50\%} \text{ of } 1{,}000 = \frac{£10{,}000}{500} = £20$$

whereas with the same fixed costs of

$$\frac{£10{,}000}{100\%} \text{ of } 1{,}000 = £10$$

By operating at a higher utilisation of capacity, the business is able to reduce its costs and become more competitive.

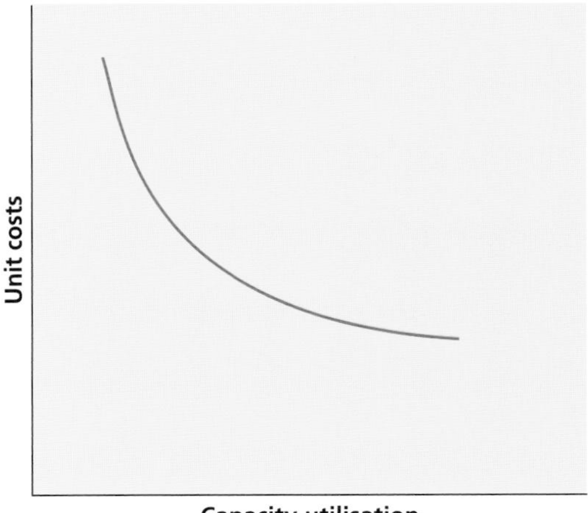

Figure 66.1 Increased capacity utilisation: unit costs fall

By reducing its unit costs, the business is more likely to be competitive.

The formula for calculating the capacity utilisation is:

$$\frac{\text{Actual or current level of output}}{\text{Maximum possible output}} \times 100$$

For example:

If a business produces 1,200 units and has the productive capacity to produce 2,000 units, the capacity utilisation equals:

$$\frac{\text{Current production level}}{\text{Maximum output}} \times 100$$

$$\frac{1{,}200}{2{,}000} \times 100 = 60\%$$

Tips and techniques

Remember, as always, to state the formula and show your working.

Table 66.1

Football club	Average attendance 2013–14	Maximum capacity	Capacity utilisation (%)
Manchester United	74,394	75,731	98.2%
Arsenal	60,013	60,355	99.5%
Newcastle United	50,395	52,404	96.2%
Manchester City	46,948	47,726	
Liverpool	44,656	45,362	98.4%
Chelsea	41,481	41,841	99.2%
Sunderland	40,117	49,000	81.9%
Aston Villa	36,080	42,788	84.3%

Source: SoccerSTATS.com

For example, with reference to Table 66.1, the average capacity utilisation of Liverpool football club for the season 2013–2014 to 1 decimal place was:

$$\frac{44{,}656}{45{,}362} \times 100\% = 98.4\%$$

Tips and techniques

Always note if a question requires you to calculate to 1 or 2 decimal places.

Whereas the capacity utilisation for Aston Villa to 1 decimal place was:

$$\frac{36{,}080}{42{,}788} \times 100 = 84.3\%$$

Reaching full capacity

There are several ways in which full capacity can be obtained.

Increase the demand for the products produced

The marketing department may undertake a variety of campaigns aimed at increasing demand and consequently more goods will need to be produced, thereby reaching full capacity. There is a danger of increasing demand beyond full capacity, which would require further investment that may or may not be possible or viable. In addition, the response to marketing may take some time and therefore reaching full capacity may also take a long time.

Produce different additional products with the same resources

If the resources are sufficiently flexible, it may be possible to produce other goods or variations to increase output and therefore reach full capacity.

Reduce capacity

Although this may appear rather drastic, in certain economic circumstances it is a viable option. It is sometimes achieved by 'mothballing'. This is when some of the capacity is kept but is taken out of usage. It may be literally wrapped up and stored ready for any upturn in the economy or demand for the given products.

On other occasions, the productive capacity is actually reduced. This is often the case when the economic climate or demand for the given product falls significantly.

Constraints on reaching full capacity

- The level of competition within the market in relation to the size of the market: if there are many competitors all competing for a limited number of consumers there is less likelihood that full capacity will be obtained.
- The stage of the product life cycle: if demand for the product is declining, operating at full capacity is unlikely.
- If the product is seasonal, there will be occasions when demand is lower and therefore production levels will be below full capacity.
- New, superior alternatives have entered the market, therefore reducing demand and therefore the level of production.

- Increased capacity will reduce the ability to reach full capacity, especially if too much investment has taken place.
- Outsourcing will reduce the utilisation of capacity.

Benefits of operating at full capacity

- As capacity utilisation increases, the average unit cost will fall, as the cost will be spread across more sales. See Figure 66.1.
- The fixed costs are spread over more goods and the variable costs may benefit from economies of scale such as bulk buying.
- Less wastage of resources.
- Profits increase, as a result of falling unit costs.
- Employees are busy, therefore occupied and possibly more motivated. A full order book may offer employees certainty of prolonged employment.
- Opportunities for employee bonus payments through overtime or profit sharing.
- More competitive due to reduced costs, enhancing business survival and market domination opportunities.
- Stakeholders will view the business in a favourable light. Bankers, shareholders, suppliers and consumers will all see full capacity in a positive manner.

Costs/disadvantages of operating at full capacity

- There is little or no opportunity for maintenance and therefore the consequences of any breakdowns will mean 'downtime', which is when the production stops so that no goods are being produced.
- Any additional orders will either be impossible to meet (especially in the short run) or will require significant additional costs in overtime. This will mean that the profit on any additional orders will be less.
- Working at full capacity may put pressure on the employees who may become stressed, leading to an increase in the level of absence. This will put even more pressure on the rest of the employees.
- As the emphasis is on producing the goods with all resources being fully employed, there is little or no time for in-house training.
- There is the possibility that the level of quality is affected. There may be occasions when, in an attempt to satisfy as many orders as possible, certain processes are hurried which lead to mistakes being made and may affect the quality of the finished product. This may lead to a fall in sales as the reputation of the product is damaged.

Over-utilisation of capacity

This can only be a short-term factor, when resources are pushed beyond their normal levels. Workers may be asked to work additional shifts or hours or some work may be subcontracted to satisfy a surge in demand. However, employees can only work additional hours occasionally before any detrimental effect on output occurs.

Tips and techniques

It is important for students to consider carefully the nature of the product and its market, in an attempt to assess the likely consequences of, or abilities to achieve, full capacity. The context of the question is crucial.

Further sources

www.growthbusiness.co.uk

Your turn

Questions marked in red are for A Level candidates only.

Multiple-choice questions

1 A business produces 600 units a week with a capacity of 750 units; the capacity utilisation is:

A 60%
B 75%
C 80%
D 90% *(1)*

2 If the capacity in Q1 above were to increase by 20% and production increased from 600 to 700, the capacity utilisation would now be:
   A 180%
   B 75%
   C 77.7%
   D 85.5% (1)

3 As capacity utilisation increases:
   A units costs rise
   B unit costs fall
   C average costs rise
   D average costs remain the same. (1)

4 Which of the following is NOT a constraint on reaching full capacity?
   A a seasonal product
   B new competitors join the market
   C outsourcing
   D product life cycle at growth stage. (1)

Revision questions

1 Explain what is meant by the term 'capacity utilisation'. (4)

2 Calculate the capacity utilisation if a factory is capable of producing 6,500 units but is presently producing 5,000 units (to one decimal place). (2)

3 If production is 200 units and the capacity utilisation is 80%, calculate the maximum level of production (to one decimal place). (2)

4 Analyse two likely benefits for a business of operating at full capacity. (4)

Total (12)

Case study

Yeovil Town football club

When promoted to the Championship in 2013, Yeovil had a ground capacity of 9,665 of which 5,212 were seats.

As a consequence its revenue from match day attendances was well below the average for the league.

1 The average ground attendance was 4,072 (based on season 2012–13). Calculate the capacity utilisation to one decimal place. (2)

2 If the average attendance increased to 5,500, calculate the new capacity utilisation to one decimal place. (2)

3 Explain how Yeovil Town's capacity utilisation could be increased. (4)

Total (8)

Source: www.footballgroundguide.com/yeovil_town

Chapter 67

Stock control

AS / Year 1

Both AS and A Level students must know all of the content in this chapter.

The quantity of stock held by a business is vitally important. Insufficient stock may mean that the business runs out of stock and cannot satisfy orders for its products. Too much stock will mean that the business is not being efficient, as too much cash will be tied up in stock. It is therefore essential that the right amount of stock is held; enough to meet orders from customers, but not so much as to incur unnecessary costs. How much stock needs to be held depends upon the type of business. Supermarkets will need large quantities of stock as they sell FMCGs (fast-moving consumer goods), while a garage selling cars would not need to hold much stock.

Production businesses will hold varying amounts of stock depending upon the type of productive process used. Where just-in-time is operated less stock will be held, whereas where job production is used, only sufficient stock to produce the single or low level of production will be held. There is no set amount of stock that will be held by a business and the type of production process is only one factor that will influence the level of stock (see below).

What is stock?

Stock is usually one of the following:

1 raw materials
2 work-in-progress
3 finished goods.

Raw materials

This is stock that includes all the raw materials or components that are needed to produce a finished good such as steel for cars. Many businesses will only buy in stock once an order has been gained.

Work-in-progress

This includes the raw materials and components that are partly assembled or used to produce the finished good. At any one time much of the stock may have already been used in the production process, but it is not as yet a finished product that consumers would be willing to buy.

Finished goods

This is the completed product that has yet to be delivered to the consumer. Some products are stored and then delivered. How much stock will be in this form will depend upon the nature of the product and the size of a given order. The business may be storing the finished goods until the number required by the consumer has been completed, which are then delivered in one despatch. This is often the case when products are to be exported.

For many products, the amount of finished goods stock is minimal, because the finished goods have already been sold and are therefore transported out of the factory immediately. This is particularly true for a business with a high rate of stock turnover (see financial efficiency ratios, **Chapter 38**).

The major issue is trying to decide on the right level of stock, balancing the benefits and the costs of holding stock.

Benefits of holding stock

Satisfying demand

It is important to be able to satisfy a demand for the products that are produced by a particular business. Creating a demand that cannot be satisfied often leads to a loss of goodwill, with potential customers turning elsewhere for their goods. This leads to a loss of revenue.

Coping with fluctuations in demand

This is similar to the previous benefit; however, being able to take advantage of a surge in demand, for whatever reason, may lead to further sales and a potential increase in orders and revenue. Furthermore, if orders increase due to the business's ability to meet the sudden increase in demand, the business may be able to reduce costs, as the additional production costs may benefit from the savings due to economies of scale.

Buffer stock to meet late deliveries

Not only does buffer stock ensure that there is sufficient stock available before a delivery is due, it ensures that there is no disruption to the production line. Stopping a production line because there is insufficient stock could cost thousands of pounds in 'downtime' (when production is not taking place).

Cost savings due to economies of scale purchases

Purchasing a large quantity of stock may allow for cost savings due to buying in bulk. Providing that the cost of holding the stock is not greater than the savings made by buying in bulk, it may be worthwhile. It also assumes that there is adequate space to store such quantities.

Costs of holding stock or inventory

Storage costs

Using warehouse space is expensive. The actual costs of purchasing the warehouse to hold stock, or the cost of rent, has to be covered either immediately, or if rented, on a regular basis regardless of any sales patterns and subsequent revenue.

It is not only the actual warehouse that needs to be provided, but also some sort of storage facilities even if it is just shelves. In many factories the stock storage is computerised and uses automotive equipment for stocking and distributing; all of which is an additional cost to the business. Depending upon the nature of the products or raw materials to be stored, there may be heating or freezing costs.

Opportunity costs

Paying for stock prevents the business from undertaking alternative expenditure.

Depreciation/obsolescent costs

Stock may depreciate over time, especially if it is perishable and reaches its sell-by date. It may also be damaged and will therefore lose value.

Stock can also suffer from becoming obsolete. While in storage, stock can become redundant as tastes change, or a new product arrives on the market that supersedes the stored item. Although the stock has been paid for, it is unlikely that a return in the form of sales revenue could be gained.

Security costs

Most goods will require some form of security. CCTV cameras or security guards are both expensive. The level of security will depend upon the nature of the products and raw materials involved.

Administrative costs

These costs are related to the costs of obtaining the stock. Raising orders, agreeing transport delivery times and checking the stock on arrival all incur costs.

Insurance costs

As the risks of holding stock increase, the cost of insurance will increase. Insuring the stock is an unavoidable cost.

Out-of-stock costs or stock-out costs

Although the above points highlight the often significant costs of holding stock, there are additional costs of not having sufficient stock which are usually referred to as out-of-stock costs.

If a business runs out of stock and is therefore unable to continue to produce goods, the inevitable loss will be the inability to complete and satisfy the order. Although this cost can be calculated by taking the value of the order, what is harder to gauge is the value of any future orders that may have been lost as a result of not meeting the existing order.

Traditionally, businesses would hold sufficient stock on the basis of 'just-in-case'; however, this can also be costly as often too much stock is held. Finding the optimum stock level can be achieved by considering the cost of holding stock and the cost of a stock-out. Figure 67.1 weighs up the cost of holding stock against the cost of not having stock. (See economic order level below.)

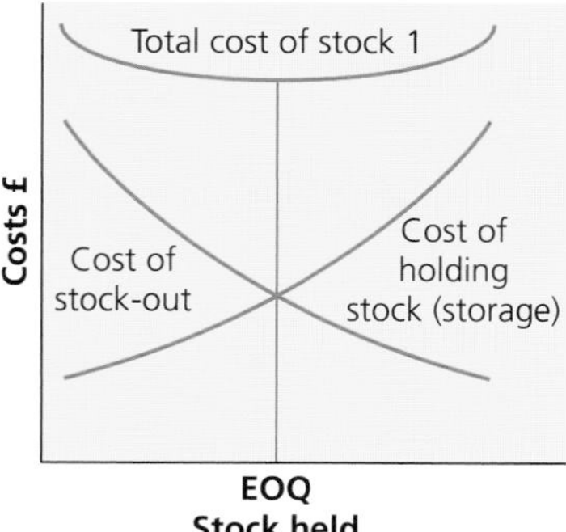

Figure 67.1 Optimum stock level (economic order quantity)

Stock control charts

Once a level of stock has been decided upon, the management of that stock needs consideration. Stock control charts are often used to monitor the levels of stock. They show the total cost of the stock on an annual basis, once both costs have been taken into consideration.

Figure 67.2 shows some of the key aspects and terms found in stock control charts.

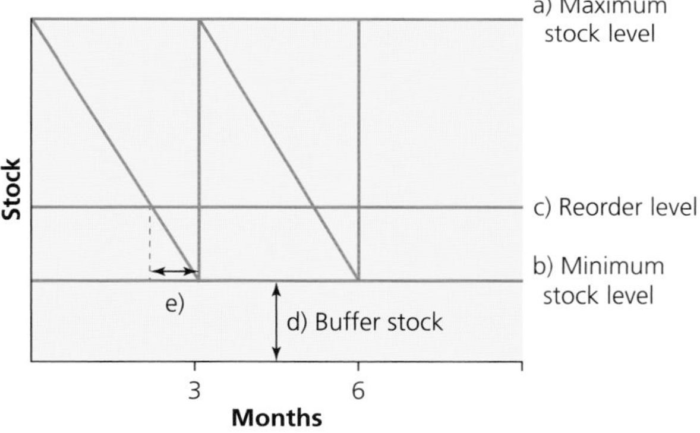

Figure 67.2 Stock control chart

Maximum stock level

This is represented by a) on Figure 67.2. This amount will be determined by several factors:

Storage capacity of the factory or warehouse

The larger the storage capacity, the more likely the business will be able and willing to hold more stock. Additional storage space may be available for expansion in the future.

Product

The characteristics of the product in terms of its rate of turnover (stock turnover levels), its size and value are all factors that will affect the level of maximum stock.

Level of sales

A high level of sales will often mean that the maximum stock level will be higher.

Cost of storage

Storage space will probably incur costs.

Degree of competition

If the market is competitive and there is an opportunity to gain more sales, the business will probably have a higher maximum stock level to be able to cope with any unexpected surge in sales. However, the cost of holding such stock levels will still need to be considered, if costs are to be kept under control.

Timing of marketing campaigns

If a business has launched a marketing campaign to introduce a new product or improve sales of an existing product, it may decide to hold a higher level of stock in the hope of increased demand.

Time of the year (seasonal sales)

Businesses involved with selling seasonal products may have to stock-pile products, so a higher maximum level of stock will be required to satisfy the surge in demand whenever it occurs.

Minimum stock level

This is represented by b) on Figure 67.2. This will be determined by the following factors:

Level of sales

If stock is sold quickly, the minimum stock level is likely to be higher.

Amount of time taken to deliver new stock

If the lead time is substantial, then a higher minimum stock level will probably be used.

History of unforeseen circumstances

If stock has run out previously, the business is more likely to have a higher minimum stock level.

Reorder level

Represented by c) on Figure 67.2, this is determined by the following factors:

- The amount of time that is taken from reorder to the actual delivery, which is known as the lead time.
- How near the supplier is to the factory.
- The sales records to date; if the trend of sales has been increasing, the business is more likely to have an earlier reorder level.

Fixed time reordering

This is exactly what it says. A business will reorder at a given fixed time, either every week or month depending on needs. This method allows the business to have a regular delivery of stock and will know how long it needs to last.

However, having a fixed reorder time would not be suitable for a business where demand for its products varies considerably.

Economic order level

This represents the result of attempting to 'balance' the difficulty of, on the one hand, weighing the cost of holding stock (storage, insurance, space and money being tied up in stock) and, on the other hand, the amount of stock that is ordered. The more stock that is ordered; normally it can be purchased at a lower price.[query Usually The level of stock that is seen as a balance between the two is known as the economic order level.

Buffer stock

Buffer stock is represented by d) on Figure 67.2, and is the difference between the minimum stock level and holding no stock. It should be viewed as emergency stock. The level of the buffer stock will be determined by:

- the likelihood of delays with deliveries
- the speed of the production process
- reliability and location of suppliers
- the level and pattern of demand.

Lead time

This is shown as e) on Figure 67.2 and represents the length of time between reordering the stock and its arrival (see Figure 67.3).

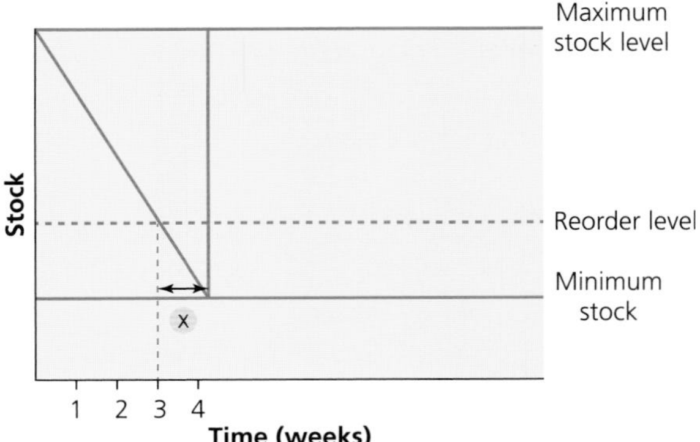

Figure 67.3 Lead time

The gradient of the line indicates the rate of sales. The steeper the gradient, the faster is the rate of sales. Figure 67.4a shows a steep gradient that is typical for a FMCG; Figure 67.4b shows a less steep gradient, typical for a slow-selling product such as furniture.

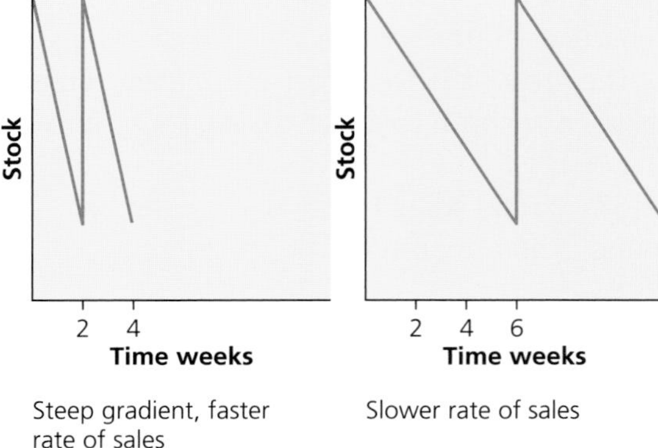

Figure 67.4a and b The rate of sales

However, there is an assumption that the rate of sales is constant (hence the straight line). In reality, the rate of sales will vary according to the time of year and because of other business environment factors that affect sales.

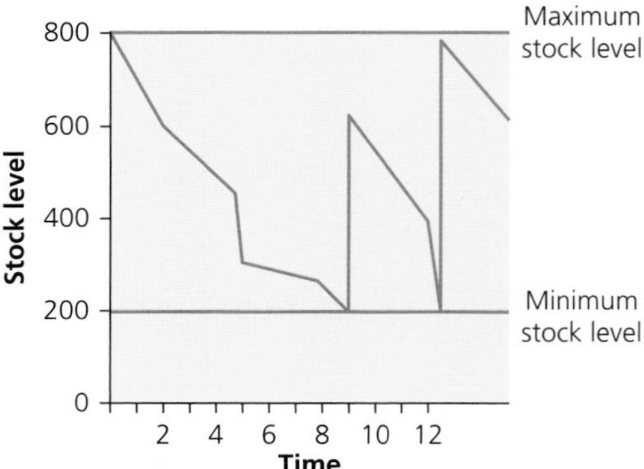

Figure 67.5 Variable sales pattern

Figure 67.5 shows that sales are more likely to vary over time. The amount of stock ordered varies. Even though the maximum stock level is 800 units, if a business knows its sales trends, it may not reorder quantities to ensure that maximum stock is held.

As lean production has been adopted within the UK (see **Chapter 68**), the level of stock has been one obvious area of concern. The utilisation of just-in-time (JIT) has led to significant falls in the overall levels of stock held. Consequently, a typical stock control chart has also changed. (For more details on JIT, see **Chapter 68**).

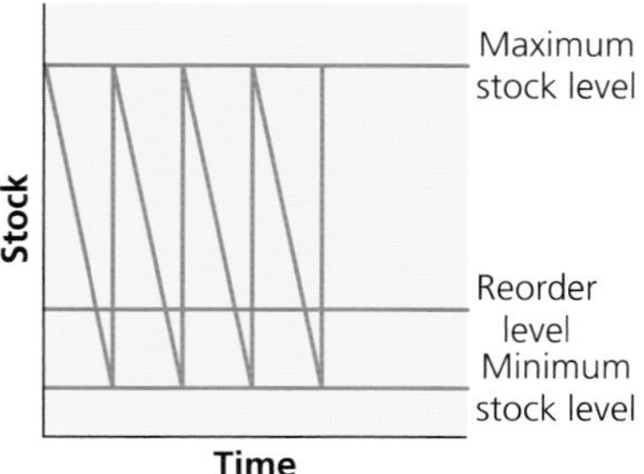

Figure 67.6 Just-in-time (JIT)

In Figure 67.6 it is clear to see that the maximum stock, the minimum stock and the reorder level of stock have all changed. This is because JIT is an attempt to reduce costs in order to be 'leaner' and therefore more competitive.

Tips and techniques

It is unlikely that you would have to draw a stock control chart in full. However, understanding how the stock control chart would change when circumstances change would be helpful.

Examples

If a business is growing in size, it will no doubt need more stock. It will therefore need to consider the consequences for its reorder and buffer stock levels, as well as the maximum stock levels. Ensuring that supply is maintained is vital to the business and therefore a higher buffer stock may be needed to avoid any stock-out situations.

Seasonal products may require more frequent deliveries and in larger quantities at certain times of the year, to coincide with the peak selling periods. A firework manufacturer is likely to hold much greater levels of stock in the run up to bonfire night, and New Year celebrations, than in the summer months.

The weather, the dates of public holidays and special events can trigger a change in stock levels. A business selling soft drinks will watch the long-range weather forecast with interest. Knowing that a heatwave is on the way will mean an increase in the level of stock held, in order to meet the potential surge in demand.

Calculating the average level of stock

To calculate the average level of stock:

$$\frac{\text{Maximum stock level} + \text{minimum stock level}}{2}$$

= average stock

For example, if the maximum stock level is 15,000 items and the minimum stock level is 4,000 items, the average stock is:

$$\frac{15{,}000 + 4{,}000}{2} = 9{,}500$$

Tips and techniques

As for any calculation, always show your workings, including any formula(e) you may use.

Control of stock levels

Concern over the levels of stock held has encouraged businesses to persuade suppliers to hold the stock until required (roughly how JIT operates); or alternatively, to persuade the customer to take the stock and store it. In this case, the supplier usually will not charge the customer until the stock is used or sold.

Apart from JIT, there are other ways in which the level of stock can be both monitored and controlled. The obvious method of controlling stock levels is by careful stock rotation.

LIFO and FIFO

These acronyms stand for last in, first out (LIFO) and first in, first out (FIFO). LIFO and FIFO are stock control terms that are also used for accounting valuations. The terms are related to the order in which stock is sold and how restocking takes place.

If new stock is simply placed on the shelves in front of the old stock, it will be sold first; hence, first in first out! Such a system is acceptable if the products in question have a long shelf-life such as paint or canned foods.

However, it would not be an appropriate way of controlling stock if the products were perishable and therefore have a short shelf-life. If this is the case, a more stringent system needs to be used. LIFO is a better system for the control of stock if waste is to be avoided or reduced. Selling the older stock before any new stock will help to ensure that stock does not go beyond the sell-by date. This system does, however, assume that shelves are stacked correctly. If staff do not bring all the old stock to the front of the shelves and then stack the new stock at the back, the system breaks down. Some stores are able to fill some cabinets from the back to ensure that the old stock is sold first; however, this is not possible on supermarket shelves, and therefore the success of FIFO relies on the efficiency of the employees.

Using EPOS

Just as the Kanban system is necessary to effectively operate JIT, EPOS (electronic point of sale) is invaluable in ensuring stock levels and the reordering of stock is done efficiently. The EPOS information is scanned by bar codes. Each product has a unique bar code number which is read electronically at the checkout desk, and the information is passed via electronic data interchange (EDI) to a computer that will automatically reorder stock at the required level.

Further sources

www.thebarcodewarehouse.co.uk

Your turn

Questions are suitable for all AS and A Level candidates.

Multiple-choice questions

1 If a business has a minimum stock level of 5,000 units and a maximum stock level of 35,000 units the average stock level is:
- A 30,000 units
- B 40,000 units
- C 20,000 units
- D 15,000 units *(1)*

2 Buffer stock level is the:
- A number of units between 0 and the minimum stock level
- B stock level when there is a need to reorder
- C maximum stock level minus the minimum stock level
- D average stock level. *(1)*

3 The lead time for stock may be calculated by the time:
- A between reordering stock and it being received/delivered
- B to reorder stock
- C to utilise the stock before the next delivery of stock
- D taken for the supplier to receive the order. *(1)*

4 Operating JIT will mean that the stock control chart will have:
- A a longer lead time
- B a lower maximum stock level and a higher minimum stock level
- C a higher maximum stock level and a lower minimum stock level
- D more frequent deliveries of stock. *(1)*

Revision questions

1 State two factors that would affect the maximum stock level held by a business. *(2)*

2 Explain how a stock control chart would change if the rate of sales changed. *(3)*

3 Explain the difference between LIFO and FIFO. *(4)*

4 If the maximum stock level was 25,000 units and the minimum stock level was 4,000 units, calculate the average stock level. *(2)*

5 State four 'out-of-stock costs'. *(4)*

6 Draw a diagram to show the economic order quantity. *(4)*

Total *(19)*

Case study

Numatic International (manufacturer of Henry vacuum cleaners)

Numatic International is based in Chard, Somerset and produces around 3,500 'Henry' vacuum cleaners a day. There are over 300 varieties of the Henry vacuum cleaner available. It also produces a wide range of cleaners for the domestic and industrial markets. The business has expanded rapidly with Employment Officer, Paul Stevenson, stating that the business 'just keeps growing and growing'.

All the components of Numatic's products are manufactured individually prior to assembly, which is undertaken by a combination of robotics and manpower at the Chard factory.

The impressive sales warehouse facility covers over 16,000m^2. This allows the business to hold higher levels of stock for fast-moving and selected specialised products, ensuring it provides its customers with fast availability.

Many of Numatics' products are sold abroad, helping to ensure that the 800 plus workforce are kept busy.

1 Evaluate the stock control factors that Numatic International will need to consider as it continues to expand. *(20)*
2 State two likely issues for Numatic in having over 300 varieties of Henry vacuum cleaners. *(2)*

Total *(24)*

Chapter 68

Lean production

AS / Year 1

Both AS and A Level students must know all of the content in this chapter.

Globalisation has increased the level of competition for many manufacturers. Ensuring that the best possible product is produced at the lowest possible price is now of paramount importance if a business is to survive in the international marketplace.

In order to remain competitive, it is essential that businesses find ways to reduce costs and to improve their productive efficiency.

What is lean production?

Lean production originated from Japan, and is an approach in which all employees are involved in putting into operation a series of working practices that will help the business to meet the demands of the consumer in an efficient and effective manner.

Apart from the price of a good, the consumer now expects a reliable product that has quality built in as standard and can be delivered on time. By operating lean production, the above requirements of the consumer are more likely to be met.

Lean production is a whole-business approach to achieving and maintaining a competitive product in the highly competitive markets of the world. It concentrates on the elimination of waste in its broadest sense. It not only looks at how a business can reduce its waste in terms of materials used, but waste in terms of time. Reducing the amount of energy used helps to reduce costs and thus contributes to the competitive edge for a business. Anything that helps to reduce the time it takes to introduce a new product, produce a new product and deliver a product is related to the lean approach. By reducing waste in its broadest sense, the business should be able to reduce its costs and therefore become more competitive.

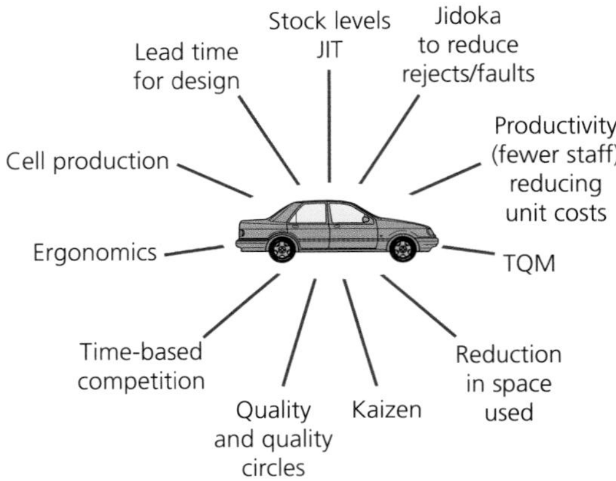

Figure 68.1 Different aspects of lean production

Depending on the sources used, there are between three and seven principles for lean production (see Further sources).

Car manufacturer Toyota followed the original ideas that had been used by Ford, and improved on them to increase productivity further and gain the maximum output from the minimum inputs. The Toyota Production System is seen today as the benchmark for the industry.

The main elements of lean production are set out below.

Time-based competition

This is an attempt to reduce the time taken between the generation of the idea for a product and it going into production (lead time).

This can be speeded up by the usage of computer-aided design (CAD) and virtual design techniques that can eliminate the need to build prototypes. Instead, any new designs can be tested virtually before the actual product is put into production. This saves valuable time and the cost of building prototypes.

Total quality management (TQM)

Total quality management considers the efficient usage of all the resources used within the production process, whether directly or indirectly related to the actual production process. The word 'total' is the significant factor, as it is considered vital that all employees are responsible for the well-being of a business, and not just those that produce the product. Employees are empowered to take the responsibility for the work they do. It is a different approach to the control of quality within a business. The emphasis is on finding ways to prevent mistakes rather than inspect for mistakes.

Jidoka

This is a process for building into the production process an ability to detect and reject faulty goods and components at the earliest possible moment in the production of the good. It is essential to try to keep the production line operating. If it stops, this is known as downtime, and means that no production on this line is taking place. The cost of downtime can be very expensive and is therefore to be avoided if at all possible. Jidoka is an aid to prevent defects occurring, which may eventually mean that the production process has to be stopped.

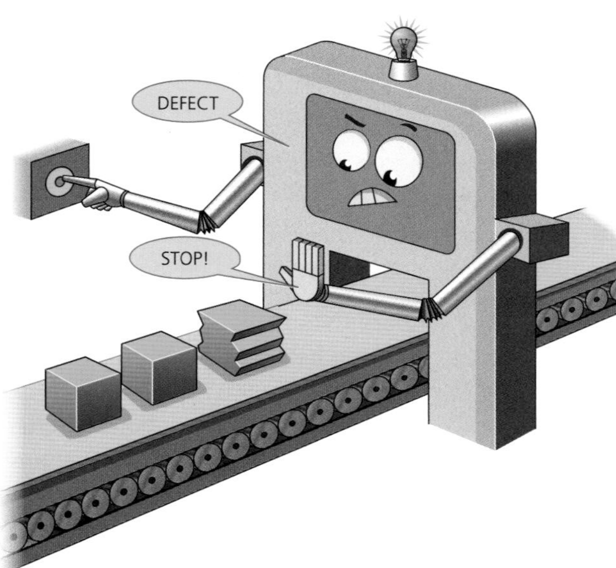

Figure 68.2 Jidoka in process

The Andon lights signs which are usually displayed alongside every line enable management and supervisors to check the progress of each section of the assembly line. Each number refers to a particular workstation, and the status of the problem can be shown with amber and red lights. This enables a quick response to the right part of the line, in an attempt to keep the line moving and thereby avoid any downtime.

Figure 68.3 Andon lights. Amber light: warning if a problem on the line is being dealt with; red light: line stopped, downtime

Kaizen

Kaizen is a philosophy which regards improvements in quality as an ongoing phenomenon, and not just something that takes place occasionally.

Striving for 'continuous improvement' is the key factor for the Kaizen approach. It is also achieved more easily if all employees are encouraged to take part in the process, and not just the management. Often, the people best placed to make suggestions for improvements are the production workers who know what the job actually entails.

At JCB, founder Mr Joseph Cyril Bamford suggested: 'I am never content. I'm always looking for improvement'.

Improving one part of the production process often encourages improvements in other parts of the process. If flow production is taking place, the saving of several seconds in an early process in the production line will mean that other processes will have to find time savings, otherwise bottlenecks on the line will occur. This acts as an incentive to find improvements further down the production line in order to facilitate the smooth flow of the whole process.

However, if continuous improvements are being made, eventually jobs may be affected;

consequently, employees may be reluctant to make too many suggestions on how to improve the production process, for fear of losing their own jobs. There is also a view that continual improvement programmes put great pressure upon the employees, who then tend to suffer either from accidents or stress. It has been suggested that job rotation helps reduce such concerns.

The alternative viewpoint is that without improvements, the business will become uncompetitive and jobs will be lost due to a falling demand for the products.

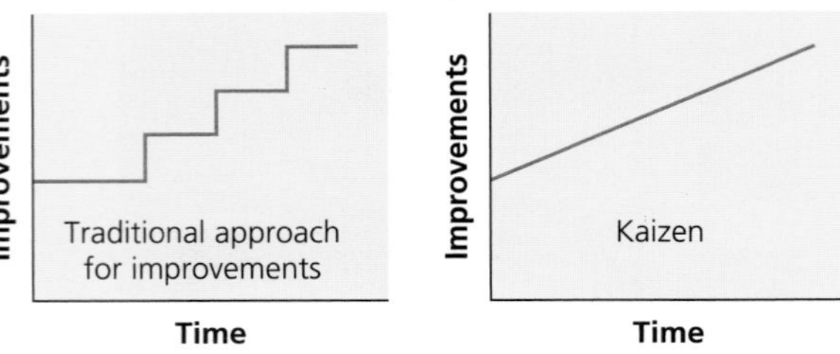

Figure 68.4 Kaizen

Quality and quality circles

As quality is now considered as something that needs to be built into the product that is produced, the business needs to focus on how quality can be improved and maintained (see also **Chapter 70**).

To complement the Kaizen approach, some manufacturers have adopted quality circles. This is a voluntary scheme where employees, often between four and ten in number, are allowed to meet in working hours to discuss problems related to their working environment and workstations. They will also aim to create solutions to problems, and pass on these suggestions to management. By involving the employees, there are motivational benefits that may contribute to an improvement in the level of productivity for the business.

Just-in-time (JIT)

This is a method whereby levels of stock are kept low in order to reduce the amount of space required for storing stock. By ordering stock in smaller quantities but with more frequent deliveries, the business is able to hold less stock with all the related advantages. (See **Chapter 67**).

Kanban

In order to operate JIT successfully, a Kanban system needs to operate.

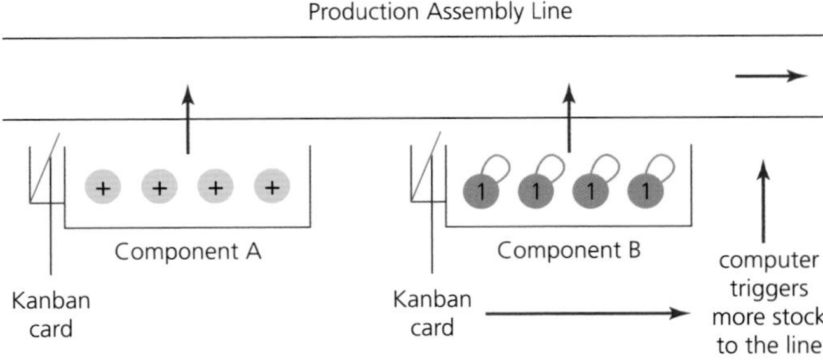

Figure 68.5 Kanban system to operate JIT

A Kanban system helps to organise the flow of components onto the production line at the right place at the right time. In Figure 68.5, the production assembly line is fed with components A and B. As the components are used, the level of stock by the line falls and, at a predetermined quantity, the Kanban card is removed and 'posted'; the details of the Kanban are within the bar code, so a computer will recognise the type of component, the quantities required and where the component is required on the production line.

The main benefits of JIT are:

- Reduced costs due to less stock being held.
- Less cash is tied up in stock whether it is stock or work in progress.
- As less stock is held there is less likelihood of damage, or it becoming out of date and therefore wasted.

However, there are risks to operating a JIT system:

- With less stock being held any delay from suppliers could halt production.
- Any serious errors within the production system may affect the level of production as again there is little spare stock to utilise.
- There is a substantial set-up cost in order to operate JIT (e.g. Kanban technology).

Figure 68.6. A Kanban card barcode

The computer will automatically trigger a withdrawal of additional stock to be fed on to the line at the correct point in the process. It will also help organise the production and timing for any sub-assembly that takes place within the factory, so that these parts are ready in time to be used at another stage of the production process. The new stock will have a Kanban so that the process can start all over again. Automatically, additional stock from the suppliers will arrive on time, just-in-time to be used on the line (with the usage of EDI – electronic data interchange).

For the Kanban system to work effectively:

1 All components must have a Kanban attached to the parts or the container of the parts.
2 No parts should be moved without a Kanban.

Naturally, there is a significant initial set-up cost if JIT and the associated Kanban system are implemented. However, the long-term benefits far outweigh these capital costs.

Example

Car manufacturer Jaguar holds only two hours' stock of many of its components. At its plant in Castle Bromwich, Birmingham, the Kanban cards have, for some components, been replaced with an electronic push-button kanban. This sends the message for additional stock automatically, therefore saving more time as the Kanban does not have to be collected and delivered to a computer. The push-button Kanban is located at the workstation related to a particular part or raw material.

Cell production

Cell production is a form of teamwork. Employees are placed in different teams, with each team responsible for a particular part of the production process. Their responsibility includes the control of quality for their particular part of the production process, and ensuring that the parts that are delivered to their area or part of the process are of an acceptable standard.

The team is also responsible for the health and safety of their area, and for deciding who performs the tasks and when they are to be completed. As long as the particular process is completed in time to be passed to the next stage of the production process, and the tasks have been completed to the right standard, the employees within the cell can rotate their jobs to enhance job satisfaction.

Allowing employees some responsibility and involvement (Herzberg and Mayo's theories) contributes to a more contented workforce and consequently a higher level of productivity.

Ergonomics

Ergonomics looks at the relationship between the employee and the capital equipment (machine or tool) being used. An effective ergonomic design is one where the minimum amount of time is wasted in using the machine or equipment. In many car plants, drills and such tools are deliberately hung on spring coils so that workers can literally let go when the task involving that particular tool is complete, saving valuable seconds in not having to walk to place the tool back on a bench. Although such savings appear minute, when multiplied by the number of times a repetitive process is undertaken, they become significant in terms of both time and costs.

Summary

All of the above will help the business to become 'leaner' and therefore more cost effective and, in turn, may aid its ability to remain or become competitive.

There are of course cost implications in the short term, which may make total implementation difficult; nevertheless, ensuring a business is 'lean' ought to enhance its ability to survive and prosper.

Tips and techniques

Assessing whether adopting 'lean' approaches will depend upon:

- the individual business
- its budget
- its objectives
- the market it operates within
- the economic climate.

Further sources

www.leanuk.org
http://freeleansite.com: for information on The Toyota Production System 1996
www.cio.com (three principles for lean manufacturing)
www.cardiff.ac.uk/lean/principles (five principles)
www.kcprofessional.co.uk: (seven principles)

Your turn

Questions are suitable for all AS and A Level condidates.

Multiple-choice questions

1 To operate JIT successfully requires:
   A cell production
   B ergonomic production
   C Kanban system
   D a quality circle. *(1)*

2 Jidoka is a process for:
   A detecting and rejecting faulty goods
   B assessing the level of production
   C JIT to be implemented
   D improving the ergonomic layout of the production process. *(1)*

3 Kaizen is:
   A continuous improvement
   B used to prevent stoppages in production
   C requires JIT to be used
   D a time-based competitive element. *(1)*

4 JIT is often referred to as a process to ensure components:
   A are fitted correctly
   B reach the line when needed
   C are not faulty
   D are fit for purpose. *(1)*

Revision questions

1 Explain two reasons why Jidoka may save the business money in reduced costs. *(4)*

2 Explain two reasons how Kaizen is a benefit to a business. *(4)*

3 State two ways in which time-based competition can be improved. *(2)*

4 Explain two reasons why the use of cell production may increase the motivation of the employees. *(4)*

Total *(14)*

Case study

JCB

JCB was set up at the end of the Second World War and in 1945 built agricultural tipping trailers.

Today, it manufactures industrial excavators in nearly 30 plants around the world, with a worldwide workforce of over 11,000.

JCB produced its first 'backhoe loader' as long ago as 1952, with its millionth machine being produced in May 2013. Its headquarters remain at Uttoxeter in Staffordshire.

A JCB Backhoe

Concern for lean production was clearly evident in 2010, after which it enhanced its machine efficiency and productivity to higher levels with the introduction of its 'EcoMax' machines when full production started in 2012. The fuel-efficient technology means the fuel is burnt in a clean manner, thus reducing the need for high-maintenance exhausts, which in turn reduce the running costs of the engines.

The production line operates JIT and its ergonomic layout enables savings to be made both in terms of time and costs.

On the line 'kitting trollies' serve each station with around 480 required components, readily available for the assembly workers to use when needed and within easy reach. The tools needed to aid the assembly process are also strategically placed to enable easy usage for the assembly workers.

A kitting trolley

Careful consideration has been given to the production line and assembly order. The actual backhoe itself is fitted at a very late stage of the production process so the assembly line can be narrower and therefore increase the amount of productive space within the factory.

The factory operates a form of the Andon lights system. The lights are strategically placed above the assembly lines. Green indicates all is well, amber indicates there is a minor problem on the line and red means there is a stoppage on the production line. This approach allows for a visual management of where a problem exists and the extent of its seriousness. This usage of a Jidoka system allows faults to be spotted and hopefully rectified with a minimum delay to production.

JCB also has a signboard stating what the planned output is to be and what the actual output is. This can act as a spur to the employees and also allows management to see if the target or planned output is being reached.

The production line operates a 'no fault forward' approach. This means that the next stage of the assembly line will not 'accept' anything that is faulty, as this will save money in terms of costs.

1 Explain two ways savings in terms of both time and costs are achieved because of the ergonomic layout of the production line. *(4)*

2 Explain two reasons why the form of Jidoka with the Andon lights saves JCB costs. *(4)*

3 By operating a 'no fault forward' system, analyse how this will save JCB money in the long run. *(6)*

4 The signboard stated that the planned output for the shift was 13 and the actual output was 11; if this variance was repeated over 15 shifts, calculate the total variance for the 15 shifts. *(2)*

Total *(16)*

Chapter 69

Location and logistics

> **Year 2**
>
> A Level students must know all of the content in this chapter.
>
> This chapter is not applicable for AS students.

Location

Location decisions are important because they are not easy or costless to reverse. The decision where to locate a business will depend on a variety of factors.

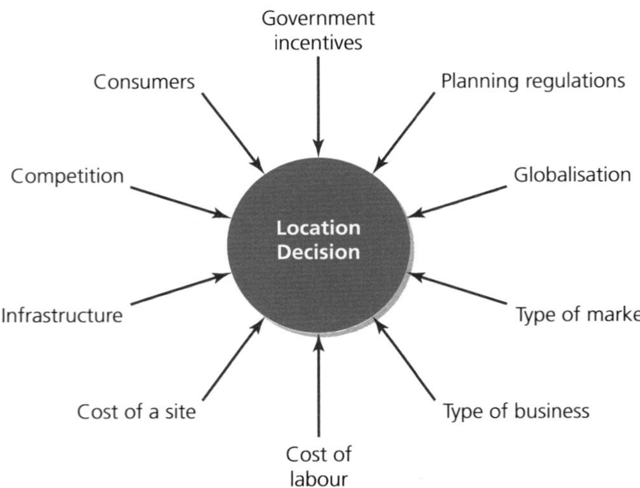

Figure 69.1 Factors influencing the location of industry

Type of market and significance of costs

The greater the degree of competition within a market, the more likely it is that any locational decisions will be cost-orientated.

Type of business and its product/service

If the business is in the primary sector of the economy, it may have little or no choice about where to locate, as the raw material it uses will govern its location; for example, a coal mine will be located wherever the coal seams are.

The nature of the product is important if bulky raw materials are required. Reducing the cost of transporting the raw materials, especially if the product is in a competitive market or is a low value product, will be a key objective. For both, minimising costs will be a factor affecting location. Crisps are a good example of a low-value product that is also bulky to transport.

While there has been a steady fall in the level of activity within the primary and secondary sector the tertiary sector has expanded rapidly. Providing a service to consumers usually means that the location of such services is vital to achieve success. Ensuring that consumers are served in a convenient way is crucial. Consumers want to access services quickly and so location for personal services (such as a gym or a cinema) becomes even more important.

Cost of labour

The significance of the cost of labour will again depend upon the nature of the business, and the level of labour required. If the business is labour-intensive, then locating near a cheap and plentiful supply of labour will be paramount. Selecting an area where unemployment is high may mean that there is a high supply of workers, which will make the cost of labour cheaper. However, if particular skills are required, an area where such skills exist will be a significant factor in the choice of location.

Cost of a site

The cost of any site is determined by the forces of demand and supply. Any increase in the level of demand for a particular site will increase its price (see Figure 69.2).

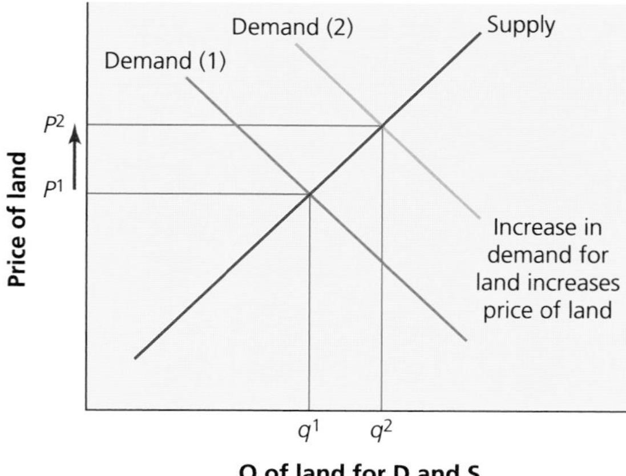

Figure 69.2 Cost of site affected by demand

Similarly, any increase in the level of supply of appropriate sites will tend to reduce the cost of the sites (see Figure 69.3).

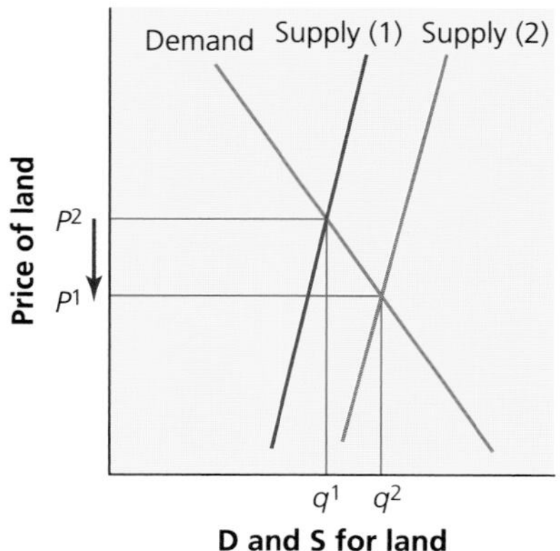

Figure 69.3 Cost of site affected by supply

Infrastructure

Businesses will look carefully at the infrastructure within the area. Transport links are an important part of an area's infrastructure; a business needs to ensure that it can move its inputs 'in', and its finished goods 'out' quickly and easily.

Infrastructure also includes the facilities within the area such as transport links, schools, health services and the ability to 'link up' with other firms. If a business is to relocate to a new area, it may want to take some or all of its employees with it. The employees will want to be sure that there is a good range of housing and good educational and health facilities within the area before contemplating any move.

Key term

Infrastructure: the structures that support a society, such as transport links, telecommunications, education and health facilities, water supply, sewers, and so on. If these are poor it will deter business location.

Degree of competition

The greater the degree of competition within a market, the more likely it is that any locational decisions will be cost-orientated. A monopolist may not be as concerned about costs due to the lack of competition, and therefore will not view locational decisions in the same manner as a firm under competitive pressure.

Businesses will usually want to locate away from their competitors. However, there are occasions when it will deliberately choose to locate alongside them. In Birmingham, jewellery shops are all located together in what is called 'the jewellery quarter'. This may seem strange, but consumers will make a conscious decision to go the jewellery quarter, knowing that there will be a vast amount of choice within a small area of the city.

Location of consumers

Depending on the nature of the product or service, being close to the consumers can be significant. For those involved in retailing, being close to the consumer is often the most significant factor. Local shops provide a range of products and services for locals. Consequently, there is a real need to be located in a convenient location for the consumers. Local corner shops such as the Spar chain survive because they meet a consumer need in a convenient manner.

Similarly, a supplier to the car industry may want to be near to its consumer (the car plant) in order to deliver the components when required. With the heavy reliance on just-in-time (JIT) production, suppliers tend to locate as near to the consumer as possible.

Some international businesses choose a new location because of the access it gives to new customers. Nissan and Toyota both located within the UK in order to access consumers in the EU. This locational decision allowed these businesses to avoid the import duties that would have to be paid if the cars were made outside the EU. This benefit needed to be evaluated against the problems related to any currency fluctuations that may occur which could create uncertainty about costs and revenues (see **Chapter 16**).

Government incentives

For Nissan and Toyota, both locations (Sunderland and Derby) had the added incentive of financial inducement to locate there which was provided by the UK Government.

The government has for many years attempted to alleviate unemployment by offering incentives to industry to locate in areas where the level of unemployment is high. Ever since the 1960s when Development Areas were introduced, and in the 1980s when Enterprise Zones were established, governments have offered financial help to industry.

Currently, government assistance is administered through the Regional Growth Fund. As well as trying to achieve balanced growth around the UK, the aims of Regional Aid are to safeguard jobs in order to support communities and encourage new businesses into the area to create new jobs within them. The amount of assistance given to a business depends on the extent to which it will help meet these aims. A project that creates a lot of jobs that are likely to be permanent will receive more assistance than one that creates a few jobs that may only be short term. Some of the funds for this sort of aid come from the European Union.

Planning regulations

A business cannot simply locate wherever it likes – or indeed extend its current facilities. The impact on the environment and neighbouring residential areas has to be considered. Certain smaller scale commercial building projects do not require planning permission. These projects have what is known as 'permitted development rights'. However, as a general rule, if a business wants to build something new, make a major change to its existing building, or change the use of the building, it will need planning permission. Each area of the UK has a local planning authority which is responsible for considering and granting local planning permission. Approval for a new development can take quite a long time, especially if the application is contested for some reason. If a project needs planning permission and the business does not obtain it, an 'enforcement notice' ordering it to undo all the changes it has made will be issued.

Globalisation

Globalisation has meant that the level of competition has increased as businesses face a much larger (world) market. The main consequence of globalisation is the need to be highly competitive. This in turn has encouraged businesses to locate where costs are at their cheapest. Many call centres are now located in the Far East because of the low labour costs. Also ICT means that there is no need to be located within the market country. Some manufacturers have benefited from locating in eastern European countries to take advantage of cheap land and labour.

Special requirements

There are some businesses that require special conditions or requirements for their operations to take place. A port obviously needs to be located by the sea. However, airports will not only require a large amount of land to provide all the facilities expected, but also have to try to avoid populated areas because of noise pollution. At the same time, airports need to be near to good transport links and sufficient population to warrant their usage. This therefore presents a dilemma. On the one hand, being near to the population is important but, on the other, being too near will create pollution problems for those people who live nearby.

Tips and techniques

A wide range of factors affect a business's location, but in the examination it will be important to select and evaluate the relevant factors for the firm in the case study, rather than write out a list of possible locational influences.

Logistics

Logistics is concerned with supply chain management. It includes the integration of the procurement of supplies, production, warehousing and transportation. A crucial part of effective logistics management is therefore reduction of the costs involved at each stage of these processes. Ineffective or outdated logistics can add significantly to a business's costs which will lower profits and so affect its stakeholders in a negative manner. The flow of finished goods from the business to the customer is particularly important.

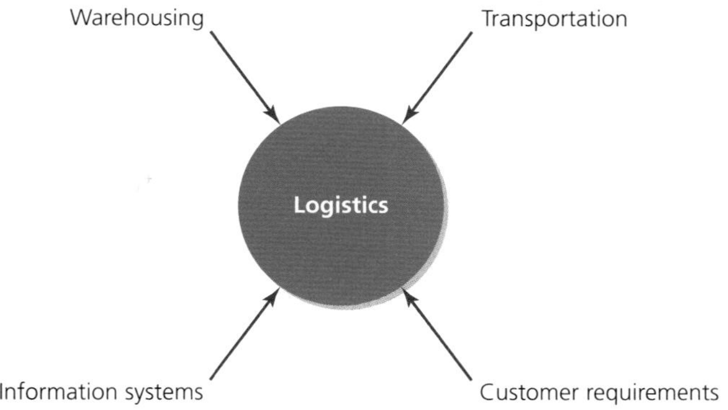

Figure 69.4 Key factors affecting logistical decisions

> **Key term**
>
> **Supply chain management (SCM):** the strategic co-ordination of business functions within a firm and with other businesses in its supply chain. The aims of SCM are to co-ordinate supply with demand and lower costs.

- Warehousing: if the firm has its own storage depots it can have stocks of raw materials or finished goods ready to use, which lowers the possibility of production problems or customer disappointment. However, it will incur large fixed costs for the purchase of the building, security costs to protect the stock, employees to work there. Would a JIT system of stock management for raw materials be more appropriate? (See **Chapter 68.**)
- Customer requirements: how important is it for products to reach the consumer at a specified time? If a business is selling industrial cleaning products to another business, delivery at a specific time on a specific day may not be particularly important. However, if products are perishable (e.g. flowers) there is much more urgency in getting them to the retailer.
- Information systems: it is essential to have an ICT system that connects departments of the business internally to co-ordinate operations. It is also important, especially if demand varies, to communicate externally with other businesses to find out about their requirements.
- Transportation: how should the products be delivered to the customer? There are a variety of choices (road, rail, air, etc.) all with different cost and handling implications. If the business owns its own vehicles then products can be moved 'from door to door', which is not the case with rail transportation. This will, however, mean there is the cost of buying and operating the vehicles.

A business can undertake its logistical functions 'in house' or it can choose other ways to manage them.

Outsourcing

Outsourcing occurs when a business contracts a specialist company with expertise in a particular area to provide activities and/or services that would otherwise be performed 'in-house' by its own employees. In the case of logistics this may be the transportation of finished products. At first sight it might seem strange to hand over such a crucial element of the business's operation to a third party but there is, hopefully, going to be an advantage in terms of cost reduction.

If a business decides that it wants to have its own vans and lorries to transport finished goods, there will be an initial capital cost. In addition, the vehicles have to be taxed, insured and serviced. There is the labour cost of the drivers, along with the potential human resource problems such as sickness and absenteeism. Outsourcing means that these issues are no longer the concern of the business that produced the products. There will be no need for a transport manager to organise the drivers and their routes. In addition, if staff are off sick or involved in a dispute this is not a problem for the company that has outsourced the service; the other firm now has the (contractual) responsibility to deliver on time.

Another advantage is that managers can now concentrate on important core issues such as improving productivity or expanding into new markets. However, there is always the possibility that the company responsible for the outsourced function fails to deliver on its promises, or there is a dispute over the contract. An argument over exactly what has been agreed could lead to payment being withheld and subsequently the creditor company refusing to provide the delivery service which, in turn, would mean consumers not getting the products. Consumers are not interested in the finer details of a dispute, they want the products. If these are not delivered on time there is an immediate negative effect on the reliability of the company that produced the goods, which could jeopardise future orders and profit.

The decision to outsource a business function such as transportation needs careful evaluation. Issues such as the extent of the cost saving, the reliability of the company now undertaking delivery, and the nature of a contingency plan if the other company lets you down will have to be considered. The same sort of issues would apply to the outsourcing of warehousing.

Subcontracting

Subcontracting can often form part of a business's logistics. It refers to the production of a particular product or service and usually occurs where a project is complicated and the main contractor does not possess the skills and capabilities to undertake the whole task. A common example of subcontracting occurs in the construction industry. If a large new office block is being built, the main contractor is responsible for the project's completion in accordance with contractual deadlines but is unlikely to undertake all of the work. The main contractor may subcontract tasks such as painting, electrical work or plumbing to another business, which in turn has to adhere to contractual deadlines. In this respect, it is similar to outsourcing and the reasons for subcontracting (lowering costs or the inability to perform the service 'in-house') and the disadvantages associated with it (a failure to provide the agreed service on time to the desired standard) are the same.

A disadvantage of subcontracting is that if certain tasks are always subcontracted, the business never develops the expertise itself to perform that particular task. Another issue is that those who are working for a subcontractor are usually paid higher rates than 'regular' company employees, since they are not receiving the benefits that regular employees are in terms of (say) holiday or sickness pay. This might cause resentment and discontent.

Offshoring

Offshoring is the relocation by a business of an operational process, such as the manufacturing of its products abroad. It could also refer to the production of services such as customer support via a foreign call center. Offshoring has been very popular for the past few decades. An article in *The Economist* noted:

> *The original idea behind offshoring was that Western firms with high labour costs could make huge savings by sending work to countries where wages were much lower. Offshoring means moving work and jobs outside the country where a company is based... For several decades that strategy worked brilliantly.*

Logistically, the cost-saving potential is enormous which, in turn, should lead to improved profitability.

There are, however, disadvantages. The article continued:

> *Many American firms now realise that they went too far in sending work abroad and need to bring some of it home again . . . Firms are now discovering all the disadvantages of distance. The cost of shipping heavy goods halfway around the world by sea has been rising sharply, and goods spend weeks in transit . . . And a succession of wars and natural disasters in the past decade has highlighted the risk that supply chains a long way from home may become disrupted.*

Source: http://www.economist.com/news/special-report/21569572-after-decades-sending-work-across-world-companies-are-rethinking-their-offshoring.

Reshoring

In the light of the problems that some businesses have encountered when 'offshoring', the process of 'reshoring' has accelerated in both the UK and the USA. The term 'reshoring' refers to the returning of production operations back to the original country. Offshoring works well when large volumes of standardised products are demanded by customers on a regular basis. However, when customer needs change in terms of quantities or the nature of the product itself then offshoring can mean that the business's logistical system is ill-equipped to deal with these. Reshoring can mean an ability to respond much more quickly to customer needs – one of the key aspects of logistics. It also means that small production runs of new products can be market tested much more easily and then redesigned to meet customer requirements than if the product was manufactured abroad.

Clearly, in some countries such as China, India or Brazil there will still be advantages in 'offshoring' to those countries because labour costs are lower and there is a huge demand for standardised products, but where the products are to be marketed in advanced economies the advantages of offshoring may not be as significant as they once were.

Wherever goods are made, they need to be sold. Effective and efficient distribution is therefore essential. Distribution management – the process of managing the movement of goods to the point of sale – is therefore of crucial importance. There is little point in establishing what the consumer wants and then making the product if it is not delivered where and when it is required. Consumers who are disappointed by a failure to deliver will switch to an alternative and this can create poor publicity and a reputation for a failure to deliver. This can affect future sales.

Sometimes a business will own its own distribution centre. Essentially, a distribution centre is a warehouse (which may be a specialised building, e.g. a refrigerated unit for food products) in a strategically important location so that the business's retail outlets can be quickly and easily supplied, according to the level of demand. However, the problem for many businesses is that they do not own the final retail outlets where the product is sold. It can therefore be difficult and expensive to distribute the products directly to a large number of final retailers and therefore a distribution center in the form of an independent wholesaler may be used. This means that 'the customer' is actually the wholesaler, not the final consumer.

Key term

Distribution management: the process of managing the movement of goods to the point of sale. It includes activities such as stock control, warehousing and transportation.

Summary

Logistics need just as much consideration and planning as any other business activity. In addition, as with all major business decisions, decisions regarding logistics should not be considered in isolation but rather as an integral part of an overall plan for the firm to reach its strategic objectives. Logistics impact directly on costs and therefore profits.

Further sources

www.gra-ukgrants.com/Areas_red2.html: a map showing the Assisted Areas of the UK and information about the assistance that is available.

www.gov.uk/planning-permission-england-wales: a guide to planning permission and building regulations in the UK.

www.noa.co.uk: the National Outsourcing Association. Information about the benefits of outsourcing.

www.gov.uk/government/publications/businesses-are-coming-back/businesses-are-coming-back: a government policy paper on reshoring.

Your turn

Multiple-choice questions

1 Which of the following is NOT part of an area's infrastructure?
- A availability of skilled workers
- B electricity supply
- C road networks
- D telecommunications. *(1)*

2 A fall in the quantity of industrial units being built in a particular area is likely to:
- A raise the price of industrial units in the area and increase the demand for them
- B raise the price of industrial units in the area and reduce the demand for them
- C lower the price of industrial units in the area and increase the demand for them
- D lower the price of industrial units in the area and reduce the demand for them. *(1)*

3 Outsourcing occurs when a business:
- A contracts another firm to provide a service rather than employing its own staff to do it
- B moves production of a good abroad
- C is unable to provide a particular business function
- D is short of funds. *(1)*

4 Which of the following best describes the term 'the supply chain'?
- A the effective marketing of a product
- B moving a product or service from supplier to customer
- C the transportation of raw materials
- D ensuring that a business has sufficient stock *(1)*

Revision questions

1 State two ways in which the UK government may affect the location decisions of a business. (2)
2 Explain two advantages of a business outsourcing a service such as transportation. (2)
3 Explain two reasons why a business might decide to 'reshore' its products. (2)
4 Explain two reasons why a business may decide to subcontract some of the products it has agreed to supply. (2)
5 Evaluate the likely factors that could affect the location of a new Tesco supermarket. (15)

Total (27)

Case study

Dyson

In 2002 the entrepreneur James Dyson announced that he intended to relocate the manufacturing of his company's vacuum cleaners to the Far East; a move that would result in the loss of 800 jobs in the UK. Dyson himself admitted it was a sad day, both personally and for the company. Employees at the company were devastated and Brian Wilson, the Minister for the Department of Trade and Industry at the time, described the Dyson announcement as 'very disappointing'. Dyson did state that the company's research and development facility at Malmesbury in Wiltshire would remain and would continue to expand.

Sir James Dyson plans to invest £250m in the expansion of his company headquarters in Wiltshire, creating jobs for 3,000 engineers.

Under the plans, Sir James will double the size of his base in Malmesbury and triple the number of engineers he employs. It would mark the largest expansion in the company's history. Sir James plans to invest £250m in the expansion of his company headquarters in Wiltshire, creating jobs for 3,000 engineers.

Under the plans, Sir James will double the size of his base in Malmesbury and triple the number of engineers he employs. It would mark the largest expansion in the company's history.

In 2014 Dyson announced a huge expansion at that location. The *Telegraph* reported:

Sir James Dyson plans to invest £250 million in the expansion of his company headquarters in Wiltshire, creating jobs for 3,000 engineers and scientists. Under the plans, Sir James will double the size of his base in Malmesbury and triple the number of engineers he employs. It would mark the largest expansion in the company's history. Dyson's research and development (R&D) facility has been based in the Wiltshire town for 20 years, and seen the development of hugely successfully products including vacuum cleaners and fans. It currently boasts 1,000 engineers.

The company has been working on plans for the new site for the past two years and is close to securing planning permission. 'If that goes ahead, we hope to build it by 2015,' he said.

'We would also like to be well on the way to our 3,000 engineer target by then. But we need help from the Government to make that happen.... It will not be impossible to find an additional 3,000 if the Government makes engineering a more attractive career choice,' said the entrepreneur.

Sir James is keen to keep his R&D headquarters in the UK because of the calibre of our academic institutions. 'We have established close links with universities and have created a really exciting pipeline of new products,' he explained. 'We have lots of top-secret plans that look as much as 25 years into the future.'

Source: Adapted from: http://www.telegraph.co.uk/finance/2752100/800-jobs-to-go-as-sad-Dyson-moves-factory-to-Far-East.html

http://www.telegraph.co.uk/finance/newsbysector/industry/engineering/10590729/Sir-James-Dyson-to-create-jobs-for-3000-engineers.html

The *Telegraph*, 22 January 2014, Rebecca Burn-Callander.

1 In 2002 the Minister for the Department of Trade and Industry described the Dyson announcement as 'very disappointing'. Analyse two reasons why the government might be disappointed with Dyson's relocation decision. *(4)*

2 James Dyson said, 'We would also like to be well on the way to our 3,000 engineer target by then. But we need help from the Government to make that happen.' Analyse two reasons why the government offers assistance to businesses in certain areas of the UK. *(4)*

3 Evaluate the possible reasons for the expansion of the Malmesbury site rather than also relocating the research and development facility to the Far East. *(15)*

Total *(23)*

Chapter 70

Internal and external quality standards

AS / Year 1

Both AS and A Level students must know all of the content in this chapter.

Consider this very simple quality control test.

Statistical Quality Control

100% Inspection Exercise

Consider the letter 'f' – capital or lower-case – as a defect. How many defects in the following text?

'Effective quality control in manufacturing enterprises, in office operations, in service functions and in job shops, has undergone many innovations of late. From early times it has been presumed that if you had a few inspectors and they were on the ball, your quality of product would be okay. If your firm still adheres to this outmoded concept, you may be missing an immense potential for quality improvement and defect elimination for your operation. If this test demonstrates anything, it should show the difficulty of finding all defects, even if you have 100 per cent inspection. Far better to never build defects into the product in the first place. How can this be done? Many firms have found the total approach to quality control is the only systematic way to achieve perfection in quality, but it does mean that from first to last you'll have covered most of the possible loopholes in purchasing, receiving, material control, process design, and shipping and packing, at which key points final product quality are checked out. Above all, quality control is a team effort, which should energise the entire organisation toward a common goal.'

Your count: ______________________

Actual number: ______________________

Conclusion:

This is a very simple test of quality, and you attempted it just once, without pressure or distractions; yet, you may have missed some of the 'faults' and failed to think carefully about what was written. It may now be easier for you to understand how mistakes are made and why they are not always spotted and subsequently rectified. It is important to try and ensure that any quality checks do not rely solely on those made by people.

What is quality?

Quality is concerned with:

- the design of the product
- the reliability of the product
- ensuring that the product is properly checked while in production and not only when completed.

Being fit for purpose

Quality includes ensuring that the product is fit for purpose and is safe to use, will be reliable and last an appropriate time (durable).

Quality is also important for services. A survey in 1993 by Mintel suggested that consumers looked for an efficient service, with helpful and knowledgeable staff.

Satisfying legislation

Legislation is passed which sets the standard for certain products. Toys have to be manufactured within several legal guidelines on the material used, the type of paint used and the way in which parts are assembled. Food has to be fit for human consumption; cars have to pass several crash-safety tests.

Why is quality important?

Quality has become more important in today's markets because consumers now expect it as standard and not an optional extra. Any good that is purchased and then has to be returned because it is faulty brings bad publicity for the business and may lead to a loss of goodwill. When a business has to recall products because a major fault has been discovered, not only are sales lost, but the reputation of the business is damaged. Recovering a good reputation requires time and money, and if a good reputation is lost irretrievably, sales will be lost for ever.

Consumers are now more likely to complain and publicise their complaints on consumer television programmes and social media. They will often select a product because of its perceived quality and its reputation for reliability.

Quality assurance

Quality assurance is concerned with the way in which a business sets out its procedures to assure its consumers that the products produced are of the right quality. Systems should be in place to ensure that quality is appropriate.

Quality control

Key term

Quality control: this is a process in which a business reviews the quality of all the factors involved in the process of production.

Inspection versus cost of rejects/returns

For the business, the cost of inspecting products for quality must be balanced against the cost of the consequences of poor-quality products. See Table 70.1.

Table 70.1 Costs of inspection and returns

Costs of inspection	Cost of poor-quality products
Installing procedures to improve quality	Wasted materials
Time taken to check and inspect	Cost of repairing
Employing people to inspect, or requiring employees to use part of their time to inspect instead of producing	Production losses to rectify faults
	Damage to reputation of the business and loss of sales

This creates a dilemma for most businesses. It may not be possible or economically worthwhile to check that every pencil made in a factory is exactly the same length; the value of the end product has to be considered. However, ensuring that a particular part of a car engine is exactly the right size may be crucial if all the other components are to fit correctly. In other words, the decision on whether or not to inspect products for faults will depend upon the product and its function. The degree of tolerance depends upon the nature of the product.

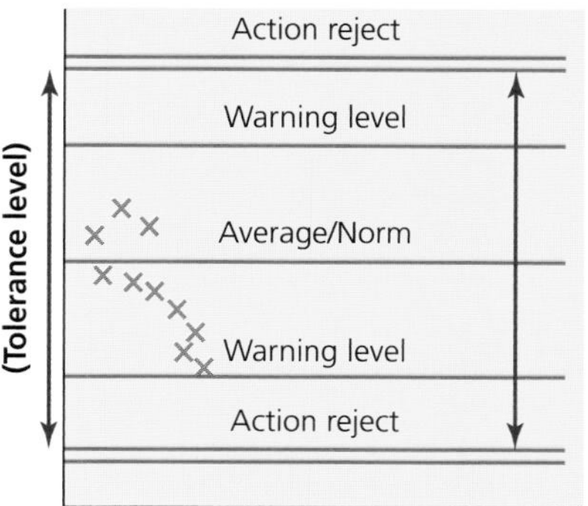

Figure 70.1 Control chart tolerance levels

Figure 70.1 shows the tolerance levels for a given product. Every time a product or part of a product is tested, it must fall within the tolerance levels (between the arrowed lines). If a test discovers a product outside of the permitted tolerance level, it should be rejected as a defect (action level).

Every time a test is undertaken, the actual reading is usually plotted, and it is possible to plot a trend that may indicate that something is going wrong and can be rectified before it is too late. Each 'x' represents a test result, and the trend of the tests in Figure 70.1, although within the tolerance levels, suggests that it is getting close to the warning level. If the warning level is reached, it should trigger questions about why the test results are moving towards and beyond the warning level.

How much tolerance is allowed will depend upon the sophistication of the product and its function. Many of today's factories prefer prevention rather than cure (see Dr Deming and P. Crosby's views below).

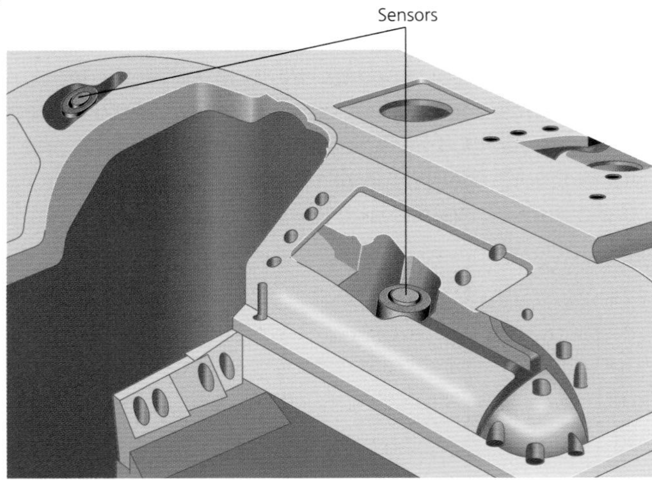

Figure 70.2 Sensors to prevent damage and loss of materials

Figure 70.2 shows sensors on a machine that prevent a fault occurring while building a car. Before the press comes down to cut and shape the various panels of a car, the sensors detect whether the steel or aluminium is aligned correctly. If it is not, the press will not come down, therefore preventing serious damage to the steel, aluminium or even the press itself.

Statistical quality control

Dr Deming, a quality guru, suggested fourteen factors to improve quality performance; see Table 70.2.

Table 70.2 Dr Deming's plan for improving quality performance

1	The message about quality should be consistent throughout the business.
2	There should be a commitment to improve continuously.
3	Improvements are not just about the product itself.
4	Encourage employees not to fear improvements; they are not negative.
5	Remove any barriers within the organisation that may prevent the improvement of quality.
6	Ensure that the organisational structure of the business supports all of the other thirteen points.
7	Ensure that all suppliers are concerned about quality, and award business to them on this basis.
8	Encourage everyone to be involved in quality, and train employees to think in this way.
9	Training is vital.
10	The role of supervising employees needs to change to one of training and helping.
11	Switch from the detection to the prevention of faults.
12	Remove barriers that prevent employees from having a pride in their work.
13	Dispose of slogans and unrealistic targets.
14	Dispose of work quotas.

Another guru, Philip Crosby, has only four items on his list to aid quality management.

Table 70.3 Philip Crosby's four points

1	Meeting conformance requirements: standards either meet the requirement or fail to do so.
2	Prevention not detection: build quality into the product.
3	The standard for performance is zero defects.
4	Improved quality is free (no costs of repairing or correcting), therefore the cost of good quality pays for itself.

As you can see by looking at Tables 70.2 and 70.3, what constitutes quality and how to achieve it, varies. However, there is one constant theme that arises: prevention of faults is preferable to detecting faults. As a consequence, sampling completed products is now not the main approach or method of achieving a good quality product. Sampling is still used, but as part of a range of procedures.

Wastage rates

A measure of employee performance that could be used alongside labour productivity is the level of waste and/or rejects produced. A business will seek to minimise these because a high percentage is very inefficient; costs are higher than they should be.

Whether measured on an individual or departmental basis, the calculation is straightforward:

$$\frac{\text{Number of rejects produced (by employee or department)}}{\text{Total number of products produced}} \times 100$$

Therefore, if the number of rejects produced by employees on a particular factory shift was 543 and the total output was 7,500, the wastage calculation is:

$$\frac{543}{7{,}500} \times 100$$

The reject rate = 7.2%

Waste and reject rates need to be minimised in order to maximise business efficiency. High rates can be due to poor quality inputs from suppliers or from outdated capital equipment, but they can also be indicative of an indifferent attitude by employees. If high rates are identified, the cause needs to be investigated.

Training

Training of employees is important in the process of ensuring quality because workers who are not adequately trained are likely to make mistakes. This can lead to higher wastage rates or poor quality products entering the market. A reputation for poor quality will quickly earn a business reputation for unreliability and is likely to reduce sales.

Tips and techniques

Quality control is the process of checking the factors involved throughout the production process to ensure that there are no defects. Quality assurance is a process of preventing mistakes and defects in the production process.

Total quality management

This approach became extremely popular in the 1980s. Total quality management (TQM) considers the efficient usage of all the resources used within the production process, directly or indirectly related to the actual production process. The word 'total' is the significant factor, as it is an essential part of this practice that all employees are responsible for the well-being of a business and not just those that produce the product. Employees are empowered to take the responsibility for the work they do.

It is a different approach to the control of quality within a business. The emphasis is on finding ways to prevent mistakes rather than inspect for mistakes. This approach fits with the philosophy of both Dr Deming and P. Crosby.

Toyota, the car manufacturer, adopted a TQM approach within its car plants. The components of TQM are listed within its 'house', shown in Figure 70.3.

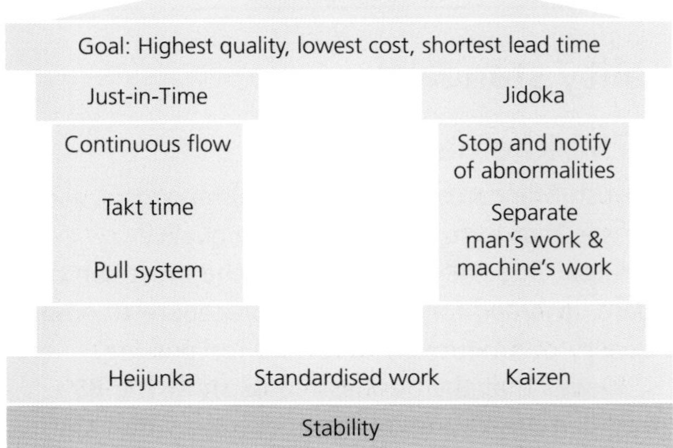

Figure 70.3 Toyota production system 'house'

TQM helps a business to:

- focus on the needs of the consumer
- improve quality in all its departments
- encourage a team approach by its employees
- encourage employees to be involved
- find ways to improve performance and quality
- seek out waste and any inefficiencies.

However, TQM may take time to implement, as employees may have to learn a new way of thinking and operating. It will require financing to pay for the training and installation of new procedures and approaches to organising the business.

Benchmarking

In its simplest form, benchmarking is achieved by comparing a business with that of a competitor that is usually the market leader, in order to improve its own practices. It involves setting standards for the performance of the business.

Benchmarking is concerned with the identification of the 'best practice'. This is done by comparing the products produced and how they are produced, with other businesses in the same industry. By improving its practices within the business, costs may be reduced, quality should be improved and a business should aim to improve standards on a constant basis.

There are several stages to effective benchmarking:

1. Decide which products or activities/processes are to be benchmarked.
2. Be aware of the existing processes in the business (to enable a comparison to be made).
3. Conduct an analysis of those operating 'best practice' (if accessible).
4. Make a comparison and identify gaps or areas for improvement.
5. Take action to improve where necessary, to ensure that the practice of the business is close to being 'best practice'.
6. Ensure process is ongoing (as for Kaizen, see below).

Types of benchmarking

There are of different types of benchmarking:

- External benchmarking: this is the most common type, where comparisons of performance are made between one business and another.
- Internal benchmarking: is when comparisons are made within a business, usually between one department and another.

- Competitive benchmarking: A comparison is made with the best competitor. Although gaining information from a competitor may not be easy, some exchange of information may be available through the trade association for that type of industry.
- Functional benchmarking: Comparisons are made between businesses with similar processes, though not necessarily for similar products. It could involve comparing how businesses collect their research data, or how they undertake the design processes.
- Strategic benchmarking: This is not related to a specific process but is concerned with the overall strategies that businesses use. If a business needs to improve its overall performance, considering the various strategies used by successful businesses is a good way forward.

Limitations of benchmarking

- limited access to sensitive material (trade secrets)
- difficult to find which business offers 'best practice'
- difficult for a business to implement improvements to reduce gaps between itself and 'best practice' business; this may be due to insufficient employees of the right calibre, a lack of finance or an inflexible workforce.

Kaizen

Kaizen is the philosophy of attempting to gain 'continuous improvement' (see also **Chapter 68**). The days of occasionally managing to find a way to improve the process of producing a product have gone. No business can afford to stand still if it is to remain competitive. 'Continuous improvement' refers to the production of the product and how to improve the quality of the product.

This approach is achieved more easily if all the employees are encouraged to take part in the process, and not just management. Often, the people best placed to make suggestions for improvements are the production workers, who know what the job actually entails.

Quality circles

Quality circles are a voluntary scheme where employees meet within the working day to consider problems affecting their work (see also **Chapter 68**). Quality circles were established in Japan in 1962, and their main functions are to identify, analyse and attempt to solve problems within the workstation. Quality circle groups tend to be concentrated within manufacturing companies.

Management are consulted but rarely involved within the actual quality circle. This is because operating a quality circle for workers provides a sense of responsibility (Herzberg) and a sense of involvement (Mayo), and therefore provides an obvious source of motivation for the employees. The consequence for the business when quality circles operate is an increase in productivity, less absenteeism and an increase in the morale of the workforce.

There may, however, be disadvantages. If suggestions to improve workstations involve a reduction in the number of jobs that are performed and even a possible reduction in the number of employees required, such ideas will conflict with the employees' basic need for a job.

Evidence shows that such fears are unfounded, and that quality circles have been adopted by many businesses.

Example

The concept of quality circles was introduced at Wedgwood, the pottery business, as early as 1980. It was an ideal type of business to adopt this process for improving quality and dealing with specific problems that arose on the shopfloor/workplace. A variety of problems were tackled, including:

- the elimination of clay waste
- a reduction in the level of dust
- a redesign of several workstations
- a better method of maintaining specialist equipment used to paint pots and plates
- a redesign of the paintbrush holder and paint bowl used for gold paint.

Quality standards

BS 5750 Kitemark

The British Standards Institution (BSI) rewards businesses that have adopted certain quality procedures. Originally, BS 5750 was the most common standard, awarded for operating a procedure to ensure the quality of products. The reward for 'passing' BS 5750 was that the business could show the BS symbol, demonstrating to potential buyers that the products from this particular business were likely to be of a high standard because the procedure for ensuring quality was practised. Many businesses insisted that their suppliers were registered as 'BS 5750' standard.

The international version of BS 5750 is ISO 9000.

ISO 9000, European standards (EN)

European Standards are documents that have been ratified within the European Union. They oblige the member states to make the standards national ones and to remove any other standards that might conflict.

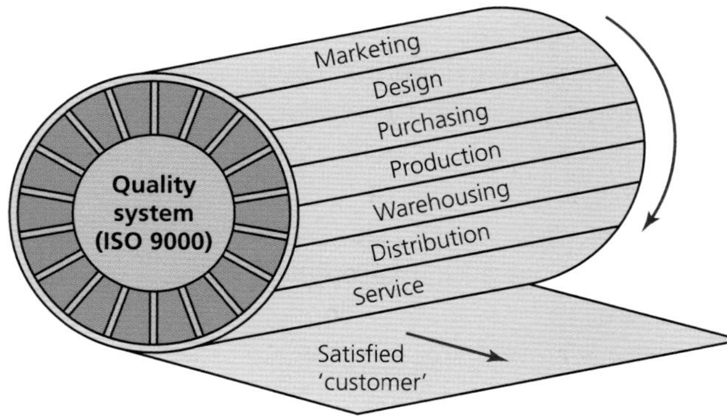

Figure 70.4 Quality system for ISO 9000

Source: Total Quality Management (1989) J. S. Oakland

These relate to a series of quality management systems. There are various different standards that can be awarded:

- ISO 9000: introduces the user to the concepts behind the management systems, and specifies the terminology used
- ISO 9001: concentrates on the design and development of products
- ISO 9002: production
- ISO 9003: final inspection tests
- ISO 9004: quality management and systems.

Who is it relevant for?

ISO 9001 is suitable for any organisation that is looking to improve the way in which it operates and is managed, regardless of size or sector. However, the best returns on investment come from those companies prepared to implement it throughout their organisation, rather than at particular sites, departments or divisions.

Figure 70.5 Kitemark symbols

Being able to display this and other similar quality assurance labels is an important marketing tool. A potential consumer (another business or an end-user) knows that the business displaying the marks has achieved a particular standard or undertaken certain quality procedures. The products should be of a high standard in terms of their quality.

Zero defects

By applying the concept of zero defects, a business should be able to benefit from an improvement in quality and therefore a reduction in costs, as fewer defects equals less waste. If a policy of zero defects is to be successful, the business needs to ensure that the right conditions are in place.

The needs of the consumer are paramount and the product is then built with these needs in mind. If the needs of the consumer are met, this should increase consumer satisfaction and lead to further orders or consumption. This in turn may lead to brand loyalty, and allow the business to establish its market share and even benefit from economies of scale as orders increase. If the expectations of the consumer are not met, this could have a damaging effect upon the image of the business.

However, the cost of achieving zero defects needs to be considered carefully against the likely benefits.

Further sources

www.asq.org A website for 'people passionate about quality'; up-to-date issues and examples

Your turn

Questions are suitable for all AS and A Level candidates.

Multiple-choice questions

1 Total Quality Management:
 A ensures the efficient use of all resources
 B involves all employees
 C involves checking every item
 D seeks to prevent faults rather than find them. *(1 mark)*

2 The benchmarking process involves all of the following except:
 A using best practice
 B making comparison with competition
 C actions to achieve improvement
 D finding faults in the production process. *(1 mark)*

Revision questions

1 State two limitations of benchmarking. (2)
2 Explain what is meant by 'Kaizen'. (2)
3 State two characteristics a 'Quality Circle'. (2)
4 Explain what a Kitemark signifies for a business? (2)
Total (8)

Case study

Emma Bridgewater Ltd and Bullers Rings

The Emma Bridgewater pottery was opened in Stoke-on-Trent in 1985 and now employs almost 200 people. The company produces a range of tableware that it describes as 'quintessentially English' and the business has managed to thrive and grow at a time when other pottery firms have struggled and many well-known names have gone out of business.

Emma Bridgewater uses a product called Bullers Rings to measure and monitor the amount of heat that is produced in the kilns during the firing process. Before the business introduced Bullers Rings, the company found that it continually experienced problems with uneven firing. This led to problems of rejection of a large number of items, the production of too many seconds and inconsistent products throughout all the ranges. The Quality department at the business decided that this situation was unacceptable if the company wanted to establish a reputation for a quality product, for which it could charge a relatively high price.

The company uses the Bullers Rings to 'map' the temperature throughout the kiln. If any of the reading is outside the agreed tolerance, the Quality department will check that the kiln is working accurately.

The use of this process has helped to improve the quality of production considerably, leading to lower costs, fewer 'seconds' and less time used in the use of quality control at the end of the process.

1 Explain what is meant by Quality Control and how it differs from Quality Assurance for Emma Bridgewater. *(4)*
2 Analyse one problem that poor quality in the finished product created for Emma Bridgewater. *(4)*
3 Evaluate the benefits for Emma Bridgewater of using the Bullers Rings system to improve quality control. *(9)*

Total *(17)*

Acknowledgements

Every effort has been made to trace all copyright holders, but if any have been inadvertently overlooked, the Publishers will be pleased to make the necessary arrangements at the first opportunity.

p.1 Dan Martin, 'What is an entrepreneur? A brilliant definition' (http://www.businesszone.co.uk/blogs/dan-martin/dan-martin-editor039s-blog/what-entrepreneur-brilliant-definition); **p.6** The Startups Team, 'Dame Mary Perkins: Specsavers' (http://startups.co.uk/dame-mary-perkins-specsavers/); **p.17** The Co-operative Group, 'The Co-operative Group Purpose' (http://www.co-operative.coop/corporate/aboutus/ourvisionandaims/); **p.31** Ian Weinfass, 'Tube strike called off', Oxford Mail, 5 May 2014 (http://www.oxfordmail.co.uk/news/11192118.print/); **p.52** 'Definition: Crisis management', (http://whatis.techtarget.com/definition/crisis-management, Accessed 24 April 2014); **p.54** Zoe Wood, 'Tesco pays the full price for failure to offer discounts', Observer, 13 April 2014 (http://www.theguardian.com/business/2014/apr/13/tesco-full-price-discount-philip-clarke); **p.79** Réka Blazsek, 'Why 'Me-Tailing' is The Future of Retail', 4 October 2013 (www.onsmb.com/2013/10/04/tailing-future-retail/); **p.84** Ofgem, 'How we work', www.ofgem.gov.uk/about-us/how-we-work; **p.85** Adapted from 'Store Wars: A new hope', Stephen Springham, Planet Retail, 24 Mar 2014 (http://www1.planetretail.net/news-and-events/press-release/discount-store-wars-%E2%80%93-reshaping-uk-grocery-landscape); **p.107** World Trade Organisation, 'Understanding the WTO' (https://www.wto.org/english/thewto_e/whatis_e/what_we_do_e.htm); **p.116** UK Trade & Investment and UK Trade & Investment in the USA, 'UKTI helps Wheathills carve out a future in international trade', 19 March 2014 (https://www.gov.uk/government/case-studies/ukti-helps-wheathills-carve-out-a-future-in-international-trade); **p.127** Barclays, 'Our approach' (http://www.barclays.com/citizenship/our-approach.html); **p.142** Bank of England, 'How does monetary policy work?' (http://www.bankofengland.co.uk/monetarypolicy/Pages/how.aspx); **p.167** 'Adnams receives top honour', 21 April 2014 (http://adnams.co.uk/about/news/company-news/doing-the-right-thing/adnams-receives-top-honour/); **p.168** Sir John Harvey Jones, Making it Happen, Profile Books: London, June 2003; **p.194–195** (i) Adapted and quoted from Oliver Shah, 'Tesco Shambles', The Sunday Times, 28 September 2014; (ii) Adapted from 'Culture has to change at Tesco, new boss Dave Lewis tells staff', 26 September 2014 (http://www.thisismoney.co.uk/money/markets/article-2771317/Culture-change-Tesco-new-boss-Dave-Lewis-tells-staff.html); **p.204** Graham Ruddick, 'Milkmen and dairy farmers - victims of the supermarket price war', 9 October 2014; **p.216–217** Secret Compass (http://www.secretcompass.com/); **p.243** The Times, 'Third of tiddlers have just £500 in reserve', 11 August 2014; **p.278** J. Ficenec, 'News for Investors', The Sunday Telegraph, 23 November 2014; **p.295–296** Rob Dabrowski, 29 September 2014 (www.rcm.org.uk); The Guardian, 'NHS strike: midwives take to picket lines with 'very heavy hearts'', 13 October 2014 (http://www.theguardian.com/society/2014/oct/13/nhs-strike-midwives-picket-lines-very-heavy-hearts); **p.318–319** Jo Faragher, '"Appraisals don't work," says former BBC HR director Lucy Adams', (http://www.personneltoday.com/hr/appraisals-dont-work-says-former-bbc-hr-director-lucy-adams, Accessed 20 May 2014; **p.320** Simon Caulkin, Observer, 20 September 2014; **p.320** The Times, 20 September 2014; **p.339** Tom Peters, 'Tom Peter's True Confessions', Fast Company, Issue 53, November 2001 (http://www.fastcompany.com/44077/tom-peterss-true-confessions); **p.342** Anne Wollenberg, 'Wellbeing is the key to keeping employees motivated', 14 March 2014 (http://www.theguardian.com/careers/wellbeing-key-to-employee-motivation); **p.342** Weightmans, 'Why work for Weightmans?' (http://www.weightmans.com/working-for-us/); **p.345** Trade Union Congress (TUC) (www.tuc.org.uk); **p.348** Acas, 'Consultation' (http://www.acas.org.uk/index.aspx?articleid=675); **p.349** 'Collective Conciliation Explained', (http://www.acas.org.uk/media/pdf/k/9/Collective_conciliation_explained_%28June_2009%29.pdf); **p.350** Acas, 'Mediation' (http://webarchive.nationalarchives.gov.uk/20070108123845/acas.org.uk/index.aspx?articleid=1011); **p.352** HR Zone (http://www.hrzone.com/engage/employees, Accessed 14 February 2014); p.357 Acas, 'Managing in difficult times' (http://www.acas.org.uk/index.aspx?articleid=2143); **p.380** Acorn, (http://acorn.caci.co.uk/); **p.381** Macrumors.com; **p.429** Sweetart.co.uk; **p.460** www.soccerstats.com; **p.462** 'Yeovil Town' (http://www.footballgroundguide.com/leagues/england/league-two/huish-park-yeovil-town-fc.html, Accessed 28 May 2015); **p.480** Tamzin Booth, 'Here, there and everywhere', The Economist, 19 January 2013 (http://www.economist.com/news/special-report/21569572-after-decades-sending-work-across-world-companies-are-rethinking-their-offshoring); **p.482** Robert Uhlig, The Telegraph, '800 jobs to go as 'sad' Dyson moves factory to Far East' 6 February 2014 (http://www.telegraph.co.uk/finance/2752100/800-jobs-to-go-as-sad-Dyson-moves-factory-to-Far-East.html); **p.482** Rebecca Burn-Callander, The Telegraph, 'Sir James Dyson to create jobs for 3,000 engineers', 22 January 2014 (http://www.telegraph.co.uk/finance/newsbysector/industry/engineering/10590729/Sir-James-Dyson-to-create-jobs-for-3000-engineers.html)

Photo credits

p.5 © Sarah Morgan/Getty Images; **p.9** © Ingram Publishing Limited; **p.11** © Simon Dack / Alamy; **p.13** © Scott Patterson – Fotolia; **p.16** © Photoshot; **p.18** © Paul Thomas/Bloomberg via Getty Images; **p.21** *l* © Digital Vision/Thinkstock, *r* © lassedesignen – Fotolia; **p.29** © PHB.cz – Fotolia; **p.33** © Matt Cardy/Getty Images; **p.70** © Matt Champlin/Getty Images; **p.73** © Jonathan Hordle/ REX Shutterstock; **p.80** © Laiotz – Fotolia; **p.86** © Frank Boston – Fotolia; **p.91** *l* © Cultura RM/Paul Burns/Getty Images, *r* © Okssi - Fotolia; **p.96** © Gudellaphoto – Fotolia; **p.100** © Reflekcija – Fotolia; **p.103** © BABU/Reuters/Corbis; **p.115** © anekoho – Fotolia; **p.119** © IRStone – Fotolia; **p.127** © Peter Macdiarmid/Getty Images; **p.134** © Edward Salter – Fotolia; **p.143** © Ray Tang/REX Shutterstock; **p.153** © Kadmy – Fotolia; **p.155** © Karen Roach – Fotolia; **p.161** © Tolga Akmen/Anadolu Agency/Getty Images; **p.164** © Ivonnchen – Fotolia; **p.170** © seraphic06 – Fotolia; **p.196** © Bernd Settnik/Picture Alliance/Photoshot; **p.204** © FLPA/REX Shutterstock; **p.209** © Jenny Thompson – Fotolia; **p.216** Secret Compass; **p.218** © Marina Lystseva/Photoshot; **p.226** © Encore / Alamy; **p.230** © Hans Strand/ Corbis; **p.250** © Digital Catwalk/Retna/Photoshot; **p.286** © Stefan Kiefer/Imagebroker/Photoshot; **p.296** © Jonathan Nicholson/ NurPhoto/Photoshot; **p.303** © Ollie Millington/Redferns via Getty Images; **p.311** © Media Bakery – Fotolia; **p.313** © zimmytws – Fotolia; **p.315** © tigger11th – Fotolia; **p.316** © Rido – Fotolia; **p.344** © Peter Hayman/Evening Standard/Getty Images; **p.345** Trade Union Congress; **p.354** © martincp – Fotolia; **p.364** © Chad McDermott – Fotolia; **p.365** © Roger Cope / Alamy; **p.370** © PA Photos / TopFoto; **p.372** © AndreyPopov/iStock/Thinkstock; **p.383** © Tatty - Fotolia; **p.407** © View Pictures/UIG via Getty Images; **p.408** © Imagestate Media (John Foxx); **p.411** © SFL Travel / Alamy; **p.412** © Michele Eve Sandberg/Corbis; **p.413** © sturti/Getty Images; **p.422** © Matt Champlin/Getty Images; **p.428** © Marijan Murat/UPPA/Photoshot; **p.429** / © Heather Sweet-Moon / Sweetart.co.uk; *r* © dp3010 – Fotolia **p.436** © Getty Images/Atlantis, The Palm; **p.437** © tuayai – Fotolia; **p.438** © David H. Seymour – Fotolia; **p.442** © Heather Sweet-Moon / Sweetart.co.uk; **p.456** © PA Photos / TopFoto; **p.458** © Art Directors & TRIP / Alamy; **p.471** © Benjamin Haas – Fotolia; **p.475** *both* © JCB; **p.489** © British Standards Institution; **p.490** © OLI SCARFF/AFP/ Getty Images.

Index